THE PRINCIPLES AND PRACTICE OF INTERNATIONAL AVIATION LAW

The Principles and Practice of International Aviation Law provides an introduction to, and demystification of, the private and public dimensions of international aviation law. Unlike other global sectors, the air transport industry is not governed by a discrete area of the law but rather by a series of disparate transnational regulatory instruments. Everything from the routes that an international air carrier can serve to the acquisition of its fleet and its liability to passengers and shippers for incidents arising from its operations can be the object of bilateral and multilateral treaties that represent diverse and often contradictory interests. Beneath this multilayered treaty infrastructure are hundreds of domestic regulatory regimes that also apply national and international rules in disparate ways. The result is an agglomeration of legal cultures that can leave even experienced lawyers and academics perplexed. By combining classical doctrinal analysis with insights from newer disciplines such as international relations and economics, this book maps international aviation law's complex terrain for new and veteran observers alike.

Brian F. Havel is Distinguished Research Professor of Law, Associate Dean for International Affairs, and Director of the International Aviation Law Institute at DePaul University College of Law. From 2011 through 2013, Professor Havel served as the Keeley Visiting Fellow at the University of Oxford, Wadham College. He also holds appointments as visiting professor of law at Leiden University and University College Dublin. His publications have an interdisciplinary focus and include *Beyond Open Skies: A New Regime for International Aviation* (2009) and *In Search of Open Skies: Law and Policy for a New Era in International Aviation* (1997).

Gabriel S. Sanchez is Senior Research Fellow at the International Aviation Law Institute and previously served as the Institute's FedEx/United Airlines Resident Research Fellow from 2007 to 2011. His most recent work on international aviation law and policy has featured in the *Catholic University Law Review*, the *Virginia Journal of International Law*, and the *Harvard Environmental Law Review*.

The Principles and Practice of International Aviation Law

BRIAN F. HAVEL

DePaul University College of Law

GABRIEL S. SANCHEZ

DePaul University College of Law

CAMBRIDGE
UNIVERSITY PRESS

32 Avenue of the Americas, New York NY 10013-2473, USA

Cambridge University Press is part of the University of Cambridge.

It furthers the University's mission by disseminating knowledge in the pursuit of education, learning and research at the highest international levels of excellence.

www.cambridge.org
Information on this title: www.cambridge.org/9781107697737

First published 2014

A catalogue record for this publication is available from the British Library

Library of Congress Cataloguing in Publication data
Havel, Brian F., author
The principles and practice of international aviation law / Brian F. Havel, DePaul University School of Law, Gabriel S. Sanchez, DePaul University School of Law.
  pages   cm
1. Aeronautics – Law and legislation.   I. Sanchez, Gabriel S., author.   II. Title.
K4095.H385   2014
343.09′7–dc23   2013030435

ISBN 978-1-107-02052-8 Hardback
ISBN 978-1-107-69773-7 Paperback

Contents

Preface   *page* ix

Acknowledgments   xiii

List of Abbreviations and Acronyms   xv

1   **What Is International Aviation Law?**   1

   1.1.   Introduction: A Book About International Aviation Law   1
   1.2.   The Distinctiveness and Content of International
          Aviation Law   4
   1.3.   A Quick Look at Legal Theory   7
   1.4.   Public and Private International Aviation Law   11
   1.5.   The Sources of International Aviation Law   16
   1.6.   The Role of International (and a Few National)
          Organizations   23

2   **The Foundations of Public International Aviation Law**   28

   2.1.   Introduction to the Chicago Convention   28
   2.2.   The "Prehistory" of the Chicago Convention   30
   2.3.   The Cosmopolitanism of the Chicago Convention   33
   2.4.   The Historical Impact of the Chicago Convention   36
   2.5.   The Core Elements of the Chicago Convention   40
   2.6.   The International Civil Aviation Organization   55

3   **The International Law Regime for Trade in Air Services**   69

   3.1.   Introduction to the Bilateral System   69
   3.2.   Aviation Trade After the Chicago Convention   72
   3.3.   The Freedoms of the Air   76

3.4.	The Nationality Rule	86
3.5.	The Core Elements of Air Services Agreements: The Open Skies Model	95
3.6.	Looking Beyond Bilateralism	109
3.7.	Remaining Challenges to Trade in Air Services	115
3.8.	Some Concluding Comments on Trade in Air Services	122

4   The International Law Regime for Airline Investment and Global Alliances · **123**

4.1.	Introduction	123
4.2.	The (Airline) Nationality Rule in Action	125
4.3.	A Quick Look at How International Law (Normally) Regulates Foreign Investment	131
4.4.	An Emerging International Investment Regime for Airlines	137
4.5.	Circumventing the Nationality Rule: Global Alliances	148
4.6.	The Legal (and Policy) Framework for Global Alliances	151
4.7.	Ongoing Issues of Law and Policy for Alliances: "Metal Neutrality" and "Spillover"	159
4.8.	A Survey of U.S. and EU Antitrust Oversight of the Three Global Alliances	163
4.9.	Beyond the Alliance System	171
4.10.	Conclusion: A New EU Initiative	172

5   The International Law Regime for Aviation Safety and Security · **173**

5.1.	Introduction	173
5.2.	The Basic Principles of International Air Safety Regulation	175
5.3.	Ensuring International Aviation Safety Through ICAO Harmonization and State Obligations	176
5.4.	The Basic Principles of International Aviation Security Regulation	182
5.5.	The Role of ICAO in International Aviation Security	185
5.6.	Exercising State Criminal Jurisdiction in International Law	189
5.7.	The Tokyo Convention (1963)	194
5.8.	The Hague Convention (1970)	201
5.9.	The Montreal Convention (1971)	205
5.10.	Beyond the ICAO Treaty Regime	208

5.11. Preventing Aviation Crimes and Other Hostile Incidents
        Within the Limits of Law   212

6 **The International Law Regime for Aviation
    and the Environment**   217
    6.1. Introduction   217
    6.2. An Overview of International Environmental Law   222
    6.3. The Role of ICAO in Environmental Issues Affecting
          International Aviation   228
    6.4. The Chicago Convention and Aviation Emissions
          Regulation   235
    6.5. The Role of Air Services Agreements in Environmental
          Regulation   241
    6.6. The Legal and Political Prospects for a Multilateral
          Aviation Emissions Treaty   242
    6.7. The International Regulation of Noise Abatement   246
    6.8. Conclusion   249

7 **The International Law Regime for Air Carrier Liability
    and Surface Damage**   251
    7.1. Introduction   251
    7.2. The Choice Between Private and Public Oversight of Air
          Carrier Liability   255
    7.3. The Warsaw System   257
    7.4. Reforming the Warsaw Convention (1): The Treaty
          Instruments   262
    7.5. Reforming the Warsaw Convention (2): Government
          and Non-Government Initiatives   268
    7.6. The Warsaw Convention: Conclusion   274
    7.7. The Montreal Convention (1): Introduction   275
    7.8. The Montreal Convention (2): The Basic Principles   277
    7.9. The Montreal Convention (3): Activating the Liability
          Regime (Accidents, Death, Injury)   283
    7.10. The Montreal Convention (4): The New Liability Regime   293
    7.11. The Montreal Convention (5): Expanding the Bases for
          Jurisdiction   303
    7.12. The Montreal Convention (6): A Final Miscellany
          of Provisions   306
    7.13. Conclusion   313
    7.14. The International Law Regime for Surface Damage
          Liability   315

8   **The International Law Regime for Aircraft Financing
     and Aircraft Nationality**   325
     8.1. Introduction   325
     8.2. A Quick Look at International Aircraft Financing   328
     8.3. The Third-Party Effects of Secured Financing of Aircraft   332
     8.4. An Overview of International Aircraft Leasing   337
     8.5. The International Law Regime for Aircraft Nationality   340
     8.6. An Overview of International Aviation Law and Aircraft
           Financing   345
     8.7. The Geneva Convention (1948)   347
     8.8. The Cape Town Convention (2001) (1): Background
           and Overview   351
     8.9. The Cape Town Convention (2): Application and Scope   358
     8.10. The Cape Town Convention (3): The Registration and
           Priority System   363
     8.11. The Cape Town Convention (4): Remedies in Default   366
     8.12. The Cape Town Convention (5): Insolvency   371
     8.13. The Cape Town Convention (6): Jurisdiction
           and Choice of Law   375
     8.14. The Cape Town Convention (7): The Convention's
           Impact on Aviation Financing and on International Law   377
     8.15. An Overview of the Governmental Role in Aircraft
           Financing   380

Afterword by Ulrich Schulte-Strathaus   393
Select Bibliography   399
Table of Authorities   417
Index   435

Preface

In the age of online search engines, virtually all of international aviation law's primary (and many secondary) materials are now only a few keyboard clicks away. Nevertheless, given the fact that international aviation law, particularly in its private dimension, is also bound up with more than 190 domestic legal systems, the sheer amount of documentation to be sifted through can quickly prove overwhelming to even the most curious and enterprising individual. Of course, there is nothing wrong with getting into the details, and for practitioners, it is a necessity; but without first having a sure guide to the whole terrain, it is all but impossible to find one's way to the proper sources. With that in mind, *The Principles and Practice of International Aviation Law* is set primarily at a cruising altitude of 30,000 feet. By taking the reader from one end of international aviation law's "cosmos" to the other (and all necessary points in between), we hope to satisfy the need for an overview before the detailed work of specialization begins.

In addition to breadth of coverage, however, we seek to give the reader a broader conceptual *context* for every area of international aviation law that we consider. Thus, on the public side, we present the regulatory structure of the international air transport industry against the backdrop of economic and political history as well as insights from general doctrines of public international law and from rational choice theory (Chapters 1, 2, and 3). We look at the highly charged issues of foreign investment in airlines and the emergence of global airline alliances by exposing the reader to the governing principles of modern international investment law (Chapter 4). We frame international safety and security issues in the wider context of the effectiveness of certain kinds of multilateral collaboration, and we analyze security issues in particular within current understandings of the nature of global piracy and evolving concepts of State criminal jurisdiction (Chapter 5). We examine the impact of climate change issues on the global aviation industry as part of the wider evolution of international environmental law (Chapter 6). On the private side, we scrutinize airline passenger and cargo liability law through lenses of corrective justice and the rise of consumerism (Chapter 7). And finally, still on the private side, we offer a solid foundation in transnational aircraft financing law and practice that reveals how and why international treaty making in this area is focused primarily on the protection of creditors (Chapter 8). As we progress through these discussions, the reader will notice that we also engage critically with the present state of international aviation law in the hope of igniting further debate about its future development.

There are two further dimensions to our study. A glance at such important collections as the *United Nations Treaty Series* or *International Legal Materials* reveals only that international law (including international aviation law) *exists*; what is not revealed in their pages is the question of how international law *functions*, particularly in a State-centric world that lacks strong, centralized mechanisms of oversight and enforcement. We will keep that question in mind and study it from a number of perspectives including theories of international relations, rational and public choice, and economics. But we will not neglect more traditional doctrinal approaches as typified by comparative, historical, and teleological analysis. Indeed, our approach to the subject does not mean that we have dispensed with detailed exegesis of particular treaties – on the contrary, too abstract a view of the Cape Town Convention on aircraft security interests, for example, would leave the reader more puzzled than enlightened as to why its drafters pursued its completion with such ardor. Nor does it mean that we have not on occasion landed in a particular national (or regional) legal system in order to provide a closer look at how it has influenced the development of the international order. That is true, for example, of the open skies policy of the United States as well as of the grant of antitrust immunity to global alliances involving a U.S. airline, and also of the wholesale replacement of Member State control over national market access attempted by the European Union. We also take careful note of innovations and developments in other regions, including some dramatic shifts in thinking about the issue of foreign investment in national airlines that are taking place in Latin America, the Middle East, and Australasia. Once the reader has completed the journey with us through any of the eight themed chapters that make up the book, further voyages lie ahead using the guideposts placed in the notes, the tables of abbreviations and authorities, and the detailed bibliography.

Like all works on law, this book has been written "in the middle of things." The philosopher Eric Voegelin once likened law to Zeno's paradox: every time you think you have reached where you think the law has been, you still have further to go. International law, no less than domestic law, is constantly expanding. Fresh accords, amendments to shopworn treaties, new interpretations of existing policy, political brinkmanship – the practice of "aeropolitics" keeps international aviation law dynamic. Recognizing these challenges, we cannot do better than to invoke Professor Andreas Lowenfeld's modest claim, opening the 1981 second edition of his treatise, *Aviation Law*, that although "[y]ou will not find instant answers – and certainly not definitive answers – between these covers[,] ... you will find a good deal of information, a good many explanations, and [we] hope a few useful insights."[1]

Finally, we have not included an appendix of documents. As the opening sentence of this Preface implies, and we now confirm, there is no document mentioned in this text that cannot be downloaded by a simple online search.

We have attempted to provide an account of international aviation law as it "rested" on December 31, 2013.[2] Any remaining errors or inaccuracies are entirely the responsibility of the authors.

Brian F. Havel
Gabriel S. Sanchez

---

1 ANDREAS F. LOWENFELD, AVIATION LAW xiv (2d ed. 1981).
2 The book's cover design, by Wendy Bedenbaugh, juxtaposes a Leonardo da Vinci drawing of a mechanical wing device (circa 1485) with an image of the jet age version.

Acknowledgments

We would like to express our sincere gratitude to a number of persons and institutions for their help in bringing this book to fruition. First on the list is our editor, John Berger, whose enthusiasm for the project was boundless and who has kept us to a fairly tight schedule from contract to proofs. Finola O'Sullivan, well known to many Cambridge legal authors, was also solicitous of the book's progress. We offer our appreciation to two deans of DePaul University College of Law, Warren D. Wolfson and Gregory Mark, for their continuing support. Brian F. Havel would also like to acknowledge his colleagues at Wadham College, University of Oxford, where he spent two happy years working on this book as the Keeley Visiting Fellow.

Portions of the book were inspired by lectures we have given at DePaul, at Leiden University's International Institute of Air and Space Law (IIASL), at the International Air Transport Association (IATA) and McGill University's Institute of Air and Space Law (IASL) in Montreal, and under the auspices of the Centre for Aviation (CAPA) in Mumbai. We are especially grateful to Professor Pablo Mendes de Leon, the Director of IIASL, for creating an enduring link between his institute and DePaul's International Aviation Law Institute and for all of the academic opportunities that he has made available to us over the years.

Several leading figures in international aviation law contributed their time and skill to reviewing and critiquing selected parts of the book. For the liability chapter, we had the expert input of Harold Caplan, former Legal Advisor of the International Union of Aviation Insurers, and Richard Gardiner, University College London. On aviation finance, we were able to call on the expertise of Dean N. Gerber (Vedder Price, Chicago), Dr. Donal Hanley (Vice President, Legal Aviation Capital Group Corp., Newport Beach, California), and B. Patrick Honnebier (Of Counsel, Gomez and Bikker, Aruba and Amsterdam).

We also wish to recognize the contributions of our colleagues in the International Aviation Law Institute at DePaul. John Q. Mulligan, FedEx/United Airlines Resident Research Fellow, showed his characteristic attention to detail and accuracy in the research and refinement he provided for every chapter of the book, and we owe him prodigious thanks for his dedication. Stephen B. Rudolph, Executive Director of the Institute, served as project manager for the book and was indispensable to its completion. Our peerless proofreader, Alice Rudolph (Steve's wife), cast her usual meticulous eye over the whole text. Our thanks also to our student research assistants, Eli Judge and Jessica Katlin, who gave us many hours of their time and considerable talents.

We are indebted to John R. Byerly, former U.S. Deputy Assistant Secretary of State for Transportation Affairs, a loyal friend of our Institute, who has always been available with counsel and support during the writing process. Rush O'Keefe, Senior Vice President and general counsel of FedEx, and Hershel Kamen, Senior Vice President, Alliances, Regulatory and Policy at United Airlines, have also been strong allies of the Institute and of its work, and this book could not have happened without their material and moral encouragement. And our thanks finally to Ulrich Schulte-Strathaus, former secretary general of the Association of European Airlines and now Managing Director, Aviation Strategy and Concepts, for his Afterword to the book – an unflinching view of the economic issues that will influence the future of the international aviation industry and of its governing rules.

Brian Havel dedicates this book to his parents, Miroslav and Betty, to his partner Graeme, and to his family. Gabriel S. Sanchez dedicates this book to his sons Jonah, Manuel, Iohan, and Eliyah, and most of all to his dear wife, Laura, without whose love, patience, and support his contribution to this work would not have been possible.

List of Abbreviations and Acronyms

A4A	Airlines for America (formerly Air Transport Association of America (ATA))
AAPA	Association of Asia Pacific Airlines
ACSA	Central American Agency for Aeronautical Safety
AEA	Association of European Airlines
AFRAA	African Airlines Association
ALTA	Latin American and Caribbean Air Transport Association
APG	Aircraft Protocol Group
ASA	Air Services Agreement
ASAM	ASEAN Single Aviation Market
ASEAN	Association of Southeast Asian Nations
ATAG	Air Transport Action Group
AWG	Aviation Working Group
BAGASOO	Banju Accord Group Safety Oversight Organization
BIT	Bilateral Investment Treaty
BRIC	Brazil, Russia, India, and China
CAA	Civil Aviation Authority
CAEP	Committee on Aviation Environmental Protection
CASSOS	Caribbean Aviation Safety and Security Oversight System
CJEU	Court of Justice of the European Union
COMAC	Commercial Aircraft Corporation of China
DGComp	Directorate General for Competition
DOJ	United States Department of Justice
DOT	United States Department of Transportation
DSB	World Trade Organization Dispute Settlement Body

DVT	Deep Vein Thrombosis
ECAA	European Common Aviation Area
ETS	Emissions Trading Scheme
EU	European Union
ExIm	Export-Import Bank
FAA	Federal Aviation Administration
GATS	General Agreement on Trade in Services
GATT	General Agreement on Tariffs and Trade
GIACC	Group on International Aviation and Climate Change
GRC	General Risks Convention
IACA	International Air Cargo Association
IACA	International Air Carrier Association
IASA	International Aviation Safety Assessments (FAA)
IATA	International Air Transport Association
ICAN	International Commission for Air Navigation
ICAO	International Civil Aviation Organization
ICJ	International Court of Justice
IDERA	Irrevocable Deregistration and Export Request Authorization
IGO	International Governmental Organizations
IPCC	Intergovernmental Panel on Climate Change
KLM	Koninklijke Luchtvaart Maatschappij
LAN	Línea Aérea Nacional
MAAS	Multilateral Agreement on Air Services
MALIAT	Multilateral Agreement on the Liberalization of International Air Transportation
MBM	Market-Based Measures
MFN	Most Favored Nation
MOU	Memorandum of Understanding
NASA	National Aeronautics and Space Administration
NGO	International Nongovernmental Organizations
OAA	Open Aviation Area
PANS	Procedures for Air Navigation Services
PNR	Passenger Name Records
RSOO	Regional Safety Oversight Organizations
SAFA	Safety Assessment of Foreign Aircraft
SARI	South Asian Regional Initiative
SARPs	Standards and Recommended Practices
SAS	Scandinavian Airlines
SCM Agreement	Agreement on Subsidies and Countervailing Measures

SDR	Special Drawing Right
TACA	Transportes Aéreos del Continente Americano
TFEU	Treaty on the Functioning of the European Union
TSA	United States Transportation Security Administration
UIC	Unlawful Interference Convention
U.K.	United Kingdom
U.N.	United Nations
UNFCC	U.N. Framework Convention on Climate Change
U.S.	United States of America
USOAP	Universal Safety and Oversight Audit Program
WTO	World Trade Organization

1

What Is International Aviation Law?

1.1. INTRODUCTION: A BOOK ABOUT INTERNATIONAL AVIATION LAW

1.1.1. *Introducing Aviation Law in Its International Dimension*

In his landmark casebook-treatise *Aviation Law*, Professor Andreas Lowenfeld set out to answer the challenge of his friend, Judge Henry Friendly, that there would only be value in giving the rules and regulations governing air transport separate treatment if "the heads of [the] given subject can be examined in a more illuminating fashion with reference to each other than with reference to other branches of law."[1] Despite Judge Friendly's negative appraisal of the possibility, Lowenfeld prevailed. *Aviation Law* – expanded considerably with the publication of its second edition in 1981 – provided an integrated overview and analysis of the broad, and occasionally disparate, "heads" (e.g., economic, safety, and tort) of U.S. aviation law to a generation of students, practitioners, and academics before tumbling into obsolescence as its author abandoned further updates in favor of new research agendas.[2] As the size and format of the book you currently hold in your hands (or have downloaded to your eReader) make apparent, *The Principles and Practice of International Aviation Law*[3]

---

[1] ANDREAS F. LOWENFELD, AVIATION LAW: CASES AND MATERIALS xiii (1972) (internal quotation marks omitted).

[2] *See, e.g.,* ANDREAS F. LOWENFELD, INTERNATIONAL ECONOMIC LAW (2d ed. 2008); ANDREAS F. LOWENFELD, INTERNATIONAL LITIGATION AND ARBITRATION (3d ed. 2005); THE HAGUE CONVENTION ON JURISDICTION AND JUDGMENTS (Andreas F. Lowenfeld & Linda J. Silberman eds., 2001).

[3] We prefer the term "international aviation law" to "international air law." Other authors have a different view, *see, e.g.,* I. H. PH. DIEDERIKS-VERSCHOOR, AN INTRODUCTION TO AIR LAW (Pablo M. J. Mendes de Leon ed., 9th rev. ed. 2012). Our preference, which follows that of Professor Andreas Lowenfeld's treatise (discussed in the main text), is motivated only by our view that the word "aviation" can be used independently of the word "law" to describe the industry we

is not a direct descendant of Lowenfeld's work. It is not a thousand-page
hybridization of scholarly treatise and casebook. Neither is it a recitation of
the "black letter" of any single jurisdiction's aviation law. Rather, what follows
is a fully up-to-date critical introduction to aviation law in its *international
dimension* that addresses those elements of national and inter-State legal and
political cultures that continue to have the greatest impact on the development of international aviation law.

1.1.2. *Complexity of International Aviation Law*

The choice of a global perspective on aviation law in place of a jurisdiction-
specific analysis is not accidental. For more than sixty years the air transport
industry has functioned as probably the world's most visible services sector and
(despite, as we will see, the irony of its own legal inability to "globalize" across
borders) as one of the principal catalysts for globalization. Revenues from
international air passenger and air cargo carriage hugely overshadow those
from domestic air transport – a differential that is expected to widen even
further in the coming decades.[4] And, although domestic aviation regulation

are discussing: the term "air" does not appear to have the same autonomy (the "air industry"
seems a nebulous idea; a Google search of that term quickly defaults to "airline" or "air transport"
industry). For an early consideration of the question of nomenclature, see DANIEL GOEDHUIS,
AIR LAW IN THE MAKING (1938) (arguing that "air law" is favored also in France (*Droit Aérien*)
and Germany (*Luftrecht*) but noting Italian jurist Antonio Ambrosini's use of the even wider term
"aeronautical law"). Another approach to naming the subject is taken in the International Civil
Aviation Organization's MANUAL ON THE REGULATION OF INTERNATIONAL AIR TRANSPORT
(Doc. 9626, 2d ed. 2004), at (iv) [hereinafter ICAO MANUAL], which draws a distinction between
"air transport" as a more specific term, referring to those aspects related to carriage by air (usually
commercial air transport), and "aviation" as a more generic term that includes topics such as
military, state, and private flying, aircraft manufacturing, and air navigation. Although in this
book we focus primarily on international commercial air transport, we also consider legal and
regulatory issues that affect other participants in the modern "aviation" value chain (including
airports, air navigation service providers, manufacturers, computer reservation systems, and
ground-handlers). Accordingly, we still prefer to adopt the wider term.

4   Despite the current weak economic conditions, especially in the West, global air transport
over the long term is expected to grow by 5% annually until 2030, a compound increase of
more than 150%. Differential growth rates, however, will see a relative shift to areas outside
the United States and the European Union with Asia and the Middle East in particular
expected to become the focus of international air traffic flows. Fully half of the world's
new traffic added during the next 20 years will be to, from, or within the Asia-Pacific
region, which may therefore overtake the United States as leader in world traffic by 2030
(reaching a market share of 38%). *See* European Commission, Communication from
the Commission to the European Parliament, The Council, The European Economic
and Social Committee and the Committee of the Regions, *The EU's External Aviation
Policy: Addressing Future Challenges*, COM(2012) 556 final, at 5 [hereinafter European
Commission Communication, *External Aviation Policy*].

(especially in the United States) certainly exhibits the complexity that no doubt captivated Lowenfeld, the regulatory governance of international air transportation – which of course includes *national* governance of inbound and outbound international air services – is by an order of magnitude even more complex. Indeed, while the tempo of regulatory change has fluctuated between intrusive and light-handed, complexity is *always* implicated when one considers the task of regulating air transport within, across, and beyond the borders of more than 190 sovereign States. Comprehending this legal labyrinth without a modern foundational text is a formidable challenge for a dedicated academic and almost impossible for students and practitioners who must, by necessity, compartmentalize their time. We hope that this book will serve all of these potential readers.

1.1.3. *Enduring Role of Domestic Law*

Nevertheless, it must be obvious from the foregoing statements that domestic aviation law retains an important place in this study even though our principal focus is international. As this chapter introduces, and as the remainder of the book elucidates, there is a dynamic relationship between aviation law's "classically" international components (e.g., the corpus of bilateral and multilateral agreements) and the State (or, in the case of the European Union (EU), supra-State) legal systems that regulate air transport. For example, although almost every country has laws addressing the civil liability of air carriers for any damage they may cause to their passengers, cargo, or to third parties on the ground, to the extent that a flight responsible for the damage can be identified as international, one or more multilateral treaties will set the baseline rules for the responsible carrier's liability, the choice of jurisdiction for any lawsuits, and the carrier's available defenses.[5] In those situations, domestic courts will have direct jurisdiction over claims arising from damages caused by an air carrier's performance of international services, yet much of the procedural and substantive disposition of those claims will be, depending on your perspective, aided or constrained by the international legal obligations contracted by the carrier's home State.

1.1.4. *Definitions, Sources, and Organizations*

In the next part, we will define more precisely what we mean in this book by the term "international aviation law." We will then discuss the book's

---

[5]   For further discussion, see *infra* Chapter 7.

interpretive approach – one that relies not only on traditional doctrinal scholarship, but also at times on economic analysis and on other so-called rational choice methodologies. Next, we will review the sources of international law and briefly explain how they intersect with international aviation law in both its public and private dimensions. Finally, we will consider how international aviation law is applied through a number of governmental and nongovernmental bodies and explore how those organizations (both public and private) continue to help shape legal developments in the field. More detailed exposition of all of these topics will be found throughout the remaining chapters.

1.2. THE DISTINCTIVENESS AND CONTENT OF INTERNATIONAL AVIATION LAW

1.2.1. *A Discrete Object of Study?*

It is not necessarily obvious what is meant by "aviation law" or, more specifically, "international aviation law." Is there really a distinct body of the law of *aviation* that stands comparison with "organic" subjects like the law of *contracts*, the law of *property*, and the law of *torts*? To restate the question in stronger terms, is international aviation law simply an academic illusion open to Judge Frank Easterbrook's charge of being patently absurd like his mythical "law of the horse" and thus "doomed to be shallow and to miss unifying principles"?[6] Lowenfeld's case for aviation law as a discrete object of study was made easier by the fact that he grounded his materials in the legal culture of the United States. A designated segment of Title 49 of the *United States Code*, for instance, specifically covers aviation. At the same time, however, laws as sectorally panoramic as the Sherman and Clayton Antitrust Acts and the Railway Labor Act[7] have undeniably powerful effects on the functioning of the U.S. aviation industry. To cut a line that demarcates "pure" aviation statutes from "aviation-related" legislation would not only render an account of this area of law woefully incomplete, but would also be needlessly artificial. Still, to legal conservatives who may be suspicious of *sui generis* bodies of law that depart from the ideal of a set of foundational principles covering all of

---

[6] Frank H. Easterbrook, *Cyberspace and the Law of the Horse*, 1996 U. CHI. LEGAL F. 207.

[7] The Sherman Antitrust Act and Clayton Antitrust Act provide the basis for most U.S. competition regulation including the air cargo and airline industries. The Railway Labor Act was amended to include aviation in 1936. *See generally* Duane E. Woerth, *Airline Labor Law in the Era of Globalization: The Need to Correct a Misreading of the Railway Labor Act*, ISSUES AVIATION L. & POL'Y (CCH) ¶ 30,011, at 16,011 (2001).

life's events, *international* commercial aviation offers a compelling response as to why it can and should support a separate body of law: it is a massive industry, heavily regulated, structurally borderless, and treated by governments (e.g., through creation of a separate United Nations (U.N.) organ to frame common global aviation rules) not as an ordinary part of international trade but as singular and exceptional.[8]

1.2.2. *Content of International Aviation Law*

Simply stated, then, international aviation law is comprised of the rules and regulations (whether domestic, bilateral, or multilateral in their origin) that affect global air transport. The fount of this body of law includes not only the widely recognized sources of international law, but also the national and supra-national legal and political cultures of the world community of States. At the level of international law, it is possible to identify aviation-specific multilateral treaties that govern global airline safety, security, and liability, and lately even aircraft financing, as well as the rights and duties of States with respect to control of their sovereign airspaces. From there, the mass of bilateral instruments that directly regulates the international aviation industry's commercial environment (routes, fares, capacity, etc.) can be located, aggregated, and analyzed to draw out general, but reliable, conclusions concerning the privileges and limitations that apply to air carriers' abilities to access foreign markets. Only a handful of "general" treaties (those not specific to any sector) have any bearing on aviation. And, consistent with aviation's exceptionalism, even some of those include whole or partial exemptions for air transport. For example, the North American Free Trade Agreement, which dismantled many of the trade and investment barriers between the United States, Canada, and Mexico, does not embrace their aviation sectors.[9] Similarly, the Kyoto Protocol to the U.N. Framework Convention on Climate Change singles out emissions produced by international aviation for separate consideration under the auspices of the U.N.'s aviation body, the International Civil Aviation Organization (ICAO).[10]

---

[8]   As always, there are exceptions to the exceptional. Those who reject an autonomous concept of aviation law might concede, at most, that aviation is just a special instance of the broadly similar transport rules that cover maritime and rail. Some evidence exists for this assertion. Italy, for example, has combined its aviation and maritime rules into a single code, *Il Codice della Navigazione* [C. nav.] (It.).

[9]   *See* North American Free Trade Agreement, art. 1201(2)(b), U.S.-Can.-Mex., Dec. 17, 1992, *reprinted in* 32 I.L.M. 289 (1993).

[10] *See* Kyoto Protocol to the United Nations Framework Convention on Climate Change, art. 2(2), *opened for signature* Dec. 11, 1997, 2303 U.N.T.S. 162; *see also infra* Chapter 6 (discussing more fully the implications of the Kyoto Protocol for the control of international aviation emissions).

1.2.3. *Aviation's Exceptionalism*

By examining the provisions of all of these specific and general treaties, together with their historical and negotiating contexts, a unified (though not always coherent) picture of aviation's exceptionalism emerges. With due respect to Judge Easterbrook, the treatment of aviation law as distinct – in its international dimension no less than in its Lowenfeldian domestic dimension – is not just an academic indulgence. To illustrate: the near-universal prohibition on States granting foreign airlines "cabotage rights," that is, the privilege to move passengers or cargo between two points within a single domestic territory, makes little sense without reference to what the 1944 Convention on International Civil Aviation (the "Chicago Convention")[11] says about the practice. An international dimension also applies when it comes to domestic laws limiting foreign investment in airlines. Those laws are designed, in large part, to ensure that States comply with requirements in their bilateral air services treaties that their airlines remain "substantially owned and effectively controlled" by their own nationals as a prerequisite for access to foreign markets.[12]

1.2.4. *Influence of National Regimes on International Aviation Law*

Just as States have national laws to regulate domestic aviation, so too do they have rules governing air services to or from their respective territories. Is that international aviation law as well? To the extent that States are engaging in regulation of transnational activity, of course the answer is yes. Trawling through the particulars of each national regime, however, would require several volumes and has been usefully done elsewhere.[13] Even so, a few

---

[11] Convention on International Civil Aviation, *opened for signature* Dec. 7, 1944, 61 Stat. 1180, 15 U.N.T.S. 295 (entered into force Apr. 7, 1947) [hereinafter Chicago Convention]. The ninth and latest edition of the quadrilingual text (English, French, Spanish, and Russian) is available from the ICAO, Convention on International Civil Aviation, ICAO Doc. 7300/9 (9th ed. Dec. 3, 2010). As of March 1, 2013, ICAO reported 191 contracting States, making it one of the most "universal" of modern treaties. *See* Status of Convention on International Civil Aviation Signed at Chicago on 7 December 1944, http://www.icao.int/secretariat/legal/List%20of% 20Parties/Chicago_EN.pdf. As discussed *infra* Chapter 2, the Chicago Convention is the centerpiece treaty of international aviation law and also the constitutive document for ICAO.

[12] Cabotage and airline investment restrictions are discussed in detail *infra* Chapters 2, 3, and 4.

[13] *See, e.g.*, AVIATION LAW REPORTER (1947–2013) (semi-monthly update on U.S. aviation law, especially tort liability rulings); EUROPEAN AIR LAW (Elmar Giemulla et al. eds., 1992–2013) (regularly updated loose-leaf compilation of EU legislation and decisions affecting air transport).

powerful jurisdictions have had a substantial and quantifiable impact on the evolution and direction of the general body of international aviation law. The United States, which convened the negotiating conference for the Chicago Convention in November 1944, later pioneered the international air transport liberalization agenda known as "open skies," provoked the modernization of the international aircraft accident liability regime, and (through the Boeing Company and the Federal Aviation Administration (FAA)) has until recently been the sole decider of global best practices for safe and reliable aircraft manufacture. The EU, now with twenty-eight Member States, legislated a single EU aviation market in 1992. The single market combined the Member States' commercial airspaces into a unified sovereignty somewhat analogous to U.S. federal airspace and thereby (albeit without prior intent on the part of the legislators) caused the rise of the "low-cost" carrier phenomenon represented by Ryanair, easyJet, and others.[14] The EU has since externalized its commitment to liberalization by pursuing an Open Aviation Area policy (OAA) (its more muscular version of open skies) with several third countries, most notably the United States.[15] Where specific States (and subglobal organizations of States) have significantly shaped international aviation law, their influence will be discussed throughout the book.

1.3. A QUICK LOOK AT LEGAL THEORY

1.3.1. *Dominance of Doctrinalism*

This book is not wedded to any particular "theory" of law to explain (or speculate) why international aviation law has developed as it has, but we have chosen to refer to legal theory wherever it seems helpful to the reader's understanding. It must be said that neither international law in general nor international aviation law in particular has been the object of much introspective theorizing by the academy. Both fields have been dominated by doctrinal experts skilled in explicating the content of the law.[16] Most doctrinal

---

[14] Low-cost carriers now represent 40% of intra-EU capacity, a figure projected to reach between 45% and 53% by 2020. *See* European Commission Communication, *External Aviation Policy*, *supra* note 4, at 6.

[15] *See generally Developing the Agenda for the Community's External Aviation Policy*, COM (2005) 79 final (Mar. 11, 2005). For more on the OAA, see *infra* Chapter 3.

[16] This is not an unworthy pursuit given that the "teachings of the most highly qualified publicists of the various nations" are deemed by the Statute of the International Court of Justice to be a "subsidiary means for the determination of the rules of [international] law." Statute of the International Court of Justice art. 38(1)(d), Jun. 26, 1945 [hereinafter ICJ Statute], http://www. icj-cij.org/documents/. *See also* Michael Peil, *Scholarly Writings as a Source of Law: A Survey of the Use of Doctrine by the International Court of Justice*, 1 CAMBRIDGE J. INT'L & COMP. L.

scholars probably share the idealism of the late Columbia law professor Louis Henkin, who famously observed that "almost all nations observe almost all principles of international law and almost all of their obligations almost all of the time."[17] A domestic tax lawyer would recoil from such a proposition if its tenets were applied to the taxpaying citizenry of a State,[18] but for international lawyers it actually reflects a comforting assumption about the degree to which, and the reasons why, States comply with rules of international law.[19] Sometimes even doctrinalists, especially those working in general international law, are tempted to cross over from observation to promotion and to proselytize or advocate for the merits of their field and its usefulness to humanity. After the "realist" school of international relations emerged during the second half of the twentieth century,[20] it was left to pioneering doctrinalists such as Ian Brownlie to rebuff claims that international law was little more than impotent rhetoric.[21] Brownlie and others distilled a body of international law doctrine that was assumed, more often than proven, to serve as an exogenous constraint on State behavior. "Advocates" like Brownlie professed their faith in international law as *law*, ambitiously hoping that more international law or the "right" kind of international law (no matter how ill-defined) would yield positive outcomes ranging from universal respect for human rights to uninterrupted international peace and security.[22]

1.3.2. *Issue of State Compliance*

In the field of international aviation law, Henkin's assessment is probably close to the truth, although his statement lacks the power to explain a strong culture of State compliance.[23] Do States obey international aviation law because of a sense of moral obligation, or because the efficient and secure coordination of

---

136 (2012). For a comment on the authoritativeness of the writings of publicists, *see infra* note 74.

[17] LOUIS HENKIN, HOW NATIONS BEHAVE 47 (2d ed. 1979).

[18] A tax law professor who announced with satisfaction to students that "almost all citizens observe almost all principles of tax law and almost all of their tax obligations almost all of the time" might be accused of condoning tax evasion.

[19] *But see* John Strawson, *Introduction, in* LAW AFTER GROUND ZERO xi, xix (John Strawson ed., 2002) (arguing that, after the World Trade Center attacks, international law became a post-Westphalian "contested arena").

[20] *See generally* JACK DONNELLY, REALISM AND INTERNATIONAL RELATIONS (2000).

[21] *See generally* IAN BROWNLIE, PRINCIPLES OF PUBLIC INTERNATIONAL LAW (7th ed. 2008).

[22] *See id.*

[23] *See generally* Harold Koh, *Why Do Nations Obey International Law?*, 106 YALE L.J. 2599, 2655 (1997) (explaining several schools of thinking on the methods by which international law binds State actors).

transborder aviation operations simply cannot occur without it? As we will see, defectors from international air transport law regimes, whether the governing instruments are bilateral or multilateral, will suffer immediate economic and other consequences that cannot easily be remedied. That said, there are certain theoretical domains, beyond legal positivism (i.e., doctrinal law from identifiable sources), that a contemporary analysis of international aviation law should consider.

1.3.3. *Use of Economic Analysis*

Aviation law, at least in its domestic iteration, has long been the subject of economic analysis.[24] Starting with Michael Levine's pioneering 1965 critique of the now-defunct U.S. Civil Aeronautics Board's approach to economic regulation of the airline industry,[25] economics added coherence to aviation law scholarship during the 1970s and 1980s before eventually petering out.[26] This is not to say that economists did not continue to comment on aviation, only that the formal legal academy took little interest in attempting to make economics its primary analytical tool once the era of U.S. regulation had ended and eyes turned toward the international arena and the liberalization of cross-border air transport services. Some aspects of international aviation law always received scant attention from economists, particularly the private realm governing air carrier liability, despite the obvious economic consequences these rules have for the air transport industry as a whole.[27] In this book, we endeavor to include insights from the field of economics when they seem to explain the emergence (and shortcomings) of international aviation law, but we leave the strictly commercial aspects of airline economics to the side.[28] In Chapter 4, for instance, we look at the potential anticompetitive effects of international airline alliances that have received immunity from national

---

[24] The application of economic analysis to aviation law and policy emerged alongside the "Law & Economics" (L & E) movement of the 1960s and 1970s. Despite significant resistance within the legal academy, L & E remains the most successful interdisciplinary partnership between academic law and another academic field. *See generally* RICHARD POSNER, ECONOMIC ANALYSIS OF LAW (8th ed. 2011).

[25] *See* Michael E. Levine, *Is Regulation Necessary? California Air Transportation and National Regulatory Policy*, 74 YALE L.J. 1416 (1965).

[26] *See, e.g.,* ALFRED E. KAHN, THE ECONOMICS OF REGULATION: PRINCIPLES AND INSTITUTIONS (1981).

[27] *See infra* Chapter 7.

[28] For a useful introduction to commercial planning and business economics in the airline industry, see RIGAS DOGANIS, FLYING OFF COURSE: AIRLINE ECONOMICS AND MARKETING (4th ed. 2010).

antitrust rules. We do not, however, look closer at the complex revenue-sharing and marketing agreements that sustain these alliances.

1.3.4. *Rational Choice Theory*

More recently, a new generation of international law scholars has taken its cue from international relations theorists rather than from the orthodox, but theoretically limited, thinking of the doctrinalists.[29] Leveraging economic analysis and other rational choice methodologies, the new scholarship attempts to provide instrumental accounts of international law and compliance without recourse to traditional (but vague) concepts such as "legality" or "morality."[30] Rational choice adherents believe that in order to understand international law, scholars and students alike must go "behind" it to track, explain, and predict what they see as the largely self-interested behavior and motivation of States. Given the unavoidable economic and other State-interest implications of international aviation, rational choice theory opens up a richer methodology to understand and critique international aviation law. For example, the principle of "international Paretianism" – one of the conceptual products of this new literature – holds that States will not enter into international agreements unless they believe that they are made better off as a result of the transaction.[31] When applied to international aviation, the principle helps to clarify why, for example, an aviation power like the United States has eagerly entered open skies treaties that expand market access opportunities for its airlines, but is hesitant to commit to a global aviation emissions reduction agreement that would impose heavy financial burdens on those same carriers.[32] Moreover, as we will illustrate throughout the following

---

[29] For an early example, see Kenneth W. Abbott, *Modern International Relations Theory: A Prospectus for International Lawyers*, 14 YALE J. INT'L L. 335 (1989).

[30] Or, at least, this is the explanation for the field offered by neo-rationalists Jack Goldsmith and Eric Posner in *The New International Law Scholarship*, 34 GA. J. INT'L L. 463 (2006). Other scholars in the rational choice "mode" have attempted to offer more nuanced views that retain some of the "old thinking" on international law. *See, e.g.*, JOEL P. TRACHTMAN, ECONOMIC STRUCTURE OF INTERNATIONAL LAW (2008). For further examples of the different applications of rational choice theory in the field of international law, see ECONOMICS OF PUBLIC INTERNATIONAL LAW (Eric A. Posner ed., 2010); Symposium, *Rational Choice and International Law*, 31 J. LEGAL STUD. S1 (2002).

[31] *See* ERIC A. POSNER & DAVID WEISBACH, CLIMATE CHANGE JUSTICE 6 (2010). International Paretianism is derived from "Pareto efficiency" in normative economics, namely, the proposition that "[a] change is said to be superior if it makes at least one person better off and no one worse off." RICHARD A. POSNER, THE ECONOMICS OF JUSTICE 54 (pbk. ed. 1983).

[32] For further explanation, see Brian F. Havel & Gabriel S. Sanchez, *Toward a Global Aviation Emissions Agreement*, 36 HARV. ENVTL. L. REV. 351, 372–75 (2012).

chapters, rational choice can contribute also to a fuller understanding of other international aviation legal phenomena, ranging from the shortcomings of the Chicago Convention's dispute settlement machinery[33] to the loopholes that emasculate the "aviation crimes" treaties.[34]

1.3.5. An Integrated Approach

Despite some of the perceived shortcomings of rational choice theory, notably its alleged under-appreciation of the effects of government inertia and of the higher motivations of individual government officials,[35] our sense is that the benefits of its insights into a highly mercantile business like international aviation far outweigh the potential costs associated with its some of its simplifications. At the same time, we strongly resist the temptation to dispense with orthodox doctrinal analysis altogether. Only by understanding in the first place what the law of international aviation actually is, for example, through close inspection of its treaty provisions, can we or other scholars in this field begin to test the extent to which rational choice analysis – or any kind of interpretive theory – assists or hinders a more robust understanding of those rules.

1.4. PUBLIC AND PRIVATE INTERNATIONAL AVIATION LAW

1.4.1. Public International Aviation Law

Most of the content of international aviation law is generated by public international law, the legal system that governs the conduct of States and intergovernmental organizations. Public international law determines, *inter alia*, States' control over the airspace above their territories, their duties and powers to prevent and punish crimes aboard or against aircraft, and the level of market access they provide to foreign air carriers. The sources of public international law (reviewed in more detail below) include custom, treaties, general principles of law,[36] and, to a lesser extent, the decisions of international adjudicatory bodies.[37] These sources are sometimes referred to as "hard" international law on the assumption that they intrinsically carry

---

[33] *See infra* Chapter 3.
[34] *See infra* Chapter 5.
[35] *See generally* MICHAEL P. SCHARF & PAUL R. WILLIAMS, SHAPING FOREIGN POLICY IN TIMES OF CRISIS (2010).
[36] *See* RESTATEMENT (THIRD) OF FOREIGN RELATIONS LAW OF THE UNITED STATES § 102(1) (1987) [hereinafter RESTATEMENT (THIRD)].
[37] *See id.* § 103, cmt. B; *see also* ICJ Statute, *supra* note 16.

binding force. Hard law is sometimes contrasted with so-called soft law
international instruments, such as the U.N. Universal Declaration of Human
Rights, political statements, and agreements between States, that disclaim legal
effect. Soft law is generally not seen as having legal effect, although some
international jurists have argued that soft law still has normative force and
can be used to track State practice with respect to adducing customary international law. Others have argued that the hard/soft distinction is irrelevant with
respect to agreements between States and that the choice of one instrument
over another other is more likely to be informed by the perceived importance of
the proposed agreement, its effect on the internal legal systems of the parties,
and the costs of compliance.[38]

1.4.2. *More on Distinction Between Hard and Soft International Aviation Law*

While we will call attention to the hard law/soft law distinction at relevant
points throughout the book, readers should be aware that the distinction is in
practice sometimes more illusory than real in the realm of international
aviation. For instance, memoranda of understanding (MOUs) and diplomatic
notes, both of which are typically assumed by international jurists to be nonlegal instruments,[39] are routinely used by States to update or amend terms in
their aviation trade treaties (commonly referred to as air services agreements
(ASAs)).[40] Despite their alleged "sub-legality," these instruments have proven
to be an expedient and durable means of coordinating the terms of aviation
trade between States, mainly because defection by one party from these terms
would surely induce defection by the other to their mutual detriment. It is
unclear what compliance gains would accrue from "legalizing" such soft law
exchanges, especially because States have recourse in any event to several
mechanisms to modify, suspend, or terminate their hard law commitments.

---

[38] *See* JACK L. GOLDSMITH & ERIC A. POSNER, THE LIMITS OF INTERNATIONAL LAW 81–106 (2005).

[39] *See* Anthony Aust, MODERN TREATY LAW AND PRACTICE 20–22 (2000).

[40] Article 83 of the Chicago Convention provides that any contracting State can "make arrangements not inconsistent with the provisions [of the Convention]," that any such "arrangement" should be registered with the ICAO Council, and that the Council "shall make it public as soon as possible." Chicago Convention, *supra* note 11, art. 83. The vast majority of contracting States "do not consider [that] the requirement [in Article 83] extends to MOUs." THE OXFORD GUIDE TO TREATIES 59 (Duncan B. Hollis ed., 2012) (noting also that ICAO's registration rules include State/airline arrangements, a few of which have been registered). Nevertheless, ICAO has criticized the practice of States not filing air transport MOUs. *See* ICAO MANUAL, *supra* note 3, at 2.3–3 (emphasizing that "[f]ull compliance with the requirement of the Chicago Convention to file all agreements with ICAO could significantly increase badly needed transparency").

1.4.3. *Private International Aviation Law*

"Private international aviation law" is a handy but mildly misleading descriptor. It is intended to convey the idea that when certain legally significant transnational events – a catastrophic aircraft accident or the financing of a Boeing aircraft, for example – are affected by instruments of public international law (the Warsaw and Montreal conventions[41] for international aircraft accidents or the Cape Town Convention and Aircraft Protocol[42] for certain cross-border aircraft financing transactions), they are principally enforced or activated by non-State entities operating within national legal systems. The term is misleading because public international law instruments like the Chicago Convention also affect the operating privileges and commercial choices of non-State entities (where airlines are in private ownership, for example). The distinction lies in the identity of the parties and the ultimate forum for enforcement. Public international law instruments provide for State-to-State cooperation or dispute resolution, sometimes through bilateral treaties and sometimes at the multilateral level. In contrast, for "private" international law instruments (a lawsuit against an airline manufacturer for negligence, a creditor's action against a debtor or third party based on a registered security interest), the contracting States delegate enforcement to those parties directly involved in the underlying event and to those national courts that can claim jurisdiction under the relevant treaty.

1.4.4. *Private International Aviation Law and Airline Liability*

Thus, if a passenger on an Air Canada flight originating in Toronto and bound for Chicago is involved in an onboard accident outside Detroit, the applicable rules covering standard of liability, jurisdiction, and available defenses are not found in Michigan law or in U.S. federal rules, but rather have appeared in a series of international treaties and amending protocols that date as far back as 1929.[43] Although domestic courts are ultimately charged with adjudicating

---

[41] *See* Convention for the Unification of Certain Rules Relating to International Carriage by Air, *opened for signature* Oct. 12, 1929, 49 Stat. 3000, 137 L.N.T.S. 11 (entered into force Feb. 13, 1933) [hereinafter Warsaw Convention]; Convention for the Unification of Certain Rules for International Carriage by Air, *opened for signature* May 28, 1999, 2242 U.N.T.S. 350 (entered into force Nov. 4, 2003) [hereinafter Montreal Convention].

[42] Convention on International Interests in Mobile Equipment, Nov. 16, 2001, 2307 U.N.T.S. 285; Protocol to the Convention on International Interests in Mobile Equipment on Matters Specific to Aircraft Equipment, Nov. 16, 2001, S. Treaty Doc. No. 108–10, http://www.unidroit.org/english/conventions/mobile-equipment/aircraftprotocol.pdf.

[43] *See supra* note 41.

international air carrier liability claims, they do so under the provisions of international instruments. But those international agreements are not comprehensive. Jurisdiction-specific rules of procedure and evidence, along with canons of interpretation, are present in domestic proceedings as well. So, too, are jurisdiction-specific interpretations of key concepts that have been incorporated into international treaties: for example, the meaning of the term "accident" that appears in both the Warsaw and Montreal conventions.[44] Over the course of eight decades, the result has been contradictory rulings among courts in different States and operating within different legal traditions. At times, this quagmire of inconsistency has challenged fundamental conceptions of justice.

1.4.5. *Terminological Confusion*

There is considerable confusion about the use and meaning of the term "private international law." "Private international law" (generally the preferred term in civil law jurisdictions) is used interchangeably with "conflict of laws" or "choice of law" (generally the preferred terms in common law jurisdictions) to refer to the laws of a domestic legal system that determine which of two or more applicable State legal systems will apply to a given dispute between or among private parties where more than one legal system might apply. The study of transnational commercial relations between private parties and sometimes between private parties and sovereign States or State entities (i.e., legal relations other than those between sovereign States) has complicated the terminology. Some scholars have posited that those arrangements are most appropriately defined as a subset of private international law, distinguishable from the term's traditional application to conflict of laws.[45] Others have argued that legal instruments governing international transactions between private commercial actors are best described as a diluted or "privatized" version of "public international law" that in no way alters the traditional "conflict of laws" meaning traditionally attributed to "private international law."[46] Recognizing the differing viewpoints, in this book we

---

[44] *See infra* Chapter 7, Part 7.9.

[45] *See* John A. Spanogle, Jr., *The Arrival of International Private Law*, 25 Geo. Wash. J. Int'l L. & Econ. 477 (1992) (using the phrase "international private law" to distinguish the new subset of "private international law" from the traditional concepts associated with "conflict of laws").

[46] Ralf Michaels, *Public and Private International Law: German Views on Global Issues*, 4 J. Private Int'l L. 121 (2008) (observing that Germany has preserved a more rigorous demarcation between "public" and "private" international law than other States, many of which have allowed the two concepts to merge, despite maintaining the pretense of separation in Restatements and academia).

have chosen (when useful) to house this area of law under the much less contentious heading of "private transnational aviation law."[47]

1.4.6. Gray Zones of Public Regulation and Private Effects

Switching between public and private lenses to scrutinize international aviation law, while conceptually helpful, can also sometimes be distorting. The Warsaw/Montreal treaty-based liability system, for example, shows how public international aviation law and private transnational aviation law emerge from the same *public international law* instrument. Were it not for those treaties, classical "private" international aviation law would otherwise have developed organically within the legal culture of each State: domestic courts would have taken jurisdiction under locally based rules that apply to liability claims arising in both domestic and international air transport. The conflict of laws rules of the forum State (the *lex loci delicti*,[48] for example) would then apply the law and jurisprudence of another State, where appropriate.[49] But that idea of separate State liability rules has not shaped international aviation law.[50] And, even in areas where one would expect traditional private-party litigation (and traditional "private" international law) to predominate, such as in passenger disputes seeking restitution for cancellations, delays, or denied boarding, the United States and EU have moved away from private resolution of these disputes to

---

[47] Although private transnational aviation law today enjoys more coherence than at many points in its history, new proposals for an updated international instrument covering third-party surface damage arising from international air transport have again raised questions about the desirability of incursions by international law into private liability cases. *See infra* Chapter 7, Part 7.14.

[48] Literally, "the law of the place of the harm."

[49] Indeed, as discussed *supra* in Section 1.4.5, private international law is often considered to be no more than the application of a State's conflict of laws (or choice of law) rules, and this classical system is what applies internally to aircraft liability, for example, in the United States. *See* JOSEPH STORY, COMMENTARIES ON THE CONFLICTS OF THE LAW 10 (1834). But even stronger models of "extraterritorialization" of national laws can be imagined. Some authors have proposed that national courts apply an "amalgam" of domestic and foreign laws: *see generally* Graeme B. Dinwoodie, *A New Copyright Order: Why National Courts Should Create Global Norms*, 149 U. PA. L. REV. 471 (2000). The Court of Justice of the European Union seems recently to have endorsed the same kind of creativity. *See* Joined Cases C-509/09 & C-161/10, eDate Advertising v. X and Olivier Martinez v. MGN Limited (25 Oct. 2011), http://curia.europa.eu/juris/liste.jsf?language=en&num=C-509/09. Conflict of laws rules play a very minor part in the Warsaw/Montreal liability system, doing little more than recognizing that the procedural rules of the adjudicating (forum) court must govern. The system's substantive legal rules all come from the conventions.

[50] *See* GOEDHUIS, *supra* note 3, at 31 (noting that Warsaw Convention drafters rejected common rules regulating State conflict of laws because of difficulty of reconciling "different national legislation[]").

adopting so-called passenger rights regulations.[51] Similarly, the EU's inclusion of the airline industry in its carbon emissions trading scheme (ETS) extends a system of public regulation beyond the sovereign borders of the legislator (the EU) and affects private actors (EU and non-EU airlines and their passengers and shippers).[52] Neither the U.S. nor the EU passenger rights legislation, nor indeed the EU ETS, would be classified conventionally as an instrument of public international law. Yet each is an example of a system of public regulation (whether national or regional) that has predictable effects on the private conduct of international air transport and on the passengers and shippers who use it. Here, enforcement is by a public authority rather than by non-State private entities, but it is ultimately the latter who are affected. This arrangement is not dissimilar to the public/private arrangement that public international law establishes (through bilateral treaties) when States negotiate with foreign governments for market access and other economic privileges for their airlines. If States allowed airlines to conduct these kinds of negotiations directly with each other across borders, again we would have some difficulty in describing such a system as one that is definitively part of public international aviation law or private transnational aviation law.[53]

1.5. THE SOURCES OF INTERNATIONAL AVIATION LAW

1.5.1. *Traditional Sources of Public International Law*

As we have seen, some international aviation law rules (especially those affecting passenger and cargo liability and aircraft financing transactions) are actually the result of interpretive and adjudicative activity within national jurisdictions, but traditional public international law sources such as custom and treaties are overwhelmingly dominant in creating what this book regards as the modern body of international aviation law. Readers already familiar with the sources of public international law may still wish to examine the sections below to develop a better understanding of how international aviation law relies upon those sources. Unlike in other areas of international law, notably human rights, the role of custom in shaping the modern regulatory regime for international aviation can be assessed today as mainly historical.

---

[51] Note that the Warsaw and Montreal conventions, *supra* note 41, do have provisions on delays, but these are mostly not practicable for the average traveler. *See infra* Chapter 7, Section 7.12.7.
[52] *See infra* Chapter 6 (discussing the ETS).
[53] In the United States, such behavior would run afoul of the Logan Act, which forbids U.S. citizens from negotiating with foreign governments absent official authorization. *See* Logan Act, 1 Stat. 613 (1799) (codified as amended at 18 U.S.C. § 953 (2006)).

Just as public international law sources dominate over national sources of international aviation law, therefore, treaties dominate over custom when we assess the rule-generating capacity of public international law sources in modern international aviation law.

1.5.2. *Custom*

"Customary international law results from a general and consistent practice of [S]tates followed by them from a sense of legal obligation."[54] This belief held by States that they are acting out of an obligation imposed by international law, a belief commonly referred to by its Latin term *opinio juris*,[55] is notoriously difficult to infer and thus lies at the heart of many disputes over whether a particular practice has indeed crystallized as customary international law.[56] Further problems arise when determining the time horizon by which to determine State practice. Over a long enough expanse of time, few behaviors of States (and indeed, the existences of particular States themselves[57]) are likely to prove enduring. Changing economic, political, and social circumstances all contribute to the decision of States to act one way or another. Even so, some practices of States have more "stickiness" as custom than others.[58] For instance, the principle of State sovereignty, that is, a State's exclusive and independent control over its geographic territory, including over those persons who abide within that territory, has been recognized (with caveats) among Western States since at least the Treaty of Westphalia (1648) and by the world community since the establishment of the United Nations (U.N.) in 1945. Although modern sovereignty is increasingly defined through the perfectly rational paradox of its capacity to be given away,[59] that it exists in the first place

---

[54] RESTATEMENT (THIRD), *supra* note 36, § 102(2).

[55] Literally, the "sense of legal obligation."

[56] Unlike treaty-based norms, for example, custom is neither formally documented nor officially reported. Indeed, it is unsettlingly dependent for its articulation on the writings of international law scholars. What do these scholars (and the international lawyers who rely on them) look at to make their determinations? The catalog includes official government statements at international conferences, diplomatic exchanges, formal instructions to diplomatic agents, national and international court decisions, legislative measures, and even government press releases. *See* BROWNLIE, *supra* note 21, at 6.

[57] *See generally* NORMAN DAVIES, VANISHED KINGDOMS: THE RISE AND FALL OF STATES AND NATIONS (2012).

[58] *See* Koh, *supra* note 23, at 2655.

[59] *See* Brian F. Havel, *The Constitution in an Era of Supranational Adjudication*, 78 N.C. L. REV. 257, 327 (2000). An example of this rational paradox is the choice of a State to refrain from exercising its sovereign right to exclude foreign air carriers from its airspace by granting market access privileges in exchange for symmetrical rights for its own airlines to serve other State territories.

and is generally respected lends credence to the view that sovereignty is entrenched as customary international law. Other principles, such as the limit of territorial sovereignty over coastal waters and the duty of States to refrain from attacking and capturing another State's fishing vessels, are more ambiguous and subject to fluctuating State practices.[60]

1.5.3. *Role of Custom in International Aviation Law*

Customary international law has played a modest role in the development of international aviation law. Presumably, the principle of airspace sovereignty – captured in the medieval maxim *cuis est solum, eius est usque ad caelum et ad inferos* ("for whomever owns the soil, it is theirs up to the sky and down to the depths")[61] – is part of customary international law in that it represents a logical extension of the aforementioned principle of State sovereignty. Nevertheless, its fixed position in multilateral aviation agreements (dating back to the so-called Paris Convention of 1919[62]) obviates the need to rely on custom to assert that this doctrine actually exists in international law. Some might argue that the "nationality" rule in international aviation law, whereby airlines must be owned and controlled by citizens of their home States, is tantamount to a principle of custom. Although there are few "persistent objectors,"[63] the rule's crystallization as custom has been undermined by recent government initiatives to destabilize its operation (which include, most notably, its elimination within the twenty-eight-member EU).[64] Finally, piracy is included among a small list of nonderogable customary international law norms known as *jus cogens* ("compelling law").[65] Although piracy would seem to cover injurious attacks against air transport such as hijacking and sabotage, resistance to extending the piracy prohibition beyond maritime transport prompted a series of multilateral aviation crimes treaties beginning in the 1960s.[66]

---

[60] *See* GOLDSMITH & POSNER, *supra* note 38, at 59–78 (tracking changes in State practice in these areas over time and offering a rational choice explanation of those changes).

[61] *See* Herbert David Klein, *Cujus Est Solum Ejus Est ... Quousque Tandem?*, 26 J. AIR L. & COM. 237, 238–43 (1959).

[62] *See* Convention Relating to the Regulation of Aerial Navigation art. 1, *opened for signature* Oct. 13, 1919, 11 L.N.T.S. 173, *reprinted in* 30–1 ANNALS AIR & SPACE L. 5 (2005).

[63] If a State had persistently objected to the nationality rule's status as custom, that State presumably would not be bound by it.

[64] *See* Brian F. Havel & Gabriel S. Sanchez, *The Emerging* Lex Aviatica, 42 GEO. J. INT'L L. 639 (2011) (discussing this normative shift). *See also infra* Chapter 4, Part 4.4 (discussing recent erosion of the nationality rule).

[65] The list is contested, but at the beginning of the 21st century it likely also includes genocide and slavery, although not inarguably torture. *See* BROWNLIE, *supra* note 21, at 510–11.

[66] *See infra* Chapter 5.

1.5.4. *Treaties*

A treaty, as defined by the 1969 Vienna Convention on the Law of Treaties, is "an international agreement concluded between States in written form and governed by international law, whether embodied in a single instrument or in two or more related instruments and whatever its particular designation[.]"[67] It may seem circular that it takes a treaty to define a treaty, but the Vienna Convention is presumed to express what had become the customary international law rules governing the definition and interpretation of treaties. That is why the Vienna Convention's canons of treaty construction are generally taken as valid for all extant international legal agreements even though the Convention disclaims application to treaties ratified before it entered into force or to treaties concluded with one or more States that are not party to the Convention (including the United States[68]). While treaties share equivalent status to custom as a source of international law, in practice treaties are normatively superior in most instances because of linguistic concision and a capacity to express nuances, caveats, idiosyncrasies, exceptions, and particularities that the invariably general principles derived from custom cannot. Because the States that become parties to a given treaty likely had some input into the drafting of its terms, the instrument presumably expresses the interests of its adherents and therefore may be perceived as more legitimate than custom by the parties' internal political cultures. But this does not mean that treaties are always an ideal means to give fixity to inter-State collaboration. Broadly speaking, a treaty's effectiveness vis-à-vis a given end is inversely related to the number of its State parties. Whereas a bilateral treaty will often maximize concessions and opportunities between the two parties, multilateral agreements tend to suffer from a lowest common dominator effect that "waters down" key provisions in order to make the treaty palatable to the greatest number of potential parties.

1.5.5. *Role of Treaties in International Aviation Law*

It should come as no surprise, then, that treaties are the largest and most important source of international aviation law. The pivotal instrument is the 1944 Convention on International Civil Aviation[69] (known popularly as the

---

[67] Vienna Convention on the Law of Treaties art. 1(a), *opened for signature* May 23, 1969, 1155 U.N.T.S. 331.

[68] The United States does recognize, however, that the Convention states customary international law. *See, e.g.,* Fujitsu Ltd. v. Federal Express Corp., 247 F.3d 423 (2d Cir. 2001).

[69] *See* Chicago Convention, *supra* note 11.

"Chicago Convention"). The Convention has been ratified by more than 190 States and contains universal rules covering airspace sovereignty, aircraft registration and airworthiness, navigation, and global Standards and Recommended Practices (SARPs) for technical and safety harmonization. The Convention also creates a U.N. intergovernmental organ, ICAO, to foster technical cooperation in the international aviation industry. The Convention, however, does not organize or authorize the distribution and exchange of air traffic rights among States; that function is discharged bilaterally by a network (some have called it a labyrinth) of more than 4,000 ASAs. Nor is the Chicago Convention the only multilateral treaty that forms part of international aviation law. Multilateral agreements, some negotiated under the auspices of ICAO, cover areas as diverse as aviation security, aircraft financing, and the liability of air carriers to their passengers and cargo shippers. What may be more surprising is that these complex international agreements, which have almost always engendered significant political differences in their formation,[70] have yielded only a small quantum of inter-State legal disputes over the past sixty-plus years. From the perspective of rational choice, this relative legal quiescence may be owed to a perception of aviation's utility in a globalized world and a concomitant willingness to engage in political collaboration on issues affecting the cross-border movement of air transport.

1.5.6. *General Principles of Law*

Another recognized (albeit secondary) source of international law are "general principles common to the major legal systems of the world."[71] Recourse to general principles "may be important when there has not been practice by States sufficient to give the particular principle status as customary law and the principle has not been legislated by general international agreement."[72] It is not altogether clear, however, what criteria ought to apply in order to ascertain these principles. International law scholars and commentators generally hold to the view that conceptions of fairness and justice that are universally present in most of the world's legal systems (*e.g.*, good faith, *res judicata*, *audi alteram partem*, impartiality of judges) are general principles, though this may be

---

[70] Matthew Hoffman has described lawmaking through grandiose global agreements like the Chicago Convention, involving the majority of the world's nations, as "megamultilateralism." But he also believes that the era of megamultilateral treaty initiatives has passed. *See generally* Matthew J. Hoffmann, Climate Governance at the Crossroads: Experimenting with a Global Response after Kyoto (2011).

[71] Restatement (Third), *supra* note 36, § 102(1)(c). *See also* ICJ Statute, *supra* note 16, art. 38(c).

[72] Restatement (Third), *supra* note 36, § 102, cmt. l.

reflective of their liberal, Western democratic biases rather than a metaphysical insight into the nature of law. Often the discussion of general principles of law is limited to procedural matters within the context of international tribunals, although most international agreements that create such mechanisms (such as the Dispute Settlement Understanding of the World Trade Organization (WTO)[73]) provide a quite sophisticated set of procedural rules for their adjudicatory bodies to follow. Because formal dispute settlement plays only a minor role in international aviation law, divining the content of general principles is not a topic of importance for this field.

1.5.7. Judicial Decisions

The Statute of the International Court of Justice (ICJ) describes judicial decisions as a "subsidiary means for the determination of rules of [international] law."[74] The rapid expansion in transnational adjudicatory bodies since the close of World War II has led to a massive body of public international law jurisprudence, although not a great deal of this case law has import beyond the ruling tribunal. One possible exception might be made for the opinions of the ICJ itself (which is sometimes dubbed "The World Court"), although some commentators have perceived a marked decline in the Court's caseload and reputation in recent decades that may have impaired the persuasive force of its judgments.[75] In international aviation, a number of cases have been submitted to the ICJ – especially during the Cold War – but, for reasons discussed in Chapter 2, the Court has seldom issued a definitive ruling in aviation

---

[73] *See generally* Dispute Settlement Understanding, Ann. 2 to the WTO Agreement, *in* Final Act Embodying the Results of the Uruguay Round of Multilateral Trade Negotiations, *opened for signature* Apr. 15, 1994, 33 I.L.M. 1226.

[74] *See* ICJ Statute, *supra* note 16, art. 38(1)(d). Article 38 also lists "the teachings of the most highly qualified publicists of the various nations" as another subsidiary means. *See supra* note 16. Although some have attempted to aggressively expand this principle to mean that the *opinions* of the "qualified publicists" (i.e., international law scholars) themselves can serve as an independent source of international law, they do so in the face of long-held understandings concerning the limits of scholarly opinion in shaping international legal rules. *Cf.* Paquete Habana, 175 U.S. 677, 700 (1900) ("[T]he works of jurists and commentators . . . are resorted to by judicial tribunals, not for the speculations of their authors concerning what the law ought to be, but for trustworthy evidence of what the law really is.").

[75] *See* Eric Posner, *The Decline of the International Court of Justice*, *in* INTERNATIONAL CONFLICT RESOLUTION 111, 111 (2006) (analyzing the decline of the Court's caseload due to inconsistent application of international law and judicial bias); *see also generally* Eric Posner, *The International Court of Justice: Voting and Usage Statistics*, 99 AM. SOC'Y INT'L L. PROC. 130 (2005); Eric Posner & Miguel F. P. de Figueiredo, *Is the International Court of Justice Biased?*, 34 J. LEGAL STUD. 599 (2005).

matters.[76] Similarly, the WTO's dispute settlement body – which has jurisdiction over the few discrete aspects of trade in international air services in the WTO agreements[77] – has never adjudicated any dispute relating to that circumscribed subject matter jurisdiction.

1.5.8. *ICAO Council and Dispute Settlement*

The closest thing in international aviation law to a widely recognized dispute settlement body is the ICAO Council created under the Chicago Convention. Even so, States rarely submit disputes to ICAO, and the Organization never reached a legally binding decision in those few disputes that have been submitted. In November 2011, however, seventeen Member States submitted a complaint to the ICAO Council challenging the EU's proposed extension of its emissions trading scheme to non-EU carriers using EU airports.[78] The fact that ICAO is evidently structured as a deliberative body may explain why States have been more reluctant to initiate ICAO legal challenges than they have been, for example, in exploiting the consciously adjudicatory WTO dispute settlement body or the narrower International Tribunal for the Law of the Sea.[79]

1.5.9. *Judicial Enforcement of Private Transnational Aviation Law*

As already noted, international aviation law also has a significant "private" dimension, including the international rules on airline liability and (to a lesser extent) aircraft finance, that is adjudicated within national court systems. Accordingly, although these national decisions might not technically be part of international aviation law properly so-called, they nevertheless remain the only forum in which public international law treaties that create private transnational rights and obligations, in particular the Warsaw and Montreal conventions and the Cape Town Convention and Protocol, are judicially interpreted and applied. In examining decisions of national courts concerning liability issues, for

---

[76] *See infra* Chapter 2, Part 2.6. A notable exception is the extradition dispute between Libya and the United States following the 1988 Lockerbie bombing. *See* Questions of Interpretation and Application of the 1971 Montreal Convention Arising from the Aerial Incident at Lockerbie (Libya v. United States), Provisional Measures, 1992 I.C.J. 114, P 42 (Apr. 14, 1992).

[77] *See infra* Chapter 2.

[78] This significant dispute at the intersection of the laws affecting the environment and international aviation is considered in more detail *infra* in Chapter 6.

[79] *See* United Nations Convention on the Law of the Sea, *opened for signature* Dec. 10, 1982, 21 I.L.M. 1261. The UNCLOS Tribunal is narrower in the sense that it is a purely adjudicative body dedicated to the settlement of disputes arising under the Convention on the Law of the Sea, whereas the ICAO Council performs numerous other functions.

example, we will note those courts' willingness (or lack of it) to recognize and apply decisions by foreign domestic tribunals. This question is particularly challenging when one realizes that, in resolving conflicts between private persons, courts are looking at the same treaty terms within different legal traditions, such as Anglo-American common law and French Napoleonic civil law. To the extent that a local court will look to decisions of foreign courts for interpretive guidance, it is said to be acting on principles of international comity.[80]

1.6. THE ROLE OF INTERNATIONAL (AND A FEW NATIONAL) ORGANIZATIONS

1.6.1. *IGOs, NGOs, and "Super" National Bodies*

International (and a small number of national) organizations feature prominently in the development of both public and private international aviation law. They include international governmental organizations (IGOs) and international nongovernmental organizations (INGOs, though the "I" is typically dropped and we will follow that usage), as well as powerful national governmental authorities and trade associations (which we will call "super" national organizations) whose influence stretches well beyond their home country borders. Two prominent IGOs, the EU and U.N. (the latter through ICAO), have served as the most prolific and influential originators of modern international aviation law. NGOs like the International Air Transport Association (IATA), the Association of European Airlines (AEA), the International Air Carrier Association (IACA), the African Airlines Association (AFRAA), the Association of Asia Pacific Airlines (AAPA), the Latin American and Caribbean Air Transport Association (ALTA), the International Air Cargo Association (IACA), and the Air Transport Action Group (ATAG) have not only provided technical support for the industry but have also pioneered new ideas in transnational commercial regulation.[81] "Super" national organizations like the U.S. Federal Aviation Administration (FAA) and the U.S. airline trade association Airlines for America (A4A)[82] have been influencing the shape of law and policy not only within their significant domestic spheres but throughout the international air transport system.[83]

---

[80] *See* Hilton v. Guyot, 159 U.S. 113, 164 (1895).
[81] For a more complete listing of aviation-related NGOs, *see* ICAO MANUAL, *supra* note 3, at 3.9–1 to 3.9–3.
[82] A4A was known until December 2011 as the "Air Transport Association."
[83] The FAA sets U.S. aviation policy and is therefore naturally influential in the formation of global aviation policy. A striking example of the agency's reach was its establishment of the first national air safety oversight program for foreign airlines in 1991 (the precursor to similar EU

1.6.2. *IGOs: ICAO and the EU*

A critical taxonomic distinction can be drawn between IGOs and NGOs – the former have explicit power to adopt, through the consent of their members, binding international legal rules to govern aspects of international air transport. ICAO, for example, is empowered by its founding instrument, the Chicago Convention, to propose and negotiate not only amendments to that Convention, but also additional treaties covering aspects of international air transport not thematically present in the Convention.[84] ICAO also uses its treaty-based authority regularly to monitor and update the Convention's annexes containing SARPs for technical and safety harmonization among the Member States.[85] And although possibly outside its remit, the Organization has not been shy about convening air services trade conferences in an effort to expedite aviation liberalization.[86] The EU is even more agile in its lawmaking capacity. As a "supranational" organization,[87] its rules (adopted by EU institutions) are directly binding in the jurisdictions of its twenty-eight Member States.[88] The EU has created within its borders a single aviation market that is a commercial replica of the federalized airspace of

---

and ICAO programs): *see infra* Chapter 5, Part 5.3. The FAA's safety program expanded understandings of international aviation law to recognize that such external monitoring of non-national airlines could be consistent with the principle of airspace sovereignty and with the Chicago Convention regime.

[84] *See* Chicago Convention, *supra* note 11, pt. II (providing the rules and organizational structure of ICAO). Although the power to propose and negotiate treaties is not made explicit in the Chicago Convention, it can be inferred from a broad reading of Articles 44 ("Objectives" of ICAO) and 65 ("Arrangements with other international bodies"). *See* Chicago Convention, *supra* note 11, arts. 44 & 65. ICAO has been deeply involved in the creation of multilateral aviation crimes and air carrier liability treaties such as the Convention on Offences and Certain Other Acts Committed On Board Aircraft (Tokyo Convention) and the Convention for the Unification of Certain Rules for International Carriage by Air (Montreal Convention). *See infra* Chapters 5 and 7.

[85] The legal fog that has enveloped SARPs is discussed *infra* Chapter 2, Part 2.6.

[86] See ICAO, Air Services Negotiation Conference, http://legacy.icao.int/ican2011/. ICAO does not seem to have set any *a priori* limits to the topics for which it will provide a negotiating platform or become a treaty sponsor. For example, ICAO enrolled as the "Supervisory Authority" for the relatively arcane Cape Town Convention, establishing an international registry of aircraft security interests, despite the Organization's initial concern that the treaty was not a matter for public international aviation law. *See infra* Chapter 8, Part 8.8.

[87] *See* Wayne Sandholtz & Alec Stone Sweet, European Integration and Supranational Governance 1 (1998) (portraying the EU as a "supranational polity" that creates rules fully binding on its Member States within its domains of policy).

[88] Note that EU practice insists on capitalizing both "Member" and "State." *See* Treaty on the Functioning of the European Union art. 2, Sept. 5, 2008, 2008 O.J. (C 115) 47, *reprinted in consolidated form at* 2010 O.J. (C 83) 47. Croatia signed a Treaty of Accession to the EU on December 9, 2011, and became the 28th EU Member State on July 1, 2013.

the United States.[89] Eventually, it is likely that the EU will take autonomous responsibility for all international aviation relations with non-Members, but in the meantime it has already acted on behalf of all the Member States to negotiate a number of far-reaching ASAs with selected partners.[90] Additionally, the CJEU – which is responsible for adjudicating disputes arising under EU law – has handed down a number of landmark rulings that have dramatically influenced the direction and content of EU aviation law.[91]

1.6.3. *Other IGOs*

Other IGOs play a less direct role in injecting normative content into international aviation law, but are nonetheless influential within their respective spheres. The WTO, through its General Agreement on Trade in Services, technically has oversight over a handful of small subsectors of aviation-related services (repair and maintenance, sales, and ground-handling[92]), but remains excluded from applying its trade disciplines to "hard" economic areas such as airline market access and cross-border investment.[93] Despite these restraints, the WTO is nonetheless making a more meaningful contribution to the development of international aviation law through regular studies of trade in global air services and an interactive online ASA database guaranteed to fascinate aviation policy wonks.[94] The Organization for Economic Co-operation and Development (OECD) – an intergovernmental policy forum dedicated to liberalizing global trade[95] – has extensively analyzed the

---

[89] Unlike in the United States, however, air traffic management within the EU is not yet "federalized."

[90] Although many legal sources still refer to the "European Community" when discussing the EU's legal personality, the distinction was rendered obsolete following the Dec. 1, 2009 implementation of the Treaty of Lisbon, 2007 O.J. (C 306) 1, which affirmed the existence of a single juridico-political entity: the European Union. *See generally* Consolidated Version of the Treaty on the Functioning of the European Union, 2008 O.J. (C 115) 47. Throughout the course of the book, we will rely solely on the term "European Union" (or its EU abbreviation) and red-flag any substantive or cosmetic changes the Lisbon Treaty made to preexisting legislation or to CJEU case law.

[91] *See infra* Part 3.5.

[92] In reality, these subsectors await further inter-State agreements, and the practical effect of the WTO's oversight has been minimal. *See infra* Chapter 3, Part 3.6.

[93] *See* General Agreement on Trade in Services [GATS], Annex on Air Transport Services, Marrakesh Agreement Establishing the World Trade Organization, Annex 1B, Legal Instruments – Results of the Uruguay Round, *opened for signature* Apr. 15, 1994, 1869 U.N. T.S. 183, *reprinted in* 33 I.L.M. 1125, 1167.

[94] *See* WTO, Air Services Agreements Projector, http://www.wto.org/asap/index.html.

[95] The OECD is often labeled a "rich States' club" by virtue of its primarily American and Western European membership, but ironically it originated as the implementing organ for the

regulatory patterns of international aviation, and has been especially vocal in advocating liberalization of air cargo services.[96] In the Asia-Pacific region, the ten-member Association of Southeast Asian Nations (ASEAN) has been developing a series of treaties and protocols intended to create a free-trade zone for intraregional aviation services that is in part modeled on the EU template, although the project is deliberately incremental and is not expected to be complete before 2015.[97] Similarly, the African Union (AU) has attempted to foster air services liberalization on the African continent through the so-called Yamoussoukro Declaration, with mixed success.[98]

1.6.4. NGOs as Sources of "Law-Generating" Activity

It would be wrong to imagine, however, that only organizations comprised of governments and their representatives are capable of developing (and enforcing) normative standards for the international aviation industry. If law is considered in its broadest sense to include alternative or concurrent sites of law-generating (or at least "quasi" law-generating) activity,[99] then such behavior can also be identified among NGOs and even among consortia of private airlines. Indeed, there is a spirited debate among academics as to the normative power of these sites, and international aviation offers a number of telling examples supporting the idea that private actors can choose to self-regulate in ways that emulate the authority of a State-backed legal system.[100] To some extent, IATA, the global airline industry's most visible representative

---

U.S.-funded Marshall Plan to revive Europe's shattered economies after World War II. *See generally* Richard Woodward, The Organization for Economic Co-Operation and Development (2009). The OECD is self-conscious about its "rich" and geographically narrow reputation and has latterly added States from outside its dominant hemisphere, such as Chile. *See* Press Release, OECD, Chile Signs Up as First OECD Member in South America (Jan. 11, 2010).

[96] *See, e.g.*, OECD, Principles for the Liberalisation of Air Cargo (2000), http://www. oecd.org/dataoecd/7/9/1806687.pdf.

[97] *See* Alan Khee-Jin Tan, *The ASEAN Multilateral Agreement on Air Services: En Route to Open Skies?*, 16 J. Air Transp. Mgmt. 289 (2010).

[98] *See* Charles E. Schlumberger, Open Skies for Africa: Implementing the Yamoussoukro Decision (2010). For other examples of regional multilateral agreements, *see* ICAO Manual, *supra* note 1, at 3.2–5 to 3.2–6.

[99] *See* Roderick Macdonald, *Unitary Law Re-form, Pluralistic Law Re-Substance: Illuminating Legal Change*, 67 La. L. Rev. 1113, 1140 (2007).

[100] The legal literature abounds with speculation as to the emergence of a modern *lex mercatoria* ("law merchant") resembling the autonomous system of legal norms and courts evolved by medieval merchants plying their trade across the European continent. While dissenters argue that a modern *lex mercatoria* is simply a fancy reworking of the law of contracts, and therefore ultimately dependent on the State for its authority, the more impressive point is surely that private actors use their party autonomy to bind themselves into specific (and mutually

organization,[101] has at various times in its history provided a normative infra-structure for the pricing and routing of international air services that had at least tacit support from governments which saw no alternative to its ratemaking and interlining functions.[102] IATA has also straddled the lawmaking divide between IGOs and NGOs by brokering agreements between its member airlines and the U.S. Government to waive liability caps once found in international treaty law.[103] With a self-proclaimed tripartite mission to "represent, lead, and serve the airline industry," the Association has evidently developed a unique relationship with world governments that has allowed it to operate in significant ways as a site for autonomous regulatory activity.[104] Sometimes, too, aviation NGOs have tried to occupy a space where they were clearly not acting normatively but which allowed them to nudge government officials into fundamentally rethinking how international aviation should be regulated. The most prominent example of this kind of influence was the AEA's policy paper in 1999 calling for a single U.S./EU airspace. The paper set the early negotiating agenda for what became the game-changing 2007 U.S./EU Air Transport Agreement.[105] Other aviation and nonaviation NGOs that continue to make important contributions to regulatory policy for international aviation include the Airports Council International, the Air Line Pilots Association, the International Chamber of Commerce, and the Transatlantic Business Dialogue. We conclude by noting the work of the World Economic Forum, host organization of the famous Davos conference, which has promoted several important initiatives in international aviation policy (including a biofuel response to reducing aviation carbon emissions and a so-called smart visa to encourage tourist-driven air travel) through its Global Agenda Council on New Models of Travel and Tourism.[106]

enforceable) commercial relations across entire swathes of private enterprise. The phenomena of code-sharing (*see infra* Chapter 4, Part 4.6) and global airline alliances (*see infra* Chapter 4, Part 4.5) have been mentioned as representative examples of a modern *lex mercatoria*. *See* Havel & Sanchez, *supra* note 64, at 659–61.

[101] *See* Brian F. Havel & Gabriel S. Sanchez, *International Air Transport Association, in* Handbook of Transnational Economic Governance Regimes 755, 755–64 (Christian Tietje & Alan Brouder eds., 2009).

[102] *See* Brian F. Havel, In Search of Open Skies 120–21 (1997).

[103] *See infra* Chapter 7, Part 7.5.

[104] More recently, IATA persuaded a number of governments to initial an IATA-generated document that arguably committed them to ignoring their own treaty rules on ownership and control of foreign airlines with any other State that agreed to do so on a reciprocal basis. *See infra* Chapter 4, Section 4.4.8.

[105] *See* AEA, Towards a Transatlantic Common Aviation Area: AEA Policy Statement (1999).

[106] *See* World Econ. F., Global Agenda Council on New Models of Travel & Tourism 2012, http://www.weforum.org/content/global-agenda-council-new-models-travel-tourism-2012.

2

The Foundations of Public International Aviation Law

2.1. INTRODUCTION TO THE CHICAGO CONVENTION

2.1.1. *Background to the Chicago Convention*

The cornerstone instrument of public international aviation law is the 1944 Convention on International Civil Aviation, popularly known as the "Chicago Convention" in honor of its birthplace.[1] Even as the Second World War was reaching its fiery climax in the European and Asian theaters, United States (U.S.) President Franklin D. Roosevelt – responding to a British initiative – brought fifty-four Allied and neutral States to Chicago during the winter months of 1944 with the goal of developing an ordering mechanism for the world's airspace and the nascent international air transport industry.[2] The United States hoped that it could steer the negotiations toward affirming a (relatively) free market in aviation services, one which would give the U.S. airline industry – at the time the most developed and technologically sophisticated in the world – the opportunity to dominate the global marketplace. That ambition was not to be realized. Instead, the Convention's scope was curtailed to solve technical coordination problems relating to, among other things, aircraft registry, air traffic management, cross-border recognition of licensing certificates, and the kinds of taxes and charges that could be imposed on international air services.

---

[1] Convention on International Civil Aviation, *opened for signature* Dec. 7, 1944, 61 Stat. 1180, 15 U.N.T.S. 295 (entered into force Apr. 4, 1947) [hereinafter Chicago Convention]. Popularizing treaties through use of the names of the cities in which they were signed is a common practice in international aviation law, as we will see in the course of this book. But the name of the city may not appear in the treaty itself (*cf.* the Cape Town Convention discussed in Chapter 8).

[2] Alone among the Allied Powers, Saudi Arabia and the USSR did not participate in the Conference. It is also worth noting that 72% of the current Convention signatories were not present in Chicago in 1944.

2.1.2. *States, Not Airlines, Define Chicago's Commercial Environment*

Where the Convention does directly implicate economic rights for air carriers, it is typically in an illiberal key. States, not their airlines, are vested with the right to define international aviation's commercial environment. That fact is not terribly surprising if one recalls the Chicago Convention's historical context. Memories of the 1929 worldwide economic collapse were still fresh, and economic advisors on both sides of the Atlantic were flirting with the supposed benefits of a Soviet-style command economy.[3] Even the United States, eventually a bastion of neoliberalism and globalization, tempered the market freedoms of its industrial sectors in the late nineteenth century when Congress passed the Sherman Antitrust Act[4] and established the Interstate Commerce Commission.[5] That regulatory impulse spread to the privately owned U.S. air transport industry, which since 1938 had been placed under the economic supervision of a public agency, the now-defunct Civil Aeronautics Board (CAB).[6] European States, on the other hand, opted to couple regulation of their major airlines with outright public ownership.

2.1.3. *Overview of Topics*

In this chapter we detail the Chicago Convention's most salient features, including its provisions for the establishment and operation of the ICAO. Throughout, we will also note how the Convention is augmented by national aviation regimes, particularly those of the United States and European Union (EU). We will also delve further into how modern public international aviation law developed in the aftermath of the ideological clashes at the conference that framed the Chicago Convention. By giving context to international aviation law's foundational treaty, we seek to provide a better understanding of its compromises and limitations. The same holds true for ICAO. Despite its endurance as one of the longest-standing international governmental organizations (IGOs), ICAO has had only limited effect on liberalization of the international air transport market. But that does not mean that ICAO is a failing or superfluous

---

[3] *See generally* Daniel Yergin & Joseph Stanislaw, The Commanding Heights: The Battle for the World Economy (rev. ed. 2002).

[4] On the economic, political, and social background to the Sherman Act, see 1 Philip E. Areeda & Herbert Hovenkamp, Antitrust Law ¶ 100–04 (3d ed. 2006).

[5] *See generally* Richard D. Stone, The Interstate Commerce Commission and the Railroad Industry: A History of Regulatory Policy (1991).

[6] *See generally* Paul Stephen Dempsey, *The Rise and Fall of the Civil Aeronautics Board – Opening Wide the Floodgates of Entry*, 11 Transp. L.J. 91 (1979).

institution. It has assiduously developed universal safety and technical standards for air transport while serving as a forum for the Chicago Convention's 191 contracting States to engage each other on international air transport concerns. We begin, however, by glancing back at what we might call the prehistory of modern international aviation law.

2.2. THE "PREHISTORY" OF THE CHICAGO CONVENTION

2.2.1. *From Paul Fauchille to the Paris Convention of 1919*

We should not flatter the delegates at the 1944 Chicago conference by intimating that their Convention, the most ambitious and comprehensive aviation treaty in history, sprang Athena-like from their heads in December 1944. International jurists had been at work on the problem of regulating transborder aerial movements since as early as 1900 when the French jurist Paul Fauchille suggested that a code of air navigation be created by the Institut de Droit International (one of those rare instances where the legal profession was *ahead* of technological innovation).[7] That same year, The Hague Peace Conference promulgated the International Declaration Prohibiting Launching of Projectiles and Explosives from Balloons[8] – demonstrating that States even in aviation's earliest days were already sensitive to its national security and sovereignty implications. Fauchille's concerns gained new traction in 1903 following the Wright Brothers' historic flight in Kitty Hawk, North Carolina. The French Government subsequently followed up on The Hague Declaration by summoning a conference in 1910 specifically to examine the question of airspace sovereignty. Although the Paris conference was considerably influenced by Fauchille's ideas, the delegates reached no consensus, and indeed the participating jurists felt hamstrung by a lack of guiding scholarship.[9] Ultimately, it took World War I – the first major conflict to involve aircraft as instruments of aggression – to spur European

---

[7]   *See* Arthur K. Kuhn, *The Beginnings of Aerial Law*, 4 AM. J. INT'L L. 109, 111 (1910). The Institut de Droit International was founded in Ghent, Belgium, in 1873.

[8]   *See* Declaration Prohibiting Launching of Projectiles and Explosives from Balloons, *opened for signature* Jul. 29, 1900, 1 Bevans 270 (entered into force Sept. 4, 1900). The Declaration, which placed a five-year moratorium on the practice of using balloons as military bombers, was renewed by the International Declaration Prohibiting the Discharge of Projectiles and Explosives from Balloons, *opened for signature* Oct. 18, 1907, 1907 A.T.S. 14 (entered into force Nov. 27, 1909). For a recent case discussing whether "balloons" still qualify as "aircraft" in international aviation law, *see infra* note 12.

[9]   A quite different context prevailed for international maritime law, where even before the era of global conventions a settled consensus developed around Grotius's concept of the *mare liberum*, the free access of all nations to navigation of the high seas. *See infra* note 34.

powers in 1919 to draft an international treaty on air transport. The indelible legacy of the Convention Portant Réglementation de la Navigation Aérienne ("Convention Relating to the Regulation of Aerial Navigation"), dubbed the Paris Convention, was the codification of airspace sovereignty: "[t]he High Contracting Parties recognize that every Power has complete and exclusive sovereignty over the airspace above its territory."[10] Although the United States declined to ratify the Convention, opting instead for aviation treaties covering its "near abroad" in Latin America,[11] thirty-two States eventually ratified – a remarkable circle of recognition given the technological and territorial limitations of air transport at that time.

2.2.2. Novel Features of the Paris Convention

Despite its brief life span, the Paris Convention had lasting effects on public international aviation law, including the Chicago Convention. The Convention, for example, introduced the concept of global technical uniformity that would also underpin its Chicago successor, pioneering the use of special annexes dedicated to standards of airworthiness for airlines and certificates of competency for pilots. It also established ICAO's institutional antecedent, the *Commission Internationale de Navigation Aérienne*, an independent body charged with fostering cooperation and harmonization in technical matters, disseminating information on air navigation, and rendering advice on matters submitted by the contracting States. The Paris Convention is notable, also, for containing the first internationally accepted definition of "aircraft," indicating that such devices as airships, gliders, free balloons, and helicopters were also covered by the terms of the treaty. The Chicago Convention later telescoped the definition, dropping the list of aerial conveyances in favor of a simple affirmation that an aircraft is "any machine that can derive support in the atmosphere from the reactions of the air."[12] ICAO – at the behest of its member States – honed this

---

[10] *See* Convention Relating to the Regulation of Aerial Navigation art. 1, *opened for signature* Oct. 13, 1919, 11 L.N.T.S. 173, *reprinted in* 30–1 ANNALS AIR & SPACE L. 5 (2005) (entered into force May 31, 1920) [hereinafter Paris Convention].

[11] *See generally* Brower V. York, *International Air Law in the Americas*, 3 J. AIR. L. 411 (1932) (discussing the history and terms of the 1926 Ibero-American Convention and 1928 Havana Convention).

[12] Chicago Convention, *supra* note 1, Annex 1. *See also* Laroche v. Spirit of Adventure (UK) Ltd., [2009] EWCA (Civ) 12 (Eng.) (in which Lord Justice Dyson held that the "natural and ordinary meaning" of the word "aircraft" would include a recreational hot air balloon under U.K. legislation applying the Warsaw Convention liability system (*see infra* Chapter 7) to domestic carriage by air; responding to the objection that hot air balloons could not realistically be used for international air transport as that form of carriage is understood in the Warsaw Convention,

phrasing even further in 1967 by defining an aircraft as "any machine that can derive support in the atmosphere from the reactions of the air *other than the reactions of the air against the earth's surface.*"[13] In layperson's terms, therefore, a hovercraft is not an "aircraft" under international law.[14]

2.2.3. *Regionalism of the Paris Convention*

The Paris Convention should not be adjudged a failure despite the manifest regulatory advances that the Chicago Convention would make slightly more than two decades later. Two U.S.-backed aviation accords – the 1926 Ibero-American Convention and the 1928 Havana Convention – transplanted the Paris Convention's terms to a pan-American setting,[15] and as noted, Chicago's intent and broad design were substantially indebted to its French forerunner.[16]

Lord Justice Dyson observed that "[b]efore the invention of the aeroplane, [balloons] were *the* means of transport by air, sometimes across borders").

[13] *Id.* Annex 13 (emphasis added). *See* I. H. Ph. Diederiks-Verschoor, An Introduction to Air Law 6 (8th rev. ed. 2006). For ICAO's most recent endorsement of this definition, see International Civil Aviation Organization, Proposal for Annex 19 and Related Consequential Amendments to Annexes 1, 6, 8, 11, 13, and 14, Letter of the Secretary General of the Air Navigation Commission and Attachments, Ref. AN 8/3–12/42 (Jun. 29, 2012), at A-13.

[14] *See* Chicago Convention, *supra* note 1, Annex 7. ICAO has not, however, produced a decisive answer as to how many angels can dance on the head of a pin. On how to answer this centuries-old conundrum, see Dorothy L. Sayers, The Lost Tools of Learning (1961), http://www.gbt.org/text/sayers.html.

[15] Unlike the Paris Convention, the Havana Convention had no annexes or continuing supervisory commission or regulatory body. *See* Robert M. Kane, Air Transportation 361 (2003). The Ibero-American Convention contemplated an independent commission, but such an entity never materialized, in part because Spain, along with Argentina and other Latin American States, gained admission to the Paris Convention's regulatory body. Unlike the Paris Convention, the Havana Convention had no annexes or continuing supervisory commission or regulatory body. *See* Kane, *supra.*

[16] Although under Article 2 of the Paris Convention all contracting States undertook (in peacetime) "to accord freedom of innocent passage" above their territories to the aircraft of all other contracting States, in reality Article 15 of the Convention limited that apparently broad grant by requiring (as the Chicago Convention would later) that States must "consent" to the establishment of all international airways. *See* Paris Convention, *supra* note 10, arts. 2 & 15. Admittedly both provisions appeared to be confined to "flyover" rights, but the requirement of consent was still narrower than what otherwise might have been accorded: a right of passage (including stops) subject only to restrictions a State might consider necessary in the interests of safety. In any event, the Chicago Convention made the concessionary principle of prior State consent for all flight operations (including transit over airspace) explicit. For background on the possible meanings of Articles 2 and 15 of the Paris Convention, see Daniel Goedhuis, Air Law in the Making 22–27 (1938) (condemning Article 15 as a restraint on the general principle of free passage and likely to impede "the increasing economic importance of air traffic"). Incidentally, the Paris Convention (like the Chicago Convention) contained no indication of the legal mechanism by which States should exchange commercial access to each other's airspaces.

Although some commentators criticized the United States for weakening the Paris Convention by withholding ratification and opting instead to support regional aviation compacts, the technological reality of the 1920s and 1930s understandably limited the vision of policymakers as they looked at air transport's international commercial potential. Cross-border air transport was entirely intra-regional, and the United States had little interest in compromising its international aviation interests to make treaty deals with faraway European States. With the coming of World War II and heavy investment in substantially improving the size and range of aircraft (investment that would lead eventually to the jet age), regionalism could no longer be an effective option. The Paris Convention, along with its inter-American stablemates, had to yield to a new order.

2.3. THE COSMOPOLITANISM OF THE CHICAGO CONVENTION

2.3.1. *A Cosmopolitan Tenor*

In a tenor that can be described as "cosmopolitan," the Chicago Convention's Preamble announces the treaty's intents and purposes:

> WHEREAS the future development of international civil aviation can greatly help to create and preserve friendship and understanding among the nations and peoples of the world, yet its abuse can become a threat to the general security; and
> WHEREAS it is desirable to avoid friction and to promote that co-operation between nations and peoples upon which the peace of the world depends;
> THEREFORE, the undersigned governments having agreed on certain principles and arrangements in order that international civil aviation may be developed in a safe and orderly manner and that international air transport services may be established on the basis of equality of opportunity and operated soundly and economically;
> Have accordingly concluded this Convention to that end.[17]

Thus, the Preamble reflects an ascendant faith in international institutions held by many governments in the West after two global wars. Peace would be the dividend of strengthened cooperation, especially in trade and economic

Presumably, as in the post-1945 period, bilateral agreements between the contracting States would be the "default" norm. In fact, few intergovernmental agreements were concluded in the period between the Paris and Chicago treaties, in part because of the small volume of international air transport activities and in part because commercial flights virtually ceased during World War II. *See* ICAO, Manual on the Regulation of International Air Transport 2.0–1, Doc. 9626 (2nd ed. 2004).

[17] Chicago Convention, *supra* note 1, pmbl.

matters. Even the United States, reflexively isolationist since rejecting Woodrow Wilson's project for a League of Nations,[18] was finally willing to champion levels of international cooperation unimaginable at any other point in human history. While the United Nations (U.N.), the Bretton Woods institutions,[19] and the General Agreement on Tariffs and Trade (GATT) would become the most visible emanations of the new mid-century internationalism, the Chicago Convention came first. Unlike preceding public international aviation law treaty instruments, the Convention is distinguished by its universality. With 191 State parties and its own U.N.-affiliated organization (ICAO) to steer technical cooperation and (to a limited extent) to resolve disputes, the Chicago Convention is surely one of the most effective multilateral agreements in the modern era of international law.

2.3.2. A Successful Treaty

The success of the Chicago Convention may appear surprising, given international aviation's fraught history of inter-State disagreement (a history that we will revisit many times in this book). But the vitality of the Convention becomes easier to understand in light of its substantive scope. Unlike human rights treaties, for example, the Convention imposes no burden on States to produce a "public good" for their own citizens;[20] there is no legal obligation under the treaty for countries to provide their citizens with a certain quantum of international air services. In other respects, the Convention reaffirms behaviors and recognitions already adhered to by its State parties, notably the principle of airspace sovereignty.[21] Where the Convention does impose positive duties on its parties or requests that they refrain from certain behaviors, their willingness to do so is perhaps best explained by the relatively low costs of these impositions compared to their manifest benefits.[22]

---

[18] U.S. involvement in the Second World War was driven more by the attack on Pearl Harbor and President Franklin D. Roosevelt's political maneuvering than by any national desire for military engagement. *See generally* ANDREW ROBERTS, THE STORM OF WAR: A NEW HISTORY OF THE SECOND WORLD WAR (2009); *see also* John M. Schleusser, *The Deception Dividend: FDR's Undeclared War*, 34 INT'L SECURITY 133–65 (2010).

[19] These institutions include the International Monetary Fund and the five financial and development organizations that comprise the World Bank Group.

[20] *See generally* Eric A. Posner, *Human Rights, the Laws of War, and Reciprocity* (John M. Olin L. & Econ. Working Paper No. 537 (2d ser.), Sept. 2010).

[21] *See* Chicago Convention, *supra* note 1, art. 1.

[22] The premise of our argument here, as the reader will quickly suspect, is largely that of rational choice theory. The treaty's longevity can be explained by the theories of other jurists, of course, including the so-called global legalists who have been criticized as having "an excessive faith in

A State that adheres to the Convention presumably wants to offer its citizens (and the citizens of other States) access to international air transport services that serve its territory. The State will therefore be interested in resolving baseline coordination problems that may hinder the provision of those services.[23] Thus, for example, to the extent that the inward and outward operations of foreign States' air carriers are allowed (and that, again, is a choice for each State to make), the legal standard in the Convention is broadly to provide air navigation and airport services to meet ICAO's common technical standards, and to do so in accordance with basic principles of nondiscrimination in the provision of such services[24] or in levying takeoff and landing charges.[25]

2.3.3. *A Logic of Coordination*

That logic of coordination (and harmonization) is especially apparent in the Convention's treatment of pilot licenses and airworthiness certificates for airlines.[26] If each State were unsure whether its licensing provisions would be recognized by foreign governments or were forced to customize licensing criteria to meet the diverse (and perhaps idiosyncratic) standards of other States, the cost of the licensing regime would inflate precipitously while yielding few, if any, benefits. By working through ICAO to install a universal licensing framework, States bypass many of these costs. While the process of norm-creation in international law can sometimes risk making "universal" synonymous with "lowest common denominator," in the context of the Chicago Convention, those States that hold to the highest standards in matters such as licensing and safety (e.g., the United States and the EU Member

---

the efficacy of international law," believing it to have "value for its own sake" independent of any instrumental value to States. ERIC A. POSNER, THE PERILS OF GLOBAL LEGALISM xii (2009). Among other things, global legalists would invoke the moral necessity of States keeping their promises to one another, *see generally* Eric A. Posner, *Do States Have a Moral Duty to Obey International Law?*, 55 STAN. L. REV. 1901 (2003) (arguing against this assumption), or that adherence to the treaty is part of the "cosmopolitan duty" of its parties, *see generally* Jack L. Goldsmith, *Liberal Democracy and Cosmopolitan Duty*, 55 STAN. L. REV. 1667 (2003) (analyzing and critiquing that point of view). Global legalists, in other words, do not shirk from conflating moral and positivist analysis. They are less likely, however, to be able to add to the putative moral imperative of obeying treaties a richer secular explanation of *why* States adhere when they adhere and defect when they defect.

[23] *Cf.* JACK L. GOLDSMITH & ERIC A. POSNER, THE LIMITS OF INTERNATIONAL LAW 86–87 (2005) (applying this logic to international communications standards).
[24] *See* Chicago Convention, *supra* note 1, art. 28.
[25] *See id.* art. 15.
[26] *See generally id.* art. 33.

States) have historically wielded the economic power and influence to align the treaty's common standards with their own.[27]

2.4. THE HISTORICAL IMPACT OF THE CHICAGO CONVENTION

2.4.1. *Conflicting Agendas and the Triumph of Managed Trade*

The two overarching purposes of the Chicago conference when it convened on November 1, 1944, were to make arrangements for the establishment of provisional world air routes and services and to set up an interim council to collect, record, and study data concerning international aviation. The participants arrived at the conference with different agendas. The Americans, supreme in civil air transport, advocated open competition. The British proposed an international organization to coordinate air transport, to apportion the world's air routes, and to decide on frequencies and tariffs.[28] Australia and New Zealand offered the most imaginative solution, which Professor Michael Levine treated with retrospective alarm as a harbinger of "international socialism": the creation of a single world airline.[29] But by the time the delegates had finished their parleys in Chicago, their Convention would have very little to say directly on the shape of a new commercial order. As we will discuss at length in Chapter 3, hard economic rights and privileges ("traffic

---

[27] Sometimes even this is not enough. The EU, for example, has unilaterally developed a "blacklist" for airlines that fail to meet not only the safety standards established by the Chicago Convention, but also those established under "relevant [EU] law." *See* Commission Regulation 2111/2005, Establishment of a Community List of Air Carriers Subject to an Operating Ban within the Community and on Informing Air Transport Passengers of the Identity of the Operating Air Carrier, and Repealing Article 9 of Directive 2004/36/EC, 2005 O.J. (L 344) 15; *see also* Commission Regulation 473/2006, Laying Down Implementing Rules for the Community List of Air Carriers Which Are Subject to an Operating Ban within the Community Referred to in Chapter II of Regulation (EC) No. 2111/2005 of the European Parliament and of the Council, 2006 O.J. (L 84) 8. Whether this practice is compatible with EU Member State commitments under the Chicago Convention is, at best, ambiguous. The U.S. approach mirrors that of ICAO: instead of blacklisting individual airlines, the Federal Aviation Administration (FAA), under its International Aviation Safety Assessment (IASA) program, evaluates the compliance of foreign civil aviation authorities with ICAO standards. States that receive a Category 2 (noncompliant) rating from the FAA are prohibited from expanding services to the United States, but existing services are not affected.

[28] *See* BRIAN F. HAVEL, BEYOND OPEN SKIES: A NEW REGIME FOR INTERNATIONAL AVIATION 100 n.5 (2009). Ambitious projects for global or pan-regional airline operating companies or intergovernmental public bodies were not a new idea in 1944: *see, e.g.,* ROBERT NEALE LAWSON, A PLAN FOR THE ORGANIZATION OF A EUROPEAN AIR SERVICE (1936).

[29] Michael Levine, *Scope and Limits of Multilateral Approaches to International Air Transport, in* ORGANISATION FOR ECONOMIC CO-OPERATION AND DEVELOPMENT, INTERNATIONAL AIR TRANSPORT: THE CHALLENGES AHEAD 75, 87 n.6 (1993).

rights") were relegated to two ancillary accords also negotiated at the Chicago conference, the so-called Two Freedoms and Five Freedoms agreements.[30] The latter of these two treaties, which would have opened up a transnational network of traffic rights allowing air carriers to freely move passengers, cargo, and mail across the globe, failed to receive more than a handful of ratifications. As such, international air services became the subject of tightly managed bilateral trade – a practice that in large measure continues to this day.

2.4.2. *Clashing Interests of the United States and Europe*

The clash of interests at the Chicago conference was unsurprising. "VE Day" (Victory in Europe) was still five months away when the delegates convened; Europe was still enduring the ravages of war. The industrial sectors of the European Allied Powers were in ruins, and those parts that did function were geared almost exclusively toward the war effort. The U.S. industrial base, on the other hand, managed to exit the war largely unscathed. Military aircraft could easily have been retooled for commercial air services, providing U.S. airlines with an enduring structural advantage over the Europeans. That advantage can be framed in the language of economic theory as "absolute," and was built on U.S. access to key inputs like aircraft and mechanical support.[31] To catch up, European airlines would need sustained subsidization. European States feared (perhaps rightly) that their airlines would never match those of their U.S. competitors, an especially unpalatable outcome at a time when air carriers were being viewed as embodiments of State prestige rather than just commercial actors. Larger macroeconomic concerns were also at work. The world had not yet fully recovered from the impact of the Great Depression when World War II began and, for Europe in particular, the magnitude of the conflict exacerbated the effects of a lingering economic

---

[30] *See generally* International Air Services Transit [Two Freedoms] Agreement, *opened for signature* Dec. 7, 1944, 59 Stat. 1693, 84 U.N.T.S. 389; International Air Transport [Five Freedoms] Agreement, *opened for signature* Dec. 7, 1944, 59 Stat. 1701, 171 U.N.T.S. 387.

[31] The concept of absolute advantage should not be confused with the theory of "comparative advantage." The former is a measure of what a particular State is best at from a production standpoint; the latter concerns where a State can most efficiently direct its productive resources given the existence of international trade. For instance, the United States may have had an absolute advantage over every State in the world in providing international air services, but could possibly have used a certain portion of its productive inputs for air services (e.g., technology and labor) in other, more lucrative, sectors. As such, the United States would be better off reducing its production of international air services and allowing other countries' airlines to meet the market demand. *See generally* CONCISE ENCYCLOPEDIA OF ECONOMICS (David R. Henderson ed., 2007); *see also* INTERNATIONAL ENCYCLOPEDIA OF THE SOCIAL SCIENCES 1–2 (William A. Darity ed., 2d ed. 2008).

malaise. Under the sway of economist John Maynard Keynes, Europe was disposed toward a model of central planning or control over key segments of its industrial base, the "commanding heights" in Vladimir Lenin's resonant phrase.[32] Indispensable sectors like coal, steel, and transportation were thought to be so integral to State prosperity that they simply could not be left to the "perennial gale of creative destruction" wrought by the free market.[33] In Europe, that ideological leaning led to direct public ownership over international airlines. The United States, although insouciant about the idea of private ownership of its aviation providers, kept custody of their commercial operations (what routes they could fly, how frequently, and with what capacity) through the regulatory artifices of the CAB. To the extent that U.S. air carriers could deliver international services that conformed to the amorphous standard of the "public interest," regulators were willing to tolerate their functioning as (relatively) independent participants in the market. The challenge that the United States faced at the Chicago conference was how to transform commercial potential into actual market dominance.

2.4.3. *Deflecting Criticisms of the Chicago Convention's Outcome*

As already noted, strong opposition to the U.S. pro-market position resulted in a treaty that mostly avoids the hard task of creating a universal structure for the distribution of economic rights and privileges. Thus, there would be no global commercial airspace analog to the *mare liberum* ("freedom of the high seas").[34] That fact has prompted many analysts over the past six decades to

---

[32] *See* YERGIN & STANISLAW, *supra* note 3, at xii.

[33] CHARLES A. SCHUMPETER, CAPITALISM, SOCIALISM, AND DEMOCRACY 84 (1975).

[34] Early advocates of a *mare liberum* regime for airspace would have granted balloons and aircraft the right to travel freely anywhere, including above sovereign territory, allowing sovereign control only of airspace proximate to the surface for purposes of self-defense. The difference is largely contained in the contrasting views of the nature of property rights in airspace. Under *mare liberum*, Grotius's idea is that the sea cannot be occupied, and therefore cannot be possessed. It is common property to be used by all. Some analogized the concept to airspace, arguing that it is impossible to occupy and therefore possess an expansive portion of airspace, even if it is directly above land over which a State does exert territorial control. Stuart Banner's book argues that the analogy to the sea fell out of favor because of safety and security concerns, suggesting that aircraft flying above populated land present certain risks and dangers to those below the aircraft (including State military installations) that are not present in maritime travel. Thus, it was concluded that a State's sovereign authority over land should extend upward to the airspace above the territory the State controls. *See generally* STUART BANNER, WHO OWNS THE SKY?: THE STRUGGLE TO CONTROL AIRSPACE FROM THE WRIGHT BROTHERS ON 42 (2008) ("[W]as the atmosphere like the ocean, a zone through which anyone could pass, regardless of nationality? Did the sovereign power of the nation-State extend upward, or was it confined to the surface of the earth?").

condemn the Chicago Convention as a failure and, even more critically, as an enduring hindrance to international air transport liberalization. The first charge is overstated, as discussed in Part 2.3: the final treaty instrument negotiated in Chicago resolved (or attempted to resolve) a number of key coordination problems for air safety and navigation that are fundamental to the operation of global air services.

2.4.4. *The Chicago Convention Did Not Hinder Later Liberalization*

The second charge, however, is spurious. Although it is true that the post-Chicago world saw the rise of a highly restrictive bilateral trade in air services, that outcome was not foreordained by the Chicago Convention itself. States, not the Convention, created the bilateral system[35] – a point that will receive more elucidation in Chapter 3. Further, the U.S. decision to compromise with conference participants and to relegate traffic rights to supplementary treaty instruments (the aforementioned Two and Five Freedoms agreements) was not an irrational concession to protectionist trade pressures. Resolving the coordination challenges addressed in the Convention, along with establishing ICAO, were goals worth pursuing for their own sake; insisting that trade concessions be made part of the bargain could have doomed the Chicago conference to deadlock or yielded a document so freighted with compromises as to be valueless. From a present-day vantage point, the absence of comprehensive economic provisions from the Chicago Convention appears providential. Given the inherent complications involved in renegotiating or amending multilateral treaties, had the Convention specified the level of air services trade concessions States must provide to the other contracting parties (likely a low threshold given the economic attitudes that prevailed at the time), it might have been extremely difficult for the United States and EU to pursue their bilateral international aviation liberalization initiatives in the 1990s and 2000s.[36] In other words, the Chicago Convention might have had the effect of adopting only a particular set of substantive *minima*[37] that would have survived long after the market skepticism evident at the time of its drafting.

---

[35] *Cf.* Peter P. C. Haanappel, *The External Aviation Relations of the European Economic Community and of the EEC Members into the Twenty-First Century, Part II,* 14 Air L. 122, 141 (1989).

[36] *See supra* Chapter 1, n. 70, commenting on how the Chicago Convention comes from an era of "megamultilateralism" that has probably ended.

[37] The notion of substantive *minima* has been primarily used in international intellectual property law, but it occasionally appears in other contexts. *See* Dinah Shelton, *Human Rights and the Environment: What Specific Environmental Rights Have Been Recognized,* 35

2.4.5. *The Chicago Convention's Significant Economic Impact*

Nor did the Chicago conference entirely fail in its principal treaty to specify terms with significant economic implications for the international aviation industry. Rather, as we will discuss, the delegates agreed on a number of fundamental propositions related to, for example, airspace sovereignty, the scope and nature of State regulatory authority, cross-border recognition of aircraft registration and markings, international safety and technical harmonization, and the formation and functioning of ICAO. All of these components of the Chicago Convention continue to bear upon the conduct of global airline operations. Without universal standards related to air traffic management procedures, for instance, it would be enormously costly (as well as dangerous) for airlines to fly across national and regional boundaries. By articulating a framework for solving flight coordination challenges, the Chicago Convention facilitates global air services. The Convention does not, however, provide a comprehensive economic regulatory schema for the industry.

2.5. THE CORE ELEMENTS OF THE CHICAGO CONVENTION

2.5.1. *Airspace Sovereignty: Articles 1 and 2*

Like its antecedent, the 1919 Paris Convention, the Chicago Convention gives primacy to the principle of airspace sovereignty. That principle, which is a presumptive extension of the customary international law doctrine of State sovereignty, has often been expressed through the maxim *cujus est solum, ejus est usque ad caelum et ad inferos* ("for whomever owns the soil, it is theirs up to Heaven and down to Hell"[38]). Oftentimes misidentified as a part of classical Roman law, the phrase's origins are, in fact, medieval.[39] It is important not to take the expression too literally (it does, after all, have absurd consequences if

---

DENV. J. INT'L L. & POL'Y 129, 164 (2006). Its meaning is constant in all contexts, however: it refers to a minimum level of substantive rights or protections required by an international treaty. In the intellectual property setting, the term refers to the minimum protections that a treaty requires to be inserted into domestic legal systems, whereas here we are using the term more expansively to refer to a minimum level of concessions that could have been granted directly by the treaty itself, that is, the Chicago Convention.

[38] The quote, minus the *et ad inferos* (which is often omitted), is probably best cited to *Bury v. Pope*, Cro. Eliz. 118, 78 Eng. Rep. 375 (1587). Banner has described how the established common law concept provided an intellectual basis upon which the State sovereignty regime was constructed, largely for safety and security reasons. *See generally* BANNER, *supra* note 34, at 4–41 (2008).

[39] *See* JAMES W. HARRIS, PROPERTY & JUSTICE 76 (1996).

one does so[40]) or assume that it serves as a colorful substitute for what is in the text of the Convention itself. Article 1 declares only that "every State has complete and exclusive sovereignty over the airspace above its territory"; there is no extension "up to Heaven," which is the province of the 1967 Outer Space Treaty.[41] As to where a State's airspace ends and outer space begins, although international law has furnished no definitive answer, the Karman Line – which lies at an altitude of 62 miles above the Earth and represents the point where the atmosphere becomes too thin for aeronautical purposes – has been asserted as the upper limit of airspace sovereignty.[42] The actual scope of a State's territory under the Chicago Convention is defined in Article 2 as "the land areas and territorial waters adjacent thereto under the sovereignty, suzerainty, protection or mandate of each State."[43] Further clarity is provided to that open-ended description by the U.N. Convention on the Law of the Sea, which limits a State's territorial waters to twelve nautical miles off its coast.[44] For the airspace "[o]ver the high seas," where no sovereign control is exercised, Article 12 of the Chicago Convention notes that the treaty itself provides the rules in force.[45]

2.5.2. *A Concessionary Principle of Market Access: Article 6*

Article 6 of the Chicago Convention perfects the restrictive logic of the airspace sovereignty principle through a concessionary principle of market

[40] *See* BANNER, *supra* note 34, at 89 (quoting Chicago lawyer Carl Zollmann's observation that, taken literally, the *cujus est solum* maxim would make the center of the earth "the most disputed territory imaginable" because all property rights on the earth's entire surface would eventually converge when extended far enough downward; in addition, the maxim would grant rights to owners of land that extended upward to include distant planets).

[41] *See* Treaty on Principles Governing the Activities of States in the Exploration and Use of Outer Space, including the Moon and Other Celestial Bodies, *opened for signature* Jan. 27, 1967, 610 U.N.T.S. 205. The related question of where a landowner's airspace rights end and the State's begin has never been definitively answered, although landowners surely possess air rights. *See* BANNER, *supra* note 34, at 252–58 (discussing *United States v. Causby*, 328 U.S. 256 (1946), in which the U.S. Supreme Court for the first time imposed a uniform nationwide rule of aerial trespass).

[42] *See* Dean N. Reinhardt, *The Vertical Limit of State Sovereignty*, 72 J. AIR L. & COM. 65 (2007).

[43] Chicago Convention, *supra* note 1, art. 2.

[44] *See* United Nations Convention on the Law of the Sea (UNCLOS), art. 3, *opened for signature* Dec. 10, 1982, 21 I.L.M. 1261. In the 18th and 19th centuries, the territorial waters were defined more or less by the distance of a cannon shot, the customary line being three nautical miles.

[45] Article 12 of the Chicago Convention requires that States establish and enforce rules of flight for aircraft operating above their territory. It provides further that "[o]ver the high seas, the rules in force shall be those established under this Convention." Because flights operating over the high seas will not be subject to the rules of operation established by any State, rules pertaining to such operations are set out in Annex 2 of the Convention.

access. Thus, "[n]o scheduled international air service may be operated over or into the territory of a contracting State, except with the special permission or authorization of that State, and in accordance with the terms of such permission and authorization."[46] This is not only an application of *noli me tangere* ("touch me not")[47] sovereignty by States to the airlines of the world, however.[48] There is also a strong national security component to the Article. Given aviation's capacity to penetrate the territorial integrity of a State as no mode of transportation had heretofore allowed, governments understandably wanted to limit access to the airspace over their territories to prevent activities such as unauthorized photographing of military installations. In the intervening decades, that concern has lost much of its salience. Satellites and high-resolution photography make aerial photography less important; anyone with an Internet connection has free access to global satellite imagery on websites such as Google Earth. Additionally, improvements in air traffic management technology have proven sophisticated enough to monitor and keep aircraft away from sensitive areas.[49]

2.5.3. *Restricted or Prohibited Zones: Article 9*

Even so, States still have a compelling interest in maintaining national security and in protecting their citizens. Hence, Article 9 of the Chicago Convention allows States – "for reasons of military necessity or public safety" – to establish restricted or prohibited zones above their territories so long as these limitations are applied uniformly to the airlines of the Convention's contracting parties.[50] In exceptional circumstances or where public safety demands it, Article 9 also permits a State to "temporarily restrict or prohibit flying over the whole or any part of its territory," again on the condition that

---

[46] Chicago Convention, *supra* note 1, art. 6. The use of the term "scheduled" in Article 6 is not accidental. Article 5 of the Convention provides rights for nonscheduled (i.e., charter) services "to make flights into or in transit non-stop across" the territory of another contracting State "and to make stops for non-traffic [i.e., noncommercial] purposes without the necessity of obtaining prior permission, and subject to the right of the State flown over to require landing." States may still, however, place restrictions on where nonscheduled services may fly for reasons of safety.

[47] *John* 20:17 (Vulgate).

[48] *See generally* MARK MAZOWER, GOVERNING THE WORLD: THE HISTORY OF AN IDEA (2012) (discussing how traditional "Westphalian" sovereignty is arguably curtailed by a modern doctrine of intervention by other States when a State abuses its sovereignty by subjecting its own population to violations of global humanitarian norms).

[49] *See* U.S. GEN. ACCOUNTING OFFICE, AIRLINE COMPETITION: IMPACT OF CHANGING FOREIGN INVESTMENT AND CONTROL LIMITS ON U.S. AIRLINES, GAO/RCED-93-7, at 14–15 (1992).

[50] Chicago Convention, *supra* note 1, art. 9.

the limitation is applied uniformly to all contracting States' airlines.[51] Two of the most visible deployments of Article 9 authority were the shutdown of U.S. airspace following the 9/11 terrorist attacks and the closure of large segments of EU airspace after the "Volcanic Ash Crisis" in April 2010.[52]

2.5.4. Reasons for a Treaty-Based Airspace Sovereignty

None of the provisions discussed up to now is controversial. Some might argue that they are superfluous given that the customary international law doctrine of State sovereignty seems, with only modest tweaking, to provide States with plenary control over their respective airspaces. Even so, there are still good reasons for States to use a treaty like the Chicago Convention to crystallize the doctrine of airspace sovereignty. In a bilateral scenario, for example, State A may subjectively believe that airspace sovereignty applies only with respect to landing or taking off from the territory of another State and therefore authorize its airlines to overfly State B – while State B, taking a more robust construction of the principle as its guide, may interpret the overflight as an encroachment upon its sovereignty and use military force to deter any further "intrusions." By entrenching airspace sovereignty, the Chicago Convention allows States to avoid these pitfalls of ambiguity, although it must be said that the Convention's approach to sovereignty is not (ultimately) absolutist. Article 9, for instance, imposes some modest restrictions on the scope for discrimination among third States that is afforded to a State that desires to close part or, in cases of emergency, all of its airspace. State A cannot close the airspace over a particular area to States B and C while allowing State D's airlines to continue flights over the excluded zone. That curbing of sovereign choice makes sense given that States do not want their own airlines to be subjected to discriminatory airspace closures by other States.[53]

2.5.5. Regulatory Scope and Harmonization: Articles 11 and 12 and the Annexes

While providing contours to the concept of sovereignty, the Chicago Convention also contains provisions that purport to clarify the regulatory

---

[51] *Id.*

[52] Both actions clearly fell under the terms of Article 9 of the Chicago Convention. *See* Ruwantissa I. R. Abeyratne, *Responsibility and Liability Aspects of the Icelandic Volcanic Eruption*, 35 Air & Space L. 281, 283 (2010) (confirming that the EU volcanic ash shutdown was an exercise of Article 9 powers).

[53] *See generally* Peter P. C. Haanappel, Law and Policy of Air Space and Outer Space: A Comparative Approach 45 (2003) (discussing closure of U.S. and Canada airspaces under Article 9 after the World Trade Center attacks in September 2001).

reach of a State over aircraft registered in its territory and also to establish territorial and substantive limits on the regulations that may be imposed on another State's aircraft operating in its airspace. Article 11 of the Convention grants each State the authority to devise "laws and regulations" relating to "the admission to or departure [of aircraft] from its territory" and the "operation and navigation of such aircraft while within its territory," subject to the limitations that such laws and regulations cannot conflict with any provision of the Convention itself and that they are applied "without distinction as to nationality."[54] Article 12 requires a State to ensure that all aircraft operating within its territory – foreign or domestic – obey these aviation laws and regulations while also ensuring that all aircraft registered in its territory obey the regulations of any other State over which they are flying. Article 12 further obligates all contracting States "to keep [their] own [aviation] regulations ... uniform, to the greatest possible extent, with those established from time to time under [the] Convention."[55] The referenced Convention regulations are the rules, standards, and recommended practices set forth in its eighteen annexes.[56] Additional articles covering the permissible scope of customs searches, entry and clearance regulations, and preventive measures to limit the spread of diseases are contained in the Convention as well.[57]

2.5.6. *Tax Treatment of the International Airline Industry: Article 15*

There is no controversial issue that divides government tax collectors and the modern international airline industry more than the industry's apparently favorable tax treatment under Articles 15 and 24 of the Chicago Convention. Article 15, which covers "airports and similar charges," has moved to the foreground as States have adopted so-called eco-charges or green taxes to offset the purportedly harmful environmental effects of aircraft carbon emissions.[58] Article 15 permits States to levy nondiscriminatory charges for the use of airport and air navigation (air traffic management) facilities, subject to a

---

[54] Chicago Convention, *supra* note 1, art. 11.

[55] Chicago Convention, *supra* note 1, art. 12. For a more detailed account of how Articles 11 and 12 function in relation to the EU's attempt to regulate global airline emissions, see Chapter 6, Section 6.4.2.

[56] A full list and description of the annexes is available in ICAO, THE CONVENTION ON INTERNATIONAL CIVIL AVIATION: ANNEXES 1 TO 18 (no date given), http://www.icao.int/ icaonet/anx/info/annexes_booklet_en.pdf. Although a detailed treatment of each annex is beyond the scope of this book, those that are relevant to particular topics will be given further treatment in the appropriate sections of the work. For discussion of the forthcoming Annex 19, *see infra* Chapter 5, Section 5.3.6.

[57] *See* Chicago Convention, *supra* note 1, ch. II *passim*.

[58] *See infra* Chapter 6, Section 6.4.2.

general exception which provides that "[n]o … charges [i.e., other than charges imposed for the use of airports and air navigation facilities] shall be imposed by any contracting State in respect solely of the right of transit over or entry into or exit from its territory of any aircraft of a contracting State or persons or property thereon."[59] Although not a paragon of clear draftsmanship, the text of Article 15 has been interpreted by the Convention's State parties, acting through ICAO, to permit only the imposition of charges (which may also be called dues, fees, or taxes) specifically to recover the costs to the charging State of providing facilities and services to international civil aviation.[60] A general charge, such as a "green" tax, that is unrelated to the provision of services would arguably be a charge imposed in respect "solely" of the right of transit over or entry into or exit from the State, and thus would be impermissible under the Convention.[61] In Chapter 6 we will return to Article 15, which was scrutinized closely by the Court of Justice of the European Union (CJEU) in a recent case challenging the legality of the EU emissions trading scheme.[62]

2.5.7. *Another Rule on Tax Treatment: Article 24*

Article 24, which sits among a small group of provisions that deals with common customs and immigration procedures, provides an excise tax exemption regime for fuel, lubricating oils, spare parts, regular equipment, and aircraft stores that arrive in a State on board an international flight and are retained on the aircraft

---

[59] Chicago Convention, *supra* note 1, art. 15.

[60] *See* ICAO, *ICAO Policies on Charges for Airports and Air Navigation Services*, para. 1, ICAO Doc. 9082/7 (7th ed. 2004).

[61] Problematically, economically pressed States feel free to designate airline or aircraft charges as "eco" or "green" taxes but to sweep revenues into the general treasury rather than using them to offset environmental pollution, which would be a purpose that arguably might satisfy the "facilities and services" test in Article 15. Even the EU emissions trading scheme has been accused of being a mere revenue-gatherer for the EU Member States. In a speech before the Association of Asia Pacific Airlines, Brian Simpson MEP, Chair of the European Parliament's Committee on Transport and Tourism, is reported to have said the following: "And yet, within the EU, governments are keen to press ahead because they desperately need the money. They won't say that – oh no – they will claim it's to help the environment, just as they do with [the U.K.] Air Passenger Duty [APD]. But let's be under no illusions here – both [the EU emissions trading scheme] and APD are being used as revenue streams for hard-up governments and not for environmental protection measures." *See* Karen Walker, *EU MP: Europe Will Not Back Down on ETS*, Air Transport World Daily News, Nov. 7, 2011, http://atwonline.com/operations-maintenance/news/eu-mp-europe-will-not-back-down-ets-1104.

[62] Case C-366/10, The Air Transport Ass'n of America, American Airlines, Inc., Continental Airlines, Inc., United Airlines, Inc. v. the Sec'y of State for Energy and Climate Change, 2010 O.J. C-260/12, referred by U.K. High Court of Justice, Q.B. Div. (Admin. Ct.).

until its departure from the State.[63] After many decades of quiescence, Article 24 was also thrust into the spotlight by the recent CJEU judgment. The Court ruled, in effect, that Article 24 is not infringed by an emissions trading scheme where airlines surrender a quantum of emissions allowances that is determined for each flight by the amount of fuel consumed. We will return to Article 24, in the context of emissions trading schemes, in Chapter 6.

2.5.8. *Facilitating Air Navigation: Articles 25–28*

Articles 25–28 of the Convention address various coordination problems with respect to facilitating international air navigation. A State is obligated to provide air traffic navigation services to any aircraft of another contracting State it allows to transit to, from, or over its territory and to harmonize such services "in accordance with the standards and practices *recommended or established* from time to time" in the Convention's annexes.[64] Where aircraft are in distress or an accident occurs, the State that is the *situs* is obligated to provide assistance and to institute an accident inquiry.[65] To the extent that these universal standards are properly applied, they not only reduce the need (and cost) for air crews to master variant air traffic management practices, but also minimize the risk and expense of accidents. Airlines will feel confidence in international route development if they can plan for the absence of idiosyncratic air navigation systems and the presence of reasonable emergency support in each contracting State. Pilot inability to communicate effectively with air traffic controllers can have disastrous consequences. The 1977 Tenerife airport disaster involved a runway collision of two Boeing 747s and the deaths of 583 passengers and crew. The accident was caused, in part, by a breakdown in communications protocols between local controllers and the pilots.[66]

---

[63] Chicago Convention, *supra* note 1, art. 24.

[64] *See* Chicago Convention, *supra* note 1, art. 28 (emphasis added). Although the "established" and "recommended" terminology clearly exists in the text of the Article, in practice ICAO has chosen "standards" and "recommended practices," collectively known as SARPs, as the distinguishing terms for ICAO guidelines. Standards are those specifications considered necessary for the safety or regularity of international air navigation, while recommended practices are those deemed merely desirable. *See infra* text accompanying notes 119 & 120. Contracting States that fail to conform to an existing standard are compelled by Article 38 of the Convention to report the noncompliance to ICAO. Neither compliance, nor reporting of noncompliance, is compulsory for recommended practices. For more on ICAO Standards and Recommended Practices, see *infra* Part 2.6.

[65] *See* Chicago Convention, *supra* note 1, arts. 25–26.

[66] *See* Final Report and Comments of the Netherlands Aviation Safety Board on the Investigation into the Accident with the Collision of KLM Flight 4805, Boeing 747–206B, PH-BUF and Pan American Flight 1736, Boeing 747–121, N736PA at Tenerife Airport, Spain on 27 March 1977,

2.5.9. *Uniform Documentation, Technical Specifications, and Licensing: Articles 29–33*

The Chicago Convention, in its fifth chapter, creates uniform rules with respect to the type of documents aircraft are required to carry when engaged in international services, establishes technical specifications for aircraft radio equipment, and provides for the establishment of minimum universal standards for and mutual recognition of aircraft and personnel (pilot) licensing.[67] One of the chief incentives for promulgating these international standards was to reduce duplication costs. Imagine if a major international air carrier such as United were compelled to have its aircraft licensed by each country to which, from which, or over which it flies. Even though United could likely bring itself into compliance with multiple licensing regimes, the process would still raise its costs and those of its passengers. Moreover, once the initial congregation of States that negotiated the Chicago Convention ratified the treaty and agreed to baseline rules and standards on licensing (rules and standards are adjustable over time in the relevant annexes to the Convention), little incentive remains for these founding parties or for States acceding later to the treaty to defect. Doing so would deny a defecting State's airlines the cost-saving benefits of the universal rules and sour the defector's aeropolitical relations with all other States that are parties to the Convention.[68]

2.5.10. *Aircraft Registration and Nationality: Articles 17–21*

Chapter 8, in the context of aircraft financing, offers a detailed discussion of the registration and nationality of aircraft. The discussion will also examine the conceptual misalignment, briefly noted at the end of this section, that attributes potentially separate "nationalities" to airlines and aircraft.[69] For now it is useful to provide a summary of the Chicago Convention's relevant provisions on

---

http://www.project-tenerife.com/nederlands/PDF/finaldutchreport.pdf. *See generally Nova: The Deadliest Plane Crash* (PBS (U.S.) television broadcast 2006).

[67] *See* Chicago Convention, *supra* note 1, ch. V *passim*. Although ICAO has pursued its charge under the Chicago Convention to promulgate global standards in these technical and licensing areas, there has been a number of issues on which individual contracting States (or a regional organization of States) were the initial movers and ICAO then acted more in a responsive, harmonizing role. One current example is the recent action by regulators in the United States and EU to implement new scheduling rules to combat pilot fatigue. *See* Press Release, European Aviation Safety Agency, EASA Proposes New Harmonized Rules to Avoid Flight Crew Fatigue (Oct. 1, 2012); Press Release, Federal Aviation Administration, FAA Issues Final Rule on Pilot Fatigue (Dec. 21, 2011).

[68] *Cf.* GOLDSMITH & POSNER, *supra* note 23, at 86–87.

[69] Chicago Convention, *supra* note 1, art. 17.

aircraft registration. The Convention's core doctrine with respect to aircraft is contained in Article 17: "Aircraft have the nationality of the State in which they are registered."[70] Although the Convention does not quite go so far as to say that an aircraft registered in a particular State's territory is part of that territory, the importance of attaching the nationality of an aircraft to a State cannot be overstated. An aircraft, no matter where it is operating across the globe, remains under the regulatory control of its home State of registry, subject to the proviso inserted by Article 11 that once the aircraft enters the sovereign airspace of another State, it must adhere also to that State's navigational and operational rules.[71] Although some might see the aircraft nationality rule as a legally appropriate extension of long-standing maritime "flagging," whereby ships must bear the flag of their country of registry, Article 17 is supported also by a freestanding rationale. Imagine if Article 17 did not exist – or, rather, that the Convention mandated that an aircraft should absorb the nationality of any State over which it happens to be flying. That could subject the United fleet (along with passengers and crew on board), for example, to one body of criminal, civil, and social law and legislation when a United aircraft is departing Chicago and to an entirely different set of legal rules when it passes over United Kingdom (U.K.) airspace on approach to London. And what about flights over the high seas? Does the airspace above the high seas constitute a "lawless zone"? Subsequent chapters of this book will discuss other tenets of international aviation law that sometimes limit or qualify the regulatory principle implicit in Article 17, but the consequence of embedding that provision in the Convention is that there is never a moment in the life of an aircraft where it escapes a governing body of law. At the same time, Article 17 provides a (sometimes contentious) basis for States to intervene abroad on behalf of aircraft registered in their territory. An extreme example of such an intervention involved the botched 1985 storming by an Egyptian special forces team of an Air Egypt flight that had been hijacked to Malta, resulting in fifty-six civilian and two crew deaths.[72]

2.5.11. *State-Based Aircraft Registration: Articles 18–19*

With respect to the rules governing aircraft registration itself (including the transfer of registrations from State to State), the Convention cedes regulatory

---

[70] *Id.*

[71] *See* Chicago Convention, *supra* note 1, art. 11.

[72] Clearly, one ostensible legal justification for that Egyptian military action within Maltese territory was that the plane was registered in Egypt, although presumably the on-board presence of Egyptian citizens and the fact that the aircraft belonged to the Egyptian government were also relevant. *See* U.S. v. Rezaq, 134 F.3d 1121, 1126 (D.C. Cir. 1998) (recounting the tragic outcome of the raid).

authority and latitude to the contracting States.[73] As with vessels operating subject to maritime law, aircraft must "bear [their] appropriate nationality and registration marks,"[74] while States must furnish ICAO or any other contracting party "information concerning the registration and ownership of any particular aircraft registered in" their territory, according to the reporting standards ICAO prescribes.[75] And although Article 18 of the Convention states that "aircraft cannot be validly registered in more than one State,"[76] that should not be taken to mean that airlines, that is, the commercial enterprises that provide air services through the use of aircraft, must have all of their aircraft registered in a single State. For example, British Airways (BA), which is incorporated in the U.K., operates a wholly owned subsidiary established in France called OpenSkies. The aircraft operated by OpenSkies are registered in France, whereas BA's mainline fleet is registered in the U.K.[77] Article 18 by itself, therefore, does not disallow airlines from having a multinational presence in the global marketplace. Ownership of airlines, however, is a different matter from registration of aircraft. The absence of multinationally owned airlines is a consequence of a different rule, the nationality rule, which is not in the Convention at all: as we will see in Chapter 3, the nationality rule is included in the restrictive bilateral air services treaties that dominate the exchange of air traffic rights across the world.

2.5.12. *Introduction to Cabotage*

As already emphasized, the Chicago Convention is not a comprehensive economic regulatory charter despite the fact that many of its provisions affect the commercial operations of airlines. There exists, however, one major exception to that proposition: the doctrine of cabotage that excludes foreign airlines from providing domestic point-to-point air services. Although the doctrine is applied internationally through bilateral air services treaties (often backed by domestic legislation), its international legal foundation actually rests in the Chicago Convention. As such, we explicate the doctrine here and review some of the legal and policy questions that cabotage continues

---

[73] *See* Chicago Convention, *supra* note 1, arts. 18–19. Article 19, for example, provides that the registration or transfer of registration of aircraft in any contracting State "shall be made in accordance with [that State's] laws and regulations."

[74] *Id.* art. 20.

[75] *Id.* arts. 20–21. Information reported under ICAO's standards will be made available to other States upon request.

[76] Chicago Convention, *supra* note 1, art. 18.

[77] The following is a link to the French Registry listing BA's three OpenSkies aircraft: http://www.immat.aviation-civile.gouv.fr/immat/servlet/aeronef_liste.html.

to raise. Cabotage within the framework of trade in international air services will be discussed further in Chapter 3.

2.5.13. *History and Legal Basis of Cabotage*

The doctrine of cabotage has a venerable pedigree: it is a phenomenon of the history of trade, invented with the deliberate mercantilist purpose of protecting domestic commerce from foreign competition. Originally, cabotage was a creature of maritime law, and described a State reserving to itself the right to restrict all coastal navigation between two points within its territory for the exclusive use of its own subjects.[78] In the international aviation milieu, cabotage has been defined neutrally as the carriage of passengers, cargo, and mail between two points within the territory of the same State for compensation or hire, but also peremptorily as a sovereign right that has traditionally been reserved to the exclusive use of that State's national carriers.[79] It is in this *preceptive* sense that Article 7 of the Chicago Convention acknowledges the right of each State "to refuse permission to the aircraft of other contracting States to take on in its territory passengers, mail, and cargo carried for remuneration or hire and destined for another point within its territory."[80]

2.5.14. *Cabotage and Article 7 of the Chicago Convention*

Taken in isolation, the segment of Article 7 quoted in the preceding section seems superfluous given the Convention's earlier provisions related to airspace sovereignty (Article 1) and the acknowledged right of States to allow scheduled foreign carriers to access their territory on a concessionary basis only (Article 6). But Article 7 goes on to reinforce the peremptory nature of cabotage by decreeing that "[e]ach contracting State undertakes not to enter into any arrangements which specifically grant [the privilege of cabotage] on an exclusive basis to any other State or an airline of any other State, and not to obtain any such exclusive privilege from any other State."[81] Under a strong reading of that passage, States that are parties to the Chicago Convention are barred from treating cabotage as a coin of exchange in international air services trade.

---

[78] *See generally* PABLO M. J. MENDES DE LEON, CABOTAGE IN AIR TRANSPORT REGULATION (1981).

[79] *See generally* Douglas R. Lewis, *Air Cabotage: Historical and Modern-Day Perspectives*, 45 J. AIR L. & COM. 1059 (1980); W. M. Sheehan, Comment, *Air Cabotage and the Chicago Convention*, 63 HARV. L. REV. 1157 (1950).

[80] Chicago Convention, *supra* note 1, art. 7.

[81] *Id.* art. 7.

A weaker reading holds that Article 7 does not bar States from trading cabotage privileges so long as they are not offered or obtained "on an exclusive basis." Chile, for example, has abolished its cabotage restriction and stands ready to offer domestic market access on a reciprocal basis to airlines representing any of its bilateral air services partners.[82] That liberal approach does not offend Article 7 so long as none of Chile's agreements includes a rider prohibiting Chile from offering the same concession to any other countries. Regardless of which reading is adopted or is ultimately correct as a matter of law, the conclusion is the same: Article 7 is not simply a scenario-specific reiteration of the principle of airspace sovereignty, but rather a restraint on the degree of sovereignty the Convention's State parties can trade away. But why would States have agreed to such a condition? From a strategic trade perspective, economically powerful States may have feared that other parties to the Convention with strong airlines could lock down potentially lucrative exclusive cabotage rights for their airlines in third countries with weak air transport markets. The second sentence of Article 7 keeps that possibility in check, regardless of whether a strong or weak reading of the provision is accepted. Economically weaker States, on the other hand, may enjoy the protection that Article 7 affords: external pressure from strong States for (exclusive) cabotage rights can be mitigated by reference to the fact such concessions (may) violate international law. And all States, whether motivated by national pride or by a protectionist impulse to repel foreign competitive incursions, can avail themselves of Article 7 in its entirety in order to maintain closure of their home transport markets. The United States is the world's largest cabotage market, representing over a quarter of global air traffic movements; and U.S. domestic airlines, both passenger and cargo, are shielded from foreign competition on

---

[82] The Chilean law permitting cabotage is Ley 2.564 de 1979, art. 1. Reciprocity is contained in Ley 2.564 de 1979, art. 2 (In fact, the relevant legislation also grants Chile's Civil Aviation Board the power to offer cabotage rights on a nonreciprocal basis.). Why has Chile offered to trade away its cabotage restriction? The reason has something to do with geography and a desire to attract more air service to a country that is three times the length of California but is isolated at the end of the South American continent. *See* David Knibb, *Chile Trades Cabotage for "Precedent Setting" Deal*, AIRLINE BUS., Apr. 1, 2003, at 14. Chile also freely grants fifth (beyond) and seventh (stand-alone) freedom rights for the same reason (although its available fifth freedom connections have been described as air services for the penguin community, since its closest geographical neighbors are Antarctica and Easter Island). But Chile's liberality is also strategic: the cabotage, fifth, and seventh freedom concessions are also being offered to mollify critics who point out that its largest carrier, LanChile, is engaged in a continent-wide airline acquisition spree that at least in some cases may be incompatible with the terms of the nationality rule. *See generally* José Ignacio García-Arboleda, *Transnational Airlines in Latin America Facing the Fear of Nationality*, 37 AIR & SPACE L. 93, 100–112 (2012). For fuller explanations of the fifth and seventh freedoms, *see infra* Chapter 3, Part 3.3.

internal U.S. routes by Article 7 of the Chicago Convention and supporting federal law.[83]

2.5.15. *Current Concerns About Cabotage*

With the singular exception of Chile's unilateral renunciation,[84] cabotage remains heavily embedded in public international aviation law. According to a recent study by the World Trade Organization's Council for Trade in Services, "[t]he granting of cabotage rights is an extremely rare feature" in international air services trade – so rare that the Council was only able to identify two agreements worldwide that made cabotage concessions.[85] As noted in the preceding section, the United States stands firm on refusing cabotage rights despite its record during the past two decades as a bastion of international air transport liberalization. The closest the world aviation market has come to a "cabotage-free zone" is the EU, where the establishment of a common air transport market between and within the twenty-eight EU Member States necessitated dismantling the doctrine (albeit only for air carriers licensed under EU law). Australia allows foreign-owned airlines to provide internal services, and a number in fact do,[86] but they must be incorporated and licensed in accordance with domestic law and cannot

---

[83] *See* Chicago Convention, *supra* note 1, art. 7; 49 U.S.C.A. § 41703 (West 2008). Although there is no U.S. federal statute that *expressly* forbids cabotage, the Department of Transportation is only authorized to provide cabotage privileges to foreign air carriers for limited periods of time in cases of a national air transportation emergency. *See* 49 U.S.C.A. § 40109(g) (West 2012).

[84] *See* Ley 2.564 de 1979, art. 1.

[85] Council for Trade in Services, *Quantitative Air Services Agreements Review (QUASAR): Part B: Preliminary Results*, at 43, para. 120, S/C/W/270/Add.1 (Nov. 30, 2006). The two identified agreements are China-Albania and New Zealand-Brunei Darussalam, which cover very little traffic: http://www.wto.org/english/tratop_e/serv_e/transport_e/quasar_partb_e.pdf. The Review goes on to add that "[c]abotage traffic has not been identified as such by the Secretariat. In view of the low number of agreements involved, given the appropriate data sets it might be possible to identify whether such rights are used, and it might even be feasible to estimate the traffic. Further analysis could include at least one additional agreement . . . which covers significant traffic (*i.e.*, Australia-New Zealand, with between 3.5 and 4 million passengers). Moreover, several plurilateral agreements covering several million passengers contain cabotage rights implicitly or explicitly (*e.g.*, [the European Economic Area], [the European Common Aviation Area])." Subsequent to the conclusion of the Council's analysis, the United Kingdom and Singapore finalized an air services agreement (ASA) offering reciprocal cabotage rights. *See* Alan Khee Jin Tan, *Singapore's New Air Services Agreements with the E.U. and U.K.: Implications for Liberalization in Asia*, 73 J. Air L. & Com. 351, 362–64 (2008). As noted in the main text, Chile has also offered reciprocal domestic traffic rights to interested foreign airlines.

[86] As well as Virgin Australia, Skywest is owned by a Singapore-based company and Tiger Airways Australia is a subsidiary of a Singapore company partially owned by Singapore Airlines.

serve international destinations as designated Australian carriers.[87] Strictly speaking, that is not cabotage as contemplated under Article 7 of the Chicago Convention, but rather the provision of a "right of establishment" to foreign investors to allow them to participate in Australia's domestic aviation sector.[88] Were Australia to allow British Airways to fly domestic routes despite maintaining its principal place of business and country of incorporation in the United Kingdom, and without establishing a new Australian subsidiary for that purpose, then "true" cabotage would be implicated. (We will explore this distinction further in Chapter 3 when we examine the legal and policy challenges surrounding foreign investment in airlines.) There are two final matters to consider. First, the commercial value of cabotage rights remains a matter of contention among airlines, government officials, and industry analysts. Even if States with large domestic air transport markets conceded cabotage privileges to foreign air carriers, a lack of brand presence or status as an "alien competitor" might make those carriers unappealing to consumers. More importantly, there is only a small number of domestic markets in the world that are lucrative enough to entice foreign carriers to

---

[87] That is a privilege currently protected under the terms of Australia's bilateral ASAs with third countries. *See, e.g.,* Air Transport Agreement, U.S.-Aus., Mar. 31, 2008, http://www.state.gov/documents/organization/168386.pdf/. Domestic legislation also applies: *cf.* Air Navigation Act, 2002, § 11A (Austl.). As a general matter, if other Australian-based air carriers were to be permitted to operate internationally, they would need an international license. Eligibility requirements for the international license are typical of ownership and control requirements – a minimum of 51% Australian ownership, Australian citizens must make up at least two-thirds of the board, and an Australian citizen must serve as the Board chairman. *See* http://www.infrastructure.gov.au/aviation/international/ial/intro.aspx#1. Creative airlines have found ways to work around this restriction. A recent increase in the quantum of foreign ownership of Virgin Australia, which has been operating international flights since 2004, has caused it to adopt a complicated corporate structure under which its international operations are placed with a separate holding company with majority Australian ownership and an independent board of directors. The international operations holding company has long-term loan and service agreements with the foreign-owned domestic operations division of Virgin Australia. *See* Press Release, Virgin Australia, Virgin Australia Announces Proposed New Structure (Feb. 23, 2012), http://www.virginaustralia.com/us/en/about-us/media/2012/VIRGIN-AUSTRALIA-NEW-STRUCTURE/.

[88] In the context of aviation, a right of establishment would allow foreign investors not only to take majority ownership and control of domestic carriers, but also to set up new airlines or subsidiaries of foreign airlines in a domestic market as well as (if compatible with bilateral ASAs) to be designated to serve international routes. The right of establishment would also mandate that the foreign-owned entity must operate as a domestically regulated carrier employing "localized" workers and abiding by local labor, tax, immigration, registration, safety, security, and other laws. *See generally* Brian F. Havel & Gabriel S. Sanchez, *The Emerging Lex Aviatica,* GEO. J. INT'L L.639, 668–71 (2011); *see also infra* Chapter 3, Section 3.3.9.

park their planes abroad in the hope of capturing incremental revenues.[89] Second, States – for social, political, and economic reasons – have a compelling interest in regulating the airlines that operate within their territory. In a situation where BA, using aircraft registered in the U.K., sought to provide cabotage services between Sydney and Melbourne, the U.K. would arguably remain the State with primary regulatory jurisdiction over BA in its provision of that service,[90] hardly a palatable prospect for the local Australian civil aviation regulators. Under Articles 11 and 12 of the Chicago Convention, it is true, Australia exercises regulatory authority over the operation and navigation of the flight,[91] but Australian labor and environmental laws, for instance, might not (technically) apply.[92] A State that is willing to tolerate a foreign-owned carrier operating within its domestic sphere would find its regulatory interests better served by following Australia in providing a right of establishment rather than unadulterated cabotage.[93]

---

[89] Even within the EU, very few "true" cabotage services have materialized precisely because of a lack of competitive passenger numbers on even the largest domestic routes. (It is arguable whether the cabotage services referred to here should even be considered true "cabotage" services, because the EU is considered a single aviation market and any carriers flying between points within EU Member States are now "Union" carriers and not foreign carriers.) As a commercial matter, cabotage rights are much more valuable in large landmass countries such as Australia, Canada, China, and the United States.

[90] *See* Havel, Beyond Open Skies, *supra* note 28, at 48 n.92.

[91] Under Article 11, foreign aircraft need only comply with "[t]he laws and regulations of a Contracting State relating to the admission to or departure from its territory of aircraft engaged in international air navigation, or to the operation and navigation of such aircraft while within its territory. . . ." Chicago Convention, *supra* note 1, art. 11. Article 12 requires contracting States to ensure compliance with local navigational rules by aircraft holding their nationality. *See id.* art. 12.

[92] Neither the Chicago Convention nor the substance of ASAs speaks to issues such as which State's labor law would govern in those circumstances. In most cases, it is likely that the airline's employees would operate under the labor law of the State of registration. It is fair to assert that this question of regulatory jurisdiction remains unsettled. In any event, a State that felt concerned by the regulatory regime affecting cabotage could endeavor to eliminate or minimize the apparent split in regulatory responsibility through specific arrangements in its relevant ASAs. Although some might argue that this form of bilaterally mandated regulatory specification violates the express terms of the Chicago Convention, it is a generally agreed-upon principle of international treaty law that two or more States that are party to the same multilateral agreement may take on or waive rights and obligations supplied by the multilateral so long as they do not affect the rights and privileges of third-party signatories to the multilateral. *See* Vienna Convention on the Law of Treaties, art. 58, May 23, 1969, 1155 U.N.T.S. 331.

[93] As we will see, *infra* Chapter 3, cabotage also provides two of the "freedoms of the air" (traffic rights): the eighth freedom occurs at the end of an existing international service (e.g., passengers or cargo could be picked up in New York on a London/New York flight for onward transit to Los Angeles), and the ninth freedom (which is "true" cabotage that connects domestic points without being an extension of an international service). We have been advised of a draft

2.6. THE INTERNATIONAL CIVIL AVIATION ORGANIZATION

2.6.1. *The Chicago Convention as a Charter for ICAO*

As well as being a repository of solutions to the problems of multilateral coordination, the Chicago Convention also functions as the charter for ICAO – the official U.N. intergovernmental agency charged with "develop[ing] the principles and techniques of international air navigation and foster[ing] the planning and development of international air transport" so as to:

(a) Insure the safe and orderly growth of international civil aviation throughout the world;

(b) Encourage the arts of aircraft design and operation for peaceful purposes;

(c) Encourage the development of airways, airports and air navigation facilities for international civil aviation navigation;

(d) Meet the needs of the people of the world for safe, regular, efficient and economical air transport;

(e) Prevent economic waste caused by unreasonable competition;

(f) Insure that the rights of contracting States are fully respected and that every contracting State has a fair opportunity to operate international airlines;

(g) Avoid discrimination between contracting States;

(h) Promote safety of flight in international air navigation;

(i) Promote generally the development of all aspects of international civil aeronautics.[94]

2.6.2. *Tensions Between Some ICAO Goals*

These goals amplify the cosmopolitan sentiments expressed in the Preamble to the Convention quoted earlier in this chapter. The list of ICAO's goals, however, includes some that are in obvious tension with one another. Most glaringly, subparagraph (e) – the handiwork of States that were unwilling to sacrifice their inefficient air carriers to the vagaries of the free market and

master's thesis at Leiden University's International Institute of Air and Space Law that postulates a tenth freedom (related to cabotage): this freedom would allow a suborbital space flight – for example, by Sir Richard Branson's U.K.-owned Virgin Galactica – to depart from and return to the same launch site in another country (e.g., in the U.S. state of Arizona). (As told to Professor Brian Havel by distinguished U.K. aviation lawyer Mr. John Balfour, Leiden, Nov.25, 2011.)

94 Chicago Convention, *supra* note 1, art. 44.

"unreasonable" competition – sits uneasily beside the economic efficiency and "economical" availability of international air services mentioned in subparagraph (d). Without dwelling on the Convention's polemical use of the term "unreasonable," if one assumes that competition on routes, quality of service, and pricing will best accomplish the Convention's goal of greater efficiency and economical availability of services, then an operating environment where firms do not have to compete meaningfully for their customer base will erode efficiency and reduce availability by tolerating monopolistic or oligopolistic pricing as well as declining service. It is also difficult to imagine how "competition" (whether reasonable or unreasonable) can flourish while States are encouraged by subparagraph (f) to sponsor their own international airlines under a benign regime of "fair opportunity" for all carriers.[95] As we know from the history of trade in international air services, States have acted to protect their international airlines by heavy regulation of the degree of foreign competition they will allow into their markets. And, as we also know, ICAO has done relatively little over the course of its history to dethrone that system of managed trade. Only since its first Worldwide Air Transport Conference in 2003 has ICAO shown signs of acknowledging U.S. and EU initiatives to liberalize the international air transport market by calling on States to give "as much economic freedom as possible [to airlines] while respecting . . . the need to ensure high standards for safety, security, and environmental protection."[96]

2.6.3. *Assessing ICAO's Roles in Economic Regulation and Technical Coordination*

The Chicago Convention, having effectively devolved stewardship of market access to its member States, assigns no determinative role to ICAO in the

---

[95] That is precisely why much of the European aviation marketplace in 2013 remains essentially uncompetitive: there are too many State-sponsored airlines that have never achieved scale and scope efficiencies. But some smaller European States may be willing to allow their carriers to disappear, as demonstrated by toleration of recent bankruptcies of State-dominated airlines – most notably Hungarian national carrier Malev, which had been the recipient of government subsidies that were determined to be illegal under EU law. *See* Nicola Clark & David Jolly, *Hungarian National Airline Halts Flights*, N.Y. TIMES, Feb. 3, 2012. Other European governments, namely, Ireland and Portugal, have been attempting to sell their stakes in struggling national carriers Aer Lingus and TAP, respectively. Portugal and Hungary are each smaller geographically than the U.S. state of Indiana and have smaller populations than the U.S. state of Ohio. One might well wonder how the competitiveness of the U.S. domestic aviation market would look if each mid-sized state were to have its own air carrier.

[96] *See* ICAO, *Consolidated Conclusions, Model Clauses, Recommendations and Declarations*, at 19, ATConf/5 (Mar. 31, 2003) (revised Jul.10, 2003), http://www.icao.int/icao/en/atb/atconf5/.

realm of air services trade regulation.[97] Arguably, neither the Organization's relatively recent embrace of an agenda of regulatory liberalization nor its involvement in developing a global regime to limit aircraft carbon emissions has any sound textual basis in the Convention and should instead be the concern of regional economic groupings.[98] In the traditional areas of its remit, notably technical cooperation, ICAO has had a much better track record. Charged under the Convention with developing and updating the treaty's annexes containing Standards and Recommended Practices (SARPs) for, *inter alia*, air traffic management, aircraft and personnel licensing, airport operations, and aeronautical information services, ICAO is optimally viewed as the facilitator of the Chicago Convention's implicit goal of resolving the coordination challenges that we have noted throughout this chapter. Because later chapters will provide more specific detail on ICAO's engagement in matters of safety, security, and the environment, and also in discrete areas of economic regulation such as the registration of international security interests,[99] we confine ourselves here to surveying the Organization's structure and its primary responsibility to promulgate SARPs. We also examine ICAO's tightly circumscribed role as a dispute settlement body and argue that those limitations, coupled with the fact that States have a rational interest in adhering to the Convention without the (soft) threat of sanctions, renders ICAO an uncongenial (and unnecessary) forum in which to resolve disputes occurring in international aviation.[100]

---

[97] Through six ICAO Worldwide Air Transport Conferences since 2003, ICAO has injected itself into economic regulation of the industry. Indeed, ICAO now sponsors annual "speed-dating" Air Services Negotiation (ICAN) Conferences for States interested over the course of a few days in making more liberal arrangements to exchange air market access with like-minded States. A description of those conferences can be found here: http://legacy.icao.int/ICAN2009/docs/ICAO_Journal_ICAN2008_Vol64Num01_p21.pdf.

[98] Nevertheless, as noted in the preceding main text, the aims and objectives of the Organization include the orderly growth of air transport (Article 44(a)), the provision of efficient and economical air transport (Article 44(d)), and allowing States a fair opportunity to operate international airlines (Article 44(f)). Cumulatively, these provisions could offer a broad justification of ICAO's involvement in economic regulation.

[99] This last engagement has been achieved in the context of the Convention on International Interests in Mobile Equipment (the Cape Town Convention), which will be covered *infra* in Chapter 8.

[100] A full analysis of ICAO's legal and extralegal functions is well beyond the scope of this book. Readers seeking a detailed introduction to the Organization should see LUDWIG WEBER, INTERNATIONAL CIVIL AVIATION ORGANIZATION: AN INTRODUCTION (2007). A prolific commentator on ICAO is one of its senior officials, Ruwantissa Abeyratne. *See, e.g.,* Ruwantissa Abeyratne, *The Role of the International Civil Aviation Organization (ICAO) in the Twenty-First Century*, 34 ANNALS AIR & SPACE L. 529 (2009); Ruwantissa Abeyratne, *Reinventing ICAO's Role in Economic Regulation – A Compelling Need*, 13 ISSUES AVIATION

2.6.4. ICAO's Structure (1): The Council

Organized as a triptych, ICAO features a Council as its main executive body, along with a Secretariat and a General Assembly comprised of representatives from the 191 States parties to the Convention.[101] In harmony with the practice of the U.N. General Assembly, all member States have an equal right to representation (i.e., one vote).[102] The Council elects a President and appoints a Secretary General.[103] It comprises thirty-six State party representatives who are elected by the Assembly on a triennial basis. Although the Council elections are open, Article 50(b) of the Convention stipulates that membership preference should be given to "(1) the States of chief importance in air transport; (2) the States . . . mak[ing] the largest contribution to the provision of facilities for international air navigation; and (3) the States . . . whose designation will insure that all major geographic areas of the world are represented[.]"[104] Once its membership is established, the Council's primary responsibility (discussed below) is the development and adoption of the SARPs listed in the Chicago Convention annexes. To that end, the Council receives assistance from a series of subject-specific bureaucratic support bodies that operate under its direction, including the Air Navigation Commission (technical harmonization and

---

L. & POL'Y 9 (2013). For a list of Abeyratne's ICAO-related publications, *see* http://www.mcgill. ca/files/iasl/PUBS_Ruwantissa_Abeyratne.pdf.

[101] *See* Chicago Convention, *supra* note 1, Ch. VII.

[102] *See id.*, art. 48(b). *See also* Charter of the United Nations art. 18, *opened for signature* Jun. 26, 1945, 3 Bevans 1153 (entered into force Oct. 24, 1945).

[103] The descriptions of both positions are vague, and indeed it is unclear how the processes of "election" and "appointment" differ with respect to the two positions. While the Chicago Convention does not vest the Council President with the right to vote, he or she is charged with convening and overseeing meetings of the Council, the Air Transport Committee, and the Air Navigation Commission, as well as with serving as the Council's representative to the rest of ICAO and carrying out any specific duties that the Council may assign to him or her. *See* Chicago Convention, *supra* note 1, art. 51. The Secretary General, on the other hand, acts to oversee the Secretariat that provides technical, legal, and administrative support to the Council and the Assembly, including the Secretariat's five main divisions: the Air Navigation Bureau, the Air Transport Bureau, the Technical Co-operation Bureau, the Legal Affairs Bureau, and the Bureau of Administration and Services. The Chicago Convention does not mention the Secretariat, but its development is in keeping with the evolution of the modern administrative State. ICAO, like any governing authority, recognized the need for a professional staff to evaluate, analyze, research, and report on treaty amendments and SARPs that would eventually be submitted for approval to the Organization's member States.

[104] *See* Chicago Convention, *supra* note 1, art. 50(b). Newly elected Council members for the 2014–2016 term are: Australia, Argentina, Bolivia, Brazil, Burkina Faso, Cameroon, Canada, Chile, China, Dominican Republic, Egypt, France, Germany, India, Italy, Japan, Kenya, Libya, Malaysia, Mexico, Nicaragua, Nigeria, Norway, Poland, Portugal, Republic of Korea, Russian Federation, Saudi Arabia, Singapore, South Africa, Spain, United Arab Emirates, United Kingdom, United Republic of Tanzania, United States, and Venezuela.

safety), the Air Transport Committee (economic regulation), the Legal Committee (comprising legal experts appointed by the member States), and the Committee on Unlawful Interference (aviation security).[105] Although Article 54 of the Convention briefly mentions the appointment of an Air Transport Committee among the mandatory functions of the Council,[106] without further guidance on the Committee's precise scope of duties, its current focus on economic regulation has evolved entirely at the discretion of the Council. The Air Navigation Commission, in contrast, has a more elaborate textual footing in the Convention: Article 56 discusses its appointment and composition, and Article 57 endows it with specific SARP-generating responsibilities.[107] Finally, the ICAO Council is also vested with limited dispute settlement powers that are considered below.

2.6.5. *ICAO's Structure (2): The Assembly and Secretariat*

The Assembly, which convenes every three years at ICAO's headquarters in Montreal, Canada,[108] acts as a reviewing mechanism for the work of the Organization as a whole. In addition to electing the Council members, the Assembly approves ICAO's budget and passes resolutions addressing pertinent matters affecting international civil aviation.[109] The Assembly's resolutions are not a species of binding international legislation, however. ICAO member States that accept the resolutions are not bound to their terms and, in practice, the language used in these statements is hortatory. Where the Assembly does exercise some degree of international legal authority is in evaluating amendments to the Convention proposed by the Council. But even here the Assembly's "legislative" powers are subject to the high bar that a minimum of two-thirds of the Convention States must ratify any approved amendment before it enters into force (and even then the amendment binds only the countries that have ratified it).[110] The ICAO Secretariat's role is less exalted

---

[105] The Air Navigation Commission is expressly authorized by Chapter X of the Chicago Convention. *See* Chicago Convention, *supra* note 1, arts. 56, 57. The Council's authority to establish other subordinate commissions derives from Article 55. *See* Chicago Convention, *supra* note 1, art. 55(a). The ICAO Legal Committee was established by the ICAO Assembly in May 1947 as a permanent successor to the *Comité International Technique d'Experts Juridiques Aérien* (CITEJA), a group of independent legal experts that (among other achievements) prepared the draft of the 1929 Warsaw Convention on passenger and cargo liability. *See infra* Chapter 7, note 6.

[106] *See id.* art. 54(d).

[107] *See id.* arts. 56, 57.

[108] These meetings are referred to as the ICAO Triennial Assembly.

[109] *See* Chicago Convention, *supra* note 1, art. 49.

[110] *See id.* art. 94.

than that of either the Council or the Assembly.[111] Its functions are chiefly administrative and limited to managing the Organization's subordinate units such as the Air Navigation, Air Transport, and Legal Affairs Bureaus. These bodies discharge useful auxiliary functions. The Legal Affairs Bureau, for instance, researches private and public international aviation law and has drafted a number of multilateral agreements related to air carrier liability and security. The Bureau also acts as the secretariat for the ICAO Legal Committee and facilitates ICAO's role as a depositary for a number of international aviation treaties.

2.6.6. *Binding Nature of SARPs*

At the core of ICAO's role and utility is the promulgation of the SARPs listed in the annexes to the Chicago Convention. Article 54(1), in tandem with Article 90 of the Chicago Convention, grants the Council the power to adopt, at its discretion, new or amended annexes by a two-thirds majority vote of its membership. Once adopted, the new or amended annexes take effect after three months (or longer if the Council so specifies) unless they are rejected by a majority of the contracting States.[112] All of that is straightforward enough. Interpretive complications arise, however, with respect to the legally binding nature of SARPs. Recall that Article 12 of the Chicago Convention stipulates that a contracting State "undertakes to keep its own [aviation] regulations . . . uniform, to the greatest possible extent, with those established from time to time under [the] Convention."[113] Although the phrasing here is strong, Article 12 falls short of an unambiguous duty on

---

[111] As indicated *supra* note 103, the Secretariat is not explicitly mentioned in the Chicago Convention.

[112] This is a legislative mechanism sometimes referred to as a "negative consensus." Once the initial adopting event has taken place (the two-thirds Council vote in favor of a new annex or amendment of an existing annex), the new annex or amendment does not require further affirmative action, such as ratification by a majority of the contracting States. Rather, the change will inevitably take effect unless a majority of contracting States rejects the new measure. A comparable procedure exists in the World Trade Organization's Dispute Settlement Body (DSB). There, in a context that operates through a stronger sense of unanimity than exists in ICAO, the DSB automatically adopts a dispute settlement decision (ruling) unless all 159 State parties to the Organization vote to reject it. In practice, that means that even the victorious party to a dispute settlement proceeding would have to vote against a decision in its favor for the ruling to be rejected. *See generally* WTO, THE WTO DISPUTE SETTLEMENT PROCEDURES: A COLLECTION OF THE RELEVANT LEGAL TEXTS (2012).

[113] Chicago Convention, *supra* note 1, art. 12.

States to implement SARPs. Moreover, Article 37 of the Convention, which has a preliminary listing of eleven SARP subject categories, also appears to step lightly on State sensibilities, providing only that "[e]ach contracting State undertakes to collaborate in securing the highest practicable degree of uniformity" on matters addressed in the SARPs.[114] To "undertake" is not the same thing as to "adhere," nor is the imperative form "shall" present in the text. Even if "undertakes" is read strongly, the "undertaking" in question is only to "collaborate," and not even (for example) to "follow." The impression that SARPs are not obligatory (even if compliance is strongly encouraged) is underscored dramatically by the peculiarities of Article 38 of the Chicago Convention. That provision, ironically, strips Article 37 of any residual possibility of mandatory effect by imposing an obligation on all member States to alert ICAO of any intention on their part *not* to comply with a Council-approved "standard."[115] Thus, a State that finds it "impracticable" to comply with a new or amended standard (or "deems it necessary" to adopt separate standards) "shall" notify the Council of any differences between its national regulations or practices and standards adopted under the annexes.[116] Once notified, the Council must inform the other contracting States, but it possesses no *direct* powers under Article 38 to punish or demand compliance from recalcitrant States (nor to sanction States that simply ignore the requirement to notify).[117] But some measure of *indirect* enforcement remains possible. Article 84 – to be discussed in more detail in the following section – provides that "any disagreement between two or more contracting States relating to the interpretation or application of [the Chicago] Convention and its Annexes ... shall ... be decided by the Council."[118] Article 84 is so compendiously drafted that it would seem to allow an ICAO member State that is relying on an Article 38 exception nevertheless to be summoned before the Council by any other member State.

---

[114] *Id.* art. 37.

[115] *See supra* note 64 (explaining that this reporting requirement only relates to standards and not to recommended practices).

[116] *Id.* art. 38.

[117] *Id.* It is on the basis of ICAO's notification that other States must determine how to respond. Article 39 allows an aircraft's airworthiness certificate to be endorsed (presumably by its State of registration (*cf.* Article 31) with an enumeration of details of how that aircraft has "failed in any respect" to satisfy an international standard of airworthiness or performance. Chicago Convention, *supra* note 1, art. 39. It might have been useful to link this procedure to Article 38 by requiring an endorsement on the certificate indicating that the registering State has itself departed from international standards in a particular respect, but Article 39 does not provide for such self-policing.

[118] Chicago Convention, *supra* note 1, art. 84.

2.6.7. *Differences in Legal Effect Between Standards and Recommended Practices*

A further difficulty that arises with respect to the binding force of SARPs is the distinction between "standards" and "recommended practices."[119] A standard, according to the ICAO Air Navigation Bureau, is defined as "any specification for physical characteristics, configuration, *matériel*, performance, personnel or procedure, the uniform application of which is recognized as necessary for the safety or regularity of international air navigation and to which [c]ontracting States will conform in accordance with the Convention[.]"[120] Despite the Bureau's sanguine expectation that States "will conform" to a standard because of its indispensability to international air navigation, its definition goes on to recognize both that deviations are possible under Article 38 and also that (concurrently) standards are always subject to a mandatory notification requirement.[121] A recommended practice, on the other hand, is defined by the Bureau as only "any specification for physical characteristics, configuration, *matériel*, performance, personnel or procedure, the uniform application of which is recognized as desirable in the interest of safety, regularity or efficiency of international air navigation, and to which contracting States will endeavor to conform in accordance with the Convention."[122] The Bureau adds that contracting States are "invited," but not required, "to inform the Council of non-compliance" with recommended practices.[123] The Bureau's

---

[119] Frankly, the Convention's use of these terms is not a model of clarity. Just examine Article 38 to see a range of labels, including repeated invocation of an "international standard or procedure" in addition to Article 37's extended lexicon of "standards and recommended practices *and procedures*." *See also supra* note 64 (discussing the Convention's additionally confusing use of the terms "recommended" and "established" standards and practices).

[120] ICAO, Air Navigation Bureau, *Making an ICAO Standard*, Assembly Res. A1–31, ICAO Doc. 4411 (A1-P/45) (1947), http://legacy.icao.int/icao/en/anb/mais/index.html. For ICAO's most recent endorsement of this definition, see International Civil Aviation Organization, Proposal for Annex 19 and Related Consequential Amendments to Annexes 1, 6, 8, 11, 13, and 14, Letter of the Secretary General of the Air Navigation Commission and Attachments, Ref. AN 8/3–12/42 (Jun. 29, 2012) [hereinafter ICAO, *Proposal for Annex 19*].

[121] *See supra* text accompanying note 115.

[122] ICAO, Air Navigation Bureau, *Making an ICAO Standard*, *supra* note 120. For ICAO's most recent endorsement of this definition, see ICAO, *Proposal for Annex 19*, *supra* note 120, at A-8.

[123] The Bureau's argument that the Article 38 notification requirement applies only to international standards is arguably correct, even though Article 38 regrettably opens with a befuddling reference to an "international standard *or procedure*" (emphasis added) before defaulting to the term "international standard." *See supra* note 119. But the notion that States are "invited" to report deviations from recommended practices is wholly an invention of the Bureau and has no textual support in the Convention. *See also infra* Chapter 5, Part 5.3 (noting that ICAO has recently reiterated its invitation to report deviations from recommended practices in the context of Annex 19, its new consolidated safety annex). There is no notification requirement that attaches to ICAO's copious output of policies and guidance materials.

differential treatment of standards and recommended practices under Article 38 places recommended practices beyond whatever zone of normativity has been established by the Chicago Convention, although they may represent an instance of soft law. In other words, recommended practices possess some strong measure of aspirational power, but nothing more. But if recommended practices are arguably soft law, does that mean that standards are hard (binding) law? Despite the deconstruction of the texts of Articles 37 and 38 of the Chicago Convention set forth above, ICAO appears to believe so, although once again the absence of a strong sanction to punish scofflaws surely militates against an unambiguous assertion of hard law.[124] While that fact may vex legalists, in practice the absence of a sanction may be inconsequential. States that fail to adhere to the SARPs promulgated by the Council – whether standards or recommended practices – are likely to incur losses to reputation, especially if their defections are habitual or severe. Even if those reputational losses do not affect the nonadhering States' international relationships as a whole,[125] they could undermine other States' confidence in the safety of the defectors' airlines, in the suitability of their air traffic management systems, or in their capacity properly to screen passengers and cargo in order to stop terrorist threats.[126] Countries may issue warnings to their airlines and passengers not to fly to defecting States or to avoid deepening aeropolitical ties with the defectors until they prove they are capable of adhering, or do adhere, to the SARPs. Both the United States and EU, for example, have audit programs that monitor international compliance with SARPs and, in the event of serious shortfalls, allow their civil aviation authorities to freeze, reduce, or suspend the traffic rights of airlines originating from defecting States.[127] Adherence to

[124] A principal reason why standards, unlike recommended practices, might be said to constitute hard law is the requirement in Article 38 of the Convention that noncompliance with standards must be reported to ICAO, which then must inform other contracting States of that noncompliance. Chicago Convention, *supra* note 1, art. 38; *see supra* text accompanying note 115. To assert that ICAO standards have binding force would minimally require that those tasked with enforcing the standards – the contracting States themselves – be made aware of instances of noncompliance.

[125] *See generally* George W. Downs & Michael A. Jones, *Reputation, Compliance, and International Law*, 31 J. LEGAL STUD. S95 (2002) (describing how State reputational loss limits defections from international law); *see also* ROBERT O. KEOHANE, AFTER HEGEMONY: COOPERATION AND DISCORD IN THE WORLD POLITICAL ECONOMY 97 (1984) (discussing how participation in international "regimes" raises "the costs of deception and irresponsibility" for States).

[126] All of these matters are covered in one or more of the Chicago Convention Annexes.

[127] The U.S. program is known as the International Aviation Safety Assessment (IASA) Program. Begun in 1992, the program authorizes the FAA to assess the civil aviation authorities of foreign States (not individual carriers) with respect to their capacity to adhere to ICAO standards and recommended practices for aircraft operation and maintenance. The United States does not

SARPs is strongly incentivized, therefore, even in the absence of a direct sanction under the Convention.

2.6.8. *ICAO Dispute Settlement: Article 84*

In addition to its SARPs-related "legislative" authority, the ICAO Council is also permitted to settle disputes arising under the Chicago Convention. According to Article 84 of the Convention:

> If any disagreement between two or more contracting States relating to the interpretation or application of this Convention and its Annexes cannot be settled by negotiation, it shall, on the application of any State concerned in the disagreement, be decided by the [ICAO] Council. No member of the Council shall vote in the consideration by the Council of any dispute to which it is a party. Any contracting State may ... appeal from the decision of the Council to an ad hoc tribunal agreed upon with the other parties to the dispute or to the [International Court of Justice [ICJ]].[128]

To help facilitate the dispute settlement process, ICAO devised procedural rules that, *inter alia*, govern the nature of submissions to and hearings before the Council.[129] Notably, those rules privilege the settlement of disputes through negotiation over relying on the Council to sort out and settle the contending claims of the parties.[130] That approach is unsurprising given the internal defects of Article 84. The Article, for instance, vests the ICAO Council with all of the Organization's dispute settlement powers without regard to what (if any) competence that body has to settle international legal claims. The ICJ, which is granted only "appellate jurisdiction" for Chicago Convention disputes, and despite its many perceived flaws,[131] has the experience and resources to adjudicate State-to-State legal entanglements.

2.6.9. *A Critique of Dispute Settlement Under Article 84*

Moreover, Article 84 raises legitimacy concerns by denying Council members whose States may be party to a dispute the right to vote on the outcome. As a

blacklist States it classifies as noncompliant, but works with them to improve their standards and practices and will deny expansion of traffic rights until compliance issues have been addressed. The EU Member States inspect individual carriers and have a common blacklist banning noncompliant carriers from flying to any EU State. *See also supra* note 27.

[128] As a U.N. body, ICAO is permitted under Article 96(2) of the U.N. Charter to submit legal questions to the ICJ for an advisory opinion. It has yet to avail itself of this privilege, however.

[129] *See* ICAO, *Rules for the Settlement of Differences*, ICAO Doc. No. 7782/2 (1975).

[130] *See id.* arts. 6 & 14.

[131] *See generally* Eric A. Posner, *The Decline of the International Court of Justice*, in INTERNATIONAL CONFLICT RESOLUTION 111 (Stefan Voigt et al. eds., 2006).

matter of *Realpolitik*, we may wonder why any State would leave itself exposed to a negative finding by the Council if it lacks the right to have a meaningful say in the decision. This enforced abstention is strange given that the ICJ grants a State party to a case before it the right to have one of its nationals on the bench.[132] Further, given that any Council decision can be appealed to a non-ICAO body (the ICJ or an *ad hoc* arbitral tribunal), which is under no obligation to respect the Council's findings, it may be queried what forensic purpose the Council's intervention serves. If anything, the Council seems shoehorned into a political role that lies somewhere between initial accusations of legal violation and more legitimate and purposive fora for international adjudication. It is also likely that States that are assessing particular disputes (either as complainant or respondent) will in part determine their view of the value or threat of the Convention's dispute settlement process by an assessment of the practical effects of the available sanctions. Should a State find itself on the losing end of a Council decision and subsequent appeal, it forfeits voting power in the Council and the Assembly.[133] The most important powers of those organs are, as we have seen, to propose and accept amendments to the Chicago Convention – amendments that must then be ratified by the member States before they become enforceable and which bind only ratifying States.[134] If amendments to the Convention alone are considered, a State that has forfeited its voting powers typically need not fear the imposition of new legal obligations under Convention amendments to which it has not specifically assented.[135] But more problematical is the process of SARP and annex adoption and amendment, where new rules can take effect for every member State unless a majority of States rejects them.[136]

---

[132] *See* Statute of the International Court of Justice, art. 31, Jun. 26, 1945, 3 Bevans 1153, 33 U.N. T.S. 993.

[133] *See* Chicago Convention, *supra* note 1, art. 88.

[134] *See id.* art. 94(a).

[135] Note, however, that Article 94(b) does allow the Assembly to designate an amendment such that nonratification will result in a State's expulsion from ICAO and make that State no longer a party to the Convention. *See id.* art. 94(b). Thus, the inability to vote on Convention amendments is not always without consequence.

[136] *See supra* note 112 (discussing the "negative consensus" procedure). Thus, if a State with a Council vote were penalized with loss of voting power under Article 88, that State would also presumably lose its ability to influence the adoption or amendment of SARPs and annexes. Whether or not SARPs constitute a binding legal obligation, States may still view that loss of influence as a serious consequence of forfeiting voting power. Although the exact meaning of "voting power" has never been defined in ICAO practice, it is unclear that a State stripped of its vote would still be allowed to participate in the development and consideration of a SARP or an annex (in the same way that non-Council States are permitted to do under Article 53 of the Convention). Moreover, while such participation would mitigate the effect of the loss of a vote, any member State deprived of voting power might find its contributions to the development of

2.6.10. *Another Available Remedy: Article 87*

A facially potent remedy contemplated under Article 87 of the Convention involves situations where *an airline of a State party*, rather than the State itself, is found to have failed to comply with the outcome of the Convention's dispute settlement process. In such instances, *all* 191 contracting States must bar that air carrier from flying into, out of, or over their territory.[137] But third-party enforcement of international agreements can be difficult to coordinate and monitor, particularly because every potential enforcer has an incentive to "cheat" and to rely on other enforcing States to bear any costs associated with the punishment. If the potential gains and losses of a dispute are confined only to a select number of States, other contracting States have little or no interest in expending resources on enforcement. Enforcing States, after all, may damage relations with the rogue airline's home country, compromising opportunities to strengthen existing ties. Banning a major network carrier like British Airways or United could have untold aeropolitical fallout, antagonizing major economic powers while losing the benefits those airlines provide to the enforcing States' economies.

2.6.11. *A Brief Proposal on ICAO Dispute Settlement*

More reasonably, the Chicago Convention ought to (but does not) emulate the later-evolving WTO dispute settlement model by allowing aggrieved States to take retaliatory measures against nonconforming States (or, in appropriate cases, their airlines). That way, only those countries with a vested interest in the dispute (and thus the incentive to enforce the outcome) would be committed to doing so.[138] As it stands, however, the Convention's enforcement provision against noncompliant airlines is impractical and politically imprudent.[139]

---

norms to be unwelcome within the rest of the ICAO community. Although the hard legal penalties for noncompliance mentioned in the main text may not appear overly stringent, therefore, much of ICAO's work, like most international lawmaking, involves less formal mechanisms for norm-generation, and States will not want to be shut out of that process.

[137] *See* Chicago Convention, *supra* note 1, art. 87.

[138] *See* POSNER, THE PERILS OF GLOBAL LEGALISM, *supra* note 22, at 154–56 (discussing the effectiveness of this dispute settlement enforcement method).

[139] For a proposal to reinforce relatively weak intergovernmental bureaucracies like ICAO by collective member State action that would exclude violators from the benefits of membership, see Oona Hathaway & Scott J. Shapiro, *Outcasting: Enforcement in Domestic and International Law*, 121 YALE L.J. 252 (2011).

2.6.12. *ICAO's Continuing Mission*

This survey of ICAO and its most legally related functions hardly captures all of the Organization's activities. Criticism of ICAO's role in international economic regulation or in dispute settlement should not be taken as an indictment of the institution as a whole. It is important to bear in mind that the promulgation of SARPs is now only one dimension of ICAO's mission to promote technical cooperation and safety harmonization at the international level. In 1999, the Organization launched its Universal Safety and Oversight Audit Program (USOAP) with the aim of fostering greater global transparency with respect to State adherence to the Convention and its annexes. ICAO circulates the reports produced through these audits to all contracting States. Although USOAP cannot directly compel States to fall into line with the Convention, negative audits can inflict reputational losses on States and in turn lead to breakdowns in aeropolitical relations with, or even sanctions by, other State parties to the Convention.[140] As later chapters will reveal, ICAO has been active also in securing global cooperation to prevent and combat aviation crimes, including hijackings and other terrorist challenges to international civil aviation. More recently, the international community entrusted ICAO with the responsibility to develop global standards on aviation carbon emissions. The Organization continues to encourage its members to collaborate on projects that expand the reach of international air transport, for example, by channeling assistance to developing countries in modernizing their air transport sectors.[141] Another key initiative – the Cooperative Development of Operational Safety and Continuing Airworthiness Programmes (COSCAP) – has sought to devolve aviation technical and safety cooperation to regional groupings, leaving ICAO as a framework organization tasked with promoting a region-based approach to air transport issues.[142]

---

[140] ICAO uses the USOAP to help bring noncompliant States up to its global standards, but the EU, for example, has included USOAP audits in its decision-making process for banning third-country operators. *See* European Aviation Safety Agency, Opinion 05/2012, Nov. 22, 2012, http://easa.europa.eu/agency-measures/docs/opinions/2012/05/EN%20to%20Opinion%2005-2012%20(TCO).pdf. ICAO maintains a special website for the USOAP, http://www.icao.int/safety/CMAForum/.

[141] ICAO has a variety of programs and mechanisms by which it provides technical expertise as well as financial support for safety and modernization projects. *See generally* Jason R. Bonin, *Regionalism in International Civil Aviation: A Reevaluation of the Economic Regulation of International Air Transport in the Context of Economic Integration*, 12 SINGAPORE Y.B. INT'L L. & CONTRIBUTIONS 113 (2008).

[142] *See* ICAO, 2011: STATE OF GLOBAL AVIATION SAFETY 24–25 (2011). This process is intended to go further than just the coordination of ICAO's regional offices. By itself, regionalism is not a new development for ICAO: the regional offices were established shortly after ICAO was created. But in recent years ICAO has begun to reach out to other regional organizations such

Finally, ICAO continues to act as a global advocate for States to achieve interoperability as they undertake the costly task of modernizing their air traffic management systems.[143]

2.6.13. A More Muscular ICAO?

While legalists hold out hope for the eventual emergence of a more "muscular" ICAO, equipped with unambiguous international legislative powers or more clout in dispute settlement, the likelihood of that transformation in the foreseeable future is not promising. This is not a counsel of despair, however. As the last six decades have shown, the smooth functioning of the Chicago Convention does not require a strong dispute settlement mechanism. The treaty's instrumental value in solving international coordination problems provides strong incentives for States to adhere to its provisions and to avoid defections. As for ICAO's powers, although they may lack formal normativity, they remain adequate for the Organization's primary task of developing and amending the Convention annexes. And it is not clear that any of ICAO's other functions, such as promoting safety and security or working as a legal advisory body, would be significantly enhanced by an upgrade of ICAO's legal authority. In fact, as with other international organizations that depend on maintaining equipoise in its members' interests, an expanded or more intrusive role in international aeropolitical affairs could compromise ICAO's legitimacy and capacity to function.

---

as the EU and hosted a joint EU/ICAO symposium on regional organizations in Montreal in April 2008. *See generally* http://legacy.icao.int/icao/en/ro/roresp.htm.

[143] *See* Brian F. Havel, *A US Point of View on European ATM Developments, in* ACHIEVING THE SINGLE EUROPEAN SKY 107 (Pablo M. J. Mendes de Leon & Daniel Calleja Crespo eds., 2011); *see also Ensuring the Safety and Efficiency of Global Aviation*, 66 ICAO J. 3 (2011).

3

The International Law Regime for Trade
in Air Services

3.1. INTRODUCTION TO THE BILATERAL SYSTEM

3.1.1. *Parallel Frameworks: The Chicago Convention and ASAs*

As will now be clear, there are parallel frameworks that organize international air services. One is the product of the Chicago Convention and focuses primarily on setting the terms of international technical cooperation and harmonization. The other is a much more specific economic system that is based on bilateral exchange where two States negotiate an air services agreement (ASA) that grants each party's airlines the privilege to carry passengers, cargo, or a combination of both to points to, from, over, or beyond their respective territories. These market access privileges (commonly referred to as "traffic rights") have historically been subject to a number of protectionist conditions, including, *inter alia*, caps on the number of flights flown over a given time period (frequencies), predetermined limits on the amount of passengers and/or cargo carried (capacity), and rate of return (pricing or air fare) regulations.

3.1.2. *The Nationality Rule*

No restrictive condition has been more conspicuous than the pervasive requirement, stitched into virtually all ASAs, that an airline must be substantially owned (and often also effectively controlled) by its home State (or by the citizens of that State) before it is eligible to perform international air services under that State's ASAs. Referred to by aviation lawyers as the "nationality rule,"[1] the extraordinary consequence of that restriction is that the world's

---

[1] In this book, the nationality rule includes both ASA nationality clauses (requiring States to designate for international service only airlines owned and controlled by the designating State

airlines are effectively barred from fully accessing global equity markets,[2] from establishing foreign subsidiaries, and from consummating cross-border mergers. As a result, there is no such thing as a true global airline, although Australia and New Zealand had aspirations to build such a Colossus at the Chicago conference in 1944.[3] To borrow a slogan favored by the International Air Transport Association (IATA), the nationality rule prevents airlines "from doing business like any other business."[4] In a phrase, the industry that helped to globalize the world has not itself become globalized.

3.1.3. *Recent Liberalization Initiatives*

In the last two decades, however, the bilateral system (known as the "Chicago" system even though it evolved after the Chicago Convention[5]) has undergone a paradigm shift from overt protectionism to an increasingly widespread tolerance, even enthusiasm, for reducing barriers to international trade in air services. The United States, through its open skies policy,[6] has secured liberal reciprocal market access concessions from more than 100 partner States, including a landmark agreement in 2007 with all 27 Member States of the European Union (EU).[7] The EU, in turn, has developed an external aviation

---

or its citizens), and domestic laws that cap foreign ownership and control of home State airlines).

[2] Ironically, airlines' access to foreign *debt* markets is usually unrestricted, unless a foreign bank or investor acquires so much debt in a carrier that the home State or the home State citizens lose effective control over the airline. For example, in 2011 the Royal Bank of Scotland (RBS) sold all of its aircraft leasing operations to Sumitomo Mitsui of Japan for $700 million. Sumitomo is not barred by the nationality rule from financing aircraft leases for U.S. or U.K. airlines that previously relied on RBS. *See infra* Chapter 8, Section 8.2.2.

[3] *See* Michael E. Levine, *Scope and Limits of Multilateral Approaches to International Air Transport, in* OECD, INTERNATIONAL AIR TRANSPORT: THE CHALLENGES AHEAD 75, 87 n.6 (1993) (describing the proposal as a harbinger of "international socialism").

[4] The slogan has appeared in a number of settings. *See, e.g.,* INT'L AIR TRANSP. ASSOC., *Agenda for Freedom,* http://www.agenda-for-freedom.aero/.

[5] *See* BRIAN F. HAVEL, BEYOND OPEN SKIES: A NEW REGIME FOR INTERNATIONAL AVIATION 9 (2009).

[6] Open skies received official imprimatur in a policy statement issued by the U.S. Department of Transportation in 1992; *see generally* In the Matter of Defining "Open Skies," Dkt. No. 48130, Order 92-8-13, 1992 DOT Av. LEXIS 568 (Dep't of Transp. Aug 5, 1992). The policy principles were reaffirmed three years later in the Department of Transportation's Statement of United States International Air Transportation Policy, Dkt. No. 49844, 60 Fed. Reg. 21,841 (May 3, 1995). Although the term originated as a piece of U.S. policy nomenclature, it is now broadly applied to any liberal ASA.

[7] *See* Air Transport Agreement, U.S.-EU, Apr. 30, 2007, 2007 O.J. (L 134) 4, 46 I.L.M. 470 [hereinafter U.S./EU Air Transport Agreement]. The Agreement entered into provisional force on March 30, 2008, and was subsequently modified by the Protocol to Amend the Air Transport Agreement, U.S.-EU, Jun. 24, 2010, 2010 O.J. (L 223) 3. For a consolidated version of the 2007

policy aimed at exporting its *internal* model of a single aviation market among EU Member States to countries in the Union's geographic neighborhood. Simultaneously, the EU is pursuing strategic bilateral partnerships (such as the aforementioned agreement with the United States) to create an Open Aviation Area (OAA) between the EU and leading aviation powers that is intended to go even further than the U.S. open skies model in its efforts to liberalize trade in air services.[8] Regional accords, such as the Yamoussoukro Declaration/Decision among members of the African Union and the aviation agreements finalized among the member States of the Association of Southeast Asian Nations (ASEAN), have also pressed air transport liberalization forward, although in a piecemeal and incomplete manner. Meanwhile, despite the fact that the international community has come to embrace trade in goods and services at the multilateral level under the auspices of the World Trade Organization (WTO), the "hard" economic elements of air services, notably the exchange of traffic rights, have been excluded from that regime.

3.1.4. *Overview of Topics*

In this chapter, we overview the most salient features of the legal regime that has evolved to regulate international trade in air services. For conceptual simplicity, we build our analysis around the substantive elements of the U.S. open skies template,[9] but with frequent reference to important distinctions

and 2010 instruments, see Air Transport Agreement as Amended by Protocol to Amend the Air Transport Agreement Between the United States of America and the European Union and Its Member States, *reprinted in* U.S. Dep't of State, *Eighth Meeting of the US-EU Joint Committee: Record of Meetings, Attachment 2* (Nov. 17, 2010), http://www.state.gov/docu ments/organization/151670.pdf. Unless otherwise noted, all references to the U.S./EU Air Transport Agreement are to the *amended version* of that treaty.

[8] The OAA concept is derived conceptually from the Transatlantic Common Aviation Area (TCAA) initiative proposed by the Association of European Airlines (AEA) in 1999. *See* Ass'n of Eur. Airlines, Towards a Transatlantic Common Aviation Area: AEA Policy Statement (1999). Although it is sometimes compared with the U.S. open skies policy, the OAA (like the TCAA) embodies a more robust agenda for air transport liberalization – one that includes unrestricted traffic rights, cross-border investment in airlines, and comprehensive regulatory harmonization. No third State has yet entered into a full OAA with the EU (the agreement with Canada includes four progressive steps to full OAA status that depend on uncertain future Canadian legislative changes: *see* Agreement on Air Transport Between Canada and the European [Union] and its Member States, Dec. 17, 2009, 2010 O.J. (L 207) 32). On the future of the EU's external aviation policy, including proposals for future agreements, *see infra* Section 3.5.4.

[9] *See generally* U.S. Dep't of State, Air Transport Agreement Between the Government of the United States of America and the Government of [Country] (Jan. 12, 2012), http://www.state. gov/documents/organization/114970.pdf [hereinafter Model Open Skies Agreement]. An alternative model is the "Full liberalization" Template Air Services Agreement (TASA) of the

that exist in the bilateral aviation trade relationships of other countries and regions. With more than 4000 ASAs in existence,[10] along with thousands of additional hard and soft law instruments modifying those agreements,[11] it is impossible for a single chapter (or even a single volume) to capture all of the nuances, particularities, and exceptions that clutter the landscape of aviation trade. Even so, once readers are familiar with the system's principal juristic elements, the idiosyncrasies of specific agreements can be readily deciphered. We will conclude with a look at international aviation's attenuated presence within the WTO system and discuss how that organization's trade disciplines do not align easily with the key substantive rights exchanged under bilateral ASAs. We begin with a brief retrospective look at the history of trade in air services, including the emergence of its resolutely bilateral character and its embrace of certain unique ideas in international commercial regulation.

3.2. AVIATION TRADE AFTER THE CHICAGO CONVENTION

3.2.1. *Concessionary Regime of the Chicago Convention*

As discussed in Chapter 2, delegates at the 1944 Chicago conference failed to agree on a single global market system for international aviation. Ideological differences between the United States, on the one hand, and the Western European States, on the other, over the degree of market freedom that ought to be afforded the still fledgling industry drove negotiations about the "proper" aviation economic environment to stalemate. As we noted, the multilateral treaty that was finalized at the conference – the Chicago Convention[12] – is not devoid of economic impact. The principle of airspace sovereignty,[13] allied with the affirmation of the rights of States to regulate commercial airspace access on a concessionary basis[14] and to reserve domestic air transport ("cabotage") to their

---

ICAO. ICAO also provides both "Traditional" and "Transitional" templates. *See* ICAO, Air Transport Bureau, Economic Policy & Infrastructure Management Section, Economic Regulation Template Air Services Agreement, http://legacy.icao.int/icao/en/atb/epm/Ecp/Tasa.htm.

[10] *See* WTO, *Air Services Agreements Projector* (2010), http://www.wto.org/asap/index.html.

[11] *See* Cornelia Woll, *The Road to External Representation: The European Commission's Activism in International Air Transport*, 13 J. EUR. PUB. POL'Y 52, 56 (2006) (stating that if one takes into account all informal exchanges, additions, and writings, the global number of extant bilateral ASAs may be as high as 10,000).

[12] *See* Convention on International Civil Aviation, *opened for signature* Dec. 7, 1944, 61 Stat. 1180, 15 U.N.T.S. 295 (entered into force Apr. 4, 1947) [hereinafter Chicago Convention]. As of March 2013, 191 States are parties to the Convention. *See supra* Chapter 1, n. 11.

[13] *See id.* art. 1.

[14] *See id.* art. 6.

own air carriers,[15] produced powerful economic implications. An obsessive focus on sovereignty displaced any notion of creating a commercial airspace analog to the *mare liberum* (freedom of the high seas).[16] Thus, before an airline serving international routes is permitted to operate any service that crosses the sovereign airspace of a foreign State (or to land in, depart from, or enplane or deplane passengers or cargo within that territory), its home State must negotiate a concession from the foreign State that allows it do so. The Convention, however, did not predetermine how negotiations for such concessions might be conducted. The world's States (or a group of like-minded States) *could*, in theory, have subscribed to a multilateral and generous distribution of uniform traffic rights. In practice, protectionist impulses ruled.

3.2.2. *Failure of Multilateralism: The Two Freedoms and Five Freedoms Agreements*

Nevertheless, even though hard economic provisions were mostly stripped out of the Chicago Convention, the United States and some other participants still advocated for side agreements exchanging traffic rights at the multilateral level. To that end, the Chicago delegates did prepare two ancillary accords, the International Air Services Transit Agreement ("Two Freedoms Agreement")[17] and the International Air Transport Agreement ("Five Freedoms Agreement").[18] Those agreements instituted the "freedoms of the air," actually a series of restrictions that sought to confine market access rights within an ascending scale of relative openness (discussed below). Of the two instruments, only the Two Freedoms Agreement – with its provisions limited to flyover and noncommercial landing rights – managed to win wide assent in a world suspicious of unbridled market forces.[19] The Five Freedoms

---

[15] *See id.* art. 7; *see supra* Chapter 2, Part 2.5.

[16] *See generally* HUGO GROTIUS, THE FREEDOM OF THE SEAS (Ralph Van Deman Mogoffin trans., Oxford Univ. Press 1916) (1608). French scholar Paul Fauchille was the best-known advocate for an aviation regime modeled on Grotius's principles. He observed that the air was, like Grotius had said about the oceans, capable of being occupied but not of being possessed. *See* STUART BANNER, WHO OWNS THE SKY?: THE STRUGGLE TO CONTROL AIRSPACE FROM THE WRIGHT BROTHERS ON 48–50 (2008); *see also supra* Chapter 2, n. 34.

[17] International Air Services Transit Agreement, *opened for signature* Dec. 7, 1944, 59 Stat. 1693, 84 U.N.T.S. 389 (entered into force Jan. 30, 1945) (129 State parties as of January 2013) [hereinafter Two Freedoms Agreement].

[18] International Air Transport Agreement, *opened for signature* Dec. 7, 1944, 59 Stat. 1701, 171 U.N.T.S. 387 (entered into force Jan. 30, 1945) (11 State parties as of January 2013) [hereinafter Five Freedoms Agreement].

[19] The Two Freedoms Agreement has been ratified by 129 States since 1944. When set beside the mere 11 ratifications received by the Five Freedoms Agreement, it is incommensurably the

Agreement held the potential to allow airlines to develop deeper transnational route networks by generally granting an airline of a State party the privilege not only to carry traffic back and forth between any point in its home State and any point in a foreign State party to the Agreement,[20] but also to move traffic "beyond" that foreign State to serve points in any third State party.[21] But the Five Freedoms Agreement attracted few adherents and quickly became moribund. Arguably, at the inception of the Agreement only the U.S. airline industry was poised to take full advantage of its multilateral liberalizing provisions. From an economic standpoint, that "first mover" advantage of U.S. carriers was not necessarily problematic. If they enjoyed the resources, technology, and initiative to provide international air service at a level superior to that of foreign competitors, no *economic reason* disqualified them from doing so. States with less nimble air transport sectors would, theoretically, have been better off switching resources into services (or goods) where they held a comparative advantage while their consumers used U.S. airlines for international travel.[22] Such a happy destiny for the U.S. airline industry was utopian, of course, because pure-form Darwinian economic thinking was trumped in the 1940s and later by a mix of ideological factors that included national pride, deep-seated suspicion of unregulated economies, and a belief that airlines were primarily public utilities rather than autonomous actors in the marketplace. Another half-century would pass before the major aviation powers (especially those of Western Europe) would take economic theory as normative in framing policy for international air transport.

3.2.3. *Rise of Bilateralism and Managed Trade*

After the failure of the Five Freedoms Agreement to prompt a multilateral exchange of even minimally liberal market access privileges, States began to use bilateral ASAs as the principal diplomatic and political vehicle for

---

more successful of the two agreements. For more on the early history of these treaties, see Charles S. Rhyne, *International Law and Air Transportation*, 47 MICH. L. REV. 41 (1948).

[20] These back-and-forth privileges are called the third and fourth freedoms; *see infra* text accompanying note 36.

[21] Under the fifth freedom, *see infra* text accompanying note 41, an air carrier can bring passengers (and cargo) back and forth between a foreign State (the bilateral partner State) and a third State, but the flight must always remain an extension of a sequence that will end in the home State. There is (as yet) no generally available privilege to move traffic back and forth between a foreign State and a third State without a home State connection. *See infra* text accompanying note 49.

[22] On the distinction between comparative and absolute advantage in international trade, see *supra* Chapter 2, n. 31.

these trades.[23] As an object of purely bilateral exchange, however, market access privileges were now to be conceded only on the basis of defensive reciprocity. A State could choose to tighten or loosen any number of operating restrictions, including constraints on pricing, capacity, frequencies, and traffic rights, in line with the recalcitrance or generosity of its bilateral partners. A principal motivation for a managed trade strategy was that a State, by not "giving away" too much market access to other States, could secure for its own airlines what it perceived to be an equitable share of any given trans-national market. Other restrictions, which have long been endemic in this system, could then be utilized to freeze each partner's carriers in artificial commercial parity. For instance, in a two-State scenario where State A's airline has a higher cost structure than the airline of State B, State A may insist on pricing controls for routes between the two countries in order to ensure that its own airline is able to recover its costs (plus, most likely, any additional capital necessary to attract equity investments),[24] despite the fact that State B's more efficient carrier may be able to set lower prices while still recovering its costs. Similarly, where State A's airline has more available capacity to dedicate to routes between the two countries, State B may insist on capacity limits to ensure that its airline is able to carry a roughly equal share of the traffic.

3.2.4. *Bilateralism Is Not Ordained in the Chicago Convention*

Although this system of piecemeal give-and-take, as already noted, is often labeled the "Chicago system," bilateralism is in no way ordained by the Chicago Convention itself. Delegates at the conference did adopt Resolution VIII, captioned "Standard Form of Agreement for Provisional Air Routes," which recommended a model nonexclusive bilateral agreement that States were free to adopt during a transitional period (the immediate postwar period) "in order to obtain practical experience for giving effect to more permanent arrangements at a later date."[25] Divisions among the delegations

---

[23] The idea of bilateralism was actually considered at the Chicago conference and a model agreement emerged from delegate discussions. *See* main text *infra*.

[24] In instances where an airline was owned by its home State and thus was not under the same market pressures as private enterprises to return profits to its investors, pricing controls could still be used to protect the nationally owned airline (and hence its State owner) from the embarrassment of ceding large portions of its market share to foreign competitors. This "national pride" component of aviation policy still exerts a powerful influence in the realm of trade in air services.

[25] *See* Resolution VIII, *in* Resolutions for the Final Act of the International Civil Aviation Conference (Dec. 7, 1944), *reprinted in* 3 Av. L. Rep. (CCH) ¶ 28,012, at 25,063–66.

at Chicago ensured that no such "more permanent arrangements" ever materialized. The result, a massive case-by-case negotiation and exchange of
literally thousands of international air routes, has been colorfully described
by a leading commentator as a "labyrinthine legal grotto."[26]

3.3. THE FREEDOMS OF THE AIR

3.3.1. *At the Core of All Aviation Trade Agreements*

The substantive content of ASAs, present and projecting into the future, will
shortly occupy our attention for the remainder of this chapter. In this part we
examine one of international aviation's most visible deposits of jargon and
conceptual confusion: the nine freedoms of the air.[27] Entry into the domain of
international aviation law, somewhat ironically, demands fluency in the nine
freedoms despite the fact that almost no ASAs characterize their exchanges of
traffic rights using terminology such as "first freedom," "second freedom,"
"third freedom," and so on. Yet the content of these freedoms lies at the core of
all aviation trade agreements and remains a contentious element in air services
negotiations. It is not difficult to see why. An airline's right to carry international traffic (passengers, cargo, or both in combination) over, to, from, within,
or beyond points in a foreign State can seriously affect its economic viability.
When the United States and China initialed a new ASA in 2007 that increased
daily round-trip flight opportunities for U.S. carriers to Beijing, Shanghai, and
Guangzhou over a period of five years from ten to twenty-three,[28] every major
U.S. carrier petitioned the U.S. Department of Transportation (DOT) for
authorization to serve one or more of the new routes.[29] With China's sizzling
economy and growing reputation as a tourist destination, market access to
major Chinese cities had become a source of substantial potential revenues for
U.S. airlines. Although technically this improvement in U.S./China aviation
relations did not confer new freedoms of the air *per se* between the parties, the

---

[26] BIN CHENG, THE LAW OF INTERNATIONAL AIR TRANSPORT 491 (1962).

[27] A tenth freedom has been posited: the privilege of a foreign-owned enterprise to launch
     suborbital space vehicles from inside another State's territory and to return the vehicle to
     earth within the same territory – a trajectory that might otherwise be prohibited by the cabotage
     rule. *See supra* Chapter 2, n. 93.

[28] *See* Ariana Eunjung Cha & Del Quentin Weber, *U.S., China Agree to Double Flights*, WASH.
     POST, May 24, 2007, at D1, http://www.washingtonpost.com/wp-dyn/content/article/2007/05/
     23/AR2007052301120.html. On the definition of frequencies, see *infra* text accompanying
     note 134.

[29] *See U.S. Airlines Fight For New Routes*, SHANGHAI DAILY, July 25, 2007, http://www.china.org.
     cn/archive/2007-07/25/content_1218468.htm. Under open skies agreements, however, there are
     no *a priori* limitations on route availability.

easing of restrictions on the use of the existing five freedoms was itself commercially significant.

3.3.2. *The "Noncommercial" First and Second Freedoms*

The Two Freedoms Agreement, as previously mentioned, received wide ratification after the close of the Chicago conference in December 1944. One explanation for that outcome is that the Agreement does not exchange hard economic (i.e., traffic) rights, but rather resolves sovereignty issues that impinge on the ordinary functionality of international air services. Thus, the first freedom of the air allows foreign airlines to operate services that pass over the granting State's territory (hence its description as the "flyover" privilege). The second freedom permits landings for "non-traffic" (i.e., noncommercial) purposes, such as technical, maintenance, or refueling stops.[30] Neither privilege[31] appears to have much direct economic effect on the grantor's air transport market, and both are typically regarded as "transit" privileges. As one observer has noted, "a commercial enterprise ... would not get very far if ... limited to the exercise of these two privileges."[32] On the other hand, a commercial enterprise would likely not get very far without these privileges either. Despite its technical nature, the first freedom in particular can have substantial economic consequences. Without overflight rights, States such as Canada and Russia, which control large blocks of the world's airspace, could impede direct international routes. Russia has long exploited its jurisdiction over the shortest air routes from Europe to East Asia (the trans-Siberian corridor) to levy what most observers regard as excessive overflight fees on EU airlines.[33] At the same time, Russia capped the number of U.S. air carriers that can overfly the corridor, although an agreement reached

---

[30] *See* Two Freedoms Agreement, *supra* note 17, art. I.

[31] In view of the sovereignty principle in Article 1 of the Chicago Convention, it would be more accurate to speak of the freedoms as "privileges," which is the word used in both the Two Freedoms and Five Freedoms agreements. Nevertheless, the expression "freedoms of the air" has attained wide currency in the law of international air transport.

[32] R. M. Forrest, *Is Open Competition Preferable to Regulation?*, 6 Air L. 7, 8 (1981).

[33] Russia has allegedly used these "rents" to prop up its own national carrier, Aeroflot. Indeed, EU airline executives report that overflight fees were often paid directly to Aeroflot's bank account. For years the EU protested these charges and negotiated with Russia to curtail them. EU negotiators appeared finally to have succeeded as a condition of Russia's accession to the WTO, and in 2011 Russia and the EU signed a set of "Agreed Principles on the Modernization of the Siberian Overflight System." *See* Press Release, Europa, Air Transport: Commission Welcomes Agreement on Siberian Overflights (Dec. 1, 2011). But the European Commission is skeptical of Russia's willingness to honor the terms of that agreement. *See* European Comm'n, Communication from the Commission to the European Parliament, The Council, The European Economic and Social Committee and the Committee of the Regions, *The EU's External Aviation Policy: Addressing Future Challenges*, COM (2012) 556

with the United States in 2005 aimed to remove these numeric caps and to limit charges imposed on U.S. air carriers to navigation costs only.[34] The second freedom's allowance for refueling stops has, admittedly, lost some relevance in light of technological enhancements to the range of aircraft, but no airline would want to risk an aircraft being stranded in the air because of a technical emergency until it could return to its home State. In sum, the first and second freedoms are not anachronisms. Even late-model ASAs, such as the 2007 U.S./EU Air Transport Agreement, embed these transit rights in the negotiated package of commercial access privileges.[35] Knowing that their airlines' other privileges could be vitiated without the first two freedoms, States are unwilling to rely solely on the original Two Freedoms Agreement.

3.3.3. *Traffic Rights (1): The Third and Fourth Freedoms*

The Five Freedoms Agreement, considered earlier, includes the two transit rights in the Two Freedoms Agreement and three additional freedoms called "traffic rights." These traffic rights (or, more accurately, traffic "privileges"[36]) grant permission to pick up and discharge passengers and cargo (or both) and accordingly have a much more direct bearing on the commercial choices airlines make in building their international markets.[37] For ease of explanation, we will take as examples the commercial flight activities of two major international air carriers, United Airlines (United) and British Airways (BA), airlines designated to provide international air service by their respective aeropolitically powerful home States, the United States and the United Kingdom (U.K.).[38] The third freedom bestows upon United, as a designated

---

final (Sept. 27, 2012), at 13, 17 [hereinafter European Comm'n, *External Aviation Policy*]. There have been rumblings that the controversy over extension of the EU's emissions trading scheme to non-EU airlines (*see infra* Chapter 6) could once again make Siberian overflights an issue. *See* Jens Flottau & Robert Wall, *Russia May Block EU Carriers from Siberian Overflight in Emissions Trading Battle*, AVIATION DAILY, Feb. 23, 2012, at 1, http://www.aviationweek.com/Article.aspx?id=/article-xml/avd_02_23_2012_p01-01-428477.xml.

[34] *See* Protocol between the Government of the United States of America and the Government of the Russian Federation to Amend the Jan. 14, 1994 Air Transport Agreement, annex IV, secs. 5–6, U.S.-Rus., Oct. 5, 2005, *reprinted in* 3 Av. L. Rep. (CCH) ¶ 26,474d, at 22,977.

[35] *See, e.g.,* U.S./EU Air Transport Agreement, *supra* note 7, art. 3(1)(a) –(b).

[36] *See supra* note 31 (on the distinction between "freedoms" and "privileges").

[37] *See* Five Freedoms Agreement, *supra* note 18, art. I.

[38] We will also assume that these airlines carry passengers only, although in reality most long-haul international airlines operate as combination carriers, supplementing passenger traffic by carrying cargo in their aircraft hulls. All-cargo carriers, such as FedEx and DHL, typically enjoy not only the same freedoms of the air under their respective States' bilateral agreements as combination carriers, but additional privileges as well. *See infra* text accompanying note 53.

U.S. carrier,[39] the privilege to carry passengers from the United States to the U.K. The mirror image of that right is the fourth freedom, which permits United to enplane passengers in the U.K. for transit back to the United States. BA, in turn, carries passengers to the United States using U.K. third freedom privileges, and flies passengers back to the U.K. employing the fourth freedom.[40] The commercial value of the third freedom would be eviscerated without the fourth freedom: for United or BA to fly empty aircraft back across the Atlantic without enplaning new traffic would be economic madness.

3.3.4. *Traffic Rights (2): The Fifth Freedom*

The fifth freedom is optimistically known as the "network-building" freedom despite its scope limitations. This freedom allows United, on arrival in the U.K. under the third freedom, to enplane passengers or cargo for further transit to a point in a third State (such as France or Germany) with which the United States maintains a bilateral air services relationship *that also permits this freedom to be exercised.*[41] Thus, fifth freedom "beyond" traffic requires the United States to have the permission of *both* the U.K. *and* the third State,

---

[39] "Designation" has come to be used as a term of art in international aviation law. The term refers to the airline of a given State that is authorized under that State's internal regulations and the provisions of its ASAs to perform international air services as a designated airline of that State. Restrictive bilateral agreements will sometimes carry designation restrictions limiting the number of airlines the signatory States may authorize to serve points in their respective territories. For example, under the highly restrictive U.S./U.K. ASA known as Bermuda II (which replaced an earlier agreement known, in similar eponymous tribute to the place of negotiation and signature, as Bermuda I), the United States could designate only two air carriers to serve points between U.S. territory and London's Heathrow Airport. *See generally* Agreement Concerning Air Services, U.S.-U.K., Jun. 22 & Jul. 23, 1977, 28 U.S.T. 5367 [hereinafter Bermuda II] (superseded by the U.S./EU Air Transport Agreement, *supra* note 7). For more on the restrictive nature of this infamous treaty, see Bin Cheng, *The Role of Consultation in Bilateral International Air Services Agreements, as Exemplified by Bermuda I and Bermuda II,* 19 Colum. J. Transnat'l L. 183 (1981); Harriet Oswalt Hill, Comment, *Bermuda II: The British Revolution of 1976,* 44 J. Air L. & Com. 111 (1978).

[40] Because the principle of nationality is so endemic in international aviation law, it is worth emphasizing that, in the context of picking up passengers either in the home State or in any other State where an airline exercises traffic "rights," that airline can carry passengers of any nationality. Readers may find this obvious, but at the same time might have been incredulous to learn that under international aviation law airlines themselves can only fly internationally if they have an ownership profile that ties them to the nationals of a particular State (or to ownership by that State itself). *See infra* Part 3.4. Interestingly, and relatedly, many States (and airlines) hold to the view that airlines have a primary commercial claim on the custom of their home State nationals. *See infra* note 136.

[41] The situations described here are hypotheticals based on historic aeropolitical relations. Because of the 2007 U.S./EU Air Transport Agreement, *supra* note 7, the 28 EU Member States no longer have separate bilateral agreements with the United States.

whether France or Germany.[42] If United enplanes no additional passengers or cargo in the U.K., but merely carries U.S.-origin traffic to additional points outside the U.K., this is treated as so-called blind sector transit and does not require additional negotiated permission. If the beyond point is a second destination in the U.K., however, United will need to rely upon a negotiated "coterminalization right."[43] When United carries traffic from the United States to the U.K. using an *intermediate* stop in France or Germany, discharges some U.S. passengers or cargo, and picks up new passengers or cargo in France or Germany bound for the U.K., this carriage, known as "intermediate" fifth freedom traffic, also requires the United States to have the permission of *both* the U.K. *and* the intermediate third State, France or Germany. Again, fifth freedom privileges exercised by BA replicate those of United: having flown London Heathrow to New York JFK, for example, as part of that service BA might pick up passengers or cargo at JFK for onward transit to Canada, or make an intermediate stop in Toronto en route to New York to discharge passengers or cargo from the U.K. and to enplane new traffic bound for the United States. Of course, once again, the exchange of fifth freedom rights on a strictly bilateral basis "may become entirely valueless if traffic rights are not also granted by the third country concerned"[44] (France, Germany, and Canada in the foregoing examples). That "network" precondition to the exercise of fifth freedoms causes most complications in practice, and was one the major reasons that the Five Freedoms Agreement failed to attract State adherents. The route-building potential of the bilateral system is circumscribed still further by the general rule that the exercise of traffic rights contained in most ASAs must be tied to specific route patterns between the home State and any foreign State with which it is contracting bilaterally. In other words, United and BA are not allowed to create long chains of intermediate connections that have only incidental (or theoretical) origin and termination points in their home territories. To illustrate, United would not be able to use a fifth freedom to carry passengers from Chicago to Toronto, then enplane new passengers in Canada for onward transit to London and

---

[42] As expressed by the former Chairman of the U.S. Civil Aeronautics Board, John Robson, "[b]eyond [i.e., fifth freedom] rights are essentially prisoner to whatever arrangements can be made with the second, the beyond point." *Quoted in* HAVEL, BEYOND OPEN SKIES, *supra* note 5, at 106.

[43] Coterminalization rights should be distinguished from cabotage rights. The latter implicates enplaning new traffic at the first destination in a foreign State's territory for transit to a second destination point; the former simply implicates two "drop off" points with no new traffic taken aboard.

[44] Z. Joseph Gertler, *Order in the Air and the Problem of Real and False Opinions*, 4 ANNALS AIR & SPACE L. 93, 119 (1979).

then "link" the service into fifth freedoms conceded under the U.S./U.K. (or, more accurately, U.S./EU[45]) ASA by enplaning new traffic in London for additional beyond transit to, say, Istanbul or Moscow under U.S. ASAs with Turkey and Russia, respectively. Accordingly, the network potential of the fifth freedom is typically exhausted after only a single exercise.

3.3.5. *Nuances in the System (1): The Sixth Freedom*

In counterpoint to the prevailing philosophy of closure in the air services trade system, State practice has introduced some nuances that increase airline flexibility (although, historically, they have not usually been a part of the formal bilateral agenda). It is possible, for example, for air passenger or cargo traffic to originate from a country *other than* the United States, to transit through the United States, and to continue to the U.K., where that traffic is set down. This complex of access privileges, known as the sixth freedom, conflates the fourth and third freedoms (in that order). Using our existing U.S./U.K. model, fourth freedom (inbound) traffic moves from, say, Mexico to the United States (United's home State) under the U.S./Mexico ASA. Some of the U.S./Mexico passengers or cargo continue as third freedom (outbound) traffic from the United States to the U.K. under the U.S./U.K. (now U.S./EU) air services bilateral agreement. From BA's point of view, passengers or cargo in France flying to New York via London on BA flights would be sixth freedom traffic, combining two streams of fourth and third freedom traffic (i.e., Paris/London and London/New York). In practice, sixth freedom traffic can be very difficult for either the origin or the destination State to control.[46] Where sixth freedom traffic *is* carried with the knowledge and consent of the origin State (here, Mexico or France) under its respective ASAs, the term "anterior fifth freedom" can be substituted for "sixth freedom."[47] In sixth freedom scenarios, the home State of the carrier performing the service is itself an intermediate or swivel point between two other origin and destination States: for example, Dubai is the swivel point for Emirates' air services from the U.K. and Germany to points in southeast Asia and Africa. Put another way, the home State's carrier exercises fifth freedom rights out of *its own* territory. U.K. and German competitors are aware of Emirates' revenue-enhancing conflation of fourth

---

[45] *See supra* note 41 (indicating that the examples used here are historical in light of the 2007 U.S./EU agreement).

[46] *See* DANIEL A. KASPER, DEREGULATION AND GLOBALIZATION: LIBERALIZING INTERNATIONAL TRADE IN SERVICES 53 (1988).

[47] *See* PAT HANLON, GLOBAL AIRLINES: COMPETITION IN A TRANSNATIONAL INDUSTRY 87 (2d ed. 2002).

and third freedoms, yet there does not appear to be a legal basis for obstructing it. Although it is conceivable that a State could insist on sixth freedom limitations in its ASAs, international aviation's present trade regime has, for better or worse, made peace with the existence of this "rogue" freedom even if a select number of air carriers have not.[48]

3.3.6. *Nuances in the System (2): The Seventh Freedom*

In recent years, the sixth freedom has been augmented by a seventh freedom, namely, sixth freedom traffic as in the above examples, but *without* a stop at the transit point in the home State. Thus, United could offer direct service from Mexico to the U.K. without a U.S. swivel point; or BA could operate a direct Frankfurt/New York route, without touching U.K. territory. The latter scenario is now legally feasible under the U.S./EU ASA, which provides that any airline licensed in accordance with the Union's common licensing criteria (and, thus, owned and controlled by any EU Member State or by nationals of any EU Member State) can be designated to carry passenger and/or cargo traffic between the geographic territory of the EU and all points in the United States.[49] The grant of seventh freedom (so-called stand-alone) privileges, particularly for passenger traffic, is a rarity.[50] Japan, for example, will not readily jeopardize the market shares of its two international airlines (Japan Air Lines (JAL) and All Nippon Airways (ANA)) by allowing United or BA to operate direct seventh freedom (as

---

[48] See *infra* text accompanying note 108. In fact, sixth freedom privileges are explicitly included in some agreements. *See* Model Open Skies Agreement, *supra* note 9, art. 2. For an interesting analysis of the origin of the sixth freedom right as "homeland bridge carriage" by States well situated on a reasonably direct routing between other States that originate or terminate significant traffic volumes, *see* International Civil Aviation Organization (ICAO), Manual on the Regulation of International Air Transport 4.1-12 to 4.1-14, ICAO Doc. 9626 (2d ed. 2004) [hereinafter ICAO Manual] (noting that, for example, airlines based in southern Africa, southern South America, and Australia have virtually no sixth freedom opportunities because there is "literally no place for them to find or take traffic behind their homelands").

[49] See U.S./EU Air Transport Agreement, *supra* note 7, art. 3(1)(c), art. 4. Seventh freedom privileges for U.S. carriers under the Agreement, however, are limited to all-cargo carriers and include only access to third State points beyond the Czech Republic, France, Germany, Luxembourg, Malta, Poland, Portugal, and the Slovak Republic. For example, while FedEx could carry seventh freedom cargo between Toronto and Paris, it could not do so between Mexico City and London. No U.S. passenger carrier, not even a combination carrier such as United, is afforded seventh freedom privileges under the Agreement.

[50] See WTO, Council for Trade in Services, *Quantitative Air Services Agreements Review (QUASAR): Part B: Preliminary Results*, at 42, para. 118, S/C/W/270/Add.1 (Nov. 30, 2006) (describing seventh freedom rights as a "marginal feature" of ASAs).

opposed to indirect fifth freedom) services from Tokyo to points in Asia that JAL and ANA already serve.[51] Indeed, looking again at the new U.S./EU arrangement, rather than an authentic grant of liberty to operate air services entirely independent of their home territories, the seventh freedoms enjoyed by all EU airlines under the U.S./EU ASA and other Union-brokered agreements are best portrayed as the result of a common aviation market that obliterates national distinctions between EU Member State airlines in favor of the supranational legal construct of a "Union air carrier."[52]

3.3.7. *All-Cargo Services and the Seventh Freedom*

Seventh freedom privileges have, however, become increasingly prominent as part of bilateral exchanges of traffic rights for all-cargo airlines. The U.S. open skies policy, for instance, has made extension of these privileges an important (albeit optional) part of U.S. liberal ASAs.[53] For express delivery carriers such as FedEx, UPS, and DHL,[54] seventh freedoms are critical to their business model. By exploiting these privileges in U.S. ASAs with China and the EU, FedEx is able to fly packages from its hub in Guangzhou directly to its hub in Frankfurt without a time-consuming and expensive "backhauling" of traffic

---

[51] As we will see, *see infra* text accompanying note 61, allowing foreign airlines to use hubs as autonomous commercial staging-posts creates regulatory concerns. If United offers a seventh freedom service from Tokyo to Hong Kong, it is still operating as a U.S.-regulated enterprise; incorporation or "establishment" in Japan is not required under international aviation law.

[52] Under its common rules governing air transport, the EU has implemented a common licensing system for airlines that have their "principal place of business" in the territory of any Member State and that are owned and controlled by any EU Member State or by any EU Member State nationals. *See* Common Rules for the Operation of Air Services in the European [Union], Council Regulation 1008/2008, 2008 O.J. (L 293) 3, art. 3(1) [hereinafter Common Rules]. The common licensing system is administered in each Member State by national authorities that apply common EU criteria to determine the financial fitness of airlines seeking an "operating license." *See id.* art. 5. Referred to in the legislation as "Community air carriers," EU airlines are afforded full market freedoms within the entire territory of the European Union. Following the ratification in December 2009 of the Treaty of Lisbon ("Treaty of Lisbon Amending the Treaty on European Union and the Treaty Establishing the European Communities"), Dec. 13, 2007 O.J. (C 306) 1, which abolished the long-standing distinction between the European Union and the European Community in favor of the former, it appears more appropriate to refer to airlines licensed in the EU as "Union air carriers."

[53] *See* Model Open Skies Agreement, *supra* note 9, art. 2.

[54] *See generally* Brian F. Havel, *Rethinking the General Agreement on Trade in Services as a Pathway to Global Aviation Liberalization*, 44(1) IRISH JURIST 95 (2009) (discussing just-in-time business model of the express logistics industry, and its contingent reliance on air transport as the speediest means of shipment: if Olympic runners could deliver goods and parcels faster, the industry model would substitute athletes for airplanes).

to its U.S. hub in Memphis, Tennessee, for onward routing to Germany. The willingness of States to afford wider freedoms to foreign all-cargo carriers than for passenger and combination services is likely tied to the positive economic effects that emanate from this key subsector of air services. Major express delivery operators already have large international route networks available – networks that are difficult (and wasteful) for most States' air carriers to duplicate. Countries with businesses that want to integrate into the global economy can rely on established express carriers, and are ready to set aside objections to the foreign nationality of the providers.[55] Additionally, isolated regions such as Oceania (primarily Australia and New Zealand) depend heavily on air cargo operators for imports as well as exports. Easing the terms of foreign provider access rather than protecting market share for home airlines takes priority in this area of trade in air services. Governments, it seems, no longer see cargo carriage, unlike passenger traffic, as politically troublesome.[56]

3.3.8. *Cabotage (Again): The Eighth and Ninth Freedoms*

Even more contentious than either the sixth or seventh freedoms are the two additional freedoms that fall under the rubric of cabotage. The eighth freedom gives a foreign carrier so-called fill-up rights as it transits between two or more gateways in a foreign State. BA, on a coterminalized London/ New York/Los Angeles route,[57] for example, would be permitted to board new passengers or cargo in New York for the New York/Los Angeles segment only. Ninth freedom traffic is cabotage in its pure form, the privilege to pick up and set down passengers or cargo between two domestic points (New York and Chicago or London and Glasgow), neither of which is the end-point of a flight sequence that began in a foreign State. As we noted in the prior chapter, the cabotage privilege is a rare bird in the realm of air services trade.[58] U.S. open skies agreements, despite their broadly liberal cast, specifically exclude cabotage.[59] A notable outlier is the 2006 U.K./

---

[55] China has even begun to allow foreign express delivery carriers to operate within its domestic market on a limited basis. *See* Bob Sechler, *FedEx, UPS Get a Toehold in China's Express Delivery*, WALL ST. J., Sept. 11, 2012, at B1.

[56] In part this is because, unlike passenger transport, no users (customers) ever personally "experience" the shipment process for cargo services.

[57] *See supra* note 43.

[58] *See also* Council for Trade in Services, *supra* note 50, at 43, para. 120 (observing that "[t]he granting of cabotage rights is an extremely rare feature" in ASAs and identifying only two such agreements worldwide).

[59] *See* Model Open Skies Agreement, *supra* note 9, art. 2(4) ("Nothing in this Article [granting traffic rights] shall be deemed to confer on the airline or airlines of one Party the right to take on

Singapore ASA exchanging reciprocal cabotage access, although the commercial opportunities the rights provide to both parties' airlines are, admittedly, few.[60]

3.3.9. *Distinction Between Cabotage and the Right of Establishment*

Some commentators have (mistakenly) suggested that Australia has awarded cabotage routes to foreign carriers when, in fact, what Australia offers is a right for foreign nationals to *establish* commercial airlines within its territory for the *sole* purpose of serving domestic routes (Virgin Australia, for example).[61] BA, in contrast, does not have any authority under the Australia/U.K. ASA to carry traffic between Melbourne and Sydney. The distinction is not unimportant. By requiring foreign-owned carriers to have a substantial legal and commercial presence within its territory, Australia is able to exert the same regulatory control over the airline's operations that it does over its "indigenous" air carriers such as Qantas. If, however, Australia were to concede cabotage access under its ASAs, its regulatory control over foreign airlines utilizing those privileges might be compromised (although it is unclear how much) in areas such as application of local labor and environmental laws.[62] In fact, labor concerns have long driven resistance to opening cabotage routes to foreign competition. Labor unions contend that a foreign-owned, foreign-based airline providing lucrative cabotage services would be at liberty to use nondomestic staffing and to skirt or avoid local social regulations. Home-based rivals, on the other hand, may have to recognize the right to unionize, and also observe local caps on pilot and crew hours and contribute to social security programs.[63] Other objections, such as the threat that cabotage access may pose to national security, are also touted in the public arena,

---

board, in the territory of the other Party, passengers, baggage, cargo, or mail carried for compensation and destined for another point in the territory of that other Party.").

[60] *See* Alan Khee-Jin Tan, *Singapore's New Air Services Agreements with the EU and the U.K.: Implications for Liberalization in Asia*, 73 J. Air L. & Com. 351, 362–64 (2008). Otherwise put, Singapore Airlines can now fly between any two points in the U.K., a somewhat more appealing concession than reciprocally allowing BA to fly between any two points in Singapore.

[61] *See* Henry Ergas & Christopher Findlay, *New Directions in Australian Air Transport*, 10 Agenda 27, 35 (2003). The right of (commercial) establishment, which subjects the carrier to full regulation by the host foreign State, will be considered further *infra* in Chapter 4, Part 4.3. As previously discussed, Virgin Australia appears to circumvent these limitations by structuring itself so that Australian citizens own and control its international operations. *See supra* Chapter 2, n. 87.

[62] *See supra* Chapter 2, Section 2.5.15 (discussing effects of cabotage on regulatory control by the cabotage-granting State including its labor laws).

[63] *See* Havel, Beyond Open Skies, *supra* note 5, at 129 n.140 (noting, however, that a "right of establishment" would circumvent these alleged drawbacks of cabotage).

but ultimately it seems that States refuse cabotage privileges primarily because of a chauvinistic preference to have their own airlines serving domestic routes.

3.3.10. *Cabotage in the U.S./EU Negotiations*

As discussed in Chapter 2, Article 7 of the Chicago Convention has been invoked by States as a legal barrier to yielding on cabotage access in their ASAs.[64] Although this is certainly an overly narrow (but politically convenient) reading of the Convention, the juristic and practical debates surrounding cabotage are unlikely to subside anytime soon. Recently, during negotiations for the 2007 U.S./EU ASA, the Member States made a *de facto* comparison between fifth freedom privileges that U.S airlines enjoy to serve other EU points from hub destinations such as London and Frankfurt, and a hypothesized eighth freedom privilege to allow EU airlines to serve London/New York/Los Angeles, for example, with new traffic enplaned in New York for onward transit to Los Angeles. The United States rejected that "mirror image" argument, reminding its European partners that the federalization of U.S. airspace still contrasts with multiple separate Member State airspace jurisdictions. U.S. point-to-point services, therefore, are domestic while EU fifth freedom flight movements are international. *De jure* the two sets of privileges are unrelated.[65]

3.4. THE NATIONALITY RULE

3.4.1. *Restrictive Logic of Bilateralism*

One of the most commercially damaging results of the doling-out of piece-meal and uneven traffic privileges under the bilateral system is that no single air carrier with its principal place of business in a single State (i.e., its home State) can develop an autonomous transnational route network.[66]

---

[64] *See supra* Chapter 2, Section 2.5.14.

[65] *See* HAVEL, BEYOND OPEN SKIES, *supra* note 5, at 69. For the U.S. negotiators, the EU was not a genuine "cabotage" jurisdiction but a network of fifth freedoms connecting sovereign States, each of which enjoys a separate voice in ICAO. *See id.* Moreover, in an era of code-sharing and alliances (*see infra* Chapter 4), no U.S. carriers have directly provided intra-Union air passenger services since at least 2002. *See* HAVEL, *id.*

[66] We will refer several times to the notion of a "principal place of business" of airline enterprises. According to ICAO, a principal place of business of an airline is predicated on the following: the company is established and incorporated in accordance with relevant national laws and regulations in the territory of the State that designates it under ASAs to provide international services; it has a substantial amount of its operations and capital investment in physical facilities in that territory; it pays tax, registers, and bases its aircraft there; and it employs a significant

The enduring precondition for the award of traffic rights under ASAs (setting aside narrow grants of seventh freedoms for cargo operations) is the existence of an origin/destination connection to the home State. Within the logic of that system, if either United or BA, for example, desired to create a freestanding network, each would have to pick up traffic rights as designated carriers under as many ASAs as possible within and between the regions the airline wished to serve. To do *that*, United or BA would have to set about acquiring existing airlines or establishing wholly owned subsidiaries in other States, in each case parachuting into the bilateral treaty privileges secured by those States for their designated home carriers. Thus, United and BA could circumvent the bilateral system's home State-centered distribution of traffic rights and effectively "string together" a workable network of market access privileges.[67] If that course of action were permissible, it would allow the airlines to handle, not perfectly but workably, the patchwork of market access privileges required by bilateralism. Strategic trade planning of that kind is commonplace in a globalized world. Unfortunately, however, what is conventional practice for many transnational commercial enterprises is legally prohibited in the exceptional context of international aviation. Because of the nationality rule, as a general matter airlines can neither acquire air carriers nor establish air carrier subsidiaries in foreign States.

3.4.2. *Citizenship Purity and the Absence of Multinational Airlines*

The Chicago conference delegates inserted a formulation of the nationality rule into both the Two and Five Freedoms Agreements that persists with little variation to the present day. Under the original formulation, a State reserves the right to revoke, limit, or suspend traffic rights in respect of any foreign airline designated to operate service under one of its ASAs if that airline is not

---

number of nationals of that territory in managerial, technical, and operational positions. *See* ICAO Manual, *supra* note 48, at 4.4-5.

[67] For example, BA could move passengers from London to New York under the U.S./EU ASA before transferring them to a BA subsidiary established in the United States for final transit to points within U.S. territory. Or BA could use a wholly owned U.S. subsidiary to move passengers to points beyond the United States like São Paulo under the U.S./Brazil treaty. Likewise, BA could operate a subsidiary in Brazil that would move its passengers onward to Chile or Peru under the Brazil/Chile or Brazil/Peru ASAs. But in reality, as the main text clarifies, BA can only assemble these successive networks by "contracting out" many of the flight segments to airlines based in other States. The means by which airlines cooperate in this way are explained further when we consider interlining, code-sharing, and alliances *infra* in Chapter 4. For an explanation of how these international trade principles work in sectors that are not constrained by the nationality rule that governs the airline industry, see *infra* note 90 and accompanying text.

"substantially owned" and "effectively controlled" by the carrier's home State (or by the citizens of that State).[68] It is this insistence on what we polemically call the requirement of "citizenship purity,"[69] inserted into thousands of post-Chicago bilateral air services treaties, that is commonly referred to as the "nationality rule" (or sometimes as the "nationality clause" as situated within a bilateral treaty[70]). Nationality, in other words, has for six decades been the organizing principle of international air commerce. The very names of the oldest airlines in the world – Air Canada, Air France, British Airways – conflate a commercial and national affiliation. There are, it would seem, *American* carriers, *British* carriers, and *Canadian* carriers, but not a single authentically transnational carrier. Because of the nationality rule, there is no *international airline* properly so called; the concept of a multinational enterprise remains unknown in global air transport, even in the twenty-first century.[71]

3.4.3. *Reasons for the Nationality Rule: Security and Strategic Trade Policy*

The nationality rule was motivated originally by the national security concerns of a world emerging from total war. The fear (genuine or otherwise) was that enemy or ex-enemy States could attain indirect market access to the airspace of victorious countries by acquiring airlines in third States upon which traffic rights had been conferred as part of friendly foreign relations. To be sure, bilateral partners could have relied on less draconian measures to assuage security concerns, such as providing a list of "rogue" States whose investments in a partner's airlines would trigger the power of revocation. But the "one size

---

[68] *See* Two Freedoms Agreement, *supra* note 17, art. I, § 5 ("Each contracting State reserves the right to withhold or revoke a certificate or permit to an air transport enterprise of another State in any case where it is not satisfied that substantial ownership and effective control are vested in nationals of a contracting State"); *see also* Five Freedoms Agreement, *supra* note 18, art. 1, § 6. (The Chicago Convention itself contains no provisions on airline (as opposed to *aircraft*) nationality. Even the European Commission has mistakenly assumed otherwise. *See* European Comm'n, *External Aviation Policy, supra* note 33, at 11.)

[69] *See* Brian F. Havel & Gabriel S. Sanchez, *Restoring Global Aviation's "Cosmopolitan Mentalité"*, 29 B.U. Int'l L.J. 1, 16 (2011).

[70] As we previously indicated, *see supra* note 1, in this book we generally use the term "nationality rule" more broadly to encompass both the nationality clauses in ASAs and the many internal State laws that are designed to prop up the nationality clauses by limiting inward investment in national airlines.

[71] This precise point was reiterated in a recent European Commission report on the EU's external aviation policy. *See* European Comm'n, *External Aviation Policy, supra* note 33, at 10 ("[T]here is not a single truly global airline in the way that other industries have global companies.... [The] three global airline alliances ... have come to play a role as the nearest proxy to global airlines.").

fits all" expression of the nationality rule remains embedded in over 90% of extant ASAs.[72] Coupled with defense and security considerations was a strategic trade component to the nationality rule: its applicability ensures that the concessions exchanged between two States cannot be captured by a third State not a party to the deal. This intended result is not dissimilar to the "rule of origin" requirements in free trade agreements whereby concessions, such as zero tariffs on select goods, are contingent on the imports being produced or, in the language of the WTO, having their "last substantial transformation"[73] in the territory of a free-trade partner.[74] If the United States, pursuing market access privileges for its airlines in East Asia, exchanges liberal reciprocal concessions with, for example, South Korea, it would not want investors from a more restrictive State, such as neighboring Japan, to "free ride" on those privileges by either acquiring or establishing an air carrier in South Korea. Japan's incentive to offer new market concessions to U.S. air carriers would be correspondingly diminished so long as its airlines enjoyed asymmetrical market access privileges to the United States through the U.S./South Korea bilateral agreement.

3.4.4. *Protectionist Effects of the Nationality Rule*

At the same time, however, it is important to bear in mind the broader protectionist effects of the nationality rule. It effectively reserves the primary origin/destination air traffic between any two States to the home airlines of those States irrespective of the economic attraction of third-country air carriers that may offer lower cost structures, sleeker aircraft, or superior perquisites, and are therefore better placed to satisfy consumer demand. In other words, "who can perform transport services most efficiently is secondary; what matters is whether [that person] is a foreigner or a national."[75] Additionally, and as noted earlier, the nationality rule chokes off foreign capital flows and disables routine mergers, acquisitions, or consolidations.[76]

---

[72] *See* Council for Trade in Services, *supra* note 50, at 33, para. 61.

[73] *See* Agreement on Rules of Origin art. 3(b), Apr. 15, 1994, Marrakesh Agreement Establishing the World Trade Organization, 1867 U.N.T.S. 397 (1994).

[74] For further discussion of rules of origin, including their strategic trade and overtly protectionist elements, see STEFANO INAMA, RULES OF ORIGIN IN INTERNATIONAL TRADE (2009).

[75] Jürgen Basedow, *Verkehrsrecht und Verkehrspolitik als Europäische Aufgabe, in* EUROPÄISCHE VERKEHRSPOLITIK 1, 7 (Gerd Aberle ed., 1987) (Brian Havel translation).

[76] For further discussion of these shortcomings, and economic arguments for change, see DANIEL YERGIN et al., FETTERED FLIGHT: GLOBALIZATION AND THE AIRLINE INDUSTRY (2000); InterVISTAS-ga, THE ECONOMIC IMPACT OF AIR SERVICE LIBERALIZATION (2006); Roberta Piermartini & Linda Rousová, *Liberalization of Air Transport Services and Passenger Traffic* (WTO Staff Working Paper ERSD-2008–06 Dec. 2008).

3.4.5. *Interplay of the Nationality Rule with Domestic Law*

The rampancy of the nationality clauses in ASAs is only half of the protection-ist equation. Domestic law is also highly relevant.[77] Even prior to the emergence of international trade in air services, States kept tight regulatory controls on the ownership complexion of their airlines through either owning all of the capital or by a numerical ceiling (often statutory) on foreign inward investment where enterprises were held privately. As early as 1926, the United States adopted a legislative cap on foreign ownership of its airlines of 49%,[78] lowering the cap to 25% in 1938 (where it remains).[79] But the EU, which has chosen a somewhat softer stance toward foreign airline ownership than the Americans, has yet to pass legislation allowing unrestricted ownership of its air carriers by non-Member States or their nationals.[80] Other significant aviation powers, including Australia, Brazil, Canada, China, India, and Japan, impose similar foreign ownership caps.[81] While many of these national laws serve explicitly protectionist purposes, the sheer ubiquity of the nationality rule locks States into a kind of prisoner's dilemma where no State seems willing to cooperate in its wholesale extinction.

3.4.6. *Operation of the Nationality Rule*

Under the U.S./Canada ASA, for example, Air Canada is eligible to receive market access privileges to the United States so long as that airline is not in transgression of the nationality rule at the time it is designated by the Canadian Government to provide international services under the treaty.[82] If, however, the German carrier Lufthansa acquires Air Canada after the initial designation, the United States may (or may not) impose conditions on access to its airspace by Air Canada-owned-and-controlled-by-Lufthansa, up to and including a full

---

[77] *See supra* note 1.

[78] *See* Air Commerce Act, ch. 344, §§ 3(a) & 9(a), 44 Stat. 568, 569, & 573 (1926).

[79] *See* 1938 Civil Aeronautics Act, ch. 601, § 1(13), 52 Stat. 973, 978. The current provisions on airline ownership and control are available in 49 U.S.C.A. §§ 40102(a)(15) & 41101(a) (West 2010).

[80] *See* Common Rules, *supra* note 52, art. 2(9) (requiring an air carrier to be at least 50.1% owned by nationals of an EU Member State to be eligible for designation as a Union air carrier under the common operating license regime).

[81] *See* Chia-Jui Hsu & Yu-Chan Chang, *The Influence of Airline Ownership Rules on Aviation Policies and Carriers' Strategies*, in 5 Proceedings of the Eastern Asia Society for Transportation Studies 557, 557 tbl.1 (2005).

[82] *See* Air Transport Agreement, U.S.-Can., art. 3(2)(a), Mar. 12, 2007, *reprinted in* 3 Aviation L. Rep. (CCH) ¶ 26,246a.

revocation of traffic rights.[83] Under the conventional double-pronged test – which blends a quantitative test ("substantial ownership")[84] and a qualitative one ("effective control")[85] – even something *less than* a majority acquisition of Air Canada's voting shares could precipitate a U.S. revocation.[86] A mere 25% stake in Air Canada (the upper limit tolerated under present domestic Canadian law) could allow the United States to assert, if various indicia of corporate intervention by Lufthansa in Air Canada's management and operations are also present, that Lufthansa had acquired sufficient leverage to exercise "effective control" of the airline, particularly if the stake makes Lufthansa the single largest investor. On the one hand, Lufthansa (or any other foreign investor) would likely not consummate a full merger or acquisition that risks forfeiture by Air Canada of its traffic rights to serve the largest transborder aviation market in the world. On the other hand, Lufthansa or any foreign carrier would be leery of buying a stake that would (in the view of local regulators) grant "effective control" to the foreign investor. Under either scenario, the domestic airline's capital-raising ability has been compromised. And yet it is precisely these investment barriers erected under national law that hold an airline in conformity with the nationality clauses in bilateral treaties and allow it to maintain its traffic rights to other countries.

3.4.7. *External and Internal Components of the Nationality Rule: A Double-Bolted Lock*

The nationality rule, it must now be clear, has a double-bolted "locking" mechanism: the external nationality clause in each State's ASAs that typically speaks to substantial ownership and effective control, to which we can now add the internal national investment caps in its domestic laws that ensure compliance with the ownership and control requirements of the nationality clause. This double locking system also rules out foreign airline subsidiaries – the right

---

[83] *See id.* art. 4(1)(b).

[84] Though specific numeric benchmarks are not set out in the Two Freedoms or Five Freedoms agreements, nor in any formulation of the nationality rule itself, municipal law limits on foreign ownership (which vary from 25% to 49.9%) provide strong guidance as to the range of foreign investment that will be permissible under ASAs.

[85] What constitutes "effective control" is ambiguous at best and lends itself to an impressionistic, case-by-case analysis of an airline's ownership structure, contractual commitments, branding and licensing activities, financial arrangements, and management. *Cf.* DHL Airways, Inc. (ASTAR), Dkt. No. OST-2002-13089, 2003 DOT Av LEXIS 1086, *72–79 (Dep't of Transp. Dec. 19, 2003) (discussing the interpretation of "control" in U.S. administrative law); Common Rules, *supra* note 52, art. 2(9) (containing one of the rare instances where "effective control" is explicitly defined).

[86] *See infra* Chapter 4, Part 4.2, for further discussion of ownership and control issues.

of establishment that is otherwise uncontroversially exchanged in normal bilateral investment relations.[87] If Lufthansa were permitted by Canada to establish Lufthansa-Canada and were then to seek official designations to serve Montreal/New York or Toronto/Beijing, the Canadian Government could not award Canadian designations to a German-owned-and-controlled airline under the nationality clauses in its Canada/United States or Canada/China bilateral air transport agreements. At most, the Chicago Convention Article 7 provisions on cabotage do not seem to preclude Canada from conceding opportunities to foreign subsidiaries to serve wholly domestic traffic points in Canada.[88] Cabotage rights, however, are of limited value to a big carrier like Lufthansa that is more interested in building robust international route connections.[89] The airlines' enfeebled right of establishment represents another denial of commercial opportunities that are routinely swapped in ordinary trade diplomacy. As noted above, they cannot circumvent market access limitations in the way that manufacturing or services firms that are not bound by a nationality rule overcome trade barriers such as tariffs and quotas by establishing subsidiaries (or acquiring locally based producers) in more favorable locales.[90]

3.4.8. *Destabilizing the Nationality Rule*

Despite its ubiquitous place in the history of trade in air services, in recent times the external bolt of the nationality rule has begun to loosen. While we will discuss the erosion of the rule in greater detail in Chapter 4, for now it is useful to signal some of the changes that are occurring. Like many "first-order"

---

[87] *See generally* Jeswald W. Salacuse, The Law of Investment Treaties 196–204 (2010) (discussing the various approaches to the right of establishment in international investment treaties).

[88] Countries may still be hesitant, however, to grant cabotage privileges to the subsidiaries' (foreign) parent carriers because these airlines will remain beyond the comprehensive regulatory control of the State. *See* Havel, Beyond Open Skies, *supra* note 5, at 47–48 n.91; *see also supra* Chapter 2, note 92 and accompanying text.

[89] "Limited value" is not synonymous with "valueless." A right of establishment providing access to lucrative internal markets in countries such as China, India, and the United States would no doubt hold some attraction for foreign carriers or foreign investors.

[90] This circumvention can be accomplished in one of two ways. The first is for an enterprise facing export restrictions by a foreign State to set up a subsidiary within that State's territory in order to sell its products or services without the added cost of a tariff or quota limits. The second option is for an enterprise to establish a subsidiary in a host State that enjoys more liberal trade concessions with third countries than the enterprise's home State and then to export under the more favorable regime. Understandably, a foreign-owned enterprise is typically barred from profiting from the trade concessions of its host State if the subsidiary is a "shell company" or the enterprise's home State lacks diplomatic relations with the third countries' governments. *See* Salacuse, *supra* note 87, at 188–89; *see also supra* text accompanying note 66.

structures, the nationality rule is contingent and can be superseded. Although the United States still insists on embedding nationality clauses in its open skies bilateral agreements,[91] *de facto* U.S. policy has been to refrain from enforcing the rule against open skies partner States if their airlines become owned and controlled by nationals from third countries with which the United States has also signed open skies agreements.[92] Meanwhile, the focal point of the EU's massive project for a single aviation market was the removal of the discriminatory apparatus of airline nationality that once governed air transport relations among its Member States:[93] within the twenty-eight-member Union, the nationality rule is disapplied by the device of a single airline identity, the "Union air carrier," which may be owned and controlled by any EU State or nationals of any EU State and which may (at least under EU positive law) serve any traffic points inside or outside the EU.[94] As such, cross-border investment within the geopolitical territory of the EU (e.g., British Airways/Iberia, Air France/KLM, Lufthansa/Austrian Airlines) can *theoretically* escape the shadow of the "substantial ownership and effective control" duality.[95] The penumbral effects of the EU assault on the nationality rule have included a U.S./EU agreement, reached within talks to amend their 2007 ASA, to refrain from applying the nationality clause against select third countries in which ownership and/or control of an airline becomes vested in U.S. or EU citizens.[96] A more modest, but still influential, reform appears in the EU/Chile ASA that allows nationals of several Latin American States to own or control

---

[91] *See* Model Open Skies Agreement, *supra* note 9, art. 3.

[92] *See* John R. Byerly, Deputy Assistant Sec'y for Transp. Affairs, Dep't of State, Opening Remarks at the London AirFinance Journal Conference (May 18, 2009).

[93] *See supra* note 52.

[94] *See id.* Thus, the EU has put in place arrangements that would allow British Airways, for example, to be designated by France to serve Paris/Tokyo routes under the France/Japan bilateral agreement. But although these routes are theoretically available to BA, they do depend on the acquiescence of the third State, Japan. As we will see, EU negotiations are continuing at both Commission and State level to persuade third countries to accept the so-called Union designation. Not all third States have agreed to the new EU orthodoxy. *See infra* Chapter 4, Section 4.4.3.

[95] These intra-Union mergers are dependent on third countries refraining from invoking the nationality rule. Russia, for example, threatened to retract Austrian Airlines' access rights following the carrier's acquisition by Lufthansa. *See* Pilita Clark, *Russia Threatens to Ban Austrian Airlines*, FIN. TIMES, Mar. 1, 2010, at 1. *See also infra* Chapter 4, text accompanying note 63.

[96] *See* U.S./EU Air Transport Agreement, *supra* note 7, annex 6. According to the agreement, before either party will abstain from enforcing the nationality clause with respect to third-country airlines that are *controlled* by EU or U.S. citizens, both parties must agree that the third country "has established a record of cooperation in air services" with them. *See id.* paras. 3–4. With respect to *ownership* alone, however, no such record of cooperation needs to be demonstrated. *See id.* para. 1.

Chilean airlines without jeopardizing those airlines' market access to EU Member States.[97] It is also possible that the members of ASEAN will eventually align their respective ASAs to replicate the EU single market approach.[98] Additionally, in 2010, the United States and EU introduced a proposal before the ICAO Assembly for a new multilateral agreement that waives the nationality clauses in the ASAs among its State parties.[99] Although the treaty is still in the early stages of negotiation, its ratification by ICAO's membership would be the most momentous step toward global (as opposed to regional) liberalization of trade in aviation services since the Two Freedoms Agreement.

3.4.9. *Reasons for Destabilization*

What accounts for the reframing of State policy toward citizenship purity in airline ownership? Undoubtedly States perceive the waning strategic value of aggressive aerodiplomacy based on the nationality rule. Except for a few notable holdouts such as China and Russia, the United States – and, to a lesser extent, the EU – have managed to entice most aviation powers, including each other, into liberal ASAs.[100] Under this new regime of amplified (albeit incomplete) liberalization, the two aviation powers that together represent approximately 60% of world air traffic have each built networks of treaties that offer fundamental market freedoms in respect to pricing, frequencies, capacity, and (with important caveats) traffic rights. Given the number of liberal ASAs existing today, there is much less discernible need for States to use the hammerlock of the nationality rule to prevent their partners from allowing third-country nationals from more restrictive jurisdictions to free-ride on open market concessions. And States with strong air transport industries now have much to lose if their actions unleash an aviation trade war. The tilt toward

---

[97] *See* Agreement on Certain Aspects of Air Services art. 2(4), Chile-EU, Oct. 31, 2006, 2006 O.J. (L 300) 46. The Latin American States in question are those that are members of the Latin American Civil Aviation Commission.

[98] *See* Tan, *supra* note 60, at 368.

[99] *See infra* Chapter 4, Section 4.4.5; for a more detailed discussion of the draft treaty, see Brian F. Havel & Gabriel S. Sanchez, *The Emerging* Lex Aviatica, 42 GEO. J. INT'L L. 639, 665–67 (2011).

[100] The EU continues to operate on two tracks, Member State and supranational, in negotiating external ASAs. The EU Commission needs a specific mandate from the EU political body, the Council of the European Union, to undertake negotiations for a comprehensive liberalized agreement with specific aeropolitical powers such as the United States. Currently, the EU has concluded comprehensive agreements, displacing separate Member State ASAs, with the United States, Canada, and Brazil, and plans for further such agreements have been announced. *See infra* Part 3.5.

liberality should not be overstated. With some exceptions, the loosening of the external bolt of the nationality rule has not been accompanied by a disabling of its internal equivalent. The United States stridently rejects calls from the EU to open its airlines to foreign investment – a historical irony when set against the European rebuff of U.S. calls for a free market approach to air services at the Chicago conference.[101] Emerging powerhouses, such as the BRIC economies (Brazil, Russia, India, and China), have not hastened to relax caps on foreign investment in their respective aviation sectors. But until the external bolt of the nationality rule is fully disarmed, States will remain hesitant to allow substantial foreign capital in-flows that might put their airlines' traffic rights in jeopardy.

3.4.10. *Returning to the Nationality Rule*

We will return to the nationality rule in Chapter 4, where we will revisit some of the themes presented here (including the destabilization of the rule) and also consider the right of establishment and the emergence of international airline alliances. In the next part, we will survey some of the main features of bilateral ASAs and turn then to explain the narrow space that international trade in air services occupies in the WTO trading system.

3.5. THE CORE ELEMENTS OF AIR SERVICES AGREEMENTS: THE OPEN SKIES MODEL

3.5.1. *Content of ASAs*

Although the sheer number and variety of ASAs militates against a comprehensive account of their provisions, in this part we discuss the principal components of ASAs using the U.S. open skies model. These components include provisions that cover routes, capacity, pricing, frequency, safety, and "doing business" restrictions. ASAs also typically provide rules covering commercial opportunities, competition, security, and allowable charges or fees. Lastly, ASAs routinely include mechanisms for settling disputes, but do not award private rights of action (against States) to aggrieved airlines.[102]

---

[101] *See infra* Chapter 4, Part 4.10 (describing a new EU initiative to seek liberalization of U.S. domestic laws on foreign ownership of U.S. airlines).

[102] *See infra* text accompanying note 152.

3.5.2. *Grant of Traffic Rights: The First Five Freedoms*

At the core of all ASAs is a grant of traffic rights.[103] Although, as we noted, ASAs rarely use international aviation law's vernacular of the "freedoms of the air," they do rely on its underlying conceptual framework.[104] In addition to the "noncommercial" first and second freedoms, the commercial third, fourth, and fifth freedoms are swapped without numeric limits on capacity, frequency, or designations so long as each contracting State's designated passenger and cargo airlines remain compliant with the nationality rule.[105] It is these liberal exchanges of unrestricted, reciprocal traffic freedoms that are now synonymous with open skies and that have been emulated by other States. In current trading of international air services, the third, fourth, and fifth freedoms are unexceptional, although their exercise may be restricted by other negotiated provisions.[106]

3.5.3. *Grant of the Sixth and Seventh Freedoms*

The sixth and seventh freedoms are not typically exchanged, under the open skies template or otherwise. The sixth freedom presents conceptual difficulties as an object of exchange: why would Dubai, for example, seek to add an exchange of sixth freedom privileges with Germany when that Gulf State's flag carrier, Emirates, already enjoys the necessary fourth freedom privilege to fly passengers from (say) Dusseldorf to Dubai and then to transit them onward, using third freedoms negotiated with third States such as India or Japan, to an array of other destinations including Mumbai and Tokyo? Germany may be troubled by Emirates' cheaper one-stop air services over Dubai that compete with Lufthansa's nonstop services from Dusseldorf to Mumbai or Tokyo, but technically Emirates' legal capacity to offer those services already exists under third and fourth freedoms that are granted separately and independently of any effort to exchange (or withhold exchange of) a sixth freedom.[107] The seventh freedom, in contrast, cannot exist at all without a specific bilateral exchange because it breaks entirely with the home State connection that defines the other six freedoms: in the scenario just considered, Emirates would use a seventh freedom

---

[103] *See supra* note 31 (commenting that these rights are actually "privileges").

[104] For a more detailed conspectus of how route rights are actually described in ASAs, we recommend consulting ICAO's Manual on the Regulation of International Air Transport, *supra* note 48, at 4.1-2 to 4.1-5.

[105] *See* Model Open Skies Agreement, *supra* note 9, arts. 2–3.

[106] For example, China's frequency limitations (*see supra* text accompanying note 28) or Japan's restrictions on airport slots (*see infra* text accompanying note 191).

[107] *See supra* text accompanying note 46.

privilege to fly directly from Dusseldorf to Mumbai or Tokyo[108] with no segment connecting that service to Dubai (and Lufthansa, similarly, could operate a nonstop direct service to those cities from Dubai without being required to route its service through Germany[109]). The "stand-alone" seventh freedom, as already discussed, is almost never granted for air passenger traffic but is gradually being conceded to all-cargo (but not combination passenger/cargo) carriers. Protectionism is easy to detect here: seventh freedom privileges invite additional foreign competition that may be superior to domestic providers, especially those carrying passenger traffic, in meeting the demands of local consumers. Finally, eighth and ninth freedom privileges (cabotage) remain off the negotiating table in all but the most exceptional cases.[110]

3.5.4. *EU Single Aviation Market: Exchange of All Nine Freedoms*

The most panoramic exchange of traffic rights in international aviation history occurred in building the EU's single aviation market. All twenty-eight Member States enjoy all nine freedoms – without restriction – among themselves, although the matter becomes more complicated at the external level. A series of rulings by the Court of Justice of the European Union (CJEU) in 2002 found that the nationality clauses in individual Member State bilateral agreements, which prevented ASA designation by each Member State of airlines owned and controlled by nationals from any other Member State, violated EU treaty law that guarantees freedom to provide services (including, in this case, seventh freedom services operated using any airport in any Member State and serving any destination outside the EU).[111] After much political wrangling, the European Commission, as the central executive body of the EU, received authorization from the EU's political steering body, the Council of the European Union, to enter so-called horizontal agreements with selected non-EU States that simultaneously modify all of the nationality clauses in

---

[108] As the reader will by now fully appreciate, *exercise* of that seventh freedom right will depend on bilateral consent not only under the Germany/Dubai agreement, but also under Dubai's separate agreements with India and with Japan.

[109] Such a routing (Dubai/Germany/Mumbai or Dubai/Germany/Tokyo) would, in fact, be sixth freedom!

[110] *See, e.g., supra* Chapter 2, Part 2.5 (discussing Chile's abolition of cabotage).

[111] The targeted ASAs comprised a series of open skies agreements that seven Member States had concluded with the United States, but the reasoning of the Court applied to *all* ASAs between all Member States and all non-EU States. *See* Cases C-467/98, C-468/98, C-469/98, C-471/98, C-472/98, C-475/98, and C-476/98, Comm'n v. Denmark, Sweden, Finland, Belgium, Luxembourg, Austria, and Germany, 2002 E.C.R. I-090519 *et seq.* An eighth defendant, the U.K., was named even though the U.S./U.K. relationship had never produced an open skies agreement. *See* Case C-466/98, Comm'n v. U.K., 2002 E.C.R. I-09427.

all of the different Member State agreements with those States in order to comply with the CJEU rulings.[112] Under the recast nationality clause, non-EU States accept Member State designations of any "Union air carrier,"[113] regardless of the specific ownership and control profile of the carrier and provided only that it is substantially owned and effectively controlled by a Member State or by nationals of a Member State.[114] Under the bargain struck between the Commission and the Council, Member States may still conduct their own separate negotiations for new or amended bilateral agreements with non-EU countries, but the outcome of the negotiations must also respect the CJEU judgments and must not encumber the freedom of airlines owned and controlled by EU Member States or their nationals to provide stand-alone (seventh freedom) services to or from non-EU points using airports in any Member State. While the Commission's horizontal agreements allow, but do not by themselves assure, additional external traffic rights for EU airlines,[115] by "Unionizing" the nationality clause they remove the greatest legal barrier to the exercise of those rights. Horizontal agreements are narrowly focused on bringing EU ASAs into compliance with CJEU jurisprudence on free movement of services. Beyond that, the Commission's surrogacy is carefully restricted. It cannot act as a super-negotiator to obtain full ASAs with a non-EU State on behalf of all of the Member States *unless* the Council of the EU endows it with a so-called vertical mandate. To date, only a handful of such mandates has been granted, although the cluster of so-called global partners with which the Commission has completed treaty arrangements (the United

---

[112] As of 2013, 117 non-EU States (and nearly 1000 ASAs) had recognized the principle of EU designation, 55 of them through horizontal agreements. *See* European Comm'n, *External Aviation Policy, supra* note 33, at 3. *See* HAVEL, BEYOND OPEN SKIES, *supra* note 5, at 485 nn.546 & 547 (describing additional clauses in horizontal agreements that relate to pricing – including a prohibition on lower fares by non-EU carriers on all intra-EU air routes that was preserved in the U.S./EU ASA – as well as ground-handling services, taxation of aviation fuel, safety, and so on).

[113] *See supra* note 52.

[114] For the textual content of the clauses, see Comm'n Decision 29/03/2005, *Approving the Standard Clauses for Inclusion in Bilateral Air Service Agreements Between Member States and Third Countries Jointly Laid down by the Commission and the Member States,* 2005 O.J. (C 943) 1.

[115] Each Member State's designation selection process still has to be undertaken for third countries outside the EU, and not all foreign partners will accept an open skies-style unlimited designation of any Union air carrier that wishes to serve a foreign market. Accordingly, EU Member States can now *consider for designation* a much larger number of airlines, but the number of airlines that *can be designated* remains subject to the relevant ASAs. EU legislation seeks to ensure nondiscriminatory treatment of any Union carrier (regardless of its ownership/control profile) that seeks designation in each Member State's process. *See generally* Council Regulation 847/2004, 2004 O.J. (L 157) 7.

States, Canada, and Brazil[116]) is a significant one.[117] Otherwise, the EU Member States continue to tolerate the piecemeal system of bilateral ASAs in their aeropolitical relations with third countries.[118]

3.5.5. *Regional Exchanges of Traffic Rights*

Despite the endurance of bilateralism, however, the EU's external aviation policy cannot be branded a failure. Although the global partners initiative has moved slowly, the Union has adopted a livelier pace in expanding the single aviation market to a network of some thirty-seven States located in the EU's eastern and southern neighborhoods, as well as in parts of the Middle East and North Africa. In its optimal expression (from the EU's perspective) all of these States would fully accept the *acquis*[119] of the single aviation market through their membership of the EU-sponsored European Common Aviation Area (ECAA).[120] Exchanging traffic rights through regional aviation integration, in fact, has been voguish in the wake of the EU project, but none of the imitators has replicated the Union's multi-State exchanges of traffic rights. Members of the African Union, working under the Yamoussoukro Decision, have not overturned the stringent traffic restrictions that have long governed their aeropolitical relations.[121] The ASEAN

---

[116] Negotiations with Australia and New Zealand are ongoing: *see infra* note 117.

[117] Brazil, however, has not yet signed its March 2011 comprehensive agreement with the EU. *See* European Comm'n, *External Aviation Policy, supra* note 33, at 11, 18. In addition, the Commission has a mandate for talks with Australia and New Zealand, and those talks are still in progress. *See id.* at 4, 11, 18. The Commission has indicated its desire for further vertical mandates for negotiations with China, India, Japan, Russia, and Turkey. *See id.* at 11.

[118] The dual EU/Member State responsibility for external ASAs continues to be a source of "confusion" among non-EU partners. The Commission has noted that, as a result, the EU still lacks a "comprehensive common ... external aviation policy" and that its own work is hamstrung by "national interests" and also by "*ad hoc* initiatives based on individual authorizations to negotiate." *See* European Comm'n, *External Aviation Policy, supra* note 33, at 4.

[119] That is, the cumulative corpus of EU treaties, legislation, and judicial and administrative decisions that relate to the air transport area. *See* European Comm'n, *A Community Aviation Policy Towards Its Neighbours*, COM (2004) 74 final (Feb. 9, 2004), para. 35.

[120] The ECAA integrates contracting neighboring States into the legal regime governing the commercial airspace of the EU Member States with respect to issues such as market access, competition rules, safety, and air traffic management. *See* Ruwantissa Abeyratne, *The Decision of the European Court of Justice on Open Skies – How Can We Take Liberalization to the Next Level?*, 68 J. AIR L. & COM. 485, 504 (2003). As of September 2012, the European Commission reported "solid progress" in developing the ECAA, having signed agreements with the Western Balkans, Morocco, Jordan, Georgia, and Moldova. *See* European Comm'n, *External Aviation Policy, supra* note 33, at 10.

[121] The Yamoussoukro Declaration, adopted Oct. 7, 1988, set a goal of airline integration, joint operation of international routes, and removal of internal traffic restrictions among the

economies, on the other hand, have agreed a series of "staged" accords that grant comprehensive traffic rights at the subregional, then regional, levels.[122] The absence of a central enabling and enforcement agency (akin to the European Commission) or of a legally binding adjudicatory body (such as the CJEU) has impeded ASEAN liberalization. Most countries in the bloc have yet to commit to waiving nationality restrictions either in their internal laws or in bilateral treaties.[123]

3.5.6. Authorization/Designation Requirements

As a general proposition, the paramount requirement that a home State's airlines must satisfy before being eligible to provide air services under that State's ASAs is the nationality rule, that is, that the airlines are substantially owned and effectively controlled by the home State or by its nationals. U.S. ASAs typically frame the citizenship "purity" demands of the nationality rule as a *precondition* for authorization of the airlines designated by partner States.[124] For example, when Canada designates Air Canada to provide service under its ASA with the United States, U.S. authorization symmetrically requires that Air Canada must be owned and controlled by Canadian nationals. If, however, *subsequent* to that authorization, the Canadian Government were to permit BA to take a controlling stake in the Canadian carrier, it becomes incumbent upon the United States, if it so wishes, to notify Canada under the U.S./Canada bilateral ASA that the United States intends to "revoke, suspend, limit or impose conditions on the operating authorizations or technical permissions" granted to Air Canada.[125] The extinction of privileges, in other words, requires an affirmative act by the grantor, the United States. In addition, late-model U.S. open skies agreements like the

---

participating States. The Declaration was nonbinding but has been credited with initiating air transport liberalization in Africa and leading to the 1999 Yamoussoukro Decision granting the first five freedoms to the contracting parties and contemplating removal of frequency and capacity restrictions. *See* CHARLES E. SCHLUMBERGER, OPEN SKIES FOR AFRICA: IMPLEMENTING THE YAMOUSSOUKRO DECISION 9–12 (2010). Although the Decision entered into force in 2000, its implementation is not yet complete. *See id.* 29–31.

[122] The ASEAN economies have proposed a fully liberalized ASEAN Single Aviation Market by 2015. Moreover, Singapore has presented itself as a "pathfinder" for the EU to develop deeper interregional collaboration with the new ASEAN arrangements. *See* European Comm'n, *External Aviation Policy, supra* note 33, at 13.

[123] *See infra* Section 3.6.7.

[124] A foreign government's designation will usually be determinative. On U.S. practice, see HAVEL, BEYOND OPEN SKIES, *supra* note 5, at 282–83.

[125] *See* Model Open Skies Agreement, *supra* note 9, art. 4(1); *see also* Air Transport Agreement, U.S.-Can., *supra* note 82, art. 3(2)(a).

U.S./Canada 2007 air services treaty reinforce the nationality connection with a provision obligating designated carriers to have their principal place of business in the designating State.[126] Even if Air Canada were to remain owned and controlled by Canadian citizens but, for reasons of economic expediency, were to relocate its principal place of business to Mexico, the United States may also (but need not) revoke or limit Air Canada's traffic rights. As such, it is *possible* that Air Canada could undergo a transformation of its ownership profile from "citizen-owned" to "foreign-owned," or conduct business operations from a headquarters city other than its present base, Montreal, without forfeiting its U.S. traffic rights. Nevertheless, the mere risk of revocation, not to mention the likelihood of Canadian Government resistance, would certainly chill potential foreign investments.[127]

3.5.7. *Designation Requirements*

Additional criteria making authorization contingent upon a designated airline's compliance with ICAO air navigation, safety, and security regulations are understandably common as well.[128] What has faded out of open skies ASAs, however, are preset limits on the number of designations each State may make among its eligible air carriers. Historically, States restricted the number of designations by its partners in an effort to shield their home carriers from what they characterized as "excessive" or "ruinous" competition. States with only one international airline were reluctant to thrust their flagships into open competition with the phalanx of U.S. international carriers, for example, on the natural assumption that their national economic interests would suffer. Under the terms of the now-defunct U.S./U.K. ASA known as "Bermuda II," the United Kingdom limited access to London's principal hub, Heathrow Airport, to two U.S. airlines (first TWA and Pan Am, and later American Airlines and United as the respective successors to those airlines' routes[129]). The U.K. Government hoped not only to armor-plate BA's dominance at "the

---

[126] *Compare* Model Open Skies Agreement, *supra* note 9, art. 1(4) (defining "Airline of a Party" as an airline that is "licensed by and has its principal place of business in the territory of that Party"), *with* United States: Model Bilateral Air Transport Agreement ("Open Skies Agreement") art. 1, 35 I.L.M. 1479 (1996) (providing no such definition). *See infra* Chapter 8, note 72 (mentioning ICAO's approach to determining the "principal place of business").

[127] *See infra* Chapter 4, Part 4.2 (offering further analysis of the consequences of these investment changes).

[128] *See* Model Open Skies Agreement, *supra* note 9, arts 4–7.

[129] *See* Memorandum of Consultations and Draft Exchange of Notes Concerning Modifications to the U.S./U.K. Air Services Agreement, *reprinted in* 3 Av. L. Rep. (CCH) ¶ 26,540j, at 23,923 (Jan. 2007).

gateway to the world," but to prevent other U.S. airlines from gaining a foothold in the highly competitive transatlantic aviation market. In reality, designation limits merely heighten the advantages of incumbency by freezing out the disciplining effects of more efficient and more price-competitive new entrants.

3.5.8. *Pricing Freedom*

The freedom to set prices (fares and rates[130]) is critical to the success of any commercial venture. International airlines are no exception. Despite that, States long insisted on the right to regulate air fares on routes between their home territories and the territories of their bilateral partners. One of the earliest bilateral agreements, the U.S./U.K. ASA known as "Bermuda I," created a system of "double approval" pricing whereby all fare modifications by airlines operating under the terms of the treaty required advance filing with and approval by the aeronautical authorities in both partner countries.[131] The converse procedure, "double disapproval" pricing, allows a filed fare to stand unless it is rejected by both parties' aeronautical authorities. That more relaxed standard has itself been further liberalized under open skies through the abandonment of any bureaucratic requirement to file fares and reliance solely on consumer demand to influence the pricing decisions of airlines.[132]

---

[130] Both international and domestic tariffs are divided into these two categories: a "fare" is a tariff for the carriage of passengers, and a "rate" is a tariff for the carriage of cargo. *See* ICAO MANUAL, *supra* note 48, at 4.3-2.

[131] *See* Agreement Between the Government of the United States of America and the Government of the United Kingdom Relating to Air Services, annex, sec. 2, U.S.-U.K., Feb. 11, 1946, 12 Bevans 726 (no longer in force) [hereinafter Bermuda I].

[132] *See generally* Model Open Skies Agreement, *supra* note 9, art. 12. States have, however, used domestic competition law or trade law to raise the specter of foreign airlines "dumping" excess capacity into their markets through price-cutting, thereby driving prices below the cost-recovery level for national carriers. Potentially beneficial effects on airline consumers are noticeably absent from State assessments of each of these perceived threats. The EU, for example, ensures that all ASAs with non-EU States include a prohibition on "price leadership" on all intra-Union routes by carriers designated by those States. *See supra* note 113. In fact, where both "predation" (a contentious concept: *see generally* Frank Easterbrook, *Predatory Strategies and Counterstrategies*, 48 U. CHI. L. REV. 48 (1981)) and "dumping" are occurring, consumers benefit – at least in the short run – from pressure to lower fares. Consumers will only be harmed in the outside chance of successful post-predation or post-dumping supracompetitive pricing. That, in turn, assumes the unlikely event that that the new pricing structure will not be competed back down by new or returning market entrants looking to skim some of the monopoly profits made available by these allegedly countercompetitive acts.

3.5.9. *Capacity and Frequency*

In two other aspects of airline operations, capacity and frequency, ASAs have historically been restrictive (favoring "managed" trade[133]). But full liberalization of each aspect has also been a feature of open skies. Capacity refers to the total number of passengers carried (usually on a daily basis) on an individual flight segment.[134] Under Bermuda I bilateralism, airlines were at liberty to increase capacity on international routes subject to *ex post facto* review by the aeronautical authorities of the two contracting States. For its time, that was a relatively liberal formula because, like double disapproval pricing, it assumed some level of bureaucratic inertia. By the time of the highly illiberal U.S./U.K. Bermuda II agreement three decades later,[135] some ASAs had begun to insist on 50/50 capacity splits whereby the designated airlines of each party were limited (or, some might argue, entitled) to a more or less equal share of the bilateral marketplace.[136] With effects similar to price controls, capacity restrictions artificially raised fares on international routes by holding down supply. Capacity controls stifled competition by keeping aloft less competitive airlines that failed to invest in new, larger aircraft or were unable to attract the capital to expand market presence. Frequency refers to the number of flights per day that an airline will assign to a particular flight segment.[137] In the open skies era frequency caps have mostly been lifted, but conspicuous exceptions still persist. The current U.S./China ASA (which is *not* an open skies agreement) "topped out" in 2012 with twenty-three daily frequencies for U.S. airlines serving the limited number of point-to-point U.S./China routes specified in the ASA.[138] With frequency limitations, as indeed with an ASA where only certain

---

[133] "Managed trade" is the use of protectionist artifices such as preset restrictions on imports by or from a foreign supplier to favor proportionally the weaker domestic supplier.

[134] *See generally* PETER P. C. HAANAPPEL, RATEMAKING IN INTERNATIONAL AIR TRANSPORT: A LEGAL ANALYSIS OF INTERNATIONAL AIR FARES AND RATES 1 (1978); ICAO MANUAL, *supra* note 48, at 4.2-1.

[135] Bermuda II, *supra* note 39.

[136] The notion that an airline has the primary claim on the custom of its own nationals is part of a "managed trade" mindset in the supply of international air transport services. *See supra* note 40. The opposite idea is expressed in the Latin phrase *suum quoque*, "to each [its] own" – that is, to each air carrier should belong the trade that it is able to attract and build, rather than the trade that its sponsor State (whether the airline is in public or private ownership) is able to secure based on mutating aeropolitical bargains with its fellow States. *See* HENRY A. WASSENBERGH, PUBLIC INTERNATIONAL AIR TRANSPORTATION LAW IN A NEW ERA 153 (1976).

[137] Flight frequencies are effectively another way to indicate capacity. *See generally* HAANAPPEL, *supra* note 134, at 1.

[138] *See supra* Section 3.3.1.

point-to-point routes are available, air carriers typically must "bid" for authorization to be designated for the available routes and for a share of the frequencies on those routes. In the United States, administrative proceedings to obtain routes and frequencies are immensely costly and require evidence to demonstrate that the award of these privileges to a particular carrier will satisfy an amorphous "public interest" standard.[139] Even if the criteria for winning a frequency are well drawn, the problem remains that regulatory authorities are not omniscient. As Ludwig von Mises famously remarked, "the market is a process";[140] as such, only the market yields the information necessary to determine which airlines are best positioned to serve it. Regulatory authorities, charged with selecting airlines and determining the minutiae of frequency, can make mistakes. Ultimately, it is the consumer who must pay.

3.5.10. *"Doing Business" Assurances*

To exploit fully the privileges acquired under bilateral ASA diplomacy, airlines also need legally binding assurances that they will be able to conduct normal business operations in foreign States. That governments give these kinds of assurances is by no means unique to the international aviation industry: all kinds of foreign investment activities would be undoable without them.[141] "Doing business" provisions in bilateral ASAs may include a broad guarantee of national treatment (i.e., that foreign airlines will be treated at least as well as their domestic competitors by local rules and regulations),[142] but more specifically will feature a right to establish business offices and to conduct commercial operations, a "self-handling" right that allows an airline to use its own ground-handling crews at foreign airports, and the right to convert and remit its earnings.[143] These basic concessions are complemented in the open skies model by permission to enter cooperative marketing

---

[139] *See* 2007, 2008, and 2009 US-China Air Services and Combination Frequency Allocation Proceeding, DOT-OST-2007-28567.

[140] LUDWIG VON MISES, HUMAN ACTION: A TREATISE ON ECONOMICS 257–58 (4th ed. 1996).

[141] *See infra* Chapter 4 (discussing bilateral investment treaties).

[142] The U.S. Model Open Skies Agreement does not include such an explicit guarantee in its clauses on "Commercial Opportunities," although it seeks to ensure that foreign airlines can *inter alia* establish offices, sell air transportation, perform their own ground-handling services (i.e., services for an aircraft's arrival and departure, but excluding air traffic control), remit earnings to their home States, and enter commercial arrangements such as code-sharing. *See* Model Open Skies Agreement, *supra* note 9, art. 8. On the unresolved question of whether foreign air carriers can rely on national treatment provisions in general bilateral investment treaties, see *infra* Chapter 4, note 25.

[143] *See* Model Open Skies Agreement, *supra* note 9, art. 8; *see also supra* note 142.

arrangements with local carriers.[144] As we will consider in detail in Chapter 4, these arrangements have escalated into full-scale international airline alliances as large carriers have sought to circumvent the nationality rule's embargo on cross-border investment. Alliances in the international aviation industry, no matter how sophisticated they have become, are all based on the rather simple device of the code-share: two or more airlines place their IATA identifier codes[145] on the same flight segment, regardless of which airline is providing the "metal" for the service.[146] Alliances allow airlines that are established as separate companies and in different States to integrate their services and, subject to regulatory approval, to cooperate on pricing, routes, and perquisites. Today, three major alliances – SkyTeam, Star, and oneworld – have developed interlocking air transport networks using partner airlines around the globe. As we will see, because alliances exist primarily to slide past the effects of the nationality rule, they are only imperfect imitations of true mergers. Moreover, their continued existence is contingent on toleration by State authorities of what are, after all, the kinds of route, price, and capacity collaborations among competitors that would normally attract scrutiny under antitrust and competition laws.[147] The current U.S. open skies negotiating process, in particular, anticipates an award of immunity to shield alliances among U.S. and foreign international carriers designated under the ASA from the reach of U.S. antitrust laws.[148]

---

[144] Under the U.S. Model Open Skies Agreement, cooperative marketing arrangements include blocked-space, code-sharing, and leasing arrangements. *See* Model Open Skies Agreement, *supra* note 9, art. 8(7). "Blocked space" means that one carrier purchases a number of passenger seats and/or specified cargo space for carriage of its traffic on an aircraft of a second air carrier. *See* ICAO MANUAL, *supra* note 48, at 4.1-7. For a fuller explanation of code-sharing, see *infra* Chapter 4, Sections 4.6.2, 4.6.3.

[145] *See id.*

[146] "Metal" is industry argot that refers to the aircraft that is actually performing the service to which a code-share is being applied. *See infra* Chapter 4, Section 4.7.1, for further analysis.

[147] The U.S. Department of Transportation's grant of antitrust immunity to the three big alliances (*see infra* Chapter 4, Part 4.6) may also smack of a kind of "industrial policy" to allow U.S. international carriers like American, Delta, and United to generate enough revenues in global markets to ensure their viability in the U.S. domestic market against lower-cost carriers like Southwest. *See* HAVEL, BEYOND OPEN SKIES, *supra* note 5, at 206.

[148] But a pledge of antitrust immunity is not textually a part of the U.S. Model Open Skies Agreement. Since its inception, the U.S. open skies policy has been tightly interwound with U.S. administrative grants of antitrust immunity to international airline alliances. Immunity has been justified as a means of securing open skies agreements, and the agreements have been negotiated with an implied promise to other countries that immunity will also be forthcoming for alliances that include their carriers. *See infra* Chapter 4, Part 4.6, for more detailed consideration of U.S. policy on antitrust immunity.

3.5.11. *Customs, Duties, and Charges*

As we discussed in the previous chapter, Article 15 of the Chicago Convention prohibits contracting States from applying discriminatory charges against foreign air carriers while also mandating that any charges applied should be imposed only to recover the costs of providing air traffic management and airport services.[149] These progressive charging principles have been reinforced and expanded upon in bilateral aeropolitical diplomacy. U.S. open skies agreements, for example, provide detail on the acceptable range of charges that may be imposed upon U.S. carriers and those of bilateral partners. These agreements also schedule reciprocal exemptions from taxes, levies, fees, and other charges that may be applied to ground equipment, spare parts, fuel and lubricants, and promotional and advertising material introduced into U.S. territory by a foreign air carrier.[150] Moreover, in memorializing the key principles of Article 15, ASAs (including the open skies model) allow States to contest discriminatory charges on behalf of their carriers using bilateral dispute settlement proceedings outside ICAO. This is not an unimportant option given the amount of time it may take for two States to settle their differences through ICAO's vaguely defined and (as discussed in the previous chapter) inadequate dispute settlement machinery. Aggrieved States can rely on the dispute resolution provisions set out in ASAs to attempt more expedient relief of their air carriers from illicit charging schemes.

3.5.12. *Dispute Settlement*

ASA dispute settlement, including the open skies model, offers an admixture of consultations and arbitration. U.S. liberal bilaterals usually provide that, where consultations fail to yield a mutually satisfactory result, either State may request an arbitration tribunal.[151] Each party is entitled to nominate an arbitrator, and the nominated officials, in turn, select the third arbitrator (who will also chair the tribunal). Majority decision making prevails, and the parties are expected to fully implement the tribunal's findings to the extent consistent with their national laws.[152] Unlike ICAO Council determinations, bilateral arbitral decisions typically are not appealable to an additional *ad hoc* body or to the International Court of Justice (ICJ). And, unlike the ICJ and other permanent adjudicatory bodies, arbitral tribunals constituted under ASAs are not bound *a*

---

[149] Chicago Convention, *supra* note 12, art. 15.
[150] *See* Model Open Skies Agreement, *supra* note 9, art. 9.
[151] *See id.* art. 14.
[152] *See id.* art. 14(7).

priori to the standard sources of international law (e.g., custom, treaties, and general principles).[153] Moreover, they are "entitled to decide the extent of [their] jurisdiction . . . [and] establish [their] own procedural rules."[154] The findings of the few known bilateral arbitral tribunals are rarely released publicly.[155] Even if they were, they would have little or no precedential effect.[156] The paucity of bilateral arbitral proceedings results not only from States' strong preference for aerodiplomacy, but also from dissatisfaction with the dilatoriness of traditional arbitration. More stringent models are available, including the WTO's time-sensitive principle of "automaticity,"[157] but aviation arbitration has shown little innovation even in the era of open skies. A very modest step toward tightening the format appears in the U.S./EU open skies treaty, which creates a standing Joint Committee that is charged, among its many substantive responsibilities, with mediating and ultimately seeking to settle potential disputes before arbitration can be triggered by either party.[158] In practice, this may amount to little more than the usual aerodiplomatic consultations, and indeed critics have suggested that the Joint Committee merely adds yet another procedural step that will make eventual arbitration even less efficient.[159]

---

[153] See *supra* Chapter 1, Part 1.5.

[154] See Model Open Skies Agreement, *supra* note 9, art. 14(3).

[155] Notable bilateral disputes include the arbitration between Belgium and Ireland in 1971 over Belgium's allegation that the Brussels/Dublin route suffered from overcapacity, in which the sole arbitrator agreed that the frequencies of both the Irish and Belgian carriers should be reduced to ensure the viability of each airline on the route (*see* Jacques Naveau, *Arbitral Award in the Dispute between the Belgian and Irish Civil Aviation Authorities over Services between Brussels and Dublin by Sabena and Aer Lingus, given at Dublin July 17, 1981*, 8 AIR L. 50 (1983)), and the U.S./U.K. arbitration under Bermuda II (*see supra* note 39) concerning airport user charges levied at London Heathrow, in which the three-person arbitral tribunal found that the charges did not reasonably reflect the cost of airport services (*see* Samuel M. Witten, *The U.S.-U.K. Arbitration Concerning Heathrow Airport User Charges*, 89 AM. J. INT'L L. 174 (1995)).

[156] See Gilbert Guillaume, *The Use of Precedent by International Judges and Arbitrators*, 2 J. INT. DISP. SETTLEMENT 5 (2011) (noting that the doctrine of binding precedent does not exist in international law and that this is even more true in international arbitration, in which tribunals lack the permanence that is characteristic of a court with formal jurisdiction). Although arbitrations under ASAs are technically inter-State, in reality they are likely to be commercial disputes involving aviation enterprises and therefore less likely to be concerned with extensive citation of or reliance on precedent.

[157] The WTO dispute settlement procedure gives governments an automatic right to bring their legal complaints before a dispute settlement tribunal, makes legal rulings by tribunals automatically binding on the parties, and gives complaining parties an automatic right to impose retaliatory trade sanctions. See Robert E. Hudec, *The New WTO Dispute Settlement Procedure*, 8 MINN. J. GLOBAL TRADE 1, 3 (1999).

[158] See HAVEL, BEYOND OPEN SKIES, *supra* note 5, at 82.

[159] See *id.*

3.5.13. *Strategic Considerations in Dispute Settlement*

Like all bilateral agreements, ASAs thrive or fail according to the strategic interests of their parties: a defection by one side from some (or all) of the terms of the agreement is likely to ignite a reciprocal defection by the other party or even an alternative retaliatory measure. Dispute settlement is therefore most relevant in bringing both parties face-to-face to discuss what does or does not count as a defection. The United States, for instance, may believe that under its open skies agreement with Canada the maintenance of a telephone answering machine in a rented office in northern Saskatchewan will not qualify Air Canada as having a principal place of business in Canadian territory where that airline is simultaneously in full business occupation of a twenty-floor office building in Mexico City. The United States may attempt to revoke Air Canada's traffic rights, triggering a call for consultations by Canada under the ASA. If consultations fail, an arbitration tribunal may be constituted to clarify the matter. But, if the stakes for its carrier are too high, Canada may simply bypass arbitration and retaliate with its own traffic restrictions, regardless of whether or not they are legitimate under the terms of the ASA. Canada may incur a reputational loss internationally (a debatable point). More probably, its actions would undermine friendly aeropolitical relations with the United States. Canada would thus have to weigh the benefits and disadvantages of defection. The United States, too, would have to balance its legal right to revoke Air Canada's traffic authorization against potential damage to its other aeropolitical interests including the Canadian market access of its own airlines. None of this means that ASA dispute settlement is superfluous; it suggests only that tougher and tighter arbitral procedures will not necessarily serve as exogenous restraints on State behavior. Dispute settlement, even if it never reaches formal arbitration, provides an additional path to clarification and, in moments of serious disagreement, may prompt new negotiations to realign the parties' expectations. Easily the most famous historical example of such behavior can be found in the historically fraught context of U.S./U.K. aeropolitical relations. When the U.K. Government no longer believed that its interests (or, rather, the interests of BA) were being served under Bermuda I, it denounced the treaty and contemplated consultations that led to the classically restrictive Bermuda II bilateral agreement.[160] The United States ceded much economic ground by its acquiescence to

---

[160] More precisely, the U.K. invoked the termination provision in Article 13 of the Bermuda I Agreement (*see supra* note 131), which provided for formal termination one calendar year after receipt of notice by the other contracting State.

Bermuda II, but a trade war, whether confined to the aviation sector or waged across other industrial sectors, would not have been to either party's advantage.[161]

3.6. LOOKING BEYOND BILATERALISM

3.6.1. *Preparing for Multilateralism*

The bilateral slant of the trade environment for international aviation is omnipresent, but it is not invulnerable. Multilateralism as enjoyed by other globally minded service sectors like telecommunications and finance remains imaginable, although unlikely to materialize in the foreseeable future. Greater market freedoms have secured their place in open skies–style bilateralism, but States remain hesitant to submit their air services trade even to modest multilateral arrangements. Muscular regional trade pacts like the North American Free Trade Agreement (NAFTA) continue to exclude hard economic air traffic rights from coverage.[162] To explain why that is the case, but also to prepare the reader for future shifts beyond bilateralism, we turn to the treatment of air services trade within the WTO and briefly consider the challenges of adapting the WTO's multilateral legal principles to the anomalies of the Chicago bilateral system. We also examine some other regional initiatives and how they, too, are constrained by bilateralist thinking.

3.6.2. *Air Services and the World Trade Organization (WTO)*

Bilateralism marks international air services as an outlier from a trend toward multilateral trade liberalization. That exceptionalism is confirmed when we examine how international aviation is treated within the WTO General Agreement on Trade in Services (GATS).[163] Unlike all other service sectors,

---

[161] ICAO has criticized bilateral dispute settlement procedures as "inadequate" and has proposed mediation by impartial experts working to rapid timetables as an alternative to traditional arbitration clauses. *See generally* ICAO, *Policy and Guidance Material on the Economic Regulation of International Air Transport*, ICAO Doc. 9587 (3rd ed. 2008).

[162] *See* North American Free Trade Agreement art. 1201(2)(b), U.S.-Can.-Mex., Dec. 17, 1992, *reprinted in* 32 I.L.M. 289 (1993) (limiting coverage to "aircraft repair and maintenance services during which an aircraft is withdrawn from service" and "specialty air services," e.g., aerial mapping, surveying photography, advertising, etc.). *See also, e.g.,* Free Trade Agreement, art. 10.1(4)(c), U.S.-Austl., May 18, 2004, 118 Stat. 919 (excluding air services from coverage).

[163] *See* General Agreement on Trade in Services [GATS], Annex on Air Transport Services, Marrakesh Agreement Establishing the World Trade Organization, Annex 1B, Legal Instruments – Results of the Uruguay Round, *opened for signature* Apr. 15, 1994, 1869 U.N. T.S. 183, 33 I.L.M. 1125, 1167 (1993).

none of which is *a priori* blocked from coverage under GATS disciplines, the Agreement's Annex on Air Transport Services excludes all but a narrow trio of ancillary services comprising aircraft repair and maintenance, selling and marketing of air transport services, and computer reservation systems.[164] On the principle *inclusio unius est exclusio alterius*,[165] the Annex therefore denies GATS coverage to the "hard" currency of ASAs such as traffic rights (the freedoms of the air), foreign investment opportunities, and other market access privileges. Moreover, GATS treatment of the few included subsectors has been further eroded by a passel of exemption mechanisms that are hardwired into the Agreement.

3.6.3. *Challenges of Liberalizing Aviation Under WTO Trade Rules: "Most Favored Nation"*

Understanding the exclusion of hard economic rights requires knowing something about what the GATS trade disciplines are intended to do. Like its older analog in the trade of goods, the General Agreement on Tariffs and Trade (GATT), the GATS regime rests on two core principles: most favored nation (MFN) and national treatment (NT). MFN, in Article II(1) of the Agreement, instructs each member State to "accord immediately and unconditionally to services and service suppliers of any other Member State treatment no less favorable than it accords to the like services and service suppliers of any other country."[166] Applied strictly to trade in aviation services, MFN would require a State to offer its most liberal ASA concessions (e.g., under open skies agreements) to *all* WTO State parties on a *nonreciprocal* basis. The United States would be compelled to grant Air China and other Chinese carriers the same

---

[164] *See generally* ICAO, Economic Commission, *Regulation of International Air Transport Services, Report by the Council on Trade in Services*, at 2, A33-WP/7 (Jun. 6, 2001) (describing GATS Annex on Air Transport Services). It is not clear how the GATS negotiators, in their zeal to obtain *some* coverage of air transport, determined that sales and marketing would be treated as conceptually distinct from the provision of air services as such. As Tissa Abeyratne has argued, "[a]ir traffic rights that result from the Chicago Convention's provisions are the tool with which the selling or marketing of air transport services can be carried out and the two are inextricably linked to each other." Ruwantissa Abeyratne, *Trade in Air Transport Services: Emerging Trends*, 35 J. WORLD TRADE 1133, 1145 (2001). Resting in part on this premise, Abeyratne suggests that the explicit exclusion of air traffic rights from the GATS is necessarily "ambivalent." *Id.* In any event, "selling and marketing" does not include *pricing*, which remains outside the agreement.

[165] "The inclusion of one means the exclusion of the other."

[166] For all relevant WTO texts in a concise presentation, *see* World Trade Organization, *GATS Training Module*, http://www.wto.org/english/tratop_e/serv_e/cbt_course_e/signin_e.htm. No prior training in the esoterica of international trade law and policy is required for this interactive tutorial.

generous seventh freedom access to U.S. gateways that it concedes to EU airlines under the U.S./EU ASA. Although China, as a WTO member, would also be expected to grant nonreciprocal MFN to the United States, the restrictive market access provisions that the U.S./China ASA imposes on U.S. airlines would be preserved to the extent that China does not have more liberal arrangements with other States. In fact, China's ASAs are considerably less liberal than open skies-model ASAs; its GATS-induced concessions would fall far short of those that the MFN principle would allow it to extract from open skies adherents like the United States, the EU, Australia, and Canada. Nonreciprocal MFN would have had such a disruptive effect on the aviation trading environment that States were simply not interested in GATS coverage of the sector. Even though the GATS allows MFN exemptions to avoid free rider problems,[167] few States were inclined to risk the integrity of the bilateral system by opening up even the possibility of a fully loaded MFN.

3.6.4. *"National Treatment"*

Likewise, a preference for strategic (and hence discriminatory) trade practices in their home markets caused States to shun the NT principle. GATS Article XVII requires contracting States to deliver NT by "accord[ing] to services and service suppliers of any other [State party], in respect of all measures affecting the supply of services, treatment no less favorable than it accords to its own like services and service suppliers." Strictly applied, NT would prohibit the most discriminatory terms of aviation trade, including reservations of cabotage routes to national airlines as well as the nationality rule. While NT under the GATT is generally applicable, however, under GATS the principle applies only to those concessions (and for those services) in respect to which a WTO member State makes a specific scheduled (i.e., listed) commitment. Even if air services had been generally submitted to GATS treatment, no State party would have had to schedule a single NT commitment for the sector. But States were once again unwilling to risk the disruptive effects that NT *could have had* in the future on their managed bilateral approach to international air services.[168]

---

[167] Arguably the availability of MFN exemptions under GATS is not time-limited despite language in the Agreement suggesting a technical 10-year expiration. *See* HAVEL, BEYOND OPEN SKIES, *supra* note 5, at 533.

[168] The global aviation industry is governed by a variety of discriminatory rules that violate the assumptions of the NT principle. Examples include discriminatory rules that are explicitly nationality based such as restrictions on foreign ownership and control of domestic airlines, reservation of cabotage routes to nationally owned airlines, insistence on the home nationality of crew members on internal routes, the Fly America program for U.S. Government employees, prohibition on inbound wet leasing (aircraft plus crew) from foreign carriers,

3.6.5. A GATS Counterfactual

The GATS was finalized in 1995, just three years after the United States officially launched open skies and two years before the EU ended its full transition to a single aviation market. The world's major aviation powers simply may have been unprepared for the implications of applying the new GATS disciplines to an industry that was just emerging from decades of strict mercantilism. Although counterfactuals are not always useful, it is worth thinking about what the Annex on Air Transport Services would look like (or whether it would exist at all) had the GATS been negotiated today. After recruiting more than 100 partners to its open skies policy, the United States has made the idea of international air transport liberalization palatable to a majority of the world's countries. Were the United States compelled today to grant nonreciprocal MFN for air services, its strategic costs would be much less than in 1995 when the only Western European States it could attract to open skies were the Netherlands and Germany and when it still had restrictive ASAs in place with major aviation trading partners such as the United Kingdom, Australia, Canada, and Japan. A critical mass of WTO members may eventually lobby for expansion or excision of the Annex on Air Transport Services.[169] Meanwhile, the Annex mandates the WTO – through its Council on Trade in Services – to regularly evaluate international air services trade and to chronicle the results in writing. While providing useful fodder for academics, the WTO's reporting duties have confined it to the role of an information clearinghouse. To many, that is a waste of resources.[170]

---

discriminatory preferences favoring national airlines in the assignment of airport slot privileges, and so on. Strictly speaking, the GATS does not prohibit any of these features of the bilateral system. Contracting States can simply list them in the relevant schedule as "conditions and qualifications." For example, States could schedule existing foreign ownership restrictions in the form of a GATS commitment and in that way use the GATS formula as a mechanism to *freeze* existing restrictions. Had the United States done so, it would not have been able legally to impose even more restrictive conditions on foreign control in 2003. *See* Brian F. Havel, *Mixed Signals on Foreign Ownership: An Assessment*, ISSUES AVIATION L. & POL'Y (CCH) ¶ 25,341, at 13,125 (2005) (discussing amendment of U.S. air carrier ownership statute to include explicit requirement of actual control of a U.S. airline's stock by U.S. citizens).

[169] The EU, Australia, New Zealand, and Chile all supported expanding the GATS to cover air transport during the first Review of the GATS Annex on Air Transport Services. *See* Cecilia Decurtins, The Air Transport Review at the WTO: Bilateralism versus Multilateralism (Jun. 14, 2007) (unpublished Ph.D. thesis, University of Geneva), http://www.unige.ch/cyberdocuments/theses2007/DecurtinsCG/these.pdf.

[170] Hamid Mamdouh, Dir., Trade in Services, World Trade Org., address at Sustainable Aviation Policies for America and the World: A Leadership Summit (Oct. 19, 2006).

3.6.6. *Multilateralizing Liberalization: The MALIAT*

Since the inception of the U.S. open skies policy, several efforts have been undertaken to multilateralize its unlimited commercial freedom to set prices, capacity, and frequency, as well as its unrestricted granting of third, fourth, and fifth freedoms for passenger and/or cargo traffic (along with occasional grants of seventh freedoms for all-cargo carriage). The only ostensibly multi-lateral ASA finalized by the United States is the 2001 Multilateral Agreement on the Liberalization of International Air Transportation (MALIAT), in which the United States joined a group of nine other countries including Brunei Darussalam, Chile, New Zealand, and Singapore.[171] MALIAT makes some minor but interesting modifications to the open skies template, such as replacing the traditional ownership and control benchmarks in favor of a more plastic standard of "effective control" by citizens of the designating contracting State accompanied by (instead of substantial ownership) incorpo-ration and principal place of business in that State.[172] The revised standard might allow a foreign investor to take a large equity stake in a MALIAT-party airline, but otherwise the agreement does little more than regulate the bilat-eral aviation relations of its signatories. For instance, an authentically multi-lateral feature, such as collective enforcement of the treaty's terms against a scofflaw party, does not exist within the agreement.[173] Similarly, MALIAT does not provide an open investment regime among its members, nor does it facilitate cross-border regulatory harmonization. In reality, MALIAT amounts to little more than a "pooled" open skies accord.

3.6.7. *Other Multilateral Initiatives*

Other groups of States, moreover, have partnered regionally to develop liberal multilateral ASAs. The EU, as previously noted, has evolved an ambitious structure – the ECAA – that seeks to export its single aviation market to the wider Union "neighborhood."[174] Using agreements with targeted aeropolitical powers beyond its region, the EU is also seeking progressive dismantlement

---

[171] *See* Multilateral Agreement on the Liberalization of International Air Transportation, *opened for signature* May 1, 2001, 2215 U.N.T.S. 33, *reprinted in* 3 Av. L. Rep. (CCH) ¶26,018, at 21,121 (Nov. 15, 2000) [hereinafter MALIAT]; *see also* the MALIAT homepage, www.maliat.govt.nz.

[172] *See* MALIAT, *supra* note 171, art. 3.

[173] The idea of collective sanctions against a recalcitrant member of an international organization, to deter commercial or trade actions rather than in a context of belligerency, has recently regained currency. *See, e.g.*, Oona Hathaway & Scott J. Shapiro, *Outcasting: Enforcement in Domestic and International Law*, 121 YALE L.J. 252 (2011).

[174] *See supra* Sections 3.1.3, 3.5.5.

of the most pernicious restrictions of bilateralism, including cabotage and the nationality rule, as evidenced by its aspirational 2009 ASA with Canada[175] and its ongoing comprehensive aviation trade talks with Australia and New Zealand.[176] The aforementioned 2007 U.S./EU Agreement has also taken on a multilateral flavor insofar as the accord is able to function as a plurilateral treaty whereby additional parties can be added if they agree to accede to all of its terms.[177] In 2009, Iceland and Norway, neither of which is an EU Member State, joined the Agreement, bringing the total State parties to thirty.[178] Whether or not more States will petition to join remains to be seen. Beyond the European theater, ASEAN continues to pour negotiating resources into the establishment of an "ASEAN Single Aviation Market" (ASAM) by 2015. The ASAM platform envisions far-reaching regulatory harmonization in areas such as competition law, consumer protection, and airport charges while also replacing the traditional nationality rule requirements to allow citizens of any ASEAN member to own and control an airline established in the territory of another ASEAN member.[179] Currently, however, ASEAN air services relations are governed by the more conservative 2008 Multilateral Agreement on Air

---

[175] *See* Agreement on Air Transport Agreement between Canada and the European [Union] and its Member States, Dec. 17, 2009, 2010 O.J. (L 207) 32, http://ec.europa.eu/transport/air/international_aviation/country_index/doc/canada_final_text_agreement.pdf. The EU/Canada agreement is best characterized as "aspirational," given the fact that its most progressive features, namely, reciprocal full investment rights and the reciprocal elimination of cabotage restrictions, will only come into effect after both parties take the necessary internal legislative steps to put those provisions into effect. The agreement establishes no time horizon for such major reforms, however.

[176] Australia and New Zealand began working toward their own single aviation market (the Trans-Tasman Single Aviation Market) in 1996, and have so far granted each other such advanced features as unrestricted seventh freedom cargo rights, cabotage privileges, and competition law convergence. Despite the advanced stages of air transport liberalization between the two States, they continue to conduct external relations separately. Both States have independently been negotiating liberalized air transport agreements with the EU since 2008, but completion appears blocked over differences concerning cross-border investment. *See* David Stone, *New Zealand May Beat Australia to an Open EU Aviation Agreement*, N.Z. HERALD, Aug. 24, 2009, http://www.nzherald.co.nz/business/news/article.cfm?c_id=3&objectid=10592719.

[177] *See* U.S./EU Air Transport Agreement, *supra* note 7, art. 18(5) (extending the Agreement to third parties following the development of conditions and procedures and necessary amendments). A "plurilateral agreement" is an agreement that might initially be bilateral but is capable of being expanded to involve additional parties, although typically the later parties cannot alter the basic terms of the original treaty. *See* ICAO MANUAL, *supra* note 48, at 2.4-1.

[178] The EU itself is also a party. For the text of the U.S./EU (Iceland, Norway) Air Transport Agreement of June 21, 2011, *see* http://www.state.gov/e/eb/rls/othr/ata/i/ic/170684.htm.

[179] The most expansive of these reforms are targeted for discussion, rather than listed as agreed-upon principles, in the most recently available ASAM policy document. *See* Ass'n of S.E. Asian Nations (ASEAN), Implementation Framework of the ASEAN Single Aviation Market (Dec. 16, 2011), http://www.asean.org/images/archive/documents/111219-17th%20ATM_Agenda%20Item%208%20ASAM%20Implementation%20Framework.pdf.

Services (MAAS) and 2010 Multilateral Agreement on Full Liberalisation of Passenger Air Services (MAFLPAS), which still contain restrictions on cross-border airline investment along with limitations on market access privileges.[180] For instance, neither agreement allows for seventh freedom rights nor for any form of cabotage.[181] Moreover, despite the ambitious nature of the ASAM platform, there remains strong reason to doubt that its agenda for strong liberalization will be in place by 2015. Similarly, the African Union has not succeeded in liberalizing air transport through its own multilateral, the Yamoussoukro Declaration and Yamoussoukro Decision.[182] Although modeled on the U.S. open skies template, and therefore far less radical than the proposed ASAM, few African States have demonstrated the political will to bring its liberalizing terms into effect. That has prompted some members, such as Ethiopia and Gabon, to pursue liberalization at the bilateral level.[183]

3.7. REMAINING CHALLENGES TO TRADE IN AIR SERVICES

3.7.1. *Overview*

In this final part, we highlight three matters that trade in air services has insufficiently addressed and yet which are regularly identified by industry stakeholders as major challenges to the ongoing project of air transport liberalization. None of these matters is yet covered materially in ASAs, although some, particularly harmonization of competition laws, have begun to make their way into the conduct of aviation trade relations. The reader, however, should be attentive to the fact that this small list of challenges by no means covers all of the pressure points on the international air transport industry. Environmental regulation has recently come to the forefront of international aeropolitical relations, and while some ASAs now seek to address cross-border convergence in this area (albeit at a high level of generality), we reserve further discussion on this challenge for Chapter 5. Similarly, security concerns are also included in many ASAs, but are reserved for later treatment in Chapter 6.

---

[180] *See* ASEAN Multilateral Agreement on Air Services, *opened for signature* May 20, 2009, http://www.aviation.go.th/doc/public/MAAirServices-Eng.pdf.; ASEAN Multilateral Agreement on the Full Liberalisation of Passenger Air Services, *opened for signature* Nov. 12, 2010, http://cil.nus.edu.sg/rp/pdf/2010%20ASEAN%20Multilateral%20Agreement%20on%20Full%20Liberali sation%20of%20Passanger%20Air%20Services-pdf.pdf.

[181] *See id.*

[182] *See generally* Schlumberger, *supra* note 121.

[183] *See, e.g.,* Air Transport Agreement, U.S.-Eth., May 17, 2005, *reprinted in* 3 Av. L. Rep. (CCH) ¶ 26,300a; Air Transport Agreement, U.S.-Gabon, Aug. 23, 2004, *reprinted in* 3 Av. L. Rep. (CCH) ¶ 26,310a.

3.7.2. *Capacity Constraints*

The biggest public policy issue in U.K. aviation today is not market access rights, domestic cabotage, or whether foreign investors should have the ability to own and control British Airways. It is, rather, the related facts that London Heathrow, the world's busiest international airport, operates suboptimally with only two runways and that the U.K. Government will not countenance construction of any more.[184] Airport congestion is an enduring challenge to the orderly development of a competitive international air transport market. Finite capacity conflicts with the demand created by rising liberalization. Moreover, many of the world's highest-demand airports are in dense urban areas like west London where geographic conditions, environmental concerns, and the lack of political will make significant expansion problematic. Even authorized projects take many years before new capacity comes on-stream: Heathrow's owners predict a lengthy timescale to construct a new runway even if the government were to reverse itself.[185] A competing plan to move London's principal aviation hub to an island in the Thames estuary would take twenty years to complete.[186] In response to the problem of scarce capacity, States (or their municipalities) have devised two remedial mechanisms: congestion pricing and slots. Both are imperfect instruments that can be, and have been, used to undermine the promise of liberalization.

---

[184] The issue of U.K. airport capacity (and, specifically, expansion of Heathrow) continues to be a treacherous political issue. The current Conservative/Liberal Democrat coalition government campaigned against a third runway in the 2010 general election, but the business community has subsequently applied considerable pressure to reconsider that position. *See* Gwyn Topham, *Transport: There's Only Room for One Hub, Says Heathrow*, THE GUARDIAN, Nov. 15, 2012, at 34 (reporting on a new study promoted by Heathrow claiming that capacity limitations could cost the U.K. £14 billion annually in trade revenues). The government had promised to address the capacity problem as part of a new aviation policy to be released in 2012, but instead temporarily punted the issue to a special commission that produced an interim report in December 2013 but will not render a final decision until 2015 (after the next general election). *See Heathrow: Government to Study Airport Expansion Plans*, BBC NEWS, Sept. 5, 2012, http:// www.bbc.co.uk/news/uk-politics-19484126. *See also* Brian F. Havel & Jeremias Prassl, *Reforming Civil Aviation Regulation in the United Kingdom: The Civil Aviation Bill 2011–12*, 11 ISSUES AVIATION L. & POL'Y 321 (2012).

[185] Estimates vary, but planning objections could delay construction of a third Heathrow runway by up to a decade. *See* http://www.ft.com/cms/s/0/96241ba6-f33e-11e1-9ca6-00144feabdco. html#axzz2JDichBVH (estimating 6 to 10 years).

[186] A new four-runway airport for London, even if it wins the support of the airport capacity commission and the next U.K. government (*see supra* note 184), would probably not be completed until at least 2028. *See id.*

3.7.3. *Congestion Pricing and Slots*

Under congestion pricing, airports scale their takeoff and landing charges in accordance with the peaks and valleys of demand. The economic logic is that the airlines that most value "prime-time" access will pay higher charges; the remainder will redirect their services to off-peak hours or, in some instances, forego flying to the congested airfield altogether. Although straightforward, congestion pricing raises a number of concerns. First, it is often difficult to price properly in line with demand. If prices are set high, too many airlines may be dissuaded from using the airport and capacity is wasted. If prices are set too low, then the problem of congestion continues. Second, and more importantly, congestion pricing can be used by public authorities to collect rents from airlines. Unless there are preset rules mandating that revenues collected from congestion pricing are to be used to expand capacity at the airport or, at least, invested in airport facilities, airlines may find that their higher fees are being used to fund nonaviation projects. Worse, in States where the airlines are still publicly owned, revenues collected from congestion pricing may be used to subsidize those carriers. Finally, the costs of congestion pricing are often merely passed on to airline consumers in the form of higher fares.[187]

3.7.4. *Slot Mechanisms*

An alternative to congestion pricing – one that has been widely adopted in the EU – is the creation of airport slots. A "slot" is simply an authority to take off or land at an airport during a given period of time.[188] The slot mechanism, too, is subject to abuse. Because States have historically reserved slots to their national carriers, it can be difficult for new (including foreign) entrants to acquire prime slots at high-demand airports. British Airways, for example, has accumulated over 40% of the slots at Heathrow, and other large U.S. and EU

---

[187] *See generally* Michael E. Levine, *Airport Congestion: When Theory Meets Reality*, 26 YALE J. ON REG. 37 (2009) (proposing a "blind" slot auction that avoids monopolistic and inefficient effects of government slot allocation procedures and forces slot owners to consider the value they place on a slot); Jan K. Brueckner, *Price vs. Quantity-Based Approaches to Airport Congestion Management*, 93 J. PUB. ECON. 681 (2009).

[188] According to the U.S. Federal Aviation Administration, slots are "an operating privilege" subject to its absolute control. 14 C.F.R. § 93.223(a) (West 2008). Nevertheless, it is well known that airlines sometimes carry their slot treasuries on their books as assets and have used them as security for loans or bond flotations. *See infra* Chapter 8, n. 20 (describing a recent aborted bond issue by British Airways using some of its takeoff and landing slots at London Heathrow as collateral).

carriers have similarly colonized the majority of slot times at their principal hubs. For protectionist reasons, States may be hesitant to release new slots even when an airport can handle the additional capacity. One way to avoid adjusting a fixed supply of slots is for States to allow a secondary or "gray" market in the existing stock, so that incumbent holders are able to sell or lease their slots to airlines that value them more. Unfortunately, a gray market lacks transparency and makes it difficult for airlines to assess the value of their slots and the opportunity costs associated with holding on to them. Another approach, favored in both the United States and EU, is to establish a "use-or-lose" requirement that requires an airline to utilize a given slot at a given threshold of frequency (say 80% of available peak-time flights) over a given period – or forfeit its right to the slot. Once forfeited, the slot is redistributed to a rival carrier, although the terms of redistribution can also pose problems. The EU, for instance, has favored awarding forfeitures to new entrants despite the fact that incumbents may value the slot more and would have an incentive to exploit it more efficiently.[189] An auction system, letting the forfeited slot go to the highest bidder, could resolve this dilemma: but then the challenge would once again be presented of what to do with auction revenues. If the revenues must be earmarked for airport upgrading or capacity expansion, there is little to fret about. If, however, slot auction revenues are remitted to the general public treasury, airports (or, more specifically, the States and municipalities that own and control them) have a perverse incentive to make an inefficient number of slots available for auction in order to collect rents from bidding air carriers. As things stand, few ASAs contain direct provisions covering slots, although the pressure of the congestion issue, as well as the propensity of governments to use it as a plausible rationale for denying foreign carriers full exploitation of their market access rights, may cause this state of affairs to change. The 2009 U.S./Japan ASA, for example, granted U.S. carriers only a small number of slots at one of Tokyo's two heavily trafficked international airports, Haneda.[190] Critics, labeling the ASA as "open skies lite," were quick to note that the Japanese concessions fell far short of U.S. carrier demands for access.[191] Further, the U.S./Japan ASA did not

---

[189] The most recent proposal for amending slot allocation procedures within the EU would allow airlines to sell and buy slots and possibly incur penalties for delinquent return of unused slots. *See* Press Release, Council of the European Union, Transport, Telecommunications and Energy: Transport Items, PRES/12/447 (Oct. 29, 2012).

[190] For the text of the 2009 U.S./Japan ASA, see http://www.state.gov/e/eb/rls/othr/ata/j/ja/133510.htm.

[191] Defenders of the agreement would likely argue that the progress made toward liberalization should not be discounted given how protectionist Japanese air transport policy had been until

incorporate a mechanism for acquiring additional slots, other than the usual channels of aerodiplomacy.

3.7.5. *Public Subsidies*

The problem of State aid (or public subsidies) is endemic across all sectors of international trade. Within the EU, a supranational code of behavior seeks to ensure that industrial and services enterprises, including airlines, cannot be artificially propped up by their home States. Numerous exceptions to this regime exist and, with respect to the airline industry, some Member States appear to have openly defied it.[192] International events such as the September 11, 2001, terrorist attacks and the Icelandic Volcanic Ash Crisis in 2010 can provoke (sometimes unheeded) calls for fiscal support to airlines in the name of safe-guarding national transportation infrastructures. While, at the global level, the WTO has attempted to construct a protocol that defines and protects legitimate subsidies,[193] for example, those granted to underdeveloped regions, the decision to partition off most aspects of international air services from WTO coverage means that States are not generally dissuaded from assigning public funds to sustain weak carriers. It remains unclear what, if anything, should be done about this reality. The rise of the Gulf carriers, and suspicions that they benefit in numerous ways from the largesse of rich patron States, has added to the vexation of privately owned airlines about government handouts.[194] Yet it is indisputable that certain kinds of public funding can produce positive outcomes for

very recently. *See 5Q with Former State Department Official John Byerly*, Bus. Travel News, Nov. 10, 2010, http://www.businesstravelnews.com/Strategic-Sourcing/5Q-With-Former-State-Department-Official-John-Byerly/?a=trans (describing the U.S.-Japan agreement as "sort of a miracle agreement").

[192] *See* Havel, Beyond Open Skies, *supra* note 5, at 495–502 (describing the EU's "battle" against national subsidies for airlines like Olympic, Alitalia, Aer Lingus, and others). More recently, the European Commission has investigated the growing phenomenon of State aid to attract airlines to regional airports in several EU Member States. *See* European Comm'n, *External Aviation Policy, supra* note 33, at 8.

[193] *See* Agreement on Subsidies and Countervailing Measures, Apr. 15, 1994, Marrakesh Agreement Establishing the World Trade Organization, Annex 1A, 1869 U.N.T.S. 14.

[194] The European Commission has expressed its concern about these matters in a recent study. *See* European Comm'n, *External Aviation Policy, supra* note 33, at 7, 13 (observing that sustainable competitiveness in the international air transport industry requires elimination of subsidies and unfair practices, as well as transparency in financial reporting, and proposing new "fair competition clauses" for ASAs with non-Member States). The Commission has announced that it will strengthen Council Regulation 868/2004, Protection Against Subsidisation and Unfair Pricing Practices Causing Injury to Community Air Carriers in the Supply of Air Services from Countries Not Members of the European Community, 2004 O.J. (L 162) 1, which was intended to combat subsidization and unfair pricing practices causing injury to EU air carriers but which, because the tools it uses are more suitable to dealing with goods rather

consumers, including greater service opportunities and more competitive fares. Emirates, the Dubai carrier, has entered secondary airports in the United Kingdom and Germany to offer a plethora of new one-stop connections over Dubai, at ticket prices that compete strongly with direct flights by British Airways and Lufthansa, to points in India and East Asia.[195] As the Nobel laureate economist Paul Krugman is said to have quipped, the best policy response to foreign State subsidies is "to send a thank-you note to the [local] embassy."[196] Perhaps more importantly, there is an ideology of national pride that continues to swaddle national carriers and also the still-prevalent bias that airlines remain public utilities and not solely independent market actors (part of an airline "system" rather than an airline "industry"[197]). In those circumstances, States are unwilling to forego absolutely a sovereign right to bail out a national airline if the need should arise.[198] The prevailing bilateral order and the nationality rule make such attitudes more understandable. Airlines are largely shut out of international capital investment and cannot entertain genuine cross-border mergers or acquisitions. Until the nationality rule is banished, it seems almost perverse to demand total fiscal self-reliance from the air transport industry.

3.7.6. *Competition Law Harmonization*

If aviation trade liberalization deepens to the point where airlines will be able to acquire or establish foreign subsidiaries and consummate cross-border mergers, the question of "globalizing" competition oversight and enforcement for the international air transport industry will take on refreshed relevance. Whether any kind of global competition code is desirable or even possible is a subject that has preoccupied many legal scholars over the past two decades and is beyond

---

than services, has never been used. *See id.* A striking example of the acrimony that has existed between Emirates and the large international airline alliances can be seen in a 2011 Emirates publication, *Aviation at the Crossroads*, available at www.emirates.com. The publication accuses alliance members *inter alia* of coordinating competitive attacks on Emirates as a viable "independent alternative." Interestingly, while still eschewing the multicarrier global alliance model, in September 2012 Emirates announced that it would seek regulatory approval to pursue a 10-year "global aviation partnership" with Australia's Qantas. *See* http://www.qantas.com.au/travel/airlines/media-releases/sep-2012/5440/global/en.

[195] For a presentation of Emirates' current route development strategy, see *Aviation at the Crossroads, supra* note 194.

[196] *Quoted in* Alan O. Sykes, *International Trade: Trade Remedies, in* RESEARCH HANDBOOK OF INTERNATIONAL ECONOMIC LAW 62, 106 (2007).

[197] *See* HAVEL, BEYOND OPEN SKIES, *supra* note 5, at 376–77 (discussing, but rejecting, possible reregulation of the U.S. airline industry).

[198] *See* Tyler Brûlé, *Embassies with Wings*, FT.COM, Feb. 24, 2012 (advocating that States help their airlines for reasons of pride and tourism).

the scope of this book.[199] A handful of ASAs, most notably the 2007 U.S./EU Air Transport Agreement, contain open-ended provisions calling for "cooperation" on competition issues, although what that means in practice is hazy.[200] ASEAN's vision for regional air transport liberalization, the ASAM, makes competition law harmonization one of its pillars. But, given the uncertainty over whether or not the ASAM will come into effect, it is impossible to judge at this point what positive (or negative) effects that projected level of regulatory cooperation will have. Industry stakeholders have suggested that a "one-stop shop" for competition oversight of transnational airline merger activity would eliminate duplicative costs and offer more legal certainty, but those advantages would exist for any commercial activity that crosses borders. None of this is to say that competition law harmonization is impossible. In a limited number of bilateral circumstances, where both parties already share a similar competition code and policy, cross-border cooperation is certainly feasible.[201] But stakeholders must be wary of calls for competition harmonization that are in reality just intended to stymie further investment liberalization. There is no compelling evidence that the absence of unified global competition laws has thwarted foreign investment in industries ranging from automobiles to pharmaceuticals. Even if overlapping competition laws add costs to future potential airline merger transactions, the parties to the deal are fully capable of taking such costs into account when deciding whether or not to proceed.

---

[199] *See, e.g.,* Eleanor M. Fox, *Toward World Antitrust and Market Access,* 91 AM. J. INT'L L. 1 (1997); FREDERIC M. SCHERER, COMPETITION POLICIES FOR AN INTEGRATED WORLD ECONOMY (1994); for a more skeptical perspective, *see* Paul B. Stephan, *Global Governance, Antitrust, and the Limits of International Cooperation,* 38 CORNELL INT'L L.J. 173 (2005); Diane Wood, *The Impossible Dream: Real International Antitrust,* 1992 U. CHI. LEGAL F. 277 (1992).

[200] But some potentially extraordinary conceptual alignments have nonetheless happened. Thus, Article 20 of the 2007 U.S./EU Air Transport Agreement, *see supra* note 7, binds both sides to U.S. judicial precedent (and to a shared philosophy) when it confirms that the parties "apply their respective competition regimes to protect and enhance overall competition and not individual competitors." *See also infra* Chapter 4, Part 4.8.6 (discussing some evidence of convergence in U.S./EU treatment of international airline alliances).

[201] As a general matter, U.S./EU cooperation on competition and antitrust enforcement long predates the 2007 U.S./EU Air Transport Agreement. *See* Agreement between the Government of the United States of America and the [EU Commission] Regarding Application of Their Competition Laws, 1995 O.J. (L 95) (Sept. 23, 1991), *as corrected by* 1995 O.J. (L 134) 1, *reprinted in* 4 Trade Reg. Rep. (CCH) ¶ 13,504, at 21,233-9. The Agreement speaks in the language of diplomacy rather than normative obligation, inviting each party to demonstrate "comity" in its relations with the other, either *positive comity* (to act on the request of the other party) or *negative comity* (when each party acts, to take into account important interests of the other). *See also infra* Chapter 4, Part 4.8 (discussing cooperation in review of international airline alliances).

3.8. SOME CONCLUDING COMMENTS ON TRADE IN AIR SERVICES

3.8.1. *Assessing the Progress of Liberalization*

For those committed to the often frustrating project of trade liberalization generally, the history of trade in international air services offers a mixed record. Having largely been exempted from WTO trade disciplines, international aviation has had to evolve (and liberalize) within the much more limited framework of bilateralism. Despite this, progress continues to be made. Even with widespread restrictions on market access, passengers and cargo now move across borders under increasingly liberal regimes of routes, capacity, and fares. Code-shares and alliances have dramatically expanded the availability of seamless travel to thousands of new connecting cities. The U.S./ EU Air Transport Agreement has offered a dramatic "demonstration" model for regional liberalization and is likely to produce even further new competitive opportunities in the transatlantic marketplace. Similar multilateral regional projects are likely to follow in the Asia-Pacific, Latin American, and African regions. These emerging regions are keenly aware of the stakes: in today's sophisticated transnational economy, development is tied inextricably to new aviation market opportunities.

3.8.2. *A Continuing (and Vulnerable) Project*

Still, there is much more work to be done, especially if the global air transport sector is to enjoy the efficiencies that accompany open foreign investment and untrammeled access to global capital markets. At the same time, there is concern that managed trade could return as emerging aviation powers such as China seek to win parity with their developed State rivals. International aviation law has, and will continue to have, much to contribute to shaping aviation's trade landscape in the future. As this chapter has shown, however, law is constantly in thrall to the demands of politics and the unrelenting pressure of special interests.

4

The International Law Regime for Airline Investment and Global Alliances

4.1. INTRODUCTION

4.1.1. *The Nationality Rule Excludes Single-Carrier Networks*

As we noted in Chapter 3, the trade environment for international aviation is bedeviled by the requirement that airlines designated by a State under its bilateral air services agreements (ASAs) must be "substantially owned" and "effectively controlled" by that State or by its citizens. Moreover, that requirement has been tightened in recent years in many ASAs by making explicit what had always been an implicit assumption in bilateral aviation relations: that the designated airline must also be legally established and have its principal place of business in the designating State.[1] To reinforce these treaty-based provisions, most States have enacted domestic laws that prohibit foreign ownership and control of their national air carriers. All of these restrictions, bundled together as the "nationality rule,"[2] mean that no single air carrier is legally able to generate a freestanding global route network using any combination of wholly owned subsidiaries in strategic locales or cross-border mergers or acquisitions involving foreign partners.[3] Airlines, in a phrase, do not do business like any other business.[4]

---

[1] *See* Air Transport Agreement Between the Government of the United States of America and the Government of [country] art. 1(4) (Jan. 12, 2012), http://www.state.gov/e/eb/rls/othr/ata/114866.htm [hereinafter Model Open Skies Agreement] ("'Airline of a party' means an airline that has received its Air Operator's Certificate (AOC) from and has its principal place of business in the territory of that Party").

[2] Technically, the nationality rule refers only to the treaty-based restraints on designation (the so-called nationality clauses), but domestic laws limiting foreign ownership are just as responsible for circumscribing transnational airline investment. In our view, the "nationality rule" encompasses both treaty and domestic law restrictions, and we use the term with that more comprehensive meaning. *See supra* Chapter 3, note 1.

[3] *See supra* Chapter 3, Section 3.4.1.

[4] *See* International Air Transport, Agenda for Freedom, *Frequently Asked Questions*, http://www.agenda-for-freedom.aero/Pages/faq.aspx. Anomalously, perhaps, companies that provide

4.1.2. Rise of Strategic Alliances

As we will see, however, there is some evidence that the high-water mark of the nationality rule has passed, and that States in some regions are showing tolerance for transnational airline mergers that do not conform to the rule. In the meantime, many international carriers have sought to trump the nationality rule by forming single-identity strategic commercial alliances with foreign partners. By collaborating on fares, routes, marketing, and consumer perquisite programs, airline alliance partners can replicate, with varying degrees of intensity, the unified brand identity and service that a hypothetical "globalized" airline would be able to offer. These collaborations are not without controversy, however. As a former Qantas Airlines chief executive observed, airline alliances involve "sitting in a room to plan your business with your competitors."[5] Strategic alliances among companies that are normally in full-throated competition with each other are bound to attract antitrust scrutiny. But, as we will see, a vestigial power of antitrust exemption inherited by the U.S. Department of Transportation (DOT) from the era of airline regulation has enabled the three global alliances that include U.S. airlines to operate mostly outside that kind of scrutiny. The Department's approval of the alliances seems to have influenced competition law enforcers in other regions to take a similarly benign view.

4.1.3. Overview of Topics

In this chapter, we seek to state the contours of international investment and competition law as they relate to the airline industry. As with international environmental law (the subject of Chapter 6), the rules that affect transnational competition and investment in international aviation remain far from unified. Given that the United States and the European Union (EU) have largely set the regulatory tempo on matters of international airline competition and investment, and particularly in relation to alliances, our focus in this chapter will be on the legal arrangements and policy choices that have found favor in those two jurisdictions. But we will pay attention also to emerging trends in other regions, especially as they affect relaxation or even abandonment of the nationality rule. We will look at airline investment from three

---

ancillary services to airlines, such as aircraft leasing companies, airports, ground-handling companies, catering suppliers, and so forth, are not subject to the nationality rule.

[5] Yet in September 2012 Qantas announced a "global aviation partnership" with the Gulf-based carrier Emirates: see http://www.qantas.com.au/travel/airlines/media-releases/sep-2012/5440/global/en. See *also supra* Chapter 3, note 195.

perspectives. First, we will discuss the operation and effects of the nationality rule in current international aviation law and practice. Second, we will fit our analysis of airline investment into the wider context of how international law normally regulates foreign investment. Third, we will examine a perceptible trend toward destabilization of the nationality rule as evidenced by changes in State laws and practices and by the effects of private sector advocacy. Finally, we will explore how the international airline industry has attempted to circumvent the commercial limitations imposed by the nationality rule, and we will focus primarily on the emergence of the international airline alliance. We will review the legal and policy framework that has developed to support the three global alliances, and we will consider how U.S. and EU antitrust regulators are dealing with an industry-created system that binds competitors into potentially risky collaborative behavior. The chapter closes with a brief reflection on a new EU initiative that seeks to challenge the nationality rule within a broader context of U.S./EU trade diplomacy.

4.2. THE (AIRLINE) NATIONALITY RULE IN ACTION

4.2.1. *Operation of the Nationality Rule in ASAs*

The nationality rule has been part of international aviation law since the signing in 1944 of the Convention on International Civil Aviation[6] (the "Chicago Convention") and its subsidiary accords, the Two Freedoms and Five Freedoms agreements.[7] Although the rule's placement within literally thousands of ASAs demonstrates slight levels of variance, for the most part it is articulated as a condition precedent for States that designate one or more of their air carriers to take advantage of the terms of market access provided in each ASA. Under the Canada/U.S. ASA currently in force, Air Canada – Canada's flag carrier – must be owned and controlled by Canadian citizens before it is legally authorized under the ASA to serve destinations to, from, or beyond the United States.[8] Should Air Canada's ownership profile shift, for example, through a cross-border merger with Germany's Lufthansa, the

---

[6] *See* Convention on International Civil Aviation, *opened for signature* Dec. 7, 1944, 61 Stat. 1180, 15 U.N.T.S. 295 (entered into force Apr. 4, 1947) [hereinafter Chicago Convention].

[7] *See* International Air Services Transit Agreement, *opened for signature* Dec. 7, 1944, 59 Stat. 1693, 84 U.N.T.S. 389 (entered into force Jan. 30, 1945) (129 State parties as of January 2013) [hereinafter Two Freedoms Agreement]; International Air Transport Agreement, *opened for signature* Dec. 7, 1944, 59 Stat. 1701, 171 U.N.T.S. 387 (entered into force Jan. 30, 1945) (11 State parties as of January 2013) [hereinafter Five Freedoms Agreement].

[8] *See* Air Transport Agreement, U.S.-Can., art. 2(a), Mar. 12, 2007, 3 Aviation L. Rep. (CCH) ¶ 26,246a.

United States could, by the terms of the ASA, reduce or suspend Air Canada's market access privileges.[9] Even so, neither prong of the nationality rule – "substantially owned" and "effectively controlled" – is accompanied in ASAs by clarifications or benchmarks; what will satisfy either test seems left to be sorted out, as a matter of treaty law at least, on an *ad hoc* basis should a designated airline from an ASA partner receive a capital injection from a foreign-owned airline.[10] Would taking a mere 25% ownership stake elevate Lufthansa to "substantial ownership" of Air Canada?[11] On its face, probably not. But if Lufthansa ratchets up its stockholding to more than 50%, its ownership would certainly be perceived as legally "substantial." Yet there is no language in the U.S./Canada ASA explicitly regulating that possibility.[12]

4.2.2. *Meaning of Effective Control*

"Effective control" is an even more ambiguous measurement of foreign domination. Whereas 25% of an airline's voting share capital may not by itself reflect "substantial ownership," if 25% represents the single largest fraction of that capital, spreading the remaining 75% among a diluted mass of small shareholders may not prevent the 25% owner from exercising effective control. The imprecision of the nationality rule's two key components gives States ample latitude to enforce or (in a growing number of cases) not to enforce the rule against their ASA partners.

4.2.3. *Origins and Purpose of the Nationality Rule*

Why the nationality rule infiltrated international aviation law is itself an interesting question, the answer to which sheds light on its slow but perceptible retreat over the past decade. Recall that the Chicago Convention and its accompanying treaties were negotiated and signed before the end of World War II hostilities. The United States and its allies feared that enemy or ex-enemy States could gain control of a third State's airline and thereby indirectly enter U.S. or other airspace even though those States' own airlines might be blocked from doing so for political and military reasons. States

---

[9] *See id.* art. 4(b); *see also* supra Chapter 3, Section 3.5.6.

[10] *See supra* Chapter 3, Section 3.4.7.

[11] Canadian domestic legislation currently places a 25% cap on foreign investment in the shares of Canadian airlines. *See* Transportation Act, S.C. 1996, c.10, §§ 55, 61(a)(1) (Can.), http://laws. justice.gc.ca/PDFF/Statute/C/C-10.4.pdf. In addition, Canadian airlines must also be "controlled in fact" by Canadian citizens. *Id.*

[12] Nevertheless, as mentioned *supra* note 11, Canadian domestic law limits foreign ownership of the voting stock of Canadian airlines to a maximum of 25%.

understandably wanted to ensure that only the States – and their citizens – to which market access concessions were awarded could take advantage of those preferential terms. But there was also a strong protectionist coloring to the nationality rule. By keeping airlines tethered to their home States and to the citizen-investors of those States, the nationality rule contributed to maintaining a degree of parity in the international marketplace; no single carrier could hope to take advantage of cross-border capital infusions that might allow it to build the fleet capacity and resources to overpower specific international markets. Likewise, the rule thwarted the establishment of foreign subsidiaries that would allow airlines to assemble global networks. Hence, on the general premise that national third and fourth freedom traffic (the basic passenger and cargo traffic between any two States) "belonged" to the flag carrier in the first instance,[13] the system was effectively rigged to give national airlines the opportunity to capture business from passengers and shippers in their home States looking to access foreign destinations. Under that framework, for example, a passenger flying from Grand Rapids, Michigan, to Warsaw, Poland, would travel on a U.S. airline to Chicago and likely board the same or a rival U.S. carrier for transit to Frankfurt. From there, Poland's LOT airline would serve the final segment to Warsaw. The journey would include at least two and possibly three airlines providing successive carriage at high "interline" rates.[14] As we will see, the global alliances (while remaining bound by the limitations of the nationality rule) offer at least the promise of a more rationally integrated service.

4.2.4. *Foreclosing the Techniques of Cross-Border Investment*

The push toward airline deregulation within particular economies promised greater consumer choice and, for the airlines, much improved efficiency. The nationality rule prevented delivery of those boons at the international level. Not only were airlines prevented from creating autonomous transnational networks, but their legal inability to consummate mergers or acquisitions or to create subsidiaries across national borders disqualified them from exploiting the basic investment techniques that other industries use to elude high tariffs and discriminatory regulatory barriers. A manufacturer established in a State with high labor standards and other costly regulatory requirements may be unable to price its products competitively for export to a protected overseas

---

[13] *See supra* Chapter 3, note 136.
[14] *See infra* note 111 (defining interlining as occurring when different segments of a trip are flown by different airlines and the passenger and his or her luggage are transferred from the aircraft of the first carrier to that of the second; interlining typically does not involve a code-share.).

market. But, if the manufacturer obtains the right to establish a facility in the foreign market, localized manufacturing avoids inward tariffs, and more competitive localized pricing will build market share. Reduced transportation costs might also encourage the manufacturer to export from its new overseas base to the wider region within which its new facility is located. Finally, the manufacturer can benefit from any trade concessions negotiated by its new host State with other States in the region, such as preferential tariff treatment within a trading bloc.[15] A similar logic can be applied to international aviation. For example, were it not for the nationality rule in the U.S./Japan ASA or inward investment caps in Japan's domestic laws, a U.S. carrier such as United, frustrated by market access restrictions in Japan, might decide to establish a subsidiary – call it "United-Asia" – in Japan in order to claim a slice of Japan's international aviation market (and perhaps of its domestic market as well). Assuming that Japan has counterpart ASAs (i.e., without the nationality rule) with other Asian States, United-Asia could use the market access rights under these ASAs to offer seventh freedom (stand-alone) services from Tokyo to Beijing, Hong Kong, Seoul, Singapore, Sydney, or Ho Chi Minh City. In cooperation with its U.S. parent, United-Asia could develop Tokyo (or any Japanese "aerotropolis"[16]) as a pan-Asian hub that not only sidesteps market access restrictions, but also loops together traffic rights on the way to amassing a transpacific route network attractive to both American and Asian passengers.

4.2.5. *Domestic Enforcement of the Nationality Rule*

The nationality rule chokes off these possible market scenarios because States are fearful that allowing foreign carriers to invest in domestic airlines risks jeopardizing the latter's market access rights under ASAs with other States. Even under the right of establishment strictly so called, where only a foreign subsidiary is created,[17] if the new subsidiary applies for designation under a State's ASA, other States will have the right to deny the designation

---

[15] *See supra* Chapter 3, note 90.
[16] "Aerotropolis" is a term coined by Professor John Kasarda to refer to the concept of planning a city around an airport, with emphasis on maximizing the city's effectiveness as a business and shipping hub. *See* JOHN KASARDA & GREG LINDSAY, AEROTROPOLIS: THE WAY WE'LL LIVE NEXT (2011).
[17] Under a right of establishment, an airline would have the ability to establish a subsidiary within a foreign market. The foreign subsidiary concept is referred to as "secondary establishment" in EU law. *See generally* Benjamin Angelette, Note, *The Revolution That Never Came and the Revolution Coming – De Lasteyrie Du Salliant, Marks and Spencer, SEVIC Systems and the Changing Corporate Law in Europe*, 92 VA. L. REV. 1189 (2006).

on the ground of foreign ownership and control. States, therefore, frequently ensure the "purity" of their air carriers' citizenship (and eligibility for designation) through domestic laws that regulate the quantum of share ownership and sometimes also the stringency of foreign managerial control. The United States, for example, has a federal statute that requires all U.S. air carriers to remain 75% owned by and under the "actual control" of U.S. citizens.[18] Most other States have equivalent laws, but with different calibrations of ownership or control. The EU allows foreign (i.e., non–EU Member State or non–EU citizen) entities to hold up to 49.9% of the voting equity of its air carriers – one of the more liberal investment ceilings currently in existence.[19] The EU has also legislated one of the few definitions of "effective control."[20]

4.2.6. *Viewpoint of Organized Labor*

Special-interest groups, particularly organized labor, have passionately opposed dismantling restrictions on foreign investment in national airlines – including the right of establishment, which labor unions fear will lead to the same "flag of convenience" problem that plagues global shipping.[21] According to U.S. labor, open investment rights would entice U.S. airlines into keeping only a "shell" identity in the United States while moving their true commercial operations to low-regulation, low-tax, low-wage third countries, converting those low regulatory hurdles into significantly lower cost structures while maintaining their market access privileges in the United States. Thus, the hypothetical United-Asia, instead of serving as a partner to United's U.S. parent, could become the sole corporate presence of the entire airline and still hold intact the original parent's domestic and international hub-and-spoke system within the United States. Even more vexing to U.S. labor is the

---

[18] *See* 49 U.S.C.S. §§ 41101(a)(1), 41102(a), 40102(a)(15) (LexisNexis 2012).

[19] *See* Common Rules for the Operation of Air Services in the European [Union], Council Regulation 1008/2008, art. 4(f), 2008 O.J. (L 293) 3 [hereinafter Common Rules].

[20] Article 2(9) of the (EU) Common Rules, *see supra* note 19, defines "effective control" in the EU aviation law context as (in summary) a relationship – formed by rights, contracts, or otherwise – that confers the possibility of directly or indirectly exercising a "decisive influence" on an air carrier, in particular by (a) the right to use all or part of the carrier's assets, and/or (b) rights or contracts that grant a "decisive influence" on the composition, voting, or decisions of the governing body of the air carrier or on the running of its business.

[21] In the international shipping industry, merchant vessel owners register (or "flag") their ships in foreign States with lighter regulatory burdens than the owners' home States. *See generally* H. Edwin Anderson III, *The Nationality of Ships and Flags of Convenience: Economics, Politics, and Alternatives*, 21 TUL. MAR. L.J. 139 (1996).

contingency that United-Asia would take down its U.S. employee base and replace it with cheaper foreign workers. These objections from a powerful stakeholder suggest that a replacement investment regime for States with high labor standards would retain some prophylactic restrictions on foreign investment.[22] Such a regime would include a requirement that no airline would be eligible for designation under an ASA unless its principal place of business remained in the designating State.

4.2.7. *Viewpoint of Other Interests*

As well as labor, other interests have been uncomfortable with relaxing or abolishing the airline nationality rule. The national security bureaucracy, for example, remains a potent constituency. But whatever merit once attached to the fear that enemy States could poach the market access rights of third States, concern about the dangers of "peddling" air routes seems anachronistic in the modern era. States have not only shifted to open investment regimes covering major infrastructure industries from automobiles to telecommunications, but they have also put in place review mechanisms to screen proposed inward investments where a national security objective seems implicated.[23] Other stakeholders, such as consumer groups, may fear that cross-border mergers will reduce competition, elevate fares, and cut service. The best policy response to such concerns is vigilant antitrust enforcement, including the premerger review procedures that now occur in major air transport markets like the United States and EU. Ironically, it is a measure of how the nationality rule unsettles normal commercial practice that the instrument invented by the international airline industry to bypass the rule – the strategic alliance – relies entirely on the willingness of States to refrain from applying their competition codes.[24]

---

[22] For a response that challenges these arguments (and that advocates the importance of requiring a broad spectrum of strong legal, regulatory, and commercial links to the licensing State), see BRIAN F. HAVEL, BEYOND OPEN SKIES: A NEW REGIME FOR INTERNATIONAL AVIATION 168–71 (2009).

[23] Under the U.S. Foreign Investment and National Security Act of 2007 (FINSA), for example, the President of the United States has broad powers to block or suspend investments in and/or acquisitions of U.S. companies and assets by foreign entities if the transaction presents a "credible" threat to national security. *See* 50 U.S.C.S. § 2170 (LexisNexis 2012). *See* Joseph Mamounas, *Controlling Foreign Ownership of U.S. Strategic Assets: The Challenge of Maintaining National Security in a Globalized and Oil Dependent World*, 13 LAW & BUS. REV. AM. 381, 395–96 (2007) (concluding that the aviation industry qualifies under FINSA as a "symbolic national asset" with serious security implications).

[24] *See infra* Part 4.5.

4.3. A QUICK LOOK AT HOW INTERNATIONAL LAW (NORMALLY) REGULATES FOREIGN INVESTMENT

4.3.1. *A Regime to Encourage Foreign Capital*

For the moment, the nationality rule holds sway in the international airline industry. Yet, in the broad context of how States frame policies on inward investment, there is nothing surprising about a State giving preference to its own nationals when determining the desired ownership profile of particular (or all) sectors of its economy. The right to exclude foreign investment, after all, has always been just as much a principle of sovereignty as the right to permit it – protectionism and mercantilism have ancient pedigrees. Nevertheless, the global market turmoil since 2008 has not yet capsized the policy choice made by virtually all developed and developing States over the past two decades that access to foreign capital should be encouraged and economic sovereignty limited accordingly. A body of "foreign investment law" has developed to allow States to offer an investment-friendly climate that fosters economic growth through capital importation. Whether legal stability alone would drive investment is, of course, open to question, but the existence of a functioning State, functioning institutions, and the rule of law will certainly be major factors in weighing a State's competitiveness as a prospective site for foreign investment.[25]

4.3.2. *Another Bilateral Treaty System*

The international airline industry, in any event, has stood aside from this body of investment law and is covered only incidentally by it.[26] Foreign investment

---

[25] "[I]nvestors primarily make their decision to invest dependent on the credibility of [S]tates to ensure a predictable and stable legal framework, *i.e.*, to effectively implement the rule of law." International Investment Law and Comparative Public Law 178 (Stephan W. Schill ed., 2010) [hereinafter SCHILL] (citing 1997 World Bank report).

[26] Thus, it is possible that a foreign airline that takes only a minority shareholder position in a host State airline (to the extent that such an investment is permitted by the host State's domestic law) will benefit from protections accorded under a bilateral investment treaty. The treaty may also give independent standing to the investing airline, as it will to all minority shareholders, to pursue a claim before an international arbitral tribunal even though the local airline corporation cannot strictly be characterized as foreign-owned. There is strong arbitral support for this proposition. *See* Rudolf Dolzer & Christoph Schreuer, Principles of International Investment Law 58 (2008) (citing decisions of various international tribunals). A more dramatic argument appears in a recent article suggesting that airlines which conduct traffic operations in a host State could invoke investment treaty protections, including investor-State arbitration, in situations where the host State has acted unfairly – for example, where a government imposes steep fees on foreign airlines landing at its airports,

law does resemble international aviation law, however, in that it has developed since the early twentieth century almost entirely through the medium of bilateral treaties between States. These treaties are designed to protect the interests of private corporate investors.[27] The directory of investment treaties now exceeds 3000,[28] making the field dense enough to not only merit consideration as a separate object of legal study but also to support a number of overarching principles of fair treatment that could be described as customary international law.[29] In the past two decades, also, foreign investment law has far surpassed the adjudicatory scope of international aviation law in repeatedly using autonomous international tribunals to resolve both inter-State and investor-State disputes. These tribunals have published a body of more than 300 decisions[30] that, while not binding beyond the immediate parties to the dispute, have shown appreciable cross-fertilization in how they interpret the legal rules and standards that are increasingly common to all bilateral investment agreements.

---

without relation to any identifiable costs in receiving those aircraft. Arguably, that fee structure would be in violation of Article 15 of the Chicago Convention, *supra* note 6, which permits recoupment of airport or navigational costs but does not permit "in gross" charges for overflight, takeoff, or landing *per se. See supra* Chapter 2, Section 2.5.6. But the argument rests on the as yet-untested (and undoubtedly controversial) proposition that "doing business" activities (such as providing flight service into and from a host State) could qualify as an "investment" for purposes of invoking a bilateral investment treaty between the host State and the airline's home State. Moreover, many bilateral investment treaties exclude air transport activities from their coverage. *See generally* Andrew B. Steinberg & Charles T. Kotuby, Jr., *Bilateral Investment Treaties and International Air Transportation: A New Tool for Global Airlines to Redress Market Barriers*, 76 J. AIR L. & COM. 457 (2011).

[27] Government investors not acting in a sovereign capacity but as commercial enterprises are also covered. To determine the nationality of a corporation, legal systems typically use tests of "incorporation" or (and sometimes in addition) the *siège social* (the principal place of business). *See* DOLZER & SCHREUER, *supra* note 26, at 49. The relevant bilateral investment treaty will likely specify which test or tests will be preferred. Article 1 of the U.S. Model Bilateral Treaty defines an "enterprise" as "any entity constituted or organized under applicable law . . . including a corporation, trust, partnership, sole proprietorship, joint venture, association, or similar organization; and a branch of an enterprise." *See* U.S. State Dept., U.S. Model Bilateral Treaty (2004), art. 1, http://www.state.gov/documents/organization/38710.pdf [hereinafter U.S. Model BIT]. As noted, *see supra* Section 4.2.1, in the international aviation industry the tests of nationality are extremely stringent, because they require not just majority share ownership by a State's nationals but also "effective control" by those nationals.

[28] *See* Jeswald W. Salacuse, *The Emerging Global Regime for Investment*, 51 HARV. INT'L L.J. 427, 436 (2010). It is best not to describe these bilateral treaties on investment as a "network," since they are not necessarily connected to one another despite their repeated use of similar provisions and conditions. *Id.* at 430.

[29] *See* DOLZER & SCHREUER, *supra* note 26, at 124–28.

[30] *See* Salacuse, *supra* note 28, at 460.

4.3.3. *Potential Mechanisms for Investment in Foreign Airlines*

A "foreign investment," as we use the term here and as it is generally understood, means more than a simple one-off trade transaction because it involves the rights and obligations that flow from a permanent relationship between the investing enterprise and the foreign State.[31] As the world's airline executives are keenly aware, that kind of relationship can take one of two forms: either it is a nonnational investor taking a controlling share in an existing domestic corporation (e.g., if United were to buy Lufthansa), or, under the doctrine known as the right of establishment, a nonnational investor using local laws to set up a subsidiary corporation that must be compliant with the full sweep of tax, social, labor, environmental, and other regulatory rules that apply also to domestically owned companies (e.g., if United were to establish United/Germany).[32] Occasionally, especially with respect to large-scale utility investments such as power generation plants or oilfield or gas generation infrastructure, a foreign investor may reach a separate agreement, called an "investment agreement," with the host State.[33] Because of the role of airline companies as both profit-seeking commercial enterprises and also critical components of national transportation infrastructure, it is conceivable that some States would enter special agreements with investing foreign airlines if the nationality rule were scrapped but those States still felt that certain questions of national policy needed to be clarified: a good example would be the U.S. Government's requirement that all of its airlines remain available to provide auxiliary airlift capacity during military engagements.[34]

---

[31] "Permanency" is a term of art and may mean as little as a couple of years depending on the circumstances. The important point is that the relationship has a certain measurable duration and is not simply a one-off transaction. Note that the kind of foreign investment discussed here is also distinguishable from so-called portfolio investment where the foreign investor simply invests in corporate stocks but plays no role in the actual management of the corporation. *See* DOLZER & SCHREUER, *supra* note 26, at 64.

[32] *See supra* note 17 (noting similar EU concept of "secondary establishment").

[33] Agreements of this kind may include complex formulas to divide revenues between the parties to the investment agreement. *See generally* DOLZER & SCHRUER, *supra* note 26, at 72–73.

[34] Under the Civil Reserve Air Fleet (CRAF) program, U.S. air carriers commit to supply airlift capacity to the U.S. defense forces in the event of a military emergency. The carriers receive peacetime U.S. Government business as a *quid pro quo* for their wartime availability. The Department of Defense has expressed concern that foreign-owned U.S. carriers could no longer be relied upon to honor their CRAF commitments and may be less likely to participate in CRAF. *See* HAVEL, *supra* note 22, at 48.

4.3.4. *Foreign Investors and National Treatment*

Investment, therefore, is a broad and flexible term that is well understood in international law.[35] Also well understood is that a foreign corporate investor, like its counterparts in the host State of the investment, acts with an expectation of profit and must likewise bear the risk of business failure. But foreign investors will not expect or want to endure the collateral political risks that could follow an inward investment, for example a sudden reversal of government policy or replacement of a friendly regime by one hostile to alien rights. At that point, the investor's bargaining power recedes and "the commitments received [are at risk of] becoming obsolete in the eyes of the host government."[36] The foreign investment law found in bilateral treaties uses a number of well-recognized principles to calm investors' fears of political interference. In the first place, these treaties assure what is effectively "national treatment" (that is, treatment identical to that afforded to domestic enterprises) to prospective nonnational investors.[37] The foreign investor will be guaranteed rights and privileges (including, for example, nondiscriminatory recourse to national courts and freedom to select its own personnel and not just local managers[38]) that its host State competitors enjoy.

4.3.5. *"Better than National Treatment" (Dispute Settlement)*

Sometimes, moreover, a nonnational investor will receive "better than national treatment," as may occur where a special tax regime is offered or recourse to an international arbitration panel is conceded instead of or in addition to access to host State courts.[39] Supranational dispute settlement, in

---

[35] Bilateral treaties typically contain their own definitions of "investment," some of which can be quite extensive and include representative lists of categories. *See, e.g.*, art. 1 of the U.S. Model BIT, *supra* note 27, which defines an investment (in summary) as every asset owned or controlled by an investor that involves the commitment of capital and the expectation of profit, and which may take the form of an enterprise, shares or stock, bonds and other debt, turnkey contracts, intellectual property rights, licenses, and so on.

[36] Salacuse, *supra* note 28, at 451. Strong dispute settlement, therefore, is intended to deal with what Salacuse refers to (citing an earlier authority) as the "obsolescing bargain" between the investor and the host State. *Id.*

[37] "National treatment" is the standard embodied in the U.S. Model BIT, although some States' treaties do not envisage that existing laws which may discriminate against foreign investors will necessarily be changed. Bilateral investment agreements also frequently provide for "most favored nation" (MFN) treatment, ensuring that the State parties treat each other's investors in a manner at least as favorable as they treat investors from third States. *See also supra* Chapter 3, Part 3.6.

[38] Article 9 of the U.S. Model BIT, *supra* note 27, provides that neither State party "may require that an enterprise of that Party [i.e., an investment that qualifies as an investment under the treaty] appoint to senior management positions natural persons of any particular nationality."

[39] As early as 1965, a transnational investment dispute settlement system appeared under the Convention on the Settlement of Investment Disputes Between States and Nationals of Other States, *opened for signature* Mar. 18, 1965, 17 U.S.T. 1270, 575 U.N.T.S. 159 [hereinafter ICSID

fact, is the "hardest" concession that a State can make to a foreign investor. The radicalism of this shift toward private-party standing can be appreciated by simple comparison with the much later dispute settlement machinery of international agreements such as the treaties establishing the World Trade Organization (WTO): in that venue, just as in the Chicago Convention, all disputes are State-to-State.[40] For nonnationals, the value of State-investor international arbitration is magnified by the willingness of international arbitrators to crystallize certain common treaty assurances, such as "fair and equitable treatment" and "full protection and security," as customary international law.[41] These standards of required State behavior may appear vague when applied in domestic contexts, but, in the hands of experienced tribunals, they can be (and are) textured to provide robust protection for an aggrieved foreign national.[42]

Convention]. At present, the Convention has been ratified by 147 States. The Convention established the International Centre for the Settlement of Investment Disputes (ICSID), which allows foreign enterprises and individuals to bring an arbitral suit directly against an expropriating State. More and more bilateral treaties refer to ICSID as a forum for dispute settlement, and the Geneva-based organization is probably now the main forum for this kind of transnational dispute resolution. Features of the system include the fact that international law is applied, State immunity is restricted, the usual requirement to exhaust local remedies rule is abrogated, and awards are directly enforceable. *See* DOLZER & SCHREUER, *supra* note 26, at 20.

[40] For capital-exporting States, investor-State arbitration reduces governmental transaction costs arising out of investments made by their nationals. *See* Salacuse, *supra* note 28, at 462–63 ("[I]n effect, [investor-State arbitration] allows [governments of capital-exporting States] to say to their nationals and companies aggrieved by host government acts that 'you have your own remedy in the treaty. Use it if you wish. Go away and don't bother us.'").

[41] *See* decisions cited in DOLZER & SCHREUER, *supra* note 26, at 124–28. The general standard of "fair and equitable" treatment in effect provides an overarching commitment of good faith on the part of the host State that informs the application of more specific treaty clauses. Salacuse describes "fair and equitable treatment" as the "basic norm" of the international investment regime. *See* Salacuse, *supra* note 28, at 453. Another standard that often appears in investment treaties alongside fair and equitable treatment is that of "full protection and security." *Id.* at 452. As noted in the main text, these standards are flexible enough to be given substantive content in specific cases through the work of arbitral tribunals.

[42] There is no principle of customary international law that denies States the power to expropriate the interests of foreign nationals, nor could there be as a matter of State sovereignty. Despite occasional rogue actions, for example, Argentina's attempt to refuse compensation after seizure of a Spanish oil subsidiary in 2012, outright expropriations are rare, and in any event will normally be accompanied by what is arguably a customary international law standard of "prompt, adequate, and effective compensation." *See* SCHILL, *supra* note 25, at 762 ("Notwithstanding some variations in language, the overwhelming majority of [bilateral investment treaties] provide for prompt, adequate and effective compensation, based on the market or genuine value of the investment"). This standard is usually also included in bilateral investment treaties. *See, e.g.,* U.S. Model BIT, *supra* note 27, arts. 5, 6. The requirement of "prompt, adequate, and effective" compensation has also been extended (by both treaty law and tribunal decisions) to the more controversial issue of "effective" or "regulatory" expropriations, whereby State policies deprive foreign investments of their value through heavy-handed regulatory measures (e.g., environmental, health, safety, or social laws).

4.3.6. *Bilateral Investment Treaties (BITs)*

The current diplomatic and trade practice is to refer to a bilateral investment treaty as a BIT, pluralized as BITs. The BIT system continues to evolve.[43] Many States, including the United States, have adopted "model" bilateral treaties that they use serially to establish reciprocal investment environments with partner States. It has been argued that the nationality rule for airlines could be liberalized using "sectoralized" BITs, thereby respecting the industry's habitual preference for exceptional treatment in international trade matters. The U.S/EU open skies agreement,[44] for example, has an annex on airline ownership that focuses solely on mutual recognition of investments by airlines of each party in nonparty airlines, but that could have promoted an open investment regime between the two aeropowers using the BIT rules and standards discussed earlier.[45] More recently, a new generation of regional free-trade agreements (such as NAFTA) has overlapping coverage with BITs, but once again without any easing of the rules limiting transborder airline investment.[46]

---

[43] Interestingly, in the last decade BITs between developing States have started to outnumber those between developed and developing States. *See* Steinberg & Kotuby, *supra* note 26, at 462.

[44] *See* Air Transport Agreement, U.S.-EU, Apr. 30, 2007, 2007 O.J. (L 134) 4, 46 I.L.M. 470 [hereinafter U.S./EU Air Transport Agreement]. The Agreement entered into provisional force on March 30, 2008, and was subsequently modified by an amending Protocol. *See* Protocol to Amend the Air Transport Agreement, U.S.-EU, June 24, 2010, 2010 O.J. (L 223) 3, http://www. state.gov/documents/organization/143930.pdf [hereinafter U.S./EU Protocol].

[45] At the least, the Agreement could have presented a road map for future events of liberalization (including events that would be contingent on eventual changes in U.S. domestic law), as the EU negotiated in its new open skies treaty with Canada. *See* Brian F. Havel & Gabriel S. Sanchez, *Restoring Global Aviation's Cosmopolitan* Mentalité, 29 B.U. INT'L L.J. 1, 31–35 (analyzing how the 2009 EU/Canada open skies agreement, *see infra* note 70, has four successive phases leading, after changes to national legislation, to 100% cross-border ownership and unlimited traffic rights including cabotage; at each stage, liberalization of restrictive investment rules is accompanied by wider grants of traffic rights). The reader may have noted, *supra* in Chapter 3, that the EU has created an open investment regime for aviation within its own borders, technically permitting cross-border ownership of airlines within the EU by EU nationals. These changes were accomplished by EU supranational legislation, not by BITs. Outside EU territory, however, the nationality rule still prevails and airlines from non-EU States must still abide by EU laws limiting inward airline investment into EU carriers. Many EU States have existing BITs with non-EU States that will remain in effect unless replaced by agreements negotiated by the EU on behalf of the entire Union. Member States will still be permitted to negotiate BITs with EU supervision. Council Regulation 1219/2012, Transitional Arrangements for Bilateral Investment Agreements between Member States and Third Countries, 2012 O.J. (L 351) 40.

[46] *See* North American Free Trade Agreement, U.S.-Can.-Mex., art. 1201(2)(b), Dec. 17, 1992, 32 I.L.M. 289 (1993) (limiting coverage to "aircraft repair and maintenance services during which an aircraft is withdrawn from service" and "specialty air services such as aerial mapping,

4.3.7. *No Single Global Investment Treaty*

What has not occurred, however, is the creation of a single global treaty to establish international standards (beyond customary international law standards) of investment protection and a permanent international arbitral tribunal empowered to adjudicate disputes under the treaty and to impose penalties on States including sanctions.[47] The most ambitious project to date, the Multilateral Agreement on Investment (MAI) drafted by the Organisation for Economic Co-operation and Development, was toppled by huge political opposition.[48] Thus, the foreign investment regime today is characterized by the absence of a universal treaty and the dominance of bilateral treaties. For some commentators, however, the bilateral investment treaties themselves constitute, as a group, "an emerging global regime for investment."[49]

4.4. AN EMERGING INTERNATIONAL INVESTMENT REGIME FOR AIRLINES

4.4.1. *Is There a Regime for Foreign Airline Investment?*

It may seem strange to speak of a regime for foreign airline investment,[50] even an emerging one, when the nationality rule remains so ubiquitous. But, as

---

surveying photography, advertising, etc."); *see also* Free Trade Agreement, U.S.-Austl., art. 10.1 (4)(c), May 18, 2004, 118 Stat. 919 (excluding air services from coverage).

[47] Developing States within the WTO have strongly opposed the inclusion of foreign investment in multilateral trade negotiations, obstructing any path toward a multilateral agreement. *See* Leon E. Trakman, *Foreign Direct Investment: Hazard or Opportunity?*, 41 GEO. WASH. INT'L L. REV. 1, 14–16 (2009).

[48] Why did the MAI fail? Salacuse mentions two reasons: the practical difficulties of a multilateral approach to accommodating diverse interests, and the political rationale that motivates developed States to leverage their bargaining power with capital-importing States through one-on-one negotiations rather having their power diluted through a bloc-based approach. *See* Salacuse, *supra* note 28, at 464. The MAI was also met with fierce resistance from a collection of NGOs that were able to turn public opinion, and consequently political leaders, against it. Some of the most active NGOs referred to their anti-MAI education campaign as the "Dracula strategy," meaning that they intended to kill the agreement by exposing its details to light. *See* Katia Tieleman, *The Failure of the Multilateral Agreement on Investment (MAI) and the Absence of a Global Public Policy Network* (2000), http://www.gppi.net/fileadmin/gppi/Tieleman_MAI_GPP_Network.pdf.

[49] Salacuse, *supra* note 28, at 431.

[50] "Nations create and join regimes out of a desire to reduce the relative costs of desired transactions." Salacuse, *supra* note 28, at 435. Salacuse proposes the use of "regime theory," a construct developed in international relations studies, to reach beyond the static legal analysis of treaty texts in order to understand the dynamism and fluidity of the "system" that bilateral treaties have created. *Id.* at 436. *But see supra* note 28 (noting that Salacuse still believes that bilateral investment treaties are not yet a wholly coherent "network" and that their provisions must be individually assessed).

already mentioned, the rule is beset by ambiguity and variation, and its transborder application has been destabilized by an admixture of legal and nonlegal instruments, policy choices by States, and commercial practices that have been adopted by the airline industry itself. Some might also object to the characterization of a regime on the ground that there is no global body of airline investment law, but our discussion of foreign investment law revealed that, just as with international aviation law, a "regime" can exist even when it is the product of consistent language placed in thousands of separate, mostly bilateral, agreements.[51] The nationality rule makes an excellent case in point: no global treaty or principle of custom governs its existence and yet, according to a recent WTO survey, the rule exists in some form in over 90% of all extant ASAs.[52] Even the U.S. Model Open Skies Agreement requires ownership and control of designated airlines by the designating party or its citizens, and the U.S./EU Air Transport Agreement, to date the most liberalized manifestation of open skies, does likewise.[53] Arguably, a kind of "path dependence" may be preserving citizenship restrictions as a *pro forma* provision of ASAs regardless of whether States have actually assessed their continued usefulness (even as protectionist devices).[54]

4.4.2. *Destabilizing the Nationality Rule (Continued)*

Whatever the reasons for the endurance of the nationality rule, it has remained a stable component of international trade in air services. As a regime, however, it is under assault from liberal shifts in aviation trade policy that are now visible enough to warrant further analysis here. The new mood, if one can call it that, may ultimately change how government officials and industry stakeholders think about the international airline investment regime. Although it is too soon to speak of the demise of the nationality rule in its traditional form, its replacement by new normative standards that are generally closer to the standards of foreign investment law can now be anticipated.

---

[51] See *supra* note 28 (*but see supra* note 50, noting one commentator's view that investment treaties must still be individually assessed).

[52] See World Trade Organization, Council for Trade in Services, *Quantitative Air Services Review* (*QUASAR*): *Part B: Preliminary Results*, at 33, para. 61, S/C/W/270/Add. I (Nov. 30, 2006) [hereinafter QUASAR].

[53] See Model Open Skies Agreement, *supra* note 1, arts. 3–4; U.S./EU Air Transport Agreement, *supra* note 44, arts. 4–5. But the United States developed habits of waiver of the nationality rule in its bilateral aviation relations, see *infra* Section 4.4.6.

[54] To some extent States may become victims of "path dependence," a term used in social science, history, and economics to describe how the set of decisions one faces in any given circumstance is limited by the decisions made in the past, even though past circumstances may no longer be relevant.

4.4.3. *EU Common Licensing Regime*

Nowhere has the nationality rule come under more sustained *legal* assault than within the supranational legal space of the EU. Beginning with the so-called third package of air transport liberalization in 1997,[55] the EU defied the then-prevalent investment regime by permitting the airlines of any EU Member State to be owned and controlled by any other Member State or the citizens of any other EU Member State.[56] Under the new common licensing regime for EU airlines that applies in all Member States,[57] in order to qualify as a "Union air carrier,"[58] an airline must be at least 50.1% owned by a Member State or by the nationals of any Member State and must also be under the "effective control" of such State or nationals.[59] After 2000, a succession of high-profile mergers and acquisitions occurred within the Union, including the marriage of two long-standing flag carriers, Air France and the Dutch airline KLM.[60] Germany's flagship airline,

---

[55] All three reforming packages were consolidated into a single Regulation 1008/2008, Common Rules for the Operation of Air Services in the [EU]. *See supra* note 19. The new regulation incorporates a number of revisions and clarifications.

[56] Legislatively, this was done by redefining the concept of the "EU [formerly Community] air carrier" for purposes of the commercial operating licensing of airlines by Member States. (The safe operation of aircraft is the subject of the Air Operator's Certificate (AOC), issued also by the licensing State once the airline has been found financially fit and is granted an operating license.) Thus, the relevant regulation requires the would-be licensee to have its principal place of business located in the licensing Member State, but in effect *multilateralizes* the nationality rule by requiring that more than 50% of the voting equity as well as effective control of the undertaking be held by any Member State and/or by any nationals of any Member States. *See* Common Rules, *supra* note 19, art. 4(f). In other words, if Air France/KLM organizes a subsidiary in the U.K. that is owned and controlled by French citizens, that subsidiary must be given a U.K. operating license – and may in certain circumstances apply to serve U.K. international routes under U.K. bilaterals with third countries. *See infra* note 63. Here a hallmark feature of the "Chicago system," the nationality rule, is converted into a general principle of EU law through the insertion of EU-wide (as opposed to *national*) restrictions on ownership and control.

[57] *See supra* note 56 (distinguishing operating license from AOC). A major defect of the common licensing regime is that it lacks a central EU-wide licensing agency. Moreover, the Member States refused the Commission's fallback alternative to a central agency, namely, the grant to the Commission of full review authority and revocation power over licenses actually awarded by Member State authorities. Common rules, after all, do not guarantee common enforcement of those rules.

[58] Following the ratification of the Treaty of Lisbon, 2007 O.J. (C 306), in December 2009, and the abolition of the distinction between the European Union and the European Community, it is now more appropriate to refer to airlines licensed in the EU as "Union air carriers." *See* E-mail from Daniel Calleja, former Director for Air Transport, European Commission, to author Brian F. Havel (Mar. 18, 2010, 17:49:00 CST) (on file with authors).

[59] Common Rules, *supra* note 19, art. 4(f).

[60] A complex legal structure makes this merger more of a merger-in-fact that preserves KLM's separate brand identity. A "holding company" holds two publicly traded air carrier subsidiaries,

Lufthansa, acquired a number of smaller non-German carriers[61] and British Airways finalized a merger with Spain's Iberia in 2011.[62] In order to safeguard these new investment opportunities from becoming ensnared by the nationality rule in the ASAs of EU Member States with non-EU States, the Union has entered into horizontal agreements that add new provisions to those ASAs recognizing "EU citizen ownership and control."[63] A few States, notably Russia, have balked at being asked to acknowledge the EU's *novus ordo*.[64] Despite threatening to invoke the nationality clause in the Russia/Austria ASA to rescind the traffic rights of Austrian Airlines after its purchase by Lufthansa in 2009,[65] Russia ultimately acquiesced. Other aviation markets such as Brazil and China that traditionally resisted air transport liberalization have nevertheless chosen to honor the EU's internal displacement of the nationality rule.[66]

4.4.4. *Rolling Back of Domestic Ownership Restrictions*

More modestly, some States have rolled back their national law limitations on inward air carrier investment, paving the way for foreign-owned *domestic* airlines. Australia, for example, legislated in 1999 to give foreign carriers a right of establishment to provide air services on cabotage routes. The new law enabled the U.K.-based Virgin Group to launch its own wholly owned

Air France and KLM. The resulting organizational model has been described as "one group/ two air carriers/three businesses" (the three businesses are air passenger transport, air cargo transport, and aircraft maintenance and repair). For a fuller account of the Air France/KLM merger model, see HAVEL, *supra* note 22, at 457.

[61] *See, e.g.*, Lufthansa's acquisition of Swiss International Air Lines in 2005, British Midland (BMI) in 2009 (subsequently resold to International Airlines Group in 2012), and Austrian Airlines in 2009.

[62] The two carriers merged into a new multinational holding company, International Airlines Group (IAG), headquartered in London.

[63] Horizontal agreements allow the European Commission to act on behalf of all Member States in negotiations to amend simultaneously all ASAs between the Member States and a specific third State. But Member States are also free to act bilaterally to amend their ASAs with any third State so long as the negotiation leads to recognition by the third State of the new EU rules on ownership and control. *See* Council Regulation 847/2004, art. 1, 2004 O.J. (L 157) 7.

[64] Whenever a non-EU State has limitations in its ASA with a Member State on the number of airlines the Member State may designate for service to the third State, EU legislation provides that the Member State must ensure a nondiscriminatory distribution of designations among the Member State's own licensed carriers and all other interested carriers that are owned by citizens of other Member States. *See* Council Regulation 847/2004, *supra* note 63, arts. 5 & 6. The U.S./EU Air Transport Agreement, *supra* note 44, has no such designation limitations.

[65] *See* Pilita Clark, *Russia Threatens to Ban Austrian Airlines*, FIN. TIMES, Mar. 1, 2010, at 1.

[66] *See* European Commission, Mobility and Transport, Air, International Aviation: Brazil, http:// ec.europa.eu/transport/modes/air/international_aviation/country_index/brazil_en.htm.

Australian subsidiary, Virgin Blue (renamed Virgin Australia in 2011).[67] Chile has completely abolished all of its caps on foreign investment in its air carriers.[68] Chile has also joined Argentina and Brazil in allowing cross-border mergers of international carriers, subject only to the constraints of competition law.[69] More promising still is the blueprint for future liberalization in the 2009 Canada/EU ASA, which for the first time in a bilateral air services treaty sets out a program for eventual reciprocal rights of full investment, including a right of establishment.[70]

4.4.5. *Multi-State Initiatives*

The 2010 amending protocol to the landmark 2007 U.S./EU Air Transport Agreement opens the door to both parties' airlines acquiring or establishing airlines in an agreed-upon list of third States without compromising the traffic rights of airlines from any listed State to either the United States or the EU.[71]

---

[67] But Australia's legislation deliberately avoided any problematic third-country designation issues. As applied, the legislation generally permits foreign investors to establish a new air transport business in Australia, provided that the airline remains incorporated and headquartered in Australia and serves only internal routes. *See supra* Chapter 3, Section 3.3.9. Following its decision to launch international services in 2004, Virgin Blue/Australia was forced to comply with Australia's foreign ownership cap of 49% by way of a complicated corporate structure under which its international operations are placed with a separate holding company that has majority Australian ownership. *See* Press Release, Virgin Australia, Virgin Australia Announces Proposed New Structure (Feb. 23, 2012), http://www.virginaustralia.com/us/en/about-us/media/2012/VIRGIN-AUSTRALIA-NEW-STRUCTURE/. *See also supra* Chapter 2, n.87 and accompanying text.

[68] *See* IATA, Agenda for Freedom, The Impact of International Air Service Liberalisation on Chile (2009), http://www.iata.org/SiteCollectionDocuments/ChileReport.pdf. *See also* Chapter 2, Section 2.5.14 (discussing Chile's abolition of cabotage).

[69] *See* Daniel Michaels & Susan Carey, *More Airline Mergers Leap Borders*, WALL ST. J., Jun. 28, 2012, at B10. *See also supra* Chapter 3, Section 3.4.8.

[70] The EU/Canada ASA sets up a series of "staged" concessions giving both sides more traffic privileges in exchange for loosening their restrictions on ownership and control (e.g., once Canada raises its ownership cap to 49% vis-à-vis EU air carriers, its carriers will receive intra-Union fifth freedom rights). Subsequent phases of the agreement envisage reciprocal rights of establishment and the removal of cabotage restrictions. *See generally* Agreement on Air Transport Between Canada and the European [Union] and its Member States, Dec. 17, 2009, 2010 O.J. (L 207) 32 [hereinafter Canada/EU Air Transport Agreement]. *See supra* n. 45.

[71] *See* U.S./EU Protocol, *supra* note 44, Annex 6. Note, however, that before either party will abstain from enforcing the nationality clause with respect to third-country airlines that are *controlled* by EU or U.S. citizens, both parties must agree that the third country "has established a record of cooperation in air services" with them. *See id.* paras. 3–4. With respect to ownership alone, however, no such record of cooperation needs to be demonstrated. *See id.* para. 1.

A British Airways/Qantas linkup, for example, would not oust Qantas from its designation under the U.S./Australia ASA.[72] The United States and the EU have also laid a proposal before the ICAO for a "Multilateral Convention on Foreign Investment in Airlines" – a single treaty that, if it came into effect, would commit signatory States to waiver of the nationality rule in their ASAs (but in each case on condition of reciprocity).[73] While the draft treaty does not (and cannot) suppress national laws that limit inward investment, it may encourage States to facilitate foreign takeovers of their domestic carriers knowing that key foreign aviation markets have renounced enforcement of nationality restrictions.

4.4.6. *Effective Waivers and Waning Enforcement*

But even without a multilateral treaty some States have acted bilaterally to deliver waivers of the nationality rule. Whether those actions should be characterized as legal or political is an open question. Because they occur frequently through official passivity rather than reasoned rulings, they can be plausibly construed either as political decisions or as examples of a kind of international law estoppel.[74] Waivers are highly likely to occur when all of the States involved in a particular transaction share an open skies ideology. In 2011, for example, the U.S. Government apparently indicated that it would not withdraw traffic rights following a merger between the flag carriers of Trinidad

---

[72]   But Qantas might well encounter resistance to its continued designation under other bilateral agreements, for example, the Japan/Australia ASA. In any event, this hypothetical has become even more far-fetched since Qantas entered a new partnership with Emirates (*see supra* note 5).

[73]   The last publicly available draft can be found at http://legacy.icao.int/icao/en/assembl/a37/wp/wp190_en.pdf. The draft treaty would require signatories to provide a list of partner States against which they will not enforce the nationality clauses in their ASAs: only signatories to the treaty could avail themselves of its benefits. For a more detailed analysis of the draft treaty, see Brian F. Havel & Gabriel S. Sanchez, *The Emerging Lex Aviatica*, 42 GEO. J. INT'L L. 639, 665–67 (2011).

[74]   In international law, estoppel is a rule that bars a State from going back on its previous representations when those representations have induced reliance on the part of other States. The ambiguous and contestable doctrine of promissory estoppel in international law may be one basis for indicating that a State is legally bound by such an act of waiver. Although a species of estoppel might in theory deter a State from treating its waiver statement as merely hortatory (nonbinding), the prospect that another State would seek to enforce these statements before the International Court of Justice must be reckoned as weak. *Cf.* RESTATEMENT (THIRD) OF FOREIGN RELATIONS LAW OF THE UNITED STATES § 301 cmt. c. It is unclear to what extent a State must *rely* on a unilateral statement before the declaring State can be legally bound to it, although as one classic study of the doctrine states, "[t]he more pronounced the reliance upon considerations of good faith the more sympathetic a tribunal may be expected to be in the face of arguments based on the concept of estoppel." I. C. MacGibbon, *Estoppel in International Law*, 7 INT'L & COMP. L.Q. 468, 507 (1958).

and Tobago and Jamaica, so long as the former State entered a liberal (i.e., open skies) ASA with the United States.[75] U.S. officials sent a similarly robust signal to Brazil in 2010 during negotiations for a new ASA that incrementally liberalized U.S./Brazil aeropolitical relations. Subsequently, Brazil's Government approved a merger of the country's primary international carrier TAM with the Chilean flag carrier LAN.[76] In its relations with the EU, U.S. policy even before the landmark 2007 agreement had been one of acquiescence in intra-Union mergers, notably the 2004 Air France/KLM combination.[77] The EU itself has also begun to moderate its insistence on the nationality rule, and indeed has departed from U.S. practice in actually memorializing a more nuanced policy in some of its recent aviation trade accords.[78] No doubt an open skies ideology has persuaded each of these States to stay its hand when confronted with evident breaches of the nationality rule. The United States, however, had a record of sporadic enforcement of the rule even before it ramped up its open skies program. During the 1980s, several Latin American airlines came under foreign ownership and control without U.S. objection.[79] Smaller European carriers, such as Luxembourg's Cargo Lion, were awarded full market access to the United States despite questionable citizenship profiles: Cargo Lion, for example, lacked a single Luxembourg owner or control by any Luxembourg national.[80] When U.S. officials warned in 2000 that the United States would repeal KLM's market access rights if the company consummated a planned takeover by British Airways, that threat represented a clear and intelligible exception to the

---

[75] Trinidad and Tobago signed an open skies agreement with the United States in May 2010, *reprinted in* 3 Av. L. Rep. (CCH) ¶26,522b, at 23,164.

[76] To facilitate that arrangement, which technically violates the nationality rule, LAN took inspiration from the Air France/KLM corporate structure (*see supra* note 60) and created the LATAM Airlines Group to act as a "multinational" holding company for the two airlines. *See* Centre for Aviation, *New LAN-TAM Parent Latam Emerges as a Leader Globally and a Powerful Force Across South America*, Jun. 28, 2012, http://centreforaviation.com/analysis/new-lan-tam-parent-latam-emerges-as-a-leader-globally-and-a-powerful-force-across-south-america-76917.

[77] Although, again, U.S. forbearance was based on an open skies trading climate. In 2000, U.S. officials advised their U.K. counterparts that the United States would consider suspending KLM's air traffic rights in the event of a contemplated British Airways takeover – the U.S./U.K. ASA was still the notoriously illiberal Bermuda II. *See* 28 U.S.T. 5367 (1977); *see* HAVEL, *supra* note 22, at 116 (describing how Bermuda II met *"none* of the open skies criteria" then being proposed by U.S. international aviation policy (emphasis in original)).

[78] *See, e.g.*, the "staged" liberalization contemplated in the Canada/EU Air Transport Agreement, *supra* notes 45, 70.

[79] *See* QUASAR, *supra* note 52, at 34, para. 68 (noting several examples of foreign airlines retaining their traffic rights despite foreign acquisition).

[80] *See Translux International Airlines, Notice of Action Taken*, Dkt. No. OST-98-4329 (Dep't of Transp. Nov. 25, 1998).

usual *de facto* mildness of U.S. policy on foreign ownership and control.[81] The U.K. Government, after all, had long opposed open skies with the United States. The nationality rule presented itself as a strategic opportunity to reverse U.K. implacability. In contrast, the equally game-changing Air France/KLM arrangement, set within an open skies framework between the United States and the home States of each merger partner, drew no U.S. resistance. The (apparent) U.S. approach of benign tolerance but occasional obstinacy is easily understood as a cost/benefit calculation. Clearly, U.S. officials had little to lose in using the nationality rule to oppose the British Airways/KLM merger: having kept Heathrow underserved by U.S. airlines since the 1970s, the U.K. could not retaliate without the risk of a further loss of U.S. traffic rights for British Airways. Invoking the rule against Air France/KLM, on the other hand, would not only have upset established open skies relationships but could also have triggered retaliatory denunciations of the U.S./France and U.S./Netherlands liberal ASAs. Given that those ASAs represented (for the moment) as much as U.S. carriers wanted from aviation relations with both States, wielding the nationality rule would have produced no important benefits.

4.4.7. *Liberalizing Breezes from Latin America and Asia*

In Latin America, too, the region's strong historical, political, and economic ties to the United States have softened U.S. reaction to the spreading cross-border absorption of smaller flag carriers by big regional carriers like Chile's flag carrier LAN[82] and the Brazilian-owned, El Salvador–based conglomerate TACA.[83] But there is also a large measure of self-interest. Latin American airlines, it should be

---

[81] *See supra* note 77. Of course, rival carriers may "whistleblow" against such official passivity. This has happened several times in the United States, most recently when Alaska Airlines made a complaint to the U.S. DOT accusing Virgin America of being under the control of the U.K.-based Virgin Group. *See* Virgin America, *Petition of Alaska Airlines for Review of Citizenship*, Dkt. No. OST-2009-0037 (Dep't of Transp. Feb. 10, 2009).

[82] LAN is Chilean-owned and -controlled, but has successfully persuaded the governments of a number of Latin American States to alter their foreign ownership rules to allow LAN to acquire larger stakes in air carriers in those States, including some flag carriers. Thus, LAN has apparently acquired majority control of LAN Argentina after the local law on ownership was changed (but the airline still operates routes to and from the United States). LAN also owns significant stakes (again, in some cases possibly majority stakes) in LAN Colombia, LAN Ecuador, and LAN Peru, and other affiliates. We have previously noted its takeover of the Brazilian flag carrier, TAM (*see supra* note 76 and accompanying text).

[83] The other large Latin American carrier, TACA, which merged with the Colombian airline Avianca in 2009, is Brazilian-owned but primarily based in El Salvador. Like LAN, *see supra* note 82, both TACA and Avianca have similar complex ownership and control arrangements with local carriers outside their home States, and again it is possible that majority shareholdings are involved.

noted, do not (as yet) represent a potent enough competitive threat to the interests of U.S. (or EU) carriers in the region. But the continuing realignments in Latin America could yet disturb existing commercial relationships, especially if LAN or TACA should affiliate with one of the big Gulf carriers like Emirates. Although developments in Latin America have attracted recent focus, liberal breezes can also be detected in the Southeast Asia region. The Association of Southeast Asian Nations (ASEAN) has crafted a Multilateral Agreement on Air Services (MAAS) that attempts to transplant the "EU air carrier" concept. The Agreement provides for designated air carriers to be incorporated and have a principal place of business in the designating State, but any carrier of an ASEAN member State can be owned and effectively controlled by any number of ASEAN States or their nationals in the aggregate.[84] While the MAAS has been beleaguered by problems of implementation,[85] the leading players in the region have found innovative ways to structure and expand their operations. The pioneering Malaysian low-cost carrier, AirAsia, has established subsidiaries in Thailand and Indonesia that are technically separate from the parent carrier. The airlines – Thai AirAsia and Indonesia AirAsia – are majority-owned by local Thai and Indonesian interests respectively, with the parent holding only a minority stake. Although scrupulously faithful to the requirement of local ownership and control, AirAsia's affiliated carriers utilize the operating rights available under Thai and Indonesian ASAs with third countries. Even so, entrepreneurs in the region have been pushing to cast off the odd ownership structures that result from compliance with the nationality rule and are seeking a more "normalized" investment regime. But when other carriers have tried to replicate the AirAsia franchise model, for example, the efforts by Tiger Airways to set up related companies in South Korea and the Philippines, local carriers have blown the whistle and prevented government agencies from blessing the new arrangements.[86]

---

[84] *See* ASEAN Multilateral Agreement on Air Services, *opened for signature at Manila*, May 20, 2009, art. 3(2)(a)(ii) [hereinafter ASEAN MAAS]. *See* Philippa Dee, *Services Liberalization Toward the ASEAN Economic Community*, in TRACING THE PROGRESS TOWARD THE ASEAN ECONOMIC COMMUNITY 28, 33–46 (Shujiro Urata & Misa Okabe eds., 2010) (chronicling the aspiration of and challenges to creation of a common ASEAN air transport market). Unlike in the EU single aviation market, however, under the MAAS air carriers would still need to be designated by their home States to serve intra-Agreement markets, and that is by no means an automatic process: any State party to the MAAS must approve any designation of an air carrier that is owned and controlled by interests outside the designating State. *See* ASEAN MAAS, art. 3(2)(a). *See also supra* Chapter 3, Section 3.6.7.

[85] The MAAS has yet to be ratified by all ten ASEAN Member States.

[86] *See* Centre for Aviation, *Incheon Tiger Airways Under Attack from Competitors; License Applications Plans on Hold Indefinitely*, Aug. 29, 2008, http://centreforaviation.com/analysis/incheon-tiger-airways-under-attack-from-competitors-licence-applications-plans-

4.4.8. *Air Transport Industry Advocacy*

The international airline industry itself has also acted through its representative trade group, the International Air Transport Association (IATA), to unseat the nationality rule. At successive "summit" conferences in Istanbul in 2008 and in Montebello, Canada, in 2009, IATA and a small number of motivated governments[87] encouraged States to declare unilaterally that they would no longer apply the nationality rule in their bilateral aviation relations with any State that offered a reciprocal undertaking to do likewise.[88] The quasi-diplomatic Montebello summit issued a series of principles, under the brash banner of an "Agenda for Freedom," as a political, though probably not a legal, capstone to the process.[89] While some major aviation markets, including (somewhat ironically) the host State of Canada, declined to sign on to the Montebello "Statement of Principles," the two IATA conferences arguably set the tone for legally binding steps to be taken in the investment area. For example, the previously mentioned draft multilateral agreement on airline investment was circulated for discussion at the Montebello summit before being formally presented to ICAO by the United States and the EU in September 2010.[90] Other aviation trade groups have also lobbied against the nationality rule. As early as 1999, the Association of European Airlines (AEA) issued its landmark briefing paper, *Toward a Transatlantic Common Aviation Area* – one of the first stakeholder documents to propose an open investment regime between the two transatlantic aeropowers.[91] In the United States, the leading industry trade

---

on-hold-indefinitely-3635; Centre for Aviation, *Thai Airways Delays Launch of Thai Tiger Airways Again; Thai AirAsia Preparing Strategies to Compete*, Nov. 25, 2010, http://centreforaviation.com/analysis/thai-airways-delays-launch-of-thai-tiger-airways-again-thai-airasia-preparing-strategies-to-compete-40478.

[87] In Canada, representatives attended from Chile, the EU, Malaysia, Panama, Singapore, Switzerland, the United Arab Emirates, and the United States. Canada itself, however, was not represented.

[88] The so-called Agenda for Freedom, however, only proposed waiving the "external" treaty-based component of the nationality rule. Thus, the United States could reciprocally waive the nationality clauses in all of its ASAs and still maintain its internal rule (part of federal law) that mandates at least 75% ownership and actual control of its airlines by U.S. citizens. The treaty waiver is only a first step – albeit a necessary one – toward eliminating the nationality rule altogether.

[89] On the operation of the international law of promissory estoppel, which seems implicated by the IATA proposal, see *supra* note 74.

[90] For a detailed analysis of how the IATA reciprocal waiver process would operate, see Havel & Sanchez, *supra* note 73, at 662–65.

[91] The paper called on the governments of the United States and the EU to embrace a "unified system that on the one hand gives airlines full commercial opportunities on an equal basis and on the other ensures that their activities will be governed by a common body of aviation rules, avoiding any unnecessary regulation." Among these "full commercial opportunities" would be removal of all airline ownership restrictions and acknowledgment of a right of establishment.

association, Airlines for America (formerly the Air Transport Association), has consistently advocated a dual-track approach for U.S. airline investment policy that would scrap the nationality rule in the U.S. ASAs and also revoke the federal law limiting foreign ownership and control of U.S. airlines.[92] Some air carriers have acted independently to champion investment reform. Gulf-based Emirates is only one of several large international carriers seeking to build a global brand presence without recourse to the multicarrier alliance system.[93]

4.4.9. *A Note on Rational Interests and the Nationality Rule*

If, as Jack Goldsmith and Eric Posner contend, international law serves an instrumental purpose in States' foreign relations, and lacks freestanding, exogenous force,[94] then the discussion in this chapter so far seems to confirm that States will adhere to or defect from international law based on their rational interests. Arguably, the defection of Latin American and Southeast Asian States from the strict application of the nationality rule provides some evidence of the Goldsmith/Posner thesis at work. Especially in Latin America, many States have small air transport markets and a history of unsustainable air carriers. Smaller markets, therefore, have simply abandoned strict policing of the ownership profiles of their carriers in favor of the consumer benefits that larger entities – operating a series of smaller affiliates as "feeders" – can offer. It no longer makes economic sense (if it ever did) for every Latin American State to ring-fence its home air transport market and to repel foreign investors. Brazil's pursuit of liberalization, also in the vein of rational self-interest, is heavily influenced also by economic growth and the infrastructural challenges

---

ASSOC. OF EUR. AIRLINES, TOWARDS A TRANSATLANTIC COMMON AVIATION AREA: AEA POLICY STATEMENT 1, 8–10 (1999). The AEA paper provided the negotiating template for the 2007 U.S./EU Air Services Agreement (*see supra* Chapter 1, Section 1.6.4). *See* HAVEL, *supra* note 22, at 40–43.

[92] *See, e.g.*, Glen Tilton, Air Transp. Ass'n Chairman, Speech to U.K. Aviation Club (Feb. 11, 2010).

[93] Emirates had sponsored a public campaign against the alliance system and antitrust immunity, ostensibly to enhance global airline competition. In September 2012 Emirates announced plans for a more limited ten-year "global partnership" with Australia's Qantas. *See supra* note 5. In March 2013, the Australian Competition and Consumer Commission granted conditional authorization to the partnership, albeit for a modest period of five years. *See* Australian Competition and Consumer Commission, *Determination: Applications for Authorisation Lodged by Qantas Airways Limited and Emirates in Respect of a Master Coordination Agreement* (Mar. 27, 2013).

[94] *Cf.* Jack L. Goldsmith & Eric A. Posner, *Moral and Legal Rhetoric in International Relations: A Rational Choice Perspective*, 31 J. LEGAL STUD. 115, 121–33 (2002).

of the soccer World Cup in 2014 and the Olympic Games in 2016. Rapid economic growth, and the need to serve millions of new airline consumers, may explain as well why Southeast Asian governments continue to respond flexibly to efforts by entrepreneurs like AirAsia's Tony Fernandes to dilute the full strength of the nationality rule.

4.5. CIRCUMVENTING THE NATIONALITY RULE: GLOBAL ALLIANCES

4.5.1. *Antitrust Immunity for "Mergers Without a Transfer of Ownership Rights"*

With a new investment regime still in its earliest stages, the international airline industry itself has adhered to its own well-established tradition of *lex mercatoria* to escape some of the commercial limitations of the existing order.[95] Based initially on simple code-sharing arrangements,[96] the international airline alliance in its present advanced form can be described as a merger without a transfer of ownership rights. But any collaboration between or among competitors will attract scrutiny from antitrust and competition regulators. Beginning in 1992, several U.S. and EU airlines began to avail themselves of a little-used power of antitrust immunity that the DOT had inherited from the Civil Aeronautics Board, the agency that directed the U.S. airline industry during the era of regulation. The first of these joint ventures, involving an investment by Dutch flag carrier KLM in the now-defunct U.S. carrier Northwest Airlines, enabled the two airlines in certain respects to impersonate a single merged carrier even though an authentic business

---

[95] In its original meaning, the *lex mercatoria* ("law [of the] merchant") was a body of pragmatic rules and principles laid down by medieval merchants to regulate their dealings and that displaced the various feudal laws and Roman law, which were not sufficiently responsive to the growing demands of commerce. *See* Havel & Sanchez, *supra* note 73, at 658–59; *see also supra* Chapter 1, note 100. Here, we use the term *lex mercatoria* more loosely as a convenient descriptor for sets of norms, procedures, and institutions (such as code-sharing and alliances or the operation of computer reservations systems) which, while they may ultimately need State law to ensure their enforceability, nonetheless evolved from the customs and practices of the international aviation industry itself. The Montebello "Statement of Principles," *see supra* text accompanying note 89, exemplifies this developing narrative of converging public and private action. *See* Havel & Sanchez, *supra*, at 659. For a recent essay on a modern *lex mercatoria*, *see* Leon E. Trakman, *The Twenty-First Century Law Merchant*, 48 Am. Bus. L.J. 775 (2011) (detecting glimmerings of a new law merchant in the work of transnational arbitration tribunals).

[96] Code-sharing, as discussed later in this chapter, is the practice of two or more airlines listing their separate connecting flights in a computer reservations system and on e-tickets under a single two-letter code identifier as if a single carrier were providing the entire flight. *See infra* Sections 4.6.2, 4.6.3.

merger was precluded by the combined effects of the external and internal bolts of the nationality rule.[97] The DOT, in granting immunity, expressly acknowledged that the Netherlands had just become the first treaty partner in the new U.S. open skies program.[98] The grant of immunity to Northwest/KLM changed the face of global air transport.[99] To start with, the availability of U.S. antitrust immunity in exchange for open skies had a honeypot effect on other European governments and their airlines: sixteen European States concluded open skies ASAs with the United States between 1992 and 2006.[100] By the turn of the century, open skies with Germany (1996) and France (2001) had spawned alliance deals led by Lufthansa and United and by Delta Air Lines and Air France. For more than a decade, however, the U.K.'s unwillingness to move beyond Bermuda II chilled efforts by British Airways and American Airlines to win immunity for their rival combination.

4.5.2. *Consolidation of Alliances After the 2007 U.S./EU Agreement*

The 2007 U.S./EU Air Transport Agreement[101] converted all Member State ASAs with the United States (including the U.K. agreement) into a common open skies relationship. Since then, the alliance system has consolidated into three global joint ventures – SkyTeam, Star, and oneworld – each with a core constellation of major carriers and a tail of smaller carrier satellites. Although not all of the partner airlines in each alliance enjoy U.S. antitrust immunity, most of them do – a fact that has dismayed antitrust enforcers in the U.S.

---

[97] *See supra* Chapter 3, Section 3.4.7 (explaining how these concepts describe, respectively, the ASA-based requirement that an airline performing international services on behalf of a State must be owned and controlled by that State or by its nationals, and the domestic laws restricting ownership and control of national airlines by foreign carriers).

[98] *See* Northwest Airlines, Inc. & KLM Royal Dutch Airlines, *Joint Application for Approval and Antitrust Immunity of an Agreement Pursuant to Sections 412 and 414 of the Federal Aviation Act, As Amended*, Dkt. No. 48342, Order 92-11-27 to Show Cause (Dep't of Transp. Nov. 16, 1992), at 2 [hereinafter Joint Application of KLM/Northwest] (explicitly finding approval and immunity to be "consistent with the [open skies] accord" with the Netherlands). U.S. airlines, not pleased by the new treaty, unkindly (and accurately) pointed out that the U.S./Netherlands open skies ASA gave KLM the right to fly to all points in the United States in exchange for allowing U.S. airlines the right to fly to all points in the Netherlands. The economic value to U.S. carriers, however, lay in *beyond* rights from Amsterdam (the fifth freedom). For definitions of the "freedoms" of the air, including the fifth – the network-building – freedom, *see supra* Chapter 3, Part 3.3.

[99] Immunity allows the alliance members to "live in sin," according to former KLM executive Paul V. Mifsud (who is also the founder of the "Mifnet" that electronically links thousands of aviation professionals in daily discourse on the industry).

[100] *See* HAVEL, *supra* note 22, at 33.

[101] *See supra* note 44.

Department of Justice as well as some economists. Critics attack the alliances' deepening coordination of pricing, routes, and other service offerings as an affront to the ethos of protecting competition, not competitors.[102] Similar concerns have rung out in the EU, where the principal regulator, the European Commission, enjoys comparable powers of exemption. With the integration of major Asia-Pacific airlines into the alliances, competition authorities in Australia and Japan have also asserted jurisdiction over alliance behavior, but as yet without making negative findings.[103] Only Canada's enforcers have seemed willing to push back against the alliances, and even they have permitted Air Canada to participate in a joint venture with United and Continental subject to conditions.[104] It seems unlikely, however, that the Canadian investigators would wish to add Air Canada to the small list of major carriers that have taken the hard route of expanding their international market presence outside the fold of the alliance system.

4.5.3. *Why Global Alliances Exist*

While no alternative structure has as much upside as a flawlessly executed merger or acquisition, alliances nevertheless deliver substantial benefits to participating carriers. They represent, in the first place, a unique opportunity to bring network economies to a global industry forced by the citizenship purity rules into a fundamentally regional structure.[105] In a system where market access rights are distributed bilaterally and inefficiently by government fiat, alliances also help to break barriers to competitive entry that even open skies agreements leave unaddressed. As summed up by former DOT Under Secretary for Policy Jeffrey Shane (now general counsel of IATA), the global alliance system has three advantages in exploiting the bilateral system: first, an

---

[102] Article 20 of the 2007 U.S./EU Air Transport Agreement, *supra* note 44, in a sense binds both sides to U.S. judicial precedent (and now to a shared competition "philosophy") when it confirms that the parties will "apply their respective competition regimes to protect and enhance overall competition and not individual competitors." *See also supra* Chapter 3, note 200.

[103] The Australian Government seems to have taken a relatively positive view of more locally focused alliances. Its Competition and Consumer Commission (ACCC) has recently authorized alliances between Delta/Virgin Blue (2009), Virgin Australia/Singapore Airlines (2011), Virgin Blue/Etihad (2011), and in March 2013 granted conditional authorization to a Qantas/Emirates alliance. Conversely, the ACCC in 2009 rejected an agreement between Air New Zealand and Air Canada.

[104] The agreement between the carriers and the Canadian Competition Bureau prohibits Air Canada and United from coordinating on fourteen specified routes between Canada and the United States.

[105] *See* Warren L. Dean, Jr. & Jeffrey N. Shane, *Alliances, Immunity and the Future of Aviation*, 22 Air & Space L. 1, 17–18 (2010).

alliance allows a carrier to create domestic feeder flights in the home States of its partner carriers without violating their domestic laws;[106] second, an alliance allows a carrier to offer flights to points beyond the territories of the home States of its partner carriers, when those points are otherwise restricted in its own home State's bilateral treaties; and third, an alliance allows its members to fill up seats throughout the alliance system with traffic to a variety of destinations, even where the "last segment" operations take place on other airlines.[107] The alliances balance any potential losses to consumer welfare against coordination benefits such as global online route networks with thousands of new city-pairs as well as pooled perquisite programs including frequent flyer programs and business lounge access. There is no question that alliances are adept at providing connections that would otherwise be commercially infeasible. Omaha, Nebraska, for example, could not sustain online service to Bologna, Italy. The Star Alliance, however, can lace together a series of connections that links those two small to midsized markets: a passenger can fly United Express from Omaha to Chicago, transfer to United or Lufthansa to Frankfurt, and then fly Lufthansa's wholly owned regional airline Air Dolimiti for the final segment between Frankfurt and Bologna. Despite having to mount services of that complexity, alliance members assert that the cost efficiencies of coordination are passed to consumers in lower fares.[108]

4.6. THE LEGAL (AND POLICY) FRAMEWORK FOR GLOBAL ALLIANCES

4.6.1. *U.S. and EU Regulatory Approaches*

As noted, the legal framework that allows the alliance system to operate is either national or, in the case of the EU, a blend of national and supranational, but it is not (as yet) in any sense either transnational or global. As we indicated earlier, several States apply their own competition codes to alliance behavior; there is no serious proposal to unify or harmonize those rules. Even so, international aviation law as expressed in bilateral ASAs undoubtedly shapes the course of alliance

---

[106] *See infra* Sections 4.6.2, 4.6.3 (discussing code-sharing).

[107] *See* Dean & Shane, *supra* note 105, at 17–18.

[108] A recent joint report on transatlantic alliances by the DOT and European Commission took a broadly positive view of their competitive effects, while calling for further study. *See* Eur. Comm'n & U.S. Dep't of Transp., Transatlantic Airline Alliances: Competitive Issues and Regulatory Approaches (2010), http://ec.europa.eu/competi tion/sectors/transport/reports/joint_alliance_report.pdf [hereinafter "Transatlantic Airline Alliances Report"]; but, for a strongly contrary view, see Hubert Horan, *"Double Marginalization" and the Counter-Revolution Against Liberal Airline Competition*, 37 Transp. L.J. 251 (2010).

decision making. We have seen how the DOT in the United States conditions antitrust immunity for alliances involving U.S. carriers on the existence of an open skies relationship with the home States of any intended foreign partners. Memoranda accompanying open skies agreements typically intone that "sympathetic consideration" as well as "fair and expeditious consideration" of immunity will flow from a successful negotiation.[109] Indeed, alliance members applying for immunity have lately been making the bold representation that open skies partner States now rank immunization for their airlines' commercial involvement with U.S. carriers as a deal-breaking condition for acceptance of a liberalized ASA. Japan's international carriers, All Nippon Airways and Japan Air Lines, stated as much in their applications for immunity with Star and the Delta-led SkyTeam alliance, respectively.[110] EU officials are more constrained by their treaty-based antitrust code (which no longer has special provisions for the airline industry) and have not been able to emulate a more dogmatic U.S. approach that comes close to trading immunity for open skies. Unlike the DOT, however, the EU has been willing to withhold exemptions unless the alliance partners surrender slots at congested airports to nonalliance members. The EU, which as we will see now applies *ex post* scrutiny to potentially anticompetitive agreements, has imposed serial review as commercial circumstances change rather than adopting the "evergreen" status that the DOT typically confers after its first inquiry.[111]

4.6.2. *Code-Sharing*

We begin with the most basic technical device to connect airlines in an alliance arrangement, the code-share. Code-sharing is the practice of two or more

---

[109] Both parties to the 1992 U.S./Netherlands open skies agreement signed a Memorandum of Consultations on September 4, 1992, consenting to give "sympathetic consideration" to commercial cooperation and integration of commercial operations between each other's airlines and "to provide fair and expeditious consideration to any such agreements or arrangements filed for approval and antitrust immunity." Joint Application of KLM/Northwest, *supra* note 98, at 3. *See also* United Air Lines, Inc. and Asiana Airlines, Inc., *Joint Application for Approval and Antitrust Immunity for an Alliance Expansion Agreement, Order Granting Approval and Antitrust Immunity*, Dkt. No. OST-03–14202, Order 2003–5–18, 2003 DOT Av. LEXIS 357, *3 n.5 (citing the Memorandum of Consultations to the U.S./Republic of Korea open skies agreement).

[110] *See, e.g.*, All Nippon Airways Co., Ltd., Continental Airlines, Inc. & United Airlines, Inc., Joint Application, Dkt. No. OST-2009–0350 (Dep't of Transp., Dec. 23, 2009) at 6 n.9 (stating that, in the recent Japan/U.S. negotiations, "the Japanese delegation unambiguously communicated that U.S. approval [of the ANA/Continental/United] Joint Application [for antitrust immunity] on terms acceptable to the Japanese government is a condition precedent to entry into force of Open Skies").

[111] But U.S. congressional opponents of immunity attempted (unsuccessfully) to sunset alliance immunity after three years. *See* Ensure Adequate Airline Competition Between the United States and Europe Act, H.R. 831, 111th Cong. (2009).

airlines listing their separate connecting flights in a computer reservation system and on e-tickets under a single two-letter code identifier as if a single carrier were providing the entire service. The code identifier is each airline's IATA designator code (UA for United, LH for Lufthansa, and so on). Importantly, the participating airlines are not combining to offer a single service: in reality, each airline *pretends* that it is offering an integrated service that is in fact partly operated by one or more of its partner carriers. Code-sharing allows airlines to connect traffic to and from foreign cities, to which they do not fly themselves, with their own flights. In that way, airlines within an alliance system create the commercial impression (accentuated by service features such as common access to airport lounges) that they are offering "online" service to destinations that would otherwise be uneconomical to serve with their own aircraft and crew. Code-sharing, as noted above, also allows airlines to serve routes that their home States have not secured in ASA negotiations. Code-sharing has attracted the attention of regulators, especially with regard to consumer deception, but is typically pre-cleared in bilateral ASAs.

4.6.3. *U.S. DOT Recognizes Two Types of Code-Sharing Authority*

In the United States, two types of code-sharing authority are recognized. The first type is linked exclusively to international services and simply combines each carrier's existing international route authority. Consequently, it involves no access to cabotage routes and is readily conceded in U.S. ASAs. British Airways (BA), for example, might advertise a London/Cancún service under its own two-letter airline code (BA), even though the service requires a connection over Miami that involves changing to a Miami/Cancún segment operated by BA's oneworld alliance partner, American Airlines (AA). This coding device makes use of the fact that U.S. and U.K. carriers enjoy unlimited "blind sector" rights, that is, rights to fly to points beyond each other's territory (normally the "fifth freedom" if new passengers are enplaned in the other's territory) but without being permitted to pick up new passengers.[112] BA's Cancún service combines a preexisting privilege (to fly from Miami to Cancún without picking up new passengers in Miami) with a code-share.[113] U.S. regulators also recognize a second type

---

[112] Open skies agreements have made these rights less relevant, but in earlier bilaterals, blind sector rights were expressly granted. *See* Air Transport Agreement Between the Government of the United States and the Government of Canada, Feb. 24, 1995, http://www.state.gov/documents/organization/114328.pdf.

[113] Similarly, United can place its code on service from Chicago to Amsterdam and Brussels, connecting in London with BA's flights to those cities.

of code-share authority that clearly implicates the cabotage doctrine but that is essential to full integration of routes within a global alliance. That authority allows internal U.S. points to be connected to a foreign carrier's international system and thereby potentially provides feeder traffic to the foreign carrier for its long-haul services. As with the first type, the foreign carrier must have the economic authority, independently of the code-share, to serve the entire code-shared itinerary. Thus, a BA service advertised as London/Houston may involve a transfer at New York to a New York/Houston service operated by AA. BA must therefore have independent authority to serve London/Houston. That is a sensible restriction, because both carriers to a code-share will be applying their respective codes to the service as if they were actually performing the service with their own aircraft. The U.S. DOT readily grants any additional authority that a carrier needs to close the code-sharing deal.[114]

4.6.4. *DOT's Antitrust Immunity Power in International Aviation*

In the United States, federal antitrust review of collaborations among competitors is the responsibility of the Department of Justice (DOJ) and the Federal Trade Commission.[115] Exceptionally, however, in 1978 Congress transferred to the DOT the discretionary authority of the Civil Aeronautics Board (the industry's enforcement agency under regulation) to exempt certain inter-airline conduct from the antitrust laws. Domestic airline mergers, acquisitions, and intercarrier agreements came under the jurisdiction of the DOJ from January 1, 1989. But the DOT still retains the power to approve and immunize intercarrier agreements in international aviation.[116] The DOT and DOJ jointly convinced Congress that the anomalous regime for competition in international *aviation* – related to and the product of a diplomatic negotiating process using bilateral air services treaties – made it necessary for the DOT to continue to wield the immunity power in order to react flexibly to industry developments and to move U.S. aviation partners coherently toward a market-based pro-competitive regime.[117]

---

[114] 14 C.F.R. § 212 (2008).

[115] The Federal Trade Commission has the task of preapproving mergers under the Clayton Act. *See* 15 U.S.C. § 18a. Meanwhile, antitrust authorities at the U.S. state level are preempted from regulating air carriers. *See* 49 U.S.C. § 41713(b)(1) (2012).

[116] *See* 49 U.S.C. §§ 41308–41309 (2006). Mergers and acquisitions in international aviation, of course, were (and continue to be) foreclosed by the nationality rule. *See supra* Section 4.1.1.

[117] *See* U.S. DOT, REPORT TO CONGRESS: ADMINISTRATION OF AVIATION ANTITRUST FUNCTIONS 4 (1987).

4.6.5. *DOT's Ex Ante Evaluation of Alliances: 49 U.S.C. Sections 41308 and 41309*

The DOT evaluates alliances for *ex ante* approval and immunity under two sections of the U.S. transportation code, 49 U.S.C. Section 41308 and 49 U.S.C. Section 41309.[118] The sections are chronologically inverted: approval under Section 41309 then triggers immunity review under the earlier section, 41308. Section 41309 requires a finding that the proposed "cooperative arrangement" (i.e., alliance) is "not adverse to the public interest" and is "not in violation of" other parts of the U.S. code on air commerce and safety (e.g., provisions requiring that the relevant U.S. air carriers are 75% owned by and in actual control of U.S. citizens and possess valid aircraft operator certificates).[119] If so, the regulator must answer three questions affirmatively. First, does the alliance "substantially reduce[] or eliminate[] competition"?[120] Because an alliance always makes partners out of competitors, the answer to this question is almost invariably "yes." Second, is the alliance necessary to meet a serious transportation need or to secure important public benefits, including "international comity and foreign policy considerations"?[121] If the answer to that question is negative, the approval fails. Otherwise, the regulator proceeds to a third question, asking whether the benefits of an anticompetitive agreement can be secured by "reasonably available alternatives that are materially less anticompetitive."[122] Here, if the answer is affirmative, again approval is withheld. If the answer is "no," the alliance wins approval. In practice, an alliance that successfully navigates the tripwires of Section 41309 will likely be given immunity. Technically, Section 41308 contains its own additional "public interest" test and a mandate that immunity will be awarded only "to the extent necessary . . . to proceed with the transaction."[123] Nevertheless, it has been apparent from DOT rulings that immunity mechanically succeeds approval and that satisfaction of the public interest test in Section 41309 will carry the applicant alliance through the similarly worded test in Section 41308.

---

[118] *See* 49 U.S.C. §§ 41308–41309 (2006).
[119] 49 U.S.C. § 41309(b).
[120] 49 U.S.C. § 41309(b)(1).
[121] 49 U.S.C. § 41309(b)(1)(A).
[122] 49 U.S.C. § 41309(b)(1)(B).
[123] 49 U.S.C. § 41308(b).

4.6.6. *DOT's Pro-Immunity Record*

There is some degree of travel between the DOT's rhetorical position on the grant of antitrust immunity and the decisions that the agency actually renders. In its first opinion in the SkyTeam "show cause order" in 2005,[124] the Department admonished the applicants that the antitrust laws are a "fundamental national economic policy" and that immunity must be considered the exception and not the rule. Accordingly, before immunity is granted, a "strong showing on the record" would be required to demonstrate that the alliance is in the public interest and that the parties will not proceed without immunity.[125] The SkyTeam submission was extraordinarily brief and facially weak, lacking empirical evidence and analysis; the applicants seemed to treat immunity as a regulatory entitlement or a boon. Later, on receipt of hundreds of pages from the SkyTeam members, the DOT reversed itself and immunized what was essentially the same alliance configuration.[126] Even where the DOJ has made on-the-record submissions exposing what it argues are the negative antitrust effects of particular combinations, the DOT has approved all applications by the three global alliances.

4.6.7. *European Commission's* Ex Post *System of Review*

The EU's competition code on intercarrier agreements appears in Article 101 of the Treaty on the Functioning of the European Union (TFEU).[127] Article

---

[124] *See* Alitalia-Linee Aeree Italiane-S.p.A., Czech Airlines, Delta Air Lines, Inc., KLM Royal Dutch Airlines, Northwest Airlines, Inc., and Société Air France, *Joint Application for Approval of and Antitrust Immunity for Alliance Agreements under 49 U.S.C. §§ 41308 and 41309*, Dkt. No. OST-2004-19214, Show Cause Order 2005-12-12 (Dec. 12, 2005) [hereinafter SkyTeam 2005 Show Cause Order]. The DOT will often issue an order directing the respondent to show cause why the agency should not adopt a proposed finding or conclusion. After considering responses the DOT will then issue its final order. *See* 14 C.F.R. § 302.703.

[125] SkyTeam 2005 Show Cause Order, *supra* note 124, at 33.

[126] *See* Alitalia-Linee Aeree Italiane-S.p.A., Czech Airlines, Delta Airlines, Inc., KLM Royal Dutch Airlines, Northwest Airlines, Inc., and Société Air France, *Joint Application for Approval of and Antitrust Immunity for Alliance Agreements under 49 U.S.C. §§ 41308 and 41309*, Dkt. No. OST-2007-28644, Show Cause Order 2008-4-17 (Apr. 9, 2008) [hereinafter SkyTeam 2008 Show Cause Order].

[127] Consolidated Version of the Treaty on the Functioning of the European Union, art. 26, 2010 O.J. (C 83) 47 [hereinafter TFEU]. Article 101 was formerly Article 81 of the Treaty Establishing the European Community and originally appeared as Article 85 of the Treaty of Rome. Traditionally, EU competition law has had three goals: first, to enhance efficiency in the sense of maximizing consumer welfare and optimizing the allocation of resources in the Union (which is also the only goal shared by all adherents of the Chicago School of Economics); second, to protect consumers and small firms from large aggregations of power (not a goal of the

101(1) prohibits "agreements between undertakings" as well as "concerted practices" that have as their "object or effect the prevention, restriction or distortion of competition within the internal market." Article 101(2) provides that arrangements that violate Article 101(1) are "automatically void." Cooperative airline alliances that allow competitors jointly to reduce capacity, fix schedules, or coordinate prices should be illegal under the plain terms of Article 101(1).[128] But Article 101(3) permits an "exemption" for arrangements that (among other things) improve the distribution of goods and promote economic progress, while giving consumers a "fair share" of the resulting benefit.[129] Prior to May 1, 2004, the EU had no direct competency to investigate alliances that included non-EU airline partners.[130] Regulation 411/2004 now makes Article 101 "directly applicable" to all air transport that touches the Union,[131] and Regulation 1/2003 gives the Union (through the European Commission) the right to displace national competition authorities and courts that otherwise have co-competency to conduct competition investigations.[132] The application of EU competition laws to airline alliances (as well as to all other EU industries) has been dramatically altered by Regulation 1/2003. Under Article 1, all cooperative arrangements caught by Article 101(1) of the TFEU that do not satisfy the exemption conditions of Article 101(3) are prohibited, *"no prior decision to that effect being required."*[133] On the other hand, arrangements that violate Article 101(1) but satisfy Article 101(3) are not prohibited, *"no prior decision to that effect being required."*[134] What is the meaning of the italicized language in those two legislative statements? The meaning is that now the parties (here, the members of the alliance) must establish for themselves whether their arrangement needs clearance under Article 101(3). The former DOT-style *ex ante* notification and clearance requirements have been abolished. The risk to which alliance partners are

---

Chicago School); and third, to facilitate the creation of the EU single market (a goal that is unique to the EU). In recent years the EU has increasingly emphasized consumer welfare as a predominant goal. *See* David J. Gerber, *Two Forms of Modernization in European Competition Law*, 31 FORDHAM INT'L L. J. 1235, 1246–52 (2007).

[128] All of these practices are obviously included in Article 101(1)'s representative list of violations.

[129] The arrangement also must not impose "restrictions which are not indispensable" on the companies involved or allow them "the possibility of eliminating competition in respect of a substantial part" of their business.

[130] Instead, various articles of the former treaty required the European Commission, the Union's executive agency, to work in tandem with Member State competition authorities.

[131] *See* Council Regulation 411/2004, art. 1, 2004 O.J. (L 68) 1. The term "directly applicable" appears in the recitals to the Regulation.

[132] *See* Council Regulation 1/2003, art. 11, 2003 O.J. (L 1) 1.

[133] *Id.* art. 1 (emphasis added).

[134] *Id.* art. 1(3) (emphasis added).

exposed is that failure to notify can lead in any event to a later investigation by the Commission or by national competition regulators (often as a result of a complaint by a disgruntled competitor) and consequent large fines if the alliance is ruled to be in violation of Article 101(1).[135]

4.6.8. *European Commission's Investigative Practice*

In practice, the Commission will open such an investigation (however it is prompted) by presenting the members of the alliance with a Statement of Objections that may include concerns about specific routes.[136] The Statement must be in writing and usually allows twelve weeks for a response. The alliance members can reject the Statement (which is a "reasoned opinion" that can be litigated before EU tribunals[137]) or respond with a request for an oral hearing as well as by submitting a Statement of Commitments.[138] (SkyTeam, for example, pledged in its Statement of Commitments to offer a series of benefits to new entrant rivals at key EU airports, including slots, interlining privileges, and participation in its members' frequent flyer programs. The alliance also promised to code-share with rail providers and to accept the appointment of a trustee to oversee its commitments.[139]) The Commission "market tests" the commitments, for example, by sounding out potential new entrants on alliance routes. Finally, the commitments will be approved or rejected by a Commission decision.[140]

4.6.9. *A Quick Comparison of the U.S. and EU Approaches*

Since the U.S. and EU *ex ante* and *ex post* approaches to antitrust review of alliances provide distinct regulatory paradigms for a future global approach, it is worth quickly comparing the two systems. U.S. *ex ante* review provides

---

[135] The decentralization of the exemption procedure was in part a response to the problem of the European Commission's inability to reach exemption decisions quickly.

[136] *See* Council Regulation 1/2003, *supra* note 132, art. 11(6); Comm'n Regulation 773/2004, art. 2(1), 2004 O.J. (L 123) 18. When the Commission acts under Article 11(6) of Council Regulation 1/2003, its action suspends the co-competency of Member State national competition authorities and courts.

[137] *See* TFEU, *supra* note 127, arts. 258–59.

[138] *See* Comm'n Regulation 773/2004, *supra* note 136, art. 12; *see also* Council Regulation 1/2003, *supra* note 132, art. 9(1).

[139] *See* Press Release, Europa, Antitrust: Commission Market Tests Commitments From Eight Members of SkyTeam Concerning Their Alliance Cooperation (Oct. 19, 2007).

[140] *See* Council Regulation 1/2003, *supra* note 132, art. 9(1). The decision may simply conclude that there are no grounds for further action without finding an infringement. Violation of commitments can attract fines totaling 10% of worldwide revenues. *See id.* art. 23(2).

greater certainty to applicants but is administered by an agency (the DOT) that does not overly prize economic and market analysis, although to that extent the DOT's approach gives more "wiggle room" to the airlines to make policy arguments that include appealing to international aerodiplomatic considerations.[141] EU *ex post* review risks having an alliance that has been functioning for years suddenly dethroned by a later European Commission order to divest slots or gates or even to cease operations. Moreover, appeals to vague maxims of international aviation policy will have less purchase when the relevant review section within the Commission (known as the Directorate General for Competition or DGComp) has huge competition law expertise. Finally, the DOT's *ex ante* review imposes relatively light conditions on approved and immunized alliances including the "evergreen" validity period noted earlier as well as time-limited route "carve-outs."[142] As the SkyTeam Schedule of Commitments revealed, the EU favors more intrusive sets of conditions that may include slot divestitures and independent monitoring.

4.7. ONGOING ISSUES OF LAW AND POLICY FOR ALLIANCES: "METAL NEUTRALITY" AND "SPILLOVER"

4.7.1. *Meaning of Metal Neutrality*

As the alliance system has evolved as a business model, it has brought vexing questions of both law and policy in its wake. The matter of so-called metal

[141] The DOT, in contrast to the DOJ, believes that network competition could not be duplicated by "atomistic" point-to-point competitors. The DOJ prefers the classic competition model that examines specific routes and tests whether they are contestable, that is, whether supracompetitive fares will attract timely, likely, and sufficient new competitors to discipline the price-setter (the alliance). *See* Impact of Consolidation on the Aviation Industry, with a Focus on the Proposed Merger Between Delta Air Lines and Northwest Airlines: Hearing Before the Subcomm. on Aviation of the H. Comm. on Transp. & Infrastructure, 110th Cong. 202–12 (2008) (testimony of James J. O'Connell, Deputy Assistant Attorney Gen., Antitrust Dept., U.S. Dept. of Justice), http://www.justice.gov/atr/public/testimony/233151.htm. Professor Michael Levine has argued that antitrust enforcers should recognize that pockets of monopoly will exist within the networks but are counterweighted by increased convenience of use as against stand-alone alternatives. He contends also that the ideal market profile for international aviation should be three to four competing global networks and as much non-network price discipline as the regulators can encourage. *See generally* Michael E. Levine, *Airline Alliances and Systems Competition: Antitrust Policy Toward Airlines and the Department of Justice Guidelines*, 45 HOUS. L. REV. 333, 335–39 (2008).

[142] The DOT has gone as far as arguing that carve-outs inhibit efficiencies and hurt consumers in cases involving metal neutral joint ventures (*see infra* in main text). *See* Air Canada et al., *Final Order to Amend Order 2007-2-16 so as to Approve and Confer Antitrust Immunity*, Dkt. No. OST-2008-0234, Order 2009-7-10, at 20–22 (Dep't of Transp. Jul. 10, 2009) [hereinafter A++ Final Order].

neutrality is currently preoccupying officials and stakeholders. The term is industry argot (although it has crept into DOT opinions[143]) to describe an alliance arrangement where the alliance partner best positioned commercially to serve a particular route is allowed to do so without competing or complementary services from other members: in effect, the alliance is "neutral" with respect to which partner performs the carriage.[144] The aim of metal neutrality, in fact, is to align the economic incentives of the alliance partners so that they need not compete with each other over which carrier's aircraft flies any particular segment of a service. Otherwise, there is a perceived risk of "diversion," which makes make it more profitable to keep certain segments and behind or beyond points out of reach of rival members of the alliance.[145] Whether or not revenues from the service are split evenly among the partners, the economic expectation is that no *extra* revenue will accrue to a carrier by booking a passenger on its own aircraft rather than on that of one of its partners. Typically the partner with the lowest cost base for the service will be the operator and all other alliance members will exit.[146] In metal neutral arrangements, specialized intercarrier committees of senior executives jointly plan and manage capacity, pricing, and inter-airline financial settlement in order to develop a common bottom line.[147] The U.S. DOT believes that metal neutrality amplifies the pro-consumer benefits of the alliance by allowing its members to operate services at the most efficient cost[148] as well as to synchronize schedules and optimize the end-to-end options for the passenger. Here is the DOT's precise definition of the term:

> [Metal neutrality] is an industry term meaning that the partners in an alliance are indifferent as to which [one] operates the "metal" (aircraft) when they jointly market services. Without a metal neutral sales environment, the

---

[143] *See, e.g.,* Air Canada et al., *Joint Application to Amend Order* 2007–2–16, Order 2011–11–16, 2011 DOT Av. LEXIS 492, *9 & *30 (Dep't of Transp. Nov. 14, 2011).

[144] *See* A++ Final Order, *supra* note 142, at n.48.

[145] For example, British Airways (BA) offers a nonstop service from Seattle to London. American Airlines (AA) offers a similar service but connecting over Chicago. If AA puts its code on the BA service, its own customers will likely opt for the nonstop BA service and cause a revenue transfer from AA to BA. In code-sharing arrangements, unlike in the metal neutral joint venture, each carrier to the code-share retains an incentive to optimize its own margins rather than to maximize joint revenues.

[146] There is a risk, of course, that if and when an alliance unravels, the exiting carriers will be seriously disadvantaged economically by their "physical" absence from flying the routes. Alliances do face occasional defections: Continental Airlines leaving SkyTeam for Star in 2009 was the biggest such defection in alliance history. A plan for US Airways to leave the Star Alliance in favor of oneworld following regulatory approval for its merger with American Airlines was announced in February 2013. *See infra* note 173.

[147] *See* SkyTeam 2008 Show Cause Order, *supra* note 126, at 3.

[148] Lower costs, in other words, should translate into lower fares for the passenger.

partners have a strong economic incentive to book passengers on their own aircraft in order to retain a larger share of the revenue for themselves, which may not be in the best interest of the consumer or the alliance as a whole. Metal neutrality may be achieved through revenue and/or comprehensive benefit-sharing arrangements.[149]

4.7.2. Contrasting U.S. and EU Approaches to Metal Neutrality

Metal neutrality was not a DOT prerequisite for antitrust immunity during the decade-and-a-half before 2008 (when open skies ASAs and code-sharing sufficiently justified immunity). But the ubiquity of code-sharing and the existence of more than 100 open skies agreements seem to have persuaded the DOT to require metal neutrality for deeper consolidation among alliances that already have complex code-sharing arrangements and where the home States of the foreign carrier members have stable open skies relationships with the United States.[150] As we will see, in the SkyTeam, Star, and oneworld global alliances, metal neutrality involves only select carriers within the larger alliance structure, thereby presenting the appearance of an "alliance within an alliance." The European Commission seems to consider the deeper integration of the metal neutral joint venture to be a more urgent competition concern than the broader idea of a multicarrier alliance. This is somewhat ironic, given that the DOT now *prefers* metal neutral joint ventures as a mechanism to lower fares. But these seemingly opposed viewpoints are not contradictory if they are viewed from the vantage point of each agency's execution of its mission. The Commission is probing for anticompetitive outcomes rather than granting formal immunity. It spends much of its analysis of alliances examining specific route-pairs to determine competition effects. A metal neutral joint venture will inevitably have greater anticompetitive impact than a less integrated alliance, making it logical for a competition-focused agency to prioritize scrutiny of such arrangements. The DOT, in contrast, is not actually scouring for antitrust violations (that is the job of the DOJ) but deciding whether to grant antitrust

---

[149] American Airlines, Inc., British Airways PLC, Finnair OYJ, Iberia Lineas Aereas De España, S.A., Royal Jordanian Airlines, *Joint Application under 49 U.S.C. §§ 41308–41309 for Approval of and Antitrust Immunity for Alliance Agreements*, Dkt. No. OST-2008–0252, Order 2010–2–8 at n.6 (Dep't of Transp. Feb. 13, 2010).

[150] Although the term "metal neutrality" has only recently appeared in DOT decisions, it has been argued that the existence of metal neutrality in a heavily integrated alliance agreement now appears to be an established requirement for antitrust immunity. *See generally* Gabriel S. Sanchez, *An Institutional Defense of Antitrust Immunity for International Airline Alliances*, 62 CATH. U. L. REV. 139 (2012). For a more detailed explication of the concept, see Volodymyr Bilokach & Kai Huscherlatch, *Airline Alliances and Antitrust Policy: The Role of Efficiencies*, 21 J. AIR TRANSP. MGMT. 76, 80–81 (2012).

immunity. Although part of the required statutory testing is to determine whether an alliance or joint venture will have anticompetitive effects (otherwise there is no need for immunity), the DOT's investigative emphasis is more logically placed on the benefits offered by the proposed arrangement that would justify immunizing the anticompetitive effects. Because metal neutral joint ventures are more anticompetitive yet also offer more benefits (to the DOT's eye), the U.S. agency sees them as more deserving of immunity at the same time that the European Commission views them as more threatening.

4.7.3. *Viewpoint of Organized Labor on Metal Neutrality*

U.S. organized labor attacks metal neutrality as an incentive to heavily indebted "legacy" carriers,[151] bolted to unionized contracts, to assign expensive routes (and hence staffing) to partners with much lower cost structures.[152] The reader may detect the irony that labor has tried to avoid that exact outcome in its opposition to liberalizing inward investment. Some critics have portrayed metal neutrality as a device for the big U.S. carriers to shape-shift into "virtual" airlines, deriving a revenue stream from marketing air services that are actually provided by their alliance partners.[153]

4.7.4. *Risk of Domestic and International Spillover*

A further issue with alliance antitrust immunity, detected especially by U.S. authorities, is the risk of domestic and international "spillover." The DOT is the sole federal agency that can approve and immunize intercarrier agreements affecting international air transport. Moreover, the federal deregulation statute abolished an earlier parallel power to immunize domestic agreements between carriers.[154] Before United and Continental merged in 2009, regulators were troubled that their membership of the same (technically international) alliance, Star, would allow them to share sensitive information about their domestic services. As has happened before with problematic antitrust

---

[151] The term "legacy carrier" is used in the United States to refer to those carriers with large interstate route networks that existed prior to the 1978 Airline Deregulation Act.

[152] *See, e.g.,* Answer of the Association of Flight Attendants-CWA, U.S.-Japan Alliance Case, Dkt. No. OST-2010–0059 (Jul. 9, 2010), http://www.airlineinfo.com/Sites/DailyAirline/web-content/ostpdf78/775.pdf. The flight attendants' union argued that if United and Continental were granted antitrust immunity for a proposed metal neutral joint venture with Japan's All Nippon Airways, the two U.S. carriers (now merged) would shift operation of the affected routes to All Nippon, which had lower labor costs.

[153] For labor, "the business of an airline is to fly," not to outsource flying to the lowest bidder or merely to act as a ticket agent.

[154] *See* HAVEL, *supra* note 22, at 262–263.

issues in the air transport industry, however, the spillover question has been parked by industry developments, in this case recent U.S. merger activity.[155] But internationally the question remains sensitive. Two non-U.S. alliance members that obtain immunity in an alliance with the same U.S. airline could pursue cooperative arrangements that do not include that U.S. carrier. Under the terms of their 2009 immunity application, for example, Star Alliance core members United and Lufthansa (and several other airlines) have an immunity to cooperate that does not extend outward to cover Star's Asia-Pacific members, particularly Japan's ANA.[156] Immunization for ANA/ United cooperation in the context of Star was granted in a later DOT ruling – one which, again, did not extend the immunity beyond the circle of the applicant carriers to, say, Lufthansa.[157] Even so, some analysts fear that through their separate immunized dealings with United, Lufthansa and ANA could find ways of collaborating with one another that may offend U.S. antitrust laws, but more likely that will violate EU or Japanese competition rules. The quick solution has been for non-U.S. alliance members to secure exemptions from their home States to expand cooperation beyond the U.S. context. In 2011, for example, the Japanese authorities blessed the Lufthansa/ANA cooperative agreement.[158] Even so, as the alliance system continues to take on more airlines, international spillover will remain a risk that lacks a universal remedy.

4.8. A SURVEY OF U.S. AND EU ANTITRUST OVERSIGHT OF THE THREE GLOBAL ALLIANCES

4.8.1. *Introduction*

Finally, we will look briefly at the some of the key rulings of both the U.S. and EU antitrust review authorities on various applications by the three global alliances – SkyTeam, Star, and oneworld. We start with SkyTeam, which suffered a stunning upset in 2005 when its six-carrier request for immunity was rebuffed by the DOT. Although that decision was reversed in 2008 (motivated in part by the merger of U.S. airlines Delta and Northwest, which had been

---

[155] Similarly, DOT regulation of computer reservations systems was superseded by events in the airline ticket distribution industry.

[156] *See* A++ *Final Order, supra* note 142.

[157] *See* U.S.-Japan Alliance Case, Dkt. No. OST-2010–0059, Final Order 2010–11–10 (Nov. 10, 2010).

[158] *See* Kaveri Niththyananthan, *Lufthansa, ANA Get Antitrust Clearance*, WSJ.COM, Jun. 1, 2011, http://online.wsj.com/article/SB10001424052702303657404576359620588556408.html.

separate carriers at the time of the first application), all of the alliances have drawn useful forensic lessons from a rare refusal by the DOT to grant approval and immunity.

4.8.2. *SkyTeam Alliance: DOT Review*

The SkyTeam alliance was formally created in 2000. Air France, Alitalia, Czech Airlines, Delta Airlines, and Korean Air received U.S. antitrust immunity in 2002.[159] As noted above, the DOT refused in 2005 to grant approval and immunity to a six-way alliance comprising Air France (now including KLM), Alitalia, Continental Airlines,[160] Delta Airlines, Korean Air, and Northwest Airlines. At that time, SkyTeam embraced two already-immunized alliances that each included a U.S. carrier (Northwest/KLM and Delta/Air France/Alitalia). With overlapping route networks between the existing alliances and no new online service in new markets, the applicants failed to muster a record as to what public benefits would accompany an even more comprehensive arrangement beyond those available from arm's-length code-sharing and what the distinct immunized alliances were already achieving.[161] Moreover, the involvement of the two separate U.S. carriers, albeit in separate alliances, was a troubling matter of first impression.[162] The DOT arguably did not perceive the building momentum toward three global alliances and instead was seeking at least temporarily to apply brakes to the alliance process. Further, the 2005 ruling occurred at the outset of negotiations toward a U.S./EU open skies agreement and (unlike in the Star application in 2007[163]) the DOT did not have a visible and viable diplomatic process to protect. By 2008, however, the new U.S./EU "open skies plus" treaty[164] had entered into provisional effect and included the signatures of each of the home States of the applicant non-U.S. carriers. In the DOT's view, fewer but larger alliance networks would be competing in a competitive space that would have incommensurably wider boundaries than the traditional country-pair

---

[159] Note that the United States and France signed an open skies ASA in 2001.

[160] Continental Airlines was part of the SkyTeam alliance but was non-immunized.

[161] The DOT and DOJ were in agreement on this holding, the DOJ finding that the applicants' "significant burden" had not been met. In past cases, alliances had been constructed from end-to-end networks. *See* Sky Team 2005 Show Cause Order, *supra* note 124, at 3.

[162] *See supra* Section 4.7.4 (discussing possible domestic "spillover" effects of alliances).

[163] *See infra* Section 4.8.4.

[164] The 2007 U.S./EU Air Transport Agreement, *see supra* note 44, is sometimes described as "open skies plus" because in addition to liberalization of the four major Chicago system negotiating points – routes, capacity, frequency, and tariffs – the agreement put in place a framework for collaboration on regulatory matters such as competition, security, and consumer protection, and addressed prohibitions on cross-border investment that had been complicated by the creation of the EU common aviation area.

markets (i.e., U.S./twenty-eight EU Member States as opposed to, for example, U.S./U.K. or U.S./France).[165] With new entry possible from any EU airport, the transatlantic market would be more open than ever to new business models that could use strong regional hubs to discipline incumbents. Moreover, Northwest had now merged into Delta, dissipating concerns about having more than one U.S. carrier among the applicants for common immunity. With that backdrop, the Department now felt comfortable, as it had not been in 2005, with an arrangement to "rationalize" Air France's distinct commercial relationships with Northwest (which had been in an alliance with KLM, Air France's own merger partner since 2000[166]) and Delta (Air France's current SkyTeam partner). Despite its prior reservations, the DOT agreed that the Air France/KLM merger had made the original two immunized alliances effectively unsustainable. And the public benefits it could not find in 2005 were now manifest.[167] Accordingly, immunity was bestowed not only on the original six-way SkyTeam alliance but also on an intensified four-way metal neutral joint venture among Air France/KLM, Alitalia, Delta, and Northwest.[168]

4.8.3. *SkyTeam Alliance: EU Review*

In June 2006, the European Commission sent a Statement of Objections to SkyTeam.[169] In October of the following year, the Commission "market-tested" the commitments proposed by the SkyTeam membership.[170] These were rejected (unlike in parallel proceedings for oneworld) and the probe remained open until January 2012. In that month, the Commission closed its investigation into the broader SkyTeam alliance and opened a new probe into the metal neutral joint venture among Air France/KLM, Alitalia, Delta, and Northwest.[171]

[165] *See* SkyTeam 2008 Show Cause Order, *supra* note 126, at 13.

[166] *See supra* note 60 (explaining Air France/KLM "merger-in-fact").

[167] Unlike the original SkyTeam immunity proceedings in 2002, the DOT did not condition the grant of immunity on numerous "carve-outs" (specified routes on which the alliance carriers could not cooperate).

[168] This "alliance within an alliance" was the first of the new generation of metal neutral joint ventures where the participants pool revenues and are indifferent to which carrier actually operates a particular service. *See supra* Section 4.7.1 (analyzing metal neutral alliance structures).

[169] The Statement identified 11 transatlantic route-pairs where SkyTeam members held strong market positions that would be further strengthened by reduced competition among alliance members. The effects would be compounded by scarce slots at congested hubs.

[170] *See supra* Section 4.6.8 (discussing market-testing).

[171] *See* Press Release, Europa, Antitrust: Commission Opens a Probe into Transatlantic Joint Venture between Air France-KLM, Alitalia and Delta and Closes Proceedings against Eight Members of SkyTeam Airline Alliance (Jan. 1, 2012), http://europa.eu/rapid/press-release_IP-12-79_en.htm#PR_metaPressRelease_bottom.

4.8.4. *Star Alliance: DOT Review*

The Star Alliance was officially founded in 1997 by Air Canada, United, Lufthansa, SAS, and Thai Airways and won antitrust immunity in 2007 (by which time it had been joined by LOT Polish Airlines, TAP Air Portugal, and Swiss International Airlines).[172] US Airways joined Star as a nonimmunized participant in 2004.[173] The DOT's analysis in Star's successful immunity proceeding in 2007 resembled the 2008 SkyTeam decision: the Department took favorable note of the pending U.S./EU open skies agreement and emphasized the general importance of open skies as a predicate for immunity.[174] The 2007 decision also commented that, unlike SkyTeam in 2005, the Star members were not proposing to fuse already-immunized alliances that also had overlapping networks.[175] Continental Airlines joined Star in 2009 and almost immediately applied with Air Canada, United, and Lufthansa for DOT approval and immunization of a metal neutral joint venture that they branded as "A++," another "alliance within an alliance."[176] With a new Democratic presidential administration in office, the DOJ was embarked on tough antitrust enforcement and publicly denounced the idea of two U.S. airlines (United and Continental) collaborating inside such an arrangement.[177]

---

[172] Note that the United States and Germany signed an open skies ASA in 1996.

[173] Following the announcement of a merger between American Airlines and US Airways in February 2013, US Airways has indicated that, pending all required regulatory approvals, it would leave the Star Alliance to join oneworld. *See* Doug Cameron, *U.S. Airline Merger to Affect Alliances*, WSJ.COM, Feb. 14, 2013, http://online.wsj.com/article/SB10001424127887324432004578304210189378352.html?mod=googlenews.wsj. The planned alliance transition was briefly stalled, however, following the DOJ's antitrust challenge to the merger. *See* Press Release, Dep't of Justice, Justice Department Files Antitrust Lawsuit Challenging Proposed Merger Between US Airways and American Airlines (Aug. 13, 2013), http://www.justice.gov/opa/pr/2013/August/13-at-909.html/.

[174] A U.S./Canada liberal ASA had also been negotiated. Protocol to the Air Transport Agreement between the Government of the United States and the Government of Canada, U.S.-Can., Mar. 12, 2007, http://www.state.gov/documents/organization/114887.pdf.

[175] *See* The Austrian Group, British Midland Airways Limited, Deutsche Lufthansa AG, Polskie Linie Lotnicze Lot S.A., Scandinavian Airlines System, Swiss International Air Lines Ltd., TAP Air Portugal, United Air Lines, Inc., and Air Canada, *Joint Application under 49 U.S.C. §§ 41308 and 41309 for Approval of and Antitrust Immunity for Commercial Alliance Agreements*, Dkt. Nos. OST-2005–22922 and OST-96–1434, Show Cause Order at 7 (Dep't of Transp. Dec. 19, 2006) [hereinafter Star 2006 Show Cause Order].

[176] *See* Air Canada, The Austrian Group, British Midland Airways Ltd., Continental Airlines, Inc., Deutsche Lufthansa AG, Polskie Linie Lotniecze Lot S.A., Scandinavian Airlines System, Swiss International Air Lines Ltd., TAP Air Portugal, and United Air Lines, Inc., *Joint Application to Amend Order 2007-2-16 so as to Approve and Confer Antitrust Immunity*, Dkt. No. OST-2008–0234, Show Cause Order 2009-4-5 (Dep't of Transp. Apr. 7, 2009).

[177] "United and Continental will be discussing the most sensitive competitive subjects." Comments of the Department of Justice on the Show Cause Order to Amend Order

Rather than address the DOJ's warnings about U.S. domestic "spillover,"[178] however, the DOT relied instead on international aviation policy and insisted that the unique burden of the nationality rule fully justified treating immunity for international airline alliances as something other than a rare exception.[179] To the DOJ charge that its fellow agency could not use immunity to push its liberalizing agenda any further than had already been achieved in the U.S./ EU Air Transport Agreement, the DOT countered that immunity was still needed to *maintain* as well as to reach open skies: foreign partners must be prevented from withdrawing from existing open skies agreements and thereby impeding negotiations with other States.[180] In so stating, the Department conceded a point that (as noted above) has been widely believed, namely, that open skies agreements are now negotiated with the implicit promise of immunity.[181] In terms of the applicable statutory tests, the agency took the view that ownership restrictions preclude authentic "from anywhere to everywhere" airline mergers and therefore satisfy the requirement in U.S.C. Section 41309 that the requisite transportation needs or public benefits "cannot be achieved by reasonably available and materially less anticompetitive alternatives."[182] Moreover, sufficient competitive pressure on the "A++" venture would come from other carriers, in particular city-pairs, and from other alliances with global network connectivity.[183] Finally, the DOT for the first time awarded "global immunity" to A++, covering transpacific as well as transatlantic and transborder markets.[184] The decision held that different geographic-specific

---

2007–2–16 so as to Approve and Confer Antitrust Immunity, Dkt. No. OST-2008–0234 at 29 (Dep't of Justice Jun. 26, 2009) [hereinafter DOJ Comments]. The DOJ also asserted that it was "aware of no legal challenge to the actions taken by carriers within and in furtherance of a legitimate airline alliance." The DOT retorted, however, that the DOJ was unwilling to opine that the coordinated activities planned under the joint venture might, even absent immunity, be otherwise compliant with the antitrust laws or that "the DOJ, competitors, or consumers would not challenge these activities if undertaken without immunity." *See* A++ Final Order, *supra* note 142, at 12.

[178] *See* Dep't of Justice Comments, *supra* note 177, at 28.

[179] *See* A++ Final Order, *supra* note 142, at 10–11.

[180] *See id.* at 11.

[181] *See id.*

[182] A++ Final Order, *supra* note 142, at 3.

[183] *See id.* at 10. The Department held that coordinated connecting services by integrated alliances could discipline fares on virtually all significant nonstop routes. *See id.* To assuage the DOJ, even though the DOT found no single international nonstop overlap routes between Continental and United, the final order carved out some 2-to-1 markets (where competitors were reduced from two to one) with respect to time-sensitive business travelers who were more likely to rely on nonstop services and feel the effects of reduced competition. Contrarily, however, these passengers would also gain network benefits from an integrated metal neutral joint venture. *See id.* at 18. No 4-to-3 or 3-to-2 markets were excluded from immunization. *See id.*

[184] *See id.* at 22.

protocols, each tailored to a different scope of immunity for activities in different regions, were likely to be unduly complex and burdensome.[185] The DOT/DOJ conflict over Continental's accession to a United-led Star was sharp enough to require intervention by President Obama's economic adviser, Lawrence Summers. But the agencies' disagreement was subsequently mooted (and muted) by the merger of the two airlines in 2010.[186]

4.8.5. *Star Alliance: EU Review*

The European Commission probed the DOT-immunized alliance among United, Lufthansa, and SAS (the predecessor arrangement to Star) between 1996 and 2002. The alliance surrendered slots at Frankfurt's airport as a condition of eventual approval. A new investigation began in 2009, presumably because of changes to the EU governing treaty and the additions of Air Canada and Continental to the Star Alliance.[187] Despite opening its newest probe at the same time that it was targeting oneworld, the Commission did not issue a formal Statement of Objections in its review of Star. Instead, the Commission accepted a series of voluntary market commitments made by the Star Alliance that are intended to enhance competition on the alliance's New York/Frankfurt route.[188] These commitments, which are intended to last ten years, are now legally binding on the Star carriers.

4.8.6. *Oneworld Alliance: DOT Review*

The oneworld[189] alliance was launched in 1999 by American Airlines (AA), British Airways (BA), Cathay Pacific, Canadian Airlines, and Qantas. They were joined later by Finnair, Iberia, and Royal Jordanian Airlines. The core AA/BA partnership was unable to secure antitrust immunity from the DOT until 2010, when five carriers obtained common immunity after the U.K. finally endorsed open skies as a party to the U.S./EU Air Transport

---

[185] *See id.*

[186] Similarly, the announcement of an American Airlines/US Airways merger in February 2013 will likely allay any concerns about US Airways' plan, pursuant to the merger, to leave the Star Alliance in favor of oneworld. *See supra* note 173.

[187] The Treaty of Lisbon entered into force on Dec. 1, 2009.

[188] Specifically, Star members United, Air Canada, and Lufthansa agreed to surrender New York and/or Frankfurt slots to new entrants while also allowing competing carriers improved access to the alliance members' connecting traffic. *See* Press Release, Europa, Antitrust: Commission Renders Legally Binding Commitments from Star Alliance Members Air Canada, United and Lufthansa on Transatlantic Air Transport Market (May 23, 2013), http://europa.eu/rapid/press-release_IP-13-456_en.htm/.

[189] Note the usual lower case "o" at the beginning of the name.

Agreement. As with SkyTeam and Star, the core group (AA, BA, and Iberia, which had entered a merger with BA[190]) also secured immunity for an additional three-way joint venture within oneworld, yet another "alliance within an alliance." The oneworld proceeding was the first in which the DOT explicitly acknowledged (and deferred to) the work of EU competition authorities in a published decision: the U.S. agency accepted that the European Commission's procedures for slot divestiture would meet its own objectives for a similar remedy.[191]

4.8.7. *Oneworld Alliance: EU Review*

The oneworld alliance is the only one of the three global alliances to complete the European Commission's investigation process. In July 2010, the core joint venture between British Airways, American Airlines, and Iberia received approval in its current form for ten years.[192] The Commission concluded that the core group's key "commitment" – to make available a total of forty-nine return flights a week[193] to new competitors at Heathrow and Gatwick for service to four major U.S. cities – was sufficient to remedy its

---

[190] International Airlines Group (IAG) was formed in 2011 through a merger between BA and Iberia. The multinational airline holding company is headquartered in London with its registered office in Madrid. Both BA and Iberia continue to operate under their distinct brand names. In 2012, IAG expanded with the acquisition of British Midland International (BMI).

[191] See American Airlines, Inc., British Airways PLC, Finnair OYJ, Iberia Lineas Aereas De España, S.A., and Royal Jordanian Airlines, *Joint Application under 49 U.S.C. §§ 41308–41309 for Approval of and Antitrust Immunity for Alliance Agreements*, Dkt. No. OST-2008-0252, Order 2010-7-8 at 16–20 (Dep't of Transp. Jul. 20, 2010) [hereinafter oneworld Final Order]. Slots are essentially departure and landing rights at a specified airport tied to a specific date and time. See *supra* Chapter 3, Section 3.7.4. The DOT has not typically made use of slot remedies, but found them warranted in this case because of the oneworld carriers' especially large share of available slots at Heathrow, one of the industry's most congested and economically important hubs. The DOT noted that the implementation of slot remedies, including the four Heathrow slot pairs (i.e., four new daily round-trip flights) that the DOT itself required, would be governed by procedures agreed to by the applicants and the Commission. These procedures, the DOT found, were "sufficient" to achieve the Department's objectives for a slot remedy. See *supra* oneworld Final Order.

[192] See Summary of Commission Decision of 14 July 2010 relating to a proceeding under Article 101 of the Treaty on the Functioning of the European Union and Article 53 of the EEA Agreement (COMP/39.56 – British Airways/American Airlines/Iberia), 2010 O.J. (C 278) 14, 15 [hereinafter Summary of Commission Decision].

[193] In other words, seven daily round-trips.

concerns about diminution of competition on those routes.[194] Finally, the Commission reciprocated the DOT's earlier salute in noting that it had been "in close contact" with the U.S. agency throughout the investigation.[195]

4.8.8. *A Final Appraisal of the U.S. and EU Approaches*

Having looked at DOT review of the global alliances, the reader might empathize with one critic's view that the agency believes that "market power cannot exist in any broadly defined market that has three competitors and an [o]pen [s]kies treaty."[196] The European Commission is more inclined to circumspection. Its decisions evoke parallels with the DOJ's metric of the "contestability" of specific routes and it is less sanguine than the DOT about the inherent virtues of network competition.[197] Nevertheless, is it clear that both the DOT and the European Commission apply a dose of "industrial policy" to their scrutiny of alliances. The U.S. agency sees alliances as enabling the U.S. international carriers to expand their global networks and maintain a comparative advantage over domestic low-cost carriers.[198] Similarly, the Commission views the global alliances as helping to fortify a small number of Union "champions" to perform in highly competitive world markets.[199]

---

[194] Operating as a "single entity" on these routes, the oneworld core group would benefit from high barriers to entry, especially the lack of peak-time slots at Heathrow, the alliance members' frequency advantage, and their control of most connecting traffic on the routes. The slot remedies, along with participation in oneworld's frequent flyer programs and other concessions, were aimed at lowering barriers to entry. *See* Summary of Commission Decision, *supra* note 192.

[195] The Commission referred to the DOT's "parallel review under U.S. rules." *See* Press Release, Europa, Antitrust: Commission market tests commitments proposed by BA, AA, and Iberia concerning transatlantic cooperation (Mar. 10, 2010), http://europa.eu/rapid/press-release_IP-10-256_en.htm.

[196] *See* Horan, *supra* note 108, at 262.

[197] Some commentators argue that the North Atlantic market is not contestable (i.e., liable to attract new entrants). In this view, the three global alliances enjoy an oligopolistic 92% of capacity market share that they sustain through implicit coordination to refrain from entering each other's city-pairs and hubs. *See id.* at 268.

[198] Following its acquisition of rival low-cost carrier AirTran, Southwest Airlines announced in 2012 that it would start offering international service on AirTran's former routes to the Caribbean and Mexico. The move further complicates attempts to define Southwest's status as something larger than other U.S. regional or budget carriers but distinct from the legacy carriers that participate in the alliance system and that are largely dependent upon international service for their profits.

[199] *See* TRANSATLANTIC AIRLINS ALLIANCES REPORT, *supra* note 108.

4.9. BEYOND THE ALLIANCE SYSTEM

4.9.1. *A Contingent System*

Despite being welcomed in some quarters as the most important development in the international air transport industry since the jet aircraft,[200] the immunized alliance system faced legislative emasculation in the months before the 2010 U.S. congressional elections. Proposals to limit antitrust immunity for alliances to three years, and in any event to abolish the "evergreen" grant,[201] did not survive the return of a Republican Congress.[202] Even if they have (for the moment) dodged the wrath of Congress, however, alliances arguably will always be a contingent system that will endure only so long as international airlines have to await the emergence of a global investment regime.

4.9.2. *Rise of Multinational Airlines?*

It is widely expected that such a regime would propel the leading members of the three major global alliances –SkyTeam, Star, and oneworld – to full consolidation with one another. The rise of a future "Star Airline" or "oneworld Airline" is not entirely certain, however. The present triad has been formed in part by rational calculation, but in part also by circumstance. After the establishment of Northwest/KLM and United/Lufthansa, carriers such as Air France and Delta were forced into a similar marriage in the absence of other suitors. In an open regime, none of those arrangements will continue to seem foreordained. The sheer size of the current global alliances also hints at future reluctance by competition authorities to approve a permanent merger of their current membership. But it would be wrong to close this discussion on an entirely negative note. To many commentators, the biggest advantage of alliances to its members has yet to be realized: their present existence has allowed commercial relationships to be formalized that are bound to remain strategically important when the regulatory and political environment eventually shifts toward open investment. Very plausibly, then, the core groups of the three global alliances – the metal neutral joint venturers – will settle down together to form the nucleus of three future global airlines.

---

[200] *See* Dean & Shane, *supra* note 105, at 18.
[201] *See supra* note 111.
[202] *See* Ensure Adequate Airline Competition Between the United States and Europe Act, H.R. 831, 111th Cong. (2009).

4.10. CONCLUSION: A NEW EU INITIATIVE

4.10.1. *An Emerging Normative Order*

As we have seen throughout this chapter, the emerging normative order of international aviation law has destabilized the nationality rule in bilateral air services treaties. The replacement paradigm that we have proposed here, which respects the regulatory role of the State, is the right of establishment. In the meanwhile, however, the fact that States are actually waiving the nationality clauses in their ASAs, or simply not enforcing them, continues to reveal deep dissatisfaction with the burden of a regulatory environment that cannot sustain the needs of its principal participants. The world's most economically powerful countries are actively seeking ways to repeal not only the nationality clauses in ASAs, but also the more entrenched domestic rules that limit foreign inward investment in the airline industry.

4.10.2. *A New EU Démarche on the U.S. Foreign Ownership Rule*

The European Commission's transport commissioner, Siim Kallas, announced in September 2012 that the EU will make a new effort to persuade the United States to scale back its stringent 25% foreign ownership cap for airlines. The new initiative is a strategic response to the rise of large, well-financed rivals from the Gulf States and China: fully merged U.S. and EU airlines would compete more effectively than is possible within the current system of alliances.[203] What is most interesting about the new EU *démarche* is that, for the first time, it forms part of a wider multisector dialogue between the United States and the EU on facilitation and enhancement of transatlantic investment.[204]

---

[203] *See* Andrew Parker & David Gelles, *Brussels Renews Push in U.S. for Airline Mergers*, FIN. TIMES, Sept. 26, 2012, at 6.

[204] *See* Transatlantic Economic Council (TEC), Statement of the European Union and the United States on Shared Principles for International Investment (Apr. 12, 2012), http://trade. ec.europa.eu/doclib/docs/2012/april/tradoc_149331.pdf. Moreover, in his State of the Union address in February 2013, President Barack Obama endorsed negotiations for a new U.S./EU Transatlantic Trade and Investment Partnership. Those negotiations may provide a more dynamic context for Commissioner Kallas's initiative even if it is unlikely that the agenda for the Partnership will explicitly include air transport services.

5

The International Law Regime for Aviation Safety and Security

5.1. INTRODUCTION

5.1.1. *A Collaborative Process of Ensuring Aviation Safety*

Since its inception, aviation has imbued the public mind with feelings of awe accompanied by outsized fears regarding its associated dangers. In response to these latter concerns, State and industry actors have made safety, and, in later years, security, a primary concern of global regulatory efforts. States have surrendered their sovereign authority over the subject of safety regulation to an extent far greater than has been done with regard to any other topic in this book. Although States have remained individually responsible for certifying the airworthiness of aircraft, for licensing pilots and other crewmembers, and for implementing the technical procedures and practices that the ICAO declares necessary to achieve an acceptable level of safety, for most of the world's States these activities have meant adhering to standards originating elsewhere. The institutional and legal framework for international civil aviation safety regulation, in fact, is more collaborative and less controversial, more ICAO-driven and less reliant on State-to-State negotiations and bilateral agreements, than any topic we have covered thus far. Owing in part to its quiet, steady development and in part to its highly technical nature, safety regulation tends to receive less scholarly attention than other areas of aviation law and policy, and the concise treatment with which we begin this chapter reflects that reality. But conciseness of treatment should in no way be considered a reflection on the subject's importance or on its place within the spectrum of issues commanding the attention of State and industry actors.

5.1.2. *Aviation Security and the Challenges of a Global Solution*

Global terrorism constitutes one of the greatest threats to international peace and security in the twenty-first century and, by extension, the greatest security threat to international aviation. As the savagery of the 9/11 attacks demonstrated, airlines remain at risk because of their visibility and their nationalistic intimacy with the States whose flags they bear. Although terrorism at airports and against airlines is mercifully rare, any assault imposes psychic costs on the traveling public as well as heavy economic burdens on a beleaguered airline industry. 9/11 precipitated the bankruptcies of several major U.S. airlines, as well as government-financed rescue packages in both the United States and the European Union (EU). Much stricter regimes of passenger and cargo screening have also ensued, accompanied by losses in efficiency, time, and privacy. Unlike in the sphere of technical cooperation on aircraft safety, the international response to the contemporary threat to aviation security has lacked purposiveness. Despite the adoption of no fewer than fifteen United Nations (U.N.) subject-specific international conventions or protocols, seven regional treaties, and a range of U.N. Security Council and General Assembly resolutions, all related to the prevention and repression of terrorism,[1] ambivalence about the aims of terrorists, and sometimes even about their methods, suggests that the threat is not obviously susceptible to an authentically multilateral solution.[2] In fact, none of the multilateral or regional instruments or U.N. resolutions has produced a universally accepted definition of terrorism.[3] Our goal in this chapter, however, is not to weigh political arguments about responses to terrorism but to examine, dispassionately, what has actually been achieved (or is still proposed) at the global level to address "aviation terrorism"

---

[1]   See the complete list in TERRORISM AND INTERNATIONAL LAW: ACCOUNTABILITY, REMEDIES, REFORM: A REPORT OF THE IBA TASK FORCE ON TERRORISM (Elizabeth Stubbins Bates et al. eds., 2011) [hereinafter IBA REPORT]; this list includes the international aviation crimes treaties discussed in this chapter. All of the listed instruments have in common that they proscribe specific acts of terrorism (hijacking, bombing, attacks on diplomats, etc.) and impose duties on States to criminalize and investigate those acts, and to prosecute or extradite perpetrators. *See id.* at 2.

[2]   *See generally, e.g.,* Michael A. Newton, *Exceptional Engagement: Protocol I and a World United Against Terrorism,* 45 TEX. INT'L L.J. 323 (2009); Naomi Norberg, *Terrorism and International Criminal Justice: Dim Prospects for a Future Together,* 8 SANTA CLARA J. INT'L L. 11 (2010); Alex Schmid, *Terrorism – The Definitional Problem,* 36 CASE W. RES. J. INT'L L. 375 (2004).

[3]   Thus, negotiations for the United Nations Draft Comprehensive Convention on Terrorism have stalemated in part because of disagreement on inclusion of State-sponsored or State-aided terrorism in addition to violence by non-State actors, and on whether to include armed resistance to an occupying regime. *See* IBA REPORT, *supra* note 1, at 2.

or, more generally, what we will call "aviation crimes" or "aviation security offenses."

5.2. THE BASIC PRINCIPLES OF INTERNATIONAL AIR SAFETY REGULATION

5.2.1. *Defining the Category*

Safety is a broad category that encompasses virtually every aspect of aircraft production, air transport operations, air navigation procedures, and crew licensing and behavior. ICAO has defined safety contextually as "the state of freedom from unacceptable risk of injury to persons or damage to aircraft and property."[4] A full examination of all of the specific technical instructions issued on these subjects is beyond the scope of this book. Instead, this part overviews the mix of policy and rules that is intended to deliver that "freedom from unacceptable risk."

5.2.2. *A Positive Political Attitude to Globalized Safety Standards*

Aside from the need to settle fundamental questions of sovereign authority over territorial airspace as discussed in Chapter 2, safety has been the issue most responsible for the existence and evolution of an international aviation law regime. States rightly saw the need during the industry's early years to ensure that a transformative new technology would not unduly threaten the well-being of either the commercial passengers necessary to its development and sustained viability or an unwitting citizenry newly vulnerable to dangers from above. Long after the present technological maturity of commercial air transport was attained, the public has still not adjusted its psychological perspective on air transport to align with the industry's excellent safety record when compared to other forms of travel.[5] Airplane incidents and failures garner a disproportionate share of media attention compared to analogous events in other industries.[6] Perhaps for these reasons, the establishment, harmonization, and implementation of safety norms in international civil

---

[4] ICAO Working Paper AN-WP/7699, "Determination of a Definition of Aviation Safety," Dec. 11, 2001.

[5] Following 9/11, 1.4 million people chose alternative forms of transportation to satisfy their 2001 holiday season travel needs despite the much lower risk associated with commercial air transport. The shift in modes of transportation is estimated to have led to an additional 1,000 automotive fatalities. *See* Maia Szalavitz, *10 Ways We Get the Odds Wrong*, PSYCHOL. TODAY, Jan. 1, 2008.

[6] *See id.*

aviation have provoked less conflict and enjoyed more continuous and successful collaboration than the other topics discussed in this book. Unlike with the control of aviation carbon emissions or aircraft noise pollution, or with oversight of aviation security offenses, for example, the importance of a global consensus on safety standards was politically obvious from the industry's beginning. Consequently, the necessary legal and institutional framework to promulgate those standards was the most robust creation of the 1944 Chicago Convention.[7] Safety, unlike air traffic rights, could not be perceived as a zero-sum contest, where the adoption of certain rules would provide benefits to the airlines of some contracting States while posing threats to the carriers of other States. Surrendering authority over safety regulation and agreeing to a universally applicable set of benchmarks and practices was easier to do when all States were perceived to benefit jointly from measures to ensure safe air travel.[8]

5.3. ENSURING INTERNATIONAL AVIATION SAFETY THROUGH ICAO HARMONIZATION AND STATE OBLIGATIONS

5.3.1. *Mutual Recognition in the Paris and Chicago Conventions*

Given international aviation's origins in a closed, sovereignty-based regime, it should come as no surprise that international safety regulation has relied largely on States assuming responsibility for their airspace, aircraft, and crew. The most immediate and obvious sources of risk to be managed in the industry's early years were the quality of the aircraft and of the crew flying them. States, therefore, required their air transport partners to provide assurance on both of those subjects before allowing foreign aircraft admittance to their sovereign skies. The normative effects of that demand for assurance were seen in Article 11 of the 1919 Paris Convention, which mandated that "every aircraft engaged in international aviation . . . be provided with a certificate of airworthiness . . . by the State whose nationality it possesses."[9] That requirement was accompanied by Article 12, requiring that pilots and operating crew be licensed by the State of nationality and by Article 13, which required the other Convention contracting States to recognize national certificates of

---

7   *See infra* note 11.

8   *See supra* Chapter 1, Section 1.3.4, and *infra* Chapter 6, Section 6.6.2 (discussing the equitable effects of the economic principle of international Paretianism).

9   Convention Relating to the Regulation of Aerial Navigation art. 11, *opened for signature* Oct. 13, 1919, 11 L.N.T.S. 173 (entered into force May 31, 1920) [hereinafter Paris Convention].

airworthiness and nationally issued licenses.[10] Those three articles established a system of State responsibility for two prominent safety concerns, the safety of the aircraft and the competence of the operators, that would serve as the framework for ensuring aviation safety during the next ninety years. That system would later be reincorporated into the Convention on International Civil Aviation (the Chicago Convention) via Articles 31, 32, and 33.[11] Reliance on the safety certification of partner States was also engineered into the bilateral system of traffic rights agreements that evolved after World War II.[12] In addition, States were charged with regulating the flight and maneuver of aircraft[13] and with providing the necessary air navigation services[14] for flights within their territory.

5.3.2. *ICAO Harmonization and Standard Setting*

While the Chicago Convention and the system of bilateral air transport agreements fixed State responsibility for implementing and monitoring measures to guarantee the safety of their air transport operations, neither delineates the substantive standards that airlines and States would need to meet in order to comply with their obligations. Instead, the Chicago Convention expressly assigned that responsibility to the newly created ICAO.[15] This duty has been referred to as ICAO's *raison d'être.*[16] The model of collaborative harmonization established at Chicago also had its precursor in the Paris Convention, which cast the International Commission for Air Navigation (ICAN) in the role of safety standard setter.[17] ICAO's primary method for determining safety benchmarks has been through the issuance of Standards and Recommended Practices (SARPs)[18] contained in the annexes to the Chicago Convention. Although almost all of the annexes could be said to implicate safety in some way, those most directly on point include Annex 1, which provides guidelines for personnel licensing; Annex 2, which contains guidelines for the rules of the

---

[10] *See id.* arts. 12, 13.

[11] *See* Convention on International Civil Aviation arts. 31–33, *opened for signature* Dec. 7, 1944, 61 Stat. 1180, 15 U.N.T.S. 295 (entered into force Apr. 4, 1947) [hereinafter Chicago Convention].

[12] *See* Agreement Relating to Air Services art. 4, U.S.-U.K., Feb. 11, 1946, 12 Bevans 726 (no longer in force). *See supra* Chapter 3, Part 3.2.

[13] *See* Chicago Convention, *supra* note 11, art. 12.

[14] *See id.* art. 28.

[15] *See id.* art. 37.

[16] *See* Huang Jiefang, *Aviation Safety, ICAO and Obligations* Erga Omnes, 8 No. 1 Chinese J. of Int'l L. 63, 63 (2009).

[17] *See* Paris Convention, *supra* note 9, art. 34.

[18] For a full explanation of the difference between standards and recommended practices and the legal effect of each, see discussion *supra* Chapter 2, Sections 2.6.6, 2.6.7.

air; Annex 6, which sets standards for the operation of aircraft; Annex 8, which applies to airworthiness of aircraft; and Annex 18, which deals with the safe transport of dangerous goods by air. Typically, SARPs are drafted by ICAO's Air Navigation Commission, based on research and analysis conducted by one of the Commission's various committees or subgroups responsible for the issue in question. Contracting States or international organizations may also submit proposals for SARPs to be considered by the Commission. The drafted standard or recommended practice is then submitted to the ICAO Council, and, if supported by two-thirds of the Council members, added to the appropriate annex. Some standards are accompanied by Procedures for Air Navigation Services (PANS), which are highly detailed instructions for particularly technical SARPs. The promulgation of substantive international norms by ICAO has been the dominant source of lawmaking in international aviation safety, and the longevity of ICAO's dominance makes this body of norms unique among the topics of international aviation law. By comparison, the substantive rules concerning aviation security, passenger and cargo liability, corporate finance, and the distribution of traffic rights have been determined at various times by a mix of multilateral treaties and bilateral agreements. In addition to its SARPs, ICAO publishes a variety of other documents in furtherance of its safety regulation efforts. These include agenda-setting documents, such as the Global Aviation Safety Plan adopted by the ICAO Assembly in 1998, as well as detailed manuals and circulars to guide States in their implementation of ICAO's rules. ICAO has also sought implementation of safety standards by helping to create and work with Regional Safety Oversight Organizations (RSOOs), such as the South Asian Regional Initiative (SARI), the Central American Agency for Aeronautical Safety (ACSA), the Caribbean Aviation Safety and Security Oversight System (CASSOS), and the Banju Accord Group Safety Oversight Organization (BAGASOO).[19] These organizations vary in their functions, but provide States with technical assistance and guidance on interpreting standards and updating domestic legislation and regulations to better meet international requirements.

5.3.3. *Ensuring Compliance and Enforcement*

As is common in international law, ensuring compliance and enforcement has proved to be the most difficult component of effective international aviation safety regulation. As discussed in Chapter 2, ICAO's SARPs have an uncertain

---

[19] *See* Ruwantissa Abeyratne, *Ensuring Regional Safety in Air Transport*, 35 AIR & SPACE L. 249, 255–60 (2010).

level of binding legal effect, and ICAO is constrained in its ability to enforce them.[20] Member States are required to notify ICAO of any inability to comply with standards, although no explicit penalty or response is provided for in the Chicago Convention. A failure to comply with recommended practices does not even require notification.[21] For most of the past seventy years, ICAO has perceived its role as being to provide technical expertise and financial aid to assist States that struggle to comply, rather than to police and punish States that choose not to comply. Instead, as discussed previously, the ultimate responsibility for implementing and monitoring compliance with standards has largely fallen on the individual Member States. The assignment of regulatory and monitoring responsibility to the State of registration has become problematic in recent decades with the rise of more complicated forms of aircraft financing. In cases where an aircraft was for financing purposes registered in one contracting State, but operated out of another, the State of registry often had little opportunity to effectively ensure that safety standards were being met. Article 83*bis* was added to the Chicago Convention in 1997 to correct the gap in enforcement.[22] Under that provision, the State of registration may transfer its regulatory stewardship obligations under Articles 12, 30, 31, and 32 to the State of operation if the latter consents.[23]

5.3.4. *Monitoring Safety through National Programs*

The absence of an international body with formal responsibility for sanctioning noncompliance with safety standards led the United States in 1992 to adopt its own International Aviation Safety Assessment (IASA) program.[24] Under IASA, before a foreign air carrier is granted a permit to fly into the United States, representatives of the Federal Aviation Administration (FAA) visit the foreign State that proposes to designate the carrier and assess the ability of the State's Civil Aviation Authority (CAA) to ensure compliance with ICAO safety standards, especially with regard to Annexes 1, 6, and 8.[25] If States not currently operating services to the United States are found to be compliance-deficient, they will not be able to commence services without rectifying the deficiencies. States already operating U.S.-bound services may be prohibited

[20] *See supra* Chapter 2, Section 2.6.7.
[21] *See id.*
[22] *See* Chicago Convention, *supra* note 11, art. 83*bis.*
[23] *See id.* For a fuller analysis of the effects of Article 83*bis*, see *infra* Chapter 8, Section 8.5.4.
[24] *See* Information Concerning FAA Procedures for Examining and Monitoring Foreign Carriers, 57 Fed. Reg. 38342 (Aug. 24, 1992). *See also supra* Chapter 2, note 127.
[25] *See* Federal Aviation Administration, International Aviation Safety Assessment Program, http:// www.faa.gov/about/initiatives/iasa/more/.

from expanding their operations until they become compliant.[26] The EU followed in 1996 with its own Safety Assessment of Foreign Aircraft (SAFA) program, which imposes ramp inspections on the aircraft of any foreign State that is suspected of safety deficiencies.[27] Notice that under SAFA, it is the aircraft, as opposed to the aviation authorities, that receive scrutiny.[28]

5.3.5. *ICAO's Safety Oversight Program*

The U.S. and EU programs served as a catalyst for ICAO to adopt its own formal safety oversight program, which it finally did in 1999.[29] The Universal Safety Oversight Audit Programme (USOAP), like the U.S. IASA, scrutinizes contracting States' capability for monitoring and implementing compliance with ICAO safety SARPs. ICAO assesses that capability based on performance in eight areas: primary aviation legislation and civil aviation regulations, civil aviation organization, personnel licensing and training, aircraft operations, airworthiness of aircraft, air navigation services, aerodromes, and aircraft accident and incident investigation.[30] Initially, USOAP audits were restricted to reviewing compliance with Annexes 1, 6, and 8, but by 2005 the scope of the program was expanded to include all safety-related annexes. Beginning in 2013, ICAO moved from a periodic audit schedule to a continuous monitoring approach.[31] The results of the USOAP audits are made available to all other Member States.[32] Although ICAO lacks power to penalize States for non-compliance, this information-gathering function effectively motivates compliance by potentially jeopardizing a State's access to the markets of Member States receiving the reports. In 2006, the EU created a formal program for penalizing noncompliance and established a list of carriers banned from

---

[26] *See id.*

[27] Although the SAFA program was originally created in 1996, it was only in 2004 that the EU imposed a legal obligation on Member States to perform ramp inspections on third-country aircraft landing at their airports. *See* Council Directive 2004/36/CE, Safety of Third-Country Aircraft Using [Union] Airports, 2004 O.J. (L 143) 76.

[28] *See* European Aviation Safety Agency, Assessment of Foreign Aircraft (EC SAFA Programme), http://www.easa.europa.eu/approvals-and-standardisation/safety-assessment-of-foreign-aircraft-SAFA.php. *See also supra* Chapter 2, note 127.

[29] *See* International Civil Aviation Organization, *Establishment of an ICAO Universal Safety Oversight Audit Programme*, Assem. Res. A32–11, *compiled in Assembly Resolutions in Force*, ICAO Doc. 9790 (2001).

[30] *See* International Civil Aviation Organization, 2011: State of Global Aviation Safety (2011).

[31] *See* International Civil Aviation Organization, USOAP Continuous Monitoring Approach, http://www.icao.int/safety/CMAForum/Pages/default.aspx.

[32] For recent information on USOAP compliance levels, *see* http://www.skybrary.aero/index.php/ICAO_USOAP_and_Safety_Performance.

access to EU territorial airspace.[33] The list is based on evidence gathered from its own SAFA program as well as from ICAO's audits.[34]

5.3.6. *The Coming of Annex 19*

In February 2013, ICAO adopted its first new annex to the Chicago Convention in forty years. Annex 19, which was drafted by the Air Navigation Commission (ANC), consolidates in one document all of the safety management require-ments previously scattered across various annexes.[35] Most of the SARPs con-tained in Annex 19 were already applicable because they are existing SARPs that have been transferred to the new annex.[36] The purpose of the consolidation is to provide States with benchmarks for creating a "State safety program" that comprises an "integrated set of regulations and activities established by a State aimed at managing civil aviation safety."[37] In light of our analysis in Chapter 2 of the differences in legal status between "standards" and "recom-mended practices,"[38] it is also worth noting that in its communication on Annex 19 the ANC "invites" ICAO's member States, whenever it is "impor-tant" for the safety of air navigation, to enhance their obligation to notify ICAO of any variances from standards (under Article 38 of the Chicago

---

[33] *See* Commission Regulation 2111/2005 of the European Parliament and of the Council of 14 December 2005 on the establishment of a [Union] list of air carriers subject to an operating ban within the [Union] and on informing air transport passengers of the identity of the operating air carrier, and repealing Article 9 of Directive 2004/36/EC, 2005 O.J. (L 344) 15.

[34] *See id.*

[35] *See* Chicago Convention, *supra* note 11, annex 19. *See also* International Civil Aviation Organization, Proposal for Annex 19 and Related Consequential Amendments to Annexes 1, 6, 8, 11, 13, and 14, Letter of the Secretary General of the Air Navigation Commission and Attachments, Ref. AN 8/3–12/42 (Jun. 29, 2012) [hereinafter ICAO, *Proposal for Annex 19*].

[36] *See id.* at 2.

[37] *Id.* at A-14. The benchmarks vary in detail and focus, but the overarching theme of Annex 19 is that States must *systematize* their approach to managing safety. Thus, Annex 19 requires each State to "promulgate a comprehensive and effective aviation law" that provides all personnel performing safety oversight with access to the aircraft and operations of air carriers, and also to establish "relevant authorities or agencies," supported by qualified personnel and adequate financial resources, to discharge the required safety functions. *See* Chicago Convention, *supra* note 11, Annex 19. Annex 19 lays out a multicomponent framework for a "Safety Management System" in each ICAO member State, including effective reporting of safety violations and coordination of emergency response planning. *See id.* Although it is undoubt-edly useful to develop an integrated and consolidated list of best aviation safety practices, it remains true that implementation of ICAO's existing directory of SARPs remains well below optimal levels: *see* Skybrary, ICAO USOAP and Safety Performance, http://www.skybrary. aero/index.php/ICAO_USOAP_and_Safety_Performance (presenting statistical patterns of widespread nonimplementation of SARPs).

[38] *See supra* Chapter 2, Section 2.6.7.

Convention³⁹) to include also any departures from recommended practices (as to which no requirement of notification normally exists).⁴⁰

5.4. THE BASIC PRINCIPLES OF INTERNATIONAL AVIATION SECURITY REGULATION

5.4.1. *A Conceptual Clarification: Aviation Piracy*

As we begin our discussion of aviation security, it is important as a preliminary matter not only to be clear about which acts constitute an internationally recognized criminal offense against civil aviation, but also the means of and motivation for those acts. Both within and beyond the bounds of international aviation law, there has been a temptation to refer to a number of offenses against aircraft, particularly hijacking, as forms of "aviation piracy."⁴¹ Although some may regard "aviation piracy" as synonymous with "aviation crimes" or "aviation security offences" – or, more accurately, regard "aviation piracy" as a subset of the latter two concepts – commentators are not always meticulous in their use of terminology, and conceptual confusion is the outcome.

5.4.2. *Evolution of the Universal Crime of Piracy*

Since the advent of major exploratory and commercial endeavors by sea in the sixteenth and seventeenth centuries, the concept of piracy has undergone a radical transformation. As far back as the times of Homer, the pirate (*peirate*⁴²) had the positive character of an adventurer who was free to seek fame and fortune on the seemingly endless stretch of lawless waters surrounding the continent of Europe.⁴³ Once the seas became a lucrative medium of transport and, eventually, the pathway to colonization and empire, the pirate became *hostis humani generis* (the "universal enemy of mankind"), and the pirate's activities became universally condemned. Even today, when seafaring is less

---

³⁹ *See* Chicago Convention, *supra* note 11, art. 38.
⁴⁰ *See* ICAO, *Proposal for Annex 19, supra* note 35, at A-8.
⁴¹ The United Nations Convention on the Law of the Sea defines piracy broadly enough to include aircraft hijacking. United Nations Convention on the Law of the Sea art. 101, *opened for signature* Dec. 10, 1982, 1833 U.N.T.S. 397 (entered into force Nov. 16, 1994) [hereinafter UNCLOS]. A U.S. government task force created in 1969 to study aircraft hijacking was dubbed The FAA Task Force on Deterrence of Air Piracy. *See* FED. AVIATION ADMIN., TASK FORCE ON DETERRENCE OF AIR PIRACY FINAL REPORT, FAA-AM-78-35 (1978).
⁴² The Latin word is not dissimilar: *pirata*.
⁴³ *See* CARL SCHMITT, THE NOMOS OF THE EARTH IN THE INTERNATIONAL LAW OF THE JUS PUBLICUM EUROPAEUM 43 (G. L. Ulmen trans., 2003) (1950).

integral to the fortunes of great powers, piracy still constitutes one of the few *jus cogens* or universal crimes that any State can or ought to punish, regardless of whether the piratical acts in question were undertaken by or against the State's own citizens.[44]

5.4.3. *From Piracy to Political Terrorism*

To speak of "aviation piracy," then, would be to speak of a set of crimes that is universally proscribed and therefore, as a legal matter, requires neither a formal treaty nor, presumably, domestic legal instruments in order to be lawfully sanctioned. The "aviation pirate," if that reasoning is applied, would deserve the same treatment, that is, the same forceful application of State police and prosecutorial power, that the high-seas pirate of yesteryear (or even of today[45]) warrants. Such a conceptual overstretching of the notion of piracy, however, does not hold in the face of the significant differences that exist between the pirate and the international criminal (even the international terrorist). As the German jurist Carl Schmitt explained in his 1937 article, *The Concept of Piracy*,[46] piracy is only manifested through apolitical and indiscriminate private-party acts for pecuniary gain (*animus furandi*[47]) beyond the sovereign territory of States.[48] Schmitt went on to question whether piracy remained a viable category in the modern world given the level of financial and techno-logical resources a twenty-first century pirate would need to capture motorized vessels.[49] That is especially true of aviation, given the difficulty (if not impos-sibility) of true craft-to-craft midair interception. It is unlikely that a private group of pirates would have the finances and training to operate aircraft for such

---

[44] *See infra* Section 5.6.3 (discussing the emerging concept of "universal jurisdiction").

[45] Piracy remains a phenomenon in the modern era. "Modern day pirates carry satellite phones, global positioning systems and are armed with automatic weapons, antitank missiles and grenades." ANNEMARIE MIDDLEBURG, PIRACY IN A LEGAL CONTEXT: PROSECUTION OF PIRATES OPERATING OFF THE SOMALI COAST 5 (2011). Middleburg's book includes detailed background on how the Gulf of Aden and east coast of Somalia became the most pirate-infested waters in the world after the failure of the Somali State, and currently account for over 90% of all reported acts of piracy. *See id.* at 17.

[46] After more than seven decades, the article has finally been translated into English. *See* Carl Schmitt, *The Concept of Piracy*, 2 HUMAN. 27 (2011). For the historical background to the piece, see Daniel Heller-Roazen, *Introduction to "The Concept of Piracy,"* 2 HUMAN. 23 (2011).

[47] *Animus furandi* is Latin for "the intention to steal."

[48] *See* Schmitt, *supra* note 46, at 27.

[49] With respect to intercepting commercial and leisure ships, Schmitt appears to have overstated the level of resource support necessary to accomplish these tasks. As noted in the main text, and *supra* note 45, piracy remains a very real phenomenon off the coasts of Asia and Africa even to this day. *See* MIDDLEBURG, *supra* note 45, at 26 (describing how well-equipped Somali pirates can board and subdue poorly defended cargo ships in only 15 minutes).

purposes, which is undoubtedly why "aviation piracy" is more commonly used to refer to the possibility of "pirates" boarding an aircraft prior to takeoff and subsequently assuming control by force. But hijacking is not automatically piracy. Once it is clear that the act is intended for an overtly political purpose or it becomes clear that the hijackers are acting at the behest of a State, the concept of "commercial" piracy fades away and the idea of the terrorist takes center stage. Moreover, acts that may be dubbed "senselessly violent" or driven by subjective hostility, such as a passenger attempting to wrest control of an aircraft because of dissatisfaction with the onboard service, are not acts of piracy (even if undeniably criminal under national rules and international treaty law[50]). As the history of aviation security offenses in the last seventy years attests, few hostile acts against aircraft, including hijacking, fit the standard robbery-based definition of piracy under international law.[51] Most of those acts have been undertaken with a self-consciously political motive, and a number of high-profile incidents have relied directly on the assistance of States, either as willing landing points for a hijacked aircraft or as a safe haven for the perpetrators.[52]

5.4.4. A More Expansive Conception of Piracy?

These observations do not preclude the possibility that a more expansive conception of piracy could take root in public international law. Since the 1958 Geneva Convention on the High Seas,[53] States and international law commentators have attempted to reconstitute piracy in terms of a select number of State-sponsored and nonpecuniary acts.[54] It would be incorrect, however, to assume that these marginal efforts have hardened into a new universal

---

[50] See 49 U.S.C. § 46502 (2006); Convention for the Suppression of Unlawful Seizure of Aircraft art. 1, *opened for signature* Dec. 16, 1970, 860 U.N.T.S. 105 (entered into force Oct. 14, 1971) [hereinafter The Hague Convention]; Convention for the Suppression of Unlawful Acts Against the Safety of Civil Aviation, art. 1, *opened for signature* Sept. 23, 1971, 974 U.N.T.S. 178 (entered into force Jan. 26, 1973) [hereinafter Montreal Convention].

[51] See MIDDLEBURG, *supra* note 45, at 13 (distinguishing piracy from terrorism by noting that the former is motivated by greed and shuns publicity).

[52] A notorious example took place on July 22, 1968, when members of the Popular Front for the Liberation of Palestine (PFLP) hijacked an El Al Israel Airlines flight from Rome to Tel Aviv and redirected the aircraft to the Algerian city of Algiers. Algeria had hostile relations with Israel. Once on the ground, the hijackers released the majority of the passengers but held seven crew members and five passengers hostage for weeks until the Israeli government agreed to an exchange of prisoners; the hijackers were not apprehended.

[53] Convention on the High Seas, *opened for signature* Apr. 29, 1958, 450 U.N.T.S 11 (entered into force Sept. 30, 1962).

[54] In 1970, the International Law Association proposed a definition of piracy that lacked any reference to private pecuniary gain and covered "unlawful seizure or taking control of a vessel

definition of the pirate, unmoored from the early modern conceptualization that is implicated by the *jus cogens* condemnation of piracy.[55] More importantly, as we discuss through the remainder of this chapter, the fact that States have invested negotiating resources and political capital in hammering out a series of treaties condemning aviation security offenses suggests an emerging consensus that politically motivated attacks against or on board aircraft, or against aviation infrastructure such as airports, have emerged as a new category of international crimes requiring a more tailored response.

5.5. THE ROLE OF ICAO IN INTERNATIONAL AVIATION SECURITY

5.5.1. *Background to Multilateral Legal Action*

As noted in Chapter 1, the emergence of cross-border flight raised immediate questions of peace and security with which States continue to wrestle today. The Chicago Convention is clear that civil aviation should be used for peaceful purposes only,[56] although the Convention recognizes that States have broad discretionary powers to restrict foreign flights into and within their territory in cases of emergency.[57] Surprisingly, only a few States undertook the necessary steps to proscribe aviation-related crimes in their domestic legislation, but a series of high-profile incidents in the 1950s and 1960s where perpetrators evaded punishment due to legal technicalities brought about swift legal reform.[58] At the same time that these public miscarriages of justice were transpiring in domestic

through violence, threats of violence, surprise, fraud, or other means." See INT'L L. Ass'N, PIRACY: SEA AND AIR, REPORT OF THE FIFTY-FOURTH CONFERENCE 708 (1970). *See also* Gal Luft & Anne Korin, *Terrorism Goes to Sea*, 83 FOREIGN AFF. 61 (2004) (arguing that pirates are "sea terrorists" and should be treated that way).

[55] The relevance of "private ends" to the definition of *jus cogens* piracy was confirmed in Article 101 of the 1982 United Nations Convention on the Law of the Sea. See UNCLOS, *supra* note 41, art. 101.

[56] *See* Chicago Convention, *supra* note 11, arts. 3, 4, 89. Not only are civil aircraft to be used solely for peaceful purposes, but States are expected to treat them accordingly. This was made explicit in 1984 with the addition of Article 3*bis* to the Chicago Convention that prohibits States from using weapons against civil aircraft while in flight. See Protocol Relating to an Amendment to the Convention on Civil Aviation (May 10, 1984), ICAO Doc. 9436. The Protocol entered into force in 1998 and currently has 143 State parties.

[57] *See* Chicago Convention, *supra* note 11, art. 9(b). States must apply their flight restrictions on a nondiscriminatory basis. *Id.* This provision can be read as one of the few limitations the Convention places on a State's sovereign control over its airspace. *Cf. id.* art. 1. For further discussion of Article 9 of the Chicago Convention as it relates to closure of sovereign airspace, *see supra* Chapter 2, Sections 2.5.3, 2.5.4.

[58] *See, e.g.,* United States v. Cordova, 89 F. Supp. 298 (E.D.N.Y. 1950) (in which the court was found to lack jurisdiction to prosecute because the assault in question occurred over the high seas).

courts, international air carriers increasingly became targets for hostilities from politically motivated actors, more aptly referred to in the current geopolitical context as terrorists.[59] Where these perpetrators could be readily apprehended, either by the State whose citizens or airlines were harmed or by the State where the criminals happened to reside, there was little problem. What quickly became apparent, however, were the disparities in criminal sanctions and jurisdiction that existed across the globe with respect to aviation criminals. States whose airlines or citizens had been victimized by terrorism frequently claimed, as a matter of course, that they possessed the right to punish those responsible, but that right was only as effective as the ability of those States to exercise jurisdiction by taking the offenders into custody. If foreign nationals were able to flee, either to their home States or to a third country willing to harbor them, the possibility that they would be brought to justice was often illusory. Moreover, States lacking robust legal mechanisms to deal with aviation security offenses found that even if they wanted to aid in the capture and punishment of aviation criminals, loopholes in their legal and judicial systems neutralized such assistance.

5.5.2. *ICAO's Treaty Initiatives*

To seek an end to uncertainty at the international level, the ICAO Legal Committee drafted a series of treaties intended to clothe signatory States with jurisdiction over aviation crimes that transpire on board or against aircraft registered in accordance with their national laws.[60] The first of these instruments, the Convention on Offenses and Certain Other Acts Committed on Board Aircraft, better known as the 1963 Tokyo Convention,[61] was followed by the Convention for the Suppression of Unlawful Seizure of Aircraft (The Hague Convention, 1970).[62] To these were added the Convention for the Suppression of Unlawful Acts Against the Safety of Civil Aviation (the 1971 Montreal Convention),[63] as well as two ancillary accords addressing

---

[59] *See, e.g.,* MICHAEL BURLEIGH, BLOOD AND RAGE: A CULTURAL HISTORY OF TERRORISM 153–55 (2009).

[60] Under the Chicago Convention, all aircraft must be registered in a single State and in accordance with that State's national rules. *See* Chicago Convention, *supra* note 11, arts. 17–19; *see also infra* Chapter 8, Part 8.5.

[61] *See* Convention on Offenses and Certain Other Acts Committed on Board Aircraft, *opened for signature* Sept. 14, 1963, 704 U.N.T.S. 219 (entered into force Dec. 4, 1969) [hereinafter Tokyo Convention].

[62] The Hague Convention, *supra* note 50.

[63] Convention for the Suppression of Unlawful Acts Against the Safety of Civil Aviation, *opened for signature* Sept. 23, 1971, 974 U.N.T.S. 178 (entered into force Jan. 26, 1973) [hereinafter Montreal Convention].

airports[64] and plastic explosives,[65] in 1988 and 1991 respectively. Although laudable for seeking to close the jurisdictional gap for aviation crimes, these treaties remain subject to a number of caveats that, in the view of some critics, have impaired their effectiveness. It is not surprising, then, that countries which have routinely been shadowed by the threat of terrorism, particularly the United States, have preferred to rely on an admixture of highly sophisticated law enforcement resources, their own extraterritorial statutes, and diplomatic pressure, to ensure the prosecution of aviation criminals. Moreover, as discussed later in this chapter, the United States led a coalition of States in resorting to measures outside the normal processes of international law to compel countries that prove lax in honoring their obligations under the aviation security crimes treaties to either prosecute or extradite suspected wrongdoers.[66]

5.5.3. *Other ICAO Initiatives: Interfering with Domestic Security Policy?*

Aside from brokering the aviation crimes treaties, ICAO has otherwise limited itself to hortatory declarations against terrorism. In response to the 9/11 attacks, the Organization amended Annex 17 of the Chicago Convention[67] by calling on its State parties to "ensure that principles governing measures designed to safeguard against acts of unlawful interference with international civil aviation are applied to domestic operations to the extent practicable."[68] Not only is

---

[64] Protocol for the Suppression of Unlawful Acts of Violence at Airports Serving International Civil Aviation, *opened for signature* Feb. 24, 1988, 1589 U.N.T.S. 473 (entered into force Aug. 6, 1989) [hereinafter Montreal Protocol].

[65] Convention on the Marking of Plastic Explosives for the Purpose of Detection, *opened for signature* Mar. 1, 1991, 2122 U.N.T.S. 359 (entered into force June 21, 1998) [hereinafter Plastic Explosives Convention].

[66] *See infra* Part 5.10.

[67] Annex 17, Safeguarding International Civil Aviation Against Acts of Unlawful Interference, includes provisions binding contracting States to the Chicago Convention to establish a governmental institution dedicated to aviation security. *See* Chicago Convention, *supra* note 11, Annex 17. The list of requirements and recommendations for security programs is deep and includes creation of secure areas within airports, background checks on security personnel, and so on. Although most of the requirements will seem familiar to international travelers, Article 17 sets substantive *minima*, not maxima. (On the meaning in international law of normative minima, *see supra* Chapter 2, note 37.) Annexes 6, 9, 13, 14, and 18 also contain mandatory security measures: Annex 6, for example, requires a lockable cockpit door, while Annex 14 mandates that airports be fenced in and lit and that security facilities have an independent power source. *See id.* Annexes 6, 14. Annex 9, captioned "Facilitation," seeks to balance passenger convenience, airline efficiency, and aviation security using the hopeful exhortation that aircraft clearance for security purposes must be carried out "in a manner that does not erode the inherent advantage of speed in air transportation." *Id.* Annex 9.

[68] Chicago Convention, *supra* note 11, Annex 17, amend. 10.

this statement on its face an unauthorized interference in domestic security policy, but, for the same reason, its practical effects must be negligible. A similar reproach probably could be made with respect to the various ICAO Assembly Resolutions calling on States to adopt the aviation crimes treaties[69] and "to hold accountable and punish severely those who misuse civil aircraft as weapons of destruction[.]"[70] These Resolutions are without legal effect,[71] even if they do signal the understandably low tolerance ICAO member States have for countries that shelter aviation terrorists or that fail to apprehend, prosecute, or extradite offenders found in their territories.[72]

5.5.4. *Limitations of ICAO*

It remains possible that ICAO could seek a larger role in the ongoing international effort to combat terrorism (including aviation crimes). But the Organization's present "legislative" effectiveness has been put in doubt by its inability to deliver a workable multilateral treaty to mitigate the aviation industry's carbon airprint.[73] Moreover, ICAO's parent institution, the U.N., has itself been unable to steer its membership toward a consensus on either a practical or legal definition of terrorism.[74] For the time being, what progress ICAO has made in finalizing the aviation crimes treaties remains its principal substantive contribution to thwarting aviation security offenses and terrorism.[75] We will turn shortly to consider the ICAO aviation crimes treaties mentioned earlier in this part.[76] But to understand the design of the treaties and also their

---

[69] *See, e.g., Declaration on Misuse of Civil Aircraft as Weapons of Destruction and Other Terrorist Acts Involving Civil Aviation,* ICAO Ass. Res. A33–1 § 5 (2001).

[70] *Id.* at § 4.

[71] This understanding of the legal effect of ICAO Assembly Resolutions is not universally shared. For a thorough discussion of the differing opinions on the subject, see JIEFANG HUANG, AVIATION SAFETY THROUGH THE RULE OF LAW: ICAO'S MECHANISMS AND PRACTICES 175–87 (2009). *See also supra* Chapter 2, note 109.

[72] States have reduced the number of safe harbor jurisdictions available to criminals through a web of bilateral extradition treaties. No State has an extradition treaty with all other States, thereby making safe harbors still available to hijackers.

[73] *See infra* Chapter 6. *See also* Brian F. Havel & Gabriel S. Sanchez, *Toward an International Aviation Emissions Agreement,* 36 HARV. ENVT'L. L. REV. 351, 358–60 (2012) (critically discussing ICAO's efforts in this regard).

[74] *See supra* Section 5.1.2.

[75] Other defects remain unaddressed in the years since the aviation crimes treaties were adopted. One significant lacuna is the absence of any State-backed compensation system for victims of aviation terrorism. Passengers or shippers who suffer damage from hijackings or other aviation crimes must resort to the private Warsaw/Montreal liability systems discussed *infra* in Chapter 7.

[76] In further validation of the concerns expressed in this section, we will also briefly discuss two new aviation security instruments that were concluded under ICAO stewardship in 2010, but which have not yet secured a single member State ratification. *See infra* Section 5.9.3.

limitations, it is first necessary to introduce some concepts of international State jurisdiction that are common to all three instruments.

5.6. EXERCISING STATE CRIMINAL JURISDICTION IN INTERNATIONAL LAW

5.6.1. *State Jurisdiction in Matters of Criminal Law*

Jurisdiction relates to the power of a sovereign State under international law to exercise control over a person, property, or a set of events. Naturally, in framing multilateral treaties to regulate aviation crimes, the drafters needed to ensure that the transborder character of air travel made it possible for a number of contracting States lawfully to assert jurisdiction over those crimes and the responsible offenders using established international law principles.[77] The aviation crimes treaties implicate two of the most fraught aspects of jurisdiction, exercising State judicial power over defendants (judicial jurisdiction) and doing so in matters of criminal law.

5.6.2. *At Least Two States Have Potential Jurisdiction*

The State of registration of the aircraft would normally have jurisdiction over offenses committed on board (or to) the aircraft.[78] All of the aviation crimes treaties endorse that principle, which applies also when offenses are committed over the high seas or over the territory of any other State. But jurisdiction is primarily territorial, and the State of registration may not be the territory where the aircraft departs or lands. The aviation crimes treaties accept, therefore, that a State in which an aircraft or a suspected offender is physically present will be the first State that makes a decision as to whether to initiate its own criminal proceedings or to have the offender transferred to another State that also has a jurisdictional claim (including the State of registration). International law would expect that the landing (i.e., custodial) State should have some other ground upon which to exercise jurisdiction besides mere territoriality: after all,

---

[77] A State could, of course, exercise jurisdiction based on its own domestic rules of jurisdiction, but there is always the risk that other States would not respect such an assertion of authority.

[78] The principle that the flag State has jurisdiction over its aircraft dates back to long-standing maritime practice and is considered a principle of customary international law that has also been codified in international treaties. *See* UNCLOS, *supra* note 41, art. 92. It also appears in many States' domestic statutes. *See, e.g.,* 18 U.S.C. § 7 (2006). In international civil aviation, the State of registration is the flag state. *See* Chicago Convention, *supra* note 11, art. 17; for further discussion of nationality and registration of aircraft, see *infra* Chapter 8, Part 8.5.

although it is true that the State holding the offender will have what is called "enforcement" jurisdiction simply by virtue of its having custody, the circumstances of acquiring custody may be wholly fortuitous (e.g., a forced landing).[79] It would normally be expected, therefore, that some other principle of jurisdiction (e.g., nationality or effect on national security) would also be invoked.[80] Yet none of the aviation crimes treaties actually operates on that presumption. The treaties do provide various well-understood categories of jurisdiction that States may use to justify criminal proceedings in their territories, but they manifestly do not require that the landing State rely on any of these.

5.6.3. *Can a Universal Jurisdiction Be Asserted?*

What, then, is the nature of this enhanced territorial jurisdiction that the landing or custodial State may assert? Is it, arguably, a kind of "universal" jurisdiction, a category that allows any State to exercise jurisdiction over any individual accused of especially offensive crimes against the international community *as a whole*[81] even when that State has no other connection (beyond fortuitous custody of the offender) with the alleged criminal acts? Piracy was the classical example of a general jurisdiction recognized by international law as granted to all States to combat a common scourge.[82] But universal jurisdiction has only recently been theorized as a formal category of judicial power, entirely independent of specific treaty provisions, as part of the evolution of international humanitarian law to include war crimes.[83] In its strongest form, an exercise

---

[79]   Enforcement jurisdiction is the jurisdiction to "induce or compel compliance or to punish noncompliance with its laws or regulations, whether through the courts or by use of executive, administrative, police or other nonjudicial action." RESTATEMENT (THIRD) OF FOREIGN RELATIONS LAW OF THE UNITED STATES § 401(c) (1987). Moreover, a landing State may have no interest in exercising jurisdiction when the aircraft is registered in another State, the offender is from another State, and the victim (if any) is from another State. In those circumstances, it is possible that the offender may enjoy impunity. *See* ICAO Working Paper LC/SC-MOT-WP/1, May 7, 2012, Report of the Rapporteur, Alejandro Piera, Special Sub-Committee of the Legal Committee for the Modernization of the Tokyo Convention Including the Issue of Unruly Passengers, at 13 [hereinafter Piera Report].

[80]   *See infra* Section 5.6.4.

[81]   Thus, the "crime" need not be defined within that State's own penal laws; it is instead part of a register of truly "international" crimes, however that register is defined or created. *See supra* Part 5.4 (discussing piracy as an example of such an international crime).

[82]   Piracy, discussed *supra* in Part 5.4, was the "original universal jurisdiction crime." MIDDLEBURG, *supra* note 45, at 29 (citation omitted). Pirates, as Middleburg points out, "do not discriminate among targets based on nationality and thus endanger the trade of all countries." *Id.* at 30.

[83]   Universal jurisdiction is premised on the notion that crimes such as piracy, slavery, genocide, war crimes, and torture are an affront to humanity and threaten the interests of all States.

of universal jurisdiction may not even require the territorial presence of an offender.[84] Nevertheless, a species of treaty-based State jurisdiction, resting solely on a State's custodial power over an offender, was clearly envisaged by the aviation crimes treaties discussed in this chapter. In truth, a State's jurisdiction over physically present offenders that is implied in the aviation crimes treaties is ultimately State-based rather than "universal," because it looks for its exercise to the internal processes of each State's judicial jurisdiction (and penal laws[85]) rather than to some overarching common jurisdiction of States. For that reason, the full force of the term "universal jurisdiction" has been withheld from these and similar treaties providing for the suppression of various hostile acts against the international community;[86] the term "quasi-universal jurisdiction" may be preferred.[87] Finally, some elements of the regime of treaty-based aviation crimes, notably hijacking, have arguably become international

Unfortunately, governments frequently collude in the commission of these crimes, and colluding governments are unlikely to prosecute. Universal jurisdiction vests all States with the authority to prosecute such crimes, and ideally also provides a deterrent against their commission. In 2005, the Belgian authorities used the (now-repealed) Belgian law on universal jurisdiction to charge Hissène Habré, the former president of Chad, with crimes against humanity and torture. Habré remains in exile in Senegal, which has refused to extradite him to Belgium. At the behest of the International Court of Justice (ICJ), Senegal has recently agreed to form a special court to try Habré.

[84] But such a formidable extension of jurisdiction will typically depend on national rather than international law. Belgium's law of universal jurisdiction, which was adopted in 1993, permitted victims to file complaints for atrocities committed abroad. However, the law was repealed in 2003 and is now reconfigured to require territorial presence or national affiliation on the part of potential defendants. In 2005, the Institut de Droit International rejected any exercise of universal jurisdiction, apart from acts of investigation and requests for extradition, without the territorial presence of the offender. *See* Institute of International Law, Krakow Session – 2005, Resolution of the Seventeenth Commission, Universal Criminal Jurisdiction with Regard to the Crime of Genocide, Crimes Against Humanity and War Crimes (Aug. 26, 2005).

[85] Under the aviation crimes and similar treaties, States are expected to adopt the specified offenses into their national criminal directories, or (as in the Tokyo Convention, for example) to accept the treaty's recitation of an offense as a "default" provision of their national criminal code.

[86] Among these other treaties are the Convention Against Torture and Other Cruel, Inhuman or Degrading Treatment or Punishment, Dec. 10, 1984, 1465 U.N.T.S. 85 (entered into force Jun. 26, 1987); the Convention on the Prevention and Punishment of Crimes Against Internationally Protected Persons, Dec. 14, 1973, 1035 U.N.T.S. 167 (entered into force Feb. 20, 1977); and the International Convention Against the Taking of Hostages, Dec. 17, 1979, 1316 U.N.T.S. 205 (entered into force Jun. 3, 1983).

[87] "More correct is the approach that in such circumstances international law recognizes that domestic legal orders may validly establish and exercise jurisdiction over the alleged offenders." MALCOLM N. SHAW, INTERNATIONAL LAW 673 (6th ed. 2008). Thus, Shaw describes the kind of jurisdiction envisaged in codifications like the aviation crimes treaties as "quasi-universal," or, in the language of some members of the ICJ, "the jurisdiction to establish territorial jurisdiction over persons for extraterritorial events." *Id.* at 674 (citation omitted).

crimes "of virtually universal jurisdiction in practice."[88] The same may soon be said with respect to the crime of international terrorism (whether against aircraft or in other contexts).[89]

5.6.4. *Alternative Jurisdictional Bases*

Besides the robustness of quasi-universal jurisdiction based on territorial or custodial power, the aviation crimes treaties allow States a series of alternative jurisdictional bases that will be noted in our discussion.[90] Because aircraft have their own "nationality," the State of registration of the aircraft, regardless of the nationality of the offender, has a nonexclusive jurisdictional claim that is antecedent to (but recognized by) the aviation crimes treaties and is grounded in Article 17 of the Chicago Convention.[91] But individuals, too, have their own nationality,[92] and States whose nationals are accused of offenses under the aviation crimes treaties have a claim to judicial criminal jurisdiction over their nationals under international law even if the alleged offense took place outside the State of the accused's nationality. States tend to claim that kind of jurisdiction only over the most serious crimes, otherwise deferring to the prosecuting authorities of the territorial State. Other premises for international judicial jurisdiction feature in the aviation crimes treaties, even though their international acceptance has been less secure. No doubt the "terrorist" stamp of the treaties eased international concerns about these more robust claims of jurisdiction. The "passive personality" principle, for example, allows a State to claim jurisdiction to try a foreign individual for offenses committed outside its territory that have affected or will affect that State's own nationals.[93] Relatedly, the "protective" principle would give a State the right to exercise judicial jurisdiction over aliens

---

[88]   *Id.* at 678.

[89]   *Id.*

[90]   The territorial State, of course, could select one of these alternative jurisdictional bases also if it is available.

[91]   *See supra* text accompanying note 78.

[92]   International law provides no coherent definition of an individual's "nationality" and generally leaves the matter to be decided under the domestic rules of States. *See* SHAW, *supra* note 87, at 660.

[93]   The passive personality principle has been traditionally opposed by the United States but has increasingly gained international acceptance, at least with regard to terrorist acts. *See* Geoffrey R. Watson, *The Passive Personality Principle*, 28 TEX. INT'L L.J. 1 (1993); *see also infra* Section 5.10.3. Note that, for example, Article 5 of the 1979 International Convention Against the Taking of Hostages, *see supra* note 86, includes the State of nationality of the hostages in the list of States with a valid criminal jurisdictional claim over hostage-takers.

located abroad who have committed offenses that are deemed to jeopardize that State's vital security interests.[94]

5.6.5. *Responsibility of the Landing or Custodial State: To Prosecute or Extradite?*

But if States do have these other valid premises to exercise jurisdiction, how can they do so if the custodial or landing State maintains power over the physical being of the offender? As we will see, all of the aviation crimes treaties reference the principle of "prosecute or extradite" (the equivalent Latin expression, widely used, is *aut dedere aut judicare*).[95] That principle is intended to impose a stark choice on a State that has physical power over the offender. That State must *prosecute*, that is, exercise jurisdiction by instituting criminal proceedings (if applicable, using the quasi-universal jurisdiction described earlier), or *extradite*, dispatching the offender to a requesting State. The State that requests extradition must establish its own jurisdiction under one or more of the specific categories enumerated in each treaty. All of the aviation crimes treaties provide for the offenses created under the treaty (or, where relevant, by national penal laws) to be treated as extraditable offenses in any bilateral extradition treaties concluded between the State parties. But a shared weakness of the aviation crimes treaties, as we will discuss, is that any duty to extradite appears always to be subordinated to contrary domestic laws.[96]

---

[94] *See infra* Section 5.10.3.

[95] M. Cherif Bassiouni has argued that *aut dedere aut judicare* is a principle of customary international law: "The principle is more than an ordinary norm of international law. It is a condition for the effective repression of offenses which are universally condemned. In large part, the rules prohibiting these offenses constitute *jus cogens* norms: they are rules of paramount importance for world public order, and cannot be set aside or modified in a subsequent treaty." M. Cherif Bassiouni & Edward M. Wise, Aut Dedere Aut Judicare: The Duty to Extradite or Prosecute in International Law 24–25 (1995).

[96] A novel approach to the problem of *aut dedere aut judicare* was introduced in the criminal cases that arose out of the explosion and crash of a Pan Am 747 aircraft over the Scottish village of Lockerbie in December 1988. Libya claimed that its right to prosecute the two Libyan nationals accused of planting the bombs responsible for the explosion outweighed its obligation to extradite the defendants. The United States and the U.K. objected, arguing that because the Libyan government was suspected of involvement in the bombing, Libya had to extradite the accused parties to ensure an effective and fair prosecution. A 10-year stalemate ensued before the United States, the U.K., and Libya reached an agreement to hold a trial of the principal defendants in the Netherlands (a neutral territory) and in accordance with Scottish law. *See* Michael Plachta, *The Lockerbie Case: The Role of the Security Council in Enforcing the Principle* Aut Dedere Aut Judicare, 12 Eur. J. Int'l L. 125 (2001) (suggesting that the Lockerbie case added a third alternative, *aut transferere*, giving the requested State an option involving "delivery" of the accused to a third State).

5.7. THE TOKYO CONVENTION (1963)

5.7.1. *Summary of the Tokyo Convention*

The Tokyo Convention, which finally entered into force at the end of 1969,[97] was an important, but ultimately inadequate, vehicle to address aviation security offenses. The treaty focuses on penal offenses and other acts that endanger the safety or good order and discipline on board an aircraft while the aircraft is "in flight."[98] Adopting a somewhat martial tone, Tokyo bestows upon the pilot, designated as *commander* of the aircraft, near-plenary powers to restore order. Accompanying that "microjurisdiction" of the pilot, the treaty sets forth the rights and duties of the State parties in exercising jurisdiction over and punishing offenders. To prevent impunity for aviation crimes because of defective national laws, the Tokyo Convention has also been understood to create a specific category of internationally recognized strict liability crimes.[99] In other words, even a signatory State lacking domestic criminal code provisions on crimes on board aircraft engaged in international air service can rely on Tokyo to fill the gap.[100] This is true as well with respect to jurisdiction. In the years leading up to Tokyo's ratification, a number of States' courts had found that although certain offenses on board aircraft constituted a substantive crime under their national penal laws, a jurisdictional black hole was opened once the aircraft on which the crime took place had departed their sovereign airspace.

5.7.2. *Offenses Under and Application of the Tokyo Convention*

The Tokyo Convention, as noted, applies to "acts which, whether or not they are offenses [under a signatory's penal code], may or do jeopardize the safety

---

[97] As of 2012, 185 States have ratified the Convention.

[98] *See* Tokyo Convention, *supra* note 61, art.1(2). The Convention also provides for its application when the aircraft is "on the surface of the high seas or . . . any other area outside the territory of any State." *Id.*

[99] The offenses contained in the Tokyo Convention, like those listed in The Hague and Montreal aviation security treaties, *infra*, are strict liability offenses; no *mens rea* requirement is attached. Thus, it is unnecessary for the prosecuting authorities to inquire into the defendant's mental state, intentions, or motivations in committing the prohibited actions; mere commission of the acts barred by the treaty is sufficient.

[100] This statement presupposes that the State in question is not obligated under its constitutional law to create implementing legislation for the treaty. Moreover, a State that fails to make the treaty effective under its national criminal law would still be obligated, as a matter of international law, to do so. Even so, as discussed *infra* Section 5.10.1, the Tokyo Convention, along with the other aviation crimes treaties, lacks a strong compliance mechanism.

of the aircraft or of persons or property therein or which jeopardize good order and discipline on board."[101] Although some have argued to the contrary, this provision of the Convention does not function as a limitation on the scope of covered offenses on board (or against) aircraft or their passengers. The Convention expressly states that it also applies to "offenses against penal law," interpreted to mean the criminal codes of the respective signatories.[102] What that means in practice is that a State with a directory of aviation security offenses already included in its national laws can rely on those offenses in exercising the jurisdictional powers granted under Tokyo. Given that the express purpose of the treaty is to prevent and punish aviation crimes, it would make little sense to read the text as imposing a ceiling, rather than a baseline, on the range of crimes that States can use in pursuing and prosecuting offenders. But the Convention is nevertheless not unlimited in its scope. Its substantive criminal and jurisdictional provisions only apply to "offenses committed or acts done by a person on board any aircraft registered in a contracting State, while that aircraft is in flight or on the surface of the high seas or of any other area outside the territory of any State."[103] Interestingly, the Convention does not restrict its coverage to *international* flights. In other words, it is just as applicable to a Delta Air Lines domestic flight from Atlanta to Los Angeles as it is to a United transcontinental flight from Chicago to London so long as its key temporal condition is satisfied, that is, that the aircraft is "in flight."[104] That compact phrase is unpacked in Article 1(3) of the Convention to mean the period of time "from the moment when power is applied for the purpose of takeoff until the moment when the landing run ends."[105] Until and after that stretch of time, any offenses that take place on board the aircraft

---

[101] Tokyo Convention, *supra* note 61, art. 1(b). It is unclear how much scope can be attached to the phrase "acts which . . . jeopardize good order or discipline on board," but arguably it might cover certain instances of so-called air rage. *See infra* note 217.

[102] *Id.* art. 1(a). *See* Terry Richard Kane, *Prosecuting International Terrorists in United States Courts: Gaining the Jurisdictional Threshold*, 12 YALE J. INT'L L. 294, 301 (1987).

[103] Tokyo Convention, *supra* note 61, art. 1(2).

[104] The Convention's drafters considered restricting the Convention's scope so that it would only apply in situations in which the aircraft was operating outside the territorial airspace of the State of registration, but worried that the additional language and qualifications required to accurately define the Convention's scope were making the clause confusing and opted for the simplified "in flight" language. The drafters concluded that the Convention posed little threat to the domestic sovereignty of contracting States because the text defined offenses according to the penal laws of the contracting States, the same laws that would be in effect on purely domestic flights. *See* Robert P. Boyle & Roy Pulsifer, *The Tokyo Convention on Offenses and Certain Other Acts Committed On Board Aircraft*, 30 J. AIR L. & COM. 305, 332 (1964).

[105] Tokyo Convention, *supra* note 61, art. 1(3). But note how this definition changed (and expanded) in later treaties, see *infra* in main text.

remain subject exclusively to the local laws of the State in which the aircraft is located.[106]

5.7.3. *Jurisdiction Under the Tokyo Convention*

Like its broadly painted definition of substantive offenses, the Tokyo Convention's jurisdictional provisions are an adjunct to, rather than a replacement for, State parties' domestic jurisdictional rules.[107] According to Article 3(1), an aircraft's State of registration has primary jurisdiction over any criminal offenses that take place on board.[108] But, under Article 4, any State party to the Convention is authorized in any of the following situations to intercept an aircraft in flight in order to exercise jurisdiction over an offense that has taken place on board:[109] when the offense has an "effect" in the territory of that State, or has been perpetrated by or against a national of that State, or jeopardizes that State's security,[110] or breaches that State's air navigation regulations,[111] or when that State's exercise of its jurisdiction over the offense is necessary to fulfill its obligations under a separate multilateral treaty.[112] Although these five circumstances carry the appearance of setting bounds to interference by States other

---

[106] Offenses taking place on an aircraft when the aircraft is not "in flight" are outside the scope of the Tokyo Convention, and would thus be governed by the same domestic and international rules governing criminal acts unrelated to aviation. The State of registration is only important for acts covered by the Convention, that is, those committed "in flight." Interestingly, the scope is narrower (and more clearly defined) than that of the application of the Warsaw and Montreal conventions on airline passenger and cargo liability (*see infra* Chapter 7), which in some cases has been interpreted to extend to escalators and other areas of airports that are part of the boarding or disembarkation process.

[107] *See id.* art. 3(3) (stating that nothing in the Convention "exclude[s] any criminal jurisdiction exercised in accordance with national law").

[108] See Tokyo Convention, *supra* note 61, art. 3(1).

[109] *See id.* art. 4.

[110] The first three justifications for intervention are part and parcel of the customary international law right of self-defense. Although a treaty may modify any customary international law rule except *jus cogens* norms, States have a powerful interest in maintaining their territorial integrity and security, an interest that they were unwilling to cede under the Tokyo Convention.

[111] This ground of jurisdiction is consistent with Article 12 of the Chicago Convention, which requires each contracting State "to insure that every aircraft flying over or maneuvering within its territory ... shall comply with the rules and regulations ... there in force." Additionally, Article 12 requires each contracting State "to insure the prosecution of all persons violating the regulations applicable." Chicago Convention, *supra* note 11, art. 12.

[112] Notably, this justification cannot be triggered in pursuit of obligations under a *bilateral* treaty. However, the Tokyo Convention does not expressly define the minimum number of States required to render a treaty "multilateral." Could Canada, Mexico, and the United States, for instance, sign a pact pledging to interfere with any aircraft over any of their territories where a criminal offense has taken place even if the aircraft were registered in, say, Germany? That possibility remains open, at least theoretically, under the text of the Tokyo Convention.

than the State of aircraft registration, it is difficult to imagine a scenario where at least one of the five would not be triggered.[113] Even so, the treaty does mandate that State parties "take all appropriate measures to restore control of the aircraft to its lawful commander or to preserve [the commander's] control of the aircraft."[114] In situations where an aircraft commander is compelled to land in the territory of a State party other than the one of the aircraft's State of registration, the landing State must allow the commander to disembark "any person who [the commander] has reasonable grounds to believe has committed, or is about to commit," an offense on board the aircraft.[115] The aircraft commander is also empowered to take custody of such a person and to deliver that person to the authorities of the State in which the aircraft lands if the commander has "reasonable grounds" to believe that the person "has committed on board the aircraft an act which, in [the commander's] opinion, is a serious offense according to the penal law of the State of registration of the aircraft."[116] The latter requirement appears to establish a sufficient premise under the Convention for activating certain custodial and notification duties of the landing State. Even if the act is not an offense under the penal law of the landing State, that State must still accept custody over the perpetrator and provide immediate notification of that fact to the State where the aircraft is registered, along with the home State of the detainee as well as any other interested State that the landing State believes ought to be apprised of the situation.[117] The landing State must also provide notification to those other States as to whether it intends to "exercise jurisdiction" over the detainee, in other words, as to whether it will prosecute the offender under its penal laws[118]

---

[113] Moreover, the five circumstances are in obvious tension with the right of States to set conditions on the "first freedom" overflight privilege in accordance with the Two Freedoms Agreement (*see supra* Chapter 3, Section 3.2.2). Nevertheless, Article 30 of the Vienna Convention on the Law of Treaties resolves any incompatibility between an earlier treaty and a later inconsistent treaty in favor of the latter. *See* Vienna Convention on the Law of Treaties art. 30(3), *opened for signature* May 23, 1969, 1155 U.N.T.S. 331 (entered into force Jan. 27, 1980). Given that most modern ASAs acknowledge that the parties will act in conformity with Tokyo, this is now more a historical rather than a current problem.

[114] Tokyo Convention, *supra* note 61, art. 11(1).

[115] *Id.* art. 8(1); *see also id.* art. 12. The issue of whether the passenger has committed an offense can become more complicated for passenger disturbances that do not violate the penal law of a given territory. *See* William P. Schwab, *Air Rage: Screaming for International Uniformity*, 14 Transnat'l Law. 401, 414 (2001). The problem of air rage will be discussed briefly later in this chapter: *see infra* Section 5.11.5.

[116] *Id.* art. 9(1); *see also id.* art. 13(1).

[117] *See id.* art. 13(5). Attendant to this provision is the requirement that the landing State must perform an initial inquiry into the alleged offense and notify the results to the various referenced States. *See id.* art. 13(4).

[118] This will include, as we have seen, the offenses established directly by the Convention. *See supra* Section 5.7.2.

or institute extradition proceedings to remove him or her for trial to the State of registration of the aircraft or to some other State.[119] The landing State thus becomes a third State of concurrent jurisdiction under the treaty along with the State of registration and any State empowered to intercept an aircraft under one or more of the five conditions established in Article 4. Notably, the ICAO drafting conferences were unable to impose any explicit order of priority among the States of concurrent jurisdiction. By default, therefore, the landing State's physical control, along with its discretion to prosecute or allow extradition, gives that State effective, if not actual, priority under the Convention.[120]

5.7.4. *Achilles Heels of the Tokyo Convention: No Mandatory Extradition and the Freedom Fighter Exception*

Unfortunately, the apparent strength of the foregoing sequence of jurisdictional provisions is sapped by other provisions in the treaty. First, although Article 16(1) treats onboard offenses as having been committed in the State of registration of the aircraft as well as in the "place in which they have occurred,"[121] Article 16(2) provides that nothing in the treaty should be understood as obliging any State party to extradite an offender.[122] In other words, the Tokyo Convention does not compulsorily apply the public international law principle of *aut dedere aut judicare* ("extradite or prosecute").[123] Where a Canadian national commits a crime on board a United flight that lands in Mexico City, the Mexican Government is not required *under the Tokyo*

---

[119] Although the treaty provides no time frame for these actions, it does specify that the landing State is only to hold an alleged offender for the time necessary to bring formal criminal charges or institute extradition proceedings. *See* Tokyo Convention, *supra* note 61, art. 13(2). Note, however, that the landing State may refuse entirely to admit the disembarked offender, in which case it is obligated under Article 14(1) to remit that person to his or her State of nationality or permanent residence or to the State in which that person began his or her journey. *See id.* art. 14(1). If the wrongdoer is a national or permanent resident of the landing State, no such obligations exist, but it is unclear from the text what the landing State should do in those circumstances.

[120] *See* Abraham Abramovsky, *Multilateral Conventions for the Suppression of Unlawful Seizure and Interference with Aircraft Part 1: The Hague Convention*, 13 COLUM. J. TRANSNAT'L. L. 381, 396 (1974). *See also supra* note 96 (where the Lockerbie case illustrates the same point). Note that there will be a diplomatic conference in Montreal in March 2014 to consider once again the jurisdiction of the landing State under the Tokyo Convention. The conference will also consider the status and functions of in-flight security officers under the Convention.

[121] Tokyo Convention, *supra* note 61, art. 16(1). That might be the landing or custodial State, or some other third State, or over the high seas.

[122] *See* Tokyo Convention, *supra* note 61, art. 16(2).

[123] *See supra* Section 5.6.5.

Convention to hand over the perpetrator to U.S. or Canadian authorities, even if Mexico itself decides to forego prosecution.[124] More problematically, the Tokyo Convention is subverted by a second Achilles heel: no State is required to prosecute or extradite an offender whose actions were undertaken for a political purpose.[125] The so-called freedom fighter exception emerged during the Convention's lengthy gestation in response to the political and social upheaval in the former colonial territories of many European powers. The exception gives automatic cover for any State that offers a safe haven to aviation criminals with whom it finds itself in sympathy. Because the treaty provides such broad opt-outs, States can still claim to be acting in good faith under its provisions even if they refrain from any action to apprehend, prosecute, or extradite those accused of crimes against aviation.

5.7.5. *Powers of the Aircraft Commander Under the Tokyo Convention*

For all of its shortcomings with respect to jurisdiction and extradition, the Tokyo Convention does equip the aircraft commander (and any crew or passengers recruited by the commander) with a strong package of powers for apprehension of aviation criminals and legal protection for actions taken to do so. Unlike the substantive and jurisdictional provisions of the Convention, which as we have seen apply only when an aircraft is powered-up until its landing run ends,[126] the commander's powers are activated "at any time from the moment when [the aircraft's] external doors are closed following embarkation until the moment when any such door is opened for disembarkation."[127] This amplified conception of when the aircraft is "in flight" eliminates the possibility of an anarchic zone in which the aircraft, battened down at its points of takeoff or landing and sealed-off from police authorities on the ground, is susceptible to criminal activity or a terrorist attack while the commander remains incapable (as a matter of law) of deploying his or her otherwise abundant powers to stop the offenders. Where the commander

---

[124] But there may be a preexisting *bilateral* extradition treaty that covers such offenses.

[125] *See* Tokyo Convention, *supra* note 61, art. 2 ("Without prejudice to the provisions of Article 4 and except when the safety of the aircraft or of persons or property on board so requires, no provision of this Convention shall be interpreted as authorizing or requiring any action in respect of offenses against penal laws of a political nature or those based on racial or religious discrimination.").

[126] *See id.* art. 1(2)–(3).

[127] *Id.* art. 5. The Article further provides that "[i]n case of a forced landing," the aircraft commander's powers and protections "shall continue to apply with respect to offenses and acts committed on board until competent authorities of a State take over the responsibility for the aircraft and for the persons and property on board."

is compelled to remove passengers from the flight, he or she is required to provide as much advance notice as practicable to the landing State.[128] In addition, the commander "shall furnish the authorities to whom any suspected offender is delivered . . . with evidence and information which, under the law of the State of registration of the aircraft, are lawfully in his [or her] possession."[129] Once the aircraft is "in flight" for the purposes of the commander's powers, the commander may – as noted above – restrain and disembark any passengers he or she reasonably believes to have committed or are about to commit an offense on board.[130] The commander may also "require or authorize the assistance of other crew members and may request or authorize, *but not require*, the assistance of passengers to restrain any" offender or potential offender.[131] Enormous civil, and even criminal, liability might attach to the exercise of the commander's virtually plenary authority to restrain as well as to the assistance rendered by passengers and crew in that effort. It is unsurprising, therefore, that the Convention overlays the commander's authority with an equally robust grant of legal protection against liability. Neither the aircraft commander, nor any person recruited by the commander to subdue an aviation criminal, nor the owner of the aircraft, nor the airline operating the flight, "shall be held responsible in any proceeding on account of the treatment undergone by the person against whom the actions were taken."[132] As such, the commander and his or her chosen auxiliaries are inoculated against any legal sanction so long as their actions flow from the commander's "reasonable" belief in an actual

---

[128] *See id.* art. 9(2). Although not explicitly mentioned in the Convention, the commander implicitly has some degree of power over the jurisdiction to which a restrained passenger will be assigned, should the commander deem it necessary to land before reaching the final destination in order to unload the offender.

[129] *Id.* art. 9(3).

[130] *See id.* art. 6(1).

[131] *Id.* art. 6(1)–(2) (emphasis added). Also note that Article 6(2) invests crew members and passengers directly with authority to take "preventive measures," provided that they act with "reasonable grounds," and even if they lack authorization from the commander. The broad language of Article 6(2) grants passengers and crew members almost as much authority as the commander in a true emergency situation. The primary difference is that the authority of passengers or crew to act is contingent upon their possessing a reasonable belief that such action is "immediately necessary," and they can only act to protect the safety of the aircraft, persons, or property. The commander, on the other hand, can also take measures to "maintain good order and discipline" in order to enable delivery of the offender to the competent authorities.

[132] *Id.* art. 10. This legal protection also applies to passengers and crew acting without the commander's authorization under the authority of Article 6(2). *See supra* note 119 and accompanying text. Article 10 also extends legal protection to "the person on whose behalf the flight was performed," which presumably would extend coverage to third parties connected to the flight through wet leases, code-shares, or other common business arrangements.

or impending threat.[133] This blanket impunity may appear overly permissive, even dangerous, although its justification may be found in the fact that the sealed aircraft becomes a *de facto* "state of nature."[134] Given the risk to life because of criminal or other disorderly activity on board aircraft, normal degrees of toleration for questionable behavior are understandably lower and the demand for swift, decisive action necessarily higher.[135] The insulating provisions of Tokyo diminish the prospect that a cost-benefit analysis will undermine the strongest intervention to restrain onboard criminality.

5.8. THE HAGUE CONVENTION (1970)

5.8.1. *Context of The Hague Convention*

Less than a year after the Tokyo Convention entered into force, ICAO gathered its member States in the Dutch capital to sign a new treaty addressing the proliferation of aircraft hijackings that had been occurring during the 1960s.[136] Unlike aviation crimes contemplated under Tokyo, hijacking – when successfully executed – entails gaining control of the aircraft from the commander and redirecting the flight's destination, often to States sympathetic to the hijackers' purposes.[137] Because Tokyo provides both an express right *not* to extradite offenders as well as a "freedom fighter" escape clause,

---

[133] Or, in the case of passengers or crew acting on their own, as long as their actions flow from their own possession of "reasonable grounds to believe" that the actions are "immediately necessary" to protect the aircraft or its contents. Tokyo Convention, *supra* note 61, art. 6(2); *see also supra* note 131.

[134] *See* Lon L. Fuller, *The Case of the Speluncean Explorers*, 62 HARV. L. REV. 616, 621 (1949).

[135] The common experience of air passengers, flying together for several hours in a pressurized aircraft, greatly increases "the purely statistical chances of abnormal behaviour." J. Richard Orme Wilberforce, *Crime in Aircraft*, 67 J. ROYAL AERONAUTICAL SOC'Y 175 (1963).

[136] In 1968 alone, there were 30 successful hijackings of commercial airliners, 17 of which had U.S. registration. In 1969, there were 82 hijackings, more than twice the number between 1947 and 1967. The hijackers most active as The Hague Convention was being negotiated were U.S. radicals redirecting flights to Havana, Cuba, for political purposes or to escape punishment for prior criminal acts, and Palestinians using hijacking as a political weapon to publicize their cause. With improved airport security and new laws and international agreements, as well as shifts in motivation from criminal/pecuniary to terrorism, hijackings declined substantially after 1980 but received worldwide attention once again with the 9/11 attacks. *But see infra* Chapter 7, note 206 (emphasizing that 9/11 was not an incident governed by international law).

[137] The Tokyo Convention does have a brief chapter on "[u]nlawful seizure of aircraft," but omits effective countermeasures, specifying only that States "shall take all appropriate measures to restore control of the aircraft to its lawful commander." Tokyo Convention, *supra* note 61, ch. IV, art. 11. The Hague Convention was intended to provide the legal support for States to punish hijacking.

ICAO hoped that its new treaty, The Hague Convention,[138] could further close the jurisdictional gap and eliminate safe havens for terrorists. This was not to be, however.

5.8.2. *The Hijacking Offense Under The Hague Convention*

Under Article 1 of The Hague Convention, it is an offense for any individual on board an aircraft, through either threat or use of force or by any other form of intimidation, to seize or exercise control of an aircraft or to attempt to do so while it is in flight.[139] The Convention also provides for accomplice liability and requires its signatories to make the offense punishable and to subject hijacking offenders to "severe penalties" under their national criminal codes.[140] No further guidance appears on what constitutes "severe penalties." Given major distinctions among States in their understanding of the purposes of criminal sanctions, it would have been fruitless for negotiators to insist on a specific benchmark. States are also required to notify ICAO of any hijackings that have occurred and any responsive measures taken.[141] Notably, The Hague Convention's jurisdiction *ratione loci*[142] is somewhat narrower than that of the Tokyo Convention. Article 3(3) states that the provisions of The Hague Convention "shall apply only if the place of take-off or the place of actual landing of the aircraft on board which the offense [of hijacking] is committed is situated outside the territory of the State of registration of that aircraft; it shall be immaterial whether the aircraft is engaged in an international or domestic flight."[143] In other words, where a United Airlines aircraft (registered in the United States) bound for London from Chicago is hijacked, but ultimately

---

[138] *See* The Hague Convention, *supra* note 50. The Hague Convention currently has 185 ratifications.

[139] The Hague Convention, *supra* note 50, art. 1. The Hague Convention dispenses with Tokyo's two-tiered definition of "in flight," opting to use only the broader conceptualization applied for the purposes of the aircraft commander powers and protections under Article 5 of that treaty. *See supra* note 127; *see* The Hague Convention, *supra* note 50, art. 3(1).

[140] *See* The Hague Convention, *supra* note 50, arts. 1(a) & 2. Although The Hague Convention leaves it to the contracting States to determine the appropriate punishment for hijacking, it differs from the Tokyo Convention by actually defining the offense. The Tokyo Convention only applies to acts that violate national penal codes, but suffers from the lack of statutory prohibitions against hijacking in many contracting States (although, as we observed, *supra* Section 5.7.2, the Tokyo Convention is available to serve as a "default" repository of criminal offenses where States otherwise lack local criminal statutes). Article 1 of The Hague Convention corrects this deficiency.

[141] *See id.* art. 11.

[142] The phrase is Latin for jurisdiction by reason of the place, that is, territorial jurisdiction.

[143] The Hague Convention, *supra* note 50, art. 3(3).

touches down in Newark, New Jersey, only U.S. law applies.[144] But if the same sequence of events happens to a flight operated by British Airways (registered in the U.K.), the terms of the Convention would unambiguously be in force as both the place of takeoff and place of actual landing would be outside the territory of the State of registration.

5.8.3. *Jurisdiction Under The Hague Convention*

Like Tokyo, The Hague Convention attempts to shore up any jurisdictional deficiencies that might exist at the international level. Under Article 4, a State party is required to establish jurisdiction over a hijacking offense in three situations: when the offense takes place on board aircraft registered within its territory; when the aircraft on which the offense occurred lands in its territory and the offender is still on board; or – more technically – "when the offense is committed on board an aircraft leased without crew to a lessee who has his [or her] principal place of business or, if [the] lessee has no such place of business, his [or her] permanent residence, in that State."[145] The second paragraph of Article 4 invests a broad jurisdiction *ratione personae*[146] in any State where the offender "is present in its territory" and it does not extradite that person pursuant to the Convention to any of the States mentioned in paragraph 1.[147] In other words, a third State that is otherwise not directly affected by an offense, because it is neither the State of registration of a hijacked aircraft nor the landing State for the aircraft with the offender still on board, is obligated still to apprehend hijackers who happen to be found within its territory. Article 6 furnishes a State in which an offender is present with discretion to determine whether taking custody is warranted.[148] Once the State takes custody, however, "the custody ... may only be continued for such time as is necessary to enable any criminal or extradition proceedings to be instituted."[149] Read on its own, Article 7 of the Convention appears to embrace *aut dedere aut judicare*, because if the offender is not extradited the State is

---

[144] This point is implicitly reaffirmed by Article 4(3), which states that nothing in The Hague Convention excludes the exercise of criminal jurisdiction in accordance with signatories' national laws. The Hague Convention, *supra* note 50, art. 4(3).

[145] The Hague Convention, *supra* note 50, art. 4(1). The type of lease described in Article 4 is known as a "dry" lease. The Convention adds a jurisdictional basis for the State of the lessee because in the case of a dry lease, the lessee is the operator of the aircraft and supplies the crew, making it likely that the lessee's home State will have a stronger connection to the incident than the State in which the aircraft is registered.

[146] The phrase is Latin for jurisdiction by reason of the person, that is, personal jurisdiction.

[147] The Hague Convention, *supra* note 50, art. 4(2).

[148] *See id.* art. 6(1).

[149] *Id.*

"obliged, without exception whatsoever and whether or not the offense was committed in its territory, to submit the case to its competent authorities for the purpose of prosecution."[150] But, as with Tokyo, the apparent muscularity of The Hague Convention's jurisdictional regime becomes considerably less impressive when the question of whether to extradite arises.

5.8.4. *Undermining The Hague Convention's Strong Extradition Provisions*

Article 8 does open with two strongly worded provisions on extradition. It declares generally that the offense of hijacking is extraditable and should be included in every extradition treaty between State parties to the Convention.[151] It goes on to provide that for a State where a treaty is a condition precedent for extradition but no such bilateral treaty exists, the Convention itself may serve as the legal basis for extradition.[152] Extradition in both cases, however, remains subject to either the conditions of the relevant extradition treaty or to "the other conditions provided by the law of the requested State."[153] Similarly, a State that does *not* make extradition conditional on a treaty is obligated to recognize hijacking as an extraditable offense only "subject to the conditions provided by" its internal extradition rules.[154] In practice, the deference to national rules shown in these provisions enfeebles the Convention's seemingly strong mandate of *aut dedere aut judicare*. Although there is no "freedom fighter" exception like the one enshrined in the Tokyo Convention, a State party could embed such an exception in its domestic laws and use it to block an extradition request under either The Hague Convention or a bilateral extradition treaty.[155] That latitude, while tucked into the corners of the Convention, is effectively as open-ended as the explicit text of Tokyo. Finally, because State

---

[150] The Hague Convention, *supra* note 50, art. 7. Further, "[t]hose authorities shall take their decision in the same manner as in the case of any ordinary offense of a serious nature under the law of that State." *Id.*

[151] *See id.* art. 8.

[152] *See id.* art. 8(2). The Convention thus makes itself the basis for extradition in the absence of a bilateral treaty between the relevant States. *See* Christopher C. Joyner, *International Extradition and Global Terrorism: Bringing International Criminals to Justice*, 25 Loy. L.A. Int'l & Comp. L. Rev. 493, 510–12 (2003).

[153] The Hague Convention, *supra* note 50, art. 8(2). Common national law or treaty conditions that weaken the Convention's extradition rules include exceptions for crimes considered to be "political offenses" and bars against the extradition of nationals. *See* Joyner, *supra* note 152, at 511.

[154] The Hague Convention, *supra* note 50, art. 8(3).

[155] Thus, there is nothing in the Convention to prevent a State from granting political asylum to hijackers. *See* I. H. Ph. Diederiks-Verschoor, An Introduction to Air Law 302 (8th rev. ed. 2006).

parties to The Hague Convention are ultimately responsible for judging for themselves whether or not to proceed with a prosecution, it is consistent with the terms of the treaty for a State to apprehend a hijacker and plausibly to claim that it cannot prosecute the offender in accordance with its national laws. That State can then invoke an internal rule to excuse itself from an extradition request, even where a requesting State is ready, willing, and able to carry out the prosecution of the offender. Like Tokyo, The Hague Convention includes no potent State-to-State dispute settlement mechanism other than a dilatory arbitration procedure from which any State is free to opt out. Thus, there is no functional "court of appeal" to which States may have recourse to reverse prosecutorial or extradition decisions that may be susceptible to a reasonable second guess.[156] Hijackers can still find sanctuary in sympathetic States, and the anti–aviation crimes treaties are, in truth, powerless in response.[157]

5.9. THE MONTREAL CONVENTION (1971)

5.9.1. *Summary of the Montreal Convention and Its Later Protocol*

Despite the obvious enforcement defects of the earlier treaties, the 1971 Montreal Convention[158] (and its 1988 amending Protocol, considered below) maintained the Tokyo/The Hague model of ultimate State discretion with respect to prosecution and extradition.[159] Montreal does endeavor to move beyond its predecessors by widening the scope of aviation crimes that State parties commit to punish with "severe penalties."[160] More specifically, Montreal criminalizes any act (or attempted act) of violence against a person on board an aircraft "in flight" if that act is likely to endanger the safety of that aircraft, as well as any act (or attempted act) that destroys or damages an aircraft while it is "in service,"

---

[156] Under the Tokyo and The Hague conventions, aggrieved States may submit their disputes to arbitration. If the parties involved are unable to agree on procedures for arbitration within six months, either may submit the matter to the ICJ. Each State party, however, may enter a reservation with respect to dispute settlement. *See* Tokyo Convention, *supra* note 61, art. 24; The Hague Convention, *supra* note 50, art. 12. No disputes have been referred to arbitration under either Convention.

[157] Moreover, although The Hague Convention does not include a freedom fighter exception, neither does it proscribe States from awarding asylum. Even though the United States and others argued for a ban on asylum, the drafting debates reveal concern that such a provision would conflict with rights of asylum in many States' domestic laws and in Article 14 of the Universal Declaration of Human Rights. *See* Abramovsky, *supra* note 120, at 402–05.

[158] Montreal Convention, *supra* note 63. At present, 188 States have ratified the Montreal Convention.

[159] *See* Montreal Convention, *supra* note 63, arts. 7, 8.

[160] *Id.* art. 3.

including, *inter alia*, placing an explosive device on the aircraft.[161] Other new offenses include endangering an aircraft's safety through sabotage of on-the-ground air navigation facilities or providing false information that compromises the aircraft's safety.[162]

5.9.2. *Meaning of Aircraft "in Service" Under the Montreal Convention*

The notion of an aircraft "being in service" is a further elongation of the jurisdiction *ratione temporis*[163] used in the Tokyo and The Hague treaties. Under the Montreal Convention, an aircraft is "in service" "from the beginning of the preflight preparation of the aircraft by ground personnel or by the crew for a specific flight until 24 hours after any landing,"[164] along with the period when the aircraft is technically "in flight."[165] This means that even offenses committed against a stationary aircraft during its preflight maintenance drill and for up to a day after it has landed will be covered by the Convention. Under the Tokyo/The Hague treaties, only the domestic law of the State in which the aircraft was located prior to departure or the domestic law of the landing State would be applicable outside the "in flight" sequence. Finally, Montreal makes no distinction between domestic and international flights; all that matters for the treaty to apply is that "the place of take-off or landing, actual or *intended*, of the aircraft is situated outside the territory of the State of registration" or that "the offense is committed in the territory of a State other than the State of registration of the aircraft."[166]

5.9.3. *Other ICAO Initiatives, Including the Montreal Protocol*

In the decade after the signing of the Montreal Convention, no further efforts were made to tighten the enforcement provisions of any of the aviation security treaties. At the behest of the United States and several European States, ICAO passed two resolutions calling on Chicago Convention adherents to cooperate more closely on legal enforcement against hijacking. Under the second

---

[161] *Id.* art. 1(1).

[162] *See id.* art. 1(1). The offenses contained in the Montreal Convention, like those listed in Tokyo and The Hague, are strict liability offenses; again, no *mens rea* requirement is attached. Additionally, like The Hague Convention, Montreal also provides for accomplice liability. *See* Montreal Convention, *supra* note 63, art. 1(2). *See supra* note 99 (defining strict liability offenses).

[163] The phrase is Latin for jurisdiction by reason of time, that is, temporal jurisdiction.

[164] Montreal Convention, *supra* note 63, art. 2(b).

[165] Montreal's definition of "in flight," on the other hand, is identical to that contained in The Hague Convention. *See* The Hague Convention, *supra* note 50, art. 3; Montreal Convention, *supra* note 63, art. 2(a).

[166] *Id.* art. 4(2) (emphasis added). With respect to attacks against air navigation facilities, listed in *id.* art. 1(1)(d), the Convention only applies to such facilities that are used for international air transport.

resolution, the ICAO Legal Committee was instructed to draft a new agreement (which was never produced) that would insert a uniform clause into all bilateral agreements and subsequent multilateral agreements requiring all States to enforce the provisions of the Tokyo and The Hague conventions.[167] Discussions continued also on other proposals for additional aviation crime instruments. Those discussions began to bear fruit in 1988 with the ratification of the Montreal Protocol,[168] which further expanded the list of aviation crimes to include attacks against airports serving international aviation.[169] Three years later, after the Pan Am Lockerbie bombing,[170] a new treaty governing the marking, identification, and transport of plastic explosives was signed in Montreal.[171] This second security-related Montreal Convention established a standing International Explosives Technical Commission to keep abreast of technological developments related to plastic explosives and to propose amendments to the treaty.[172] Once again, in terms of enforcement, the treaty accomplishes nothing more than its predecessor instruments. Much more recently, in September 2010, ICAO reentered the realm of security with two new instruments signed in Beijing, China. Following the 9/11 attacks, ICAO saw the clear need to reevaluate security policy, including a review of the existing aviation crimes treaties. A study group was formed in 2005 to examine how those prior treaties might be improved to address the unanticipated dangers brought to light by the 9/11 attacks. The new Beijing instruments aim, on the one hand, to replace the Montreal Convention and its Protocol and, on the other, to amend The Hague Convention.[173] Jointly, the overarching

---

[167] *Action of the Council*, 71st Sess., ICAO Doc. 8923-C/998, *reprinted in* 9 I.L.M. 1286 (1970). In effect, full enforcement in the minds of the proponents of the Resolution meant that States should neither grant political asylum nor decline extradition. *See* Paul S. Dempsey, *Aerial Piracy and Terrorism: Unilateral and Multilateral Responses to Aircraft Hijacking*, 2 CONN. J. INT'L L. 427, 440–41 (1987).

[168] The Protocol supplements the 1971 Montreal Convention, adding paragraphs to Articles 1 and 5 of the 1971 Convention. The Convention and Protocol are intended to be read and interpreted as a single instrument. *See* Montreal Protocol, *supra* note 64, art. I.

[169] *See id.* art. II. Included in the definition of offenses are attacks against persons located at airports serving international aviation and any facilities attached to the airport. The Protocol followed several bomb attacks on large European airports in the mid-1980s.

[170] *See supra* note 87.

[171] *See* Plastic Explosives Convention, *supra* note 65. At present, 147 States have ratified the Plastic Explosives Convention.

[172] *See id.* art. V.

[173] *See generally* Convention on the Suppression of Unlawful Acts Related to International Civil Aviation, *opened for signature* Sept. 10, 2010, ICAO Doc. 9960, http://legacy.icao.int/DCAS 2010/restr/docs/beijing_convention_multi.pdf [hereinafter Beijing Convention]; Protocol to the Convention for the Suppression of Unlawful Seizure of Aircraft, *opened for signature* Sept. 10, 2010, ICAO Doc. 9959, https://www.unodc.org/tldb/en/2010_protocol_convention_ unlawful_seizure_aircraft.html [hereinafter Beijing Protocol].

purpose of both treaties is to expand the catalog of aviation-related offenses to cover, *inter alia,* using civil aircraft as a weapon to cause death, injury, or damage; misusing aircraft as delivery systems for weapons of mass destruction; and using weapons of mass destruction against aircraft or those on board.[174] In that vein, the Beijing Convention adds a new offense for transporting certain dangerous materials such as explosive or radioactive materials or biological, chemical, or nuclear weapons. Although the Convention states that none of its listed crimes should be considered "political offenses,"[175] enhanced provisions relating to prosecution and extradition are nevertheless absent. As of this writing, the two Beijing instruments have received fewer than half of the twenty-two ratifications they each require in order to enter into force.[176]

5.10. BEYOND THE ICAO TREATY REGIME

5.10.1. *Inadequacies of the ICAO Treaty System*

The inadequacies of the aviation crimes treaties that entered into force during the latter half of the twentieth century did not go unnoticed by States and commentators alike.[177] None of the treaties, for example, threatens scofflaw States with expulsion from ICAO or a revocation of the traffic rights they have secured under their various bilateral air services agreements (ASAs).[178]

---

[174] *See The 2010 Beijing Convention and Protocol: Ushering in a New Legal Era for Aviation,* 66 No. 1 ICAO J. 6 (2011).

[175] Beijing Convention, *supra* note 173, art. 13.

[176] Each agreement requires 22 ratifications before it will enter into force. Beijing Convention, *supra* note 173, art. 22; Beijing Protocol, *supra* note 173, art. XXIII. Regrettably, only a quarter of ICAO's member States have fully implemented ICAO's aviation security instruments in their national legislation. *See* Piera Report, *supra* note 79, at 10, n.91.

[177] *See* Dempsey, *supra* note 167, at 429.

[178] But ICAO's Legal Committee did consider proposals in the early 1970s to amend the Chicago Convention so that States not complying with the Tokyo, The Hague, and Montreal conventions could have their traffic access rights revoked. Initially, the U.S. and Canadian delegations proposed competing plans that would have enabled the suspension of bilateral agreements as a sanction against States that refused extradition. Other States made proposals to add the provisions of the Tokyo, The Hague, and Montreal conventions to the Chicago Convention. On the other hand, it would offend the principle of sovereignty to demand that States must ratify the aviation crimes treaties as a condition of remaining in ICAO. Interestingly, many States do include in their bilateral agreements an undertaking by their partner States that they will apply the provisions of the aviation crimes treaties. *See, e.g.,* Air Transport Agreement, U.S.-EU, Apr. 30, 2007, 2007 O.J. (L 134) 4, 46 I.L.M. 470, as amended by Protocol to Amend the Air Transport Agreement, U.S.-EU, Jun. 24, 2010, 2010 O.J. (L 223) 3; Agreement Between the Government of Australia and the Government of the Argentine Republic Relating to Air Services, art. XVI (Mar. 11, 1992) (not in force); Agreement between Japan and the Republic of Uzbekistan for Air Services, art. 13, Dec. 22, 2003, U.N. Reg. No. I-48368.

Governments whose populations sympathize with the means and ends of certain terrorist organizations may find that their interests are better served by defecting from the aviation crimes treaties, or at least by availing themselves of the generous loopholes for refusing either prosecution or extradition.[179] In other cases, such as where two States are ideologically at odds, the prospects for cooperation under any of the aviation security treaties will be even less promising. These observations beg the question as to why States would bother to negotiate and ratify these instruments at all. Why not rely on good faith bilateral cooperation to apprehend and punish aviation criminals rather than expending resources to produce agreements that can be so easily emasculated? One answer is that the aviation security treaties, particularly the Tokyo Convention, provided a "quick fix" to domestic legal regimes that had inadequately defined, for substantive or jurisdictional purposes, the kinds of aviation crimes that the treaties contemplated. Additionally, by signing these international agreements, any State could send a "cheap signal" to its partner States of its willingness to cooperate *in principle*, even if circumstances might compel it eventually to defect in fact. Given the prevailing geopolitics, a State's self-interest would likely be better served by accepting the uncertain risk of future noncompliance rather than immediate branding as a haven for aviation criminals.

5.10.2. *The Bonn Declaration on Hijacking*

Not surprisingly, States that have been victimized by aviation criminals, particularly terrorists, have not allowed the inadequacies of the treaty regime to blunt their pursuit of criminal sanctions. In 1978, the then "G7" States issued the Bonn Declaration on Hijacking.[180] Although not a treaty *per se*, this "soft" statement committed its promulgators to cutting off air services to or from any State that "refuses extradition or prosecution of those who have hijacked an aircraft and/or do not return such aircraft[.]"[181] While this threat has only been applied in a handful of cases over the years,[182] the Declaration's

---

[179] Libya's refusal to extradite two suspects in the Lockerbie bombing who were believed to have ties to the Libyan government is an obvious example. *See supra* note 96 and accompanying text.

[180] Bonn Declaration on International Terrorism, Pub. Papers 1308, Jul. 17, 1978, *reprinted in* 17 I.L.M. 1285 [hereinafter Bonn Declaration]. At that time, the G7 consisted of the United States, Canada, the United Kingdom, France, Germany, Italy, and Japan. Those States represented 70% of world aviation traffic at the time.

[181] *Id.*

[182] The Bonn Declaration has been invoked on a number of occasions. In 1981 a Pakistan International Airlines flight was hijacked to Afghanistan, which refused to prosecute or to extradite the hijackers. The three parties to the Bonn Declaration with ASAs with Afghanistan

adherents have reaffirmed its principles in subsequent summits.[183] This "extra-legal" option has raised the hackles of some observers who point out that the Bonn Declaration goes beyond even the most stringent requirements in the Tokyo and The Hague conventions and may violate the terms of the declarant States' ASAs.[184] It is unclear whether that is correct. While the Tokyo and The Hague treaties do impose certain (avoidable) obligations with respect to the apprehension and punishment of aviation criminals, neither instrument proclaims any exclusive competence over this area of international law. More critically, none of the aviation crimes treaties dictates the terms by which States will adhere to their ASAs. Most ASAs contain specific clauses allowing the parties to denounce (or temporarily suspend) the agreement without further inquiry into the reasons.[185] It may be more appropriate, then, to treat the Bonn Declaration as a statement of policy rather than an attempt to abrogate existing international law.[186] Simply put, the Declaration announces to any State that harbors aviation criminals that it may forfeit commercial privileges to and from the world's leading air transport markets. The Chicago Convention creates no "natural" right to market access, and States are well within the bounds of international law when they close their airspace for reasons of national security.[187]

---

denounced those agreements under the procedures for denunciation prescribed within their ASAs. Those provisions included a one-year notice requirement, which meant that operations to and from Afghanistan did not end until the following year. Bonn was invoked again in 1981 when South Africa refused to prosecute 45 mercenaries who sought asylum after hijacking a flight out of the Seychelles. Unlike Afghanistan, South Africa relented to the diplomatic pressure brought by the United States and others.

[183] The 1986 Tokyo Economic Summit is one example. *See* Dempsey, *supra* note 167, at 449.

[184] *See* James J. Busuttil, *The Bonn Declaration on International Terrorism: A Non-Binding International Agreement on Aircraft Hijacking*, 31 Int'l & Comp. L.Q. 474, 479–82 (1982).

[185] In fact, the Bonn Declaration States shut off air services to recalcitrant States through the processes contemplated in their respective ASAs with those third States.

[186] Indeed, the Declaration may have been an attempt by the adhering States to enunciate to the international community what they believed to be principles of customary international law (namely, that hijacking is an international crime and that States have a duty to prosecute or extradite).

[187] Some have argued that cutting off air services under the Bonn Declaration violates Article 9 of the Chicago Convention, because a State's refusal to extradite does not rise to the level of "reasons of military necessity or public safety." Further, Article 9 also requires that any such restrictions be applied in a nondiscriminatory fashion, which is obviously incompatible with the targeted and punitive way in which enforcement is carried out under Bonn. *See* Busuttil, *supra* note 184, at 479–82. These criticisms would be correct if any State were to invoke Bonn to restrict an offending State's overflight privileges, but Article 9 does not (technically) apply to restriction of services to and from a State's aerodromes. On Article 9 generally, see *supra* Chapter 2, Section 2.5.3.

5.10.3. Other State-Based Approaches to Combating Aviation Crimes

In addition to the Bonn Declaration, many States have relied on bilateral Mutual Legal Assistance treaties and other international law enforcement accords to apprehend and punish air criminals.[188] Some countries have taken extraordinary measures to capture and prosecute aviation terrorists. The United States even lured a suspected hijacking perpetrator into international waters for the purpose of seizing him.[189] Again, although such actions have intruded into the comfort zones of strict legalists, they may not be entirely inconsistent with international law. Several doctrines, including the passive personality principle[190] and the protective principle,[191] allow States to exercise extraterritorial jurisdiction over certain classes of offenders (especially terrorists), regardless of whether the offender or the offender's victims are nationals of the State claiming jurisdiction. And even if invocation of these doctrines is unpersuasive, the hard truth remains that most States would prefer to see terrorists punished, even at the margins of the law, rather than allow them to shelter in the name of upholding abstract and contestable notions of legality.[192]

---

[188] *See, e.g.*, U.S.-Cuba Memorandum of Understanding on Hijacking of Aircraft and Vessels and Other Offenses, U.S.-Cuba, Feb. 15, 1973, 24 U.S.T. 737, *reprinted in* 12 I.L.M. 370 (1973); Agreement on Mutual Legal Assistance between the European Union and the United States of America, Jun. 25, 2003, T.I.A.S. 10–201.1, 2003 O.J. (L 181) 34.

[189] *See* U.S. v. Yunis, 924 F.2d 1086 (D.C. Cir. 1991). The U.S. Federal Bureau of Investigation (FBI), in cooperation with the U.S. Navy, lured a suspected aircraft hijacker, Fawaz Yunis, into international waters under the pretense of conducting a narcotics transaction; Yunis was subsequently seized, brought into U.S. territory against his will, and successfully prosecuted under several federal statutes criminalizing hijacking and hostage taking. The only connection between the hijacking and the United States was that several U.S. nationals were aboard the affected Royal Jordanian Airlines flight. The defendant's appeal, which contested U.S. jurisdiction over his offenses on the basis of international law, failed. *See* U.S. v. Yunis, 681 F. Supp. 896 (D.D.C. 1988).

[190] "Under the passive personality principle, a State may punish non-nationals for crimes committed against its nationals outside of its territory, at least where the State has a particularly strong interest in the crime." U.S. v. Yunis, 924 F.2d at 1091. *See also supra* text accompanying note 93 (noting, however, that the United States, in international law, has contested the passive personality principle despite its use in U.S. domestic court rulings such as *Yunis*); arguably, terrorist cases have changed U.S. attitudes toward the principle. *See* Watson, *supra* note 93.

[191] "The protective principle recognizes that a sovereign can adopt a statute that criminalizes conduct that occurs outside of its borders when that conduct affects the sovereign itself," including "laws that make it a crime to engage in an act that obstructs the function of government or threatens its security as a State without regard to where or by whom the act is committed." U.S. v. Zehe, 601 F. Supp. 196 (D. Mass 1985). *See also* discussion *supra* in Section 5.6.4 (noting that the principle is directed at aliens whose conduct prejudices the security interests of a State).

[192] This is certainly not the opinion of the report by the IBA Task Force on Terrorism, however, which is threaded through with warnings that States must always respect international human rights law and international humanitarian law in their counterterrorism efforts. *See, e.g.*, IBA REPORT, *supra* note 1, at 219–21.

5.11. PREVENTING AVIATION CRIMES AND OTHER HOSTILE INCIDENTS WITHIN THE LIMITS OF LAW

5.11.1. *Reactive and Proactive Approaches to Aviation Crimes*

The international legal mechanisms discussed so far in this chapter have focused on *ex post* action that States can or ought to take to apprehend and punish aviation criminals, including terrorists. A recurrent theme among the instruments we have considered is that they represent reactive rather than proactive approaches. The Hague Convention, for instance, followed a series of high-profile aircraft hijackings but lacks any provisions that foster transnational law enforcement cooperation. ICAO has promulgated SARPs to promote basic levels of airport and aircraft security, but implementation, particularly in developing countries, remains poor.[193] Most States rely on domestic intelligence units to ascertain potential terrorists and to apprehend them before they can execute their plans.[194] But these intelligence networks are far from foolproof and, indeed, have been sharply criticized.[195] The international gathering and sharing of intelligence has noticeably intensified since the 9/11 terrorist attacks, though it, too, remains imperfect.[196] In the remainder of this part, we use U.S./EU aviation security relations to exemplify the challenges of international cooperation to prevent aviation crimes and terrorism. Although these major aeropolitical powers have concluded agreements covering trade in aviation services and the interoperability of their air traffic management systems, integration of the security cultures of the two sides remains an unfinished and often controversial project.

5.11.2. *Use of Passenger Data*

One of the preventive tools in any State's security arsenal is the use of passenger data to screen for suspected terrorists. In 2004, the United States and the EU reached an agreement (pursuant to a U.S. statutory mandate) requiring EU

---

[193] Professor Paul Stephen Dempsey tells the story of his visit to the headquarters of the civil aviation authority of a central African State where he noticed a roomful of dusty unread manuals. Upon inquiry, he was told that the room was used to store "stuff that ICAO sends us." (As told to Professor Brian F. Havel, in Montreal (Can.) (Apr. 15, 2008).)

[194] *See The Plot to Bring Down Britain's Planes* (Channel 4 (U.K.) television broadcast Apr. 26, 2012).

[195] *See, e.g.,* RICHARD A. POSNER, PREVENTING SURPRISE ATTACKS (2005); RICHARD A. POSNER, UNCERTAIN SHIELD: THE U.S. INTELLIGENCE SYSTEM IN THE THROES OF REFORM (2006) (arguing that the post-9/11 reforms to U.S. intelligence agencies have made the agencies too centralized and bureaucratic).

[196] *See generally* ADAM D.M. SVENDSEN, UNDERSTANDING THE GLOBALIZATION OF INTELLIGENCE (2012).

airlines flying to or from the United States to furnish passenger name records (PNR) in their reservation and departure control systems within fifteen minutes of their departure time. The result was an immediate backlash by EU citizens concerned about how the PNR data would be used and indignant that the EU had not insisted on stronger measures to protect their privacy.[197] Following a successful challenge to the PNR agreement before the Court of Justice of the European Union,[198] a fresh (albeit provisional) agreement was reached in 2007 which, *inter alia*, provided the United States with access to data concerning passengers' race, ethnicity, and religion, and permitted the United States to distribute the PNR data among its antiterrorism security agencies. The new accord also required airlines to send data from their reservations systems to U.S. authorities at least seventy-two hours before flight departure. The European Parliament, which strongly opposed the 2004 PNR agreement, never approved the 2007 version. Instead, negotiations on another new agreement began in December 2010 as part of a new "global external PNR strategy" adopted by the European Commission.[199] That agreement was completed in December 2011 and finally approved by the European Parliament in April 2012, six months after approval of a similar PNR agreement with Australia.[200] The two sides agreed that, should the EU in the future develop its own PNR system, the parties would consult to determine any changes needed to ensure full reciprocity between the two systems.[201] Under the 2012 U.S.-EU PNR Agreement, carriers operating passenger flights between the EU and the United States must provide the U.S. Department of Homeland Security (DHS) with the PNR contained in their reservation systems.[202] The data must be transferred by secure electronic means at least ninety-six hours before the scheduled flight departure (note the stretching of the time for data transfer over the various iterations of the agreement), and the DHS may also require further data transfers "in real time or for a fixed number of routine and scheduled transfers."[203] The United States is only

---

[197] *See* Kristin Archick, Cong. Res. Serv., RS 22030, U.S.-EU Cooperation Against Terrorism 6 (2011).

[198] Joined Cases C-317 & C-318/04, Parliament v. Council, 2006 E.C.R. I-4721. The Court annulled the accord on the ground that it had not been negotiated on the proper legal basis, but did not find any violation of EU privacy rights. *See* Archick, *supra* note 197, at 9.

[199] *See id.* (noting that, under the new strategy, general requirements for all EU PNR agreements were established).

[200] Press Release, European Parliament, Parliament Gives Green Light to Air Passenger Data Deal with U.S. (Apr. 19, 2012).

[201] *See* Archick, *supra* note 197, at 10.

[202] *See* Agreement between the United States of America and the European Union on the Use and Transfer of Passenger Name Records to the United States Department of Homeland Security, art. 3, Dec. 8, 2011, 2012 O.J. (L 215) 5.

[203] *Id.* art. 15.

allowed to use the provided information "for the purposes of preventing, detecting, investigating and prosecuting" terrorist and related offenses as well as transnational crimes punishable by a sentence of imprisonment of at least three years.[204] The 2012 PNR Agreement does not specifically mention hijacking, a sign perhaps of the degree to which terrorism has superseded hijacking as international aviation's primary security concern, but hijacking is undoubtedly covered by the references to related crimes and transnational crimes. Much of the PNR Agreement is dedicated to detailing procedures for data security, access, and retention. Sensitive personal information such as the race, ethnicity, religious and political beliefs, and health of incoming passengers may only be accessed and used in exceptional circumstances.[205] The Agreement also permits individuals whose personal information has been used in violation of its terms, and regardless of their nationality or place of residence, to "seek effective administrative and judicial redress in accordance with U.S. law."[206]

5.11.3. *Passenger Screening Procedures*

Following a failed December 2009 bomb attack against a Delta Air Lines flight bound for Detroit from Amsterdam, the United States rapidly began to install full-body scanners in its major airports in an attempt to locate concealed bombs and other weapons without recourse to more time-intensive and invasive measures such as pat-downs and strip searches. Even so, the revealing nature of the body scanners and the aggressive body search tactics of the U.S. Transportation Security Administration (TSA) yielded cries of "gate rape" in the United States and intense criticism from international observers.[207] In the EU, several Member States expressed concern that body scanners constitute an automatic privacy violation and pose serious health risks. Specifically to address these concerns, the European Commission has added operational conditions for body scanners to its common rules on civil aviation security.[208]

---

[204] *Id.* art. 4.

[205] *See id.* art. 6.

[206] *Id.* art. 13.

[207] *See, e.g.,* Press Release, Am. Civ. Liberties Union, TSA Body Scanning Technology Strips Away Privacy (Oct. 1, 2009), http://www.aclu.org/technology-and-liberty/tsa-body-scanning-technology-strips-away-privacy. *See also* Bruce L. Ottley, *Airport Full-Body Scanners: Improved Security or Cause for Concern?*, 9 ISSUES AVIATION L. & POL'Y 221 (2009) (noting view of some security planners that the money used to buy body scanners would be better spent on intelligence-sharing and on behavioral screening).

[208] In 2011, the European Commission included body scanners that do not use X-ray technology on its list of approved methods for passenger screening. The Commission laid down operating conditions on the use of security scanners that would respect fundamental rights and offer passengers the possibility of alternative screening methods. *See* Commission Regulation

Although the United States and other countries have an understandable interest in the EU utilizing the most effective measures to screen passengers for weapons before they board flights bound to their respective territories, it is unlikely that an international agreement will do much to resolve the issue. Like the use of PNR data, airport searches give rise to moral concerns that cannot be negotiated away easily.

5.11.4. *Air Cargo Screening Procedures*

Air cargo screening is one area where the United States and EU have found more common ground.[209] In 2010, both sides agreed to reconsider the effectiveness of existing post-9/11 measures when terrorists from Yemen used printer cartridges to conceal bombs on board United Parcel Service and FedEx all-cargo flights.[210] In June 2012, the two powers signed an agreement for mutual recognition of their respective air cargo security regimes.[211] Under the agreement, neither the United States nor the EU will require additional or different security measures for air cargo flown into its territory from the other side's territory.[212] In an attempt to strengthen worldwide standards, as of July 1, 2011, ICAO adopted Amendment 12 to Annex 17, which adds new air cargo security SARPs focused on development of secure air cargo supply chains.[213]

5.11.5. *Meaning of "Air Rage"*

"Air rage" is a term that has been coined to refer to aggressive conduct that could fall "anywhere on a behavioral continuum from socially offensive to

---

1141/2011, Amending Regulation (EC) No. 272/2009 Supplementing the Common Basic Standards on Civil Aviation Security as Regards the Use of Security Scanners at EU Airports, 2011 O.J. (L 293) 22. Nevertheless, Member States are not required under EU rules to deploy body scanners, and some are unlikely to do so. *See* ARCHICK, *supra* note 197, at 15.

[209] Part of the U.S. sense of urgency on this matter is the need to comply with a provision in the Implementing Recommendations of the 9/11 Commission Act of 2007 (Pub. L. 110–53, 121 Stat. 266) that mandates 100% screening of air cargo transported on U.S. domestic and U.S.-bound international passenger flights equivalent to the level of security used for checked baggage. The TSA set December 2012 as the deadline by which all inbound cargo on international passenger flights would be screened. *See* BART ELIAS, CONG. RES. SERV., R 41515, SCREENING AND SECURING AIR CARGO: BACKGROUND AND ISSUES FOR CONGRESS (2010).

[210] *See* Jad Mouawad, *For Air Cargo, A Screening Conundrum*, N.Y. TIMES, Dec. 21, 2010, at B1.

[211] *See* EU-U.S. *Security Agreement Allows Cheaper, Faster Air Cargo Operations*, HOMELANDSECURITYNEWSWIRE.COM, June 5, 2012, http://www.homelandsecuritynewswire.com/dr20120605-euu-s-security-agreement-allows-cheaper-faster-air-cargo-operations.

[212] The EU has confirmed that compliance with its air cargo security measures will also meet the U.S. statutory requirement of 100% screening of all incoming air cargo. *See supra* note 209.

[213] *See* ICAO, Aviation Security Programme, http://www2.icao.int/en/avsec/pages/default.aspx/.

criminal" and that endangers other persons on the aircraft or even threatens the safety of the aircraft itself.[214] The phrase is typically applied to passenger conduct, although it could also include actions by the crew.[215] The most common examples involve passengers attacking or assaulting flight attendants or other crew members, but the term has been broadly applied to cover a variety of acts.[216] The concept has only gained significant media and scholarly attention in the past fifteen years, but the number of reported incidents has escalated dramatically over that time. The actions encompassed under "air rage" include intentional wrongs or criminal acts that can be easily be prosecuted under domestic law when jurisdiction is clear. Problematically, however, many of these offenses are not typically defined in member States' national laws, and ICAO appears to believe that an international solution may be needed to fill that void.[217] Some States have indeed attempted to address the jurisdictional gap by statute. For example, the United States has designated a "special aircraft jurisdiction"[218] to cover wrongful seizure of an aircraft by force as well as interference with flight crew members.[219] The jurisdiction includes any aircraft registered in the United States or foreign aircraft for which the United States is the next scheduled destination or last point of departure. Airlines have also taken autonomous measures to combat the problem by banning unruly passengers.

---

[214] *See* Nancy Lee Firak & Kimberly A. Schmaltz, *Air Rage: Choice of Law for Intentional Torts Occurring in Flight Over International Waters*, 63 ALB. L. REV. 1, 7 (1999).

[215] *See* Piera Report, *supra* note 79 (proposing a new terminology of "unruly/disruptive persons on board aircraft" to take account of the occasional role of crew members failing to respect the appropriate rules of in-flight conduct).

[216] In one unique and repellent example, an investment banker defecated on a food cart on a flight from Buenos Aires to New York. *See* Firak & Schmaltz, *supra* note 214, at 9 (citing Lisa Miller, *Airlines and Courts Are Cracking Down on Unruly Passengers as Assaults Rise*, WALL ST. J., Dec. 27, 1996, at A2).

[217] *See* Piera Report, *supra* note 79, at 18–19 (noting that there is a strong case for a systematic international approach to the problem of air rage (citation omitted)). Arguably, air rage offenses could be included under Article 1 of the Tokyo Convention, which refers to "acts . . . which jeopardize good order and discipline on board." Tokyo Convention, *supra* note 61, art. 1(b). ICAO is studying the possibility of amending the Tokyo Convention to better address air rage and has prepared a draft text of an amending protocol for consideration in March 2014. *See supra* note 120. In 2001, incidentally, the ICAO Assembly passed a resolution urging member States to enact national laws to exercise jurisdiction in appropriate cases to prosecute criminal acts and offenses involving unruly or disruptive passengers on board aircraft registered in other States. A model statute was attached to the Resolution. *See* International Civil Aviation Organization, Adoption of National Legislation on Certain Offenses Committed on Board Civil Aircraft (Unruly/Disruptive Passengers), Assem. Res. A33–4 (2001). The U.S. legislation mentioned in the main text is an example of the kind of national law advocated by ICAO.

[218] 49 U.S.C. § 46502(a).

[219] *See* 49 U.S.C. § 46504.

6

The International Law Regime for Aviation
and the Environment

6.1. INTRODUCTION

6.1.1. ICAO's Response to a Politically Contentious Issue

The impact of aviation on the global environment[1] has become one of the most politically contentious issues in international aviation law and policy. For that reason, it remains an inadequately addressed facet of air transport at the international level.[2] That assertion may strike some as surprising given the resources that the International Civil Aviation Organization (ICAO) has dedicated to studying the effects of aviation on the environment, including assessment of the industry's responsibility for the phenomenon of climate change or "global warming."[3]

---

[1] We do not attempt here to define the term "environment," although for international aviation the scope of inquiry is readily understandable. *See* LYNTON KEITH CALDWELL, INTERNATIONAL ENVIRONMENTAL POLICY AND LAW 170 (1st ed. 1980) ("'environment' is a term that everyone understands and no one is able to define").

[2] This is not necessarily true within the domestic spheres of many States. The United States, for instance, has enacted a series of regulations that concern aviation's environmental impact, including noise restrictions, emissions levels, and airport operations. *See, e.g.,* 14 C.F.R. § 36.103 (2012); 14 C.F.R. § 34.21 (2012); 14 C.F.R. § 153 (2012). And some jurisdictions, like the European Union (EU), are attempting to use their internal aircraft emissions regulations (including those on emissions "trading," *see infra* Section 6.1.2) to "police" the emissions levels of foreign air carriers entering or exiting their national territory. In keeping with the international focus of this book, we have limited our discussion in this chapter to environmental regulation at the international level, although some national or regional rules (especially the EU emissions trading system) will be implicated in the analysis.

[3] The Intergovernmental Panel on Climate Change (IPCC) – an international scientific body established jointly by the United Nations (U.N.) and the World Meteorological Organization – has provided substantial scientific evidence that global temperatures are on the rise due to rapid increases in greenhouse gas emissions caused by human activity; *see* IPCC, CLIMATE CHANGE 2007: SYNTHESIS REPORT: SUMMARY FOR POLICYMAKERS (2007) [hereinafter IPCC, SUMMARY FOR POLICYMAKERS]; IPCC, CLIMATE CHANGE 2007: IMPACTS, ADAPTATION AND VULNERABILITY (2007) [hereinafter IPCC, IMPACTS, ADAPTATION AND VULNERABILITY].

ICAO's Committee on Aviation Environmental Protection (CAEP), which is comprised of members from ICAO State parties, intergovernmental entities, and nongovernmental organizations, produces regular updates on aviation's environmental impact and determines whether adjustments should be made to any of ICAO's Standards and Recommended Practices (SARPs) that concern the environment.[4] In 2007, ICAO established a second environmental task force, the Group on International Aviation and Climate Change (GIACC), to find sustainable solutions to aviation's contribution to climate change. Although long-term solutions must include technological innovations such as biofuel replacement of kerosene,[5] the Group is actually focused on more immediate economic concerns, exploring, for example, how States can use so-called 'market-based measures' (MBMs), such as eco-taxes and cap-and-trade systems, to incentivize airlines to reduce emissions without inflicting serious economic harm on the sector.[6] To date, neither of these ICAO entities has produced a workable road map for the industry's approach to climate change. Nor has the Organization itself been able to engineer a global sectoral approach to cutting aviation emissions despite being charged to do so by both the U.N. multilateral treaty on global climate change and by its own membership.[7]

6.1.2. *Political Problem of the EU's Emissions Trading Scheme*

The political problem of building a global governance structure for aviation emissions was intensified by the decision of the EU to include non-EU airlines in its multisectoral cap-and-trade MBM, the "Emissions Trading Scheme" (ETS). The gist of the ETS can be quickly stated. As of January 1, 2012, the ETS regulation proposed to cap emissions from virtually all commercial flights

---

[4] ICAO, *Committee on Aviation Environmental Protection* (CAEP), http://www.icao.int/environmental-protection/pages/CAEP.aspx.

[5] World Economic Forum, *Policies and Collaborative Partnership for Sustainable Aviation* (2011).

[6] By "cap-and-trade" we mean a system where a governmental authority establishes a ceiling on the amount of carbon a particular industrial sector (or sectors) may release during a specified period of time. Firms within the capped industry are allocated a set number of discharge permits or credits that they are then free to trade in a secondary market to other firms seeking to emit beyond their allotted permits. Such schemes may allow for either "open trading," whereby firms across multiple capped industries may engage in cross-sectoral exchanges of allowances, or "closed trading," under which firms are limited to intrasectoral exchanges. *See generally* THOMAS H. TIETENBERG, EMISSIONS TRADING: PRINCIPLES AND PRACTICE (2006).

[7] As of the publication date of this book, ICAO has received the backing of its members to draft a global aviation emissions accord in time for the Organization's 39th Assembly session in autumn 2016. Assuming that the agreement is approved, it would not take effect until at least 2020. The exact terms of this potential accord have yet to be worked out. *See* Press Release, ICAO, Dramatic MBM Agreement and Solid Global Plan Endorsements Help Deliver Landmark ICAO 38th Assembly (Oct. 4, 2013).

landing in or departing from the territory of an EU Member State, regardless of the national origin of the air carrier providing the service.[8] Using a route-based rather than an airspace-based formula, the regulation was intended to cover emissions from the entire flight, including over the high seas and non-EU territory.[9] For the first year, the cap was set at 97% of the mean average of emissions released between 2004 and 2006 by airlines operating to and from the territory of the EU. Although airlines covered by the ETS would receive most of their carbon allowances free (at least in the initial stages), 15% of the allowances would be available by auction only, with the revenues going to the EU Member States. Any airline that exceeded its initial allotment[10] would have to purchase additional allowances through auction or from other airlines and industrial sectors covered by the ETS. Given that the total number of allowances was capped at a level below historic annual emissions for the industry, there was expected to be high demand for the allowances on the market. Although the ETS regulation contemplated lowering the emissions cap to 95% in 2013 with the potential for further downward adjustments, mounting international pressure compelled the EU to "stop the clock" on the regulation for twelve months beginning in November 2012. A significant

---

[8] Allowances would be required for flights by fixed-wing aircraft with a maximum takeoff mass of 5700 kg or above. Flights performed under visual flight rules and rescue flights are to be excluded, as are flights performed in the framework of "public service obligations" (i.e., on thinly served routes that rely on government subsidies in order to be viable). There is also a *de minimis* exclusion for commercial flights below a defined frequency. *See* Council Directive 2008/101, Annex, 2009 O.J. (L 8) 17. These exemptions are consistent with ICAO policy. *See* Consolidated Statement of Continuing ICAO Policies and Practices Related to Environmental Protection, ICAO Assemb. Res. A37-19, Oct. 8, 2010, at para. 15, http://legacy.icao.int/env/ A37_Res19_en.pdf.

[9] For example, on the standard flight path for a U.S. carrier flying from San Francisco and landing in London, 29% of emissions occur in U.S. airspace, 37% in Canadian airspace, 25% over the high seas, and only 9% over EU territory. *See* Oral Submissions on Behalf of the Air Transp. Ass'n of America (ATA), United Continental Airlines, & American Airlines at para. 12, Case C-366/10, Air Transp. Ass'n of Am. Inc. v. Sec'y of State for Energy & Climate Change, 2010 O.J. C-260/12 (Jul. 5, 2011).

[10] Allowances allocated to each aircraft operator would be determined by a benchmark calculated in three consecutive steps: first, the share of auctioned allowances is subtracted from the overall cap. Second, remaining carbon emissions are divided by the sum of verified ton-kilometer data for monitoring year 2010 as reported by all participating operators. Third, the specific amount of each operator's allowances is calculated by multiplying the mission distance (great-circle distance plus an additional fixed surcharge of 95 km) by the payload transported (cargo, mail, and passengers). *See* Council Directive 2008/101, Annex, 2009 O.J. (L 8) 9–11. Each passenger (including baggage) is assigned a value of 100 kg. *See* Council Directive 2008/101, Annex, 2009 O.J. (L 8) 19. Allowances not used in the first chargeable year, 2012, could be banked to the third trading period of the ETS (2013–2020). *See* Council Directive 2003/87, art. 13, 2003 O.J. (L 275) 36–37. *But see infra* note 11 (discussing postponement of effective date for including air transport in the ETS).

consortium of States, backed by ICAO, has opposed the EU's regulatory unilateralism. While the EU initially insisted that it would not relieve any foreign airline of emissions charges until its home State adopted "comparable" aviation emissions-abatement measures, the European Commission left the door open to back out of the regulation should ICAO muster the international political capital to promulgate a global scheme.[11] We will return later in this chapter to the principles of international law that may be violated by applying an ETS unilaterally to foreign airlines serving domestic airports.[12]

6.1.3. *Noise Pollution and Localized Emissions*

Hydrocarbon emissions, while undoubtedly the most politically challenging characteristic of aviation's relationship with the environment, is not the only one. Public concerns over noise pollution, particularly in high-density urban areas, have prompted ICAO to approve several SARPs and have sparked continuing aeropolitical tensions between the United States and the EU.[13] Environmentalists have also indicted the growth of the air transport industry as

[11]   The 26 States opposed to the EU scheme, led by China, the United States, Russia, and India, garnered the moniker "the coalition of the unwilling." *See* Slaughter, *supra* note 7. China, India, and the United States announced or contemplated measures to prohibit their carriers from complying with the EU regulation. See *Europe Considers Suspending Airline Emissions Charge*, ASSOCIATED PRESS, Sept. 12, 2012. As noted in the main text, in November 2012 the EU Commissioner for Climate Action, Connie Hedegaard, announced a "stopping of the clock" that would defer for one year the ETS obligation to surrender emissions allowances for all airlines serving routes between EU and non-EU airports (but not, however, for intra-Union flights). The EU would not require allowances to be surrendered in April 2013 for emissions from such flights during the whole of 2012. The monitoring and reporting obligations would also be deferred for such flights. Commissioner Hedegaard justified the deferral on the basis that ICAO was expected to adopt new multilateral carbon emissions measures at its 2013 Assembly. More cynical voices suspected that China's threatened postponement of a $14 billion order for 55 Airbus aircraft may also have played a major part in the decision. *See* Press Release, European Commission, Stopping the Clock of ETS and Aviation Measures Following Last Week's International Civil Aviation Organization (ICAO) Council (Nov. 12, 2012). As discussed *supra* in note 7, ICAO has been charged by its member States with drawing up a global aviation emissions agreement by 2016. Nevertheless, the EU appears determined to resume application of its ETS rules to foreign carriers, while (for the moment) restricting charges to emissions occurring within the airspace of EU Member States. *See* Press Release, European Commission, Aviation Emissions: Commission Proposes Applying EU ETS to European Regional Airspace from 1 January 2014 (Oct. 16, 2013).

[12]   Why did the EU pursue this unilateralist course? Certainly, there is a widespread environmentalist culture in the EU that views aviation with suspicion. Also, the ethos of the EU has long favored social policies (like welfare and diversity) over trade liberalization. And finally, it may be that the Union's long experience with integration has eroded the force of sovereignty within its borders.

[13]   *See infra* Part 6.7.

a source of "secondary causes" of pollution, such as ground-level transportation congestion to, from, and around airports. The international airline industry, ever conscious of fuel costs, has in turn blamed outmoded air traffic management (ATM) systems for being a principal cause of fuel waste, especially during airport operations.[14] Inefficient airport use management, which allows air carriers to take off and land on a "first come, first served" basis during peak use periods, exacerbates these problems. Not all of these matters can be easily addressed at the international level, however. For instance, although States may negotiate bilaterally for fair and transparent slot allocation rules at their partners' airports, it is typically conceded that local airport regulators are better placed to optimize the distribution and frequency of available slots.[15] The huge costs of upgrading national ATM systems and ensuring interoperability with other systems also demands a "bottom-up" rather than a "top-down" approach; only after a critical mass of larger markets has achieved functional interoperability will it be possible to induce strong global compliance.[16]

6.1.4. *Seeking a Global Response*

Due to the fragmentary and uncertain shape of international aviation's environmental law regime, this chapter is oriented more than other parts of the book toward the *lex ferenda* or "law-in-the-making." As such, we will pay more attention to the legal and policy hazards of formulating an authentically global response to issues such as aviation emissions reduction. The Chicago Convention,[17] though silent on environmental issues *per se*, does affirm certain principles of sovereignty and regulatory uniformity that must be respected in any negotiation for a future global aviation emissions agreement or even with respect to national emissions regulations that implicate international air transport. Discussion of these provisions, along with the role of ICAO in promulgating environmental SARPs, will be followed by consideration of additional environmental concerns such as aircraft noise. First, however, we turn to an overview of the substantive scope of current international environmental law.

---

[14] Fuel reportedly represents approximately 35% of industry operation costs. Hugo Martín, *Airlines Cut Routes as Fuel Costs Climb; Ticket Prices Will Stay High and Planes Will Stay Crowded for the Near Future, FAA Report Says*, L.A. TIMES, Mar. 9, 2012, at B1.

[15] But, as discussed *supra* in Chapter 3, Section 3.7.4, if the slot allocation mechanism can be used by municipalities to collect rents through, for instance, a slot auction, they will have a strong incentive to stretch their airport's capacity beyond an efficient level.

[16] *See* Brian F. Havel, *A US Point of View on European ATM Developments, in* ACHIEVING THE SINGLE EUROPEAN SKY 107, 117 (Pablo Mendes de Leon & Daniel Calleja Crespo eds., 2011).

[17] Convention on International Civil Aviation, *opened for signature* Dec. 7, 1944, 61 Stat. 1180, 15 U.N.T.S. 295 (entered into force Apr. 4, 1947) [hereinafter Chicago Convention].

6.2. AN OVERVIEW OF INTERNATIONAL ENVIRONMENTAL LAW

6.2.1. *Introduction*

To give context to this discussion, it will be helpful to look briefly at the broader international environmental law regime. While international aviation's exceptional status is recognized within that regime, the policy choices and rule-making processes that have both guided and impeded its development are also influencing how laws and policies, especially on climate change, can be framed for the global air transport industry.

6.2.2. *A General Obligation of States but Few Binding Global Standards*

According to the International Court of Justice (ICJ), the evolution of international environmental law has given rise to "a general obligation of States to ensure that activities within their jurisdiction and control respect the environment of other [S]tates or of areas beyond national control."[18] Nevertheless, global governance of the environment remains fundamentally incomplete, in part because of a lack of political will but also because of the complexity of aligning the interests and concerns of nearly 200 States. Thus, the global environment is not being managed by a single international supervisory authority along the lines of the World Trade Organization (WTO). There is not a single systematic global environmental treaty that matches the sweeping coverage of the 1982 U.N. Convention on the Law of the Sea or of the WTO treaty regime for international trade law. Moreover, international environmental law has evolved few global standards that could be framed as "hard" international law: the phase-out schedule for ozone toxins,[19] the health, safety, and environmental provisions adopted by the International Maritime Organization (IMO),[20] and the greenhouse gas emissions reporting

---

[18] Nuclear Weapons, Advisory Opinion, 1996 I.C.J. 226, 241–42, para. 29 (July 8).

[19] *See infra* note 23. The ozone protection regime is the first U.N. regime ever to achieve universal ratification. United Nations Blog, Most-ratified International Treaties (Sept. 24, 2012), http://blogs.un.org/blog/2012/09/24/most-ratified-international-treaties/.

[20] For example, the ban on dumping plastic garbage at sea imposed in Annex V of the International Convention for the Prevention of Pollution from Ships, Nov. 2, 1973, 1340 U.N.T.S. 184, *as modified by* Protocol, Feb. 17, 1978, 1340 U.N.T.S. 61 [hereinafter the MARPOL Convention], which covers States representing over 98% of the world's shipping tonnage. *See* Summary of Status of Conventions, International Maritime Organization, http://www.imo.org/About/Conventions/StatusOfConventions/Pages/Default.aspx.

obligations of States under the ·climate change treaty[21] may be the only principles with a secure universal footing as hard law.[22] Outside those areas, international environmental agreements tend toward a "pledge-and-review" approach (using aspirational language such as "to the extent possible") and vague timelines. Treaty standards for carbon emissions reduction, despite serial U.N.-sponsored conferences, also fall mostly within this soft law paradigm.

6.2.3. *Subject-Specific Regulatory Regimes of International Environmental Law*

International environmental law, in fact, consists primarily of the content and scope of subject-specific regulatory regimes that are in various states of legal and policy development. These regimes have been established by multilateral treaties such as the 1985 Vienna Convention for the Protection of the Ozone Layer[23] and the 1992 Conventions on Climate Change and Biological Diversity.[24] As these treaty titles suggest, international environmental lawmaking is strongly responsive to changing political moods and priorities. As a result, and even more than in other fields of international cooperation, each treaty is the product of unique political bartering within its "environmental" subject area so that the design of each treaty reflects what was politically feasible at the time of its adoption. Robust diplomacy, rather than patient codification by teams of experts, has characterized the making of international environmental law during the past two decades.

---

[21] *See infra* note 24. In contrast, the more binding emissions reduction targets and time-frames of the Kyoto Protocol (*see infra* in the main text) affect States responsible for only 25% of global greenhouse gas emissions.

[22] *See* discussion in Veerle Heyvaert, Regulatory Competition: Accounting for the Transnational Dimension of Environmental Regulation (May 16, 2012) (unpublished paper presented to the Center for Socio-Legal Studies, Oxford).

[23] Vienna Convention for the Protection of the Ozone Layer, Mar. 22, 1985, T.I.A.S. No. 11097, 1513 U.N.T.S. 293. The real achievements of ozone protection occurred in the later 1987 Montreal Protocol on Substances that Deplete the Ozone Layer, the first in a series of agreements setting specific targets for reducing and eliminating manufacture and use of a range of ozone-depleting substances. The success of ozone protection is such that global ozone losses and the Antarctic ozone hole should recover by 2068. NASA, Goddard Space Flight Center, *NASA Study Finds Clock Ticking Slower on Ozone Hole Recovery*, Jun. 29, 2006, http://www. nasa.gov/centers/goddard/news/topstory/2006/ozone_recovery.html.

[24] United Nations Framework Convention on Climate Change, May 9, 1992, 1771 U.N.T.S. 107 (entered into force Mar. 21, 1994) [hereinafter UNFCCC]; Convention on Biological Diversity, Jun. 5, 1992, 1760 U.N.T.S. 79 (entered into force Dec. 29, 1993).

6.2.4. *The U.N. Framework Convention on Climate Change (UNFCCC)*

The most comprehensive approach to addressing a single global environmental issue is the 1992 U.N. Framework Convention on Climate Change (UNFCCC).[25] For the first time in the text of an international treaty, the Convention specifically emphasizes the risk of damage to "ecosystems" in tandem with the need to protect the planet's "climate system."[26] The UNFCCC was actually the product of "package deal" diplomacy that also led to a soft law instrument, the 1992 Rio Declaration on Environment and Development of the U.N. Conference on Environment and Development.[27] The Rio Declaration and its accompanying treaties[28] are regarded by many commentators as the coming-of-age moment for international environmental law. As an example, both the Declaration and the Convention use a specialized lexicon, incorporating terms such as "common but differentiated responsibility,"[29] the "precautionary" principle,[30] the "polluter pays" principle,[31] and the notion of "sustainable development,"[32] that had become well-established in international environmental law and policy through prior international collaboration.

---

[25] UNFCCC, *supra* note 24.

[26] *Id.* art. 1.

[27] United Nations Conference on Environment and Development, Rio de Janeiro, Braz., Jun. 3–14, 1992, Rio Declaration on Environment and Development, princ. 1, U.N. Doc. A/CONF.151/26/Rev.1 (Vol. I), Annex I (Aug. 12, 1992) [hereinafter Rio Declaration].

[28] As noted, *supra* note 24, the Convention on Biodiversity was also signed at Rio in 1992.

[29] UNFCCC, *supra* note 24, art. 3; Rio Declaration, *supra* note 27, princ. 7. Perhaps the most controversial concept in the climate change accords, the principle of "common but differentiated responsibility" was intended to recognize that industrialized nations bear a greater responsibility for the carbon buildup in the atmosphere by virtue of larger historical carbon emissions than developing countries. Industrialized countries also have greater technological and economic capacity to reduce climate emissions. As a result, developed countries are held to more exacting emissions reduction standards than developing nations, which are merely charged with continuing development in a more sustainable manner.

[30] UNFCCC, *supra* note 24, art. 3; Rio Declaration, *supra* note 27, princ. 15. The "precautionary" principle holds that climate change mitigation efforts should not be impeded by concerns about any perceived or real lack of full scientific certainty regarding the causes and effects of climate change.

[31] Rio Declaration, *supra* note 27, princ. 16. According to this principle, the polluting party is made to bear the cost of the pollution, either through taxes on the pollution or regulatory schemes.

[32] UNFCCC, *supra* note 24, art. 3; Rio Declaration, *supra* note 27, princ. 7. Sustainable development utilizes resources in a way that satisfies a country's present needs while preserving resources and the environment for future generations. It is often ensnared with "common but differentiated responsibilities" as developing countries are asked to pursue "sustainable development" rather than focus on reducing current pollution levels.

6.2.5. *Competing Priorities of the Environment and Economic Growth*

The international community, however, has never authoritatively resolved the competing priorities of ecosystem trusteeship and economic growth. The Rio Declaration did not exalt the environment over economic development, affirming instead that these goals should be "integrated" but without assigning a priority between them.[33] The political consequences of that ambivalence are reflected in the making of international environmental law. Precisely because they need to be flexible in responding to changing political, scientific, and technological circumstances, environmental treaties tend to be drafted in very general terms. Rather than settling agreed standards and timetables for action, they envisage an ongoing consultative process such as a "Committee of the Parties" to elaborate more detailed rules through later protocols, amendments, and annexes. In that way, a "regulatory regime" arises to govern specific aspects of environmental concern. Of course, that incremental process is well understood by aviation lawyers because it reflects how the principles of the Chicago Convention and its annexes continue to evolve through ICAO's adoption of new and revised SARPs. In the field of international environmental law, the possibility for more detailed bargaining to follow the adoption of the main text allows a more general treaty to consolidate support and to build confidence in its principles.

6.2.6. *The UNFCCC as an Incremental Model*

As its name indicates, the UNFCCC is just such a framework or umbrella treaty that sets out some important key principles but also reflects the incremental model through a diplomatic process for reaching further and more detailed agreement on numerical targets for carbon dioxide emissions reduction. The ultimate objective of the Convention is not to reverse climate change but to stabilize carcinogenic pollution "at a level that would prevent dangerous anthropogenic interference with the climate system."[34] The Convention sets a nonbinding benchmark of a return to 1990 levels of anthropogenic emissions,[35] but otherwise appears to tolerate some degree of climate damage provided that a "time-frame" is created "sufficient to allow ecosystems to adapt naturally to climate change."[36] Consistent with the Rio Declaration,

---

[33] *See* United Nations Conference on Environment and Development, Rio de Janeiro, Braz., Jun. 3–14, 1992, Agenda 21, U.N. Doc. A/CONF. 151/26 (Aug. 12, 1992).

[34] UNFCCC, *supra* note 24, art.2.

[35] *See id.* art. 4 (although this target is assigned only to "developed" countries).

[36] *Id.* art. 2.

the Convention also recognizes that the time-frame must "enable economic development to proceed in a sustainable manner."[37]

6.2.7. The Kyoto Protocol

The 1997 Kyoto Protocol, discussed later in this chapter, was the first milestone in the serial diplomacy that has characterized the UNFCCC process.[38] In exempting aviation and maritime emissions from its national emissions reduction targets,[39] the Protocol recognized the international nature of these industries' emissions (as the EU had also done in initially exempting aviation from its emissions trading scheme[40]). But there is some concept slippage in a document that purports to regulate global emissions multisectorally yet exempts two key sectors that emit globally.[41] The reasons for the exemption were institutional: deference was paid to the fact that both international aviation and international shipping have their own intergovernmental specialized agencies (ICAO and the IMO) within the U.N. system.[42] Nevertheless, critics have pointed out that devolving responsibility for emissions reduction to those agencies carries the risk of regulatory capture of their agenda by the industries they represent: at least with respect to international aviation, ICAO's slow progress toward a multilateral aviation emissions agreement may offer some support to its critics.[43]

---

[37] *Id.*

[38] Kyoto Protocol to the United Nations Framework Convention on Climate Change, Dec. 11, 1997, 2303 U.N.T.S. 162 (entered into force Feb. 16, 2005) [hereinafter Kyoto Protocol].

[39] *See id.* art. 2. Aviation, incidentally, was not exempted from the 1987 Montreal Protocol on substances depleting the ozone layer (*see supra* note 23). This was not a major issue for the industry because most of the pollutants regulated by the Protocol were absent from kerosene emissions.

[40] *See* Brian F. Havel & John Q. Mulligan, *The Triumph of Politics: Reflections on the Judgment of the Court of Justice of the European Union Validating the Inclusion of Non-EU Airlines in the Emissions Trading Scheme*, 37 AIR & SPACE L. 3, 6 (2012) (citing Council Directive 2003/87, 2003 O.J. (L 275)).

[41] A sectoral focus, such as nuclear energy, toxic chemicals, and the law of the sea, had been the dominant approach of international environmental law until the more recent creation of broader (but still issue-specific) regimes to superintend climate change, protection of the ozone layer, and biological diversity.

[42] In July 2011, the IMO added energy-efficiency requirements to Annex VI of the MARPOL Convention, *supra* note 20. The IMO has had ongoing discussions about development of MBMs for reducing the amount of greenhouse gases produced by the shipping industry.

[43] This deficiency has certainly drawn comment with respect to the IMO experience. *See* Claybourne Fox Clarke & Thiago Chagas, *Aviation and Climate Change Regulation*, in LEGAL ASPECTS OF CARBON TRADING: KYOTO, COPENHAGEN, AND BEYOND 606–21 (David Freestone & Charlotte Streck eds.) (2009) (commenting also on close relations between CAEP and the aviation industry).

6.2.8. *Future of International Environmental Law*

Other than the continued post-Kyoto process, there is little likelihood of major new treaty initiatives in international environmental law in the coming years.[44] The focus instead will be on consolidating and improving the effectiveness and compliance record of existing regimes. Similarly, calls for a supranational environmental enforcement agency or judicial tribunal are no longer likely to be heeded, especially in an era when pallid economic growth among Western States is forcing them to reassess policy priorities such as environmental protection. But it is now apparent that international environmental law is no longer just a matter of neighboring States quarrelling over liability for smokestack contaminants leaking across borders.[45] To the extent that international aviation lawyers should be concerned about the scope of this relatively new discipline, it is to recognize that international environmental law now has a global emphasis, and focuses in particular on a preventive and precautionary approach to management of the ecosystem.

6.2.9. *Divergent Paradigms of Airspace Sovereignty and the Global Atmosphere*

Finally, international aviation lawyers watching these developments may be troubled by one possible legal consequence of the globalization of international environmental law. The UNFCCC, in its preamble, states the eye-catching premise that climate change is the "common concern of humankind."[46] The treaty also attributes climate change to "human activity that alters the composition of the global atmosphere."[47] Although the treaty makes no express

---

[44] As the Copenhagen (2010), Mexico City (2011), and Durban (2012) summits demonstrated, the UNFCCC process has been stalled and in some respects defeated by its quest for a binding, multilateral, multisectoral emissions reduction strategy. Durban produced only an agreement to pursue a comprehensive climate change treaty to be completed by 2015, but the proposed accord would not come into effect sooner than 2020. *See* Establishment of an Ad Hoc Working Group on the Durban Platform for Enhanced Action, Draft Decision CP.17 (Dec. 2011), http://unfccc.int/files/meetings/durban_nov_2011/decisions/application/pdf/cop17_durbanplatform.pdf. A full archive of videos, documents, and other statements released during the 17th Conference of the Parties to the UNFCCC is available at http://unfccc.int/meetings/durban_nov_2011/meeting/6245.php.

[45] An example of a relatively early environmental treaty addressing just such problems is the Convention on Long-Range Transboundary Air Pollution. Transboundary pollution occurs when pollution is generated in one State but crosses the border, typically via air or water pathways, and affects the citizens or environment of another State. *See* Convention on Long-Range Transboundary Air Pollution, *opened for signature* Nov. 13, 1979, 1302 U.N.T.S. 217.

[46] UNFCCC, *supra* note 24, pmbl.

[47] *Id.* art. 1. There are numerous references in the treaty's text to the "atmosphere."

appropriation of the Earth's atmosphere to the principle of "common concern" or common ownership, it is a nice question whether the Chicago Convention's doctrine of airspace sovereignty is implicated (if not actually violated) by the climate change treaty's ideation of the "atmosphere."[48] Moreover, if the atmosphere is to be treated as a "common resource," as recommended by a preparatory group of legal experts,[49] then arguably each member of the community of States has an identifiable interest under the treaty in how each of its fellow States manages the atmospheric canopy above its territory. Airspace sovereignty, in this sense, would be circumscribed by the shared responsibilities of States in accordance with treaties like the UNFCCC. Here, it seems, international aviation law and international environmental law reflect strongly divergent paradigms of global regulation.

6.3. THE ROLE OF ICAO IN ENVIRONMENTAL ISSUES AFFECTING INTERNATIONAL AVIATION

6.3.1. *ICAO'S Competence for Environmental Issues*

International civil aviation, unlike virtually all other major industries, has its own U.N. specialized agency, ICAO, and a governing treaty, the Chicago Convention.[50] The Convention does not expressly vest ICAO with custody over aviation emissions reduction (indeed, it hardly mentions environmental issues at all). But it does provide sufficient authority to the Organization, through the consent of its 191 State parties, to develop several legal mechanisms that can address this issue with varying degrees of legal bindingness. What remains in dispute is the exclusivity of ICAO's competence over international aviation emissions and whether the Organization is functionally

---

[48] Thus, the high seas are treated (in the Chicago Convention and elsewhere) as a common area beyond the reach of any State jurisdiction. *See* Chicago Convention, *supra* note 17, art. 12. The "atmosphere," on the other hand, is neither a defined term in the UNFCCC nor in general public international law. As an air mass in constant motion both above and across national boundaries, it lacks the simple conceptual clarity that the drafters of the Chicago Convention were able to assume for the term "airspace."

[49] The conception of the atmosphere as a common resource or trust has been put forth at conferences, in scholarship, and even in judicial opinions. *See* Meeting Statement from Protection of the Atmosphere: International Meeting of Legal and Policy Experts, at Ottawa, Canada (Feb. 20–22, 1989); Mary Christina Wood, *Nature's Trust: A Legal, Political and Moral Frame for Global Warming*, 34 B.C. ENVT'L. AFF. L. REV. 577 (2007); Ramit Plushnick-Masti, *Texas Judge Rules Atmosphere, Air is Public Trust*, ASSOCIATED PRESS, July 12, 2012.

[50] *See* Chicago Convention, *supra* note 17. For a detailed discussion of the Convention, see *supra* Chapter 2.

capable of facilitating a true international consensus on emissions reduction. It is worth noting, also, that the U.N. Charter contains no explicit charge to the world organization itself to act as a policymaker in international environmental matters. The environment was not a legislative issue at the time of the adoption of the Charter in 1945, nor was it when the Chicago Convention, ICAO's founding instrument, was negotiated and signed in 1944. The emergence of a U.N. environmental competency, as with ICAO, was the result of giving a broad teleological interpretation to the Charter and to the implied powers of that organization. The specialized agencies, also, were not endowed with specific powers over the environment but have evolved their own competency through interpretation and practice.[51]

6.3.2. *Path to ICAO Oversight*

International aviation's contribution to global climate change lies at the core of ICAO's current policy agenda on the environment. According to the Intergovernmental Panel on Climate Change (IPCC),[52] global temperatures are on the rise due to rapid increases in greenhouse gas emissions produced by human activity.[53] In response to global warming concerns, as we have seen, world leaders instructed their ministers and diplomats to forge several international agreements to reduce greenhouse gas emissions. As noted earlier, the Rio Conference in 1992 agreed to the UNFCCC which, *inter alia*, establishes a framework for intergovernmental cooperation and information-sharing related to emissions, national environmental regulations, and best practices; inaugurates a series of domestic and international strategies for adapting to the impact of climate change; and classifies State parties according to the level of obligations they are expected to accept in order to scale back their output of greenhouse gases.[54] Although the treaty framers chose not to address the air

---

[51] Notice that the ICJ has taken a relatively strict view of how generously the powers of the specialized agencies should be interpreted vis-à-vis the parent organization. *See* Legality of the Use by a State of Nuclear Weapons in Armed Conflict, Advisory Opinion, 1996 I.C.J. 66, 78–79, para. 25 (Jul. 8, 1996) ("[International organizations] are invested by the States which create them with powers, the limits of which are a function of the common interests whose promotion those States entrust to them").

[52] As indicated *supra* note 3, the IPCC is an international scientific body jointly established by the U.N. and the World Meteorological Organization.

[53] *See generally* IPCC, SUMMARY FOR POLICYMAKERS, *supra* note 3. For a more detailed discussion of the potential adverse effects of global warming on the environment, see IPCC, IMPACTS, ADAPTATION AND VULNERABILITY, *supra* note 3. The Panel's next inclusive report on global warming is scheduled to be released in 2014.

[54] *See* UNFCCC, *supra* note 24.

transport industry directly, the 1997 Kyoto Protocol to the UNFCCC mandates that developed States which have ratified that instrument must "pursue limitation or reduction of greenhouse gases ... from aviation [by] working through [ICAO] [.]"[55] The following year, ICAO adopted Resolution A32–8, an update to the Organization's *Consolidated Statement of Continuing ICAO Policies and Practices Related to Environmental Protection,*[56] designating ICAO's special committee on the environment, CAEP,[57] to study the effects of aviation emissions on climate change and to develop policies based on its findings.[58] At ICAO's triennial Assembly meetings in 2007 and 2010, the Organization's member States adopted Resolutions (A36-22 and A37-19, respectively) reaffirming the Organization's legitimacy as the lead international body to execute a global response to aviation's role in climate change.[59] In the 2010 Resolution, however, ICAO seemed implicitly to contemplate other fora for transnational aviation emissions initiatives, urging States to respect the annexed Guiding Principles for MBMs (see below) "and to engage in constructive bilateral and/or multilateral consultation and negotiations with other States to reach an agreement."[60] With respect to emissions reduction, the 2010 Resolution also sets a desired but nonbinding target for "global annual average fuel efficiency improvement" of 2% until 2020, and carbon-

---

[55] Kyoto Protocol, *supra* note 38, art. 2(2). The Protocol makes a division between Annex I and II parties, which are committed to reduce greenhouse gas emissions, and non-Annex parties comprised of developing countries that are not required to make emissions reduction commitments. Ironically, three of the world's leading greenhouse gas emitters – China, India, and Brazil – are not Annex I parties. *See* Larry Parker & John Blodgett, Cong. Research Serv., RL 32721, Greenhouse Gas Emissions: Perspectives on the Top 20 Emitters and Developed Versus Developing Nations 14 (2008).

[56] International Civil Aviation Organization, *Consolidated Statement of Continuing ICAO Policies and Practices Related to Environmental Protection,* Assem. Res. A32–8 (2000), *compiled in Assembly Resolutions in Force,* ICAO Doc. 9790 (2001). The Consolidated Statement of Continuing ICAO Policies and Practices Related to Environmental Protection is updated every three years at the ICAO Assembly session. The most recent update of ICAO resolutions included a separate consolidated statement on climate change distinct from the statement regarding other environmental concerns. *See* ICAO, *Assembly Resolutions in Force,* ICAO Doc. 9958 (2010).

[57] *See supra* Section 6.1.1.

[58] Resolution A32-8 has since been superseded by subsequent resolutions addressing aviation and environmental protection. *See* ICAO, *Assembly Resolutions in Force,* ICAO Doc. 9958 (2010).

[59] *See* ICAO, *Consolidated Statement of Continuing ICAO Policies and Practices Related to Environmental Protection,* app. A, Assem. Res. A36-22 (2007), *compiled in Assembly Resolutions in Force,* ICAO Doc. 9902 (2007); ICAO, *Consolidated Statement of Continuing ICAO Policies and Practices Related to Environmental Protection – Climate Change,* Assem. Res. A37-19, *compiled in Assembly Resolutions in Force,* ICAO Doc. 9958 (2010) [hereinafter ICAO Res. A37-19]. New amendments to these policies, adopted at ICAO's 38th Assembly in October 2013, have yet to be officially published as this book goes to press.

[60] ICAO Res. A37-19, *supra* note 59, para. 14.

neutral growth thereafter.[61] Curiously, unlike the methodology adopted in the UNFCCC, the Resolution imposes no binding obligation on member States to report relevant annual carbon emissions to ICAO.[62] All of the ICAO Assembly Resolutions, however, constitute soft law to the extent that they are not techni-cally binding on States and lack legal enforceability, as we will discuss later in this chapter. But they still serve as a signaling device among the State parties that reveals attitudes toward the relationship between aviation and the phenomenon of climate change, including the willingness of States to submit their airlines to potentially costly emissions reduction mandates. As this book goes to press in late 2013, ICAO has been charged by its members with developing a "hard law" solution to the aviation emissions problem no later than the Organization's autumn 2016 Assembly meetings and with an eye to full implementation in 2020. Given the Organization's mixed record on emissions abatement as well as the challenges of trying to corral more than 190 States into endorsing an agree-ment that will have widely varying effects on their respective aviation econo-mies, hortatory resolutions may be the most that ICAO will be able to muster.

6.3.3. Role of SARPs: Annex 16

Within the range of its express powers, ICAO can do little directly to regulate aviation emissions. As a historical matter, given the dearth of knowledge about climate science in 1944, this is understandable. Even so, as discussed above and in Chapter 1, ICAO – through the consent of its members – can promulgate SARPs as annexes to the Chicago Convention in order to encourage harmo-nization of critical issues in air transport, including safety standards, navigation protocols, and various technical specifications.[63] With respect to the environ-ment, Annex 16, now divided into two distinct chapters,[64] includes standards for

---

[61] *Id.* paras. 4, 6. Notice the emphasis on fuel-efficiency improvements rather than emissions targets until 2020. Discussions to date also indicate that domestic aviation will be included in ICAO's global emissions reduction efforts. *See* ICAO Executive Committee Working Paper, *Development of a Global Framework for Addressing Civil Aviation CO$_2$ Emissions*, A37-WP/ 217 EX/39 (2010). However, no specific recommendation to incorporate domestic aviation into a future ICAO-brokered emissions agreement has been announced thus far. *See gen-erally* ICAO Executive Committee Working Paper, *Consolidated Statement of Continuing ICAO Policies and Practices Related to Environmental Protection – Climate Change*, A38-WP/34 EX/29 (2013).

[62] But ICAO member States are "encouraged" to submit action plans and to report emissions. *See* ICAO Res. A37–19, *supra* note 59, para. 9.

[63] *See supra* Chapter 1, Section 1.6.2, and Chapter 2, Sections 2.6.6., 2.6.7.

[64] Annex 16 was first developed in 1971 to regulate aircraft noise. The 1972 U.N. Conference on the Human Environment led to ICAO Assembly Resolutions A18-11 and A18-12 recognizing aviation's potential to adversely impact the environment and ICAO's role in developing environmental standards. An ICAO study group identified vented fuel, smoke, and gaseous

aircraft engine design to prevent liquid fuel expulsions during operation ("fuel venting"), while also establishing requirements to limit the discharge of smoke, hydrocarbons, carbon dioxide, and nitrogen oxide. Notably, two of the largest identified contributors to the so-called greenhouse effect, dihydrogen oxide and carbon dioxide, are left untouched by the Annex.[65] The limited scope of the SARPs dealing with emissions has prompted calls for an overhaul of Annex 16 to include more comprehensive coverage of greenhouse gas standards, along with stricter requirements for airlines to phase out noncompliant engines. Little action has been taken on either front. CAEP is charged with updating Annex 16, but seems to have settled into serving primarily as a research arm and, to some degree, as a clearinghouse for aviation emissions data and best practices with respect to abatement measures.[66]

6.3.4. *Legal Status of SARPs*

Relying only on SARPs to achieve emissions reductions is problematic: they are, at best, legally ambiguous.[67] The thirty-six member ICAO Council has the power to adopt new SARPs by a two-thirds majority vote, but their adoption can be nullified if a simple majority of the ICAO membership chooses to reject them.[68] Further, depending on whether a potential emissions abatement requirement is framed as a "standard" or a "recommended practice," it is conceivable that some ICAO member States might question its mandatory status.[69] And even if a supermajority of ICAO's Council membership had the political will to enhance Annex 16's emissions measures, the Convention

emissions as subjects for regulation. In 1977, the ICAO Council added a Committee on Aircraft Engine Emissions (CAEE), which would be the precursor to the CAEP. After a decade's worth of study, standards for engine emissions were adopted in 1981, prompting Annex 16's renaming and division into two volumes: Volume I, *Aircraft Noise*, and Volume II, *Aircraft Engine Emissions. See* ICAO, INTERNATIONAL STANDARDS AND RECOMMENDED PRACTICES: ENVIRONMENTAL PROTECTION, ANNEX 16, foreword.

[65] This is because the first engine emissions standards were devised to limit the impact of smoke, fuel venting, and gaseous emissions on the immediate environments through which aircraft traveled, and not because of any concern to reduce aviation's contributions to the atmospheric greenhouse gas buildup driving global climate change.

[66] *See, e.g.,* ICAO, *Offsetting Emissions from the Aviation Sector,* ICAO Doc. 9951 (2011); ICAO, *Scoping Study on the Application of Emissions Trading and Offsets for Local Air Quality in Aviation,* ICAO Doc. 9948 (2011).

[67] *See supra* Chapter 2, Section 2.6.7.

[68] *See* Chicago Convention, *supra* note 17, art. 90.

[69] Although often discussed collectively under the acronym SARPs, standards and recommended practices are actually distinct in that compliance with standards is deemed necessary and any contracting State that is unable to comply with a standard is required to notify ICAO. Recommended practices are considered desirable and it is not mandatory to report noncompliance. *See supra* Chapter 2, Section 2.6.7.

allows States that are unable (or unwilling) to comply with a newly promulgated standard to provide ICAO with notice to that effect without incurring penalties.[70]

6.3.5. *Exclusivity of ICAO's Emissions Reduction Competence and the Issue of MBMs*

The argument that ICAO should attempt directly to regulate emissions through SARPs is motivated by the possibly mistaken belief that the Organization now holds exclusive competence over the disposition of the issue of reducing aviation emissions. We have seen how the Kyoto Protocol requires States to work through ICAO, although that mandate is restricted to developed States that are signatories to the UNFCCC (the so-called Annex I parties).[71] The early triennial Assembly Resolutions that reaffirm ICAO's leadership[72] are unspecific with respect to whether ICAO envisions an international treaty establishing MBMs (such as emissions trading or eco-taxes) or simply plans a nonbinding framework on MBMs and nothing more. The most recent Assembly Resolution, adopted in October 2013, calls upon ICAO to create a global MBM scheme by 2016. Presumably, such a scheme would require a fresh treaty instrument.[73] The 2010 and 2013 Resolutions do set forth, however, a series of "Guiding Principles" for MBMs that States can pursue both bilaterally and multilaterally. Even though ICAO member States are free (in a technical sense) to disregard these Principles, their value lies in providing a common road map to emissions reduction. The Principles advocate that MBMs support sustainable development in the international aviation sector; be transparent and administratively simple; be cost-effective; minimize carbon leakage and market distortions; and ensure the fair treatment of international aviation in relation to other sectors.[74] In addition, the

---

[70] *See* Chicago Convention, *supra* note 17, art. 38 (a State's nonconformity with a promulgated recommended practice, on the other hand, does not carry a requirement of notification to ICAO). For more on the shortcomings of the Convention's enforcement mechanisms, see *supra* Chapter 2, Part 2.6. ICAO employs the Universal Safety Oversight Audit Program as its primary enforcement mechanism for SARPs concerning aviation safety. States are audited for compliance with safety standards and the results of the audits are made public. *See supra* Chapter 5, Section 5.3.5. The audit program has not been extended to Annex 16 SARPs, however, making compliance even more uncertain.

[71] *See supra* note 55 (explaining distinction between Annex I and II parties and non-Annex parties).

[72] *See supra* note 59 and accompanying text.

[73] *See, e.g.,* ICAO Res. A37–19, *supra* note 59, para. 13. *See* Press Release, *supra* note 7.

[74] *Id.* annex. This annex of "Guiding Principles" remains unchanged by the 2013 Resolution.

Principles recommend that "where revenues are generated from MBMs . . . they should be applied in the first instance to mitigating the environmental impact of aircraft engine emissions, including mitigation and adaptation, as well as assistance to and support for developing States[.]"[75] Finally, the 2010 and 2013 Resolutions imply that States should only apply MBMs to foreign carriers on the basis of mutual consent.[76] Unilateralism, for reasons discussed shortly, is greatly disfavored.

6.3.6. *An Aviation Emissions Reduction Regime Outside ICAO?*

The Kyoto Protocol, as noted, calls upon only a select number of its signatories to "work through" ICAO, without providing further details on what this process might entail in practice. Presumably, so long as the State parties to the Protocol do not disregard the Organization's mandates as specified in the Chicago Convention and elaborated in Assembly Resolutions, there is no conflict if States should choose to negotiate a bilateral or multilateral emissions reduction treaty outside the auspices of ICAO.[77] ICAO's own pronouncements seem to suggest that it would acquiesce in complementary (or even rival) initiatives.[78] To date, it has merely exhorted its membership "to refrain from environmental measures that would adversely affect the orderly and sustainable development of international civil aviation," as well as "to continue to cooperate closely with international organizations" on climate change.[79] Importantly, however, the Organization qualifies this arguably permissive language with a warning that States should not "implement an emissions trading system on other [Chicago Convention] [c]ontracting States' aircraft operators except on the basis of mutual agreement between those States."[80] That caveat was, of course, motivated by the EU's recent incorporation of all non-EU carriers into its ETS, but the Resolution also reflects the general stance of ICAO's members against emissions unilateralism.

---

[75] *Id.* This principle is especially important to note in light of Article 15 of the Chicago Convention, *see infra* Section 6.4.2.

[76] *See, e.g.,* ICAO Res. A37-19, *supra* note 59, para. 14 (recommending bilateral or multilateral negotiations before MBMs are adopted by any State).

[77] The Court of Justice of the European Union (CJEU) has affirmed this proposition. *See* Havel & Mulligan, *supra* note 40, at 25–26; *see also infra* Section 6.4.6.

[78] *See* ICAO Res. A37-19, *supra* note 59, para. 14.

[79] Assem. Res. A36-22, *supra* note 59, paras. 9–10.

[80] *Id.* para. 1(b)(1).

6.4. THE CHICAGO CONVENTION AND AVIATION EMISSIONS REGULATION

6.4.1. *Key Principles of Multilateralism, Reciprocity, and Mutual Consent*

The issue of unilateralism, then, is central to an understanding of how the Chicago Convention and ICAO's mandates seek to reconcile the airspace sovereignty principle in Article 1 of the Convention with the imperative of making international air travel functionally possible across national borders. As we will discuss, the Convention includes prohibitions on discrimination and places limits on charges (including, it can be argued, environmentally motivated charges) to foreign carriers. These provisions reflect an understanding that while States retain control over their national airspaces, international aviation ultimately relies on a sense and pattern of comity between States. The industry has a rich history (much of it achieved through ICAO) of multilateral technical cooperation, and ICAO's rejection of unilateral emissions reduction initiatives reflects normative deference to the importance of multilateralism, reciprocity, and mutual consent.

6.4.2. *Constraints on Unilateral Action (1): Articles 1, 12, and 15 of the Chicago Convention*

The Chicago Convention, in fact, can be read as placing strong legal constraints on unilateral action. For instance, Article 1, which codifies the customary international law principles of airspace sovereignty, arguably constrains the regulatory reach of States seeking to control the emissions released by foreign carriers into the common planetary atmosphere.[81] So, too, does Article 12, which indicates (albeit in implicit rather than explicit terms) that only ICAO has the authority to regulate flights over the high seas.[82] These provisions would readily call into question the legality of, for example, an EU-imposed flight ban on U.S. airlines over the Pacific Ocean or an EU eco-tax on

---

[81] The EU's Court of Justice did not agree with that proposition. The CJEU insisted that when non-EU airlines use EU airports during any point in their journeys, they are subject to the "unlimited jurisdiction of the European Union." Case C-366/10, The Air Transport Ass'n of America, American Airlines, Inc., Continental Airlines, Inc., United Airlines, Inc. v. The Sec'y of State for Energy and Climate Change, 2010 O.J. C-260/12, referred by U.K. High Court of Justice, Q.B. Div. (Admin. Ct.), para. 125.

[82] But note that, under the Chicago Convention, the State of aircraft registration may continue to regulate the aircraft of its air carriers regardless of where they are flying in the world. Chicago Convention, *supra* note 17, art. 12.

Canadian carriers for the emissions they discharge over the Yukon. Greater subtlety and some greater complexity is introduced by a cap-and-trade system of charges whereby any U.S. or Canadian carrier operating to or from the territory of the EU is expected to pay for all of the carbon emissions discharged on its journey as a condition for entering or exiting EU territory.[83] Such a measure would seem to implicate Article 15 of the Convention, which provides that "[n]o fees, dues, or other charges [other than charges imposed for the use of airports or air navigation facilities] shall be imposed by any Contracting State in respect solely of the right of transit over or entry into or exit from its territory of any aircraft of a Contracting State[.]"[84] Article 15 was designed to ensure that an international air carrier would not be at risk of being encumbered by multiple species of taxes in any State to or from which it wished to offer air services. ICAO has glossed Article 15 to mean that the Convention permits the imposition of charges specifically (and only) to recover the costs of providing facilities and services to airlines engaged in international air transport.[85] Under ICAO's reading, MBMs directed at off-setting emissions, such as cap-and-trade or eco-taxation, but which are unrelated to the provision of airport and air navigation services to international aviation, would constitute a charge "in respect solely of the right of transit over or entry into or exit" and would be impermissible under the Convention.[86] A possible counterargument holds that Article 15 refers only to "charges" and not explicitly to a "tax," and that therefore a tax – even if imposed "solely" on the right of transit, entry, or exit – is otherwise permissible. Although it is true that the official English language version of Article 15 does not mention the word "tax," the equally valid French, Spanish, and Russian texts do.[87] Indeed, the other authoritative translations offer powerful evidence that the

[83] Indeed, this is exactly the effect of the EU's decision to bring international aviation into its Emissions Trading Scheme. For more on the EU ETS, *see supra* Section 6.1.2.

[84] Chicago Convention, *supra* note 17, art. 15.

[85] *See* ICAO, *ICAO Policies on Charges for Airports and Air Navigation Services*, para. 1, ICAO Doc. 9082/7 (7th ed. 2004). Admittedly, ICAO's understanding of the Chicago Convention carries only persuasive authority. Unlike the WTO, it does not have the power to issue binding interpretations of its own agreements. *Cf.* Marrakesh Agreement Establishing the World Trade Organization art. IX(2), Apr. 15, 1994, 1867 U.N.T.S. 154 [hereinafter WTO Agreement].

[86] A more moderate interpretation of Article 15 is that emissions-abatement measures are themselves part of the cost of providing airport and air navigation services. But we do not think that a more moderate interpretation would allow a generalized "environmental" tax, where emissions are targeted in gross without specific remediation actions.

[87] The English text of Article 15 includes a prohibition against "fees, dues or charges." The French, Spanish, and Russian translations of the Convention all use their languages' respective terms for taxation instead of "dues." *See* Chicago Convention, *supra* note 17, art. 15, multilingual text, http://www.icao.int/publications/Documents/7300_cons.pdf.

Convention drafters intended to exclude "taxes," along with "fees," "dues," and "charges,"[88] that are not imposed to recover the costs of air navigation and the use of airports. This is a sensible reading of the Chicago Convention: to argue that Article 15 does not deal explicitly with taxes, and that therefore taxes are unregulated by the Convention, would deprive Article 15 of substantive force and allow States to levy all kinds of treasury taxes without any need for cost justification. That is probably why, for example, Article 15 provides in express terms that no charges shall be imposed *solely* for the right to exit a State's airspace[89] – by definition, such activities could occur without necessarily implicating a government-provided service.[90]

6.4.3. *Constraints on Unilateral Action (2): Article 24 of the Chicago Convention*

The only other use of the term "charge" in the Convention appears in Article 24, in a separate and subsequent chapter captioned "Measures to Facilitate Air Navigation." Article 24 defines an *impermissible* charge as including "customs duties, inspection fees, or similar national or local duties or charges."[91] It is evident from the respective placement of these Articles that Article 24 is merely a specific example of the general provision on airport and air navigation

---

[88] As indicated, *supra* note 87, these are the terms used in the English language recitation in Article 15.

[89] Also, the reference in Article 15 to "overflight," in respect of which no airport charges are required, suggests that Article 15 is an absolute rule rather than, as some have argued, a nondiscriminatory rule to protect foreign carriers against their domestic counterparts. The Chicago Convention is concerned with international air transport. It is unlikely that the parties intended by the word "solely" to mean that States could impose charges on international air transport provided that they also did so with respect to domestic air transport. The parties would not have been interested in what States did with regard to air transport within their own territories. The Article 15 prohibition, therefore, cannot be vitiated simply by applying the same tax to domestic carriers.

[90] Defenders of unilaterally imposed charges may point to Article 11 of the Convention, which provides that the "laws and regulations of a contracting State relating to the admission to or departure from its territory of aircraft engaged in international navigation ... shall be complied with by such aircraft upon entering or departing from or while within the territory of that State." Chicago Convention, *supra* note 17, art. 11. Article 11, however, does not offer a *passe-partout* for all kinds of taxes to be imposed by contracting States on the basis that it requires compliance with national laws and regulations (including, presumably, national *tax* laws and regulations). In light of the obligations accepted by the contracting States in Article 15 (and in Article 24, discussed *infra* in the main text), the Convention is unlikely to support such an interpretation. Otherwise, once again, there would be virtually no restriction on a State's ability to impose taxes on international civil aviation as a condition "solely" for entry into or exit from that State's territory.

[91] *See* Chicago Convention, *supra* note 17, arts. 15, 24.

charges in Article 15.[92] Once again, that interpretation finds support in ICAO's own statement that customs duties levied by a taxing authority on fuel, lubricants, or aircraft stores cannot be imposed except to the extent that they are based on the actual costs of providing airport or air navigational facilities and services and used to finance the costs of providing them.[93]

6.4.4. *No Constraints on Curbing National Airline Emissions*

Taken together, Articles 15 and 24 most likely limit the regulatory reach of States in environmental matters while also defining the scope of regulations that involve taxes and charges. They say nothing, however, concerning the regulations – including MBMs to offset aviation emissions – that a State may impose *on its own airlines* for hydrocarbon discharges that occur within or beyond its territory. Rather, a State is barred from unilaterally imposing taxes or charges or other regulations that discriminate against or among foreign airlines operating within its territory[94] or extending such impositions (discriminatory or otherwise) to foreign airlines operating outside its territory. Under this reading of the Chicago Convention, the United States could apply an "eco-tax" to Delta Air Lines for emissions released both within and outside U.S. sovereign airspace. But the U.S. authorities could not extend such a tax to Lufthansa for its EU-based emissions. Under a strong reading of Article 15, in fact, no U.S. taxes could be imposed on Lufthansa for any emissions in U.S. airspace unless the tax were intended in its entirety as a recoupment of the cost of providing airport or air navigational facilities.[95]

---

[92] This proposition also follows logically from ICAO's own (albeit nonbinding) interpretation that the Convention "did not attempt to deal comprehensively with tax matters." ICAO, *ICAO's Policies on Taxation in the Field of Air Transport*, intro., para. 2, ICAO Doc. 8632 (1999) [hereinafter *Policies on Taxation*]. In other words, as noted *supra* in the main text, the Convention appears to define a permissible range of cost-related charges in Article 15, and later provides an illustrative example of impermissible non-cost-related charges (labeled as fees or duties) in Article 24.

[93] *See* ICAO, Council Resolution on Taxation of International Air Transport, para. 1(b)(e), *in Policies on Taxation, supra* note 92. As the Commentary on the Resolution, para. 5, in *Policies on Taxation, id.*, also makes clear, the name attached to a levy (e.g., tax, charge, emissions trading) is not dispositive of its effects. In other words, within the Convention system, there is no such thing as a permissible tax that bears no relationship to a cost incurred for service provided. Article 24, therefore, appears to be best understood as being defined ultimately by its relationship to Article 15.

[94] This is because of an earlier clause in Article 15 which states that "[a]ny charges that may be imposed ... by a contracting State for the use of ... airports and air navigation facilities by the aircraft of any other contracting State shall not be higher" than the State applies "to its national aircraft engaged in similar international services."

[95] *See supra* Section 6.4.2.

6.4.5. *The Chicago Convention and Non-ICAO Emissions Agreements*

The Chicago Convention falls silent, however, on the question of whether two or more of its State parties could agree among themselves on an emissions taxing or trading system to be applied only to the airlines of the agreement – and without regard to the site of the emissions or any connection to the provision of navigation or other services. ICAO, as discussed above, already presupposes the legitimacy of such accords, whether reached bilaterally or multilaterally.[96] So long as all parties to the agreement apply the MBMs to their own carriers and to no other party's or nonparty's airlines, there is no conflict with the Chicago Convention. That view is consistent with Article 58(1)(b) of the Vienna Convention on the Law of Treaties, which states that "[t]wo or more parties to a multilateral treaty may conclude an agreement to suspend the operation of provisions of that treaty" so long as "the suspension in question is not prohibited by the treaty," "does not affect the enjoyment by the other parties of their rights under the treaty," and "is not incompatible with the object and purpose of the treaty."[97] A murkier question is whether a party to such an aviation emissions agreement could cede regulatory control in this area to another party (or parties). For example, could the United States and EU develop a uniform emissions taxing scheme that imposed a fixed charge on both parties' airlines for all takeoffs or landings anywhere in the world, and agree further that the scheme would be administered solely by the United States? Presumably yes, so long as the rights of third parties to the Chicago Convention were not infringed. As Joost Pauwelyn has argued with respect to conflicts between WTO law and other international agreements concluded between WTO member States, so long as the obligations made under WTO law are reciprocally given, they can be reciprocally waived through the operation of another treaty. In most such cases, where third-party rights are not violated, the non-WTO treaty prevails.[98] Under Pauwelyn's interpretation, two WTO members could agree bilaterally to refrain from importing certain species of fish from each other for a period of ten years in order to help quell the effects of overfishing, but they could not agree to restrict imports of the same species from third-party members.[99] The same logic applies in our projected

---

[96] *See supra* Section 6.3.6.

[97] *See* Vienna Convention on the Law of Treaties, May 23, 1969, 1155 U.N.T.S. 331, art. 58(1)(b). The Convention adds the caveat that suspensions must be "temporary," although it fails to provide a definite timetable.

[98] *See* JOOST PAUWELYN, CONFLICT OF NORMS IN PUBLIC INTERNATIONAL LAW: HOW WTO LAW RELATES TO OTHER RULES OF INTERNATIONAL LAW 491 (2003).

[99] *See id.*

scenario: the EU could agree to cede control over emissions-related taxation of its airlines to the United States, but could not grant the United States any rights to tax non-EU air carriers, even with respect to emissions released within EU territory.[100]

6.4.6. *Absence of Authoritative Rulings*

Neither ICAO, in its guise as a limited dispute settlement body,[101] nor the ICJ, serving as a recognized tribunal for Convention-related disputes,[102] has ever issued an authoritative ruling on the issues raised in this part. Although several local courts, including the Netherlands Supreme Court and the Court of Justice for the European Union (CJEU), have confronted the application of the Convention to national (or supranational) emissions abatement regulations, their decisions carry little transnational heft.[103] The CJEU was asked to assess (among other things) whether the Chicago Convention barred the application of the EU's ETS to non-EU airlines. The Court's ruling that the Convention is in no way binding on the EU (only on its individual Member States) is not sitting well with the international community.[104] Indeed, dissatisfaction with the CJEU decision has prompted several major aeropolitical powers, including China and the United States, to contemplate a formal challenge to the ETS before ICAO.[105] Unless the matter is mediated, a final decision – assuming one is rendered at all[106] – could take years.

---

[100] The reason is simple: the tax would, arguably, still violate Article 15 with respect to all non-EU airlines.

[101] *See* Chapter 2, Part 2.6 (discussing ICAO's dispute settlement provisions).

[102] *See* Chicago Convention, *supra* note 17, art. 86.

[103] *See* Brian F. Havel & Niels van Antwerpen, *The Dutch Ticket Tax and Article 15 of the Chicago Convention*, 34 Air & Space L. 141 (2009); Brian F. Havel & Niels van Antwerpen, *The Dutch Ticket Tax and Article 15 of the Chicago Convention (Continued)*, 34 Air & Space L. 447 (2009).

[104] *See* Case C-366/10, *supra* note 81. Although it is clear that the EU is not a contracting party to the Chicago Convention, the logic of the CJEU judgment suggests that EU Member States could declare themselves unbound by the Convention when acting in concert through their EU common institutions. Similarly, if it could find willing partners, the EU could negotiate bilateral or multilateral treaties without reference to the international law principles of the Convention. *See* Havel & Mulligan, *supra* note 40, at 10, 16. That is not a sustainable framework for international aviation law.

[105] *See* Valeri Volcovici, *U.S. Airline Industry Urges Obama to Block EU Carbon Scheme*, Reuters (Sept. 18, 2012), http://www.reuters.com/article/2012/09/18/uk-airlines-eu-emissions-idUSLNE88H00C20120918. China passed legislation that would prohibit its carriers from complying with the EU scheme, as did the United States, which enacted the European Union Emissions Trading Scheme Prohibition Act, Pub. L. No. 00, 126 Stat. 1477 (2012). On the deferral of the implementation of the ETS on flights to and from the EU, *see supra* note 11.

[106] In the case of ICAO, this is not a safe assumption to make. *See supra* Chapter 2, Part 2.6. Nevertheless, ICAO has refreshed its commitment to forging an international aviation

6.5. THE ROLE OF AIR SERVICES AGREEMENTS
IN ENVIRONMENTAL REGULATION

6.5.1. *Environmental Measures in ASAs*

Even though States would prefer to establish global rules for aviation emissions, they are reluctant to wait for ICAO to invent a multilateral response. Some States, therefore, have begun to insert environmental measures into their air services agreements (ASAs), but primarily to protect the commercial interests of their airlines. For instance, while Article 15(3) of the 2007 U.S./EU Air Transport Agreement requires the parties to follow ICAO's environmental standards,[107] it also requires each party to limit the application of environmental regulations that may adversely affect the market access privileges granted under the treaty.[108] The Agreement also stipulates that both sides are to consult with one another through a novel collaborative entity, the Joint Committee,[109] in order to assess the impact that any environmental regulation may have on the terms of the accord.

6.5.2. *A Criticism of ASA Safeguard Provisions*

Safeguard provisions of this type, which are increasingly a staple of ASAs, could be criticized by environmentalists for undermining the right of States to protect the environment. On the other hand, international trade lawyers would retort that environmental and other social regulations can serve protectionist goals if the trade climate shifts.[110] It is also conceivable, of course, that environmental provisions in ASAs could be enhanced to include cooperative arrangements on environmental protection. In addition to the reciprocal imposition of MBMs discussed in the preceding part, joint programs to research and develop green technologies or to upgrade ATM systems for interoperability can also suppress the adverse impact of aviation emissions. States that are politically committed to climate change reversal may use their

---

emissions agreement, although the particular terms of such a treaty remain undetermined. *See supra* note 7.

[107] *See* Air Transport Agreement, U.S.-EU art. 15(3), Apr. 30, 2007, 2007 O.J. (L 134) 4, 46 I.L.M. 470, as amended by Protocol to Amend the Air Transport Agreement, U.S.-EU, Jun. 24, 2010, 2010 O.J. (L 223) 3 [U.S./EU Air Transport Agreement].

[108] *See id.* art. 15(2), 15(3).

[109] On the role of the Joint Committee generally, see *infra* Section 6.6.2.

[110] *See* Jonathan Baert Wiener, *On the Political Economy of Global Environmental Regulation*, 87 GEO. L.J. 749, 771–88 (1999) (describing the prevalence of attempted rent-seeking in global environmental regulation).

ASAs to "purchase" support for emissions reduction standards, even conditioning wider market access privileges on other States' compliance with agreed-upon reduction benchmarks.

6.6. THE LEGAL AND POLITICAL PROSPECTS FOR A MULTILATERAL AVIATION EMISSIONS TREATY

6.6.1. *An Alignment of Political Will*

A sectoralized emissions treaty for the international aviation industry is feasible because the principal stakeholders have acted publicly to make it so. ICAO's member States have already agreed in principle to develop MBMs to cut aviation emissions at the global level. The International Air Transport Association (IATA), the representative trade group for most of the world's international airlines, has pledged carbon-neutral growth in the sector from 2020 onward and to halve carbon emissions by 2050 compared to 2005 levels.[111] And, as discussed earlier, the EU has begun unilaterally to sweep all flight operations touching any EU airport into its carbon trading system, the world's largest.[112] Support for emissions reduction in the aviation sector from government and industry stakeholders indicates an opportune alignment of political will for a sector-specific approach rather than a global multisectoral one. No comparable alignment of interest appears to exist in any other global industry. From the perspective of the international air transport industry, although the policy drivers for an emissions reduction agreement are not entirely altruistic, they have no need to be. The airline industry has long enjoyed trade "exceptionalism," and has been comfortable with it, since the signing of the Chicago Convention nearly seventy years ago. Industry stakeholders acknowledge that a sectoralized agreement can ensure the economic sustainability of international aviation, even though the participating States must also seek an optimal level for emissions reduction. For governments, there is clear political advantage to supporting a sectoral response by the world's most visible services industry. Emissions reductions pursued by one of the great enablers of globalization would have powerful "demonstration" effects for other industries as well as for States.

---

[111] *See* IATA, Fact Sheet: Environment, http://www.iata.org/pressroom/facts_figures/fact_sheets/pages/environment.aspx. IATA's reduction targets are shared by other industry trade groups as affirmed in ICAO Resolution A37–19. *See* ICAO Res. A37–19, *supra* note 59.

[112] *See supra* Section 6.1.2.

6.6.2. *A Regional Approach to Aviation Emissions Reduction: The U.S./EU ASA*

Because of the wide disparity of State interests, however, we do not think that a *global* sectoralized airline emissions treaty embracing all of the world's States is immediately feasible.[113] In our view, one of the most promising settings for this kind of sectoral initiative is the landmark Air Transport Agreement signed by the United States and European Union in 2007.[114] The sharp divide between these two aviation superpowers on the EU's ETS did not prevent U.S. and EU negotiators from concluding a comprehensive "open skies plus"[115] treaty that scrapped decades of calcified restrictions on the exchange of air traffic access rights between their two jurisdictions. As noted earlier, the Agreement did more than liberalize air traffic rights. In a radical break with the template for bilateral air services negotiations, U.S. and EU aviation officials added several chapters to the 2007 Agreement that contemplate regulatory convergence (and even eventual harmonization) in areas such as security, safety, competition, and the environment. In another remarkable innovation, the Agreement has a standing body, the Joint Committee, to steer the process of convergence through consensus. On environmental questions, in an amending Protocol to the Agreement signed in 2010, the U.S. and EU negotiators stated their intention "to work together to limit or reduce, in an economically reasonable manner, the impact of international aviation on the environment."[116] The parties also affirmed their openness to working through the Joint Committee "to develop recommendations that address issues of possible overlap between and consistency among [MBMs] regarding aviation emissions implemented by [them] with a view to avoiding duplication of measures and costs and reducing to the extent possible the administrative burden on airlines."[117] Finally, the Joint Committee remains charged with "fostering expert-level exchanges on new legislative or regulatory initiatives and developments ... in the field [] of ... the environment[.]"[118] With

---

[113] Also, such a treaty would have to satisfy what Eric Posner and David Weisbach refer to as the principle of "international Paretianism:" all of the State parties to such a treaty "must believe themselves better off by their lights as a result of the ... treaty." ERIC A. POSNER & DAVID WEISBACH, CLIMATE CHANGE JUSTICE 6 (2010). For a fuller discussion of how this economic principle applies to a global airline emissions reduction treaty, see generally Brian F. Havel & Gabriel S. Sanchez, *Toward an International Aviation Emissions Agreement*, 36 HARV. ENVT'L. L. REV. 351 (2012).

[114] *See supra* note 107.

[115] *See supra* Chapter 4, note 164 (explaining this concept).

[116] U.S./EU Air Transport Agreement, *supra* note 107, art. 3.

[117] *Id.* art. 15(7).

[118] *Id.* art. 18(4).

60% of global air traffic movements occurring within and between these two aeropowers, the demonstration effects of a bilateral emissions reduction treaty arranged within the structures of the 2007 Agreement would be powerful. And these effects need not be static. The trade concessions delivered in the 2007 Agreement are available to third-party States to the extent that the Agreement functions as a plurilateral, that is, an international agreement that offers non-parties the opportunity to accede after it has come into effect among its founding parties, but typically requires latecomers to accept the terms of the agreement in their entirety.[119]

6.6.3. *Regulatory Features of a U.S./EU Aviation Emissions Agreement*

A U.S./EU aviation emissions agreement would be written to comply with the principles (including international law principles) that we have been considering in this chapter. Each party would impose the agreement's selected MBM (see below) on its own carriers, and the agreement could be engineered so that either party may cede regulatory control over its airlines' emissions, including discharges over the high seas, to the remit of the other party, or to a joint administrative agency. Any inconsistency between the agreement and various provisions of the Chicago Convention (e.g., with respect to deployment of revenues[120]) would be eliminated by force of the parties' mutual consent to the agreement. Which carbon reduction mechanism would a U.S./EU emissions reduction treaty apply without sacrificing industry competitiveness or distorting the global aviation market? Although such a mechanism should be effective, it might not be the most effective option available. Quick but financially damaging "solutions" could include forcibly grounding a large number of aircraft or restricting air traffic to high-volume routes utilizing the most fuel-efficient aircraft and mandating that they be at or near capacity before being cleared to fly. More strident critics of the aviation industry have even called for the abolition of aviation.[121] In this setting, MBMs (eco-taxes and carbon trading) would be the more flexible and less burdensome alternatives. Their use has been, in principle, endorsed by ICAO, its member States, and the airline industry.[122] Practically speaking, however, it may be difficult for States to know *ex ante* how to set an emissions tax at a level that will

---

[119] See *id.* art. 18(5); *see* Vienna Convention on the Law of Treaties, *supra* note 97, art. 20(2).
[120] *See supra* Section 6.4.2.
[121] *See* GEORGE MONBIOT, HEAT: HOW TO STOP THE PLANET FROM BURNING (2007).
[122] See ICAO Res. A37–19, *supra* note 59, para. 13; IATA, A Global Approach to Reducing Aviation Emissions (Nov. 2009), http://www.iata.org/SiteCollectionDocuments/Documents/Global_Approach_Reducing_Emissions_251109web.pdf.

steer airlines toward the agreed-upon reduction goals. In contrast, emissions trading (to the extent that it is allowed to function without government distortion[123]) allows the market to set the price necessary to induce emissions reduction. A carbon trading scheme would have the further advantage of smoother integration into a future global climate change arrangement where emissions credits could be cross-traded among multiple industrial sectors.[124] In conformity with the wider reading of Article 15 discussed earlier,[125] revenues from the trading system could be directed toward projects that improve air transport efficiency (such as ATM enhancement, capacity extension at congested airports, or research into "green" technologies) rather than to fill national coffers.[126]

6.6.4. Geographic Scope of a U.S./EU Aviation Emissions Agreement

There would still be sizeable gaps in the geographic scope of a U.S./EU aviation emissions agreement. Major non-Western international air carriers such as Hong Kong's Cathay Pacific, Dubai's Emirates, and Singapore Airlines would be at liberty to operate beyond the agreement's reach.[127] A possible enticement to these airlines' home States to join the agreement would be simultaneous accession to the liberal air services trade environment created by the 2007 U.S./EU Agreement and its 2010 Protocol. Although several large EU carriers would find the prospect unsettling, rising aviation powers – and growing greenhouse gas emitters – such as China, the United Arab Emirates, and India would readily see how the 2007 Agreement could generate

---

[123] For example, through manipulation of the amount of auctionable as opposed to free allowances that the scheme will offer.

[124] This already happens in the EU ETS, where airlines have joined serial industrial carbon emitters including power stations, combustion plants, oil refineries, and iron and steel works, as well as factories making cement, glass, lime, bricks, ceramics, pulp, paper, and board.

[125] See *supra* note 86 and accompanying text.

[126] Note that the EU's ETS legislation does not specify how Member States are to use revenues captured from the emissions allowance auctions. To date, only Germany has passed legislation earmarking those revenues for emissions abatement and similar purposes. See Barbara Lewis & Nina Chestney, *EU Airline Carbon Cash Should Help Fill Climate Fund*, REUTERS (May 16, 2012), http://www.reuters.com/article/2012/05/16/uk-energy-summit-hedegaard-idUSLNE84Fo 1220120516. *See also* Chapter 2, note 61.

[127] That assumes, of course, that the Chicago Convention completely bars States from unilaterally imposing emissions taxes and charges on foreign air carriers. But the Convention (as we have seen, *passim*) could be given a more flexible reading to allow such charges to be imposed on foreign carriers for the period when they are within U.S. or EU airspace. Even so, coverage would remain marginal, for example, capturing only the limited U.S./EU airspace penetration of a Cathay Pacific flight from Hong Kong to London or an Emirates flight from Dubai to New York.

substantial market access benefits for their airlines. States already pursuing liberal air services trade relations with the United States and EU, such as Canada and Australia, might be persuaded to adhere to an emissions reduction agreement as part of those States' broader cultures of international cooperation. And for States willing to commit to emissions reduction but uninterested in further liberalizing aviation trade relations, provision could be made to integrate them into the administrative operation of the new agreement's MBMs. As the circle of adherents widens, pressure will build on recalcitrant States. Although major markets like China and Russia might last some time as outliers, principled obstinacy would be unlikely to trump new market opportunities indefinitely.

6.6.5. *A Work of Governance as Much as of Economics*

Finally, if it can fairly be said that global airline carbon emissions reduction will be as much a work of governance as of economics, then the hard work of shaping an international aeropolitical governance structure has already been accomplished by the 2007 U.S./EU Air Transport Agreement. The next iteration, an aviation emissions reduction agreement generated from within that structure, can therefore more easily be imagined.

6.7. THE INTERNATIONAL REGULATION OF NOISE ABATEMENT

6.7.1. *ICAO's Benchmark Standards*

Prior to the advent of global warming concerns, States faced the problem of noise pollution caused by the rapidly growing number of large jet aircraft taking to their skies. Although States initially chose to regulate aircraft noise through local rules, ICAO introduced Annex 16 to the Chicago Convention in 1971 in order to help establish a more uniform approach to noise abatement.[128] Like most other SARPs, the methodology of Annex 16 is to benchmark a set of minimum standards – in this case, the permissible levels of noise for various aircraft classifications and types.[129] ICAO member States

---

[128] *See* ICAO, INTERNATIONAL STANDARDS AND RECOMMENDED PRACTICES, AIRCRAFT NOISE, ANNEX 16 TO THE CONVENTION ON INTERNATIONAL CIVIL AVIATION (1971).

[129] ICAO's latest noise certification standards were promulgated in February 2013. *See* ICAO News Release, ICAO Environmental Protection Committee Delivers Progress on New Aircraft . . . Noise Standards, COM 4/13 (Feb. 14, 2013). The new standards will apply to new-design aircraft entering into service from 2017.

are responsible for evaluating and then certifying that aircraft on their national registers are compliant with the appropriate ICAO standard.[130] Aircraft are expected to carry documentation proving their noise certification (some States include this information on their airworthiness certificates), and ICAO member States undertake to recognize these certifications for foreign aircraft entering their territory regardless of domestic standards for acceptable noise levels.[131] But it would be just as incorrect to view ICAO as a global regulator for aircraft noise as it would be to view the Organization as the exclusive authority overseeing aircraft carbon emissions. ICAO sets baselines for the acceptability of noise levels, and compliance has been strong. A choice by a State to waive or apply the obligations on a discriminatory basis would spark serious political tensions.

6.7.2. *Interaction Between International and State-Based Noise Regulation*

ICAO's standard-making does not mean that States are prohibited from ratcheting up noise abatement rules for their own air carriers. The issue came to a head during the 1990s when States began to phase out aircraft that failed to meet ICAO noise standards. Several airlines, particularly in the United States, sought to adopt more economical measures to reduce noise without sacrificing the utility of their older aircraft. Through the use of "hushkits," airlines could continue to rely on aging planes without violating ICAO standards. That move antagonized environmentally savvy politicians in the EU, and the Union institutions passed legislation to ban hushkitted aircraft from EU territory.[132] The European Commission insisted that aircraft upgraded through hushkits were noisier than the newer aircraft built to ICAO's current standards.[133] The United States, in response, accused EU officials of protectionism, prompting a U.S. complaint to the ICAO Council

---

[130] *See* ICAO, International Standards and Recommended Practices, Environmental Protection, Annex 16 to the Convention on International Civil Aviation, Vol. I, Aircraft Noise (5th ed. 2008) [hereinafter Annex 16, Volume I]. The noise standards have grown more stringent over time. Generally, aircraft built prior to 1977 were governed by the standards contained in Chapter 2, while aircraft built between 1977 and 2006 had to be compliant with the stricter standards contained in Chapter 3. Aircraft built after 2006 must comply with the Chapter 4 standards. *See also supra* note 129 (indicating the recent adoption of the newest set of standards).

[131] *See* Annex 16, Volume I, *supra* note 130, amend. 8.

[132] *See* Council Regulation 925/1999, 1999 O.J. (L 115) 1.

[133] *See* Press Release, European Commission, *Commission Takes Action to Combat Aircraft Noise* (Mar. 13, 1998), http://europa.eu/rapid/press-release_IP-98-251_en.htm?locale=en.

under the dispute settlement rules of the Chicago Convention.[134] The Council never issued a binding decision, but the EU withdrew its regulation.[135] The issue remains a flashpoint in U.S./EU aeropolitical relations. In negotiations for an amending protocol to the 2007 U.S./EU Air Transport Agreement, U.S. officials lobbied their European counterparts to "Unionize" the autonomy of Member State local and regional authorities to impose noise regulations in the form of night flight restrictions.[136] The

---

[134] *See* Paul Stephen Dempsey, *Flights of Fancy and Fights of Fury: Arbitration and Adjudication of Commercial and Political Disputes in International Aviation*, 32 GA. J. INT'L & COMP. L. 231, 281–82 (2004). The Article 84 filing named the EU Member States, rather than the EU, because the EU was not a party to the Chicago Convention. Surprisingly, neither the EU States themselves nor ICAO addressed whether or not the hushkit rule could be evaluated against the Chicago Convention, given that the rule was being implemented by the EU, a nonparty to the Convention. This question would later be examined by the CJEU in the emissions trading case. See *supra* note 104. Although EU nonadherence was never raised in the ICAO dispute, the English High Court of Justice ruled in a separate case that the hushkit regulation could *not* be evaluated against the Chicago Convention precisely because the EU was not a party. *See* Kriss E. Brown, Comment, *The International Civil Aviation Organization is the Appropriate Jurisdiction to Settle Hushkit Dispute Between the United States and the European Union*, 20 PENN ST. INT'L L. REV. 465, 481 (2002) (citing The Queen v. Sec'y of State for the Env't, Transp. and the Regions, *ex parte* Omega Air Ltd., High Court of Justice (England) (Queen's Bench Div., Nov. 25, 1999)).

[135] The EU Member States did submit preliminary objections, questioning the ICAO Council's jurisdiction to adjudicate the dispute and whether the United States had exhausted the required procedural remedies. The ICAO Council ruled unanimously against the EU Member States, which declined to appeal the Council's ruling on the preliminary objections to the ICJ. Instead, the United States and the EU, with the assistance of the ICAO President and Legal Counsel, resumed negotiations, ultimately resulting in the EU repealing the regulation and U.S. withdrawal of its Article 84 complaint. Not all was lost for the EU, however: the United States permitted development of ICAO Chapter 4 noise standards (*see supra* note 130), which it had previously obstructed, to proceed. Although some observers have flagged this dispute as evidence of ICAO's robust adjudicatory powers, the fact that the ICAO Council never acted as more than a mediator during the controversy indicates that settlement was a product of diplomatic, rather than legal, intervention. For more on ICAO's dispute settlement authority, see *supra* Chapter 2, Part 2.6.

[136] Night flight restrictions are one form of noise restrictions that are levied on airports, rather than directly on air carriers as with the ICAO standards. Obviously, the restrictions impact carriers who must comply in order to utilize the restricted aerodrome. The restrictions are notable in that they are based on notions of legal control over land planning or zoning and are thus perceived as a local policy question despite their impact on the industry more broadly. Night flight regulations restrict the flights in and out of a given airport during typical sleeping hours for neighboring residents. These restrictions are most prevalent in the EU Member States. In 2001 ICAO adopted Assembly Resolution A33–7, urging States to use a "balanced approach to noise management" that would include a cost-benefit analysis and that would prioritize the reduction of noise through improved land management and operational procedures before turning to regulation as a last resort. International Civil Aviation Organization, *Consolidated Statement of Continuing ICAO Policies and Practices Related to Environmental Protection*, Assem. Res. A33–7 (2001), *compiled in Assembly Resolutions in Force*, ICAO Doc. 9790 (2001).

European Commission demurred on the ground of "subsidiarity," that is, the principle (enshrined in EU treaty law) that decisions should be taken, as far as possible, by officials and authorities closest to the affected populations.[137]

6.7.3. *A Final Comment on Noise Pollution*

Noise pollution, like aircraft emissions, is a problem that will remain on regulatory agendas in the absence of a radical technological breakthrough. ICAO will probably continue to broker a degree of international consensus, but adjustments to Annex 16 are likely to be marginal and calculated not to jeopardize the economic stability of member States' air transport sectors.

6.8. CONCLUSION

6.8.1. *An Intensifying Dialogue*

It is impossible to predict the eventual stopping-place of the climate change discourse. Barring a dramatic change in climate change projections, international dialogue will intensify as we draw nearer to the "zero hour" of climate catastrophe.

6.8.2. *Two Final Observations*

We conclude this rather policy-focused chapter with two statements that we think summarize the arguments we have raised here. First, a plausible *multilateral* aviation emissions reduction agreement can ensure that international aviation "does its part" by reducing the sector's emissions to a sustainable level without sacrificing its economic viability. The international backlash against the EU ETS strongly indicates that there is a low tolerance among aviation

---

[137] *See* Treaty of Lisbon Amending the Treaty on European Union and the Treaty Establishing the European Communities, art. 3, Protocol on the Application of the Principles of Subsidiarity and Proportionality, Dec. 13, 2007, 2007 O.J. (C 306) 149–52. Even so, the amending protocol does provide a potential incentive for the EU to change its mind, namely, a grant of limited seventh freedom ("stand-alone") rights that would allow a select number of EU airlines to serve points between the United States and third States – without a home State connection to the EU – in exchange for Member States ceding full regulatory authority over noise abatement at EU airports to the European Commission. *See* U.S./EU Air Transport Agreement, *supra* note 107, art. 21; on seventh freedom traffic rights, see *supra* Chapter 3, Section 3.3.6.

powers for regulatory unilateralism on the emissions issue. Second, the convergence of stakeholder interests within international aviation will further ensure that any such agreement can serve as a lead sector for future (and wider) global collaboration on climate change. Under the canopy of a sectoral treaty among like-minded States, international aviation can responsibly reduce its environmental impact while remaining a force for dynamic economic growth in the coming decades.

7

The International Law Regime for Air Carrier
Liability and Surface Damage

7.1. INTRODUCTION

7.1.1. *A Hybridized Structure*

In the first four chapters we discussed the principal components of the public dimension of international aviation law, namely, the Chicago Convention and the bilateral system of cross-border trade in air services. In the previous two chapters we considered other significant issues of public law, including safety and security and evolving regimes to control aircraft carbon emissions and noise pollution. This chapter turns primarily to the private transnational legal rules governing air carrier liability for injury or damages to passengers and cargo on international flights as well as to the fairly rudimentary provisions that international law provides to compensate passengers and shippers for delay.[1] The system of international air carrier liability is an unusual hybrid of public international law and private transnational law:[2] the primary rules are set forth in international treaties (public international law) and in some agreements that are not, strictly speaking, treaties. But all disputes that arise under these various public international law instruments concerning the scope of the rules and liability for damages are adjudicated in the domestic court systems of the contracting States rather than by international judicial bodies. As we will see

---

[1] We also discuss international law provisions that impose liability for third-party surface ("on the ground") damage caused by aircraft. *See infra* Section 7.1.7 and Part 7.14. Airlines, of course, may potentially incur many other types of liability to a variety of third parties, including handling agents, caterers, and maintenance companies; lenders and lessors (through financing arrangements); airport authorities (e.g., cleanup expenses); government regulators (under tax and competition laws); and to their employees under labor or employment laws. But none of this wide spectrum of liability is covered under an international agreement.

[2] *See supra* Chapter 1, Section 1.4.5, discussing the relevant distinctions that we make in this book between public international aviation law and private transnational aviation law treaty instruments.

in the next and final chapter of the book, in modern international aviation law, only the Cape Town Convention (as it relates to ownership interests in aircraft) has a comparable hybridized structure that straddles both the public and private dimensions of international law.[3]

7.1.2. *The Warsaw Convention (1929)*

The applicable series of treaty and nontreaty instruments on passenger and cargo liability begins more than eighty years ago with the 1929 Convention for the Unification of Certain Rules Relating to International Carriage by Air, commonly referred to as the "Warsaw Convention" in honor of its place of signature.[4] The most prominent international aviation treaty after the Chicago Convention, it has certainly been the most litigated instrument in the field of international aviation law.[5] The terms of the Warsaw Convention, though

---

[3]   *See infra* Chapter 8, Part 8.8.

[4]   *See* Convention for the Unification of Certain Rules Relating to International Carriage by Air, *opened for signature* Oct. 12, 1929, 137 L.N.T.S. 11, 49 Stat. 3000 (entered into force Feb. 13, 1933) [hereinafter Warsaw Convention]. In some translations from the official original French text, the word "Carriage" in the title appears as "Transportation." *See, e.g.,* note following 49 U.S.C. § 40105; O'Grady v. British Airways, 134 F. Supp. 2d 407 (2001); Glenn Pogust, Note, *The Warsaw Convention – Does it Create a Cause of Action?*, 47 FORDHAM L. REV. 366 (1978).

[5]   The U.S. Supreme Court has considered issues relating to the Warsaw Convention on eight separate occasions since 1966: Trans World Airlines, Inc. v. Franklin Mint Corp., 466 U.S. 243 (1984) (upholding the decision of the U.S. Civil Aeronautics Board, after the 1978 repeal of the U.S. Par Value Modification Act – which had previously set an official price of gold within the United States – to use a $9.07-per-pound cargo liability limit for Warsaw Convention cases when converting the treaty's liability limits from gold francs to U.S. currency); Air Fr. v. Saks, 470 U.S. 392 (1985) (holding the airline not liable under the Warsaw Convention for a passenger's deafness caused by the normal operation of the aircraft's pressurization system, on the ground that the injury was not caused by an unusual or unexpected event external to the passenger, and therefore was not an accident under Article 17; *see infra* Part 7.9); Chan v. Korean Air Lines, Ltd., 490 U.S. 122 (1989) (holding that the airline did not lose the benefit of Warsaw's liability limitation when notice of the limitation was provided to passenger in 8-point instead of required 10-point type); Eastern Airlines, Inc. v. Floyd, 499 U.S. 530 (1991) (holding that Article 17 of the Warsaw Convention does not allow recovery for mental or emotional injuries unaccompanied by physical injury; *see infra* Section 7.9.8); Zicherman v. Korean Air Lines Co., 516 U.S. 217 (1996) (holding that Article 17 of the Warsaw Convention only permits recovery for legally cognizable harm as determined by domestic law, and that loss-of-society damages are not permitted under the U.S. Death on the High Seas Act); Dooley v. Korean Air Lines Co., 524 U.S. 116 (1998) (holding U.S. Death on the High Seas Act does not provide a basis for relatives to recover under the Warsaw Convention for decedents' pre-death pain and suffering); El Al Isr. Airlines, Ltd. v. Tseng, 525 U.S. 155 (1999) (holding that a passenger cannot recover under domestic law for personal injury damages for which the carrier was not liable under the terms of the Warsaw Convention; *see infra* Section 7.9.8); and Olympic Airways v. Husain, 540 U.S. 644 (2004) (holding that flight attendant's refusal to move an asthmatic passenger away from cigarette smoke constituted an accident under Article 17, *see infra* Section 7.9.3).

admirable for their time in helping to provide a fairly stable liability regime for airlines in the formative decades of international air transport, were eventually found to be outmoded as to liability. Infelicitous drafting, coupled with a tight liability cap for passenger injury and death that many plaintiffs' attorneys found unpalatable, led to a series of amending instruments that received mixed degrees of ratification. The United States, unrivaled in the international aviation market, was prepared to reject the Warsaw Convention entirely by the mid-1960s until the international airline industry's private trade organization, the International Air Transport Association (IATA), stepped in on behalf of its member airlines to broker the first in a series of private, nontreaty agreements (some involving the U.S. Government) to waive aspects of the Convention that had drawn U.S. opprobrium.

7.1.3. *The Montreal Convention (1999)*

It would not be until 1999, seventy years after the Warsaw Convention was negotiated, that a successor treaty intended to address the shortcomings of Warsaw and to consolidate the various amending instruments was finalized in Montreal, Canada. Although the Montreal Convention[6] has yet to receive universal assent, its adoption by 103 States, including the United States and all twenty-eight EU Member States, has positioned it as the controlling liability treaty for a majority of the world's international air carriage activities. As such, Montreal, not Warsaw and its amending instruments, receives the greater part of our analytical attention in this chapter.

7.1.4. *The Montreal Convention Replaces, Not Augments,* *the Warsaw Convention*

Our decision to focus principally on the Montreal Convention requires some further justification. It is not uncommon for secondary sources of private transnational aviation law to discuss "the Warsaw Convention as amended" and to speak of the "Warsaw System" as encompassing all of the governmental and private agreements subsequent to the original treaty, including internal rules adopted by States intended to modify the coverage of that regime with respect to their air carriers. Some commentators have gone so far as to conflate the Warsaw System with the 1999 Montreal Convention, treating the seven-decade legal and policy history that separates the two instruments as comprising

---

[6] See Convention for the Unification of Certain Rules for International Carriage by Air, *opened for signature* May 28, 1999, 2242 U.N.T.S. 350 (entered into force Nov. 4, 2003) [hereinafter Montreal Convention].

a unified whole. That is incorrect. The purpose of the Montreal Convention, as the language of Article 55 of that treaty makes clear, is to *replace*, not merely to augment, the old Warsaw System.[7] It is only because of recalcitrance on the part of certain States that Montreal is still compelled to live in an uneasy cohabitation with the vestiges of Warsaw. Although there may be no way of telling how long international aviation's *ancien régime* for civil liability will endure, suffice it to say that the guillotine of history awaits.

7.1.5. *Either the Warsaw or the Montreal Conventions May Apply*

Later in this chapter we will look briefly at the disposition of cases where, because of divergent State ratifications, it is possible that either Warsaw or Montreal may apply to the litigated accident.[8] Readers interested in learning more about the Warsaw System in detail, including the particularities of its rules governing liability, jurisdiction, and defenses, may consult the sources listed in the bibliography. For present purposes, we will only discuss the Warsaw System to elucidate provisions now located in the Montreal Convention or to explain the history of this area of private transnational aviation law.

7.1.6. *Terminology and Scope of the Warsaw System*

For ease of exposition, we will refer to the "Warsaw System" when discussing the Warsaw Convention *and* all of its related instruments. The term "Warsaw Convention" will be used when referring to that single treaty, although – unless

---

[7]   *See id.* art. 55, which provides that: "This Convention shall prevail over any rules which apply to international carriage by air . . . by virtue of those States commonly being Party to . . ." Article 55 goes on to list the Warsaw Convention and its subsequent amending protocols as sources of rules over which the Montreal Convention "shall prevail." Some might argue to the contrary by invoking the Montreal Convention's Preamble, which states in part that its signatories recognize "the need to modernize and consolidate the Warsaw Convention and related instruments[.]" Warsaw Convention, *supra* note 4, pmbl. Although that assertion is accurate so far as it goes, it is also true that the Montreal Convention stands autonomously: there is no need for a State to go behind the new treaty and to adopt any of the Warsaw System's instruments in order to give Montreal full legal effect. Additionally, given the Montreal Convention's "consumer-oriented" approach of providing full restitution in contrast to Warsaw's original "airline-oriented" approach of shielding carriers from anything more than nominal liability, it is problematic to frame Montreal as a mere extension or modification of its predecessor. But, as discussed *infra* Part 7.9 *passim*, courts that interpret the Montreal Convention do look for guidance to existing case law under the Warsaw Convention as a matter of prudence and to State-level jurisprudence developed under the Warsaw Convention because of the similarity of many of the provisions in the two instruments and also "so as not to result in a complete upheaval of the 'common law' surrounding the Warsaw Convention." Watts v. Am. Airlines, Inc., No. 1:07-cv-0434, 2007 WL 3019344, at *2 (S.D. Ind. Oct. 10, 2007).

[8]   *See infra* Sections 7.12.3, 7.12.4.

otherwise noted – always in light of its various amendments prior to the Montreal Convention. In the interest of economy, we have also limited our discussion of the Montreal rules relating to ticketing and carriage of cargo. In the decades between Warsaw and Montreal, detailed rubrics covering the issuance, format, and medium of airline ticketing have yielded to advances in technology and the near-universal embrace of "e-ticketing" in the airline industry. Readers interested in more advanced discussion of the history of documentation rules for international carriage by air are advised to consult the bibliography in this book.

7.1.7. *Third-Party Surface Liability*

Finally, this chapter concludes with an examination of another area of private liability where efforts have been made to apply international lawmaking: the rules that govern air carrier liability for third-party surface ("on the ground") damage caused by aircraft. The importance of this area of international law-making, however, has been reduced by the existence of effective national laws to impose liability for these rare events.

7.2. THE CHOICE BETWEEN PRIVATE AND PUBLIC OVERSIGHT OF AIR CARRIER LIABILITY

7.2.1. *Contrasting Public and Private Regulation of Liability*

To deepen the reader's appreciation of the fundamental changes in liability policy that led to the Montreal Convention, we turn now to a short discussion of the tensions involved in developing a system of private law to determine after-the-fact (*ex post*) liability instead of relying solely on before-the-fact (*ex ante*) public regulatory governance of claims arising from the provision of international air services. Advocates of private liability for air carriers[9] have long argued that the Warsaw System provides a more efficient mechanism to discipline the safety standards of the international air transport industry than

---

[9]   We do not enter the debate here as to whether the kind of liability established in the Warsaw Convention sounded (or sounds) in contract, tort, or the civil law notion of "delict." *See* Hamid Kazemi, Carrier's Liability in Air Transport with Particular Reference to Iran (unpublished Ph.D. thesis, Leiden University 2012) (analyzing how the "exceptional system" of the air carrier liability treaties required that States with different national liability principles put these aside "in order to achieve uniformity in the liability principles for air carriage"). *See also infra* at Section 7.3.3 (indicating that the Convention finesses the relevance of these distinctions by creating an automatic international liability regime).

public regulation.[10] *Ex post* liability, when strictly applied, is seen to meet the demands of corrective justice – a concept that dates back to Aristotle.[11] *Ex ante* public regulation, some critics charge, is too clumsy to meet its ends in a cost-effective manner. Even if government regulators draw safety standards to minimize the risk of air travel accidents, they impose compliance costs on the airlines that are not always aligned with the benchmarks set forth in the actual regulations.[12] The private system of recovery provides the necessary incentives for air carriers to take prophylactic measures to protect passengers and cargo. In this view, by scrutinizing past damages awards and the accidents that triggered them, air carriers are well placed to assess what modifications they need to make to their operations to avoid those costs.[13]

7.2.2. *Integrating the Private and Public Regulatory Approaches*

But it is also true that public regulation continues to play a decisive role in safety (as well as in security, as we saw in Chapter 5). ICAO's continual updating of the relevant technical annexes to the Chicago Convention, as well as that Organization's safety audits and similar programs conducted by the U.S. Federal Aviation Administration (FAA) and the European Union (EU), all demonstrate a public focus on establishing a "base level" for safety regardless of what the airlines may be prompted to do out of fear of litigation. The air carriers, in turn, insist that the Warsaw System has driven them to exceed publicly drawn international safety standards precisely because of the perpetual threat of liability. In that sense, *ex ante* public and *ex post* private systems of regulation are seen to be complementary and synergistic. The integration of those two approaches arguably keeps airlines "honest" on the front end about their commitment to safety and culpable at the back end in the unfortunate

[10] *See, e.g.,* Robert W. Poole Jr., *Toward Safer Skies, in* INSTEAD OF REGULATION: ALTERNATIVES TO FEDERAL REGULATION 207 (Robert W. Poole ed., 1982). On the other hand, there are practitioners who would argue that considerations of improving safety have never been of any concern to a pragmatic system of tort-based private regulation.

[11] *See* ARISTOTLE, ETHICA NICOMACHEA 1132a25 (L. Bywater ed., Oxford Univ. Press (1920)). For the "classic" treatment of strict liability and corrective justice in contemporary legal scholarship, see RICHARD A. EPSTEIN, A THEORY OF STRICT LIABILITY: TOWARD A REFORMATION OF TORT LAW (1980). For Epstein's latest restatement of his views on strict liability, see *Toward a General Theory of Tort Law: Strict Liability in Context,* J. TORT L., Vol. 3, No. 1 (2010).

[12] For example, airlines may be compelled to submit to direct inspections from government officials or to follow reporting procedures that are subsidiary to the practice of keeping aircraft in good repair or to making sure that pilots, crew, and repair staff are properly trained in the execution of their duties.

[13] *See* Paul A. Cleveland and Thomas L. Tucker, *Privatizing Airline Safety and Security,* IDEAS ON LIBERTY, Nov. 2002, at 6–9.

event of a crash or other incident giving rise to damages. Many would view a shift toward one to the exclusion of the other as either inadequate to maintain a high level of safety in international air transport or as failing to meet some other overarching societal value. Moreover, as the authors of this book have discovered, there are also practitioners who would question an assertion that the litigation system exists for any grander societal purpose beyond satisfying the demands of the claimants in a particular dispute.[14] In any event, whether the additional costs imposed by this dualistic system are more than what is necessary to sustain aviation safety is a debatable point. It is certainly arguable that an environment of high-octane *ex post* liability where no air carrier is permitted to fly unless its risks are fully insured could, in fact, achieve levels of safety comparable to the present mixed system but without its intrusiveness into airlines' commercial operations.[15]

7.3. THE WARSAW SYSTEM

7.3.1. *The Warsaw System Created a Unique Concept in International Law*

Instead of imposing obligations directly on States to remedy the consequences of aviation accidents and delays, the Warsaw Convention established a private legal regime that directly affects human and corporate persons. The Montreal Convention later did likewise. Although the Warsaw Convention set the

---

[14] *See supra* note 10. Within the U.S. tort bar, also, an intense focus on the rights of plaintiffs has also fostered a sense that the whole Warsaw/Montreal system of strict or absolute liability (*see infra* note 76 and accompanying text) deprives plaintiffs of an opportunity, in addition to obtaining compensation, of exposing the particular culpability and negligence of the defendant carrier. But this question of identifying "fault" may well exceed what the Warsaw/Montreal treaties were intended to provide: rather than being instruments of criminal law designed to assign guilt and to root out bad behavior, their primary goal was always the efficient compensation of the victims. This Warsaw/Montreal "mentalité" has perhaps allowed the airline industry to develop too impersonal and transactional an approach to customer dissatisfaction, leaving it vulnerable to a deluge of passenger rights legislation imposed over the last decade. The industry's singular focus on defining a monetary liability for passenger injuries, while bypassing concerns about passenger treatment (especially during long delays), left a void that savvy politicians across the world were eager to fill with new rules on passenger rights. *See infra* Section 7.12.8.

[15] Whether insurers actually have safety goals in mind when they set their premiums is also debatable, however. The airline insurance industry is fundamentally pragmatic: the cost of coverage is not established in order to encourage higher safety compliance (however that might be done) but rather is determined by an individual airline's claims record and the general geographic, economic, and regulatory environment in which that airline operates. Insurance companies no doubt assume that appropriate safety standards will be enforced by national and international regulators.

framework governing air carrier liability, it did not establish any independent or supranational judicial body to adjudicate liability actions against air carriers.[16] In the absence of such a tribunal, all Warsaw and Montreal liability actions are under the jurisdiction of the individual contracting States and depend for their efficacy on the enforcement power of the contracting States within their own territories. Thus, the separate domestic legal regimes of the ratifying States – primarily a mixture of civil and common law systems – have controlled all of the treaty's interpretation, execution, and, some would argue, expansion beyond the original intent of its framers. In that sense, the Warsaw System and its Montreal successor have occupied a unique place in international aviation law; as we have noted, only the much more recent Cape Town Convention (as it affects ownership interests in aircraft) now replicates the Warsaw/Montreal model of a private legal regime established through a public international law treaty and enforced within the contracting States' legal systems.[17]

7.3.2. A Search for a Universal Cap on Liability

At two international conferences held between 1925 and 1929, States debated the merits of constructing a system of harmonized rules governing liability for international carriage by air.[18] Although cross-border air travel was still in its infancy, States and their air carriers realized that uniform standards of liability could not exist in a legal environment where national courts applied inconsistent conflict of laws (choice of law) rules to select a governing law in a particular dispute.[19] More important, from the airlines' perspective, was the need to create a universal cap on their liability for damages arising out of international air transportation. According to the airlines, their fledgling status, combined with uncertainty surrounding the causes of many airline accidents, made them uniquely vulnerable to lawsuits. Unlimited liability would deter investors and limit the scope of services that air carriers would be able to provide. Other options besides a universal liability cap were available

---

[16] Even today, we might not encounter much State enthusiasm for some kind of "world civil aviation liability court."

[17] *See* Convention on International Interests in Mobile Equipment, Nov. 16, 2001, ICAO Doc. 9793, U.N. Doc. A/AC.105/C.2/2002/CRP.3, U.S. Treaty 108–10 [hereinafter Cape Town Convention].

[18] Although the United States sent observers, it did not participate directly in the proceedings of the conferences.

[19] *See King v. Bristow Helicopters & In Re Morris*, [2002] UKHL 7, at ¶ 63 (stating that one of the "primary objectives" of the Warsaw Convention was "to eliminate conflict of laws problems") [hereinafter *King v. Bristow Helicopters*]. *See also supra* Chapter 1, Section 1.4.5 (further explaining the equivalent terms "conflict of laws" and "choice of law").

to narrow the industry's exposure. Airlines concerned about risky cross-border transit could have negotiated liability limits or other protections into their contracts of carriage, perhaps foregoing some profit through reduced fares in exchange for the consent of passengers or shippers to a fixed level of damages in the event of an accident.[20]

7.3.3. *Integration of the Warsaw Convention with National Law and Carrier Contracts of Carriage*

It is critical to understand that the Warsaw Convention was not just a *traité-loi*[21] setting out certain key principles of airline liability that contracting States were to observe in their relations with one another. Its effectiveness lay in the fact that contracting States were undertaking to treat the Convention's provisions as the applicable domestic law in all airline liability cases in all of their national courts. Were that not the case, the absence of a uniform international law of contract and of uniform rules of conflict of laws would have meant that carriers would be required to conform their individual contracts of carriage to each system of law within which they conducted flight operations. The Warsaw Convention instead provided international airlines with a kind of "transnational" contract with respect to the matters it covered. IATA, the representative body for most commercial airlines operating at the time of the Convention's adoption, revised its "standard contract of carriage" in 1929 so that all of the Convention's provisions would become part of the contractual relationship between individual passengers and shippers and their air carriers. IATA has continued to update its standard contract ever since.[22] Because of

---

[20] Indeed, the Warsaw Convention itself envisaged precisely this alternative to a general liability cap. *See* Article 22(1), providing for special contracts between passengers and carriers allowing "a higher limit of liability." Warsaw Convention, *supra* note 4, art. 22(1). The alternative of a private bargain assumed, of course, that such contracts would be honored across national boundaries. Disparities in the law of contracts, coupled with the 20th century decline in (common law) courts upholding freedom of contract over ancillary social concerns, may have curtailed widespread reliance on contract to set liability terms. Even so, nothing prevented States from using the original Warsaw Convention as a means of tilting the scales of justice more discernibly toward a freedom of contract approach with respect to air carriage. Doing so would not have seemed unreasonable as a matter of social justice: passengers in 1929 were wealthy and could readily have self-insured.

[21] *See* V. D. DEGAN, SOURCES OF INTERNATIONAL LAW 489 (1997) (distinguishing the law-making treaty or "treaty as statute," the *traité-loi*, from the treaty as contract, the *traité-contrat*, such as a commercial sales agreement between States).

[22] Each airline has a contract of carriage with its customers that, while it will include terms additional to those of the international liability conventions, certainly includes all of those terms. The contract of carriage is actually mentioned in Article 3(2) of the Warsaw Convention, which provides that the lack of a ticket does not affect the existence or validity of the contract of

Warsaw (and subsequently Montreal), therefore, each national law of contract is integrated automatically into the international liability system by each airline's contract of carriage with its customers. Notwithstanding the arrival of the e-ticket, the fundamental principle of a common set of conditions of carriage (and of liability) remains the same today. Moreover, the automatic application of the Warsaw and Montreal conventions to any carriage falling within the term "international carriage" neatly avoids having to categorize the liability system itself as sounding in contract, tort, or delict.[23]

7.3.4. *Basic Principles of Liability Under the Warsaw Convention*

In very broad terms, the Convention sought to create a suite of exclusive remedies[24] applicable to accidents or damage occurring in all international carriage of persons, baggage, or cargo performed by air transport enterprises for payment or even without payment.[25] Articles 17 and 18 of the Convention acknowledged the heightened scrutiny that Anglo-American common law imposed on all "common carriers,"[26] making airlines *prima facie* liable for damages for death or injury to passengers or loss or damage to baggage and cargo.[27] The contracting States opted, however, to shelter their airlines from the exigencies of common carrier liability law by capping air carrier exposure

carriage, and that a carrier accepting a passenger without a ticket is not entitled to limit its liability under the Convention (presumably because the passenger would not have received the Warsaw notice required in Article 3(1)(e)). See Warsaw Convention, *supra* note 4, art. 3. In the era of e-ticketing, the full text of each airline's contract of carriage (which is considerably longer than the text historically printed on the back of ticket stock) is now more likely to be available online.

[23] *See supra* note 9.

[24] Warsaw Convention, *supra* note 4, art. 24.

[25] As we will see in our more detailed treatment of the Montreal Convention, even that one introductory sentence contains a series of terms ("accidents," "international carriage," and so forth) that would become the object of (sometimes varying) court interpretations in the legal systems of the various contracting States.

[26] English judges in the late 16th or early 17th centuries began holding common carriers strictly liable for lost or damaged goods. A variety of public policy reasons were given, including the fear that customers would have no defense against or possibility of proving fraud by carriers, a desire to promote commerce, and the belief that carriers were performing a public service. Common law courts held common carriers to an only slightly less stringent standard of liability for injuries to passengers, out of concern for public safety. For a thorough discussion of how common carrier liability evolved first in England and then in the United States, see Robert J. Kaczorowski, *The Common-Law Background of Nineteenth-Century Tort Law*, 51 OHIO ST. L. J. 1127, 1129–69 (1990).

[27] *See* Warsaw Convention, *supra* note 4, arts. 17–18. Under Article 17, injury to passengers must have been sustained "on board the aircraft" or in the process of "embarking or disembarking"; under Article 18, loss or damage to baggage or cargo must occur during the period when the carrier is in charge of the baggage or cargo. Again, these provisions contain terms of art that have been subject to extensive judicial interpretation in the courts of contracting States.

for injuries to passengers at 125,000 "Poincaré" gold francs[28] (approximately $8300 at the time that Warsaw took effect in 1933) and damage to cargo at 250 gold francs per kilogram (approximately $17 in 1933).[29] Despite the relatively modest caps, a carrier could escape liability altogether if it could prove that it had taken "all necessary measures" to avoid the alleged wrong or could show that it was impossible to do so.[30] A plaintiff seeking to break the liability caps bore the burden of demonstrating that the damage or injuries in question arose out of the air carrier's "wilful misconduct."[31] The scope and meaning of that troublesome phrase would be revisited in later State efforts to reform Warsaw. Plaintiffs could also circumvent the Warsaw liability limits altogether if the defendant airline failed to issue a ticket,[32] although (in a departure from Anglo-American common law) plaintiffs that were shown to be contributorily negligent risked foregoing some or all of their damages.[33]

7.3.5. *Surviving Early U.S. Skepticism*

The Faustian exchange of presumptive liability for a near-unbreakable damages cap proved unstable in the decades after the Warsaw Convention entered

---

[28] The Poincaré gold franc was created by French Prime Minister Raymond Poincaré in 1926 when he returned France to the gold standard. The franc was equal to 65.5 milligrams of gold of millesimal fineness .900. When the Warsaw Convention was negotiated three years later, the drafters decided to tie the compensation caps to the franc and, specifically, to the amount of gold represented by the franc. Some courts converted the Warsaw caps into their domestic currencies by referring to the market price of gold in that currency. Others used official prices of gold set by the State. *See* Kevin Kyser, *Tarnished But Still Valuable: A History and Present State of the Gold Franc*, 16 SUM CURRENTS: INT'L TRADE L. 82, 84–89 (2007); Allan I. Mendelsohn, *The Value of the Poincaré Gold Franc in Limitation of Liability Conventions*, 5 J. MAR. L. & COM. 125, 125–28 (1973).

[29] *See* Warsaw Convention, *supra* note 4, art. 22. The liability limit for cargo could be increased if the consignor of the cargo declared a value for the goods in excess of the Warsaw limits *and*, where necessary, paid additional fees to the carrier. Failure on the part of either the carrier or the consignor to abide by the Convention's esoteric rules on cargo documentation could also affect the Convention's standards of liability. *See id.* arts. 4, 9.

[30] *See id.* art. 20(1). Article 20(2) of Warsaw analogizes the traditional maritime defense of "nautical fault" to events of cargo and luggage damage: "[T]he carrier is not liable if he proves that the damage was occasioned by negligent pilotage, or negligence in the handling of the aircraft or in navigation[.]" On the history of nautical fault in liability law, see Madeleine Jansson, The Consequences of a Deletion of the Nautical Fault 12–17 (May 2007) (M.A. thesis, Department of Law, Göteborg University).

[31] Warsaw Convention, *supra* note 4, art. 25(1). The phrase "wilful misconduct" was later replaced in The Hague Protocol. *See infra* Section 7.4.1.

[32] *See* Warsaw Convention, *supra* note 4, art. 3(2).

[33] "If the carrier proves that the damage was caused by or contributed to by the negligence of the injured person the Court may, in accordance with the provisions of its own law, exonerate the carrier wholly or partly from his liability." Warsaw Convention, *supra* note 4, art. 21.

into force. The U.S. tort bar was especially vociferous in its complaints that the treaty undermined the recovery rights of plaintiffs by failing to meet even the minimum standards of corrective justice. Some U.S. lawyers also alleged that Warsaw created a moral hazard by incentivizing airlines to take unnecessary risks with their safety protocols – airline companies would never have to internalize the full costs of the damages for which they were responsible.[34] But fears of a safety free-for-all did not prove justified. As States began to intensify their regulatory oversight of airlines,[35] and in many cases to take ownership in their national carriers, *ex ante* regulations were put in place to protect against aircraft crashes and maintain consumer confidence in the industry. Arguably, Warsaw's liability shield worked (at least financially) by allowing the industry to leverage technological advances in the 1950s and 1960s to begin offering transcontinental jet transportation. With an enhanced global profile and improving financial prospects, however, a buoyant international airline industry faced intensified calls for reform to the original Warsaw Convention and a realignment of its liability rules to favor the consumer.

7.4. REFORMING THE WARSAW CONVENTION (1): THE TREATY INSTRUMENTS

7.4.1. *The Hague Protocol (1955): A Doubling of the Liability Cap*

The first concerted attempt to bring meaningful reform to the Warsaw System came in September 1955 with the adoption of "The Hague Protocol."[36] Drafted by the ICAO Legal Committee, the Protocol sought to relieve growing disquiet, especially among American plaintiffs' lawyers, about Warsaw's relatively modest liability caps.[37] After much wrangling, the drafting conference rejected a U.S. proposal to quadruple the original passenger injury cap, consenting instead to a

---

[34] *But see supra* note 14 and accompanying text (discussing U.S. tort lawyers' particularistic view of the tort system).

[35] Regulatory oversight existed in the U.K. from as early as 1919 with the establishment of the Department of Civil Aviation. The United States passed the Air Commerce Act in 1926, which included provisions for safety regulation and pilot certification.

[36] *See* Protocol to Amend the Convention for the Unification of Certain Rules Relating to International Carriage by Air, *opened for signature* Sept. 28, 1955, 478 U.N.T.S. 371 (entered into force Aug. 1, 1963) [hereinafter The Hague Protocol].

[37] Most U.S. states at the time had limits on recovery in wrongful death actions, so that caps were not a foreign concept to U.S. tort lawyers. *See* 2 STUART M. SPEISER ET AL., RECOVERY FOR WRONGFUL DEATH AND INJURY § 7.1 (3d ed. 1992) (describing U.S. states' caps on recovery for wrongful death actions).

doubling of the amount to $16,600.[38] In addition, the Protocol rebalanced Warsaw's liability rules governing cargo carriage, improving the legal positions of both shippers and carriers.[39]

7.4.2. *Reforming the Principle of "Wilful Misconduct"*

The Hague Protocol also attempted to resolve an interpretive controversy concerning the phrase "wilful misconduct" in Article 25 of the Warsaw Convention.[40] A finding of "wilful misconduct" would deprive a carrier of entitlement to rely on any liability caps: civil law jurisdictions (such as France) interpreted the term as requiring that the air carrier *intentionally* inflicted injury,[41] whereas common law systems such as the United States did not make intentionality an issue.[42] Naturally that divergence created a problem when attempting to translate the authentic French text of the Convention[43] into an English equivalent and then seeking to interpret the translated English text as if the translated concepts were synonymous with those found in Anglo-American law. Common law courts, in any event, barely troubled themselves with any misalignment between civil law concepts and common law reality. As a result, plaintiffs in common law jurisdictions more easily breached Warsaw's liability limits than those litigating under civil law regimes.[44] The compromise struck in 1955 was to integrate the two lines of interpretation, replacing "wilful misconduct" with a standard that triggers unlimited liability

---

[38] *See* Hague Protocol, *supra* note 36, arts. XI, XIII. The post-Hague liability cap was set at 250,000 gold francs ($16,600). The United States had lobbied for a much higher cap of $25,000.

[39] In particular, the "nautical fault" defense, *see supra* note 30, was deleted entirely and clearer standards were promulgated with respect to calculating cargo and baggage damage. *See* Hague Protocol, *supra* note 36, art. XI. Additionally, the Protocol provided air carriers with the right to defend themselves from cargo liability claims if they could prove that the damage was due to an inherent defect in the cargo. *See id.* art. XII.

[40] *See supra* note 31 and accompanying text.

[41] The original French text of the Convention used the words "*dol*" and "*faute . . . equivalente au dol*," both of which suggest an intention to inflict damage on another person or "gross negligence" (the latter deemed to be equivalent to intention in civil law based on the Roman maxim *culpa lata dolo aequiparatur* ("gross negligence is equal to malice")).

[42] *See* Koninkljke Luchtvaart Maatschappij N.V. KLM v. Tuller, 292 F.2d 775, 778–79 (D.C. Cir. 1960) (discussing recognition by delegates to the Warsaw Convention that "wilful misconduct," the chosen English translation of "*dol*," included acts where the harm was not intended).

[43] At the time of The Hague Protocol, only the French text was recognized as official.

[44] *See* Tuller, *supra* note 42, 292 F.2d at 779–82 (holding that under the U.S. common law interpretation of the Warsaw Convention, an airline's failure to take appropriate safety measures before and after a crash could constitute wilful misconduct); *see also* LAWRENCE B. GOLDHIRSCH, THE WARSAW CONVENTION ANNOTATED: A LEGAL HANDBOOK 152 (2d ed. 2000) (citing *Gallais c. Aéro Maritime, T.G.I. Seine*, Apr. 28, 1954, R.F.D.A. 1954, 184 (Fr.), as an example of French courts requiring intentional harm to trigger unlimited liability).

if the plaintiff proves that the damage or injury resulted from an act or omission of the carrier *either* (a) with the intent to cause damage (the civil law standard) *or* (b) done recklessly and with knowledge that such an act or omission would probably result in damage or injury (the common law approach).[45] By incorporating the more lenient demands of the common law, The Hague Protocol also expanded the options available to plaintiffs in civil law jurisdictions.

7.4.3. *U.S. Failure to Ratify The Hague Protocol*

In a harbinger of things to come, the United States refused to ratify The Hague Protocol and openly expressed dissatisfaction with the reset liability cap. Although some commentators noted the irony that the U.S. demurral continued to subject U.S. plaintiffs to Warsaw's even less savory liability limits, courts in America had already shown themselves willing to find "wilful misconduct" on the part of air carriers and thereby to avoid Warsaw's caps altogether. Failure to ratify The Hague Protocol did not significantly impede the efforts of plaintiffs' lawyers in the United States to score larger recoveries from the airlines.[46] But the uneven ratification of the Protocol marked the first in a series of incomplete ratifications of amending instruments. A decline in the coherence of the Warsaw System would be the inevitable result.[47]

7.4.4. *Problem of Successive Carriage*

The Hague Protocol tilted the scales further toward plaintiffs, but by no means addressed all of the problems associated with the original Warsaw System.

---

[45] *See* Hague Protocol, *supra* note 36, art. XIII. "Recklessness" is often proven by violation of a statute or of air safety regulations. *See* GOLDHIRSCH, *supra* note 44, at 163.

[46] In the opinion of several U.S. federal courts, the United States implicitly ratified The Hague Protocol when it ratified Montreal Protocol No. 4 of 1975 (which incorporates the terms of the earlier instrument; *see infra* Section 7.4.7). *See* Continental Ins. Co. v. Federal Express Corp., 454 F.3d 951, 958 (9th Cir. 2006); *but see* Avero Belgium Ins. v. Am. Airlines, Inc., 423 F.3d 73, 89 (2d Cir. 2005). Explicit ratification came in 2003. *See* U.S. Dep't of State, *Treaties in Force* 350 (2004). Even without U.S. participation, The Hague Protocol entered into force on May 1, 1964. As of mid-2005, it had 137 State parties. *See* ICAO Composite Table (status of treaties and status of States vis-à-vis treaties), http://www.icao.int/Secretariat/Legal/Pages/TreatyCollection.aspx.

[47] The Hague Protocol, incidentally, produced a complete amended Convention by providing that its own provisions and those of the unamended Warsaw Convention form a single instrument. *See* Hague Protocol, *supra* note 36, art. XIX. Reversing the common legislative technique of reading amendments into the original legal instrument, Warsaw's unamended provisions are, instead, read into The Hague Protocol to produce a complete regime. *See* Richard Gardiner, *Revising the Law of Carriage by Air: Mechanisms in Treaties and Contract*, 47 I.C.L.Q. 278, 281 (1998).

One of the most disconcerting technical shortcomings concerned cases involving lease, charter, or interchange of aircraft and airlines as well as the practice of freight forwarding. In those situations, a passenger or shipper may conclude a contract of carriage with one enterprise, while the actual carriage is performed by a different enterprise. Code-sharing, where an airline places its IATA designator code on a service that is actually operated by another carrier, is a more recent example of such intercarrier arrangements.[48] An austere reading of Article 1(3) of the Warsaw Convention[49] indicates that the treaty's terms (including its liability limits) apply between the passenger or shipper and the airline with which either has contracted for carriage, but *not* (unless a further specific contractual provision is made) to any additional carrier or carriers that may perform all or part of the service.[50] For example, United could avail itself of the Warsaw Convention on a ticket that it sells for a Washington, D.C./Madrid flight operated by Irish carrier Aer Lingus,[51] but Aer Lingus as the actual carrier would be exposed to unlimited liability in the event of an accident affecting the purchaser of the ticket.

7.4.5. *Successive Carriage Under the Guadalajara Supplementary Convention (1961)*

Although not all jurisdictions took such a stern view of Article 1(3) of the Warsaw Convention, a separate treaty instrument – the Guadalajara Supplementary Convention of 1961[52] – clarified that all carriers providing a single service under the ticket's contract of carriage were protected by Warsaw for those segments of

[48] "Code-sharing is a marketing arrangement in which an airline places its designator code on a flight operated by another airline and sells and issues tickets for that flight(s)." OFFICE OF SEC'Y, DEP'T OF TRANSP. & FED. AVIATION ADMIN., CODE-SHARE SAFETY PROGRAM GUIDELINES 4 (2006). Readers will probably have noticed that airlines do not actually share codes, but rather aircraft. Airport information screens continue to list "code-shared" flights under the separate code of each partner airline. Nevertheless, the term "code-sharing" has become accepted usage: for fuller discussion of the concept, see *supra* Sections 4.6.2, 4.6.3.

[49] "A carriage to be performed by several successive air carriers is deemed . . . to be one undivided carriage, if it has been regarded by the parties as a single operation, whether it had been agreed upon under the form of a single contract or of a series of contracts." Warsaw Convention, *supra* note 4, art. 1(3).

[50] A broad reading of Article 1(3), *supra* note 49, in contrast, posits that the Convention already contemplates that multiple and successive carriers may be involved in passenger transport and cargo shipments.

[51] This was an actual service (now discontinued) that was made legally possible by the offer of seventh ("stand-alone") freedoms to EU carriers serving the United States under the terms of the 2007 U.S./EU Air Transport Agreement. *See supra* Chapter 3, Part 3.3.

[52] Convention, Supplementary to the Warsaw Convention, for the Unification of Certain Rules Relating to International Carriage by Air Performed by a Person Other Than the Contracting Carrier, ICAO Doc. No. 8181 (entered into force May 1, 1964). The ICAO Legal Committee

the journey where they performed the actual carriage.[53] That would remain true even if a particular carrier's portion of an international journey were wholly domestic.[54]

7.4.6. *The Guatemala City Protocol (1971): A Failure to Set an Absolute Liability Cap*

Although the Guadalajara Convention eventually attracted eighty-four ratifying States, the United States was never among them. As we will shortly see, U.S. resistance to the whole Warsaw System would spill over into a threatened formal denunciation of the Warsaw Convention in 1965 and a parallel "private" arrangement between the U.S. Government and IATA's member airlines. But ICAO still sought to salvage Warsaw, and in 1971 its Legal Committee launched the Guatemala City Protocol, an update to The Hague Protocol and thus in legal effect a "protocol to a protocol." In its most notorious provision, Guatemala City sought to minimize litigation and expedite compensation by establishing an *absolute* liability ceiling of $100,000 that could not be broken even in instances of "wilful misconduct."[55] That proposal held little appeal for most of the Warsaw Convention's signatories. The Protocol never received enough ratifications to enter into force and remains merely a drafting relic of the Warsaw era.[56]

---

dealt with the issue of successive carriers using a new treaty rather than another amending instrument. Ostensibly the Committee's decision reflected a concern that an amending conference would be used by some States to revisit the issue of liability caps. The true underlying reason, however, was to prevent Poland – using its status as the depositary State for the Warsaw Convention – to deny ratification to States (such as South Korea) that the Polish Communist government did not recognize.

[53] The Guadalajara Convention corrected the Warsaw Convention's apparent omission of the actual carrier (which is otherwise covered by Warsaw) from being deemed a party to the contract of carriage by operation of the Convention. *See* Gardiner, *supra* note 47, at 295. The acts of the actual carrier are deemed to be those of the contracting carrier (and vice versa). *See id.*

[54] *See* Warsaw Convention, art. 1(3). For example, on a Los Angeles/New York/London flight offered under a code-sharing agreement by American Airlines (Los Angeles/New York) and British Airways (New York/London), American Airlines would still be protected under Warsaw even if the accident occurred within the territory of the United States.

[55] *See* Protocol to Amend the Convention for the Unification of Certain Rules Relating to International Carriage by Air, as Amended by the Hague Protocol, *opened for signature* Mar. 8, 1971, ICAO Doc. 8392 (1971). A detailed analysis of the ill-fated instrument is available in Rene H. Mankiewicz, *The 1971 Protocol of Guatemala City to Further Amend the 1929 Warsaw Convention*, 38 J. Air L. & Com. 519 (1972). Given that the requirement of an "accident" had proven so problematic under Warsaw (see *infra* Part 7.9), the Protocol also made the reasonable proposal to replace the Article 17 term "accident" by the term "event." *See id.* at 525.

[56] The Protocol had the cumbersome requirement that it could not come into force unless the 30 ratifying States included five States whose airlines carried 40% of international scheduled air

7.4.7. The Montreal Protocols (1975): A Basket of Changes

Undaunted by the chilly reception for its Guatemala City Protocol, or by U.S. unilateralism, ICAO pushed the rest of the international community to continued modernization of the Warsaw System. Four new legal instruments, known as the Montreal Protocols, were agreed upon in 1975.[57] The most sweeping change implemented by the Protocols was to replace the Warsaw Convention's "gold clause" monetary standard by use of the International Monetary Fund's Special Drawing Rights (SDRs).[58] Additionally, Montreal Protocol No. 3 set a new liability cap of 100,000 SDRs,[59] while Protocol No. 4 terminated Warsaw's archaic rules on cargo documentation in favor of modernized methods that rely on standard forms (the "air waybill"[60]) and electronic transactions.[61] Protocol No. 4 also raised the liability cap for cargo to 17 SDRs ($25) per kilogram.[62] Finally, Protocols Nos. 2–4 also incorporated The Hague Protocol by reference, intending thereby to allow countries such as the United States that failed to ratify that instrument to take advantage of its clarifications to the Warsaw System.[63]

traffic in 1970. *See* Guatemala Protocol, art. XX. That percentage would have required U.S. ratification, which never happened.

[57] *See* Protocols to Amend the Convention for the Unification of Certain Rules Relating to International Carriage by Air, *opened for signature* Sept. 25, 1975, *reprinted in* 22 I.L.M. 13.

[58] Montreal Protocols Nos. 1–3 all amended Article 22 of the Warsaw Convention to replace the Poincaré gold franc with the SDR. SDRs were created by the International Monetary Fund in 1969 to support the now-defunct Bretton Woods fixed exchange rate system. That change was prompted by the "demonetization" of gold, which subjected gold to the ordinary laws of supply and demand and ended its "transcendent" or "universal" value. Despite the collapse of Bretton Woods, SDRs are still used as a means of valuation in some international instruments such as the Warsaw and Montreal conventions. The value of SDRs is based on a basket of four currencies – currently the euro, the Japanese yen, the pound sterling, and the U.S. dollar. *See* International Monetary Fund, Factsheet, *Special Drawing Rights* (Aug. 24, 2012), http://www.imf.org/external/np/exr/facts/sdr.htm.

[59] Article VII of Montreal Protocol No. 3 stated that ratification would have the effect of accession to the Guatemala City Protocol for any State not already a party. Incidentally, Montreal Protocol No. 3 was the only one of the four Montreal instruments to have failed to receive sufficient ratifications to enter into force. *See supra* note 57.

[60] Air waybills are used in air cargo transport as contracts of carriage and evidence of receipt of goods. IATA is primarily responsible for the development and standardization of the air waybill, which was incorporated by Montreal Protocol No. 4 into the Warsaw System.

[61] IATA is pushing an e-Air Waybill initiative to increase the use of electronic as opposed to paper air waybills. Both the shipping and receiving States must have ratified either the Montreal Convention or Montreal Protocol No. 4 in order to allow airlines to use electronic air waybills. *See* http://www.iata.org/whatwedo/cargo/Pages/eawb.aspx.

[62] This was an increase from the previous 250 gold franc limit (approximately $17 per kilogram). *See supra* Section 7.3.4.

[63] *See* Montreal Protocol No. 2, art. IV; Montreal Protocol No. 3, art. V; Montreal Protocol No. 4, art. V.

7.4.8. *Aftermath of the Montreal Protocols*

The Montreal Protocols marked the last efforts by public international law treaty-making to modify the Warsaw System. But they did not obviate any need for further change. The Warsaw System was now plagued by inconsistent and uneven ratifications of its various instruments. The United States, as noted, had rejected all of the agreements that followed Warsaw (and had even threatened to reject Warsaw itself). Moreover, other than in the technical sense of consolidating prior agreements, the Protocols largely avoided the fraught question of moving (or removing) Warsaw's liability caps.[64] Despite enthusiastic U.S. support for the Montreal Protocols at the time of drafting, once again U.S. ratification was not forthcoming. And, as we will see, other States revealed displeasure with the Warsaw System by adopting less airline-friendly variances of the prevailing international rules for international air carrier liability.

7.5. REFORMING THE WARSAW CONVENTION (2): GOVERNMENT AND NON-GOVERNMENT INITIATIVES

7.5.1. *Continued U.S. Dissatisfaction with Warsaw*

In truth, the United States had little stake in further multilateral negotiations to modify the Warsaw System. Preservation of the concept of liability limits, however many times the caps were elevated, ran counter to its interests (or, rather, to the vocal interests of the U.S. plaintiffs' tort bar). Critics accused the United States of undermining the Warsaw System through unilateralism, but those attacks were overstated. From the beginning, after all, the Warsaw Convention presented no *textual* objection to waiving its ground rules for liability and defenses. As noted earlier, Article 22 allowed air carriers, "by special contract," to "agree to a higher limit of liability" than that codified in the treaty.[65] Added to that, Article 33 of the Convention provided that "[n]othing in [the] Convention shall prevent [a carrier] ... from making regulations which do not conflict with the provisions of the Convention."[66] Besides, few would have denied that the Warsaw System had failed to keep

---

[64] *But see supra* note 59 and accompanying text.

[65] Warsaw Convention, art. 22. *See also supra* note 20. On the question of special jurisdictional contracts under the Montreal Convention, see *infra* note 266 and accompanying text.

[66] Warsaw Convention, art. 33. At the same time, however, Article 23 stated that an airline cannot *lower* its liability or use the contract of carriage to create new defenses from liability. "Any provision tending to relieve the carrier of liability or to fix a lower limit than that which is laid down in this Convention shall be null and void . . ." Warsaw Convention, *supra* note 4, art. 23.

pace with the huge expansion of international air services during the second half of the twentieth century. The economic justifications for inoculating the airlines against high liability that were so convincing in 1929 had lost much of their directive force by the 1970s. Finally, U.S. domestic air transport had not perished as a result of decades-long exposure to the rigors of uncapped liability under common law. To U.S. critics of the Warsaw System, it was absurd that an accident befalling a passenger on a flight between Chicago and Toronto could be subject to severe liability caps while a similar event on the much longer Los Angeles/New York route would be controlled by the common law rules on common carrier liability.

7.5.2. The U.S./IATA Montreal Agreement (1966)

ICAO perceived a threatened U.S. denunciation of the Warsaw Convention (delivered on November 15, 1965) as potentially lethal to the Warsaw System.[67] But, although the Organization continued to advocate modernization, it was outflanked by the forces of (especially U.S.) unilateralism. The U.S./IATA "Montreal Agreement" signed in 1966,[68] extraordinary as it appeared to be, would not be the only public/private initiative that a State would pursue to alter the terms of international air carrier liability. Throughout 1965, IATA itself had convened a series of meetings to discuss possible reforms to the Warsaw System, including supersession of Warsaw by the local liability laws of the domicile of injured passengers. A related proposal sought to expand the jurisdictional options under Warsaw to allow more suits to be brought into U.S. courts.[69] Under the terms of the Montreal Agreement, IATA's member airlines[70] consented to an increased liability limit of $75,000 ($58,000 after deduction of legal fees and costs) for all international flights for which a point

---

[67] In fact, the United States never followed through on its Notice of Denunciation. The withdrawal of the Notice consisted of the announcement of the deal outlined in the main text.

[68] Order of Civil Aeronautics Board Approving Increases in Liability Limitations of Warsaw Convention and Hague Protocol, May 13, 1966 (approving Agreement CAB 18900), 31 Fed. Reg. 7302 (1966), *reprinted in* 49 U.S.C. app. § 1502 (1988) [hereinafter Montreal Agreement]. In fact, the IATA agreement was with the then–U.S. aviation regulatory agency, the Civil Aeronautics Board. The Agreement was named after the location city of IATA's headquarters. That usage naturally causes confusion with similarly styled public international aviation law treaties.

[69] Under Article 28(1) of the Warsaw Convention, jurisdiction may be exercised (at the option of the plaintiff) by the court of: the domicile of the air carrier; the air carrier's principal place of business; the place where the contract of carriage was made; or the place of destination. *See infra* Part 7.11.1.

[70] Non-IATA member airlines were not covered, although in 1966 there were few such carriers that operated international services.

in the United States was an agreed-upon stopping-place, point of departure, or destination under the contract of carriage.[71] Passengers would have to be notified in writing of the possible applicability of the new provisions.[72] The airlines also agreed to waive their right to the "all necessary measures" defense in Article 20 of the Warsaw Convention.[73] The IATA-brokered compromise did not, it should be noted, affect the "wilful misconduct" provision in Article 25 of the Warsaw Convention. U.S. courts continued to apply that standard in its common law (i.e., "nonintentional") meaning in cases where a plaintiff sought to shatter the Warsaw (or IATA) liability cap altogether.[74]

7.5.3. The IATA Intercarrier Agreement (1995)

IATA's nongovernmental interventions in the Warsaw System did not stop with the Montreal Agreement. The Association reentered the liability fray in the 1990s when it became clear (especially after the "Japanese Initiative" discussed below) that Warsaw was not going to hold. Acting under a grant of antitrust immunity from the U.S. Department of Transportation, sixty-seven IATA member airlines convened in Washington, D.C., to discuss the Warsaw limits. While they expressed support for preserving the Warsaw System, they acknowledged that "the existing passenger liability limits for international carriage by air [were] grossly inadequate in many jurisdictions and should be revised as a matter of urgency."[75] Hoping to break the governmental deadlock on fixing the Warsaw Convention, the member airlines confirmed the dramatic reach of their proposed reform at the IATA annual general meeting in Kuala Lumpur in October 1995.[76] Under the so-called 'IATA Intercarrier Agreement,' they agreed to take steps to waive the Warsaw Convention/Hague Protocol Article 22(1) limitation for passenger injury or death arising out of an

---

[71] *See* Montreal Agreement, *supra* note 68, ¶ 1(1). The agreement was limited, however, to cases involving passenger death or injury; it did not extend to loss or damage to baggage or cargo.

[72] In legal effect, the Montreal Agreement could be regarded as a "special contract" between air carriers and passengers under the Warsaw Convention. *See* Chubb & Son, Inc. v. Asiana Airlines, 214 F.3d 301, 307 n.4 (2d Cir. 2000). *See infra* note 266 and accompanying text.

[73] *See* Montreal Agreement, *supra* note 68, ¶ 1(2); *see also supra* Section 7.3.4.

[74] *See, e.g.*, In re Korean Air Lines Disaster of Sept. 1, 1983, 932 F.2d 1475, 1485 (D.C. Cir. 1991). It has been speculated that the United States could have "strong-armed" the airlines into accepting no liability cap at all, although the Article 20 ("all necessary measures") defense would have remained. It was probably in the interest of the U.S. tort bar, however, to get rid of the Article 20 defense in exchange for the raised liability cap. Moreover, as noted in the main text, U.S. courts were quite willing to break the cap altogether in instances of "wilful misconduct."

[75] Ruwantissa Abeyratne, *Regulatory Management of the Warsaw System of Air Carrier Liability*, 3 J. AIR TRANSPORT MGMT. 37–45 (1997).

[76] Although only 12 airlines signed the agreement initially, all U.S. carriers signed on a week later, which effectively cleared the way for a new liability regime.

Article 17 accident.[77] The 1995 Agreement introduced a universal approach to liability caps, excluding any *a priori* limits on damages for passenger injury or death and waiving defenses (including the "all necessary measures" defense) for those portions of claims below 100,000 SDRs. Where a plaintiff's "no proof of fault" (strict liability[78]) entitlement to damages no longer applied automatically, that is, for those portions of claims that exceeded 100,000 SDRs, the airlines would carry the burden of proof. Two further points should be noted. First, for those portions of claims exceeding 100,000 SDRs, the "all necessary measures" defense would continue to apply.[79] Second, the Article 25 provision on "wilful misconduct" became irrelevant because, in principle, the concept of a liability cap was no longer in play.[80]

7.5.4. *Effect of the IATA Intercarrier Agreement on the Warsaw System*

The IATA Intercarrier Agreement worked to bring the Warsaw System (albeit unofficially) closer in line with the long-standing common law presumption that common carriers (such as railroads and airlines) should bear the risks associated with their services because they are better placed than their passengers to guard against them.[81] Although that presumption originated in an era when people (and the courts) were much more circumspect about the safety of new modes of travel, it still appears intuitively correct given the fact that airline passengers (and, indeed, shippers[82]) are, for good reason, afforded no control over the operation of the aircraft in which they or their cargo will travel.[83] Even though neither the Montreal Agreement nor the Intercarrier

---

[77] International Air Transport Association, Intercarrier Agreement on Passenger Liability, Oct. 31, 1995, *reprinted in* 3 Av. L. Rep. (CCH) ¶ 27,951 [hereinafter IATA Intercarrier Agreement]. In April 1996, IATA drafted the "IATA Measures of Implementation Agreement" to give effect to the measures agreed upon in the Intercarrier Agreement. *See* International Air Transport Association, Agreement on the Measures to Implement the IATA Intercarrier Agreement, *reprinted in* 3 Av. L. Rep. (CCH) ¶ 27,952 [hereinafter IATA Implementation Agreement].

[78] A plaintiff still had to prove that the Article 17 accident caused the plaintiff's damages, distinguishing the Warsaw regime from an absolute liability system where proof of causation would be unnecessary.

[79] That defense had been suspended under the Montreal Agreement. *See supra* note 73.

[80] Unlike the 1966 Montreal Agreement, the IATA Intercarrier Agreement was not restricted to routes connected to the United States, although the Agreement still provided some flexibility. For instance, select routes were bracketed off and therefore remained subject to the Warsaw System.

[81] *See supra* note 26 and accompanying text.

[82] Although, in fact, the IATA Intercarrier Agreement did not apply to air cargo transport.

[83] Some might argue that in an era of pervasive *ex ante* safety regulation and international standards set by ICAO, governments have assumed responsibility for safety and should accept at least some of the blame if accidents occur. *See supra* Part 7.2. A more contrarian line of thought is to suggest that, in the modern age, consumers know better the risks associated with

Agreement constituted a formal treaty instrument,[84] the two IATA agreements effectively established the rules for international air carrier liability in the United States for more than thirty years. Those who take a more favorable view of these initiatives see them as remarkable examples of a private trade group having a discernible impact on the development of international law.[85] The willingness of IATA's member airlines to accept the new liability regime – no doubt fearing an even more deeply fractured and unworkable Warsaw System if States emulated the United States with threatened or actual defections – also pointed toward the possibility of further reforms. Their solidarity revealed, too, that their plea of certain economic ruin if liability caps were lifted no longer had force after the 1960s. Finally, as we will see, IATA's acceptance of a new, "post-Warsaw" model of presumptive liability would become the cornerstone of the 1999 Montreal Convention.

7.5.5. *The Japanese Initiative on Liability (1992)*

Across the Pacific, Japan had also grown dissatisfied with the liability regime established by Warsaw. The absence of a universal consensus on liability, coupled with the undeniable fact that airlines engaged in international carriage enjoyed a level of protection not afforded to carriers providing wholly domestic air services,[86] led ten Japanese airlines in 1992 to invoke Article 22 of the Warsaw Convention and to add language to their conditions of carriage altering their liability under the Warsaw System.[87] Under the new liability regime for Japanese carriers, known as the "Japanese Initiative" and which was a precursor to the IATA Intercarrier Agreement, the airlines waived their right

---

air travel and can judge for themselves whether they want to bear them. Why should the airlines "automatically" carry the burden of responsibility? Should they not have the option to negotiate narrower liability terms in their contracts of carriage? Whatever the merits of these alternatives, IATA was never ready to advocate such unprecedented flexibility.

[84] They are actually contractual agreements between carriers, at least some of which were private (i.e., non-State-owned) entities. Treaty law as set down in the Vienna Convention on the Law of Treaties only applies to agreements between States. *See* Vienna Convention on the Law of Treaties, art. 3, 1155 U.N.T.S. 331 (1969), 8 I.L.M. 679 (1969).

[85] This is hardly an uncommon occurrence, widely discussed in international law scholarship by reference to the medieval *lex mercatoria*. *See* Brian F. Havel & Gabriel S. Sanchez, *The Emerging Lex Aviatica*, 42 GEO J. INT'L L. 639, 658–59 (2011). *See also supra* Chapter 4, Section 4.5.1 (mentioning IATA's more recent initiative to encourage States to waive the operation of the nationality rule in their bilateral air transport agreements).

[86] Thus, a trigger for the Japanese Government's action was the 1985 domestic crash of a JAL 747 in which 520 people lost their lives. The average recovery in that case was $800,000, well above the Warsaw System limits. *See* Naneen K. Baden, *The Japanese Initiative on the Warsaw Convention*, 61 J. AIR L. & COM. 437, 453–55 (1996).

[87] *See id.*

to the Warsaw Convention's "all necessary measures" defense for claims up to 100,000 SDRs (i.e., allowing strict liability) in exchange for keeping the defense available for any amount in excess of 100,000 SDRs[88] (i.e., fault-based liability). There would, however, be no cap on recovery. Commentators noted, incidentally, that the Japanese Initiative may have been an emanation of a deeper sense of "moral commitment" that Japanese businesses feel toward the wider citizenry.[89]

7.5.6. *Response of the European Union (EU)*

Discontent with the Warsaw System reigned in Europe as well. With an eye to raising air carrier liability to a socially acceptable level, the EU adopted Regulation 2027/97.[90] The EU legislation, which only applied to air carriers licensed under the Union's single aviation market rules,[91] essentially duplicated the liability terms set out in the IATA Intercarrier Agreement: EU airlines would be subject to unlimited liability, but the strict/fault-based dichotomy would be retained by allowing recourse to the "all necessary measures" defense for the portion of claims that exceeded 100,000 SDRs. Regulation 2027/97 also allowed EU carriers to avail themselves of a defense of contributory negligence.[92] The EU legislation was not the first time that European States had tried to fix the Warsaw System. In 1974, several European States signed on to an informal accord known as the Malta Agreement to encourage their carriers to increase their liability caps.[93] A decade or so later, the Italian Constitutional Court exposed Italian carriers (especially Alitalia) to unlimited liability when it ruled in 1985 that the domestic law implementing the Warsaw Convention was unconstitutional insofar as it discriminated against air travelers vis-à-vis surface travelers and its liability limits constituted an offense to human life and dignity.[94] In response, the Italian Government passed Law No. 274 of 1988,

---

[88] *See* Abeyratne, *supra* note 75, at 39. Following the Japanese Initiative, Australia enacted new legislation in 1995 to unilaterally raise the liability cap to 260,000 SDRs. *See id.*

[89] Compounding that sense of obligation was the long-standing official Japanese perception of the airline industry as a public utility rather than a purely private enterprise.

[90] *See* EC Regulation 2027/97, Air Carrier Liability in the Event of Accidents, 1997 O.J. (L 285) 1.

[91] For further discussion of these rules, *see supra* Chapter 4, Section 4.4.3.

[92] For further discussion of the Regulation's other provisions, see E. Schmid and R. Giemulla, *Council Regulation (EC) No. 2027/97 on Air Carrier Liability in the Event of Accidents and its Implications for Air Carriers*, 23 AIR & SPACE L. 98 (1998).

[93] *See* I. H. PH. DIEDERIKS-VERSCHOOR, AN INTRODUCTION TO AIR LAW 163–64 (8th ed. 2006). The Malta Agreement related to carriage outside the United States; U.S.-related carriage would already have been covered by the Montreal Agreement. *See supra* note 68.

[94] *See* Coccia v. Turkish Airlines, 108 Foro It. 1 1586 (Corte Cost. 1985).

which imposed strict liability up to 100,000 SDRs and mandated compulsory insurance.[95]

7.6. THE WARSAW CONVENTION: CONCLUSION

7.6.1. *A Sustained Onslaught on the Warsaw Convention*

Although all of these reform efforts were limited in scope, they nevertheless represented a sustained onslaught on the Warsaw Convention's fundamental conceptual premise (the product of applying Articles 17 and 22) of admitting fault but capping liability. The sequence of public and public/private instruments, beginning with The Hague Protocol and culminating in the second IATA agreement, sent a powerful signal that the Warsaw System was failing to achieve its principal intended purpose, namely, to create uniform rules for air carrier liability in international transport. Moreover, the integrity and cohesion of the Warsaw System had been progressively eroded by some of the world's largest aviation markets.

7.6.2. *Need for a New Treaty*

The apparent willingness of the international airline industry to tolerate these new, sometimes conflicting rules sent its own message as well: the old protections that the Warsaw Convention bestowed were no longer necessary. The international airline industry had finally evolved to the point where it could be expected to take, and expected itself to take, full responsibility for its actions and to accept potentially unlimited liability for accidents resulting in injuries or loss of life.[96] What was needed was a fresh treaty to restore uniformity without sacrificing the new ethos. To that end, ICAO stepped forward to develop the 1999 Montreal Convention.

---

[95] *See* Law 274 of July 7, 1988. The law applied to all Italian carriers flying anywhere in the world and to any air carrier flying to or from Italy. Although some have seen the Italian legislation as novel, in truth it did little more than implement the Guatemala Protocol and Montreal Protocol No. 3. So long as the new Italian regime was consistent with the Warsaw Convention, it would not be invalidated "by this being at the behest of [a government]." Gardiner, *supra* note 47, at 299. The problem, as Gardiner notes, is that it does not appear that the special contract provisions of the Warsaw Convention (*see supra* note 20) were intended as a means of increasing limits of liability for all carriers affecting a particular State. But that State's imposition of liability limits on carriers of its own nationality would be within its legitimate sphere of regulation. *See* Gardiner, *supra, id.*

[96] The reader may have noted that most of these reforms in the Warsaw System ignored liability for baggage and cargo.

7.7. THE MONTREAL CONVENTION (1): INTRODUCTION

7.7.1. *Preserving a System of Uniform Liability*

The tolerance of the international community for the Warsaw Convention's regime of liability limits declined steadily over the course of the twentieth century. The arrival of the jet age and the vitality of the aviation industry compared with its precarious health in 1929 swept away any remaining justification for the Warsaw limits. What remained, however, was a desire to hold onto the other stated aim of the Warsaw System, namely, to create universally applicable rules governing liability. After all, in the realm of public international aviation law, the Chicago Convention had successfully anchored a stable regime for facilitating international air services (albeit one that left most economic rights to be distributed through an idiosyncratic patchwork of bilateral treaties).[97] But seven decades of amendments, criticisms, threats of denunciation, private side agreements, State-level initiatives, and a plethora of secondary studies, had made only limited progress toward modifying the Warsaw System to boost liability caps and to provide plaintiffs with more options to recover damages beyond those caps. Most of the international community kept faithful to Warsaw, relying still on the original Convention and its various amending protocols (which themselves had not been universally adopted). But the United States, the perennial voice of reform, had a sporadic record of actually accepting the amendments.[98]

7.7.2. *Role of ICAO in Creating the Montreal Convention*

The alacrity of many IATA carriers in adopting the Intercarrier Agreement put enormous pressure on ICAO to respond at the intergovernmental level and to forge a long-elusive consensus on the issue of liability limits. ICAO, in fact, defied expectations to recapture the leadership on this issue from IATA. In May 1999, the Organization convened a Diplomatic Conference of 118 States in Montreal to discuss a draft convention that would "modernize and

---

[97] *See supra* Chapters 2, 3.

[98] Eventually the United States did ratify Montreal Protocol No. 4 while also ratifying the 1999 Montreal Convention. *See* ICAO, Status of the United States with Regard to International Law Instruments, http://www.icao.int/secretariat/legal/Status%20of%20individual%20States/united_states_en.pdf. The reason for adopting the Protocol was to ensure that its liability terms, even though imperfect, still applied in situations where the international air carriage in issue involved an airline of a State that had not adopted the Montreal Convention as well, but only the Protocol. For further discussion of the applicability of different instruments depending on the circumstances of individual cases, see *infra* Section 7.12.3.

consolidate" the Warsaw System.[99] The successor instrument would integrate not only the treaty-based advances made over the decades within the Warsaw System, but also the progress achieved through the various State and public/private initiatives already noted.[100]

7.7.3. Issues of Restitution and Corrective Justice

One of the clearest indicators that the Montreal Convention inaugurated "regime change" can be found in the treaty's Preamble, which recognizes "the importance of ensuring protection of the interest of consumers in international carriage by air and the need for equitable compensation based on the principle of restitution."[101] That one line, hortatory though it may be,[102] is a far cry from the manifest intent of the Warsaw Convention (expressed through its apparatus of liability caps) to shield airlines from the risk of an "excessive" liability. The Preamble also accords with the principle of corrective justice: according to that idea, airlines *should*, as a matter of right, restore those they injure as near to the condition they were in prior to the accident as circumstances will allow.[103]

7.7.4. Basic Principles of Liability and Jurisdiction

To that end, the Montreal Convention aligns with the IATA Intercarrier Agreement and the Japanese Initiative to abolish all arbitrary limits on recovery for passenger death or injury. Like those instruments, it adopts a scheme of strict liability for *proven* damages up to 100,000 SDRs and unlimited liability beyond that amount, subject to a narrow range of defenses. Montreal sets no upper limit on the amount of damages an airline may have to pay out; the determination of damages rests with the local courts applying the Convention's rules. In certain circumstances, too, Montreal expands the bases of jurisdiction for claims relating to passenger death or injury to permit suits in the passenger's home State if certain conditions are met.[104] Additionally, Montreal updates the liability limits for baggage and cargo, setting a 1000 SDR per passenger

---

[99] Montreal Convention, *supra* note 6, pmbl.
[100] *See* Assad Kotaite, President, ICAO, Opening Address at the International Conference on Air Law on the Modernization of the Warsaw System (May 10, 1999), http://legacy.icao.int/icao/en/conf/warsaw_pres.htm.
[101] Montreal Convention, *supra* note 6, pmbl.
[102] And, indeed, the concept of "restitution" appears nowhere in the main text of the Montreal Convention.
[103] *But see supra* Part 7.2, also canvassing a more contrarian view.
[104] *See infra* Section 7.11.12.

liability cap for checked baggage[105] and a 17 SDR per kilogram cap for loss, damage, or delay of cargo.[106] Finally, Montreal preserves all of the documentary efficiencies secured for the cargo industry by the Warsaw-era Montreal Protocol No. 4.[107] In the next parts, we will examine the most important principles of the Montreal liability system in more detail.

7.8. THE MONTREAL CONVENTION (2): THE BASIC PRINCIPLES

7.8.1. *Scope of Application of the Montreal Convention*

Article 1 of the Montreal Convention, which defines the treaty's scope of application, replicates Article 1(1) of Warsaw in holding that the treaty "applies to all international carriage of persons, baggage or cargo performed by aircraft for reward," and applies equally to gratuitous carriage.[108] As in Warsaw, Article 1(2) also makes clear that the Convention governs all international carriage where the places of departure and destination are in two States that have ratified the Montreal Convention *or* are within a single ratifying State, provided in the latter case that there is an agreed-upon stopping-place in another State, whether or not it has ratified the Convention.[109] Thus, the Convention's applicability is a combination of treaty relations between States

---

[105] See Montreal Convention, *supra* note 6, art. 22(2).

[106] *See id.* art. 22(3). This matches the cargo liability cap contained in Montreal Protocol No. 4, *supra* note 57.

[107] *See supra* Section 7.4.7.

[108] Montreal Convention, *supra* note 6, art. 1. The extension of coverage to "gratuitous carriage," that is, carriage offered free of charge as a courtesy, is limited in application. Courts have read it to include airline employees who are "deadheading" (traveling free in unsold seats without working), and it would seemingly apply also to passengers who have earned a free ticket through a frequent flyer plan. The Convention, however, does not cover on-duty airline employees, nor, presumably, would it apply to stowaways. *See* GOLDHIRSCH, *supra* note 44, at 12.

[109] *See* Montreal Convention, *supra* note 6, art. 1(2). Although this language seems convoluted, it works out to be fairly straightforward in practice. Take State A, a Montreal-ratifying State, and State B, a nonratifying State that still adheres to the Warsaw System (including The Hague Protocol). A one-way trip from State A to State B will not be covered by the Montreal Convention (it will continue to be covered by Warsaw, assuming that State A still adheres also to that treaty). But if the ticket is for a State A/State B/State A round-trip journey, the Montreal Convention governs because the places of departure and destination are both in State A and the agreed-upon stopping-place is State B (even though it is not a Convention party). The reader may wonder why State A is the "destination" State rather than State B, a point that is not obvious. To determine the "destination" State, in fact, courts have focused on the objective manifestations of the parties' intent expressed by the ticket. *See In re* Alleged Food Poisoning Incident, Mar. 1984, 770 F.2d 3, 4–5 (2d Cir. 1985). *But see infra* Section 7.12.4 (adding a further complication to the fact pattern considered here).

coupled with "facts of a geographical nature":[110] it will apply when relevant States are party to it, the link between those States being provided by geographical information in the contract of carriage as to the origin and destination of the flight.[111] Cabotage (purely intra-State) services are excluded from coverage even if the flight route crosses non-national airspace.[112] Article 1(3), again borrowed virtually intact from Warsaw, addresses the oft-litigated question of when a domestic journey performed by one carrier is connected to an international journey performed by a different, "successive" carrier for purposes of securing coverage for the first carrier under the Convention. That problem of successive carriage was more significant when airlines routinely orchestrated passenger and baggage connections on flights performed by other airlines using an IATA-sponsored collaborative process called "interlining."[113] Today most airlines operate through code-sharing arrangements with partner carriers,[114] reducing the number of disputes over whether successive carriers formed a "single, undivided operation."[115]

[110] Gardiner, *supra* note 47, at 282.

[111] *See id.* As Gardiner points out, "[t]o the extent of selection of places of departure, destination and agreed stopping places (and to that extent only), what is agreed between the airline and the passenger or consignor of cargo has a bearing on whether the carriage is within the ... Convention. Beyond those choices, however, the parties to the contract have no option whether or not the ... Convention is to apply. It applies by force of law. The obligation on each State to apply the Convention's provisions to each such instance of carriage by air arises from the treaty relations between States parties to the Convention." *But see infra* note 269 (indicating that treaty relations may sometimes be completely absent and the case cannot proceed under any international agreement).

[112] For example, a United flight from Chicago to Seattle may enter Canadian airspace at various points in the journey. On cabotage generally, see *supra* Chapter 2, Part 2.5.

[113] Interlining occurs when different legs of a trip are flown by different airlines and the passenger and his or her luggage are transferred from the aircraft of the first carrier to that of the second. Although the two carriers cooperate on getting the passenger to his or her ultimate destination, they do not necessarily place their codes on the cooperating carrier's aircraft, nor does the passenger receive frequent flyer miles for the portion of the trip flown by the other carrier. This is distinct from code-sharing, where regardless of the aircraft or crew used to fly a given route, the flight will be listed and sold under the flight number of multiple partner airlines whose customers are often eligible to receive all of the miles, priority boarding, and other perks associated with flights operated by any of the airlines code-sharing on that flight. Article 36 of the Montreal Convention covers liability for interline operations. On code-sharing generally, see *supra* note 48.

[114] In 2011, approximately 80% of capacity flown across the Atlantic and Pacific oceans and between Asia and Europe was provided by the three major code-share alliances. *See* IATA ECONOMICS BRIEFING, THE ECONOMIC BENEFITS GENERATED BY ALLIANCES AND JOINT VENTURES (2012), http://www.iata.org/whatwedo/Documents/economics/Economics%20of%20JVs_Jan2012L.pdf.

[115] *See, e.g.,* Feeney v. America W. Airlines, 948 P.2d 110 (Colo. App. 1997) (determining that baggage lost by the carrier flying the Phoenix-Denver leg of a Mexico-Denver flight was covered under the Warsaw Convention because the flight was an undivided operation).

7.8.2. *Successive Carriage Through Interlining*

Nevertheless, where mere interlining, as opposed to code-sharing, is still employed, the legal consequences remain significant. Article 39 of the Montreal Convention excludes mere successive carriers, whose liability is governed by Article 36, from the provisions of Chapter V that extend the performing carrier's liability to contracting carriers in code-sharing arrangements.[116] Article 36 instead specifies that when there are successive carriers, such as in an interline relationship, a claim can only be brought "against the carrier which performed the carriage during which the accident or delay occurred" unless the first carrier expressly assumes liability for the entire trip.[117] The distinction between the liability of interlining carriers and code-sharing carriers was cogently described by the court in *Best v. BWIA West Indies Airways (BWIA)*.[118] Karen Best purchased a round-trip ticket from BWIA to fly from New York to Grenada. The trip included a stopover at Port of Spain, Trinidad, and the Port of Spain–Grenada leg was to be flown by a separate carrier, LIAT. Although the ticket Best purchased from BWIA covered both legs of the flight, there was no code-share arrangement between BWIA and LIAT, making this a simple interline arrangement. Best arrived in Port of Spain without incident, but suffered injuries after boarding the LIAT aircraft for the onward portion of the flight. While the plaintiff argued that BWIA should be liable under Article 39 of the Montreal Convention, the New York federal district court granted BWIA's motion for summary judgment, finding that the successive carrier relationship between BWIA and LIAT was not enough on its own to impose liability on BWIA.[119]

---

[116] *See* Montreal Convention, *supra* note 6, art. 39. Thus, in a code-share arrangement, the plaintiff has the option of bringing a claim against either the actual carrier or the contracting carrier. In one recent case, a French court ruled that a passenger who used accumulated Air France frequent flyer miles to purchase a one-way ticket on Kenya Airways (a partner with Air France in the SkyTeam alliance) to fly from Cameroon to China could bring a claim against Air France as the contracting carrier because of the code-sharing agreement between Air France and Kenya Airways. *See* Cour d'appel [CA] [regional court of appeal] Paris, 2001 (Kuate v. Air Fr., Kenya Airways and others).

[117] Montreal Convention, *supra* note 6, art. 36.

[118] 581 F. Supp. 2d 359 (E.D.N.Y. 2008).

[119] *See id.* at 364. "Although Article 39 provides a basis for liability for a ticket seller that did not exist under the Warsaw Convention, by its plain language this Article does not apply to the contract of carriage in this case since, as noted, it excludes from coverage successive carriage arrangements. The relationships typically covered by Article 39 include 'code share operations and operations where one carrier offers service using an aircraft and crew leased from another carrier.'" *Id.* For discussion of successive carriage under the Warsaw Convention, *see supra* Sections 7.4.4, 7.4.5.

7.8.3. Code-Sharing

Code-sharing, in fact, is more relevantly and reliably treated under the new Article 1(4) of the Montreal Convention, the first example of how the new treaty consolidates pieces of the Warsaw System. Consistent with the clarification of Warsaw by the Guadalajara Supplementary Convention, Article 1(4) now explicitly extends the treaty's coverage (via the ten Articles of a newly minted Chapter V[120]) to carriage performed by air transport "undertakings"[121] other than the contracting carrier, such as code-share partners.[122] The looped provisions of Article 1 and Chapter V serve a modern international aviation commercial environment dominated by large alliance groups such as SkyTeam, Star, and oneworld.[123] Without Montreal's extended coverage, an alliance partner might be hesitant to perform portions of international carriage for which it is not the "contracting carrier," that is, the airline that sells the ticket to the passenger.[124] The Convention also applies to carriage performed by State-run entities, although it generally excludes postal carriage.[125]

7.8.4. Cargo Carriage

Like Warsaw, the Montreal Convention also contains a number of provisions (in Articles 4 through 16) that relate to cargo carriage and which are distinct from the rules that apply to air passenger carriage. Unlike its predecessor, however, the Montreal Convention's cargo regime resists strict oversight of documentary procedures, leaving most of the technical details to be worked out between consignor and consignee.[126] Article 5, for instance, reflects a philosophy of ticket simplification (applicable also to the air passenger ticket,

---

[120] The text is not identical, but Guadalajara was cited as the precedent. *See* Letter of President William Jefferson Clinton Approving the Montreal Convention (Sept. 6, 2000), 106th Cong., 2d Sess., Treaty Doc. 106–45 (2000).

[121] As in the Warsaw Convention, this term is undefined.

[122] *See* Montreal Convention, *supra* note 6, Chapter V. For discussion of international airline alliances, see *supra* Chapter 4; on code-sharing generally, see *supra* Chapter 4, Sections 4.6.2, 4.6.3.

[123] *See In re* Air Crash at Taipei on Oct. 31, 2000, 219 F. Supp. 2d 1069 (C.D. Cal. 2002) (finding that the Star Alliance itself is not a carrier under Article 17 of the Warsaw Convention).

[124] *See* Montreal Convention, *supra* note 6, arts. 39, 40. Article 39 of the Convention distinguishes the "contracting carrier" from the "actual carrier" that performs the whole or part of the carriage "by virtue of authority from the contracting carrier."

[125] *See* Montreal Convention, *supra* note 6, art. 2.

[126] *See generally id.* art. 5. Some of the old Warsaw rules are retained, however. For example, Article 10 of Montreal retains the Warsaw mandate that the cargo shipper is responsible for the accuracy of the details related to the shipment that appear on the air waybill. Articles 12–14, which enumerate the rights of the consignor and the consignee vis-à-vis the air carrier, have also been retained from Warsaw. According to Article 14, the consignor and consignee can both

as considered below) that requires the general document of carriage, the "air waybill," to contain only one cargo-specific detail, the weight of the consignment.[127] The air waybill must also indicate the places of departure and destination and at least one foreign stopping-place if the places of departure and destination are within the same State.[128] New ground is struck for cargo in Article 18, which appears in the Montreal Convention's chapter on liability. Under that provision, a carrier can escape liability for damage to or loss of cargo if it can prove one or more of the following causal events: "(a) inherent defect, quality or vice . . .; (b) defective packaging of that cargo performed by a person other than the carrier . . .; (c) an act of war or armed conflict; and (d) an act of public authority carried out in connection with the entry, exit or transit of the cargo."[129] Only the first event, "inherent defect, quality or vice," was a traditional (common law) liability defense,[130] but Article 18 offers further sturdy excuses permitting the cargo carrier to escape liability – and might be viewed as sitting uneasily alongside the apparent consumer-friendly ethos of the new Convention. One justification for giving carriers new opportunities to avoid cargo-related liability is the fact that shippers, particularly shippers of high-volume, high-value air freight, are likely to have enough commercial sophistication to know the risks associated with using air transport to move their products.[131] Shifting too much of the liability burden to the air carriers may also force them to become self-insurers of cargo damage risks and to spike their tariffs accordingly. Also, a strict liability cargo regime, akin to the rules that now govern liability to passengers, potentially opens the door for shippers to be less careful in packing. Unlike the extreme dependency that affects

enforce all rights granted to them by Articles 12 and 13 (on the disposition and delivery of cargo), each in their own name and whether they are acting in their own interests or in the interests of another person, provided that they carry out their contractual obligations. Finally, Article 15 duplicates the same-numbered provision in Warsaw in stating that Articles 12–14 do not affect the relations of consignor and consignee with each other or the relations of third parties whose rights are derived from the consignor or consignee. *See id.* arts. 12–15.

[127] The weight of the cargo is essential because weight is the basis for the Convention's liability cap for damaged cargo.

[128] *See supra* note 109 for an explanation of the importance of indicating the foreign stopping-place if the Convention is to apply.

[129] Montreal Convention, *supra* note 6, art. 18(2).

[130] *But see* Missouri Pac. R.R. v. Elmore & Stahl, 377 U.S. 134, 137 (1964) (listing as the common law defenses for carriers, "(a) the act of God; (b) [the act of a] public enemy; (c) the act of the shipper himself; (d) [the act of a] public authority; or (e) the inherent vice or nature of the goods").

[131] While to some extent, therefore, the duty of insurance remains with the shipper, Article 18 of the Montreal Convention still imposes liability on the carrier for destruction, loss, or damage that occurs "during the carriage by air." Montreal Convention, *supra* note 6, art. 18(1). The carrier will be responsible for damage in transit caused by improper loading, storage, air turbulence, and so on. *See id.*

passengers, cargo shippers can themselves take better precautions to assure the intact arrival of their consignments.[132]

7.8.5. *Air Passenger Ticketing*

Finally, another marker of Montreal's break with the old Warsaw System appears in the provisions of Article 3 of the Montreal Convention relating to air passenger ticketing. Article 3(1) requires "an individual or collective document of carriage," that is, a ticket that indicates the places of departure and destination and must also include one stopping-place in a foreign State if the places of departure and destination are within the same State.[133] Thus, the arcane Warsaw rules relating to the nature and content of a physical ticket are discarded in favor of much simpler provisions, and indeed Article 3(2) plainly contemplates eventual full conversion to e-ticketing.[134] Also, while an airline is still required to provide passengers with written notice that the Montreal Convention's liability rules apply for international carriage,[135] failure to provide such notice no longer automatically vitiates the applicability of the Convention.[136] Having scrapped Warsaw's cumbersome requirements for a "luggage ticket,"[137] however, Montreal does require that an air carrier supply a separate "baggage identification tag" for each piece of checked baggage.[138] Although the new Montreal rule is both simpler (there are no required formalities) and slightly more complex (the requirement for multiple tags), the whole matter has become trivial. In an age when few air passengers ever

---

[132] It is interesting to note that under the revised cargo liability regime introduced in Montreal Protocol No. 4, *supra* note 57, the defenses were available only if the damage to cargo resulted "*solely* from one or more" of the listed causes [emphasis added]. *Id.* art. IV. By dropping the word "solely," the Montreal Convention allows a carrier to escape liability even if it can prove only that one or more of the enumerated events led *partly* to the damage or loss. Thus, in that sense, the Convention furnishes an even thicker set of protections for air cargo carriers.

[133] Montreal Convention, *supra* note 6, art. 3(1)(a), (b). *See supra* note 109 for an explanation of the importance of indicating the foreign stopping-place if the Convention is to apply.

[134] "Any other means which preserves [the information about departure and destination] may be substituted for the delivery of [the ticket]." Montreal Convention, *supra* note 6, art. 3(2). It can be seen that the text of Article 3(2) is capacious enough to absorb even futuristic technologies that would allow the information to be "mind-melded" into passengers' brains. Note that Article 4(2) of the Convention includes an almost identical provision for air cargo.

[135] *See* Montreal Convention, *supra* note 6, art. 3(4).

[136] *See id.* art. 3(5). The contrasting Warsaw Convention provision appeared in Article 3(2) of that instrument. *See* Warsaw Convention, *supra* note 4, art. 3(2). On the other hand, of course, the later Convention no longer has any caps on liability for passenger injury or death.

[137] Warsaw Convention, *supra* note 4, art. 4. The luggage ticket even required a declaration of value to comply with the luggage liability cap (and the available cap-breaking declaration of higher value) in Article 22 of the Warsaw Convention. *See supra* Section 7.17.7.

[138] Montreal Convention, *supra* note 6, art. 3(3).

receive a physical ticket, multiple computerized baggage tags are now the only reliable means of tracking your belongings on their journey from Des Moines to Frankfurt after you have already arrived safely at your final destination in Sydney.

7.9. THE MONTREAL CONVENTION (3): ACTIVATING THE LIABILITY REGIME (ACCIDENTS, DEATH, INJURY)

7.9.1. An "Accident" Causing Death or Injury

Unlimited liability is the cornerstone principle of the Montreal Convention, and we will return to that topic later in the chapter. But the conditions that determine air carrier liability for death or bodily injury of a passenger are the same as those articulated in the Warsaw Convention. Under Article 17(1) of Montreal, which appears in Chapter III on liability of the carrier, an exclusive cause of action arises under the Convention[139] if the "accident" that caused the death or injury takes place "on board the aircraft" or "in the course of any of the operations of embarking or disembarking."[140] Although seemingly straightforward, this is actually a polyvalent sentence that requires some unpacking.[141] Moreover, it is common ground among domestic court systems

[139] *See* El Al Isr. Airlines, Ltd. v. Tseng, 525 U.S. 155, 161 (1999) ("We therefore hold that recovery for a personal injury suffered 'on board [an] aircraft or in the course of any of the operations of embarking or disembarking,' art. 17, 49 Stat. 3018, if not allowed under the Convention, is not available at all"). *See infra* Section 7.10.10.

[140] Montreal Convention, *supra* note 6, art. 17(1). Article 17(2) of the Montreal Convention lays down related terms for carrier liability for lost or damaged checked baggage – although the embarkation/disembarkation dyad is replaced by "any period within which the checked baggage was in the charge of the carrier." Montreal Convention, *supra* note 6, art. 17(2). The airline can, however, absolve itself of liability if the loss or damage was due to an inherent defect, quality, or vice of the baggage. *See id.* For unchecked baggage, the carrier is liable if the damage resulted from "its fault or the fault of its servants or agents." *Id.* A carrier has 21 days to locate lost baggage before an enforceable claim arises. *See* Montreal Convention, *supra* note 6, art. 17(3). Carrier liability for baggage is capped at 1000 SDRs per passenger. *See id.* art. 22(2).

[141] Article 35 of the Montreal Convention (which is virtually the same as Article 29 of Warsaw) prescribes a two-year statute of limitations within which plaintiffs must commence any action for damages (whether related to passenger or cargo transportation) under the Convention. *See* Montreal Convention, *supra* note 6, art. 35; *see* Kahn v. Trans World Airlines, Inc., 82 A.D.2d 696, 709 (N.Y. App. Div. 1981). There remain unsettled questions regarding the application of the statute of limitations to actions for indemnification and contribution. *See* Motorola, Inc. v. MSAS Cargo Int'l, Inc., 42 F. Supp. 2d 952, 956 (N.D. Cal. 1998) (holding that the two-year statute of limitations applies to indemnification suits brought by one carrier against another); *but see* Chubb Ins. Co. of Eur. S.A. v. Menlo Worldwide Forwarding Inc., 634 F.3d 1023 (9th Cir. 2011); Connaught Laboratories Ltd. v. Air Canada (1978), 23 O.R. 2d 176 (Can. Ont. Sup. Ct. J.) (holding that the Warsaw and Montreal Conventions, and thus the statute of limitations, were only intended to apply to passenger and not carrier claims).

that the basic concepts used in the liability Conventions are "autonomous concepts," the meaning of which should be determined by examining the words of the Convention itself rather than by scrutinizing what they signify under individual national legal systems.[142]

7.9.2. *A Subjective Approach to Defining "Accident"*

The meaning of the term "accident" in Article 17 of the Warsaw and Montreal Conventions is ambiguous and the scope of the term has been the subject of numerous judicial interpretations.[143] The lay observer might well expect that an event labeled an "accident" must be literally and entirely outside the control of any of the parties involved, but that would leave only acts of God to be covered by the Convention. Another approach, which seems to have won favor with the U.S. Supreme Court in its famous Warsaw Convention decision in *Air France v. Saks*,[144] is to accept *a priori* that a wide spectrum of unexpected events may occur in air transport (as in any common carriage), but to use the reaction of the individual passenger as the benchmark for whether the term "accident" should apply to any specific event. Thus, the Supreme Court ruled in *Saks* that a Warsaw Convention "accident" occurs only where the injury suffered is produced by "an unexpected or unusual event or happening that is external to the passenger."[145] That definition, in turn, excludes any instance where an injury "indisputably" results from a passenger's "own internal reaction to the usual, normal and expected operation of the aircraft."[146] One cannot pretend that *Saks* is easy to apply. U.S. courts have struggled with numerous fact situations to which they have had to apply the Supreme Court's quasi-psychological analysis of external/internal passenger responses. Generally speaking, where an alleged accident flows from a passenger's consumption of alcoholic beverages on the flight, the courts have labeled such occurrences as arising from an internal response to the intoxication.[147] On the other hand, where a passenger's intoxication led to the harm of another passenger and the

---

[142] *King v. Bristow Helicopters, supra* note 19, at ¶ 16.

[143] As previously noted, Warsaw Convention precedent is regularly used to interpret the same or similar provisions in the Montreal Convention. *See, e.g.,* Baah v. Virgin Atl. Airways Ltd., 473 F. Supp. 2d 591, 596 (S.D.N.Y. 2007).

[144] 470 U.S. 392 (1985).

[145] *Id.* at 405.

[146] *Id.* at 406.

[147] *See* Padilla v. Olympic Airways, 765 F. Supp. 835 (S.D.N.Y. 1991) (passenger falling over from intoxication is not an accident). *But see* Scala v. Am. Airlines, 249 F. Supp. 2d 176, 179–81 (D. Conn. 2003) (flight attendant serving alcoholic beverage to passenger who ordered non-alcoholic beverage is an accident and passenger can recover for damage resulting from aggravation of existing heart condition).

airline personnel failed to provide assistance to that passenger, an "accident" within the scope of Warsaw occurred.[148] But, where an airline's personnel failed to provide medical assistance to a passenger, including failing to have the proper medical equipment on board, that set of circumstances was held not to be an "accident."[149]

7.9.3. *The "Characteristic of Air Travel" Approach to Defining "Accident"*

Another, less subjective interpretive approach used by U.S. courts has been to find that an Article 17 "accident" must arise from a risk "derived from" or "characteristic of" air travel.[150] Thus, an assault on another passenger would not be covered if the airline (through its employees) is not part of the causation.[151] But using the metric of what is "characteristic" of air travel has produced some startling reasoning, driven no doubt by a desire to allow passenger recovery in upsetting circumstances. In *Wallace v. Korean Air*,[152] plaintiff Brandi Wallace fell asleep aboard a nonstop flight from Seoul, South Korea, to Los Angeles, California, seated in economy class next to two men she did not know. She awoke to find one of the men sexually assaulting her. The court held this to be an accident under the characteristic risk of air travel standard, stretching the notion to encompass situations such as the plaintiff's where "the characteristics of air travel increased [the plaintiff's] vulnerability to [her fellow passenger's] assault."[153] The court cited the confined space in economy seating, the plaintiff's proximity to strangers, the dimmed lighting to allow passengers to sleep, and especially the inattentiveness of the flight attendants, as characteristics contributing to the assault.[154] Similarly, recent cases dealing with failure to render adequate medical assistance have added what might be considered unexpected burdens to the duties of air carriers and their employees. For

---

[148] Langadinos v. Am. Airlines, Inc., 199 F.3d 68, 71 (1st Cir. 2000).

[149] *See* Hipolito v. Nw. Airlines, Inc., 2001 WL 861984 (4th Cir. Jul. 31, 2001). *But see* Watts v. Am. Airlines, Inc., No. 1:07-cv-0434, 2007 WL 3019344 (S.D. Ind. Oct. 10, 2007) (airline's failure to recognize and respond to passenger's heart attack can count as accident).

[150] *See* Stone v. Cont'l Airlines, Inc., 905 F. Supp. 823, 827 (D. Haw. 1995) ("The fundamental premise in authorizing carrier liability under the Warsaw Convention 'is to include such risks that are characteristic of air travel'") (citing Price v. British Airways, No. 91 Civ. 4947, 1992 WL 170679, at *3 (S.D.N.Y. Jul. 7, 1992)). The Court in *Stone* dismissed plaintiff's claim, arising out of an assault by a fellow passenger, as "not an accident derived from air travel." *Id.*

[151] *See id.*; *see also Price, supra* note 150, (holding that a fistfight between passengers was not an accident); *Langadinos, supra* note 148 (airline only liable for assault by intoxicated passenger if crew's over-serving of passenger caused tort).

[152] 214 F.3d 293 (2nd Cir. 2000).

[153] *Id.* at 299.

[154] *Id.*

instance, in *Olympic Airways v. Husain*,[155] a passenger with an asthmatic condition was seated too close to the smoking section. The flight attendant refused to move the passenger, despite repeated requests from the passenger's wife, and the passenger ultimately died from an asthma attack. The U.S. Supreme Court held that the flight attendant's failure to act could constitute an "accident" under the Warsaw Convention.[156] A number of other cases resulted in liability for carriers where the response to an onboard medical emergency was deemed inadequate or insufficient under industry standards to the point of constituting an "accident."[157]

7.9.4. DVT Cases

There has been a spate of recent cases involving claims for damages related to deep vein thrombosis (DVT), an ailment some passengers develop on long international flights. In this series of cases, the quasi-psychological component of events external to the passenger is missing. Either the passenger has a medical predisposition, or he or she does not. Courts have primarily concluded that claims based on the development of DVT do not fall under the definition of an Article 17 accident, because the development of DVT is internal to the passenger and not caused by an unusual or unexpected event or happening.[158] A more interesting question was posed by recent litigated claims arguing that an airline's failure to warn passengers about the risk of DVT rises to the level of an external, causal action by the carrier that would constitute an Article 17 accident. Thus far, courts remain unpersuaded.[159]

7.9.5. How Does the Montreal Convention Affect the Definition of "Accident"?

It is unclear what, if any, changes ought to be made to the *Saks* exposition of "accident" now that the Montreal Convention is in force.[160] If the treaty is read

---

[155] 540 U.S. 644 (2004).

[156] *See id.* at 645, 647–48.

[157] *See, e.g.,* Yahya v. Yemenia-Yemen Airways, No. 08–14789, 2009 WL 3424192 (E.D. Mich. Oct. 20, 2009); Watts v. Am. Airlines, Inc., *supra* note 149; Fulop v. Malev Hungarian Airlines, 175 F. Supp. 2d 651 (S.D.N.Y. 2001).

[158] *See, e.g.,* Rodriguez v. Ansett Austl. Ltd., 383 F.3d 914, 917 (9th Cir. 2004); Blansett v. Cont'l Airlines, Inc., 379 F.3d 177, 180 (5th Cir. 2004); Povey v. Qantas Airways Ltd., [2005] 223 C.L.R. 189 (Australia); Deep Vein Thrombosis and Air Travel Group Litigation, [2005] UKHL 72, [2005] 1 A.C. 495 (U.K.).

[159] *See* Twardowski v. Am. Airlines, Inc., 535 F.3d 952 (9th Cir. 2008).

[160] *Saks* was cited with approval in the U.K. Court of Appeal in Chaudhari v. British Airways, [1997] EWCA Civ. 1413.

teleologically in light of its Preamble's emphasis on protecting passengers, then a broad construction of the term is indicated. An overly broad reading, however, could overburden the airlines and make them responsible for the internal reactions of extraordinarily sensitive passengers.[161] Air travel, after all, is no longer novel. Air travelers do or ought to realize that even behemoths like the A380 cannot always furnish a smooth ride; mental duress or an adverse physiological reaction may occur in response to events that are "extraordinary" in the sense that they deviate from any carrier's desire to provide a pleasant cabin experience but are not so far beyond the norm as to be wholly unexpected. The *Saks* judgment shifts some responsibility to the passenger for his or her reaction to the events of flight.

7.9.6. *Distinction Between "Bodily" and "Psychic" Injury*

Can a passenger who is frightened by air turbulence recover for the psychological trauma he or she felt and may even continue to feel after the flight?[162] At this point in the history of Warsaw/Montreal jurisprudence, the answer appears to be "no." Even though an "accident" is found to occur under Article 17 of the Montreal Convention, liability will not attach unless that accident has caused "death or bodily injury."[163] This formulation carries over from the Warsaw Convention, and once again Warsaw precedent is arguably applicable. Few phrases in either Convention have generated as much interpretive

---

[161] Such a possibility raises the specter of the "eggshell skull" common law tort rule, exemplified by Vosburg v. Putney, 80 Wis. 523, 50 N.W. 403 (Wis. 1891). Perhaps the most alarming recent example of an unexpected event that disrupted the passenger experience occurred in March 2012, when a JetBlue pilot went temporarily insane and was locked out of the cockpit by his copilot. The pilot could be observed by the passengers pounding on the cockpit door and yelling about the 9/11 attacks, and was ultimately subdued by some of the passengers while the copilot made an emergency landing. *See* Corrie MacLaggan, *U.S. Charges JetBlue Pilot for Midair Meltdown*, REUTERS, Mar. 29, 2012, http://www.reuters.com/article/2012/03/29/us-usa-crime-jetblue-pilot-idUSBRE82R1GF20120329. JetBlue settled a lawsuit brought by some of the passengers. *See* Passengers, JetBlue Settle Suit Over Pilot Rampage, Associated Press, Jun. 13, 2013, http://www.usatoday.com/story/todayinthesky/2013/06/13/passengers-jetblue-settle-suit-over-pilot-rampage/2418437/. Note that the case serves only as a hypothetical when discussing the Montreal Convention, because the incident occurred on a domestic flight.

[162] Obviously allowing recovery for psychic reactions to the many untoward events of air travel could open an "avalanche" of intangible and expensive claims against carriers both large and small. *King v. Bristow Helicopters*, *supra* note 19, at ¶ 17. An IATA position paper at the Montreal Conference in 1999 listed 17 possible such events: in addition to turbulence, the paper mentioned missed approaches, near misses, lightning strikes, accidental emergency announcements, aircraft decompression, emergency landings, aborted takeoffs, diversions to alternative airports, delayed gate departures due to announced mechanical problems with aircraft or engine, and unruly passenger behavior. *Cited id.*

[163] Montreal Convention, *supra* note 6, art. 17(1).

dissonance among national courts as "bodily injury." With respect to "injury," U.S. judges made careful efforts to develop a coherent jurisprudence under the Warsaw System that opened up the term to include both physical *and* some expressions of psychic injury (the latter is known alternatively as "mental distress"[164]). The approach adopted in 1974 by the New York Court of Appeals in *Rosman v. Trans World Airlines*[165] was to find TWA liable for "plaintiff's palpable, objective bodily injuries, including those caused by the psychic trauma of [a] hijacking, and for the damages flowing from those bodily injuries, but not for the trauma as such or for the nonbodily or behavioral manifestations of that trauma."[166] In other words, if the psychic harm *caused* bodily injury, such as (in the plaintiff's case) mental anguish giving rise to backaches, swollen feet, and leg and back discoloration, damages were recoverable under the Warsaw Convention.[167] Some courts went further. In 1975, in *Husserl v. Swiss Air Transp. Co.*,[168] the Southern District of New York found damages for "severe mental pain and anguish," including "various mental and psycho-somatic injuries, at least some of which involve[d] demonstrable, physiological manifestations," to be recoverable.[169] The *Husserl* court justified its strong reading by observing that "[t]o effect the treaty's avowed purpose [of covering air carrier liability], the types of injuries enumerated should be construed expansively to encompass as many types of injuries as are colorably within the ambit of the enumerated types."[170]

7.9.7. *Approach of Non-U.S. Courts to Psychic Injury*

Some courts in other jurisdictions accepted psychic harm without the tangled formulas resorted to in the United States. The Israeli Supreme Court, in the

---

[164] *See, e.g.*, Ruwantissa I.R. Abeyratne, *Mental Distress in Aviation Claims – Emergent Trends*, 65 J. Air L. & Com. 225 (2000).

[165] 314 N.E.2d 848 (N.Y. 1974). The case arose out of the September 1970 hijacking of a TWA flight from Tel Aviv to New York.

[166] *Id.* at 857. The definition of "accident" was not at issue in *Rosman*. Hijacking is clearly an accident under Article 17, and the airline defendant did not contest that point.

[167] *Id.* at 856–57 (finding also that the plaintiff's children could be compensated for developing boils and substantial weight loss as a result of the trauma of the hijacking).

[168] 388 F. Supp. 1238 (S.D.N.Y. 1975).

[169] *Husserl* involved a Zurich–New York flight that was hijacked to a desert area near Amman, Jordan. *See id.* at 1242–43. *See also generally* Borham v. Pan Am. World Airways, Inc., No. 85 Civ. 6922, 1986 WL 2974 (S.D.N.Y. Mar. 5, 1986) (finding that passenger's cause of action for emotional trauma without physical injury, caused by an explosion on a Pan Am flight from Hong Kong to Honolulu, was within the scope of Article 17).

[170] *Husserl*, 388 F. Supp. 1238, 1250.

1984 case of *Air France v. Teichner*,[171] read Article 17 of the Warsaw Convention broadly enough to allow recovery for purely psychic injuries unaccompanied by bodily injury or physical manifestation. Interestingly, the high court, which enjoys a reputation as a liberal reformist tribunal, was less focused on the text of Article 17 than on the evolution of the general law of liability to include recovery for psychic injury. In the court's view, "desirable jurisprudential policy" demanded that Warsaw's heads of recovery should be enlarged accordingly.[172]

7.9.8. *U.S. Supreme Court's Decisions in* Floyd *and* Tseng

Although welcomed by plaintiffs' attorneys, it is questionable whether the reasoning in *Husserl* – or, for that matter, in *Teichner* – was companionable with Warsaw's aim to put boundaries around airline liability.[173] Certainly, the U.S. Supreme Court in *Eastern Airlines v. Floyd*[174] thought not, although it still managed to leave the matter somewhat ambiguous. In *Floyd*, the plaintiff sued Eastern Airlines for intentional infliction of emotional distress as a result of engine failure and subsequent preparations for ditching the airplane.[175] The Court, after inquiry into the meaning (in French law and at the Warsaw negotiating conference) of the term *lésion corporelle* ("bodily injury") in the authentic French text of Article 17, held that "an air carrier cannot be held liable [under the Warsaw Convention] when an accident has not caused a passenger to suffer death, physical injury, or physical manifestation of injury."[176] But a unanimous Court also disclaimed, in *dictum*, any view "as to whether passengers can recover for mental injuries that are accompanied by

---

[171] Cie Air Fr. v. Teichner, 39 Revue Francaise de Droit Aérien 232, 242, 23 Eur.Tr.L. 87, 101 (Isr. 1984). *Teichner* arose from the 1976 hijacking of an Air France flight to Entebbe, Uganda. Passengers sought compensation for psychic injuries caused by that ordeal.

[172] *Id.* at 243, 23 Eur.Tr.L., at 102. The Court took a similar view in another of the cases referred to as the "Entebbe" cases, Daddon v. Air Fr., 1 S & B Av. R. VII/141 (Isr. 1984), relying on changes in the aviation industry since 1929 and the current domestic Israeli view of mental and psychological injury: *but see supra* text accompanying note 142 (indicating general view that Convention concepts should be interpreted as "autonomous").

[173] The *Teichner* court's interpretation, for instance, may have severely overstretched the treaty, which after all was intended to shield the airline industry from unlimited liability and was never designed with the general "public interest" in mind. *See* Eastern Airlines, Inc. v. Floyd, 499 U.S. 530, 546 (1991) ("In 1929 the parties were more concerned with protecting air carriers than fostering a new industry than providing full recovery to injured passengers").

[174] 499 U.S. 530 (1991).

[175] The pilot had informed the passengers after successive engine failures and altitude loss that the plane would be ditched in the Atlantic Ocean. The plane landed safely after an engine restart. *See id.* at 533. Eastern Airlines conceded that the events constituted an "accident" under Article 17 of the Warsaw Convention. *Id.*

[176] *Id.* at 552. Justice Thurgood Marshall appeared to express sympathy for the Israeli Supreme Court's policy-based reasoning that allowed recovery in *Teichner*, *see supra* note 171.

physical injuries."[177] Eight years later, in *El Al Israel Airlines v. Tseng*,[178] the Supreme Court offered up a "restatement" (in a footnote, and again in *dictum*) of *Floyd* when it declared that "[t]he [Warsaw] Convention provides for compensation under Article 17 *only* when the passenger suffers 'death, physical injury, or physical manifestation of injury.'"[179] Thus, the *Tseng* footnote tightens *Floyd* by inserting "only" before the *Floyd* list of recoverable events and by eliminating any reference to mental injuries accompanied by physical injuries.[180] Some commentators nevertheless view *Floyd* as accepting a sole instance of recovery for psychic harm, namely, when that harm results in physical injury.[181] The two *dicta* remain facially inconsistent and one cannot assume that *Tseng* intended to overrule or modify the *Floyd* holding.[182] In the

> Nevertheless, Marshall held that, because the purpose of Warsaw was uniformly to limit liability for the international airline industry, and in the absence of "convincing evidence" that the signatories intended recovery for psychic injury, Article 17 should be construed narrowly. *Id.* at 551.

[177] *Id.* at 552. That issue was not presented in *Floyd*, because the plaintiff passengers did not allege physical injury or physical manifestation of injury. *Id.*

[178] 525 U.S. 155 (1999).

[179] *Id.* at 166 n.9 (emphasis added). *Floyd* had left such confusion in its wake that lower courts issued a number of inconsistent opinions concerning psychic injury, holding in some instances that a plaintiff may recover for such harms when accompanied by physical injuries, and in others insisting that psychic injury must be linked inextricably to the physical harms suffered. For a good collection of disparate case law on this point, see John F. Easton, Jennifer Trock, & Kent Radford, *Post-Traumatic "Lésion Corporelle": A Continuum of Bodily Injury Under the Warsaw Convention*, 68 J. Air L. & Com. 665, 673–90 (2003). It seems, however, that psychic injury alone is not recoverable under the Warsaw Convention. The only known case to allow compensation for stand-alone psychic injury is the 1984 Israeli Supreme Court decision in *Daddon v. Air Fr.*, *supra* note 172.

[180] In fact, later in the opinion the Court reminded the plaintiff, who had sued El Al for assault and false imprisonment arising out of a rigorous security search, that she had not sustained "bodily injury" under Article 17 of Warsaw and "could not gain compensation . . . for her solely psychic or psychosomatic injuries." 525 U.S. at 172.

[181] *See, e.g.*, Dr. Christian Andrews & Dr. Vernon Nase, *Psychiatric Injury in Aviation Accidents Under the Warsaw and Montreal Conventions: The Interface Between Medicine and Law*, 76 J. Air L. & Com. 3, 33 (2011).

[182] Arguably, the *Tseng* footnote was an inartful summary of the holding in *Floyd* and was not intended to be a new rule to guide the lower courts. In *Weaver v. Delta Airlines*, 56 F. Supp. 2d 1190 (1999), a lower U.S. court seemed to "outflank" *Floyd* by accepting an argument that psychiatric injury or illness can in some circumstances be shown to involve physical changes to the brain and therefore can constitute a recoverable head of damages as "bodily injury" under Article 17 of the Warsaw Convention. . The use of the word "outflank" comes from the opinion of Lord MacKay in the U.K. House of Lords decision in *King v. Bristow Helicopters*, *supra* note 19, at ¶ 19. In *King*, while all five judges were satisfied that *Floyd* represents the correct analysis, three members of the panel also accepted the possibility, not present in the cases before them, that demonstrable brain damage flowing (as in *Weaver*) from a mental or psychic injury might also be compensable. Lord Nicholls held that "[i]njury to a passenger's brain is an injury to a passenger's body just as much as injury to any other part of his body." *Id.* at ¶ 4.

absence of a clear ruling, the point remains in dispute. A number of scholarly articles look hopefully to a future U.S. Supreme Court returning to Article 17, but this time under the Montreal Convention, and finally resolving the uncertainty.[183]

7.9.9. *Issue of Psychic Injury Under the Montreal Convention*

All of the foregoing jurisprudence, selected primarily from U.S. case law, evolved under the Warsaw System. How relevant is this corpus of precedent to cases arising under the Montreal Convention? Early rulings under Montreal suggest that *Floyd*-as-narrowed-by-*Tseng* remains the applied standard.[184] But if Montreal is tilted toward passenger welfare, is a broader reading of "injury" now warranted? During the drafting sessions for the Montreal Convention, delegates specifically discussed extending liability to "mental injury."[185] A consensus never formed, however, in part because some delegates appeared to believe that "injury" is a sufficiently pliable term to include both bodily and mental harms.[186] France, for instance, confirmed at the drafting conference that the term *lésion corporelle* ("bodily injury"), which appears in the official French text of the Warsaw Convention, is a legal term of art to which French courts had attached both physical and mental injury.[187] Therefore, the expression "bodily injury" in the Montreal Convention must be freighted with the

Although the point might appear reasonable, Lord Steyn did not think that the *Weaver* opinion contained any such limiting principle. He criticized his fellow judges for embracing a "too controversial" position that would sweep "mental injury and illnesses" into the Convention system and would escalate claims beyond what the drafters intended. *Id.* at ¶ 27.

[183] *See, e.g.*, Andrews & Nase, *supra* note 181, at 38, 73–75.

[184] *See, e.g.*, Schaefer-Condulmari v. U.S. Airways Group, LLC, No. 09–1146, 2012 WL 2920375 (E.D. Pa. Jul. 18, 2012) (passenger can recover for post-traumatic stress disorder if caused by physical injuries from accident).

[185] *See* Ehrlich v. Am. Airlines, Inc., 360 F.3d 366, 390–400 (2003) (discussing drafting history of "bodily injury" under the Montreal Convention). The United States delegation pushed the inclusion of psychic injury at the drafting conference. *See id.* at 399–400. *See also King v. Bristow Helicopters, supra* note 19, at ¶ 31, indicating that the U.K. Government reported insufficient support at the Montreal drafting conference for a "separate head of claim for mental injury."

[186] *See Ehrlich, supra* note 185, at 390–400. One has to treat the failure of the Montreal Convention to add mental harm recovery as at least surprising. The delegates were aware that liability law had been gradually evolving toward recognition of psychic damage unaccompanied by physical harm not only in the United States but also in other jurisdictions, including France, Germany, and Israel. *See id.*

[187] *See* McKay Cunningham, *The Montreal Convention: Can Passengers Finally Recover for Mental Injuries?*, 41 Vand. J. Transnat'l L. 1043, 1073 (2008) (citing 1 International Civil Aviation Organization, International Conference on Air Law (Convention for the Unification of Certain Rules for International Carriage by Air), Montreal (May 10–28, 1999), Minutes, Doc. 9775-DC/2, at 68 (2001)).

same meaning. It remains unclear, however, whether the drafting history of the Montreal Convention and the interpretive *acquis* of civil law jurisprudence will (or should) push courts in all contracting States to shape an expansive understanding of "bodily injury." As others have noted, even though Article 17 of Montreal repeats its predecessor virtually verbatim, that does not mean that the newer language was also intended to ratify the court-crafted jurisprudence of the old Article 17.[188] As a purely textual matter, after all, courts in the Montreal era might be expected to acknowledge that the drafters of the Montreal Convention *rejected* readings of Article 17 that included mental harm.[189]

7.9.10. *Embarking and Disembarking*

Warsaw Convention cases again supply useful precedent in defining the final element of Article 17, namely, that the "bodily injury" caused by the "accident" must occur "on board the aircraft or in the course of any of the operations of embarking or disembarking."[190] The determination of whether a passenger is "on board" an aircraft has proven unproblematic. But courts in different jurisdictions have felt a need to give greater precision to the embarkation/ disembarkation requirement. All of their various approaches are predicated on where the passenger was physically located when the injury took place, on the activity in which the passenger was engaged, but also on whose control or direction the passenger was under at the time of the accident.[191] Again, the

---

[188] *See* Cunningham, *supra* note 187, at 1076–81.

[189] On the other hand, the Supreme Court's reasoning in *Floyd* was centered on protection of the fledgling airline industry, a theory that has lost purchase under the "individual restitution" philosophy of Montreal. But no lower U.S. court has yet rejected the old jurisprudence in favor of a "fresh start" under Montreal. Also, it will be recalled that Montreal is not by its terms a "reset" of Warsaw, but was intended to "modernize and consolidate" that Convention and its related instruments. *See* Montreal Convention, *supra* note 6, pmbl; *see also supra* Section 7.1.4.

[190] Montreal Convention, *supra* note 6, art. 17(1).

[191] *See* Day v. Trans World Airlines, Inc., 528 F.2d 31, 33–34 (1975). The court in *Day* first articulated the "tripartite test" by which embarking or disembarking became based on location, activity, and control. That test has been updated by recent courts, a more current formulation being: "(1) the activity of the passenger at the time of the accident; (2) the restrictions, if any, on the passenger's movement; (3) the imminence of actual boarding; and (4) the physical proximity of the passenger to the gate." Ramos v. Am. Airlines, Inc., No. 3:11cv207, 2011 WL 5075674 (W.D.N.C. Oct. 25, 2011). The *Day* test has been subject to some criticism by courts and commentators supporting a narrower interpretation of "embarking," but that criticism has primarily been confined to *dicta* in cases where courts have ruled that plaintiffs would not recover even under the *Day* test. *See* Maugnie v. Compagnie Nationale Air Fr., 549 F.2d 1256, 1262 (9th Cir. 1977) (Wallace, J., concurring); Sweis v. Trans World Airlines, Inc., 681 F. Supp. 501, 504 (N.D. Ill. 1988).

common law rule on "common carriers" requires a high standard of care on the part of a carrier when passengers are entering into or alighting from a vehicle operated by the carrier.[192] Aligned with Article 17, the common law rule creates an expectation that a passenger waiting in line during the boarding period, but who has not yet boarded the aircraft, will be covered by the Montreal Convention. On the other hand, a passenger who is still *en route* to the terminal, or who wanders away from the boarding area to fetch a soft drink and succumbs to an injury while doing so, is probably beyond the scope of the Convention.[193] Disembarkation is measured using similar benchmarks: it appears that Montreal will cease to apply once the passenger has moved beyond the gate and is proceeding toward the airport terminal.[194] Regardless of what the articulated test may be in a given case, the courts have generally taken a flexible view of the changing circumstances of international air travel. Control is probably the most critical component in each analysis; combined with the passenger's degree of proximity to the aircraft (both physical and temporal), the control test usually yields a sensible outcome. Control is also at the core of the "zone of aviation risk" test that has evolved in some civil law jurisdictions.[195]

7.10. THE MONTREAL CONVENTION (4): THE NEW LIABILITY REGIME

7.10.1. *A Mandatory System of Liability*

The mandatory and exclusive character of the Montreal system of liability is established in Article 49 of the Montreal Convention. That provision vitiates any clause in a contract for international air carriage that purports to change

---

[192] *See generally* Woodard v. Saginaw City Lines, Inc., 112 N.W.2d 512 (Mich. 1961).

[193] These are not actual examples from case law, but rather hypotheticals that almost certainly would not satisfy the *Day* court's three-part test doctrine (*see supra* note 191) as it has developed. However, for a more expansive view of "embarking," see Matveychuk v. Deutsche Lufthansa AG, No. 08-CV-3108, 2010 WL 3540921 (E.D.N.Y. Sept. 7, 2010) (passenger who was denied boarding due to tardiness and suffered injury in restroom on way to rebooking desk found to be in process of embarking).

[194] *See generally* MacDonald v. Air Can., 439 F.2d 1402 (1st Cir. 1971); Martinez Hernandez v. Air Fr., 545 F.2d 279 (1st Cir. 1976). Courts have applied the *Day* test (*see supra* note 191) to disembarking and have generally come to the conclusion that passengers can be considered to be in the process of disembarking while still in the gate area and before reaching customs or the main terminal. For example, passengers injured on an escalator that is part of the gate area maintained by the defendant airline have repeatedly been found to be disembarking. *See, e.g.,* Ugaz v. Am. Airlines, Inc., 576 F. Supp. 2d 1354 (S.D. Fla. 2008).

[195] *See* Hailegabriel G. Feyissa, *Ethiopian Law of International Carriage by Air: An Overview*, 5 MIZAN L. REV. No. 2, 215, 234, n.114 (2011).

the law to be applied or the rules of jurisdiction.[196] Reinforcing Article 49, the Convention annuls any provision that purports to relieve the carrier of liability or fix a lower limit of liability than that laid down in the Convention[197] and stipulates that carriers may by special contract accept only higher limits of liability than those in the Convention (or no limits whatsoever).[198]

7.10.2. *Strict Liability Under the Montreal Convention*

The most salient feature of the new liability regime is its imposition in Article 21 of the Montreal Convention, consistent with later Warsaw Convention reforms, of strict liability on air carriers up to 100,000 SDRs and potential unlimited liability above that amount.[199] This regime codifies the liability reforms to which the airline industry acquiesced in the Convention's immediate historical precursors, the IATA Intercarrier Agreement and the Japanese Initiative.[200] But Article 21 is not, as some commentators have implied, synonymous with *absolute* liability.[201] Under a hypothetical system of absolute liability (which, truth be told, has probably never existed[202]), an airline would automatically have to disgorge 100,000 SDRs regardless of the nature of the injury incurred and would be unable to avail itself of *any* defenses. Under the system of strict liability in Article 21 of the Montreal Convention, a plaintiff must still *prove* damages up to 100,000 SDRs. Once proof is made, however, the airline's only backstop is to plead a defense of contributory fault by the plaintiff.[203] If a plaintiff is seeking more than 100,000 SDRs, the presumption remains that the air carrier is responsible (the same presumption that Warsaw made[204]), but Article 21(2) dismantles Warsaw's "all necessary measures" defense and substitutes a modernized negligence formula: the carrier will not be liable for damages that exceed 100,000 SDRs if it proves that "the damage was not due to the negligence or other wrongful act or omission of the carrier" *or* that "such

---

[196] *See* Montreal Convention, *supra* note 6, art. 49. A similar provision appeared in Article 32 of the Warsaw Convention.

[197] *See* Montreal Convention, *supra* note 6, art. 26; *see also supra* note 66.

[198] *See* Montreal Convention, *supra* note 6, art. 25. As to the use of special contracts, see *supra* note 20.

[199] *See* Montreal Convention, *supra* note 6, art. 21.

[200] *See supra* Part 7.5.

[201] *See* Senai W. Andemariam, *Does the Montreal Convention of 1999 Require that a Notice be Given to Passengers? What is the Validity of Notice of a Choice of Forum Clause Under Montreal 1999?*, 71 J. AIR L. & COM. 251, 270 (2006).

[202] *See generally* RICHARD A. EPSTEIN, TORT LAW (1999).

[203] Montreal Convention, *supra* note 6, art. 20; *see also infra* note 209.

[204] *See* Warsaw Convention, *supra* note 4, arts. 20, 21.

damage was solely due to the negligence or other wrongful act or omission of a third party."[205]

7.10.3. *Disproving Negligence*

The first negligence defense for claims above 100,000 SDRs – that of non-negligence by the carrier itself – is, admittedly, extremely hard to prove. The second defense, of third-party negligence, is arguably an extension of the first.[206] Third-party responsibility could arise, for example, where a terrorist detonates a device aboard an aircraft[207] or an airport fails to properly maintain its runways or landing apron. For both defenses, the problems of proof are likely to be less onerous than those of the "all necessary measures" proviso in the IATA Intercarrier Agreement and the Japanese Initiative.[208] Moreover, as noted above, the Montreal Convention still affords an air carrier the opportunity to avoid all or part of its liability by proving a plaintiff's contributory fault.[209] Finally, the Convention stipulates that all claims are subject to a two-year statute of limitations.[210]

---

[205] Montreal Convention, *supra* note 6, art. 21(2), (a), (b). This new system obviates any need for passengers to allege "wilful misconduct" on the part of the carrier: passengers are now free to recover unlimited amounts, and the burden falls on the carrier to argue its negligence defense to avoid damages greater than 100,000 SDRs.

[206] This is because it is difficult to conceive how a carrier could show that *no* negligence was involved in an accident *without* some other party being responsible. Where mixed responsibility is found, however, the airline is still liable to pay any damages proven in excess of 100,000 SDRs.

[207] But remember that the terrorist attack would have to be the sole cause of the airplane's debilitation. If the air carrier failed to properly screen its baggage or to undertake normal security precautions, it is likely that the carrier would be responsible for all of the damages arising out of the attack.

[208] Although the drafters thought that a negligence defense would be more favorable to carriers, in fact courts never applied the "all necessary measures" defense literally: if such measures had indeed been taken, the injury would not have occurred. The clause has been construed, rather, to mean "all reasonable measures." *See* Manufacturers Hanover Trust Co. v. Alitalia Airlines, 429 F. Supp. 964, 967 (S.D.N.Y. 1977), *aff'd*, 573 F.2d 1292 (2d Cir. 1977).

[209] *See* Montreal Convention, *supra* note 6, art. 20. There is a strong public policy motivation for including this defense in the Convention. No State would wish to incentivize passengers to engage in risky behavior on board aircraft in order to create the conditions where a damages recovery would redound to that passenger's benefit. At the same time, no government would want to deal with the public outcry if the family of a terrorist were to seek damages after the destruction of an aircraft. (The 9/11 terrorists, incidentally, were all aboard domestic U.S. flights and no Warsaw/Montreal issues were presented.)

[210] *See id.* art. 35(1). However, "[t]he method of calculating that period shall be determined by the law of the court seised of the case." *Id.* art. 35(2). *See also supra* note 141.

7.10.4. *Forensic Reality of the Montreal Convention Liability Regime*

Critics of the Montreal Convention have pointed out – probably rightly – that the treaty's liability defenses will rarely, if ever, come into play. Given the universality of insurance coverage, an inability to plead a liability defense may not be of great moment with respect to individual claims for events such as onboard coffee spillage or the like. But for large accident claims, it is undoubtedly true, as a practical matter, that the exact nature of what caused an accident remains difficult to prove and expose (even with advances in accident investigation techniques and reporting). The threshold demonstration that an accident was *absolutely not due to a carrier's negligence or wrongful act or omission* (terms that bear no relationship to "intentionality"[211]) is, in reality, too high a forensic bar. The choice for airlines facing litigation under the Convention may be reduced to an expeditious settlement or a dissipation of resources quarrelling over the quantum of damages.[212] But is this a bad thing? Airlines will certainly not welcome such unpalatable choices. But the Montreal Convention does more than mete out a kind of rough justice between carriers and their clients. As well as compensating passengers who suffer death or bodily harm, the Convention can arguably be presented also as a scheme for *ex post* regulation that demands (albeit retrospectively) robust safety compliance by the international air transport industry.[213] From the perspective of social utility, therefore, the treaty's exacting standards of strict liability and its narrow framing of defenses may be considerably less unpalatable. Operating in Montreal's shadow, airlines are on notice of their liability and will be rationally motivated toward best practices in maintenance, inspections, and crew training. Insurers, too, should be sufficiently risk-aware not to allow their insured carriers to degrade safety oversight. Air carriers that do so

---

[211] Again, one needs to distinguish Warsaw's treatment of the idea of "wilful misconduct;" here the intent of the carrier is not at issue.

[212] Harold Caplan, dean of the aviation liability bar in the U.K., confirms this impression. In any situation where the Montreal Convention might apply to a major event, according to Caplan, defending counsel will immediately review any possibilities for asserting Convention-based defenses. Usually counsel will conclude that the prospect of asserting a non-negligence defense seems unlikely and will instead recommend settlement of all claims while reserving the contingency of later suing the manufacturer or air traffic control provider or other third party if the air incident investigation reveals noncarrier culpability. Rapid settlement of some claims occurred in the 2009 Atlantic Ocean loss of Air France flight 447, for example, even though it could take many years to identify the technical causes of the crash. Insurers, too, are likely to support early claim settlement and to reserve for later resolution (perhaps through arbitration) any cross-liability issues for the various insured parties (airlines, manufacturers, etc.) that may result from the crash investigation.

[213] Again, we note that practitioners would not universally endorse that view of the Convention's purpose. *See supra* Section 7.2.2.

may well be forced to exit the marketplace, widening the space for those with the capital, resources, and entrepreneurship to provide an appropriate level of safe air service. And although such a self-correcting regime will not give rise to a "flawless" environment where accidents never occur, it will go a long way toward keeping unfit actors out of the marketplace.[214]

7.10.5. *The "Escalator" Clause*

A major enhancement to the Warsaw Convention's terms of liability is the review of the applicable liability limits that is provided for in Article 24 of the Montreal Convention. Under the "escalator clause,"[215] ICAO is permitted to review the Convention's SDR limits every five years if the accumulated rate of inflation among the States whose currencies comprise the SDR exceeds 10%.[216] In such instances, ICAO may revise the liability limits upward, with the changes coming into effect six months later unless disapproval is registered by a majority of the State parties to the treaty. If that happens, ICAO must convene a special meeting to consider revising the liability limits or keeping them in place. The new power of adjustment was wielded for the first time in 2009, when ICAO recalibrated Article 21 strict liability up to 113,100 SDRs. Montreal's escalator clause is significant for two reasons. First and foremost, it effectively guarantees that the treaty's liability terms will not go out of date and that passengers who suffer injury in 1999, 2009, and 2029 will all have materially equivalent opportunities to recover within the Convention's strict liability regime. And second, except in circumstances of collective discontent with upward movements of the strict liability cap, States will not have to bother with reconvening to negotiate a new treaty instrument every time the cap appears inadequate to achieve the Convention's purposes. Given the historic failure of the Warsaw System not only to adjust the old caps in a timely manner, but also to attain a consensus for any proposed adjustments, the "automaticity" of the new Montreal clause is remarkably efficient.

7.10.6. *Other Provisions for Calculating Liability*

In addition to the escalator clause, the Convention provides additional details with respect to calculating liability. Article 23, for example, establishes

---

[214] *See id.* (discussing the coexistence and utility of separate systems of *ex ante* and *ex post* regulation of air safety).

[215] The term "escalator clause" does not appear in the Convention text.

[216] *See* Montreal Convention, *supra* note 6, art. 24(1).

methodologies for converting SDRs into local currency.[217] Article 25 recapitulates Warsaw's "special contract" exceptions by providing that, as noted above, "[a] carrier may stipulate that the contract of carriage shall be subject to higher limits of liability than those provided for in [the] Convention *or to no limits of liability whatsoever.*"[218] Given the presumptive unlimited liability to which air carriers covered by Montreal are already exposed, however, the second (italicized) clause of this provision of the treaty rings strange.[219] At most, it reinforces the treaty's disavowal of the liability-capping philosophy of Warsaw.

7.10.7. *Advance Compensation*

The consumer-friendly ethos of the Montreal Convention is reflected also in Article 28's strict requirement that "[i]n the case of aircraft accidents resulting in death or injury of passengers," the airline must make, *if its national law so requires,* "advance payments without delay to . . . persons who are entitled to claim compensation in order to meet the immediate economic needs of such persons."[220] As with Article 17, "accident" is not a defined term in the Convention's advance payment requirement. Several questions are therefore presented, once again, about the scope of that critical term. If it is contestable as a matter of law whether an "accident" has occurred, is an advance payment still required? Can an airline seek to resist the payment on the ground that a Montreal "accident" has not occurred? Does the social desirability of advance payments give rise to a more flexible definition of the term "accident" in

---

[217] *See* Montreal Convention, *supra* note 6, art. 23.

[218] Montreal Convention, *supra* note 6, art. 25 [emphasis added]; *see also supra* notes 20, 65.

[219] The *first* clause ("higher limits of liability than those provided for in [the] Convention") simply allows carriers to increase their strict liability exposure above the Article 21 ceiling (as amended). In that context, airlines would also have the freedom to use potential waiver of their strict liability as a bargaining chip in their contractual arrangements. This possibility finds some support in Article 27's disclaimer that "[n]othing contained in [the] Convention shall prevent the carrier from . . . waiving any defenses available under the Convention, or from laying down conditions [in its contract of carriage] which do not conflict with the provisions of [the] Convention." In other words, carriers retain the freedom to contract terms of carriage so long as they do not run up against the purposes of the treaty itself. *Cf.* Montreal Convention, *supra* note 6, art. 26.

[220] Montreal Convention, *supra* note 6, art. 28. Article 28 also provides, however, that advance payments are not "a recognition of liability" and may be offset against any amounts subsequently paid as damages. EU Regulation 889/2002 requires Union carriers to make advance payments of not less than 16,000 SDRs. Comm'n Regulation 889/2002, amending Regulation 2027/97, 2002 O.J. (L 140) 2–5. U.S. law does not require such payments, but many carriers voluntarily make them. The largest U.S. airline trade association, formerly known as the Air Transport Association, in its 2005 Intercarrier Implementing Provisions Agreement sought to obligate its carriers to make the same minimum 16,000 SDR advance payments as required under the EU Regulation. *See* DOT Order 2006–10–14, Docket OST-2005–22617 (Oct. 26, 2006).

Article 28 than in Article 17, or should the two terms be considered inter-changeable? It has also been suggested that the use of "aircraft accidents" as opposed to simply "accidents" could signify a stricter interpretation of "acci-dents" than in Article 17.[221] Nevertheless, EC Regulation 2027/97, the original EU legislation requiring advance payments for accidents, uses a definition of "accident" that corresponds fairly closely to prevailing interpretations of the Article 17 usage of the term.[222] Practically speaking, airlines will rarely cavil at paying out advance compensation in accordance with Article 28, even if they are ultimately exonerated (an outcome that, as we have seen, may be difficult to achieve under Montreal).

7.10.8. Punitive Damages

One provision added in the Montreal Convention that potentially moderates the liability exposure of airlines is the prohibition in Article 29 of "punitive, exemplary or any other non-compensatory damages."[223] Although none of those terms is actually defined in the treaty itself, carriers may artfully resort to them as a means of barring claims or parts of claims that appear to extend beyond the compensatory damages that are axiomatic in the Montreal Convention.[224]

7.10.9. Exclusivity of Actions Under the Montreal Convention

Article 29 is otherwise a reworking of the "exclusivity clause" in Article 24 of the Warsaw Convention, providing that "any action for damages, however founded, whether under [the] Convention or in contract or in tort or otherwise[,]" must be brought under the conditions and liability limits as set out in the Montreal

---

[221] *See* Wolf Müller-Rostin, *The Montreal Convention of 1999: Uncertainties and Inconsistencies*, THE AVIATION Q. 218, 223 (2000).

[222] *See* Pablo Mendes De Leon & Werner Eyskens, *The Montreal Convention: Analysis of Some Aspects of the Attempted Modernization and Consolidation of the Warsaw System*, 66 J. AIR. L. & COM. 1155, 1178–79 (2001).

[223] Montreal Convention, *supra* note 6, art. 29.

[224] For example, Article 29 has been cited as a basis for denying claims for emotional distress from lost baggage. *See* Nastych v. British Airways PLC, No. 09 Civ. 9082, 2010 WL 363400 (S.D.N.Y. Feb. 2, 2010). Note that, with respect to the determination of *what* compensatory damages will be awarded (in other words, what "harm" will be remedied), the Convention simply provides a "pass-through" to the applicable domestic law to determine the types of recoverable compen-satory damages as well as the eligible claimants. *See* LITIGATING THE AVIATION TORT CASE: FROM PRE-TRIAL TO CLOSING ARGUMENT 31 (Andrew J. Harakas ed., 3rd ed. 2008). Thus, the Convention itself does not exclude recovery for psychic injury; as we have seen, whether that head of recovery will be permitted is dependent on the interpretations of the courts of the various contracting States. *See supra* Section 7.9.6.

Convention.[225] Although the thinking behind Montreal's liability scheme is consumer-oriented, as we have noted, Article 29 is a sharp reminder of the historical purpose of protecting international air carriers from the vagaries of local laws. Even so, it could certainly be a concern that mere contemplation of *any* action other than a claim set forth under the treaty itself could provide plaintiffs (and local courts) with a back door out of the treaty's terms entirely. Alternative bases of claim would seem to be in conflict with a uniform system of international air carrier liability across national boundaries. If some States were to allow liability actions to be premised on national laws rather than on the Montreal rules, not only would the purposes of the treaty be compromised, but other States might be tempted to defect from the regime entirely in favor of establishing their own schemes of liability.

7.10.10. *Exclusivity and the U.S. Supreme Court's Decision in* Tseng

U.S. courts divided over the controversial question of whether the Warsaw Convention (a federal treaty) displaced alternative causes of action under the separate laws of the fifty U.S. states.[226] Strangely, the exclusivity debate was not resolved until the Supreme Court's relatively recent opinion in *El Al v. Tseng* in 1999.[227] The question before the *Tseng* Court was whether, given both parties' submissions that Mrs. Tseng's aggressive body search by El Al security officials[228] was not an "accident" within the meaning of Article 17 of the Warsaw Convention, and because the Convention did not permit recovery for emotional or psychic damages,[229] she could still maintain an action for those damages under another source of law – in this case, the tort law of the state of New York. The larger legal question controlling that specific determination was whether Article 24 made the Convention the exclusive source of remedy only for claims that fall within its legal parameters (i.e., meeting

---

[225] Montreal Convention, *supra* note 6, art. 29. Note that the exclusivity language in Article 29 of the Montreal Convention does not derive *directly* from the original text of Article 24 of Warsaw, but rather from the Warsaw provision as amended and expanded by Montreal Protocol No. 4. Nonetheless, it is obvious that the Protocol language merely clarified, and did not alter, the original rule of exclusivity. *See* El Al Isr. Airlines, Ltd. v. Tseng, 525 U.S. 155, 161 (1999).

[226] *See Tseng*, 525 U.S. at 161 n.3. As to whether the Warsaw Convention itself created a cause of action under federal law, see Benjamins v. British European Airways, 572 F.2d 913 (2d Cir. 1978).

[227] 525 U.S. 155 (1999). The tribunal below, the Second Circuit Court of Appeals, had ruled that the Warsaw Convention's cause of action was *not* exclusive.

[228] Before boarding, passenger Tsi Yuan Tseng was taken to a secure room by El Al Israel personnel and subjected to what she considered to be an invasive search of her person. She was then allowed to continue on her flight to Tel Aviv. She later sued the airline for the emotional and psychological harm that she claimed to have suffered as a result of the search.

[229] On this question, see *supra* Section 7.9.6.

the Article 17 definition of accident, involving bodily injury, etc.) or for *all* personal injury claims based on events that take place between a passenger's embarking and disembarking from an aircraft. The U.S. Supreme Court adopted the latter interpretation, emphasizing that the provision of uniformity and predictability in air carrier liability was central to the Convention's purpose.[230] Given the Court's ruling, considered earlier in this chapter, that damages for purely psychic injury were not available under the Convention, disqualification from state relief would leave Mrs. Tseng without any remedy. In the Court's view, however, the Convention's uniform regulation of international air carrier liability foreclosed Tseng and similarly placed plaintiffs from venturing into alternative forums.[231] Courts in other signatory States of the Warsaw Convention have also endorsed the treaty's exclusivity vis-à-vis domestic remedies.[232]

7.10.11. *Some Further Implications of the* Tseng *Ruling*

The Court in *Tseng* exposed some anomalous consequences of allowing claims under local law. First, airlines would face unlimited liability under diverse legal regimes but would be prevented, under the treaty, from contracting out of such liability.[233] Second, passengers injured physically in an emergency landing might be subject to the liability caps of the Montreal Convention, while those merely traumatized in the same mishap would be free to sue outside the Convention for potentially unlimited damages.[234] At the very least, plaintiffs like Tseng could engage in "artful pleading" in order to opt

---

[230] *See Tseng*, 525 U.S. at 169.

[231] As in *Saks*, see *supra* note 144, the Supreme Court grounded its ruling on an inquiry into the textual meaning of Article 17 of the Warsaw Convention, including its negotiating and drafting history. *See Tseng*, 525 U.S. at 167–70, 172–76.

[232] Justice Ginsburg's *Tseng* opinion, in a footnote, cited the following non-U.S. cases in support: Gal v. Northern Mountain Helicopters Inc., Dkt. No. 3491834918, 1998 B.C.T.C. LEXIS 1351, *15–*16 (Jul. 22, 1998); Naval-Torres v. Nw. Airlines, Inc., 159 D.L.R. (4th) 67, 73, 77 (1998); Emery Air Freight Corp. v. Nerine Nurseries Ltd., [1997] 3 N.Z.L.R. 723, 735–36, 737; and Seagate Technology Int'l v. Changi Int'l Airport Servs. Pte Ltd., [1997] 3 S.L.R. 1, 9. Exceptions are confined primarily to circumstances deemed to be outside the scope of the Warsaw/Montreal conventions, such as the example of a breach of contract claim brought by passengers whose "bumping" from a flight was found to be not covered by Article 19. *See* Weiss v. El Al Israel Airlines, 433 F. Supp. 2d 361 (S.D.N.Y. 2006).

[233] Under the Montreal Convention, of course, carriers now face unlimited liability under the international treaty regime as well. But Montreal, like its predecessor, still prevents any carrier from contracting out of such liability. *See* Montreal Convention, *supra* note 6, art. 26; *see also supra* Section 7.10.1.

[234] *See Tseng*, 525 U.S. at 171.

out of the Convention's liability scheme, for example, by pleading a psychic injury cause of action that could only be litigated under local law.[235] Another hypothetical in the case imagined a passenger injured by a malfunctioning escalator in the airline's terminal: if the exclusivity of the Convention were confirmed, would that passenger have any recourse against the airline even if the airline recklessly disregarded its duty to keep the escalator in proper repair?[236] As discussed earlier, however, the Warsaw Convention "addresses and concerns, only and exclusively," the airline's liability for passenger injuries occurring "on board the aircraft or in the course of any of the operations of embarking or disembarking."[237] Finally, federal preemption law in the United States is well established and indeed much litigated under the various iterations of the Federal Aviation Act.[238] It is fair to say that federal preemption of the laws of the fifty states is disfavored, particularly in matters of health and safety. Tseng argued as much in trying to persuade the Supreme Court to allow her to pursue relief in New York state court.[239] But the Court distinguished the Warsaw Convention, addressed to nation States, from ordinary federal legislation that speaks to the "subdivisions" of a single State, here the fifty states of the Union: "Our home-centered preemption analysis, therefore, should not be applied, mechanically, in construing our international obligations."[240]

---

[235] *See id.*

[236] This scenario was postulated by the Second Circuit Court of Appeals in *Tseng*. *See* El Al Isr. Airlines v. Tseng, 122 F.3d 99, 107 (2d Cir. 1997).

[237] *See supra* Section 7.9.10. "[T]he Convention's presumptive effect on local law extends no further than the Convention's own substantive scope." *Tseng*, 525 U.S. at 172. The Court's clear implication was that the escalator hypothetical would not be pre-empted by the Warsaw Convention because it would fall outside the Convention's scope. Many courts, however, have found escalator accidents to be covered under Warsaw's "embarking and disembarking" language: *see supra* note 194. The point remains, nevertheless, that the Montreal Convention (as interpreted through Warsaw) only preempts claims for which it provides a remedy (or denies recovery, as in the case of emotional distress), and therefore passengers will not find themselves in a no-man's land with claims that are preempted by but not addressed in the Convention.

[238] Courts have swung back and forth on the question of whether the U.S. Federal Aviation Act (FAA) preempts state tort and product liability law with regard to all aviation safety matters. The most prominent case has been Abdullah v. American Airlines, Inc.,181 F.3d 363 (3d Cir. 1999), which produced an expansive ruling that the FAA preempts the entire field of aviation safety. A recent Supreme Court case on implied federal preemption has, however, called the holding in *Abdullah* into doubt. *See* Wyeth v. Levine, 555 U.S. 555 (2009).

[239] *See Tseng*, 525 U.S. at 175.

[240] *Id. See also* Sidhu v. British Airways plc [1997] AC 430, in which Lord Hope observed on behalf of a unanimous U.K. House of Lords that "[t]he idea that an action for damages may be brought by a passenger against the carrier outside the [Warsaw] Convention in the cases covered by [A]rticle 17 . . . seems to be entirely contrary to the system which [Article 17] was designed to create."

7.11. THE MONTREAL CONVENTION (5): EXPANDING THE BASES FOR JURISDICTION

7.11.1. *Five Jurisdictional Choices*

The original Warsaw Convention identified four carrier-related forums, any of which would have to be in the territory of a contracting State, where a plaintiff would have the option to bring an action for any form of damages (including cargo-related claims) under the Convention. These treaty-based jurisdictions were the State of domicile of the carrier (i.e., "where the carrier is ordinarily resident"[241]); the State of the carrier's principal place of business; the State in which the carrier has an "establishment" that made the contract of carriage;[242] and the State of final destination of the aircraft.[243] All four of these potential lawsuit venues are retained under the Montreal Convention.[244] Moreover, after intensive and prolonged discussions at the drafting conference, the Warsaw heads of jurisdiction were amplified to include a new so-called fifth jurisdiction for death and injury claims only: the State in which the passenger (not the carrier) has either his or her "principal and permanent residence" when the accident occurred.[245] The residence affiliation in addition requires that the qualifying State of residence must also be a place "to and from which the carrier operates services for the carriage of passengers by air, either on its own aircraft or on another carrier's aircraft pursuant to a commercial

---

[241] U.S. courts interpret "domicile" to mean the State in which the carrier is incorporated, but the term carries a slightly different meaning in other languages. For example, French courts have interpreted "domicile" as the location of the carrier's headquarters. *See In re* Air Disaster Near Cove Neck, N.Y., 774 F. Supp. 725, 728–30 (E.D.N.Y. 1991). It is unclear how this interpretation materially differs from the "principal place of business" forum. The redundancy is probably an accidental by-product of the drafters' intent that the "domicile" forums apply to private individuals providing air transport services and not to incorporated carriers. *See id.* at 731 n.7.

[242] This refers to the entity from which the ticket was purchased.

[243] *See* Warsaw Convention, *supra* note 4, art. 28(1).

[244] *See* Montreal Convention, *supra* note 6, art. 33(1). With the widespread use of arbitration to settle international public/private or wholly private disputes, *see supra* Chapter 4, Part 4.3, it is not surprising that Article 34 of the Montreal Convention provides an option for arbitration: this alternative forum, which must nevertheless be one of the jurisdictions mentioned in Article 33, is only available for "the parties to [a] contract of cargo." Montreal Convention, *supra* note 6, art. 34(1), (2). The Convention offers no arbitration option in relation to cases of passenger injury or death. To have done so might have been offensive to public policy in many States as well as contrary to various national constitutions that will not assign their citizens' litigation rights to an international arbitrator. Commercial arrangements involving sophisticated shippers are less likely to engage issues of fairness and "adhesion."

[245] "Principal and permanent residence" is defined in the Montreal Convention as "the one fixed and permanent abode of the passenger at the time of the accident." Montreal Convention, *supra* note 6, art. 33(3)(b). Nationality is not the determining factor. *See id.*

agreement, and in which the carrier conducts its business of carriage of passengers by air from premises leased or owned by the carrier itself or by another carrier with which it has a commercial agreement."[246]

7.11.2. *More on the Fifth Jurisdiction*

The United States had lobbied for a more expansive jurisdictional basis that would permit travelers to bring suit in their State of residence even if the contract of carriage has no other connection with the State.[247] Nevertheless, when set beside the proposal in the stillborn Guatemala City Protocol of a fifth jurisdiction comprising the State of permanent residence or principal business of the passenger so long as the defendant carrier has an establishment there,[248] Montreal's formulation is cumbersome and confusing. The Montreal Convention, in fact, sought to cabin the more generous Guatemala City approach by ensuring some rational connection between the passenger's home State and the air transport services provided by the defendant carrier. The defendant, accordingly, must operate to and from the qualifying State *and* must have a commercial presence in that State. Because the nationality rule typically prevents airlines from setting up wholly owned subsidiaries outside their home States,[249] it is unlikely that the Montreal delegates intended the strong form of commercial activity that such enterprises represent. In an era of big-carrier alliances, however, there are other forms of "doing business" that might trigger the fifth jurisdiction. If a U.S. citizen who lives and works in Chicago purchases a ticket in Germany for a Lufthansa flight from Frankfurt to Tokyo, any ensuing death or injury befalling that person might be litigable in a U.S. court on the premise that the passenger is a resident of the United States and the carrier has some appreciable "minimum contacts" with the United States that would engage the fifth jurisdiction: Lufthansa, for example, not only leases ticket counters at several U.S. airports but also has a highly integrated alliance agreement with United that includes but far exceeds a simple code-share arrangement.[250]

---

[246] Montreal Convention, *supra* note 6, art. 33(2).

[247] *See* Hornsby v. Lufthansa German Airlines, 593 F. Supp. 2d 1132, 1138–39 (C.D. Cal. 2009) (explaining that developing countries without operations in the United States resisted an unqualified passenger residence jurisdictional basis to protect their carriers from facing suit in U.S. courts).

[248] *See* Guatemala City Protocol, *supra* note 55, art. XII.

[249] On the nationality rule, see *supra* Chapter 3, Section 3.1.2. An exception would be the EU single aviation market, within which EU designated carriers are allowed to establish and own subsidiaries in any contracting State. *See supra* Chapter 4, Section 4.4.3.

[250] *See supra* Chapter 4, Parts 4.5, 4.8.

7.11.3. *More on the First Four Jurisdictional Choices*

The quartet of choices retained from Warsaw, in contrast, is each fairly straight-forward. As cases across several jurisdictions have shown, a carrier's domicile is typically viewed as the State where it is incorporated, while its principal place of business is the State where it is headquartered.[251] In an era where code-sharing is the dominant form of intercarrier cooperation, Article 46 of the Montreal Convention adds the *actual* (in addition to the contracting) carrier's domicile and place of business to the available forum choices.[252] As for the State where the "contract" (i.e., the ticket[253]) was made, courts have generally defined that expression to signify the place where the ticket was purchased rather than where it was physically issued.[254] Notice also that the State of destination has been denominated by courts to be the destination point *contracted for*, not the *actual* destination reached.[255] Additionally, passengers are not permitted subjectively to alter their "final destination." For example, on a fifth freedom flight operated by British Airways (BA) from London to Toronto and onward to Chicago, an injured passenger who seeks to disembark at the intermediate point of Toronto, despite the fact her ticket will take her through to Chicago, cannot subject BA to Canadian jurisdiction under the Montreal Convention.[256]

7.11.4. *Procedural Questions Under the Montreal Convention*

Finally, the Montreal Convention's provisions on jurisdiction also state, as the Warsaw Convention previously provided, that "[q]uestions of procedure shall be governed by the law of the court seised of the case."[257] That apparent deference to national courts has, unsurprisingly, yielded different interpretations. Within the U.S. Federal Circuits, there has been a split over whether the doctrine of *forum non conveniens* – a procedure that may allow a defendant to transfer a case to a non-U.S. jurisdiction if evidence and witnesses can be more

---

[251] *See supra* note 241 and accompanying text. *See also* Eck v. United Arab Airlines, Inc., 360 F.2d 804, 809 (2d Cir. 1966).

[252] *See* Montreal Convention, *supra* note 6, art. 46. Article 46 flows conceptually from the terms of Article 45, which allows actions for damages, at the plaintiff's option, against either the *actual* or the *contracting* carrier, or against both together and separately. If only one of the carriers is sued, the other has the right to implead the former into the lawsuit. *See id.*

[253] *See, e.g.,* Chan v. Korean Air Lines, Ltd., 490 U.S. 122, 127–29 (1989).

[254] *See* Polanski v. KLM Royal Dutch Airlines, 378 F. Supp. 2d 1222, 1229–31 (S.D. Cal. 2005).

[255] For instance, for a one-way ticket from Chicago to London, the latter is the final destination even if the aircraft is forced, for technical or safety reasons, to make an emergency landing in New York. For round-trip transportation, the final destination has been defined as the "ultimate destination," that is, the point from which the journey originated. *See* GOLDHIRSCH, *supra* note 44, at 185–86.

[256] *See id.* at 186–87.

[257] Warsaw Convention, *supra* note 4, art. 28(2); Montreal Convention, *supra* note 6, art. 33(4).

readily accessed in the foreign State – applies to cases brought under the Warsaw Convention.[258] But U.S. courts have thus far looked more benignly on the use of *forum non conveniens* under Montreal.[259] There is obvious tension when a plaintiff's right to pick the forum is frustrated by local rules of procedure such as *forum non conveniens*. A teleological reading of the Montreal Convention, not available under its predecessor, may help to slice through that Gordian knot. Using that perspective, Montreal emphasizes the rights of the plaintiff/consumer over the convenience of air carriers. Even local rules of procedure should therefore be subordinated to the goal of providing aggrieved passengers with their best available chance to prevail.

7.12. THE MONTREAL CONVENTION (6): A FINAL MISCELLANY OF PROVISIONS

7.12.1. *A Right of Recourse*

Article 37 of the Montreal Convention states, in sum, that "[n]othing in this Convention shall prejudice the question whether a person liable for damage

---

[258] *See generally* Allan I. Mendelsohn & Renee Lieux, *The Warsaw Convention Article 28, the Doctrine of Forum Non Conveniens, and the Foreign Plaintiff*, 68 J. AIR L. & COM. 75 (2003). In *Hosaka v. United Airlines, Inc.*, 305 F.3d 989 (9th Cir. 2002), the Ninth Circuit Court of Appeals ruled that airlines cannot plead *forum non conveniens*, causing a split with the Fifth Circuit Court of Appeals that found *forum non conveniens* compatible with the Warsaw Convention. *See In re* Air Crash Disaster Near New Orleans, La. on July 9, 1982, 821 F.2d 1147, 1162 (5th Cir. 1987) (en banc). The doctrine is not accepted in civil law jurisdictions, incidentally. *See* Christian G. Lang & Prager Dreifuss, *Forum Non Conveniens* in Continental Europe (unpublished paper, Aug. 2, 2009, http://www.prager-dreifuss.com/system/document_des/78/orig inal/Forum_Non_Conveniens_Cont_Europe_.pdf?1289378662) (noting that bias toward certainty and predictability in civil law systems discourages resort to discretionary doctrines like *forum non conveniens*).

[259] *See* Allan I. Mendelsohn, *Recent Developments in the Forum Non Conveniens Doctrine*, 52 FED. LAW. 45, 46 (2005) ("[T]he dearth of legislative history … is corrected by copious legislative history [for the Montreal Convention] … showing that *forum non conveniens* is available and will be employed by U.S. courts under Article 33(4) [of Montreal]"). *See also In re* W. Caribbean Airways, S.A., 619 F. Supp. 2d 1299, 1310–28 (S.D. Fla. 2007). But is U.S. adherence to *forum non conveniens* in aviation liability cases correct as a matter of international treaty law? Arguably, the *lex generalis* in Article 28 of the Montreal Convention that assigns questions of procedure to local law should always be subject to the *lex specialis* in Article 33 that grants the plaintiff noncontingent access to five potential jurisdictional fora. On the relationship between *lex specialis* and *lex generalis*, *see* Fragmentation of International Law: Difficulties Arising from Diversification and Expansion of International Law – Report of the Study Group of the International Law Commission, U.N.G.A. Doc. A/CN.4/L682 (Apr. 13, 2006) (noting that the principle that special law derogates from general law is a widely accepted maxim of legal interpretation). In any event, the U.S. delegation to the Montreal preparatory conference stated explicitly that U.S. courts would continue to apply the doctrine.

in accordance with its provisions has a right of recourse against any other person."[260] Thus, for example, an airline that has been exposed to liability and damages under the Montreal Convention may seek recovery from an aircraft manufacturer using theories of product liability. Moreover, nothing prevents the injured passengers themselves from also seeking recovery directly from third parties including the aircraft manufacturer, avoiding any limitations on recovery imposed by the Montreal and Warsaw conventions (which affect only carrier liability). Finally, Article 37 could be said to provide an independent basis for an airline to claim indemnification from a negligent third party for the 100,000 SDRs per injured party that the carrier is required to pay out even where the airline is not found to be negligent. This is not an inconsequential right given that a major international airline accident could result in hundreds of liability claims totaling tens of millions of SDRs. Without Article 37's right of recourse, Montreal would shift a potentially unpalatable burden onto non-negligent international airlines while providing a safe haven to other parties that may be responsible for passenger injuries and deaths.

7.12.2. *The Question of Insurance*

For the Montreal Convention's scheme of *ex post* liability to be effective, airlines must carry enough insurance to meet their potential exposure. According to Article 50, "State Parties shall require their carriers to maintain adequate insurance covering their liability under this Convention."[261] By the same provision, a State party is allowed to demand documentation evidencing insurance. This is not a minor matter. If airlines are not required to carry insurance in line with Montreal's liability regime, an important, market-based oversight measure – the insurance companies themselves – is removed from the equation.[262] At the same time, Article 50 does pose a conundrum: how much insurance is "adequate"? If a Warsaw-type scheme were in effect, with 100,000 SDRs as a global cap rather than serving merely as a ceiling for strict liability, air carriers could reasonably calculate a per-flight estimate of required insurance cover.[263] But because the Montreal Convention contains a rebuttable presumption of unlimited liability above 100,000 SDRs, must an air carrier contemplate an "unlimited" insurance policy? Realistically, no

---

[260] *See* Montreal Convention, *supra* note 6, art. 37.

[261] *See* Montreal Convention, *supra* note 6, art. 50.

[262] *But see supra* note 15 (observing that insurance companies probably do not see themselves as performing a societal function as safety overseers).

[263] For instance, on a 100-passenger international flight from New York to London, an airline might insure for up to 100,000,000 SDRs.

insurer would write such a policy, and passenger liability policies usually contain a limit of indemnity for each accident or "occurrence." There may also be a "combined single limit" intended to cover the combination of all claims potentially arising from one event. In fact, the risks of operating commercial aircraft are so potentially huge that the coverage must be spread among several insurance underwriters.[264] Aviation insurers may further limit their own exposure through placement of risk with so-called reinsurers (i.e., underwriters that insure insurers).[265]

7.12.3. *Legal Effect of the Montreal Convention*

In accordance with Article 53, the Montreal Convention entered into force on November 4, 2003, sixty days after the deposit of its thirtieth ratification.[266] Article 55 ordains, in an omnibus catalog of the prior international law instruments of the Warsaw System, that Montreal prevails over any rules in any of those instruments where two States are common parties to any of them as well as being parties to Montreal.[267] Nevertheless, all of the instruments of the Warsaw System remain in effect for those States that have yet to become a party to the successor treaty.[268] As discussed earlier, the applicable treaty is determined by the origin and destination points specified on the ticket.[269] Thus, while a flight from the United States to France would be covered under the Montreal Convention, as both States are contracting parties to that Convention, a flight from the United States to Russia would fall under the Warsaw System as amended by The Hague Protocol: Russia has yet to ratify the Montreal Convention, but both the United States and Russia have ratified

---

[264] There is a specialty market in aviation insurance. For more detailed information on the operation of this market, the reader should consult additional sources mentioned in the bibliography.

[265] *See* I. H. Ph. Diederiks-Verschoor, An Introduction to Air Law 342–43 (Pablo Mendes de Leon, ed., 9th rev. ed. 2012).

[266] Montreal Convention, *supra* note 6, art. 53(6); treaty status available at http://www.icao.int/secretariat/legal/List%20of%20Parties/Mtl99_EN.pdf. ICAO was designated as the depositary.

[267] *See* Montreal Convention, *supra* note 6, art. 55.

[268] As the reader can glean from this and the following section, the continued existence of the Warsaw System (not just of the Warsaw Convention!) adds considerable complexity and confusion to selection of the applicable treaty regime. The Montreal Convention does not include a required denunciation of Warsaw, and therefore allows conflicting obligations to States that are not parties to Montreal. What can now be done to reduce or remove that uncertainty? If Warsaw were no longer applicable in Montreal States, carriers from States that did not ratify Montreal would still find themselves caught by Montreal's extended liabilities whenever they performed carriage with the requisite connections. *See* Gardiner, *supra* note 47, at 289. In such situations, they would have to devise special contracts with passengers or risk a loss of international traffic and soaring insurance premiums.

[269] *See supra* note 111 and accompanying text.

Warsaw and its Hague Protocol. A flight from the United States to South Sudan would not be covered under any of the treaties discussed, as South Sudan (a recently recognized sovereign State) has not ratified any of the agreements going back to Warsaw. But a United States/South Sudan/France ticket, and even a United States/South Sudan/United States ticket, would both be governed by the Montreal Convention because the origin and destination points are both within a State that has ratified the Convention, with a stopover in another State.[270]

7.12.4. *An Anomalous Effect That May Flow from a Plaintiff's Jurisdictional Choices*

But the jurisdictional choices available to a plaintiff can upset this relatively straightforward treaty selection process and may result in different treaty regimes being applied in different jurisdictions to carriage involving the same points. To take one possible scenario: a plaintiff who purchases a ticket from Air France in Moscow for a Paris/New York flight does have the option under Article 28 of the Warsaw Convention to use Russia as a qualifying jurisdiction for the lawsuit (if, for example, Air France has an "establishment" in Moscow that sold the ticket).[271] If the dispute were litigated in Paris or New York, a court in either of those States would apply the Montreal Convention. A Russian court, in contrast, would likely apply the Warsaw/Hague rules to the same lawsuit.[272] Thus, although the origin and destination States actually trigger the application of the Montreal Convention for the Paris/New York flight, the jurisdiction provisions in the Montreal Convention do not assure that the action will be brought in either the State of departure or the State of destination or that the Montreal Convention itself will ultimately apply.[273]

---

[270] *See* Byrd v. Comair, Inc. (In re Air Crash at Lexington, Ky., Aug. 27, 2006), 501 F. Supp. 2d 902 (E.D. Ky. 2007) (ruling that the Montreal Convention governed an action on behalf of a passenger who was killed in a crash during a round-trip flight between the United States and St. Lucia, a nation that had ratified neither the Montreal Convention nor any of the Warsaw instruments; in reaching its decision, the court determined that St. Lucia was an agreed-upon stop on the flight, which had originated, and was to have ended, in the United States).

[271] Warsaw Convention, *supra* note 4, art. 28(1); *see also supra* Section 7.11.1.

[272] A case brought in Russia concerning a Paris/New York flight would be governed by the only common treaty, the Warsaw Convention, to which all three involved States (Russia, France, and the United States) remain parties. Again, we have to watch the interaction between jurisdictional provisions and the nature of the relevant treaty relations (*see supra* note 111 and accompanying text). The treaty relations that follow from a plaintiff's choice of jurisdiction will determine which treaty (or version of a treaty) is applicable. *See id.*

[273] It can happen that no common treaty relations exist between the States of departure and destination and that the case cannot therefore proceed under any international agreement, leaving the dispute (presumably) to be dealt with under the applicable local law of the forum.

7.12.5. *State Reservations to and Withdrawal from the Montreal Convention*

A State that ratifies the Montreal Convention is required to accept all of its provisions and can only enter reservations (exceptions) with respect to either or both of two matters: "international carriage by air performed and operated directly by [that State] for non-commercial purposes in respect to its functions and duties as a sovereign State"; or "the carriage of persons, cargo and baggage for its military authorities on aircraft registered in or leased by [that State], the whole capacity of which has been reserved by or on behalf of such authorities."[274] States wishing to withdraw from the Montreal Convention may do so by written notification to ICAO, but the denunciation does not take effect until 180 days following such notification.[275]

7.12.6. *Absence of a Dispute Settlement Mechanism*

As noted at the start of this chapter, the Montreal Convention (like its predecessor) does not contain any formal dispute settlement mechanism or available sanctions against violators. If the United States, for example, were to enact federal legislation in contravention of the treaty that limited the liability of U.S. international carriers for any claims brought in U.S. courts, no other party to the Convention *under the Convention* could initiate procedures to deter or punish that unilateral action.[276] That apparent impunity is not a cause for alarm, however. Like most international agreements, the Montreal Convention survives on the self-interested adherence of its signatories. If

See Chubb & Son, Inc. v. Asiana Airlines, 214 F.3d 301 (2d Cir. 2000), *cert. denied*, 533 U.S. 928, 121 S. Ct. 2549 (2001) (holding that the U.S. District Judge erred in seeking to extrapolate a "hybrid" or "truncated" treaty between the United States and South Korea based on common elements drawn from the original Warsaw Convention, to which the United States adhered, and The Hague Protocol, amending the Warsaw Convention, to which South Korea adhered; accordingly, South Korea was not in a treaty relationship with the United States under the original Warsaw Convention and the federal court did not have subject matter jurisdiction over the dispute).

[274] Montreal Convention, *supra* note 6, art. 57. Many States have entered either or both of the two available reservations. *See* ICAO, Treaty Status, http://www.icao.int/secretariat/legal/List%20of %20Parties/Mtl99_EN.pdf.

[275] *See* Montreal Convention, *supra* note 6, art. 54. Article 54 of the Montreal Convention preserves each contracting State's right to denounce by written notification to the depositary 180 days prior to the effective date of denunciation.

[276] Presumably, however, the disputant States could agree to invoke the optional jurisdiction of the International Court of Justice (ICJ) to hear the dispute. *See* Statute of the International Court of Justice, art. 36(2), http://www.icj-cij.org/documents/ (allowing States to declare their acceptance of the jurisdiction of the Court in relation to any other State making the same declaration, and without any special agreement, on all legal disputes such as interpretation of a treaty).

changed world economic conditions were to return the international air transport industry, or parts of it, to something like the structural fragility of its early decades, it is possible that airlines in affected regions would pressure their governments to defect from the treaty before formally denouncing it. Conversely, if a State were disenchanted with the capacity of Montreal's strict liability regime to compensate travelers or to discipline airline safety practices, it could follow Warsaw System precedent by building coalitions with the airline industry or with like-minded States to enlarge even the Montreal Convention's relatively pro-consumer terms of liability.

7.12.7. *Liability Regime for "Delays" Under the Montreal Convention*

The private liability scheme in both the Montreal and Warsaw conventions includes coverage of the ubiquitous phenomenon of delays in air travel. Article 19 of the Montreal Convention echoes Warsaw's terse declaration of liability for "damage occasioned by delay" in the carriage by air of passengers, baggage, or cargo.[277] Neither Convention further defines the term "delay."[278] Under Article 22(1) of the Montreal Convention, recoveries for delays to passengers are capped at 4150 SDRs, while Article 22(2) limits baggage delay claims to 1130 SDRs and Article 22(3) sets 17 SDRs per kilogram as the maximum recovery for delay in the delivery of cargo.[279] As in Warsaw, Article 19 of the Montreal Convention exonerates carriers if they have taken "all measures that could reasonably be required to avoid the [delay]" or can show that "it was impossible . . . to take such measures."[280] Arguably, such a capacious defense eviscerates carrier liability by making it too easy to justify delays. On the other hand, under Article 22(5) air carriers can still be confronted by the elimination of all liability caps if the plaintiff can prove that the delay resulted from "an act or omission of the carrier . . . done with intent to cause [delay] or

---

[277] Montreal Convention, *supra* note 6, art. 19.

[278] Naturally, the courts must step into this vacuum and create content for the term. Rather than *a priori* definitions, they generally explore whether the delay in question is "reasonable," that is, due to weather conditions or the demands of air traffic control. *See* GOLDHIRSCH, *supra* note 44, at 101–04.

[279] *See* Montreal Convention, supra note 6, art. 22(1)–(3). Although, as we have seen, *see supra* note 233 and accompanying text, carriers cannot contractually exclude themselves from the liability terms of the Warsaw or Montreal conventions (unless by offering more generous terms), Article 10 of the IATA standard "General Conditions of Carriage (Passenger and Baggage)" nevertheless includes "best efforts" language that appears designed to mitigate the liability of international airlines in instances of delay or cancellation. That phrase does not appear, however, in IATA's Conditions of Carriage for Cargo.

[280] Montreal Convention, *supra* note 6, art. 19. Montreal substitutes "reasonable" for "necessary" measures, a more realistic (and carrier-friendly) standard.

recklessly and with knowledge that [delay] would probably result."²⁸¹ Although it may stretch credulity to imagine an airline intentionally precipitating a delay, given the potential harm to its commercial reputation, the availability of this means to suppress the liability caps is again characteristic of Montreal's identification with consumer interests.

7.12.8. *Alternatives to the Montreal Convention's Delay Provisions*

Potential litigation has been discouraged by the cost and time involved in suing under the delay provisions of Warsaw and Montreal. Large cargo shippers affected by delay usually rely on insurance but also on the compensatory terms of specialized arm's-length contracts negotiated with their carriers. Passengers who are delayed or whose baggage is delayed typically rely on whatever "pastoral" arrangements their carriers are willing to make.²⁸² Government disquiet about airline treatment of passengers who experience delays and related inconveniences has produced a raft of consumer legislation aimed at regulating how carriers respond. Relatively fast administrative procedures may be available in lieu of scaling the Warsaw/Montreal edifice.²⁸³ In a recent judgment, the Court of Justice of the European Union (CJEU) ruled that the remedies for delays that are available under the Montreal

---

²⁸¹ Montreal Convention, *supra* note 6, art. 22(5).

²⁸² That care may include a willingness to offer the prescribed Warsaw/Montreal compensation without further proceedings. We are aware that some readers may find our use of the term "pastoral" to be ironic.

²⁸³ EU legislation, for example, covers cancellations, long delays, and denied boarding. *See* Regulation 261/2004, of the European Parliament and of the Council of 11 February 2004 Establishing Common Rules on Compensation and Assistance to Passengers in the Event of Denied Boarding and of Cancellation or Long Delay of Flights, and Repealing Regulation 295/91/EEC, 2004 O.J. (L 46) arts. 4–6 (EC). On March 13, 2013, the European Commission put forward a proposal for a new Regulation to amend and extend its existing regime. *See* Commission Proposal for a Regulation Amending Regulation 261/2004, COM(2013) 130 (seeking to resolve airline compliance problems with and consequent airline challenges to the existing regime by clarifying key terms, adding legislative support for financial compensation for delays, introducing passenger rerouting privileges after very lengthy delays, refining the definition of the much-litigated "exceptional circumstances" exemption for airlines from the compensation regime, and creating certain new passenger rights including free amendment of misspelt names, nondenial of boarding for passengers attempting to use only the return portion of their tickets, and a no-charge increase in the Montreal baggage loss or delay liability caps for equipment needed by passengers with limited mobility). The U.S. Department of Transportation has also introduced some regulations to cover delays in which passengers are stranded on the tarmac for more than four hours, although the rules do not apply to cancellations or delays in which the passengers are not kept waiting on the aircraft. *See* Enhancing Airline Passenger Protections, Dkt. No. OST-2010–0140, Final Rule (Dep't of Transp. Apr. 20, 2011).

Convention are not self-contained and exclusive. The individually activated liability system of the Convention, the Court held, can coexist with the new generalized EU scheme of public regulation of compensation for air carrier delays and other inconveniences.[284] With its ruling, the CJEU has challenged the prevailing orthodoxy of a treaty regime that displaces local systems of compensation within its sphere of operation.[285]

7.13. CONCLUSION

7.13.1. *An Unfinished Regime*

As important as the Montreal Convention has been to overcoming problems encountered in the Warsaw System, it is not a terminal point in the evolution of this area of law. The treaty is only a decade old and has not yet won "universal" ratification. Although its circle of adhering States is expanding (103 States had ratified as of 2013[286]), the total number is just over half that of the Chicago Convention. Thus, it is premature to declare the Montreal Convention an unqualified success or to extol it as the private law complement to the Chicago Convention. Many commentators have suggested that further work on the Convention needs to be done and that issues ranging from the amount of strict liability to more specific provisions on psychic injury will require future amendments to the treaty. Like Warsaw, Montreal fails to define several key terms including "carrier," "accident," "embarkation" and "disembarkation," and "delay." Nor does the treaty elucidate fully the role of insurance, establish uniform conflict of laws (choice of law) rules, or give detailed guidance on recoverable compensatory damages. There is concern, however, that meddling with the Montreal Convention through

---

[284] *See* Case C-344/04, International Air Transp. Ass'n v. Department for Transp., 2006 E.C.R. I-00403. Although the Court recognized that the Montreal Convention governed the conditions when, after a flight delay, passengers "may bring actions for damages by way of redress on an individual basis," it found nothing inherent in the Convention itself preempting the EU from adopting regulations mandating "standardized and immediate compensatory measures.... The [EU] system operates at an earlier stage than the system which results from the Montreal Convention." *Id.* ¶¶ 44, 46. *See also* Jeremias Prassl, *The European Union and the Montreal Convention: A New Analytical Framework*, 12 Issues Aviation L. & Pol'y 381, 402–06 (2013) (further explaining the distinction drawn by the Court between delay-related damage that is identical for every passenger and for which redress may take the form of standardized and immediate assistance, and individual damage, inherent in the reason for traveling, that requires a case-by-case assessment).

[285] On the exclusivity of the damages remedies provided under the Montreal Convention, see *supra* Sections 7.10.9, 7.10.10.

[286] *See* ICAO, Treaty Status, *supra* note 266.

amendments before wider ratification is achieved will not only slow the accession of new States, but also duplicate Warsaw's history by developing another fractured, piecemeal system that squanders global uniformity and coherence. Some States, for example, might ratify the Montreal Convention but not an amending instrument. Montreal, it is argued, was designed to unclutter the confusion of Warsaw, not to compound it.

7.13.2. *Effect of Divergent Judicial Interpretation*

It is still not entirely clear how much of the Warsaw System's thick body of jurisprudence will endure under its successor. Just as in the development of Warsaw, if national courts again divide in their rulings, it may well be necessary for States to return to the negotiating table to bolt together an amending instrument. But continued divergence of judicial interpretation could also have a more dramatic consequence for the international liability system. As we explained early in this chapter, governments are not unwilling to consider alternative forms of regulation to govern air carrier liability. There remains support for the radical view that the Montreal Convention should be discarded in favor of a "true" system of liability developed within the legal cultures of individual States. Competing claims of jurisdiction, where plaintiffs and defendants representing several nationalities are potentially involved, could be buffered through application of national conflict of laws rules and the precepts of judicial comity. Montreal's international regime would be superseded by domestic courts applying doctrines that may be (or are seen to be) better adapted to the needs of local citizens and to public sentiment on liability and safety. Indeed, a process of informal collaboration on issues of foreign law among courts from different jurisdictions also holds the potential, over time, of itself producing international convergence on applicable rules and norms of liability.[287]

---

[287] *See* Graeme B. Dinwoodie, *A New Copyright Order: Why National Courts Should Create Global Norms*, 149 U. PENN. L.R. 469 (2000) (explaining how this process could occur, for example, among a specialized community of judges in each State that deals with issues of international intellectual property law, if such judges are continuously confronted with the application of foreign law). *See also* Prassl, *supra* note 284 (discussing how, following EU accession to the Montreal Convention, the CJEU is promoting interpretive convergence among the 28 EU Member States by ruling on Convention-related legal questions that are referred to it by EU national courts; the article analyzes Case C-410/11, Pedro Sanchez v. Iberia, 2012 E.C.R. 1–0000, in which the Court ruled that if several passengers bundle their belongings into a single suitcase that is lost by the airline, they can each claim for their loss up to the relevant liability cap on the basis that while the loss triggered the carrier's liability, the entitlement to compensation under the Convention accrues to each individual passenger).

7.14. THE INTERNATIONAL LAW REGIME
FOR SURFACE DAMAGE LIABILITY

7.14.1. A "Doomed" System?

The second, but radically less effective, facet of private transnational aviation law that governs airline liability is comprised of a series of ratified and unratified treaties on air carrier responsibility for third-party surface damage. Beginning with the failed Rome Convention of 1933[288] and its 1938 protocol governing insurance,[289] States sought to establish a uniform set of rules governing surface damage caused by air carriers outside the territory of their home States.[290] Unlike the Warsaw System, which had time to ferment before it would become an object of scorn by academics and the U.S. tort bar, the so-called Rome System seemed doomed from the start. Almost as soon as the first instrument was assembled, States had already bypassed its terms with their own laws governing surface liability, while also mandating that carriers operating within their airspace carry the requisite insurance coverage to compensate damage claimants. None of this deterred ICAO from forging ahead, first with an over-hauled Rome Convention in 1952,[291] followed by an amending protocol in 1978,[292] and, more recently, with a dual set of thus-far unratified treaties that contemplate radically reforming the global surface damage liability regime.

7.14.2. Policy Challenges to a Uniform System of Surface Damage Liability

It is instructive to evaluate not only the terms of these treaties but also the policy challenges that continue to be posed to a uniform system for surface

---

[288] *See* International Convention for the Unification of Certain Rules Relating to Damage Caused by Aircraft to Third Parties on the Surface, *opened for signature* May 29, 1933, 192 L.N.T.S. 291 (entered into force Feb. 13, 1942). Only five States – Belgium, Brazil, Guatemala, Romania, and Spain – ever ratified the treaty.

[289] Protocol Supplementary to the Convention for the Unification of Certain Rules Relating to Damage Caused by Foreign Aircraft to Third Parties on the Surface, *opened for signature* Sept. 29, 1938, ICAO Doc. 107-CD.

[290] Surface damage is any damage to person or property on land or on water caused by an aircraft in flight or by a person or object falling from an aircraft in flight.

[291] *See* Convention on Damage Caused by Foreign Aircraft to Third Parties on the Surface, *opened for signature* Oct. 7, 1952, 310 U.N.T.S. 182 (entered into force Feb. 4, 1958) [hereinafter Rome Convention].

[292] Protocol to Amend the Convention on Damage Caused by Foreign Aircraft to Third Parties on the Surface Signed at Rome on 7 Oct., 1952, Sept. 23, 1978, ICAO Doc. 9257 (entered into force Jul.25, 2002) [hereinafter 1978 Montreal Protocol]. The 1978 Montreal Protocol significantly increased the Convention's per person and per accident liability caps, but did not enter into force for 24 years and has only garnered 12 ratifications.

liability. Indeed, the policy concerns that lay behind the treaties are almost identical to those that prompted creation of the Warsaw Convention system: limiting carrier liability in order not to impede industry development, while at the same time guaranteeing compensation to third parties who suffer damages. The failure of surface damage treaties (in comparison with Warsaw) suggests that they were less artfully crafted, that the international airline industry attributed much less importance to surface liability exposure than it had to limiting passenger liability, and that States were more reluctant as a matter of public policy to limit recovery for damages endured by unaware third parties as opposed to those suffered by passengers who have voluntarily assumed the risks of flying. Certainly, States may feel that they have an obligation to protect citizens living within their sovereign borders from the unassumed risks of air transport and that, moreover, they should be allowed to select the most appropriate liability regime for doing so. Unlike public regulatory systems governing, for example, commercial access rights or foreign investment, liability systems are typically imbued with a strong moral content. That moral dimension consists of a first-order duty not to injure and, where that duty is breached, a second-order duty to repair (the idea of "corrective justice"[293]). Other theories, ranging from civil court recourse to purely economic evaluations (what is the most efficient allocation of risk? which party is in the better position to bear the cost of any foreseeable harm?), have also intruded, resulting in a mixed schema of tort liability within and across borders. Some U.S. courts, influenced in part by statutory law, opted for a negligence-based system where liability for aircraft surface damage was determined by the defendant's degree of fault.[294] Other common law jurisdictions, such as Australia and the U.K., preferred strict liability where the defendant could escape responsibility only through an affirmative defense that attributed blame to the plaintiff.[295] But these are not the only liability frameworks that are available. In a fault-based system, a third-party victim of surface damage would carry the burden of proving that the airline was at fault: at the opposite extreme, a system of *absolute* liability would impose automatic responsibility

---

[293] See supra Part 7.2.

[294] Judicial interpretations of U.S. common law have shown both strict liability and negligence-based approaches. See, e.g., RESTATEMENT OF (SECOND) TORTS § 520A (1977); Margosian v. U.S. Airlines, Inc., 127 F. Supp. 464 (E.D.N.Y. 1955) (unnecessary for owner of property damaged by aircraft crash to prove negligence to recover damages for trespass under New York law). But see, e.g., Boyd v. White, 276 P.2d 92, 128 Cal. App. 2d 641 (1954) (aviation no longer considered an ultrahazardous activity, so negligence, rather than strict liability, standard applies).

[295] See Civil Aviation Act, 1949, 12 & 13 Geo. 6, c. 67, § 40 (Eng.); Damage by Aircraft Act, 1952 No. 46, § 2 (N.S.W.). Australia's current surface damage liability statute does not even include the contributory negligence affirmative defense. See Damage by Aircraft Act, 1999 § 10 (Austl.).

on an air carrier without recourse to any defense whatsoever. The moral and metaphysical, not to say economic, merits and demerits of these competing approaches to tort liability are the subject of a voluminous literature that we will not delve into here. Nevertheless, an initial awareness of the alternatives should be enough to alert any putative designer of uniform global rules for third-party surface liability that the task will not be easy. That proposition is as true today as it was when the Rome Convention of 1952 was being prepared. In any event, once the early attempts at a surface damage treaty proved less than fully successful and States established their own domestic liability regimes, the initial policy drivers behind a uniform treaty became even less persuasive. By the 1950s, the international aviation industry probably no longer needed this kind of protection. Moreover, unlike with the Warsaw Convention, States were not already bound to an international system that they would feel compelled to modify. Surface damage liability reemerged as a public policy issue in the aftermath of the 9/11 attacks, which prompted the creation of the most recent draft treaties.[296] Even so, as we will discuss, serious shortcomings in the treaties from 1952 onward have continued to block the emergence of an authentic global regime.

7.14.3. *The Rome Convention (1952)*

The 1952 Rome Convention was designed with the express purpose of rehabilitating the possibility of a uniform system for third-party surface liability that had met defeat through scant ratification of the original 1933 treaty. From the outset, however, "Rome *Redux*" faced serious obstacles, not the least being (as the previous section revealed) the divergence in liability regimes for surface damage already put in place under their national laws by potential signatories. Like its predecessor, the Rome Convention focuses on air carrier liability for damage that is external to the aircraft and inflicted on persons or property on the ground and that is caused by the aircraft itself or by any objects (including passengers) falling from the aircraft.[297] It is obviously distinct, therefore, from the instruments of the Warsaw System, which are principally concerned with damage inflicted on passengers or cargo on board the aircraft. For the Convention to apply, the damage must have occurred while the aircraft is "in flight," that is, from "the moment when power is applied for the purpose of actual take-off until the moment when the landing run ends."[298] Additionally,

---

[296] *See infra* Section 7.14.7.

[297] *See* Rome Convention, *supra* note 291, art. 1(1).

[298] *Id.* art. 1(2). *See supra* Chapter 5, Parts 5.7, 5.8, 5.9 (discussing equivalent definitions under the ICAO-backed aviation crimes treaties).

the Convention is limited in scope to damage caused in the territory of a contracting State by the aircraft of another contracting State.[299] Because of the cabotage rule, the Convention is effectively excluded from covering any domestic flights, although it is theoretically applicable to the domestic segment of a foreign-operated international flight that uses coterminalization rights.[300] Finally, the courts of the contracting State where the damage occurred are afforded exclusive jurisdiction, while claims are subject to a two-year statute of limitations.[301]

7.14.4. *The Rome Convention's Terms of Liability*

Where damage occurs while the aircraft is in flight, the operator of the aircraft is liable.[302] As to the amount of liability, the Rome Convention mimics the Warsaw Convention of 1929 in imposing a liability cap that insulates carriers from exorbitant liability risks that could compromise their ability to buy insurance and, in the event of a lawsuit, swiftly destroy their economic viability. Unlike Warsaw's "one size for all" caps, however, Rome inscribes a series of caps based on the weight of the aircraft. Following the 1978 Protocol to the Convention, the operator's liability is capped at 2.5 million Special Drawing Rights (SDRs), plus an additional 65 SDRs per kilogram if the aircraft weighs more than 30,000 kilograms.[303] Even so, death and personal injury recoveries have a relatively low 125,000 SDRs per person ceiling[304] – well below typical damages awards under most national liability regimes. The Rome Convention does allow these limits to be broken, however, in instances where the damage was caused by a deliberate act or omission by the aircraft's

---

[299] *See* Rome Convention, *supra* note 291, art. 23(1).

[300] In coterminalization, a foreign airline can serve further domestic airports after termination of an inbound international flight at the first domestic landing point, but (because of the cabotage rule) cannot pick up new passengers at that first landing point for flights to any additional domestic airports. *See supra* Chapter 3, note 43 and accompanying text.

[301] *See* Rome Convention, *supra* note 291, arts. 20–21.

[302] *See* Rome Convention, *supra* note 291, art. 2. The registered owner (e.g., the lessor) of the aircraft is presumed to be the operator unless it can "prove that some other person was the operator and, in so far as the legal proceedings permit, take appropriate measures to make that other person a party in the proceedings." *Id.* art. 2(3). Additionally, nothing in the Convention prevents an operator from having recourse against another party that may also be liable for damages. *See id.* art. 10. On the relevant legal and practical distinctions between owners and operators of aircraft, see *infra* Chapter 8, Part 8.5.

[303] *See* 1978 Montreal Protocol, *supra* note 292, art. 3(1)(d). For an explanation of SDRs, see *supra* note 58.

[304] *See* 1978 Montreal Protocol, *supra* note 292, art. 3(2).

operator or with an intent to cause damage.[305] Airlines accused of committing surface damage can, under Rome, avail themselves of several defenses to avoid some or all liability. In instances of armed conflict, public disturbance, or public appropriation of the aircraft, the air carrier can be exonerated from all liability.[306] Even aside from these extreme events, an airline can still be fully exonerated if it proves that the victim was solely at fault.[307] And even where the victim is only partially to blame, the liability exposure can still be scaled back under the doctrine of contributory negligence.[308]

7.14.5. *Rejection of the Rome Convention*

As we noted earlier, the prevalence of national liability regimes cast instant doubt on the capacity of a single treaty to synthesize these regimes and to organize a common system that would appeal to the majority of States. Of the 191 States that are party to the Chicago Convention, only 49 have subscribed to Rome.[309] More critically, some of the world's largest air transport markets, including the United States, the U.K., France, Germany, and India, either did not sign or did not ratify the treaty.[310] Others, including Australia and Nigeria, eventually denounced their ratifications.[311] At the time that the final Rome text was released for signatures, the major recalcitrant States probably believed that their domestic systems were fully able to address surface liability claims. Moreover, for many of these States it was probably unacceptable from a political and social welfare perspective that foreign airlines should be subject to a different liability regime. The differentiation imposed disparate financial burdens on domestic airlines (including those engaged in international services) vis-à-vis their foreign counterparts, which risked undermining the competitiveness of the domestic carriers in the international marketplace.[312] Further, limited liability for foreign carriers could prompt a lower level of care in other States' airspace than in States' own domestic territories.

---

[305] *See* Rome Convention, *supra* note 291, art. 12. The text of Article 12 makes clear that an intentional injurious act is necessary to avoid the liability caps in the Rome Convention. This clarity is in contrast to the debate over the meaning of the Warsaw Convention's "wilful misconduct" clause, which, until modified by The Hague Protocol, produced competing interpretations as to whether an intentional act or mere recklessness was necessary to lift Warsaw's liability caps. *See supra* Section 7.4.2.

[306] *See* Rome Convention, *supra* note 291, art. 5.

[307] *See id.* art. 6(1).

[308] *See id.* art. 6.

[309] *See* ICAO, Treaty Status, *supra* note 266.

[310] *See id.*

[311] *See id.*

[312] Strictly speaking, of course, that is also true of the Warsaw/Montreal liability system.

Finally, governments were no doubt fearful of the massive political backlash from a major surface event where a foreign carrier dodged the perceived full scope of its liability.

7.14.6. *The Montreal Protocol (1978)*

The 1978 Montreal Protocol went some way toward alleviating these concerns, primarily by raising the extremely low liability caps established in the original treaty.[313] But the revised scheme still trailed well behind the levels adopted by major airlines in order to secure insurance. Given that the Rome Convention was never widely ratified, it remains unclear what States hoped to accomplish by the amending Protocol. Arguably, States that were displeased by Rome's liability regime should have denounced the treaty and reset their domestic rules on exposure at a more politically appropriate level. The 1978 augmentation of liability caps certainly did not induce high-liability countries like the United States to join the Rome circle. Because of its disappointing history, therefore, ICAO has continued to revisit the status of the Rome System. In the aftermath of the September 11, 2001, terrorist attacks, the Organization asked its Legal Committee to accelerate plans to reengineer the entire regime in order finally to achieve that long-elusive international consensus.

7.14.7. *A New Rome Regime?*

A Special Group of the ICAO Legal Committee has spent the past decade in pursuit of a new surface liability treaty.[314] From the beginning, however, the Committee was forced to work around a set of directive principles that appeared more contradictory than cohesive. For example, the Special Group attempted to hold to a mandate of victim protection while ensuring also that the airline industry would not face undue burdens under a successor regime. As the history of Warsaw/Montreal seems to have demonstrated, only one of those goals could prevail at any one time. Now well past its infancy, the airline industry received little sympathy from the States that negotiated and ratified the Montreal Convention on passenger and cargo liability. It was apparently this attitude that also inspired the work product of the Special Group: but two new surface liability treaties introduced in 2009 – the Unlawful Interference Convention and the General Risks Convention – have received neither signature nor ratification from any significant air transport market.

[313] On the disappointing ratification history of the Protocol, see *supra* note 292.
[314] *See* Sean Gates & George LeLoudas, *From Rome to Montreal in 57 Years: Worth the Wait?*, 22 No. 3 AIR & SPACE LAW. 1 (2009).

7.14.8. *The Unlawful Interference Convention*

The first of the two new instruments, the Unlawful Interference Convention (UIC),[315] applies to damages to a third party in the territory of a contracting State caused by an aircraft in the course of an international flight that becomes the object of an unlawful interference by another party.[316] Like the Rome Convention, the UIC relies on a weight-based system and provides that aircraft weighing more than 500,000 kilograms can be liable for up to 700,000,000 SDRs ($1.29 billion).[317] That cap can be broken, however, if the damage caused is attributable to serious misconduct by the aircraft operator – such as engaging in intentional or reckless behavior with the knowledge that damage would probably result.[318] In order to relieve air carriers of some of the risks implicated by the new liability scheme, the treaty contemplates the establishment of an International Civil Aviation Compensation Fund collected from charges levied on passengers and cargo by signatory States.[319] The UIC also contemplates serving as the exclusive remedy for victims of the narrow type of liability claim that the treaty covers and excludes entities such as aircraft manufacturers, lessors, security personnel, and airport operators from all liability.[320] For the UIC to enter into effect, however, it must receive 35 ratifications from States representing at least 750 million departing passengers per annum.[321] Unsurprisingly, the UIC has received a chilly reception. Critics, including airlines, have been quick to note that "unlawful interference" with air carriers is typically the action of terrorists targeting either the home State of the aircraft or the country in which it is operating. As such, it is argued, States rather than airlines should compensate third parties harmed by terrorism. Moreover, the airlines argue that the UIC unduly burdens them financially by forcing them to carry additional insurance to protect against liability from a terrorist attack. Although the UIC does allow airlines to seek recourse from persons who committed, organized, or financed the unlawful interference that gave rise to liability,[322] it is virtually unimaginable that terrorist perpetrators would have the financial resources to indemnify damages

---

[315] The Convention on Compensation for Damage to Third Parties Resulting from Acts of Unlawful Interference Involving Aircraft, *opened for signature* May 2, 2009, ICAO Doc. 9920 [hereinafter UIC].

[316] The Convention does allow States to extend its scope of applicability to cover domestic flights also. *See id.* art. 2(2).

[317] *See* UIC, *supra* note 315, art. 4(1)(j).

[318] *See id.* art. 23(2).

[319] *See id.* art. 8.

[320] *See id.* arts. 27, 29.

[321] As of 2012, the UIC had only nine signatories. *See* ICAO, Treaty Status, *supra* note 266.

[322] *See* UIC, *supra* note 315, art. 24.

suffered by an airline. Even if they did, it would be improbable that the airlines, or even their home States, could enforce any civil judgment.

7.14.9. *State Resistance to the Unlawful Interference Convention*

Despite these defects, the promoters of the UIC continue to argue that it does more to protect airlines than States that impose strict liability for third-party surface damage.[323] They contend also that the treaty ensures that victims on the ground will receive adequate compensation even in the event of a terrorist act. Although these arguments might be attractive, it is not difficult to see why many States would prefer not to address them using an international treaty. Some States may believe that the material consequences of a terrorist attack must be borne by its populace like any adverse military strike: neither the State nor private commercial entities that are also victimized should bear responsibility for what is ultimately the act of a foreign (albeit perhaps "Stateless") aggressor. Other States may take the view that national sentiment coupled with financial realities at the time of the attack will better determine the course of compensatory action than an inflexible *ex ante* liability system. Finally, although airlines have indeed moved well past their "infancy," their financial position remains precarious. Fuel prices and substantial regulatory burdens have already placed the industry at continuing risk of ruin: adding further financial exposure to the mix can only worsen the problem. Given the position of airlines as critical elements of national infrastructure and economic systems, most countries are more inclined than not to shield their airlines from total destruction. In such contexts, a major terrorist catastrophe is more likely to induce a bailout rather than a day in court for air carriers.[324]

7.14.10. *The General Risks Convention*

The second treaty proposed by the Special Group of the ICAO Legal Committee, the General Risks Convention (GRC),[325] is intended to cover third-party surface damage liability claims that *do not* involve unlawful interference. In other words,

---

[323] *See* Gates & Leloudas, *supra* note 314, at 6–7.

[324] This is essentially how the United States responded to the 9/11 terrorist attacks. Within two weeks of the tragedy, Congress passed the Air Transportation Safety and System Stabilization Act compensating airlines for the losses the industry had suffered as a result of the attacks, reimbursing carriers for the resulting insurance increases, creating a government fund to compensate victims, and capping carriers' liability at their amount of liability coverage. *See* Air Transportation Safety and System Stabilization Act, Pub. L. No. 107–42, 115 Stat. 230 (2001).

[325] The Convention on Compensation for Damage Caused by Aircraft to Third Parties, ICAO Doc. 9919, *opened for signature* May 2, 2009 [hereinafter GRC].

it serves as the effective replacement for the original Rome Convention. Sharing many of the features of the 1999 Montreal Convention addressing passenger and cargo liability, the GRC also establishes a weight-based system of strict liability for third-party surface damage.[326] The plaintiff is free, however, to plead damages above the weight-based strict liability measure, subject only to an airline's defenses that the damage was not due to its negligence or wrongful acts or omissions or that the damage was due solely to the negligence or other wrongful act of another party.[327] Like the UIC, the GRC also requires thirty-five ratifications before it enters into force, although it does not specify that the thirty-five ratifiers must represent any preset numeric share of the international air transport market.[328] Few States have been persuaded by the GRC's willingness to blend the governing principles of the passenger/cargo liability regime with that of the surface liability system. Most major aviation markets, as we have seen, have already developed a strong suite of domestic legal remedies for surface liability and therefore remain unpersuaded that a new treaty is desirable or necessary. Still, nothing prevents those States that find virtue in the terms of the treaty from seeking to rally thirty-four like-minded partners, or even unilaterally incorporating its provisions into their domestic legal systems. Indeed, it is unclear why multilateral acceptance is critical to this project. The best argument offered thus far is that a uniform system of liability will put airlines in a better position to predict the appropriate insurance cover. Even so, where public pressure is sufficiently strong, even ratifying States may be compelled to denounce the agreement or demand revisions to the treaty's terms of liability. The result could well be piecemeal ratification accompanied by international acrimony.

7.14.11. *Outlook for Ratification of the New Surface Damage Liability Conventions*

Despite the recent completion of the UIC and GRC, the outlook for an international surface damage treaty remains uncertain. The GRC only has eleven

---

[326] The operator's total liability is capped depending on the weight of the aircraft. Ten different weight classes are specified, ranging from a cap of 750,000 SDRs for aircraft 500,000 kilograms or less to a cap of 700 million SDRs for aircraft weighing more than 500,000 kilograms. *See id.* art. 4. As with the Warsaw/Montreal system, the operator is strictly liable for damages where causation is proven. Unlike Warsaw/Montreal, however, the GRC provides greater textual clarity regarding the types of damages compensable, including bodily injury as well as mental injury that is "caused by a recognizable psychiatric illness resulting either from bodily injury or from direct exposure to the likelihood of imminent death or bodily injury." Damage to property and environmental damage are also compensable, but punitive or noncompensatory damages are not available. *See id.* art. 3.

[327] *See id.* art. 4(3).

[328] *See id.* art. 23.

signatories out of the required thirty-five contracting parties, and major aviation markets, such as the EU Member States, do not appear interested.[329] The GRC has proven most appealing to developing States that lack adequate domestic liability regimes, and continued development of the aviation industry in those markets is probably necessary for the GRC to succeed where the two Rome Conventions failed. The UIC's prospects for meeting the ratification requirements are more interesting, although also more challenging. In the wake of the 9/11 attacks, major aviation States called for a solution to the necessity for publicly funded enhancement of insurance coverage that resulted from those attacks. The process initiated at that moment led to the creation of both treaties, with the UIC specifically intended to cover damage caused by terrorist acts. Because the UIC most directly responds to the events that motivated this law-making process, it would follow that the treaty would stand a strong chance of entering into force (and that the GRC's prospects would correspondingly suffer because the primary concerns of major aviation powers are addressed by the other treaty). As more time has passed, however, the shared urgency that followed the 9/11 attacks has eroded, and States appear less inclined to overlook areas of the treaty with which they disagree. Moreover, the compensation fund and other measures contemplated in the UIC may not prove sufficient to address another event of similar magnitude to 9/11, and the very ability of the UIC to serve its basic purpose has been called into question. Additionally, the requirement that the ratifying parties represent a minimum number of passengers makes it virtually impossible for the UIC to take effect without ratification by at least one State representing a major aviation market. As noted earlier, none of the major aviation powers has signed the treaty. Thus, as of now, it appears that unification of the private transnational law governing surface damage from aircraft is little closer to being a reality than it has been for the past eighty years.

---

[329] *See* Gates & Leloudas, *supra* note 314, at 6.

8

The International Law Regime for Aircraft Financing and Aircraft Nationality

8.1. INTRODUCTION

8.1.1. *Distinction Between Equity and Debt*

Chapter 4 on investment and alliances considered the airline business model from the perspective of equity: how airlines attract and hold risk capital in their voting stock.[1] Equity, however, is not typically a secured or preferred investment as against an airline's creditors.[2] It is junior to the debt that an airline takes on from banks, financiers, and other investors. This chapter moves to the debt side of the business equation, examining the principles of public international law and private transnational law that affect how airlines typically pay for their most glamorous but also their most expensive capital asset, the large commercial passenger or cargo

---

[1] "Risk capital" is a more specific term here than, say, "investment capital," which certainly includes equity but which will also include debt. What does equity cost an airline? Unlike debt, equity typically only costs the payment of a dividend to the shareholders, and even that is at the discretion of the management. Dividends, it must be said, are rarely paid in the airline industry, and shareholders in airlines look more to stock price increases than dividends. A doubling of the stock price makes a mere 4–5% dividend interest irrelevant. On the other hand, raising funds through equity issues (i.e., more stock) may dilute the ownership of the company as held by the existing stockholders, who must therefore be offered a discount to the current share price in order to convince them to put in new money. If an airline is in good shape, the discount need not be large, but a troubled carrier may have to slash 40–50% off its share price in that situation. If equity financing is unavailable, then airlines must borrow from capital markets or other sources. Borrowing, of course, means paying interest.

[2] Once the creditors are paid, the shareholders (as owners of the residual value of the corporation) will share any remaining assets, which may produce a profit or loss for them depending on the circumstances. Applicable local law (Delaware law, EU law, etc.) will determine whether "preferred" shareholders have a relationship with a corporation that is akin to that of a creditor, while still ranking behind the "senior" secured debt as discussed in this chapter.

aircraft.[3] Today, asset-based financing, where a financier lends money based on the security of the aircraft as collateral,[4] and lease-based aircraft financing[5] constitute international businesses: transactions are inherently complex and cross national boundaries and legal systems.

8.1.2. *Private Aircraft Financing and International Aviation Law*

In this chapter, therefore, we explore what international aviation law has to say about these quintessentially private law issues of ownership of and security interests in aircraft. Certainly, the private rights of contracting parties, but especially of contracting parties who are negotiating across borders, have long been of concern to the policymakers who develop international aviation law.[6]

---

[3] This chapter does not specifically address the financing of private corporate aircraft (which may include large jets, even the Airbus A380), although the same or similar financial instruments usually apply.

[4] "The essence of secured financing is that the risk of loss to the creditor in the event of default by its debtor is reduced by access to the value of collateral." Roy Goode, Herbert Kronke, Ewan McKendrick, & Jeffrey Wool, Transnational Commercial Law: International Instruments and Commentary 468 (2d ed. 2012) [hereinafter Goode et al., Transnational Commercial Law]. Secured transactions, to the extent that they protect the creditor against rights asserted by third parties, "permit the granting of credit to borrowers unable or unwilling to finance solely on terms reflecting their commercial capacity to repay." *Id.* Any home mortgage borrower would recognize that principle.

[5] Again, we should not be too rigid in our classifications: in a sense all transactions, including leases, that have an aircraft at the root of the financing transaction are asset based. Indeed, the lessor in a lease transaction will probably have arranged its own acquisition of the leased aircraft (from a financier such as a bank) using some form of asset-backed financing. Also, as we will see, the finance (or "capital") lease can be characterized as just as much an asset-based loan as a mortgage.

[6] *See generally* Roy Goode, Official Commentary on the Convention on International Interests in Mobile Equipment and Protocol Thereto on Matters Specific to Aircraft Equipment 180 (Unidroit rev. ed. 2008) [hereinafter Goode, Commentary]. Almost from its foundation in 1926, an international expert drafting group called the *Comité International d'Experts Juridiques Aérien* (CITEJA) was at work on two international property law conventions, one concerning mortgages and other rights in aircraft and the other primarily on the recording and registration of those rights in title registries. *See Editorial, Convention on International Recognition of Rights in Aircraft: Early Ratification Desirable*, 16 J. Air L. & Com. 61 (1949). The Chicago Conference in 1944 (*see supra* Chapter 2, Part 2.1) recommended early adoption of a treaty dealing with the transfer of title to aircraft, and the Preamble to the Geneva Convention of 1948 (*see infra* note 87), which deals with international recognition of rights in aircraft, refers explicitly to that precedent. The 1948 Convention, which is dealt with later in this chapter (*see infra* Part 8.7), was spurred by the U.S. aviation industry in which private finance was already a principal feature. That Convention, as will be discussed, was primarily only a "choice of law" treaty – in part because the dominant paradigm outside the United States remained that of State financing of aircraft for publicly owned flag carriers.

Nevertheless, the treaties on which we have focused in the preceding chapters have little if anything to say on that subject. The Chicago Convention is a public law instrument that primarily promotes safe and orderly flight operations,[7] liability treaties like the Warsaw and Montreal conventions are concerned with the rights of third parties (passengers and shippers), and bilateral air services treaties give no formal legal standing to the airlines that derive traffic and other rights from them.[8] Recent treaty making has corrected some of the deficit in coverage, but there is still no *comprehensive* system of transnational substantive property law that governs the full spectrum of purchasing and financing of aircraft. On the other hand, several important rules and principles have emerged in international treaties that shape how aircraft investments are facilitated, and particularly how secured investments are accorded priority, and also how States meet their responsibility to ensure the constant presence of a State of registration to monitor safety compliance by aircraft operators. Those are the rules and principles that we will examine in this chapter.

8.1.3. *Government Aid for Aircraft Manufacturing and Financing*

The final part of the chapter switches back to public law and policy issues, examining how governments use subsidization to support both aircraft manufacturing (e.g., through tax relief) and financing (e.g., through the export credit system). We will explore various international mechanisms that have been created to restrain subsidy levels in each of those sectors, and reflect on the critical role that public aid continues to play in the production and sale of hugely expensive large civil aircraft.

---

[7] *See* Convention on International Civil Aviation pmbl., *opened for signature* Dec. 7, 1944, 61 Stat. 1180, 15 U.N.T.S. 295 (entered into force Apr. 7, 1947) [hereinafter Chicago Convention].

[8] There is one other early treaty dealing with aircraft rights that should be briefly mentioned here. The Convention for the Unification of Certain Rules Relating to the Precautionary Attachment of Aircraft, *opened for signature* May 29, 1933, 192 L.N.T.S. 289, is known as the "Rome Convention." The Convention attempted to place strong restraints on the (private) precautionary arrest of aircraft. Arrest is prohibited if the aircraft is used for governmental purposes or in a regular line of public transport or if the aircraft is ready to start on a journey. One exception to the applicability of the Convention, however, is the insolvency of the operator. The Convention was intended to benefit airlines that desired to maintain uninterrupted service at a time when a small number of carriers was serving a limited number of routes. Rome found favor with only a handful of (mainly) civil law countries, and was never ratified by the United States. Under Article XXIV of the later Aircraft Protocol to the 2001 Cape Town Convention, *see infra* Part 8.9, unless a contracting State has declared to the contrary, the Cape Town Convention supersedes the Rome Convention for all contracting States to the later instrument.

8.2. A QUICK LOOK AT INTERNATIONAL AIRCRAFT FINANCING

8.2.1. *Introduction*

All air carriers must plan for fleet purchases and renewal and that process will continue. Before looking at the relevant international law instruments, the reader may find it useful to have a conceptual overview of the sources for and also some of the animating ideas of financing in the aircraft acquisition market. Especially germane in this context are the words of Sir Roy Goode, the common law world's preeminent exponent of the law of commercial transactions. In Sir Roy's view, the theoretical framework of a subject and its fundamental concepts will endure even though its detailed rules, no matter how sophisticated, may change.[9] Our overview is constructed with that observation in mind.

8.2.2. *Aircraft Financing and the (Airline) Nationality Rule*

At the outset, it is worth mentioning that the airline nationality rule, which so pervasively inhibits cross-border equity investments including mergers and acquisitions, does *not* apply to aircraft finance transactions. In 2011, for example, the Japanese investment banking group Sumitomo Mitsui purchased the aircraft finance unit of the Royal Bank of Scotland.[10] But British Airways (BA) and other non-Japanese carriers are nonetheless free to borrow capital from Sumitomo to finance the purchase of new aircraft. If Sumitomo, however, were to take an equity stake in BA's ownership – for example, as security for a loan – U.K. regulators might scrutinize whether Sumitomo was leveraging a large debt placement to exercise *de facto* operational control over the British flag carrier. That consideration aside, however, if Sumitomo is not a shareholder of BA, then the legal impediments associated with the nationality rule will not arise.[11]

8.2.3. *Aircraft Financing and the (Aircraft) Nationality Rule*

As we will discuss in more detail below, there is another dimension to the issue of "nationality" in addition to the airline nationality rule and its effect on transborder airline ownership. The Chicago Convention requires that each

---

[9] ROY GOODE, COMMERCIAL LAW xxvi (2d ed. 1995).

[10] *See* Harry Suhartono & Tim Hepher, *Asia Plugs European Aircraft Lending Gap*, REUTERS, Feb. 17, 2012, http://www.reuters.com/article/2012/02/17/us-airshow-financing-idUSTRE81G0FU 20120217.

[11] For a more complete discussion of the nationality rule, see *supra* Chapter 3, Section 3.1.2.

aircraft have a single nationality. The intention behind that rule is to ensure that *some* State holds responsibility for the safety compliance of every aircraft on its national register. The two concepts (airline and aircraft nationality) are not conceptually linked in the Convention (in fact, the Convention itself makes no reference at all to airline nationality[12]), and we will consider some of the implications of that conceptual misalignment.

8.2.4. *Macroeconomic Climate for Aircraft Financing*

A critical variable in the choice of financing vehicles is investor confidence. Deals will get done if investors feel confident in an airline's economic prospects. Airlines are regularly able to obtain financing: even in the most challenging economic climate, leasing options are available (as discussed further below). Sometimes the manufacturer itself will participate in financing risks alongside the airline and the financier.[13] According to Boeing, banks and leasing companies will fund the bulk of an estimated $4 trillion worth of new aircraft that airlines, financing companies, and leasing companies are expected to buy over the next twenty years.[14] As has been observed, there are no airplanes parked on the tarmac in Seattle (Boeing) or Toulouse (Airbus) for want of financing.[15]

---

[12] The nationality rule on airline ownership makes appearances only in the subsidiary Two Freedoms and Five Freedoms agreements. *See supra* Chapter 3, Section 3.4.2.

[13] *See generally* DONALD H. BUNKER, 1 INTERNATIONAL AIRCRAFT FINANCING 344 (2005) (explaining that manufacturers may become "junior" lenders to an airline, make direct investments in the shares of an airline, or become involved in leasing aircraft to an airline). As Bunker points out, however, manufacturers' support of the financial risk of their purchasers is a market-driven factor that manufacturers will prefer to avoid but that is currently the result of intense competition for market share in a challenging environment. *See id.* Recently, American Airlines, although in bankruptcy, was able to benefit from approximately $13 billion of committed financing from The Boeing Corporation through lease transactions that will help maximize balance sheet flexibility and reduce risk. The financing fully covers the first 230 deliveries. *Source*: Andrew Lobbenberg, airline analyst, European Airline Equity Research, HSBC.

[14] *See* Suhartono & Hepher, *supra* note 10.

[15] The global alliance system (*see supra* Chapter 4) has encouraged airline members to integrate or collaborate on their aircraft purchasing activities. The Star Alliance sourcing committee, for example, coordinates on specifications and requirements with respect to different items that offer an opportunity for joint sourcing (e.g., onboard items, seats, jet fuel), and the Star Alliance organization executes a framework agreement that captures terms and conditions of general application and typically incorporates a volume-based principle that incentivizes the aggregation of purchase with the preferred vendor or supplier. From time to time, an airline member that enters into an agreement with a vendor or supplier may have the opportunity to include a "Star clause" that permits other alliance members to benefit from similar terms and conditions. *Source*: Star Alliance Services GmbH. *See also* BUNKER, *supra* note 13, at 130–31.

8.2.5. *Cash-Based Financing of Aircraft*

Arguably, the cheapest way to finance an aircraft purchase is by using cash.[16] Consistently profitable carriers like Southwest Airlines in the United States or Ryanair in Europe, or State-owned carriers, can afford to think in terms of all-cash transactions. Since the 9/11 tragedy, airlines all over the world have endeavored to hold an appreciable percentage of their assets in cash, 15–20% being a common benchmark.[17] Cash on the balance sheet acts as insurance against exogenous shocks like 9/11, when bank financing (such as an overdraft facility) can suddenly become more costly or even unavailable. Nevertheless, holding large cash deposits may not always be efficient from the point of view of aircraft financing. Depending on interest rate fluctuations, cash holdings could be earning a low interest rate while the airline continues to pay a high interest rate on other borrowings to buy aircraft.[18] Another option to generate cash is to use an equity flotation (i.e., issuing new shares) to raise money from existing and also from new shareholders. But most airlines simply do not contemplate cash transactions, no matter how the cash might be generated. For them, paying all at once for an aircraft would be simply unsustainable. Obtaining aircraft, therefore, becomes a question of taking on debt and of how best to structure that debt.[19]

8.2.6. *Sources of Debt Financing*

What kinds of debt financing are available? Although answering that question in detail could occupy a book by itself (and does), the principal sources can be quickly sketched. A first (but not often exercised) option is for the airline to

---

[16] We say "arguably" because there are very wealthy individuals and companies who do not want to pay cash for tax-related and other valid legal and practical reasons. Accordingly, they prefer secured lending using a variety of offshore aviation finance and lease transactions.

[17] When an airline drops below 15–20% in cash holdings, that generally indicates that it is struggling to make money. Airlines do not fail because of a lack of profitability, according to one senior investment analyst, but because "they lack cash." Astonishingly, a recent check of company reports revealed that easyJet carries 43% of its revenues in cash and Ryanair 81%. *Source*: Andrew Lobbenberg, airline analyst, European Airline Equity Research, HSBC.

[18] It may make sense, therefore, to "burn up" cash if an airline has it available, either to make larger deposits when buying or leasing aircraft or to amass a war chest that allows the airline some strategic options – it can pounce, for example, if the assets of a bankrupt or liquidated competitor come into play.

[19] Debt transactions, in any event, can be less expensive than equity flotations (e.g., issuing more stock) because of the usual tax deductibility of interest and the availability of tax shelters. *See supra* note 1 (commenting on the relative advantages of equity and debt). Of course, debt is best serviced when interest rates are competitive; airlines are especially vulnerable when economic conditions drive up interest rates.

issue unsecured corporate bonds. A bond is simply a corporate "IOU" to the purchaser of the bond and also requires the airline to pay interest to the purchaser over the lifetime of the bond.[20] After that, we enter the realm of "true" aircraft financing, where the debt is secured by the aircraft itself. The major forms of *secured* debt financing are bank debt or bond debt.[21] The repayment obligations will be secured by an instrument – a bank loan will require a mortgage, for example[22] – that gives the creditor a reversionary interest in the aircraft in the event of default. Leases are sometimes regarded

[20] Bonds are known in some jurisdictions (e.g., India) as "debentures." Unsecured bonds are more likely to be used to raise capital to reduce overall corporate debt (which in turn will include some aircraft outlays). Some carriers with poor credit ratings are compelled to issue bonds at high interest rates in order to attract investors. These are high-yield bonds that are considered below investment grade ("junk" bonds). Air Berlin, the third-largest low-cost carrier in Europe, refinanced existing debt in 2011 with an interest rate of 11.5% redeemable by investors in November 2014. The higher the interest rate, the weaker the issuing carrier. As a comparator, the average interest rate on corporate bonds tends to be in the 5% range. Interestingly, investor appetite for the Air Berlin bonds was strong: the order volume exceeded the issuing total of $100 million. *Source*: Andrew Lobbenberg, airline analyst, European Airline Equity Research, HSBC.

[21] Aircraft-backed bond issues are more common in the United States: in 2010, for example, Delta Air Lines used a purchase of 24 jet aircraft to collateralize a bond issue of $450 million. But these transactions are more likely to be used elsewhere in the future as banks cut back lending to conserve capital as required by new global rules. For a recent EU-based issue, for example, see Arno Schuetze & Andreas Kröner, *NordLB Sells First Aircraft Covered Bond in Germany*, REUTERS, July 10, 2012, http://in.reuters.com/article/2012/07/10/nordlb-aircraft-pfandbrief-idINL6E8IA8ZY20120710. Typically the bonds are issued through underwriters such as Goldman Sachs, which "place" the issue through private capital markets (comprising large corporate and institutional investors such as pension funds). Secured bonds do not usually trade on public stock exchanges, but rather on specialty bond exchanges. Bond collateral need not only consist of aircraft, however, although the proceeds may be used in part to finance aircraft, and bonds may occasionally be traded on the public stock exchanges. A recent aborted issuance by British Airways (BA) demonstrates both of these points. In 2012, International Airlines Group (the holding company for BA and Iberia) pulled plans for an innovative £250 million bond issue on the London Stock Exchange that would have used 31 takeoff and landing slots at London Heathrow as collateral. *See* News Release, International Airlines Group, Issue of Debt (Jul. 9, 2012), http://www.iagshares.com/phoenix.zhtml?c=240949&p=irol-rnsArticle_Print&ID=1712478&highlight. The scarcity value of BA's Heathrow slots (much greater than those of Lufthansa at Frankfurt or of Air France at Paris Charles De Gaulle) looked enticing to risk-takers. But almost concurrently with BA's announcement there was informed speculation that the U.K. Government might reverse its ban on a third runway at Heathrow. At a stroke, the future scarcity value of BA's slots was compromised and the flotation collapsed. U.S. bonds, on the other hand, have been more readily secured against slots and even airport gates and route rights.

[22] International law does not itself regulate the types of debt instruments that may be used in aircraft financing; while national laws must be consulted, the "basic" transactions through which national systems (but not *all* national systems) allow the creation of secured rights in aircraft include mortgages, pledges, charges, liens, and conditional sales. Most of these forms of transaction are covered elsewhere in this chapter.

as conceptually distinct from secured asset-based financing, but in fact that separation is only clear in the case of "operating" leases (whereby an airline "rents" aircraft for a period from a lessor[23]). In a "finance" or "capital" lease, where the airline agrees in advance to buy the aircraft at the expiration of the lease, arguably a secured debt relationship is created not by a mortgage but by the fact that the lender/lessor retains legal ownership until repayment is completed. Both types of lease are considered further below.

8.3. THE THIRD-PARTY EFFECTS OF SECURED FINANCING OF AIRCRAFT

8.3.1. *Distinction Between Proprietary and Contractual Rights*

It is critical to understand that the core concern of secured aircraft financing law and practice is with rights *in rem* and *erga omnes* rather than with contractual (*in personam*) rights that arise between buyers and sellers of aircraft. What does that string of Latin tags signify? Simply the following: if the acid test of a financial transaction is the successful assertion of a secured right against all third parties (*erga omnes*[24]) when the debtor goes bankrupt, it is easy to see that the creditor or lender needs to have a strong proprietary interest in the thing itself (the aircraft), that is, an *in rem*[25] claim, rather than just a personal claim (a claim *in personam*[26]) against the bankrupt debtor – a claim that may be completely useless.[27] The distinction between the "contractual effects" of a transaction and its "property effects" is well known.[28] How strong should the *in rem* claim be? Because aircraft have the capacity to land in multiple jurisdictions, and because local courts in those jurisdictions may seek to determine ownership and possessory rights in the aircraft, the creditor needs to be able to assert a proprietary claim across multiple jurisdictions. In a contest between the

---

[23] As noted earlier, the lessor itself may have obtained the aircraft through secured bank or bond financing. *See supra* note 5.

[24] Literally, "against all persons."

[25] Literally, "in the thing."

[26] Literally, "in the person."

[27] Most of the discussion in this chapter concerns the rights of secured parties (e.g., banks) in situations where a debtor, which often is the technical "owner" of an aircraft, defaults on repayments of its loan. Most legal systems recognize that the debtor is indeed the "owner," and that a bank is a mortgagee or pledgee whose rights (e.g., of repossession or resale) are not triggered until default: in the meantime, the bank is not the owner and cannot sell the aircraft whenever it wants, or lease it to a third party, or otherwise dispose of it. Mortgages in some legal systems (e.g., England) do regard the lender bank as the owner even before default.

[28] Blue Sky One Ltd. & Or's v. Mahan Air & Ano'r [2010] EWHC 631 (Comm.), 2010 WL 902909 (Mar. 25, 2010), at 27 [hereinafter *Blue Sky*].

creditor and the local insolvency administrator and other foreign claimants against the bankrupt debtor's estate and assets, can the creditor prevail? Different national laws recognize different types of proprietary interests (some States, for example, do not recognize the concept of a mortgage in aircraft[29]), adding to the complexity of enforcing rights – and to the risk that a right might simply not be enforceable. The dangers for creditors are vividly presented in a case from the English High Court that is discussed in the following sections.

8.3.2. Blue Sky *Case (1): Factual Background*

The now notorious decision in *Blue Sky v. Mahan Air (Blue Sky)*[30] illustrates exactly how challenging the diversity of national laws and the lack of a comprehensive international system of recognition of rights can be to the transborder enforceability of security interests in aircraft. The judgment, in international aviation finance lawyer Patrick Honnebier's estimation, "affirms that due to the absence of adequate national and international regimes many mortgages are ineffective when the aircraft are operated in other [S]tates."[31] In 2010, the English High Court considered the validity of certain mortgages created under English law in a number of Boeing 747–422 widebodies. The owners of the aircraft, who were also the lessors of the planes, acquired them using so-called Special Purpose Vehicles[32] established under English law. The aircraft were leased to an Armenian lessee but chartered and operated by an Iranian corporation, Mahan Air. The planes held the nationality of several States: for present purposes, however, the two significant aircraft were, respectively, English and Armenian. On December 21, 2006, the owners mortgaged the two aircraft to a U.S. financier (PK Airfinance), using mortgages that were purportedly valid under English law. At the time that the mortgages were created, one of the planes was allegedly in Iran (although that fact was never established to the Court's satisfaction) and the other was parked at Schiphol Airport in the Netherlands. After the lessee defaulted, PK Airfinance commenced proceedings in England to repossess the two aircraft. Mahan Air in

---

[29] *See supra* note 22.

[30] *See supra* note 28.

[31] B. Patrick Honnebier, *The English Blue Sky Case – Topical International Aviation Finance Law Issues*, in 2011 IIASL Alumni Book (rectified ed. 2012) (*rectification available at* www. airandspacebooks.info, at 2 [hereinafter Honnebier, *Blue Sky Case*]).

[32] A Special Purpose Vehicle (SPV) is used in these circumstances to ensure that the underlying partners remain "bankruptcy remote" in the event of the SPV's bankruptcy. If an airline sets up an SPV to lease or securitize an aircraft and then defaults, the creditor can pursue only the aircraft rather than the carrier's other assets.

turn stated that it was operating the aircraft under a lease, had no knowledge of any mortgages, and that in any event it disputed the validity of the two mortgages.

8.3.3. Blue Sky *Case (2)*: Renvoi *Doctrine*

Looking at the foregoing facts, it is apparent that the *Blue Sky* case potentially had significant connections to the laws of four legal systems (England, Armenia, Iran, and the Netherlands), each of which has different substantive property laws and different rules for the protection of security interests in property. The English High Court had to decide, when four different legal systems might potentially apply, which national law would determine the validity of the mortgages. To do so, the Court would have to apply English "choice of law" rules (also known as "conflict of laws" rules) to select the most appropriate foreign legal system to determine title to movable property (here, the two aircraft). Those rules sometimes involve an exercise in "judicial mental gymnastics" known as the *renvoi* doctrine,[33] the idea that picking a foreign legal system also involves applying that system's own choice of law rules. If those rules in turn select another State's legal system, then *that* legal system will govern the dispute (unless the selected legal system once again includes its choice of law rules, sometimes causing unpredictable consequences[34]). In *Blue Sky*, therefore, determination of the validity of the mortgage might depend on the substantive domestic property laws of a foreign State; but if the Court followed the *renvoi* doctrine to select a foreign State's choice of law rules rather than solely that State's domestic property law, then another State's laws could apply, including those of England.

8.3.4. Blue Sky *Case (3)*: *Distinction Between* Lex Registrii *and* Lex Situs

The English High Court held that, for the aircraft with English nationality, either English law as the *lex registrii* (law of the State of aircraft nationality – registration – on the date of the mortgage) or Dutch law as the *lex situs* (law of the State of location – *situs* – of the movable property on the date of the mortgage) could apply. For the aircraft with Armenian nationality, the

---

[33] *Blue Sky, supra* note 28, at 49 (citation omitted).

[34] Thus, a potentially ludicrous consequence of a true *renvoi* arrangement is that each foreign legal system that is selected, if its own conflict of laws or choice of law rules are also included in the selection, may then bounce the selection to yet another foreign legal system and *its* choice of law rules, thereby risking a chain of continuous instances of *renvoi* that conceptually resembles the back-and-forth of a ping-pong or tennis game.

alternatives were Armenian law as the *lex registrii* or Iranian law as the *lex situs*. Under English and Armenian law, both mortgages were valid and effective and transferred legal title to the aircraft to PK Airfinance as mortgagee. For both mortgages, however, the Court chose to apply only the *lex situs*, the place of the location of the movable property (the aircraft), and decided not to use the *renvoi* doctrine to include in that law the local choice of law rules that might have directed the Court back to English law or to the law of another State. The effects of the Court's preference for this strict view of the *lex situs* were remarkably different with respect to each of the two mortgages. For the aircraft with Armenian nationality, in the absence of proof that the plane was in Iran (the alleged *lex situs*) on the date of the execution of the mortgage, and in the absence of satisfactory proof of any other law, the Court applied English law to the validity of that mortgage. As to the aircraft with English nationality, the Court rejected PK Airfinance's argument that Dutch law (as the *lex situs* on the date of the execution of the mortgage) would uphold the validity of the mortgage because, under Dutch choice of law rules, a Dutch court would apply English law as the *lex registrii*. The Court refused to select Dutch choice of law rules and to trigger a possible *renvoi* to English law: under Dutch domestic property law, which the Court considered to be the sole applicable part of the *lex situs*, the mortgage was invalid. Astoundingly, the Court's interpretation meant that PK Airfinance lost the entire value of the aircraft under the mortgage ($43.1 million).

8.3.5. Blue Sky Case (4): Court Applied No Special Rule for Aircraft

The reader will note that in neither circumstance (i.e., whether the aircraft had English or Armenian nationality) did the High Court apply the law of the State of nationality of the aircraft, also known as the *lex registrii*, to adjudicate the "consensual" property rights in each aircraft.[35] Counsel for PK Airfinance argued that a Dutch court, applying its own choice of law rules, might have selected the *lex registrii* (English law) rather than simply applying Dutch law.[36] The *lex registrii*, English law, would have saved the mortgage. The U.S. financier's lawyers, evidently stunned by the Court's intention to select

---

[35] As will be explained later, "consensual rights" in property are those that arise between the parties to a proprietary transaction such as a mortgage. "Nonconsensual rights" are those that are imposed by operation of State law (including, for example, tax or repair liens). Arguably, the *lex situs* should govern nonconsensual property rights. *See* Honnebier, *Blue Sky Case*, *supra* note 31, at 6. *See infra* Section 8.10.5.

[36] According to Honnebier, a Dutch law expert, the appropriate rule in the Netherlands is in fact the *lex situs*, thereby making choice of law irrelevant. *See* Honnebier, *Blue Sky Case*, *supra* note 31, at 3.

only Dutch domestic law, also argued that the *lex registrii* should in any case be preferred as the English choice of law rule to the *lex situs*: "the special position of aircraft as a means of transport which move regularly from *situs* to *situs* means that the applicable law is the law of the place where the aircraft is registered: the *lex registrii*."[37] The Court's response gave no succor to the plaintiff: "Even recognizing that … the aim of our private international law [i.e., choice of law rules] is to identify the most appropriate law and appropriate principles to meet particular situations, this is a bold submission. It finds virtually no support in English cases or commentaries."[38]

8.3.6. Blue Sky *Case (5):* Lex Registrii *as the Better Rule*

Of course, the outcome in *Blue Sky* is pernicious for creditors. It suggests that property rights in aircraft that are validly created in one State may be invalid in another State where the asset is actually being operated. The *lex registrii*, the State of nationality of the aircraft, has a legitimate, predictable, and ultimately persuasive connection with the asset (the aircraft). Accordingly, the *lex registrii* should supply the governing law applied by the court. To insist on the *lex situs* is to offer scant predictability and security when an aircraft is so inherently, shall we say, peripatetic.[39]

8.3.7. Blue Sky *Case (6): An International Law Solution*

One of the most effective ways to overcome these collisions (and anomalies) of national choice of law principles would be to *internationalize* the recognition and enforcement of security interests.[40] That way, no matter where the dispute arose, the creditor would have an interest – an *international* uniform

---

[37] *Blue Sky, supra* note 28, at 48. PK Airfinance had to make this argument because the Court had earlier indicated that English choice of law with respect to determining title to movable property does not generally include reference to the choice of law (or "private international law") rules of the applicable foreign legal system. *See id.* at 47.

[38] *Id.* Honnebier cites some persuasive sources that call the Court's view into question. *See* Honnebier, *Blue Sky Case, supra* note 31, at 4.

[39] The English High Court believed that "practical considerations of control over movables" required regulation and protection by the State in which they are situated (*Blue Sky, supra* note 28, at 49); but the facts of *Blue Sky* itself demonstrate how transient such an affiliation can be for aircraft.

[40] Indeed, the High Court in *Blue Sky* indicated as much: "If the perceived advantage [of allowing reference to another State's choice of law rules in determining disputes as to title to aircraft] is to endeavo[u]r that like cases be decided alike wherever they are litigated … that task is *one for international conventions* and [will not be accomplished] by changing common law rules." *Blue Sky, supra* note 28, at 48 [emphasis added].

substantive property interest – that each State agreed to prioritize and protect against competing third-party claims. That is precisely how the problem is addressed by the Cape Town Convention, which is discussed extensively later in this chapter.[41] Although that Convention has yet to achieve universal participation, it already includes many States with significant aircraft finance activity. Had the Convention applied in the *Blue Sky* case, the rights of the mortgagee (PK Airfinance) would have been recognized, prioritized, and secured irrespective of the location of the aircraft or indeed of the identity of its State of nationality.[42]

8.4. AN OVERVIEW OF INTERNATIONAL AIRCRAFT LEASING

8.4.1. *Introduction*

An argument can be made that leases are not authentically part of the topic of aircraft financing, especially secured aircraft financing, because there are few third-party effects of the leasing arrangement and the lease is almost entirely a matter of the contractual terms negotiated and agreed upon between the lessor and the lessee. Although it is true that contractual terms predominate, it is also true that the lessor in both finance and operating leases will probably have obtained the leased aircraft through some form of secured financing transaction, and that, as noted earlier, the lessor's retention of full ownership in finance leases can be equated to the mortgagee's reversionary interest in the mortgaged aircraft.[43] More importantly, however, it would give the reader an incomplete impression of the current aircraft acquisition market if we were to exclude leases because they do not fit with the "asset-based" models of typical debt financing.

---

[41] *See* Convention on International Interests in Mobile Equipment, *opened for signature* Nov. 16, 2001, 2307 U.N.T.S. 285 (entered into force Apr. 1, 2004) [hereinafter Cape Town Convention]. The best way to access the full authorized text of the Convention, accompanied by an excellent set of documentary resources, is via the Unidroit website at http://www.unidroit.org/english/conventions/mobile-equipment/main.htm.

[42] As a result of *Blue Sky*, according to Patrick Honnebier, many aircraft being operated in and from other States (e.g., Russia) are flown across England or parked temporarily at English airports. While they are above or in English territory, the existing English mortgages are "restructured." Some English lawyers have suggested, Honnebier reports, that this practice would establish the "proper" legal *situs*. Naturally, this solution is costly. *See generally* B. Patrick Honnebier, *The English 'Blue Sky' Case Shows that the Aircraft Finance Practice Needs Uniform International Substantive Mortgage Laws as the Existing Conflict Rules Fail; The Cape Town Convention Solves the Existing Problems while the Geneva Convention is Obsolete*, 2011–2 TIJDSCHRIFT VERVOER & RECHT 70, at § 7.

[43] *See supra* Section 8.2.6.

8.4.2. *Growing Significance of Leases*

Airlines increasingly are relying on leases to obtain aircraft, especially as a hedge against unpredictable economic cycles.[44] After all, it is challenging and potentially very expensive to forecast fleet needs a decade or fifteen years into the future. Airlines, therefore, may have a core fleet of owned aircraft as strategic long-term assets, with the balance resting on flexible lease arrangements that they can allow to expire or sometimes extend depending on their market position. Leases allow a carrier to continue building its fleet even when access to more traditional financing sources (such as loans) becomes tighter. The lease offers great flexibility in devising its terms[45] and allows the carrier to accumulate cash reserves to weather economic downturns (including fluctuating fuel costs). Leasing also allows rapid access to new, more fuel-efficient aircraft. It is estimated that by 2015 the global leasing aircraft portfolio will swell to almost $280 billion.[46]

8.4.3. *Aircraft Leasing Companies*

The financial strength of lessor companies is critical to the success of aircraft leasing. GE Capital Aviation Services, for example, is an arm of the multinational conglomerate General Electric. In early 2011, Air Lease Corporation, a recent start-up by veterans of other major leasing companies, raised more than $900 million in an initial public offering of shares on the New York Stock Exchange. Strong leasing companies can borrow money more cheaply than economically challenged airlines like Air Berlin[47] and can charge their air carrier clients a nice premium on lease contracts.

---

[44] Although more than a quarter of the world's commercial air fleet is leased, aircraft leasing "as a discrete field of jurisprudence" has only "taken off" on a major scale since the 1980s. *See* DONAL PATRICK HANLEY, AIRCRAFT OPERATING LEASING: A LEGAL AND PRACTICAL ANALYSIS IN THE CONTEXT OF PUBLIC AND PRIVATE INTERNATIONAL AVIATION LAW 1 (2012).

[45] Thus, according to Bunker, lease payments may be varied according to the revenue expectations of lessees (e.g., using "balloon payments" at the front or back end of a lease). *See* BUNKER, *supra* note 13, at 251.

[46] *See* Press Release, Global Indus. Analysts, Inc., Global Aircraft Leasing Market to Reach $279 Billion by 2015 (Feb. 19, 2009), http://www.prweb.com/releases/2009/02/prweb2021874.htm. Bilateral air transport agreements (*see supra* Chapter 3) may have provisions on leasing. ICAO's Air Transport Committee found dozens of agreements with such provisions: three had clauses dealing with safety aspects requiring the aviation authority of the operator's State to be satisfied that airworthiness standards will be maintained. See ICAO, Study on Aircraft Leasing, Air Transport Committee, 156th Session of the Council, ICAO, 1999, 4.3–4.14. States may be concerned about leases between airlines, especially to ensure that no additional traffic rights are granted.

[47] *See supra* note 20 (noting high interest rate on Air Berlin bond issue).

8.4.4. *Distinction Between Finance (or Capital) Leases and Operating Leases*

The Cape Town Convention,[48] which is considered in more detail below, defines a lease generally as "an agreement by which one person (the lessor) grants a right to possession or control of an object (with or without an option to purchase) to another person (the lessee) in return for a rental or other payment."[49] As implied by the reference to the presence or absence of an "option to purchase," aircraft leases can be classified as "finance" (or "capital") leases or as "operating" leases. Although finance leases resemble operating leases in that the lessee is the operator of the aircraft, at the termination of the finance lease (unlike in the operating lease), there is an option to buy or even automatic ownership on the part of the lessee.[50] As we have noted above, a finance lease is therefore akin factually to a long-term mortgage loan, where the lessee as "mortgagor" eventually becomes the legal owner of the aircraft.[51] The finance lease contract will usually include a final price for the equipment that represents the unamortized balance of the initial purchase price rather than (in cases where operating leases allow the lessee to buy the aircraft after the lease) the fair market value.[52] Unlike in a mortgage, however, in a finance lease the lessor does retain title to the asset during the lease term and therefore holds a much stronger security interest than the typical mortgagee. (But one must always be aware of national law variations: the typical mortgage

---

[48] *See supra* note 41; *see also infra* Part 8.8.

[49] Cape Town Convention, *supra* note 41, art. 1(q); *see also infra* Part 8.9. As Hanley points out, the lessor is never the operator or maintenance provider. The lessor in an ordinary lease transaction "buys the aircraft, typically new from the manufacturer, leasing it first to one airline, then to another, until it sells the aircraft or the aircraft reaches the end of its economic life." HANLEY, *supra* note 44, at 47.

[50] Hanley points out that operating leases are becoming a widely used vehicle even though in their origin they were seen as "the preserve of carriers with a lower credit quality." HANLEY, *supra* note 44, at 17. The lessor, as owner of the aircraft, may have to place the aircraft with different lessees at several times in its operating life, and therefore must not only be concerned about the ongoing physical condition of the aircraft but must also project demand for aircraft at least on a medium-term (5- to 10-year) basis. Markets in aircraft coming off operating leases remain good in emerging markets with strong economic growth like China, India, and Latin America.

[51] Indeed, typically the lessor will set the rental under a capital lease as if the transaction were a straightforward loan. *See* HANLEY, *supra* note 44, at 15.

[52] Thus, Article 2(c) of the Unidroit Convention on International Financial Leasing (available on the Unidroit website at http://www.unidroit.org/english/conventions/1988leasing/1988leasing-e.htm), emphasizes that the primary characteristic of a capital lease is that "the rentals payable under the leasing agreement are calculated so as to take into account in particular the amortization of the whole or a substantial part of the cost of the equipment."

under English law, for example, requires title to be transferred to the lending bank for security purposes and title only reverts to the airline when the debt is paid in full.)

8.5. THE INTERNATIONAL LAW REGIME FOR AIRCRAFT NATIONALITY

8.5.1. *Basic Principles of Aircraft Nationality*

As we considered briefly above and also earlier in Chapter 2, an aircraft is unlike other forms of movable property in that it has a *nationality*. Article 17 of the Chicago Convention attributes a nationality to every aircraft, that is, the nationality of its State of registry.[53] The aircraft will be registered in one State, and only in one State, but may be operated in another State.[54] Article 18 allows for registration to be changed from the register of one State to that of another State, but aircraft can only be registered in *one* State at any time.[55] Article 19 devolves the form and requirements for registration to local State law.[56] Under Article 31 of the Chicago Convention, every aircraft of a contracting State engaged in international navigation must have a Certificate of Airworthiness issued (or rendered valid) by its State of registry.[57] Pursuant to Articles 12, 30, 31, and 32(a) of the Chicago Convention, a State has an obligation to ensure that the aircraft and operators on its registry are operating safely and prepared

---

[53] *See* Chicago Convention, *supra* note 7, art. 17.

[54] Thus, as can be seen in Annex 6 to the Chicago Convention (on Operation of Aircraft), *see infra* note 57, ICAO makes a distinction (which the original Convention itself does not make) between the State of Registry (or registration) and the State of Operation of the aircraft. *But see infra* Part 8.5.4, discussing Article 83*bis* of the Chicago Convention.

[55] *See* Chicago Convention, *supra* note 7, art. 18.

[56] *See id.* art. 19. The Paris Convention, which preceded Chicago, made registration of an aircraft dependent on the owners being nationals of the registry State. *See* Convention Relating to the Regulation of Aerial Navigation, art. 7, *opened for signature* Oct. 13, 1919, 11 L.N.T.S. 173, *reprinted in* 30–1 ANNALS AIR & SPACE L. 5 (2005).

[57] Article 29 of the Chicago Convention requires that the Certificate of Airworthiness (along with the Certificate of Registration) must be carried on board the aircraft. *See* Chicago Convention, *supra* note 7, art. 29. Annex 6 of the Convention provides in addition for an Air Operator's Certificate issued by the State of the Operator (although that State should also consider various approvals and acceptances by the State of registration), certifying professional ability and competence to ensure safe operations. See Annex 6 to the Convention on International Civil Aviation, *Operation of Aircraft: Part I, International Commercial Air Transport – Aeroplanes* (9th ed. July 2010), http://www.icao.int/safety/ism/ICAO%20Annexes/Annex%206.pdf. (Note that the air transport license is concerned with the overall economic and financial viability of the proposed enterprise, while the air operator's certificate – typically issued by the same authority – is concerned with safety.)

to comply with the regulatory standards of all contracting States.[58] Each State has complete flexibility, however, in deciding what requirements it will impose for registration, including whether it will insist (as the United States has) that only its own citizens may own aircraft placed on its register[59] and whether (where ownership and operation are separated, as in a lease) the registering entity should be the owner or the operator or both.

8.5.2. *Distinction Between Aircraft Nationality and Airline Nationality*

It has to be said, however, that the design of the Chicago Convention fails conceptually to link *aircraft* nationality with *airline* nationality, the latter being (as discussed earlier) a post-Convention development that requires an airline to be owned and controlled by the State (or citizens of that State) which designates it to serve international routes.[60] Surprisingly, and in part because the Convention drafters were never able to clarify their understanding of airline nationality, it is not evident from the Convention that an airline needs to register *any* of its aircraft on its home registry. Thus, it is legally acceptable *under the Convention* for British Airways (BA), for instance, to own aircraft that operate out of the U.K. but are registered in Australia or Japan or, conversely, to operate aircraft that are registered in the U.K. but are owned by Australian or Japanese lessors.[61] If the purpose of registration is to ensure that a State is held responsible for the operational safety of aircraft on its registry, in other words, that there is a "genuine link" between the State and its registered aircraft, it would be hard to argue that such a link would exist between Japan or Australia and the aircraft operated by the U.K. carrier on routes (for example) to the United States and

---

[58] *See* Chicago Convention, *supra* note 7, arts. 12 ("rules of the air"), 30 ("aircraft radio equipment"), 31 ("certificates of airworthiness"), and 32(a) ("licenses of personnel"). *See* ICAO, Guidance on the Implementation of Article 83*bis* of the Convention on International Civil Aviation, Cir. 295 LE/2 (Feb. 2003), at 4 [hereinafter ICAO, *Guidance*]. According to ICAO, these provisions represent the primary functions and duties of the State of registry. *See id.* at 5.

[59] The United States, for example, only allows aircraft to be registered in the United States by U.S. citizens, but also allows certain trust arrangements that obviate the strictness of that rule. *See generally* Dean N. Gerber, *Aircraft Financing*, ch. 7, *in* EQUIPMENT LEASING – LEVERAGED LEASING (Ian Shrank & Arnold G. Gough eds., 5th ed. 2012), at 7–9 *et seq.* [hereinafter Gerber, *Aircraft Financing*]. Determinations of ownership by the Federal Aviation Administration (FAA) in an application for registration of an aircraft are conclusive for FAA purposes only and do not prove title in any non-FAA proceedings. *See id.* at 7–9.

[60] Thus, bilateral air services treaties exchange traffic rights on the basis of designated *airlines* rather than designated *aircraft*. On the issue of airline nationality, see *supra* Chapter 3, Section 3.1.2.

[61] This situation, in fact, is quite common in international leasing transactions.

Mexico.[62] The reason why Japan or Australia will not serve as a "registry of choice" in that context (after all, an aircraft lessor might prefer how Japanese or Australian law treats lessor rights[63]) is that State licensing authorities, unlike the Chicago Convention, *do* typically impose a link between their national airlines and the aircraft they operate. Within the European Union (EU), for example, the BA "Japan or Australia registry" hypothetical is impossible because EU Regulation 1008/2008 requires that "aircraft used by a [Union] air carrier shall be registered, at the option of the Member State whose competent authority issues the operating license, in its national register or within the [Union]."[64] Indeed, as an ICAO senior legal officer Jiefang Huang points out, "the practice of ICAO has been not to focus on foreign ownership of aircraft but, rather, on the safety oversight capabilities of the States which register foreign-owned aircraft."[65]

---

[62] We are assuming, of course, that a "genuine link" to a State of nationality would by itself ensure safety oversight: but safety enforcement standards vary considerably among States. The fact that these variations exist highlights the inadequacy of the system of aircraft nationality established under the Chicago Convention.

[63] The choice is made for various legitimate legal, tax, and practical reasons and is not connected to safety considerations. In fact, the lessor and its financing bank will dictate that the aircraft must be maintained in accordance with applicable national and international laws and will not want their expensive asset to deteriorate because of poor maintenance.

[64] *See* Common Rules for the Operation of Air Services in the [Union], Council Regulation 1008/2008, 2008 O.J. (L 293) 3, art. 12(1). The Regulation also instructs all EU civil aviation authorities to accept on their national registers aircraft owned by nationals of other Member States and transfers from registers of other Member States. *See id.* art. 12(2). Hanley mentions "aircraft registries of convenience" like Aruba, Bermuda, Ireland, and Mauritius, *see* HANLEY, *supra* note 44, at 81, but exactly what this means is unclear if States typically require their national airlines to register their aircraft in the home registry. Certain lessors would no doubt prefer to have their aircraft registered in States that offer better protection for their interests, but the extent to which they can do so will be determined by whether the State of the lessee will allow such "external" registration in a State that is not the State of the operator. If the nationality rule for aircraft disappeared, of course, then the registration system would have to be reconceptualized accordingly to prevent "convenience" registers from springing up.

[65] *See* Jiefang Huang, Aviation Safety and ICAO 37 (Mar. 18, 2009) (unpublished Ph.D. thesis, Leiden University). These conceptual inadequacies of nationality and national registers are found elsewhere in international aviation law. For example, under Article 2(3) of the 1952 Rome Convention on Damage Caused by Foreign Aircraft to Third Parties on the Surface, considered *supra* Chapter 7, Section 7.14.3, where the operator is liable for damage caused to persons on the ground from an aircraft in flight, "the registered owner" of the aircraft is presumed to be the operator, and it is up to the registered owner, if it can, to prove that some other party was the operator and therefore liable. Not all States register "owners," however, because Article 17 of the Chicago Convention refers to registration not of *owners*, but of *aircraft*. Thus, the concept of "registered owner" in the Rome Convention has no direct analog in the

8.5.3. *Aircraft Nationality and Aircraft Financing*

Although the concept of aircraft nationality and registration is conceptually incomplete, it cannot be ignored in aircraft financing transactions. If a defaulting operator has registered an aircraft in the State of its principal operations, a financier or legal owner (e.g., a lessor) will want to secure not only repossession of the vessel but also *deregistration* if it has no other connection with that State and wishes to move the aircraft elsewhere and to register in a new State that requires the operator to maintain a registration in that State.[66] Some lessors and financiers have even required that the aircraft be registered outside the principal State of operation from the beginning.[67] Given that the State of registration is responsible for the safe operation of the aircraft, registration in States other than the State of operation (or of primary operation) is arguably not ideal:[68] registration implies safety oversight, even if the aircraft is not operated in the registering State,[69] and States that take their Convention obligations seriously do require their registered aircraft to be serviced and maintained under local supervision and by locally licensed technicians.[70] If aircraft are operating in a foreign State, the State of registration may legitimately instruct operators to return the vessel to the State of registry for safety and maintenance procedures or to use approved foreign repair stations as an alternative.

Chicago Convention. The 2009 Convention on Compensation for Damage to Third Parties Resulting from Acts of Unlawful Interference Involving Aircraft, *see supra* Chapter 7, Section 7.14.8, proposes under its Article 27 to impose liability only on the part of the operator with no right of recourse against the lessor or secured financier or even manufacturer. Note international aviation law expert Jeffrey Wool's comment that this is the first time a major international aviation law instrument "recognizes and advances the integrated industry principle": prior instruments equated airlines with the industry as a whole, so that the liability of stakeholders other than airlines was beyond the scope of such treaties and left to applicable (presumably local) law. Jeffrey Wool, *Lessor, Financier, and Manufacturer Perspectives on the New Third-Party Liability Convention*, 22 No. 4 AIR & SPACE LAW. 1 (2010). The same principle of operator liability appears in the related 2009 Convention on Compensation for Damage Caused by Aircraft to Third Parties (*see supra* Chapter 7, Section 7.14.10). Neither Convention is yet in force.

[66] Article 19 of the Chicago Convention implies that deregistration, as an aspect of registration, will occur under the laws and regulations of the State of registration. *See* Chicago Convention, *supra* note 7, art. 19.

[67] Thus, as considered above, an aircraft leased by BA would be registered in the lessor's home state of Australia or Japan.

[68] But, as we noted *supra* notes 54, 57, ICAO explicitly contemplates that distinction.

[69] As ICAO has emphasized in its guidance document on implementing Article 83*bis*: *see* ICAO, *Guidance*, *supra* note 58, at 4.

[70] *But see supra* note 62 (mentioning the wide variations in State enforcement practices).

8.5.4. *Article 83bis of the Chicago Convention*

Separating the States of registration and operation appears to be neither cost-efficient nor convenient.[71] Moreover, before 1997, the Chicago Convention did not have provisions governing aircraft registered in one State being operated in another State, even though situations of that kind were a regular occurrence under international leasing contracts. Article 83*bis* of the Convention,[72] which entered into force on June 20, 1997, provides for a temporary transfer of oversight authority by the State of nationality (registration) of the aircraft to the State where the aircraft operator (e.g., a lessee[73]) has its principal place of business or permanent residence.[74] An Article 83*bis* transfer will be of particular salience to a lessor where the lessee is based in a State that registers only the operator but where the lessor eventually wants to move the aircraft to another State after a default and needs to bypass the process of deregistration and to avoid issues created by a lessee's refusal to deregister.[75] Lessors will always prefer Article 83*bis* because it allows the lessor to register the aircraft in its own name in a favorable jurisdiction and of course thereafter to deregister upon a default by the lessee.[76] Because Article 83*bis* is usually put into effect through advance inter-State agreements that relate to specific aircraft and responsibilities, it is typically used only in long-term leasing situations rather than, for example, for short-term "wet leases."[77]

---

[71] *See supra* note 68 and accompanying text.

[72] The little word *bis*, fused with the number of the Article, is a treaty convention that means "again" or "twice" (it is of Latin origin).

[73] Note that Article 83*bis* does not distinguish between capital and operating leases.

[74] Before that, ICAO allowed case-by-case transfers under various annexes. According to ICAO, the operator's principal place of business is "a matter of appreciating the facts of each case and comparing the importance of the various places of business of an operator so that the main one can be selected." ICAO, *Guidance, supra* note 58, at 2.

[75] If there is no Article 83*bis* delegation, the registering State may simply refuse to allow aircraft on its register to be leased to operators in other States in order to ensure that it is in compliance with its obligations under the Chicago Convention. *See generally* ICAO, *Guidance, supra* note 58, at 5.

[76] Even if deregistration does not procure immediate repossession, Hanley points out that the ability of the lessor to deregister "means that, at least, it can prevent the lessee from operating the aircraft while not paying for it under the lease." HANLEY, *supra* note 44, at 171.

[77] A "wet lease" means an aircraft including crew. On the formalities for a transfer of duties and functions under Article 83*bis* (including an obligation in certain circumstances to register transfer agreements with ICAO), see ICAO, *Guidelines, supra* note 58, at 5. Hanley proposes improving the use and efficiency of Article 83*bis* by creating a multilateral agreement that would allow States which are satisfied with each other's safety standards to agree in advance that any aircraft on the register of any contracting State could be the object of a delegation of any or all of the responsibilities of the State of registration to the contracting State of the operator. *See* HANLEY, *supra* note 44, at 171. But note that not all States have regulations that would allow even bilateral arrangements to occur. Hanley, an experienced international aircraft leasing

8.6. AN OVERVIEW OF INTERNATIONAL AVIATION LAW
AND AIRCRAFT FINANCING

8.6.1. *Protection of Security Interests*

As Sir Roy Goode points out, no binding international legal instrument sets forth *general* rules for the creation, perfection, enforcement, and priority of security interests and other proprietary rights.[78] Nevertheless, in aircraft financing, whether asset based or lease based, it is critical that the security holder or owner be able to regain physical and legal control over the equipment (e.g., in order to sell or re-lease the secured aircraft). The key achievement (indeed, arguably the *only* achievement) of public international aviation law in the field of aircraft finance has been to recognize that ownership and operation of an aircraft can be divided between different parties and to improve the protection of the aircraft as a security for finance. Among other things, that protection includes ensuring transparency of competing claims against collateral (priority), ensuring quick enforcement of priority claims against the collateral in case of default by the debtor, and protection of the collateral in the event of bankruptcy or liquidation of the debtor.[79] The additional factor of priority among creditors based on recordation of their interests in national aircraft registries must also be considered.

8.6.2. *Problem of Aircraft Mobility*

It is obvious that taking a financial risk in a highly mobile asset like an aircraft is not like financing a fixed building.[80] In theory, the best protection for the creditor would be to register a security interest in every State to which the aircraft might fly, or indeed in every State that has "a runway long enough to accept an aircraft of the type subject to the mortgage"[81] – regardless of whether the aircraft might be expected to fly there. Although the latter is not economically feasible, nevertheless, as international aircraft leasing lawyer Donald

---

lawyer based in California, argues that the fact that Article 83*bis* is not widely availed of may be because the State of the aircraft operator "has no motivation to accept such responsibility" – even though it could not avoid such responsibility if the parties agree that the aircraft should be registered in the operator's State. *Id.* at 148.

[78] *See* GOODE ET AL., TRANSNATIONAL COMMERCIAL LAW, *supra* note 4, at 469, 476.

[79] Sir Roy Goode describes insolvency as the "acid test" of secured credit. *Id.* at 469.

[80] *See* BUNKER, *supra* note 13, at 388. As Bunker points out, the user's desire for as much operational freedom as possible is in conflict with the financier's expectation that the asset is maintained in the best possible condition and is readily accessible in the event of default or bankruptcy. *See id.*

[81] *Id.* at 77.

Bunker notes, limiting the registered security interest to jurisdictions where the borrower is based or the destinations on its scheduled routes will diminish the attractiveness of the security. Even if the creditor could get very broad registrations of its security interest, there is always the risk that the creditor might be trumped by higher-priority interests or even by a deliberate attempt to evade a State where the security is registered with a high priority, for example, by an emergency landing in a jurisdiction where no registration has been filed.[82] Moreover, the local regulations on registering security interests, as well as the complexities of local registration, vary so widely that a consistent pattern of defending the security interest will be virtually impossible to achieve.[83]

8.6.3. *Problem of Nonuniform Legal Concepts*

Further, interests can be differently characterized in different jurisdictions, so that universalizing terms like mortgages, finance leases, and other title retention devices may not make sense.[84] Moreover, as we will see, some interests that arise by operation of law, notably so-called nonconsensual interests such as repair or tax liens, can also defeat secured creditor interests and, as Sir Roy points out, may even be secret.[85] And the effectiveness of "registering" a security interest is generally (and obviously) limited to the duration of the aircraft's physical sojourn in the State of registration.[86] Bunker insists that the best security is actual ownership of the asset and that leasing, for example, allows the lender to hold the benefits of ownership while the borrower actually operates the asset.[87] But again, the value of ownership is a value that can only be expressed in a local court jurisdiction and will depend on how the local laws view the status of the owner in the context of specific proceedings. In the U.K., for example, ownership of an aircraft, even if perfected under local

---

[82] *See id.* at 78.

[83] Some States (such as the U.K.) actually have specific registers for security interests in aircraft, but most do not. The central aircraft registry maintained by the FAA in the United States is intended primarily to register the U.S. nationality of aircraft, but also allows registration of some security interests. *See* Gerber, *Aircraft Financing, supra* note 59, at 7–7. Since 2010, certificates of registration (or reregistration) granted by the FAA expire every three years. *See* 14 C.F.R. § 47.40(b) (2010).

[84] Not every State recognizes that a mortgage in an aircraft is even legally possible, for example. *See supra* note 22.

[85] *See* GOODE ET AL., TRANSNATIONAL COMMERCIAL LAW, *supra* note 4, at 469; on non-consensual interests, see *infra* Section 8.10.5.

[86] Here we are talking about registration of a security interest, not registration of an aircraft on a national registry.

[87] *See* BUNKER, *supra* note 13, at 78, 390.

security registration rules, will never prevail against an action by the Civil Aviation Authority to collect airport navigation charges and which may result in forfeiture of the aircraft.[88]

8.6.4. *Introduction to the Geneva and Cape Town Conventions*

As a practical matter, the focus of public international aviation law on instruments to better protect transnational security interests and leases has been open to debate: some aviation finance lawyers would regard protection of the security as lower in importance to the potential investor than the strength of an airline's management team, its profit history, and the soundness of its business plan. Nevertheless, cases like *Blue Sky* throw sharply into relief that protection of creditor security interests can create serious legal and practical difficulties in international aircraft financing. Two significant instruments that address those difficulties (the Geneva Convention of 1948 and the Cape Town Convention of 2001) therefore must now be considered. Although fifty years apart in their entry into force, they stand at the intersection of what is typically understood as the basic template of international law – treaties among sovereign States that regulate relations between those States – and the domain of transnational commercial law, which also involves treaties but which touches the private dealings of private citizens.

8.7. THE GENEVA CONVENTION (1948)

8.7.1. *Introduction*

Before the Cape Town Convention, the only treaty in force that sought to provide transnational assurance to holders of security interests in aircraft was the Convention on the International Recognition of Rights in Aircraft, known as the Geneva Convention, which was signed in Geneva, Switzerland, on June 19, 1948.[89] Before Geneva, aircraft finance law was predominantly domestic

---

[88] Thus, the U.K. Civil Aviation Authority (CAA) acts on behalf of Eurocontrol, the European organization for air traffic management safety, to collect route charges that fund Eurocontrol's operations. The CAA has authority under the U.K. Civil Aviation (Navigation Services Charges) Regulations 2000 to seize an aircraft without court order when the lessor or the operator is in default on the charges, and (with a court order) to sell the aircraft to recoup the charges. If the operator is in possession when the aircraft is detained, the aircraft may be sold to satisfy the entire fleet debt of the operator to Eurocontrol. *See* Gerber, *Aircraft Financing, supra* note 59, at 7–108; *see also infra* note 167.

[89] *See* Convention on the International Recognition of Rights in Aircraft, Jun. 19, 1948, 4 U.S.T. 1830, 310 U.N.T.S. 151 [hereinafter Geneva Convention].

law, much of it inadequately developed to meet the needs of a capital-intensive industry and its financiers. The Convention requires each State party to recognize only four types of consensual property rights in aircraft "constituted" and "regularly recorded" in a public record in accordance with the law of the State of nationality of the aircraft (the *lex registrii*) when the rights were made effective.[90] If the security interest (or lease) is valid and recordable under that national law, it will have a claim to be recognized in other contracting States of the Convention. Thus, rather than creating a genuine system of enforceable *international* rights for holders of a security in aircraft (a project that would only be attempted much later in Cape Town), the Geneva Convention merely attempted cross-border recognition of other States' aircraft mortgages and leases.

8.7.2. *The Geneva Convention as a Choice of Law Treaty*

The Geneva Convention offers no unified notion of a security right that is eligible for international protection. Unable to resolve systemic differences in the recognition, prioritization, and enforcement of security interests between common law and civil law traditions, Geneva served instead as a choice of law treaty that aims only to deflect automatic application of the law of the location of the aircraft (the *lex situs*[91]) and imposes a "choice of law" on the court of the *situs*. For that reason, the Geneva Convention has been described correctly as a "conflict of laws treaty that deals with recognition of rights, not a substantive treaty that creates rights."[92] Geneva's recognized rights are therefore only those established by and recognized in the State of nationality of the aircraft. In the event that an arrest or detention of an aircraft for nonpayment on a financial security interest or leasing agreement takes place outside of that aircraft's State of registry *and* that non-home jurisdiction is a party to the Geneva Convention, that jurisdiction must apply the laws of the aircraft's State of nationality. This framework was intended to clarify which domestically estab-lished rights in aircraft would be respected in the event that an aircraft were seized outside its home State for financial reasons. Only in a limited number

---

[90] *Id.* art. 1. The list of rights to be recognized is compendiously drafted, including "rights of property in aircraft," "rights to acquire aircraft by purchase coupled with possession of the aircraft," "rights to the possession of aircraft under leases of six months or more," and "mort-gages, liens and similar rights in aircraft that are contractually created as security for payment of its indebtedness."

[91] Also known as the *lex rei sitae* (literally, "law of the place of the thing"). *See also supra* Section 8.3.4.

[92] HANLEY, *supra* note 44, at 93, 144–145 (citing Honnebier); *see also* on the same point, GOODE ET AL., TRANSNATIONAL COMMERCIAL LAW, *supra* note 4, at 474.

of circumstances, such as insolvency, could the arresting jurisdiction dispense with applying the law of the *lex regstrii*.[93]

8.7.3. *Two Unsettled Choice of Law Issues*

Although the Geneva Convention appears clear on its face, confusion quickly arose over two issues of selecting the applicable law when a dispute arose between a creditor and a debtor. First, did the *lex registrii* rule refer only to the *internal substantive law* of the State of registration or to the choice of law rules of that State also (including the possible application of *renvoi*)?[94] If the latter, the law of the State of aircraft nationality is not necessarily the substantive property law of that State. Instead, the *lex registrii* becomes the law that *selects* the governing property law.[95] Second, commentators disagreed as to which State law would apply in financing and leasing transactions when an aircraft's State of nationality recognized another kind of "choice of law" – where the parties to the transaction themselves agree in their contract to apply the law of a third country. For instance, the parties to an aircraft transaction financed in Canada by a U.S. entity might choose to adopt New York's well-developed commercial rules as the governing law of the transaction.[96] Strict constructionists of the Geneva Convention, however, argued that this was an excessive genuflection to party autonomy and that Geneva was intended to allow only the law of the *lex registrii* to follow the aircraft;[97] privately selected choice of law rules that imported the law of a third country – even if that country, too, were a party to Geneva – were not perceived to be part of the bargain. Because the Geneva Convention, like the Warsaw and Montreal liability treaties discussed in Chapter 7, depends on national courts for its construction, it is

---

[93] *See infra* Section 8.7.4.

[94] *See supra* Section 8.3.3 (explaining *renvoi*); *see also* B. Patrick Honnebier, *Clarifying the Alleged Issues Concerning the Financing of Aircraft Engines*, 56 ZEITSCHRIFT FÜR LUFT- UND WELTRAUMRECHT [Z.L.W.] 383 (2007) (arguing that the legislative history of the Geneva Convention supports an interpretation that the *lex registrii* includes its choice of law or conflict of laws rules).

[95] And here again a *renvoi* question could be presented if the *lex registrii* selects a third State's law and that third State would apply its own conflict of law rules to select, once again, the *lex registrii* as the applicable law of the transaction – and so forth! *See supra* note 34.

[96] Of course, the parties cannot predetermine how any court would ultimately decide the *in rem* issue of the validity of a secured transaction or other asserted proprietary right as against third parties: to that extent, the "choice of law" might only be for purposes of their own contractual relations and would have no effect on third parties. The Cape Town Convention, as we will see below, explicitly confines party choice of law agreements to contractual matters between the parties. *See infra* Section 8.13.2.

[97] Again, we note the unresolved question of whether that law of the *lex registrii* would include the local choice of law rules.

not surprising that neither of the foregoing questions was susceptible to a uniform answer or that both remain unsettled.

8.7.4. *Problem of Insolvency*

In addition to the foregoing procedural ambiguities, the Geneva Convention suffered from a more problematic shortcoming, namely, its open-ended determination of which State's law governs during an insolvency proceeding. Although Geneva, as noted, requires that the law of the *lex registrii* is normally applied, it also states that "the proceedings of a sale of an aircraft in execution [i.e., seized for sale as part of an insolvency proceeding to pay the aircraft owner's debt] shall be determined by the law of the contracting State where the sale takes place."[98] In other words, the Convention leaves open the possibility that the law of a State *other than* the State of aircraft nationality may be applied in insolvency proceedings, a provision that seems to sabotage Geneva's ostensible purpose of serving as a straightforward choice of law treaty instrument. What happens if the rights of the interest holders in the seized aircraft are subject to a different insolvency framework from that of the aircraft's State of nationality? Neither the text nor the drafting history of the Geneva Convention provides substantive clarity on that point.

8.7.5. *An Ill-Suited Instrument*

The Geneva Convention has a patchy record of enforcement, but in any event its lack of rules for speedy enforcement of remedies[99] or for dealing with insolvency makes it ill-suited to handle the demands of modern asset-based and lease-based financing. And, even if one wishes to make the measured argument that all private transnational law instruments succumb to inconsistent application within the borders of national legal cultures, that does not obviate the fact that the Geneva Convention appears to be a poorly drafted instrument. Too much leeway has been left for inconsistent interpretation and application, thereby injecting instability into the conduct of international aircraft financing. It was with these drawbacks firmly in mind that a consortium of States turned not to revising the Geneva Convention, but to scrapping it altogether in favor of a less ambiguous (albeit customizable) treaty

---

[98] Geneva Convention, *supra* note 89, art. VII(1).

[99] The only enforcement remedy in the Geneva Convention is judicially mandated sale. *See* Geneva Convention, *supra* note 89, arts. VI–VIII. Sir Roy Goode finds the mandatory presale notice periods in the Convention to be incompatible with the mobility of aircraft. *See* GOODE ET AL., TRANSNATIONAL COMMERCIAL LAW, *supra* note 4, at 475.

framework. It is largely superseded by the Cape Town Convention for Geneva signatories where the latter applies.[100]

8.8. THE CAPE TOWN CONVENTION (2001) (1): BACKGROUND AND OVERVIEW

8.8.1. *Context of the Cape Town Convention*

As should be apparent from the preceding content of this chapter, the tremendous expense of acquiring aircraft frames and engines has left airlines almost entirely dependent upon borrowing, financing, and leasing to procure those assets. Unfortunately, airlines also have a notorious reputation as unstable investments, with high incidences of bankruptcy and widespread borrowing from multiple creditors, all of whom may have competing claims to an airline's assets should it be unable to pay its debts. As we noted at the outset, further contributing to the problem is the mobility of an airline's primary assets, the very aircraft in which the airline granted security interests or with respect to which it took on debt as the means to obtaining them. Any creditor that lends to an airline in exchange for a security interest in aircraft is confronted with the reality that the creditor has virtually no control over where its collateral may be located should it need to execute upon its security interest. If the debtor airline defaults on its obligations to a creditor while the aircraft in question is in a foreign State, the creditor must hope that the State's domestic laws and courts will permit it to exercise its priority in a timely fashion. All of the foregoing contingencies serve to raise borrowing costs. Creditors are cautious in lending, and when they do lend, they seek to extract high interest rates and the most robustly framed security interests in exchange for financing.

8.8.2. *Unidroit, the Aviation Working Group, and the Convention/Protocol Solution*

In the late 1980s, the need to facilitate greater financing for high-value mobile equipment such as aircraft led Unidroit[101] to begin working on standardizing

[100] *See* Protocol to the Convention on International Interests in Mobile Equipment on Matters Specific to Aircraft Equipment, art. XXIII [hereinafter Aircraft Protocol]. As with the Convention itself, the ideal means to access the full authorized text of the Protocol, as well as excellent related documentary resources, is the Unidroit website at http://www.unidroit.org/english/conventions/mobile-equipment/main.htm.

[101] Unidroit is an independent, intergovernmental organization of State representatives, itself established by multilateral agreement, that is dedicated to the unification of international "private" (commercial) law. *See* http://www.unidroit.org/.

the differing national regulatory approaches to security interests in such equipment.[102] Unidroit formed the Aviation Working Group (AWG) in 1994 to assist in that effort.[103] Putting together an agreement that adequately covered aircraft, railway rolling stock, space objects, ships, and offshore oil rigs proved exceedingly difficult. In 1996, Boeing, frustrated by Unidroit's lack of progress, asked ICAO and the International Air Transport Association (IATA) to work with Unidroit to prioritize finding a solution for aircraft equipment alone.[104] That initiative led in turn to the idea of the "Convention plus Protocols" approach that became the signature feature of the Cape Town Convention. Under that approach, a broader agreement, *The Convention on International Interests in Mobile Equipment* (the Cape Town Convention),[105] would serve as an "umbrella" treaty providing a framework of international rules for protecting secured interests in a variety of mobile equipment. A separate protocol would be specific to each of the different categories of mobile equipment.[106]

8.8.3. *The Aircraft Protocol*

During the next four years, Unidroit focused on the Convention and appointed a new Aircraft Protocol Group (APG) to draft the protocol specific to aircraft.[107] The APG was assisted by the AWG, IATA, and ICAO. The *Protocol to the Convention on International Interests in Mobile Equipment on Matters Specific to Aircraft Equipment* (the Aircraft Protocol)[108] was the first to be completed and the only protocol that was ready when the Convention was signed on November 16, 2001. The Convention and protocols were uniquely structured so that the Convention did not go into force until at least one of the protocols had entered into force. The Aircraft Protocol required ratification by eight States

---

[102] *See* John Atwood, *The Status of the Mobile Equipment (Cape Town) Convention – Arrival of an International Registration System*, 39 UCC L.J. 637 (2006).

[103] *See* Mark J. Sundahl, *The "Cape Town Approach": A New Method of Making International Law*, 44 COLUM. J. TRANSNAT'L L. 339, 350–54 (2006).

[104] *See* Angie Boliver, *Square Pegs in a Round Hole? The Effects of the 2006 Cape Town Treaty Implementation and its Impact on Fractional Jet Ownership*, 72 J. AIR L. & COM. 529, 530 (2007).

[105] *See supra* note 41.

[106] The Unidroit website, *see supra* note 101, includes numerous memoranda and studies prepared by various committees (including groups examining the interaction between the Cape Town Convention and public international law, insolvency, and jurisdiction, and the reports of the Drafting Committee), as well as contributions from Airbus and Boeing, that preceded the eventual draft treaty.

[107] *See* Sundahl, *supra* note 103.

[108] *See supra* note 100.

to come into force. The Aircraft Protocol and Convention took effect on March 1, 2006, when the required eight nations (Ethiopia, Ireland, Malaysia, Nigeria, Oman, Panama, Pakistan, and the United States) ratified the Protocol.[109]

8.8.4. *A Single Instrument, but the Protocol Prevails over the Convention*

Although the protocols on railway rolling stock and space objects have now been completed and incorporated into the Cape Town *oeuvre*,[110] this book naturally restricts its discussion to the two documents implicating aviation, the Cape Town Convention and the Aircraft Protocol, which are intended to be read for legal purposes as a single instrument.[111] Unusually in public international law, however, the Protocol prevails over the Convention in the event of any inconsistency between the two documents.[112] While there is a combined text of the two instruments, it is not authoritative for use in formal legal documentation. Accordingly, in this chapter we cite separately to the Convention (which uses Arabic numbering) and the Protocol (which uses Roman numbering).

8.8.5. *Use of Declarations*

In addition to the unique two-instrument structure, the Cape Town Convention fits into a modern trend in international commercial treaties in expressly allowing States to make "declarations." This is particularly important because these treaties usually have significant overlaps with existing domestic law. Unless a State allows treaties to have automatic priority over local law,[113]

---

[109] *See* Cape Town Convention, *supra* note 41, art 49(1); Aircraft Protocol, *supra* note 100, art. XXVIII. The Convention itself only required three ratifications to enter into force, but even then its effectiveness was contingent (with reference to aircraft objects) on the coming into force of the Aircraft Protocol. The 1948 Geneva Convention only needed two States to ratify before coming into force. *See* Geneva Convention, *supra* note 89, art. XX(1). An updated count of ratifying States for the Cape Town Convention and Aircraft Protocol can be found at the Unidroit website mentioned *supra* in notes 41 and 100.

[110] They have not, however, yet entered into force.

[111] *See* Cape Town Convention, *supra* note 41, art. 6(1); *see also* Aircraft Protocol, *supra* note 100, art. II.

[112] *See* Cape Town Convention, *supra* note 41, art. 6(2). Although it is fairly typical for treaties to have amending protocols – examples include the U.N. Convention on the Rights of the Child, Sept. 2, 1990, 1577 U.N.T.S. 3, and the Convention on International Trade in Endangered Species of Wild Flora and Fauna, Mar. 3, 1973, 993 U.N.T.S. 243 – the Cape Town treaty is unique in that its protocols are controlling.

[113] For example, "monist" jurisdictions like the Netherlands and Belgium. *See* THE OXFORD GUIDE TO TREATIES 368 (Duncan B. Hollis ed., 2012) (explaining how the terms "monism" and "dualism" describe contrasting theoretical perspectives on the relationship between international and domestic law). *See also infra* Section 8.8.8.

the international texts may need to be incorporated into the national legal order and commercial culture.[114] Declarations can be framed to allow a State to "opt into" (i.e., apply[115]) or "opt out of" (i.e., disapply[116]) specific treaty provisions.[117] States may also use declarations to make what Sir Roy Goode calls "legally operative statements," for example, which domestic courts have jurisdiction or to which territorial unit a treaty applies.[118] The Cape Town Convention's use of declarations is quite aggressive. The Convention includes numerous provisions where contracting States are permitted or, in some cases, required to make a declaration as to whether to adopt a certain rule, or to provide added clarification regarding the effect of the rule within that contracting State's legal system.[119] This "tailored" approach remains unusual in the general law of treaties and, combined with the two-instrument approach, gives the Convention an uncommonly flexible, customizable structure. The purported purpose was to be able to attract as many countries as possible

[114] This statement generally describes the concept of "dualism." *See id.*

[115] The opt-in declarations mean that those provisions will not have effect *unless* a contracting State affirmatively declares that they will. *See, e.g.,* Article 39 of the Convention, considered *infra* in Section 8.10.5, which allows a State to designate certain types of liens (such as for unpaid taxes) that will be prioritized within that State as a matter of public policy. *See* Cape Town Convention, *supra* note 41, art. 39(1).

[116] The opt-out declarations mean that those provisions will have effect unless a contracting State declares otherwise. *See, e.g.,* Article 54(1), under which a State can declare that the default rule in that provision, allowing creditors to re-lease an aircraft that is in default, will not apply in that State. As a matter of public policy, some States are opposed to re-leasing. Out of respect for that policy concern, Article 54(1) allows those States not to make the re-leasing remedy available. *See* Cape Town Convention, *supra* note 41, art. 54.

[117] Declarations are generally characterized as unilateral statements by a contracting State clarifying the meaning or scope of a treaty provision in its application within that State. Reservations are described as unilateral statements excluding or modifying certain provisions from even having effect within the State making the reservation. *See* Vienna Convention on the Law of Treaties, arts. 19–23, 1155 U.N.T.S. 331 (1969), 8 I.L.M. 679 (1969). The Cape Town Convention refers to all unilateral determinations under the treaty using the rubric of "declarations," although there are some that work in much the same way as reservations by essentially precluding a treaty provision from having force in the declaring State. Nevertheless, they are "declarations" by virtue of the fact that the choice of opting out of the provisions is granted to the State within the text of the very provisions affected. In essence, the State, even if it decides that the provision does not apply, is only clarifying the meaning of that provision because the provision specifies that a State must determine whether it applies. Additionally, and importantly for the "stickiness" (compliance profile) of international law, *see* Chapter 1, note 58 and accompanying text, Article 56 of the Convention prohibits States from making any reservations or declarations outside the specified provisions. *See* Cape Town Convention, *supra* note 41, art. 56. The extensive opt-in, opt-out declaration system was designed to accommodate State public policy differences while limiting the universe of exceptions to the new uniform rules, thereby granting private actors the predictability and certainty that are the treaty's primary purpose.

[118] GOODE ET AL., TRANSNATIONAL COMMERCIAL LAW, *supra* note 4, at 3.

[119] *See supra* notes 115, 116.

without falling back on the kind of vague, meaning-deprived verbiage that is often necessary to get every State to agree. The impact of these many declarations will become apparent in our discussion of the Convention's provisions.

8.8.6. *Effect of Declarations on Party Autonomy and the Availability of Financing*

The declaration system, in combination with choice of law provisions that defer to party autonomy on selection of the applicable jurisdiction that will govern their contractual relations,[120] also affords private contracting parties greater control over which set of rules will ultimately apply to their contract. Thus, the parties can choose to have the contract governed by the jurisdiction where they see the declarations as most preferable.[121] A final important note relates to the level of *State* autonomy that declarations can actually provide given the exogenous economic context of the Convention. One of the most significant benefits of ratifying Cape Town is eligibility for discounted financing fees from export credit agencies such as the U.S. Export-Import Bank. Under the 2011 Sector Understanding for Export Credits on Civil Aircraft (2011 Understanding) of the Organization for Economic Cooperation and Development (OECD),[122] eligibility for discounts is made contingent upon a State adopting a specified set of declarations under the Convention. Thus, many "borrowing" States will only enjoy the full benefits of the treaty (or only be able to assure those benefits to their airlines) if they accept limits to their autonomy by adhering to a preferred list of declarations. Those States' adherence is secured by the lure of lower rates. Additionally, when the OECD revises the 2011 Understanding with changes to the preferred declarations, as it has done a number of times, it indirectly alters the law of secured interests in many States.

8.8.7. *Role of the Cape Town Convention in Aircraft Financing*

As with any worthwhile addition to the world's canon of international laws, the Cape Town Convention emerged as a solution to an identified problem: the prohibitively high cost of borrowing and financing for aircraft equipment, especially for operators from developing countries. Creditors were reluctant to lend the vast sums necessary to finance aircraft equipment, given the

---

[120] *See* Cape Town Convention, *supra* note 41, art. 42(1); *see also infra* Part 8.13.
[121] *See id.* Of course, this statement is made in the abstract: the parties may not have equal bargaining power, and hence equal control over selection of a governing law, in a particular transaction.
[122] *See infra* Part 8.15.

frequency of airline bankruptcies and the uncertain prospects of recovery for highly mobile collateral that could be located in any number of legal jurisdictions at the time of default.[123] The Convention's purpose with regard to aviation is fourfold: (1) to create an internationally recognized security interest in aircraft in all contracting States; (2) to offer the creditor various basic default remedies and possibilities for expedited relief in the event of default; (3) to create an electronic, international registry so that interests can be filed to notify potential subsequent creditors, and which is searchable by potential creditors; and (4) through all of the foregoing means to increase the availability and decrease the costs of financing for aircraft equipment by diminishing the risks to creditors. The Convention accomplishes these purposes by establishing a legal regime for secured interests that is modeled in part on the U.S. system of recordations in Article 9 of the Uniform Commercial Code, as well as an international registry where applicable interests can be recorded.

8.8.8. *Implementation of the Cape Town Convention in Domestic Law*

The Cape Town Convention rests on the idea that a treaty among sovereign States can also govern the conduct of individuals in their daily commerce. From an enforcement perspective, however, there is an inherent tension in that idea. The main objective of the Convention is to ensure that *the international security interest derives solely from the Convention and in no way depends on national law*. Nevertheless, although that is true in the most general sense, it is also the case that the contracting States have effectively agreed with one another that they will see to it that the international interest will itself become part of a ratifying State's domestic law, and will be effective in ordinary legal and insolvency proceedings provided for by that law. Accordingly, each ratifying State must make specific decisions about what means it will use to implant this new norm of international law into its domestic law of security interests. Domestic legal systems take a variety of approaches to integrating international law. Those approaches are usually classified along a scale ranging from pure monism (where a ratified treaty automatically is part of domestic law, as in the Netherlands) to strict dualism (where, as is usually the

---

[123] These industry attitudes were concisely expressed by participants in the 1999 First Joint Session of the relevant ICAO Sub-Committee and the Unidroit Committee of Governmental Experts to consider a draft of the new treaty. A banking representative explained that the aviation industry had evolved from a traditionally government-owned and heavily regulated industry to a privatized and deregulated industry, increasingly governed by an open skies policy. That trend had increased airline defaults, giving rise to the need for new legal regimes to protect creditors. For more details on the First Joint Session, *see* http://www.unidroit.org/english/documents/1999/contents.htm.

case in the U.K., a ratified treaty must be further incorporated into domestic legislation).[124] Many States fall between the two poles, with subtle distinctions in approach too numerous to include in this general overview. Each State will need to take the required steps for implementation, if any, before individuals will be able to enforce their rights under the Convention in national courts. The Convention could be passed in its entirety as domestic legislation, making its provisions superior to domestic securities law in the event of conflict, or could be textually and substantively integrated into domestic securities statutes. The former option places added transactional burdens on domestic actors to under-stand both legal systems and their interactive implications, but the latter places in jeopardy the benefits, primarily reduced borrowing costs, that national air-lines may derive from the export credit agencies.

8.8.9. *Importance of Remedies*

With a substantive law treaty such as Cape Town, therefore, enforcement is not merely a question of ensuring compliance from contracting States; the more pressing and common problem is how an individual creditor (or debtor) enforces its substantive rights under the treaty. That is why some of the Convention's most important and complicated provisions are those concern-ing remedies. Remedies for rights created through international agreement have not always been strong or certain enough to protect the rights in question. That has been a common and regrettable failing of many human rights accords. Some agreements have provided access to international courts as a means of asserting those rights. Arbitration is also commonly used as an enforcement mechanism. For example, many bilateral investment treaties allow investors to bring claims against States in an independent arbitral forum.[125] The Cape Town Convention, however, departs from these prece-dents. Once implementation takes place within a State, the treaty offers instead an extensive commandeering of domestic legal systems to enforce its provisions. Thus, it not only establishes legal rules to be applied in domestic courts, but also sets forth explicit procedural rules and deadlines for courts to follow in the administration of judicially provided remedies. Additionally, the Convention's provision of self-help remedies stands apart, even though it can be vitiated by a State declaration, and is arguably the broadest grant of autonomy in the enforcement of individual or business rights in all of interna-tional law. The directives to State registration authorities in Article 15 are also

---

[124] *See supra* notes 113 and 114 and accompanying text.
[125] *See supra* Chapter 4, Part 4.3.

notable, demonstrating that domestic administrative agencies can also be commandeered in the service of the Convention.[126]

8.8.10. *Jurisprudential Significance of the Cape Town Convention*

Public international law and private transnational commercial law therefore emerge from the same *public international law* instrument, the Cape Town Convention. What does that mean for classifying the Convention as an instrument of public international law? Unlike traditional public international law instruments, the purpose of most international commercial law treaties is not to constrain State behavior but to facilitate private transactions through the harmonization of rules governing those transactions. As Professor John F. Coyle has observed, Cape Town is one of only two widely ratified treaties that can be classified as truly "substantive" commercial law treaties.[127] By this he means that the Convention creates its own body of legal rules to be followed in the conduct of a specified set of transactions. Arguably, indeed, treaties like Cape Town are helping to shape a modern *lex mercatoria*.[128] In particular, the Convention creates an enforceable international legal interest as well as an entirely new international institution, a registry of international security interests. Are these initiatives in the domain of public or private law? The Cape Town Convention (like the Warsaw and Montreal conventions before it) is shifting perceptions of the "ontology" of international law.

8.9. THE CAPE TOWN CONVENTION (2): APPLICATION AND SCOPE

8.9.1. *A One-Sentence Summary*

As with any legal regime, the first step to understanding its effects is to identify those situations to which it applies. The Cape Town Convention and, in particular, the Aircraft Protocol confer certain benefits, including registration,

---

[126] *See infra* Part 8.11.

[127] John F. Coyle, *Rethinking the Commercial Law Treaty*, 45 GA. L. REV. 343, 360 n.53 (2011).

[128] Latin for "law [of the] merchant," *lex mercatoria* originally referred to the body of norms that guided medieval merchants in their dealings with one another as they moved among feudal territories. But it has a modern application to international business norms, practices, and behaviors, some of which are clearly grounded in international commercial law treaties like the Cape Town Convention, that are followed by participants in globalized industries and services. *See* Brian F. Havel & Gabriel S. Sanchez, *The Emerging Lex Aviatica*, 42 GEO J. INT'L L. 639, 659 n.92 (2011). For discussion of the *lex mercatoria* in the context of developments in the international aviation industry, see *supra* Chapter 4, Section 4.5.1.

reliance on the Convention's priority rules, and access to specific remedies in the event of default, to "international interests" in "aircraft objects."[129]

8.9.2. *Three Broad Types of Covered Agreement*

Article 1(i) of the Convention defines a creditor as being variously "a chargee under a security agreement, a conditional seller under a title reservation agreement and a lessor under a leasing agreement."[130] Article 2(1) of the Convention creates an independent, registrable "international interest" that will have "priority over any other interest subsequently registered and over an unregistered interest."[131] In conformity with Article 1(i), an "international interest" can be created by any one of three intentionally broad categories: a security agreement,[132] a title reservation agreement,[133] or a leasing agreement.[134] Those three types of agreements capture most forms of security and leasehold interest

---

[129] *See* Cape Town Convention, *supra* note 41, art. 2 (defining an "international interest"); Aircraft Protocol, *supra* note 100, art. I(c) (defining "aircraft objects").

[130] Cape Town Convention, *supra* note 41, art. 1(i). *See* HANLEY, *supra* note 44, at 17. Thus, a lender who chooses either to lend under a finance lease or through the security of a mortgage over the aircraft will be protected in either instance – either as a lessor or as the holder of a charge.

[131] Cape Town Convention, *supra* note 40, arts. 2(1), 29(1).

[132] A "security agreement" is defined in the Convention as "an agreement by which a chargor grants or agrees to grant to a chargee an interest (including an ownership interest) in or over an [aircraft] object to secure the performance of any existing or future obligation of the chargor or a third person." *Id.* art. 1(ii). According to the leading lawyer's guide to the Convention, "[i]t is often tempting for practitioners to include a reference to 'international interest' in the granting clause of a security agreement, normally as part of the grant of security." The guide points out that "[t]his practice is unnecessary and without effect. . . . The eligibility of a security agreement to qualify as an international interest requires only that the specific requirements of the Convention be satisfied." THE LEGAL ADVISORY PANEL OF THE AVIATION WORKING GROUP, PRACTITIONER'S GUIDE TO THE CAPE TOWN CONVENTION AND THE AIRCRAFT PROTOCOL (rev. ed. Nov. 2012), at 12 [hereinafter AWG PRACTITIONER'S GUIDE]. We were reminded here of the *New Yorker* cartoon showing an unsmiling law firm partner returning a draft brief to the quivering junior attorney with the stern words, "[p]ut in more references to international law."

[133] A "title reservation agreement" (also often called a "conditional sale agreement") is defined by the Cape Town Convention as "an agreement for the sale of an [aircraft] object on terms that ownership does not pass until fulfillment of the condition or conditions stated in the agreement." Cape Town Convention, *supra* note 41, art. 1(ll).

[134] A "leasing agreement," as previously noted (*see supra* note 49 and accompanying text), is defined by the Cape Town Convention as "an agreement by which one person (the lessor) grants a right to possession or control of an [aircraft] object (without or without an option to purchase) to another person (the lessee) in return for a rental or other payment." Cape Town Convention, *supra* note 41, art. 1(q). The Convention makes no distinction between operating and capital leases, especially with regard to remedies. Hanley does not find this surprising, because one of the main purposes of Cape Town is to establish "clear rules to govern" asset-based financing and leasing alike. HANLEY, *supra* note 44, at 17.

and are as defined by the Convention and not by national law.[135] Certain benefits
are also extended to contracts of sale.[136] An "unregistered interest" is defined in
Article 1 to include nonconsensual rights or interests such as liens (as discussed
below[137]), and the effectiveness of the priority held by a registered international
interest can be reduced by a national opt-out in favor of such liens.[138]

8.9.3. *Creating an International Interest in Aircraft Objects*

The initial characterization of whether an interest constitutes an "international
interest" is prescribed by the Cape Town Convention itself.[139] For the underlying agreement to be recognized as constituting such an interest, it must be in
writing; the person creating the international interest must have the "power to
dispose" of the aircraft object in which the interest is created; the agreement
must enable the object to be identified; and, for security agreements, the agreement must enable the secured obligations to be identified.[140] "Aircraft objects"
are defined as airframes, aircraft engines, and helicopters meeting certain minimum size thresholds.[141] Aircraft engines, which are often financed separately
from aircraft frames,[142] are treated as distinct by the Convention regardless of

---

[135] GOODE, COMMENTARY, *supra* note 6, at ¶ 2.36. The interest of a chargor under a security
agreement derives entirely from that agreement. But the interest of a conditional seller or lessor
typically precedes and is independent of the conditional sale or leasing agreement – because
the seller or lessor is an *owner*. What the Convention protects in those cases, therefore, is not the
acquisition of ownership but its *retention* under the terms of the agreement. It is only when the
agreement is made that the international interest arises in favor of the seller or lessor and is
capable of being registered. For that reason, Article 3(1) of the Convention refers to an agreement "creating or providing for" the international interest – "creating" in the case of a security
agreement, and "providing for" in the case of a title reservation agreement (conditional sale) or
leasing agreement. Cape Town Convention, *supra* note 41, art. 3(1); *see also* Roy Goode, *The
International Interest as an Autonomous Property Interest*, EUR. REV. PRIVATE L., 1–2004, at
18–25 (2004) [hereinafter Goode, *International Interest*].

[136] Article 1(g) of the Cape Town Convention defines a "contract of sale" as "a contract for the sale
of an [aircraft] object by a seller to a buyer [but which is not one of the three agreements
referred to earlier otherwise constituting an international interest]." Cape Town Convention,
supra note 40, art. 1(g). The Protocol extends the provisions of the Convention, to the extent
they apply, to "outright sales," enabling buyers to avail themselves of the registration facilities
and priority provisions. *See* Gerber, *Aircraft Financing*, *supra* note 57, at 7–18. Including
contracts of sale adds a searchable listing that highlights the various title transfers of the relevant
aircraft object over its useable life. *Id.* at 7–20.

[137] *See infra* Section 8.10.5.

[138] *See id.*

[139] *See* AWG PRACTITIONER'S GUIDE, *supra* note 132, at 13.

[140] *See* Cape Town Convention, *supra* note 41, art. 7.

[141] *See* Aircraft Protocol, *supra* note 100, art. I(2).

[142] The interchangeability of aircraft component parts, especially engines, "heightens the sensi-
tivities of financiers to attendant legal and collateral risks." Gerber, *Aircraft Financing*, *supra*
note 59, at 7–4.

whether an engine is attached to or removed from a frame.[143] In that way, the Cape Town Convention creates an important uniform standard to rectify the uncertainty caused by the varying standards under which some jurisdictions treat engines as part of the airframes on which the engines are installed.[144]

8.9.4. *Location of the Debtor Determines Applicability of the Cape Town Convention*

Because a treaty can only govern those States that have acceded to it, the Convention covers solely those agreements involving debtors situated in a contracting State at the time of the agreement.[145] Critically, therefore, at the time when the international interest is created, the debtor must be located in a contracting State. The location of the creditor is irrelevant.[146] A debtor is "situated" in a contracting State if the debtor's (1) place of incorporation, *or* (2) registered office, *or* (3) center of administration, *or* (4) principal place of business, is located in a contracting State.[147]

8.9.5. *Autonomy of the International Interest*

The international interest may, but need not, be recognized as a protectable interest under any particular body of national law.[148] Once the conditions of the Convention have been satisfied, a fully constituted international interest comes into existence regardless of the applicable local law or even of whether

---

[143] The Protocol specifically provides that ownership of, or an interest in, any aircraft engine shall not be affected by its installation on or removal from an airframe. *See* Aircraft Protocol, *supra* note 100, art. XIV(3). *See generally* AWG PRACTITIONER'S GUIDE, *supra* note 132, at 9.

[144] *See* B. Patrick Honnebier, *New Protocols and the Financing of Aircraft Engines*, 21 No. 1 AIR & SPACE LAW. 15 (2006).

[145] *See* Cape Town Convention, *supra* note 41, art. 3(1). The Convention also applies if an *airframe* is registered on the aircraft register of a contracting State, that is, where an international interest is created in respect to an airframe (by virtue of registration) but not in respect to its engines (to which the Convention can apply only if the debtor is situated in a contracting State). *See* Aircraft Protocol, *supra* note 100, art. IV (1); *see also* Gerber, *Aircraft Financing*, *supra* note 59, at 7–22, 7–23.

[146] The creditor may be located, for example, in a noncontracting State. *See* Cape Town Convention, *supra* note 41, art. 3(2).

[147] *See* Cape Town Convention, *supra* note 41, art. 4(1). That wide range of factors gives "maximum scope" to the application of the Convention. Gerber, *Aircraft Financing*, *supra* note 59, at 7–22. The first two factors are objective and typically easy to ascertain (one need only look to the local authorities or corporate documents), but the latter two are subjective and can lead to difficulties, especially with large multinational entities. *See* AWG PRACTITIONER'S GUIDE, *supra* note 132, at 33.

[148] Sir Roy Goode defines an international interest as a creature of the Cape Town Convention that "in principle is not dependent on national law." Goode, *International Interest*, *supra* note 135, at 24.

the local law recognizes nonpossessory security interests.[149] Local law, according to Sir Roy Goode, will still determine whether an agreement exists between the parties at all.[150] Local law will also determine how a particular interest is to be characterized for purposes of certain provisions of the Convention, for example, the types of available remedies.[151] In most cases, of course, international interests and locally created interests will be coterminous (e.g., interests arising under a lease agreement), but in Sir Roy's view the international interest will be more legally powerful than a purely domestic interest because it overrides even unregistrable unregistered interests whereas the latter may not.[152]

8.9.6. *Internal Transactions Are Also Covered*

Despite the use of the term "international," the Cape Town Convention does not apply only to agreements between parties from different States. Article 50 of the Convention provides that unless a contracting State specifies otherwise through one of the treaty's many possible declarations (about which we will say

---

[149] The general rule under the Convention is that an "assignment" of a secured or leased interest also transfers to the assignee the related international interest and all interests and priorities of the assignor. See Cape Town Convention, *supra* note 41, art. 31(1). The formal requirements for an effective assignment mirror those applicable to creation of an international interest. *See id.* art. 32. See Gerber, *Aircraft Financing, supra* note 59, at 7–27.

[150] *See* Goode, *International Interest, supra* note 135, at 24. For example, local law will determine whether an agreement exists between the parties at all, and thus such questions as capacity to contract and the existence of a *consensus ad idem. See id.*

[151] *See* Cape Town Convention, *supra* note 41, art. 2(4); *see also* AWG Practitioner's Guide, *supra* note 132, at 38. For example, an agreement that meets the Convention's definition of a "leasing agreement" may be characterized under the applicable law of the forum State as creating a security interest. The agreement will therefore carry the rights and remedies applicable to a "security agreement" under the Convention. The applicable law, by the way, will be the domestic rules of the law applicable by virtue of the choice of law (conflict of laws) rules of the forum State (also called the *lex fori*). *See id.* Why did the Convention not definitively fix the characterization of all three types of agreements for all of its contracting States? The AWG Practitioner's Guide provides the answer. Most legal systems outside North America distinguish sharply between security agreements and title-retention and leasing agreements, treating a conditional seller or lessor as the full owner. The United States, Canada, and now New Zealand, adopt a functional and economic approach, treating title reservation agreements and certain leases as forms of security and the title of the conditional seller or lessor as limited to a security interest. Given these disparate approaches, the drafters recognized that it would not be possible to agree on a uniform Cape Town characterization. The solution adopted was to leave these matters to be dealt with under the applicable domestic law as determined by the conflict of laws rules of the forum State. *See* AWG Practitioner's Guide, *supra* note 132, at 38.

[152] *See* Goode, *International Interest, supra* note 135, at 24.

more later), the Convention's protections and priority rules will be applicable to internal transactions that satisfy the aforementioned definitional criteria.[153]

8.10. THE CAPE TOWN CONVENTION (3): THE REGISTRATION AND PRIORITY SYSTEM

8.10.1. *A One-Sentence Summary*

One of the primary purposes of the Cape Town Convention and of the benefits conferred upon international interests within its regime is the establishment of a clear, global priority system for competing interests in aircraft objects, as well as an international registry to record and establish priority for those interests and to provide notice of existing interests to prospective creditors.

8.10.2. *Setup of the Cape Town Convention Registry*

The governance structures for the international registry are set out in the Convention, while the specific features of the registry are in the Protocol. This allows the subsequent protocols to provide for their own registries with distinct characteristics.[154] When creating the International Registry of Mobile Assets,[155] the airlines, manufacturers, and financiers all sought to create a system that was simple, efficient, and inexpensive. ICAO initially wanted to serve as registrar and use the registry to produce revenue, but the ultimate decision was to make the registry not-for-profit.[156] Twenty States were designated to comprise a Preparatory Commission for the establishment of the registry, and ICAO was appointed as Supervisory Authority for oversight and regulation of the registry.[157] Ireland was chosen as the location, and Aviareto, a joint venture between the Irish Government and the private company SITA SC, was selected to establish the registry and to act as registrar.[158]

---

[153] *See* Cape Town Convention, *supra* note 41, art. 1(n) (defining "internal transactions"); art. 50(1) (permitting States to opt out of coverage of internal transactions under the Convention).

[154] Ronald C.C. Cuming, *Considerations in the Design of an International Registry for Interests in Mobile Equipment*, 4 UNIF. L. REV. n.s. 275, 276 (1999).

[155] *See* Cape Town Convention, *supra* note 41, art. 1(p).

[156] See Gerber, *Aircraft Financing*, *supra* note 59, at 7–17.

[157] *See* B. Patrick Honnebier, *The Fully Computerized International Registry for Security Interests in Aircraft and Aircraft Protocol that will Become Effective Toward the Beginning of 2006*, 70 J. AIR L. & COM. 63 (2005).

[158] *See id.*; *see also* Gerber, *Aircraft Financing*, *supra* note 59, at 7–17.

8.10.3. *Using the Registry*

The Cape Town registry is completely electronic and online, allowing approved users to log in and register assets and any member of the general public to search the registry. It is accessible twenty-four hours per day, seven days per week. A number of States have designated an "exclusive entry point" for accessing the international registry in order to harmonize systems for national registration of secured interests with the international registry. As an example, in the United States a party must first register an aircraft object with the Federal Aviation Administration (FAA) and receive a Cape Town transaction code that the party can then use to register the aircraft object with the international registry.[159] It is the responsibility of the parties to an international interest to register that interest. To do so, both parties to the agreement must have an account with the registry. Only one of the parties needs to submit the necessary information, but both parties will need to consent to the registration. Within moments of the parties submitting the necessary information and consents, the system will automatically assign the interest a file number, at which point the interest will be searchable on the registry and will be considered perfected. Registration is now complete.[160]

8.10.4. *Obtaining Priority Under the Registry*

The benefit of registering is that once an interest is registered,[161] the holder of that interest has priority over all subsequent registered and unregistered interests.[162] This is a departure from the priority rule in the United States, which gives the interest first registered in the FAA Registry priority over all

---

[159] *See* Frank L. Polk, *Cape Town and Aircraft Transactions in the United States*, 20 AIR & SPACE LAW. 4, 6 (Winter 2006).

[160] The framework principles for the operation of the Registry appear in the Convention. *See* Cape Town Convention, *supra* note 41, arts. 18–21.

[161] The reader may by now have appreciated that the International Registry provides for the registration of interests as against particular uniquely identifiable aircraft *objects* rather than against *parties* to a transaction. *See* Cape Town Convention, *supra* note 41, art. 2(1) ("an international interest ... is an interest in a uniquely identifiable [aircraft] object"); *see also* AWG PRACTITIONER'S GUIDE, *supra* note 132, at 53. Thus, users can perform searches with respect to aircraft objects but not with respect to transaction participants. *See id.*

[162] Consider the following scenario, for example: Debtor grants a charge (security interest) over an aircraft to Creditor 1 (C1) on February 1 and thereafter grants a charge over the same aircraft to Creditor 2 (C2) on March 1. The international interest in favor of C2 is registered with the International Registry before the international interest in favor of C1 is registered. Under the Cape Town Convention, C2 has priority over C1, even if C2 knew of the prior charge in favor of C1.

competing claims unless the registering party has actual notice of another claim at the time of registration.[163] Under the Convention's much simpler priority rule notice is irrelevant, avoiding some of the messy factual disputes over notice that occurred under the U.S. system.[164] Thus, the international interest gives a creditor stronger rights than a purely domestic interest because registration in the International Registry will override unregistered interests even if those are "of a kind not capable of registration under the Convention."[165] In contrast, the priority of an interest created under national law may depend on the law determined by the choice of law (conflict of laws) rules of the forum State.[166]

8.10.5. *Priority of Nonconsensual Rights*

The major exception to Cape Town's otherwise straightforward priority system can be found in Article 39(1) of the Convention, which permits contracting States to file an "opt-in" declaration specifying certain categories of nonconsensual rights or interests that, despite not being registered, will be given priority over international interests.[167] There are various types of priority interests that may take priority over the rights of a creditor, even a registered or secured creditor, as a matter of public policy under national law. Liens, for example, are charges or encumbrances on property that the law imposes in order to guarantee payment to the lienholder for some service rendered to the property. Mechanic's and workmen's liens, as well as repairmen's liens, fall into this category.[168] Depending on local law, a lien can be amplified into an *in rem* right to seize the aircraft and to sell it in satisfaction of the lien amount. Governments may impose tax liens: a strong example of such a lien would be statutory provisions that allow public authorities to seize and even sell aircraft

---

[163] *See* 49 U.S.C. § 44108(a)(3); *see also* Polk, *supra* note 159, at 6.

[164] *See id.* Some contracting States had argued for a "good faith" requirement with respect to knowledge of prior interests, but ICAO and Unidroit negotiators felt that the general principle of good faith in many jurisdictions was not justified in the special circumstances addressed by the Convention, which involves very sophisticated transactions and parties. In their view, a first-to-file priority rule was the cornerstone of the Convention and was needed to establish a degree of predictability sufficient to enable airlines greater access to financing alternatives and lower financing costs. Any exception to first-to-file would open up the prospect of costly litigation.

[165] Goode, *International Interest, supra* note 135, at 24.

[166] *See id.*

[167] *See* Cape Town Convention, *supra* note 41, art. 39(1).

[168] Airlines either perform maintenance in-house or contract the work out to qualified Maintenance, Repair and Overhaul (MRO) organizations. Many will do both. An MRO typically need not release the aircraft until it has been paid for its services.

where airport or navigation charges have not been paid.[169] States can only use Article 39(1) to prioritize those nonconsensual interests that are similarly prioritized under the contracting State's national law.[170] States also have the option of declaring pursuant to Article 40 that certain nonconsensual rights or interests are registrable and thus subject to the Convention's standard first-to-file priority rule.[171] If a contracting State fails to make a declaration under Article 39 or Article 40, then the nonconsensual rights and interests under the national law of that State will not have priority over registered international interests.[172]

8.11. THE CAPE TOWN CONVENTION (4): REMEDIES IN DEFAULT

8.11.1. *Certainty for Creditors and Nonexclusivity of Remedies*

Outside the registration and priority system, provisions establishing and clarifying creditors' access to remedies in the event of default or insolvency are the main mechanisms by which the Cape Town Convention provides the certainty and stability needed to reduce financing costs for aircraft. The Convention's main purpose in that context is to provide greater certainty for creditors and to strengthen their ability to assert their rights when a debtor has either defaulted on an agreement or has become insolvent. The remedies provided under the Convention are not exclusive, and parties are still free (under Article 12) to avail themselves of additional legal procedures and

---

[169] The U.K. Civil Aviation Authority, for example, has a draconian power under U.K. legislation to seize and sell aircraft to satisfy delinquent route charges that it collects on behalf of the intergovernmental organization Eurocontrol. *See supra* note 88. Moreover, Article 39(2) of the Cape Town Convention ordains that nothing in the Convention shall affect the right of an intergovernmental organization or other private provider of public services to exercise detention power. *See* Cape Town Convention, *supra* note 41, art. 39(1)(b). The Convention does not speak to a related power of sale, but the U.K. legislation does provide that authority. Some EU Member States have proposed a fleet lien for breaches of the Emissions Trading Scheme (ETS) directive (*see supra* Chapter 6, Section 6.1.2, for discussion of the ETS legislation). Thus, an airline that did not pay civil penalties, for example, for failure to report emissions, could have its entire fleet detained and sold by the appropriate ETS national regulator.

[170] *See* Cape Town Convention, *supra* note 41, art. 39(1). As an "opt-in" declaration, this provision only takes effect in States that choose it, and only for those types of liens that the State specifies in its declaration. It is worth noting, also, that unlike some of the other declarations in the Convention, a declaration under Article 39 can be made at any time and not just when the State ratifies the treaty. *See id.*

[171] *See id.* art. 40. The nonconsensual rights and interests covered by a declaration under Article 39 and the registrable nonconsensual rights and interests covered by a declaration under Article 40 are mutually exclusive. *See* AWG PRACTITIONER'S GUIDE, *supra* note 132, at 91.

[172] *See* GOODE, COMMENTARY, *supra* note 6, at ¶ 4.265.

remedies under local law as long as those procedures and remedies do not conflict with the Convention.[173] Moreover, the Convention's gearing toward contractual certainty further allows the parties (under Article 11) "to agree [on] ... what constitutes a default" and offers the parties "a certain contractual freedom to agree [on] remedies in the case of default."[174]

8.11.2. *Effect of Declarations and of Different Types of Agreement*

The subject of remedies is also complicated by the fact that it is the area of the Cape Town Convention most affected by the use of declarations, which means that the exact nature of the remedies available will vary depending on the contracting State in which remedies are pursued. In addition, the reader should be aware that there is a distinction drawn in the Convention between the rules governing the remedies available under a security agreement and those available to lessors and conditional sellers under leases and conditional sale agreements. For ease of exposition, we will focus on the remedies available to a "creditor" under a security agreement, while noting a narrower range of Convention-specific remedies available to a lessor or conditional seller.

8.11.3. *Events of Default*

The Convention defines "default" very broadly as an event substantially depriving a creditor of those expectations to which it was entitled under the agreement,[175] although, as noted above, Article 11 allows the parties to contractually define what events of default will trigger the Convention's default remedies.[176] If a default occurs, a creditor will ideally want repossession of the aircraft and possibly deregistration of the aircraft from the national register used by the debtor,[177] exporting it from the debtor's home State as quickly as

---

[173] *See* Cape Town Convention, *supra* note 41, art. 12. For example, the use of a remedy such as prejudgment attachment would fall into this category and be subject to the local substantive law requirements of the jurisdiction in which the aircraft is located. *See* AWG PRACTITIONER'S GUIDE, *supra* note 132, at 106.

[174] HANLEY, *supra* note 44, at 173 (discussing Article 11 of the Convention, which makes provision for the debtor and creditor to agree as to the events that constitute a default). *See* Cape Town Convention, *supra* note 41, art. 11(1).

[175] *See id.* art. 11(2).

[176] *See supra* note 174. Article 11(1) does not prescribe any kind of "materiality" standard for a default where the default is described or defined in an agreement. *See* AWG PRACTITIONER'S GUIDE, *supra* note 132, at 105.

[177] *See infra* note 188 (explaining how the Convention assists creditors in procuring these remedies).

practicable (especially if a threat of bankruptcy or a lien imposition is looming).[178]

8.11.4. A Range of Creditor Remedies

The Cape Town Convention recognizes, however, that immediate repossession may not always be feasible. Instead, it offers the creditor a number of options that include repossession. In the event of default, therefore, a creditor can do one or more of the following: (a) take possession or control of the aircraft object(s) in question; (b) sell or lease the relevant aircraft object(s); or (c) collect or receive any income or profits arising from the management or use of the aircraft object(s).[179] Alternatively, a creditor may apply for a court order authorizing any of the foregoing remedies.[180] In the case of leases and conditional sale agreements, the only remedies specifically provided in the Convention (and indeed the only necessary remedies because the conditional seller or lessor is the owner of the object[181]) are the taking of possession and control of the object or a court order authorizing the foregoing remedies.[182] Any of the above remedies must be conducted in a "commercially reasonable manner."[183] When exercising its right to sell or lease an aircraft object, the creditor must provide at least ten business days' notice to the debtor and any

---

[178] The lessor will want "to put the aircraft into revenue service with a new lessee with a minimum of delay." HANLEY, *supra* note 44, at 140. To do so, the lessor will need not only the aircraft and all engines and parts but also all aircraft documents, as well as dealing with all unpaid landing and parking fees when it tries to export the aircraft (an act that may itself trigger excise taxes and export duties). *See id. See supra* Part 8.5 for discussion of the concept of aircraft nationality and registration. (*Note:* State registries of aircraft, created in compliance with the Chicago Convention, must be distinguished from the International Registry under the Cape Town Convention.)

[179] *See* Cape Town Convention, *supra* note 41, art. 8(1).

[180] *See id.* art. 8(2).

[181] *See* GOODE, COMMENTARY, *supra* note 6, at ¶ 4.10l; *see also* Goode, *International Interest, supra* note 135, at 23 ("[A]s owner the seller or lessor can do what it likes with its property once the agreement has been terminated for default.").

[182] *See* Cape Town Convention, *supra* note 41, art. 10. But, as noted earlier, other remedies permitted under applicable local law may be exercised – and this is true also for creditors under security agreements. *See* Cape Town Convention, *supra* note 41, art. 12; *see also* AWG PRACTITIONER'S GUIDE, *supra* note 132, at 114.

[183] Cape Town Convention, *supra* note 41, art. 8(3). What does the term "commercially reasonable" as used in Article 8(3) of the Convention actually mean? The Official Commentary looks to "established commercial practice" and "accepted international practice" as relevant. Such industry standards and customary wording in international aircraft financing and leasing contracts should be used to support decisions as to what is commercially reasonable. *See* GOODE, COMMENTARY, *supra* note 6, at ¶ 5.46.

competing creditors with subsequent interests in the aircraft object.[184] Any sums a creditor obtains from exercise of its remedies must be used to satisfy the debtor's secured obligations, and if the sums exceed those obligations any surplus should be distributed to satisfy the claims of subsequent creditors and then the balance returned to the debtor.[185]

8.11.5. *Process of Deregistration and Export*

As noted, the process of repossession often involves the "deregistration" of the aircraft object in question[186] and its export and physical transfer from the territory in which it is situated. Both of those aircraft-specific remedies are added by Article IX(1) of the Aircraft Protocol to the general remedies in the Convention itself.[187] The prospect of deregistration gives State aircraft registration authorities the power to significantly obstruct a creditor's attempts at repossession. The Cape Town Convention attempts to deal with possible national administrative roadblocks by requiring local registry authorities to honor a request for deregistration and export submitted under a recorded "irrevocable deregistration and export request authorization" (IDERA).[188] Article XIII of the Aircraft Protocol permits the creditor to pursue both of these steps and, in tandem with Article IX, requires the registry authority within the relevant contracting State to comply with a request for deregistration if such a request is properly submitted.[189]

---

[184] *See* Aircraft Protocol, *supra* note 100, art. IX(4). The parties may, however, agree to a longer period of prior notice. *See id.*

[185] *See* Cape Town Convention, *supra* note 41, art. 8(5), (6).

[186] Because aircraft are mobile, it is easy to see that a repossessing creditor may wish to change the State of nationality by "deregistering" the aircraft and applying for registration in a different State. *See supra* Part 8.5.

[187] *See* Aircraft Protocol, *supra* note 100, art. IX(1).

[188] *See id.* art. XIII. The authorization, once it is given, cannot be revoked by the debtor without the consent of the authorized party (the creditor). *See id.*

[189] *See id.* arts. IX(5), XIII(4). The relevant registration authority is required to enforce the deregistration and export remedies without the need for court intervention or order. *See id.* Note that Article XIII requires a declaration by a contracting State to allow the IDERA procedure: *see id.* art. XIII(1). The failure of a contracting State to make a declaration allowing the IDERA does not mean that deregistration and export remedies are unavailable to creditors, only that the process for exercising those remedies will be determined by the procedural law of the State of registry rather than the Convention. *See* AWG PRACTITIONER'S GUIDE, *supra* note 132, at 101–102. In jurisdictions like the United States, where registration is made in the name of an owner, an IDERA should be made by the registered owner of the aircraft, whereas in jurisdictions where registration is in the name of an operator, the IDERA should be issued by the operator. *See generally* Gerber, *Aircraft Financing, supra* note 59, at 7–33. Honoring of the IDERA is subject to applicable safety laws, and the registry authority may also require proof of discharge of all registered interests ranking in priority to that of the requesting creditor or that

8.11.6. *Distinction Between Self-Help Remedies and Need for a Court Order*

The manner in which the remedies mentioned above can be legally pursued hinges on a declaration made by the relevant contracting State. This is the one *mandatory* declaration in the treaty: Article 54(2) requires that all contracting States, upon ratifying the Convention, make a declaration as to whether a creditor needs to obtain a court order before, for example, repossessing or selling an aircraft following a debtor's default.[190] Undoubtedly controversial, this bypassing of national court structures is probably the most creditor-friendly provision in the entire Convention. In States that permit such non-judicial remedies, or self-help, creditors are able to bypass the uncertainty and delay associated with the court process and to act immediately to protect their interests.[191] Any nonjudicial actions must still be performed in a commercially reasonable manner.[192] For interests arising from security agreements, as opposed to leases or title reservations, the creditor must have the debtor's consent before taking nonjudicial action.[193]

8.11.7. *Process of Interim or "Speedy" Relief*

To protect creditor rights even further, particularly where a State does not opt to allow self-help remedies, the Convention permits a creditor to make

those interests have consented to the deregistration and export. *See* Aircraft Protocol, *supra* note 100, art. IX(5). The *Wikileaks* website revealed that in 2009 the U.S. Government expressed concern that China's implementation of Article XIII required creditors to procure a court order before China's aircraft registration authority would deregister an aircraft. China's decision to require a court order in addition to the IDERA seems contrary to the purpose of the provision, which is to assure creditors a more certain and expedited deregistration process. China nevertheless interpreted such a requirement to be consistent with the terms of the Convention. The available evidence suggests that the only attempt to resolve this dispute was diplomatic, and that the United States indicated a reluctance to accept China's interpretation as a necessary cost of doing business in that country.

[190] *See* Cape Town Convention, *supra* note 41, 54(2). A contracting State's ratification will not be accepted by Unidroit without a declaration on this question – and such a rejection indeed occurred in the case of Costa Rica. *See* AWG Practitioner's Guide, *supra* note 132, at 111.

[191] Seizing a commercial aircraft in most airports without a court order, as a practical matter, will be challenging. Local administrative obligations, such as a legal requirement for approval by the local airport authority, must still be observed. A practitioner should proceed with extreme caution and avoid "breaching the peace." AWG Practitioner's Guide, *supra* note 132, at 112, 113.

[192] *See* Cape Town Convention, *supra* note 41, art. 8(3); *see also supra* note 183 and accompanying text.

[193] *See* Cape Town Convention, *supra* note 41, art. 10. Remedies that require the debtor's consent are usually already agreed to in typical forms of leases, conditional sale agreements, and security agreements. *See* AWG Practitioner's Guide, *supra* note 132, at 103.

use of interim or "speedy" relief before its claim against the debtor has been fully determined on the merits.[194] Interim relief involves a creditor providing a court with evidence that a default has occurred, without having to fully prove the default, and receiving a court order to prevent the value of the aircraft object from deteriorating while the debtor waits for a court to hear its claims. The judicial order may allow the creditor to do one or more of the following: (a) preserve the value of the aircraft object; (b) take possession, control, or custody of the object; (c) immobilize the object; and (d) lease, sell, or manage operation of the object and claim any resulting income. A creditor can only pursue those remedies by means of interim relief when the debtor has agreed to such relief as part of the contract establishing the international interest.[195] Again, contracting States have the ability to determine whether this "speedy relief" provision will be available and, if so, precisely how speedy the relief will be (the number of days between a creditor's filing for such relief and its receipt of a court order).[196]

8.12. THE CAPE TOWN CONVENTION (5): INSOLVENCY

8.12.1. *The Acid Test*

According to Sir Roy Goode, author of the official commentary to the Convention, insolvency (or bankruptcy) is the acid test of the efficacy of security interests under the Cape Town Convention.[197] Because of concerns about the balance of fairness between creditors and debtors, States are especially sensitive to inroads into their domestic systems of insolvency. For this reason, the rules regarding insolvency are among the most controversial and important provisions of Cape Town.

---

[194] *See* Cape Town Convention, *supra* note 41, art. 13; Aircraft Protocol, *supra* note 100, art. X. Interim relief may also be available under the laws of the forum, and the Convention does not preempt use of such local procedures. *See* Cape Town Convention, *supra* note 41, art. 13(4); *see also* AWG PRACTITIONER'S GUIDE, *supra* note 132, at 120.

[195] *See* Cape Town Convention, *supra* note 41, art. 13; *see also supra* note 193 (noting that remedies requiring debtor's consent usually are included in underlying transaction agreements).

[196] *See* Cape Town Convention, *supra* note 41, arts. 13, 55; Aircraft Protocol, *supra* note 100, art. X. Ten working days is the most common interim relief time period, and it is typical for States to select longer time periods under Article X of the Aircraft Protocol before creditors are allowed to lease or sell the secured aircraft object. *See id.*

[197] Roy Goode, *The Protection of Interests in Movables in Transnational Commercial Law*, 3 UNIF. L.R. n.s. 453, 456 (1998).

8.12.2. *National Insolvency Laws and the Cape Town Convention's Response*

Bankruptcy proceedings vary by country, ranging from regimes that allow the debtor in possession to remain legally immune from creditor claims while it reorganizes its business (and even thereafter) to much less debtor-friendly systems like that of Ireland.[198] Amendments to the U.S. bankruptcy code provide holders of security interests in aircraft in certain circumstances with an accelerated lifting of the "automatic stay" that protects the bankrupt corporation against creditor actions (including actions for repossession).[199] Moreover, while it is critical for a creditor to obtain prompt repossession of an aircraft when the debtor becomes insolvent, repossession is not *per se* regulated by international law and is dependent on local court proceedings. To protect creditors fully and to provide them with the certainty that they need to facilitate aircraft financing, the Cape Town drafters determined that creditors also need stronger protection for their rights in the event of debtor insolvency. Although the Convention virtually ignores the issue,[200] the drafters of the Protocol considered insolvency a matter of particular importance to aircraft financing and included relevant provisions in the Protocol. Because of the varied national law approaches to insolvency, reflecting differing perspectives on the proper balance between the rights of debtors and creditors, insolvency is one of those contentious areas that inspired the treaty's customization-through-declarations design.

8.12.3. *Application of the Cape Town Insolvency Rules: Alternatives A and B*

The Cape Town Convention's insolvency provisions will only have effect if the debtor's primary insolvency jurisdiction (the State that is "the center of the debtor's main interests"[201]) has made a declaration to adopt Cape Town's insolvency rules.[202] Contracting States that do so declare have to choose

---

[198] *See* Pitmans Lawyers News, Shopping for Bankruptcy?, http://www.pitmans.com/news/shopping-for-bankruptcy (remarking unfavorably on Ireland's debtor-unfriendly bankruptcy code).

[199] *See* 11 U.S.C. § 1110 (2008); *see also* Gerber, *Aircraft Financing, supra* note 59, at 7–62.

[200] *See* Cape Town Convention, *supra* note 41, art. 30, considered further *infra* note 202.

[201] Aircraft Protocol, *supra* note 100, art. I(2)(n). The term "center of main interests" is drawn from EU insolvency law, and the Protocol establishes a rebuttable presumption that the appropriate State is where the debtor has its registered office ("statutory seat") or is otherwise incorporated. *See* AWG Practitioner's Guide, *supra* note 132, at 129.

[202] *See* Aircraft Protocol, *supra* note 100, art. XI. In addition, the international interest must have been registered against the debtor prior to the commencement of proceedings. *See* Cape Town Convention, *supra* note 41, art. 30(1).

between two sets of bankruptcy provisions: Alternative A, the "hard provisions,"[203] and Alternative B, otherwise known as the "soft provisions."[204] A contracting State may elect A in its entirety, B in its entirety, or neither.[205] There are macroeconomic consequences to the choice of A or B: if A is chosen, in effect giving "greater certainty" to enforcement of the security interest,[206] a lower interest rate on export credit financing may be available.[207]

8.12.4. *Insolvency Alternative A*

Alternative A is the most generous option for creditors, providing them with more certainty and more protection. It is designed "to meet the requirements of advanced structured financing, including international capital market financing structures."[208] Alternative A resembles and is "similar in ideology" to the Section 1110 procedure in the U.S. bankruptcy code.[209] As prescribed by the Convention, this first alternative requires the debtor or insolvency administrator within the time period specified by the contracting State in its insolvency declaration[210] either to give the creditor possession of the aircraft object or to cure all defaults under the relevant agreement and agree to perform all future obligations under that agreement. Should the debtor fail to perform all future obligations, there will not be a second opportunity to cure defaults and the aircraft object will have to be transferred right away. The insolvency administrator or debtor is required to preserve the aircraft object and maintain its value until the creditor is given the opportunity to take possession.

---

[203] *See* Aircraft Protocol, *supra* note 100, art. XI.

[204] *See id.*

[205] *See id.* art. XXX(3).

[206] HANLEY, *supra* note 44, at 137.

[207] The OECD's 2011 Understanding, *see supra* Section 8.8.6, grants eligible States a discount interest rate on financing from export credit agencies if those States have made a declaration adopting Alternative A. Alternative A closely resembles the aircraft equipment provision of the U.S. bankruptcy code, after which it was modeled. *See* 11 U.S.C. § 1110 (2008); *see also supra* note 199 and accompanying text. *See infra* Section 8.15.9 (discussing export credits).

[208] *See* Gerber, *Aircraft Financing, supra* note 59, at 7–3.

[209] *See supra* note 199 and accompanying text. As to the point on ideology, *see* Gerber, *Aircraft Financing, supra* note 59, at 7–18. According to Donald Bunker, the availability of Section 1110 benefits may provide "a key" to the implementation of the Cape Town Convention. BUNKER, *supra* note 13, at 537.

[210] Or before the date on which the creditor would otherwise be entitled to possession if that is earlier than the end of the time period specified by the contracting State. *See* Aircraft Protocol, *supra* note 100, art. XI(2). Most States set the time period at 60 days when they make their declaration opting for Alternative A. The OECD's 2011 Understanding, *see supra* Section 8.8.6, offers its discount interest rate on financing from export credit agencies if eligible States have capped the waiting period at no longer than 60 days.

Additionally, under this Alternative, the creditor is entitled to apply for any of the previously discussed forms of interim relief as permitted by the relevant State's declarations. The creditor is also entitled to deregistration and export on an expedited basis, and local bankruptcy courts are barred from staying or interfering with the creditor's rights or exercise of its remedies as permitted by the Cape Town Convention and the Aircraft Protocol.[211]

8.12.5. *Insolvency Alternative B*

Rather than a definitive sequence of events leading to repossession as in Alternative A, Alternative B only requires that the debtor or insolvency admin-istrator either give notice that it will cure all defaults by the beginning of the insolvency proceedings and perform all future obligations under the agree-ment, or provide the creditor with the opportunity to repossess. The creditor also lacks the option of interim or self-help remedies should the debtor fail to provide such notice. The creditor is thus primarily at the mercy of the local bankruptcy court, which *may* allow the creditor to repossess the aircraft "upon such terms as the court may order."[212] Mexico is the only Contracting State to have selected Alternative B in its declaration and the results thus far have been unfavorable.[213] That was particularly evident in the August 2010 bankruptcy of Mexicana when many creditors, wary of the Mexican insolvency process, terminated their leases and began repossession in advance of the insolvency filings.[214] Had the creditors been more confident that their rights would have been protected in insolvency, they may have permitted Mexicana to continue to use the aircraft during an attempted restructuring.[215]

8.12.6. *Priority Differences Under Alternatives A and B*

Under Alternative A, registered international interests are guaranteed priority in insolvency proceedings over all competing interests aside from those noncon-sensual rights a contracting State has chosen to prioritize via declaration, as

---

[211] *See generally* Aircraft Protocol, *supra* note 100, art. XI. It is entirely possible that a State will already have a more creditor-friendly regime than Alternative A: that may be why the United States has not made an election under Article XXX of the Aircraft Protocol. *See generally* Gerber, *Aircraft Financing, supra* note 59, at 7–31.

[212] *See* Aircraft Protocol, *supra* note 100, art. XI (Alternative B(5)).

[213] *See* Donald G. Gray & Auriol Marasco, *The Cape Town Convention: Where is Canada?*, 24 No. 2 Air & Space Law. 1, 19 (2011).

[214] *See id.*

[215] *See id.*

discussed earlier.[216] Alternative B subjects the international interest to the priority rules of the local insolvency regime. Finally, for the Convention's insolvency
provisions to have any effect, the international security interest must be registered
with the International Registry before the insolvency proceedings begin.[217]

8.13. THE CAPE TOWN CONVENTION (6): JURISDICTION AND CHOICE OF LAW

8.13.1. *Party Autonomy on the Choice of the Forum State*

Given the Cape Town Convention's purpose to clarify legal rights and procedures governing highly mobile equipment and the lack of uniformity produced by its extensive use of declarations, the Convention had to include rules
for selecting the appropriate forum State in which creditors should seek to
enforce its provisions and by which that State's declarations will govern the
application of the Convention to a dispute. For most remedies, the parties to
the agreement are free to specify within the agreement which contracting
State they want to have jurisdiction, even if the State has no ties to either party
or even to the transaction itself.[218] Accordingly, the courts of the State chosen
by the parties can order the deregistration of an aircraft registered in another
State and the export and physical transfer of an aircraft located in another
State. Appropriate jurisdiction for interim relief varies with the form of relief
sought. An application for preservation, possession, or immobilization of the
aircraft object must be sought in the State where the object is located.[219]
Creditors seeking to lease, sell, or manage the income from a secured aircraft
object pending final resolution have to file either in a court chosen by the
parties or with a court in the State in which the debtor is located.[220]

8.13.2. *No Choice of Law Rules*

Although the parties can choose a jurisdiction, the Cape Town Convention
does not expressly provide for a choice of law (as opposed to a choice of

---

[216] *See* Aircraft Protocol, *supra* note 100, art. XI (Alternative A(12)). *See supra* Section 8.10.5.

[217] *See supra* note 202 (citing Article 30(1) of the Cape Town Convention).

[218] *See* Cape Town Convention, *supra* note 41, art. 42(1). The parties should recognize, however,
that because the Convention still allows the forum State – applying its choice of law or conflict
of laws rules – to determine the legal system that will characterize their agreement (*see infra*
next section and also *supra* Section 8.7.3, which discusses the similar rule under the Geneva
Convention), the selection of a forum could have material consequences for the availability of
rights and remedies. *See* AWG PRACTITIONER'S GUIDE, *supra* note 132, at 39.

[219] *See* Cape Town Convention, *supra* note 41, art. 43(1).

[220] *See id.* art. 43(2).

jurisdiction) by the parties for settling those issues that are unaddressed by the substantive rules of the Convention. That choice typically is made by the choice of law (conflict of laws) rules of the forum State. The Convention indicates that reference to the applicable law means "the domestic rules of the law applicable by virtue of the rules of private international law of the forum State."[221] Otherwise, however, Cape Town does not emulate Geneva in seeking to provide (however imperfectly) a clear choice of law or conflicts rule. But the Aircraft Protocol does allow contracting States to make a specific declaration whereby the contracting parties to a financing agreement may choose a law to govern their "contractual rights and obligations."[222] The law chosen must be the domestic law of the designated State (rather than its choice of law rules) and the choice will be respected in any courts of a contracting State.[223] The parties cannot, however, predetermine by their selection of a particular State's law whether their agreement will constitute a security agreement for purposes of determining applicable remedies.[224] That determination, as in the *Blue Sky* case,[225] will still be made in accordance with the choice of law (conflict of laws) rules applied by the forum court. A number of State domestic laws may therefore be implicated – the law of the *situs* of the aircraft, the law where the lessee has its principal place of business, the law of the *lex registrii*, the law identified as the governing law in the underlying transaction, possibly even the law where the lessor is located. The Cape Town Convention's lack of a universal choice of law rule regarding the property regime applicable to aircraft (and aircraft engines) "implies that uncertainty remains; the validity of a transfer of title or of a security right may be assessed differently depending on the jurisdiction where the matter is being adjudicated."[226]

---

[221] Reference to "private international law" means the choice of law (conflict of laws) rules of the forum State. *See* Cape Town Convention, *supra* note 41, art. 5(3). *See also supra* Chapter 1, Part 1.4 (discussing international law terminology).

[222] *See* Aircraft Protocol, *supra* note 100, art. VIII(2).

[223] *See id.* art. VIII(3); *see also* AWG PRACTITIONER'S GUIDE, *supra* note 132, at 39.

[224] *See supra* note 218; *see also* AWG PRACTITIONER'S GUIDE, *supra* note 132, at 111. To "characterize" a document legally, one must look to the domestic law determined by the choice of law (conflict of laws) rules of the forum State as the applicable law. That law will decide, for example, whether or not a lease or title reservation agreement is a security agreement. *See id.*

[225] *See supra* Part 8.3.

[226] I. H. Ph. Diederiks-Verschoor, AN INTRODUCTION TO AIR LAW 350 (9th rev. ed., Pablo Mendes de Leon ed., 2012) (concluding that "[i]t is regrettable that the Cape Town Convention fails to provide a clear conflict of law[] rule. . . ."). But can a uniform conflict of laws rule in aircraft financing even be created? The interests of more than one jurisdiction will always be in play. The *lex situs*, after all, will insist on respect for nonconsensual locally created rights such as tax liens and airport charges. The *lex registrii*, on the other hand, may represent the appropriate rule for consensually created rights in light of the possibility of momentary, fortuitous connections to the *situs*. It may be unrealistic to propose a single, certain conflict of

8.14. THE CAPE TOWN CONVENTION (7): THE CONVENTION'S IMPACT ON AVIATION FINANCING AND ON INTERNATIONAL LAW

8.14.1. *Ratifications of the Cape Town Convention and Aircraft Protocol*

At the time of publication of this book, the Cape Town Convention had fifty-eight contracting States (including the United States but not the U.K.), and the Aircraft Protocol had fifty-two contracting States (again including the United States but not the U.K.).[227] Each has also been acceded to by one Regional Economic Integration Organization (the EU). Nevertheless, the EU's competency regarding the Convention's various provisions is limited, and its accession is generally viewed as paving the way for individual Member States to become parties to the Convention rather than as an act binding the individual Member States.[228]

8.14.2. *Impact of the Cape Town Convention on Aircraft Financing*

The Cape Town Convention is generally seen as having succeeded in facilitating financing for operators in developing countries with poor credit ratings.[229] Export credit agencies[230] have extended lower interest rates, known as the "Cape Town Discount," to qualifying States that have ratified the Convention and made declarations adopting numerous creditor-friendly provisions including, as noted above, Alternative A of the insolvency provisions with a waiting period of no more than sixty days as well as the IDERA procedures.[231] The Convention's benefits are less pronounced for States with more readily available financing and without recourse to export credit agency

---

laws rule to govern all of the factual situations that can arise in an international aircraft financing.

[227] The U.K. signed both the Convention and the Protocol in 2001 but has not yet ratified either instrument.

[228] *See* Berend Crans, *The Implications of the EU Accession to the Cape Town Convention*, 35 No. 1 AIR & SPACE L. 1, 5 (2010). The EU's accession was necessary in order to ensure consistency between the Convention's provisions and substantive areas governed by EU rather than Member State law.

[229] *See* Vadim Linetsky, *Economic Benefits of the Cape Town Treaty* (Oct. 18, 2009), http://www.awg.aero/assets/docs/economicbenefitsofCapeTown.pdf.

[230] *See infra* Part 8.15; *see supra* notes 207, 210.

[231] *See supra* Sections 8.11.5, 8.12.4; *see also* AWG PRACTITIONER'S GUIDE, *supra* note 132, at 148. *See* Dean N. Gerber, *The 2011 Aircraft Sector Understanding: Calming the Turbulent Skies*, 24 No. 1 AIR & SPACE LAW. 1 (2011).

loans. This in part explains the dearth of EU States that have acceded to the Convention, some of which have expressed concerns that the Convention's creditor-friendly provisions may run contrary to national policy preferences in favor of debtors.[232] There has also been some concern that even though the appearance of clear, firm protections has reassured aircraft financiers, national courts may not always faithfully apply the Convention's provisions.[233]

8.14.3. *Two Models of Transnational Commercial Lawmaking*

As we noted when we introduced it earlier in this chapter, the Cape Town Convention resembles the Warsaw and Montreal conventions relating to liability in that it is an instrument that regulates private transnational commercial transactions but that has a legal status that is "firmly rooted in [public international] treaty law."[234] The Convention's actual influence on the principles and practice of transnational commercial lawmaking is interesting to contemplate. In that context, one should begin by reading Jeffrey Wool's 1997 article, *Rethinking the Notion of Uniformity in the Drafting of International Commercial Law: A Preliminary Proposal for the Development of a Policy-based Unification Model.*[235] According to Wool, international commercial law treaties have long suffered from the tension between the need to establish uniform normative rules to provide certainty and predictability, and the need to respect various policy objectives of collaborating nation States. Wool contends that, in the past, policy differences were often papered over by vague or general textual provisions that undermined the certainty and predictability that the treaty was supposed to provide. Wool refers to this as the "undifferentiated unification model," where the treaty attempts to harmonize both policy objectives and legal concepts. Wool proposes what he terms the "policy-based unification model," intended to allow the drafters to identify the basic objectives and associated underlying legal concepts of the treaty, and to draft the legal rules necessary to achieve those objectives in clear and concrete terms. These rules would make up the mandatory treaty provisions and be binding on all States. Next, the drafters would identify related policy determinations reasonably

---

[232] *See* Crans, *supra* note 228, at 7.

[233] *See* Gray & Marasco, *supra* note 213, at 20. But that may not matter. The critical rationale of the Convention is that there should be *no* national court involvement: the creditor can apply its remedies through "self-help" without leave of the court. *See supra* Section 8.11.6. The absence of cases, therefore, may signify that the Convention is working as the drafters expected.

[234] GOODE ET AL., TRANSNATIONAL COMMERCIAL LAW, *supra* note 4, at 1.

[235] 2 UNIF. L. REV. n.s. 46 (1997). Wool is secretary-general of the Aviation Working Group (*see supra* text accompanying note 103).

ancillary to the objectives of the treaty and draft appropriate rules – dubbed "precatory" provisions – that would be binding on only those contracting States that chose not to enter a reservation to those rules.[236] That would assure greater control for States over the impact of the treaty on policy matters of national importance.[237]

8.14.4. *The Cape Town Convention as a Policy-Based Model of Transnational Commercial Lawmaking*

The Cape Town Convention and Aircraft Protocol were the first test cases for Wool's concept. The policy-based treaty was accomplished through two notable innovations. The first is the unique two-instrument approach or "umbrella" structure. As explained earlier, the Convention is the broad umbrella agreement, and the sector-specific protocols fill in the details. The fact that the sector-specific protocols are controlling, rather than the Convention, adds to the uniqueness. The second innovation is the aggressive use, woven into the fabric of the Convention itself, of a system of declarations (also discussed previously). The success of Cape Town's innovative approach has been debatable. Uniformity (and certainty) is obviously sacrificed to achieve clearer, more definite treaty language, and to accommodate the different policy preferences of contracting States. Also, as mentioned earlier, export credit agencies have prescribed the declarations that developing (but also developed) States must adopt in order to enjoy the full measure of the Convention's intended benefits regarding their access to financing. And States that have public policy concerns about the Convention's provisions may hesitate to accede despite the customization options.[238] Still, the creation of

---

[236] These precatory provisions perform the function of reservations, but are not the same as the kinds of expressly contemplated reservations found in numerous commercial and economic law conventions. Reservations of that kind have not been used as a vehicle for purposeful identification *within the treaty itself* of policy matters and have not afforded States the opportunity to engage in deliberate decision-making on such matters. Wool's recast approach to reservations would arguably preserve greater control for States over the impact of the treaty on policy matters of national importance.

[237] A good example would be the insolvency provisions of the Aircraft Protocol, *see supra* Part 8.12.

[238] But many jurisdictions with sophisticated aircraft financing activities *have* acceded: the EU, Ireland, Luxembourg, the Netherlands, Norway, Switzerland, Russia, Oman, the United Arab Emirates, Brazil, Singapore, China, India, Canada, Mexico, the United States, and so forth. Presumably, despite "consumerist" concerns, these jurisdictions are also aware that the huge economic risk that attaches to aircraft financing may merit a corresponding level of special legal protection. Higher protection (i.e., legal certainty) for the financier can translate into more competitive pricing and more available financing.

substantive private transnational law, embodied in the international security interest, as well as the establishment of the International Registry, are accomplishments that represent a major conceptual advance for international aviation law beyond the 1948 Geneva Convention, which Cape Town has mostly replaced. The 2001 Cape Town Convention offers a template for future private transnational commercial law instruments that may emerge in this most global of industries.

8.15. AN OVERVIEW OF THE GOVERNMENTAL ROLE IN AIRCRAFT FINANCING

8.15.1. *Relationship Between Subsidization and Financing*

Although the Cape Town Convention is a public international law treaty, it is clear from the preceding discussion that it functions as a private law instrument that supplies information to international market actors about the prioritization and enforcement of security interests in aircraft. Because Cape Town was not designed to govern direct commercial relations among its signatory States, the treaty is wholly silent on the degree of allowable government intervention in the aircraft manufacturing and financing markets. That is not truly an oversight given that the Convention was negotiated for a limited (although important) purpose; but neither should it obscure the fact that public subsidies (or "State aid") to large civil aircraft manufacturers have become a politically contentious issue in the realm of aircraft financing. Indeed, one of the most protracted and expensive trade disputes in World Trade Organization (WTO) history – one that continues at the time of this writing – concerns the alleged subsidization of industry giants Airbus and Boeing by the EU and the United States, respectively. Although some observers might be inclined to segregate aircraft manufacturing subsidization from aircraft acquisition financing, that, in our view, would not be accurate. Subsidization, which can take the form of capital infusions, direct loans, guarantees, tax breaks, and an easing of regulatory strictures, affects the price of the finished product. An aircraft manufacturer that is spared high research and development costs because of a government grant, or which enjoys favorable below-market lending terms from public agencies, can funnel those savings to its airline customers. Those cost savings will not turn an aircraft into a "cheap" purchase so that financing is no longer needed, but certainly will ease an airline's access to affordable capital. Another way to think about the matter is to consider *how much more expensive* large aircraft may be without subsidization.

8.15.2. *The OECD and the Control of Export Credits*

Coupled with these concerns is the renewed involvement of the OECD – a loose confederation of top-tier economies without international legal personality – in a distinct, but intertwined, matter of aircraft subsidization that we have mentioned briefly in prior discussions: export credits. Even prior to the 2008 financial crisis, government (or quasi-government) entities known as export credit agencies provided assistance, typically in the form of loan guarantees, to foreign air carriers purchasing (or leasing) aircraft manufactured in the benefactor States. Two policy justifications underlie this export assistance. First, States have an understandable interest in increasing exports, particularly exports of capital-intensive products such as aircraft. Second, large swathes of the airline industry have argued, convincingly apparently, that but for the loan guarantees afforded by export crediting agencies, they would be unable to purchase or lease a sufficient number of new aircraft. Both justifications pass over the fact that these loan guarantees (or, in very limited instances, direct loans) are backed by taxpayer euros and dollars; like all forms of subsidization, the costs involved do not simply disappear. Rather, they are passed on to less politically savvy (or more disaggregated) targets.[239] Like the criticisms leveled against direct subsidies to aircraft manufacturers, critics have questioned the argument that the airlines are in any special need of such assistance.[240] A number of stakeholders, including private financial institutions and some airlines that are generally excluded from taking advantage of export credits,[241] have pressured States and the OECD into imposing tighter rules for when export credits may be granted and under what terms. This form of private lobbying for fresh public rules is not, in itself, surprising. Even the Airbus/Boeing dispute before the WTO, although brought

---

[239] Thus, industries with a strong organized labor presence are much more capable of leveraging the combined political influence of owners and workers to procure government assistance during bleak economic times. Think, for instance, of the controversial bailout of the heavily unionized U.S. automotive industry in early 2009, achieved (at least initially) at the expense of American taxpayers. The airline industry itself flexed some lobbying power when it negotiated a federal "stabilization" package in the wake of the 9/11 attacks. *See* BRIAN F. HAVEL, BEYOND OPEN SKIES: A NEW REGIME FOR INTERNATIONAL AVIATION 368–74 (2009) (noting, however, that federal intervention also carried the risk of economic reregulation of the U.S. airline industry).

[240] Donald Bunker has been highly critical of national export agencies that, in his view, "place equipment in the hands of airlines whose finance ratios cannot justify such credit." BUNKER, *supra* note 13, at 425. Bunker takes the view that, in a free market, commercial jet aircraft should (together with an equity contribution from the airline) be enough to provide adequate security to justify extending long-term credit to creditworthy airlines. Taxpayer-financed aircraft subsidies should not be needed if the private sector is sufficiently innovative. *See id.*

[241] U.S. and certain EU air carriers, resident in the two largest aircraft exporting regions in the world, are not eligible to take advantage of export credits from their home jurisdictions. *See infra* note 268.

by the manufacturers' home countries, is the result of advocacy by high-stakes private interests; the key difference is that the OECD possesses no authority to create or to adjudicate international law. Yet, as we will discuss, its 2011 Sector Understanding[242] may be as practically effective as any of the international law instruments we have reviewed in this chapter (and indeed in the whole of this book).

8.15.3. *Regulating Subsidies in International Trade*

In ranking the negative economic impact of trade distortions perpetrated by government intervention, subsidies fall near the bottom. Overt protectionist measures such as import quotas, which inflate prices by restricting supply, have long drawn the ire of trade economists, explaining why they are all but forbidden under WTO rules. Subsidies, on the other hand, have had a mixed reaction. Although domestic merchants forced to compete with foreign exporters enjoying government bounty understandably dislike them, subsidies are not an unqualified evil for all market participants. Consumers who buy foreign-produced subsidized goods and services can avail themselves of lower prices and perhaps even superior quality. Because foreign-produced subsidized goods and services are supported by revenues captured from outside the consumers' home country, they are not accompanied by the risk of distortions and inefficiencies that are supposed to be part of domestic subsidization.[243] As a matter of political economy, however, subsidies are often frowned upon as creating an "unfair" or "imbalanced" competitive environment, particularly at the international level. That is one reason why the WTO, unlike its predecessor, the 1947 General Agreement on Tariffs and Trade (GATT), has endeavored to police subsidies through its 1995 Agreement on Subsidies and Countervailing Measures ("SCM Agreement").[244] Regional trade organizations, such as the EU, have been even more strident in attempting to discipline public infusions of money into specific industries and enterprises. Through its facially rigorous (although unevenly applied) rules governing State aid, the EU has attempted (among other things) to impose a "first time, last time" rule on public subsidies in order to maintain a common market where

---

[242] For the text of the Understanding, see www.oecd.org/tad/exportcredits/aircraftsectorunder standings.htm.

[243] *See* Chapter 3, note 196 (quoting economist Paul Krugman's wry observation that the best response to a foreign State's subsidies is to send a "thank you" note to the local embassy).

[244] Agreement on Subsidies and Countervailing Measures, Apr. 15, 1994, Marrakesh Agreement Establishing the World Trade Organization, Annex 1A, 1869 U.N.T.S. 14 (entered into force Jan. 1, 1995).

entrepreneurial savvy, not government largesse, determines market winners and losers.[245] Moreover, most economically developed States seek to offset the adverse effects of foreign subsidies on domestic producers through "countervailing measures," an import duty that can be used to raise prices on foreign subsidized goods. While these trade regulatory actions, like subsidies themselves, are policed by the terms of the SCM Agreement, States are given considerable latitude in determining when to impose countervailing measures and at what levels. The time and political costs bound up with challenging a violation of the SCM Agreement before the WTO's Dispute Settlement Body (DSB) make it likely that many "illegal" countervailing measures, like "illegal" subsidies, remain unpoliced.

8.15.4. *The GATT/WTO Aircraft Agreement*

Although the WTO obviously concerns itself with far more than just the aircraft manufacturing sector, it is worth noting that the GATT established a special plurilateral accord, the 1980 Agreement on Trade in Civil Aircraft ("Aircraft Agreement").[246] The Aircraft Agreement was intended to eliminate a specific set of aircraft-related tariffs while also encouraging signatory States to make their civil (not military) aircraft purchasing decisions in accordance with commercial and technological, rather than nationalistic, interests. In 1995, the Aircraft Agreement was recast and inserted as Annex 4A to the new WTO Charter.[247] Because the Aircraft Agreement is a plurilateral,[248] and hence not part of the obligatory package for all 159 members of the WTO, its coterie of signatories is quite limited. Emerging economic powers such as Brazil, China, India, and Russia – all of which are expected to enhance their presence in the aircraft manufacturing market in the coming decades – have not signed. Moreover, from a substantive perspective, the Agreement's rules for curtailing politically driven government procurement of aircraft are perceived as

---

[245] *See generally* CONOR QUIGLEY, EUROPEAN UNION STATE AID LAW AND POLICY (2d ed. 2009).

[246] *See* Agreement on Trade in Civil Aircraft, *opened for signature* Apr. 12, 1979, 1186 U.N.T.S. 170, *reprinted as amended at* 1869 U.N.T.S. 508 (entered into force Jan. 1, 1980).

[247] *See* WTO Analytical Index: Agreement on Trade in Civil Aircraft, http://www.wto.org/english/ res_e/booksp_e/analytic_index_e/aircraft_01_e.htm.

[248] In the context of the WTO, this means that an agreement such as the Aircraft Agreement is only binding on a narrower circle of States (although all States are invited to accede). Such agreements contrast sharply with WTO multilateral instruments such as the General Agreement on Trade in Services (GATS) and Agreement on Trade-Related Aspects of Intellectual Property Rights (TRIPS), which are automatically binding on the Organization's entire membership. On the meaning of "plurilateral" under the general law of treaties, see *supra* Chapter 3, note 177.

weak.[249] That is perhaps why not a single WTO dispute, including the ongoing Airbus/Boeing feud, has invoked the plurilateral. Moreover, as we will discuss with respect to Airbus/Boeing, it appears likely that a new agreement – engineered outside the WTO – may be required to govern the permissible scope of aircraft manufacturing subsidies in the future.

8.15.5. *Airbus/Boeing Saga (1): Background*

At the commercial level, Airbus and Boeing have been spirited rivals for decades. Because they operate as a *de facto* duopoly in the large civil aircraft sector – a sector that is responsible for massive revenues and hundreds of thousands of jobs in their home States[250] – it is not surprising that their private interests have become, through the "black box" of trade policy lobbying,[251] national interests as well. Indeed, Airbus owes its very existence to the desire of several powerful EU Member States to create a strategic industrial alternative to the U.S.-based Boeing, a fact that raised the red flag of public subsidy from the beginning.[252] To forestall a major international row, the United States and EU began negotiating in the late 1980s for a bilateral agreement on the permissible scope of State support for the industry. These rules, which were designed to be more restrictive than the procurement standards sketched out in the Aircraft Agreement mentioned earlier, entered into force through the 1992 EU/U.S. Agreement on Large Civil Aircraft ("EU/U.S. Agreement").[253] Among other things, the EU/U.S. Agreement capped the amount of direct support (such as capital infusions) European States could offer to Airbus while

---

[249] *See* Nils Meier-Kaienberg, *The WTO's "Toughest" Case: An Examination of the Effectiveness of the WTO Dispute Resolution Procedure in the Airbus-Boeing Dispute Over Aircraft Subsidies*, 71 J. Air L. & Com. 191, 198 (2006) (criticizing the Aircraft Agreement as "a general declaration of principles [rather] than a specific enforceable document").

[250] For a more detailed discussion of the commercial and political history of the Airbus/Boeing rivalry, see John Newhouse, Boeing Versus Airbus: The Inside Story of the Greatest International Competition in Business (2008); Mohan R. Pandey, How Boeing Defied the Airbus Challenge: An Insider's Account (2010).

[251] Brian F. Havel, *The Constitution in an Era of Supranational Adjudication*, 78 N.C.L.R. 257, 369 (2000) (using "black box" as a metaphor for nontransparency).

[252] In fact, the United States originally sought to curtail subsidies to Airbus by bringing a dispute settlement action under the WTO's precursor instrument, the GATT. Despite receiving a favorable ruling from the panel constituted to hear the case, the EU blocked the decision through a now-extinct rule requiring all GATT parties to consent to a panel decision – including the loser. *See* Jennifer A. Manner, *How to Avoid Airbus II: A Primer for the Domestic Industry*, 23 Cal. W. Int'l L.J. 139, 148–49 (1992).

[253] *See generally* European Comm'n, Background Fact Sheet: EU/US Large Civil Aircraft (Oct. 11, 2012) [hereinafter Background Fact Sheet]. For the text of the Agreement, *see* http://tcc. export.gov/Trade_Agreements/All_Trade_Agreements/exp_002816.asp.

also regulating indirect subsidies offered by the United States, such as Boeing-directed military and National Aeronautics and Space Administration (NASA) contracts. Because of perceived imbalances in the EU/U.S. Agreement, particularly with respect to the amount of research and development (R&D) aid that Airbus was purportedly receiving, the United States unilaterally abrogated the treaty in 2004 and filed a dispute before the WTO's DSB alleging more than 300 subsidy violations, most of which are anchored in the terms of the SCM Agreement.[254] The EU quickly counterclaimed on behalf of Airbus, although the value of allegedly unlawful subsidies to Boeing identified in the complaint – $23.7 billion[255] – paled beside the more than $200 billion that the United States claimed as Airbus's largesse.[256]

8.15.6. *Airbus/Boeing Saga (2): Brief Analysis*

Although a complete analysis of the Airbus/Boeing dispute, which thus far has yielded numerous reports from the DSB (some at nearly 1000 pages apiece),[257] lies beyond the scope of this chapter, the early consensus is that each party has overstated the subsidization that the other was channeling to its respective aircraft builder.[258] Perhaps more importantly, it does not appear that either side intends to alter its subsidization behavior. Each side continues to assert that the other has failed to comply with WTO rules; additional DSB rulings on the appropriateness of retaliatory measures are expected by the end of 2013.[259]

---

[254] *See* Background Fact Sheet, *supra* note 253.

[255] *See* First Written Submission by the European Communities, *United States – Measures Affecting Trade in Large Civil Aircraft*, ¶ 2, WT/DS353 (July 11, 2007).

[256] *See* Daniel Pruzin, *WTO Panel Ruling Slams Illegal Subsidies for Europe's Airbus in Case Brought by U.S.*, 27 Int'l Trade Rep. (BNA) 1029 (July 8, 2010) (noting that the United States had originally alleged that the EU furnished $205 billion in illegal subsidies to Airbus).

[257] *See, e.g.*, Appellate Body Report, *European Communities and Certain Member States – Measures Affecting Trade in Large Civil Aircraft*, WT/DS316/AB/R (May 18, 2011); Appellate Body Report, *United States – Measures Affecting Trade in Large Civil Aircraft (Second Complaint)*, WT/DS353/AB/R (Mar. 13, 2012).

[258] Although the dispute is still ongoing, the DSB found that Boeing had received $5.3 billion in illegal subsidies – $2.7 billion of which the U.S. was asked to remove. *See* Daniel Pruzin, *WTO Publishes Final Ruling in Complaint Against Boeing Subsidies: EU, US Claim Win*, 28 Int'l Trade Rep. (BNA) 564 (Apr. 7, 2011). Airbus was found to have received in excess of $18 billion in illegal subsidies, far less than the $205 billion that the U.S. originally alleged. *See* Pruzin, *supra* note 256, at 1029.

[259] For continuing updates on the proceedings, including the most recent rulings from the DSB, see WTO, European Communities – Measures Affecting Trade in Large Civil Aircraft, http://www.wto.org/english/tratop_e/dispu_e/cases_e/ds316_e.htm; WTO, United States – Measures Affecting Trade in Large Civil Aircraft – Second Complaint, http://www.wto.org/english/tratop_e/dispu_e/cases_e/ds353_e.htm/.

8.15.7. *Airbus/Boeing Saga (3): Ineffectiveness of the WTO*

To appreciate why the WTO may not be the most effective instrument to discipline aircraft subsidies, it is necessary to recall how the DSB works. Setting aside the WTO's pretensions to be an authentic multilateral organization deploying powers of multilateral dispute settlement, we can better conceive the Organization – for adjudicatory purposes at least – as a bilateral entity. Aggrieved States file complaints against alleged defectors, and their only remedy, assuming that a violation is found, is to receive authorization (after extended hearings and consultations) from the DSB to take reciprocal retaliatory action against the scofflaw State. The WTO members that are not party to the dispute do not impose a form of collective punishment such as simultaneously withholding trade concessions. Even without collective action, bilateral retaliation is restricted, as noted, by the reciprocity requirement: as a result, retaliation resembles not so much a form of punishment as a "payoff" by a violating party to a contract. Indeed, as lawyer-economists Alan Sykes and Warren Schwartz have argued,[260] WTO dispute settlement is more akin to the contractual doctrine of "efficient breach," whereby a party that no longer believes that the contractual benefits warrant the costs will compensate the aggrieved party (albeit at a level lower than what the breaching party would pay had it been forced to complete the terms of the contract).[261] In the Airbus/Boeing dispute, the EU may be willing to "pay compensation" in the form of enduring retaliatory trade measures from the United States rather than internalizing the more (politically, although not necessarily economically) costly alternative of cutting the cord of State aid to Airbus. As past WTO cases have shown, the economic consequences of retaliatory measures are likely to be spread across industrial sectors rather than concentrated on the sector receiving subsidies; that way, while Airbus remains relatively protected, other branches of the economy may have to pick up the tab.[262]

---

[260] *See* Warren F. Schwartz & Alan O. Sykes, *The Economic Structure of Renegotiation and Dispute Settlement in the World Trade Organization*, 31 J. LEGAL STUD. S179 (2002).

[261] A simple aviation-related example would be that of an airline that sells the last ticket on a flight for $500. At the time of departure, a would-be passenger offers the airline $650 for the last seat. In such a scenario, it would be more efficient for the airline to break its contract of carriage with the first passenger and reimburse her $600 (which, we assume, is equivalent to the ticket price ($500) plus any damage that she suffers from not being on that particular flight ($100); the end result is that the airline would take in greater revenue ($550 as opposed to $500) and the passenger who valued the last seat more would obtain it.

[262] *See, e.g., European Communities – Measures Concerning Meat and Meat Products* (Hormones), Original Complaint filed by the United States, Recourse to Arbitration by the European Communities under Article 22.6 of the DSU: Decision by the Arbitrators, WT/DS26/ARB (July 12, 1999) (providing no objection to the contention of the United States that

8.15.8. A New Regime of International Regulation
of Aircraft Subsidies?

Even if the WTO is ill-equipped to compel two large industrial powers to roll back their aircraft subsidization programs, it is not clear that *all* subsidies to this sector ought to be curtailed. As discussed previously in Chapter 6, some analysts have argued that States should inject public aid into R&D for "green" aircraft technologies to help offset international aviation's carbon footprint. Fuel-efficient aircraft, along with eco-friendly biofuels, are seen by some (particularly the airline industry) to be a better economic option than scaling down international air services through taxation or regulatory artifices such as cap-and-trade systems. Critics of even this form of subsidization argue, however, that airlines have a built-in incentive – spiraling fuel prices – to demand more efficient aircraft and that the most innovative manufacturers already have a waiting market for state-of-the-art, environmentally efficient aircraft; attracting capital from private investors, therefore, should not be a problem. Whatever the merits of this debate, another powerful (though perhaps economically unsound) argument for subsidization is bound up with the so-called infant industries approach. With emerging economies such as China, Brazil, and Russia apparently anxious to enter the large civil aircraft market, it is possible that they will need (and want) to replicate the Airbus precedent by unleashing billions of dollars in launch aid. To stabilize what could quickly become a complicated and contentious environment for aircraft manufacturing, it has been suggested that the principal subsidy antagonists, the United States and the EU, return to the negotiating table to hammer out a new aircraft subsidy agreement. Others have proposed a similar move within the WTO, perhaps by expanding the current plurilateral Aircraft Agreement or, more ambitiously, by a multilateral agreement that encompasses all WTO members. Another option would be for the United States and the EU to open their talks to other interested parties, particularly those emerging powers that are interested in building a robust aircraft manufacturing base. Neither the United States nor Europe, for example, will welcome the fact that the assertive plans of their China-based competitor, the Commercial Aircraft Corporation of China (COMAC), remain unbounded by any new subsidization rules. And, while further WTO DSB litigation will remain an available option (at least for the time being), China, too, may be willing to "pay the price" for breaching the

---

any country may engage in a "carousel suspension" of concessions against the EU whereby the United States periodically changes its list of targeted products).

SCM Agreement rather than rein in further aid to COMAC.[263] Although it is true that the Airbus/Boeing duopoly has not proven detrimental to competition, and that a third or even a fourth major actor could help spur a new round of innovation while pushing prices down to a more competitive level,[264] it is not clear that the global aircraft manufacturing market can sustain more participants. The use of subsidies to promote the survival of new entrants could be a recipe for waste and excessive production. Again, however, that is likely to be a matter for resolution at the political and diplomatic level rather than in the hearing rooms of the WTO.

8.15.9. *A Regime for Export Credits*

As previously noted, another subsidization issue that affects the aircraft manufacturing sector involves the distribution of credits, such as loan guarantees, to foreign-based purchasers to improve their terms of trade and in that way to boost home State exports. These guarantees, usually administered by export credit agencies,[265] shelter financial institutions from the full risk of their loans to aircraft purchasers while driving down the cost of capital for airlines in the form of lower interest rates. Because of a domestic restriction usually referred to as the "home country rule," not all airlines, regardless of their financial status, are able to access these credits. U.S. air carriers such as United Airlines and Delta cannot use export credits offered by their country's export credit agency, the Export-Import Bank (or ExIm),[266] to purchase Boeing aircraft. Similarly, European carriers established in France, Germany, the U.K., and

---

[263] "[COMAC] can sink billions into [aircraft] projects without any concern for [the] bottom line." Andrew Parker, *Aerospace: A Dogfight for the Duopoly*, Fin. Times, Aug. 7, 2012, at 7. Moreover, China's emergence as a major player in aircraft financing "increases the likelihood that [its new C919 single-aisle passenger aircraft] will become a credible alternative to the Airbus A320 and Boeing 737." *Id.*

[264] This would likely happen as the new competitors seek to gain market footholds. COMAC, for example, "will probably secure international sales only by initially offering cut-price deals to airlines." *Id.*

[265] Direct loans from export credit agencies are rare. *See* Dean N. Gerber et al., *Aircraft Financings Involving the Export-Import Bank of the United States, in* Aircraft Finance Online (2010), at U.S. Banking-22 [hereinafter Gerber, *Export-Import Bank*].

[266] Originally established in 1934, ExIm Bank is backed by the full faith and credit of the U.S. Government. By fulfilling its mission, ExIm Bank aims to turn "export opportunities into sales that create and maintain U.S. jobs and build a stronger economy." Gerber, *Export-Import Bank, supra* note 265, at U.S. Banking-5. During the 2008 fiscal year, ExIm Bank authorized $14.4 billion in financing to support an estimated $19.6 billion in U.S. exports of goods and services. Air transport accounts for nearly 50% of ExIm Bank's exposure. *See id.* The Bank today is the largest financier of U.S.-manufactured commercial aircraft in the world, with more than $30 billion in outstanding exposure. *Id.*

Spain (the States that are home to Airbus[267]) cannot receive loan guarantees to purchase Airbus aircraft. This restriction, some charge, confers an unfair competitive advantage on carriers like Ryanair and Emirates, which are based in nonmanufacturing States.[268] Private financial institutions, too, claim that export credit agencies are retarding their recovery from the 2008 financial crisis by providing an alternative and more favorably priced financing product. Moreover, these institutions claim that although airlines may have had some justification to seek export credits after 2008 when financial sector liquidity dried up, that problem is no longer acute.[269]

8.15.10. *The OECD 2011 Understanding on Export Credits*

To address what was fast becoming an international trade problem, in 2010 the OECD convened a new working group to set standards on export credits that would bring their terms of engagement more into line with regular market rates.[270] The 2011 Understanding is a nonbinding document that commits the Organization's thirty-four members (along with China and Russia, should they choose to join[271]) to a unified set of terms, conditions, and procedures with respect to official support for large and regional aircraft exports. The intent of the Understanding is to drop the level of export credit support from its apparent high of 30% of all aircraft deliveries in 2009 to more modest levels[272] by increasing the minimum premium rate of export credit financing by at least double.[273] Airlines, arguably, would therefore be more apt to seek financing from commercial banks rather than relying on export credits as a

---

[267] Technically, Airbus is a wholly owned subsidiary of the multinational European Aeronautic Defence and Space Company (EADS).

[268] The "home country" rule is actually an *unwritten*, informal understanding among the major export credit agencies supporting the manufacturers of large commercial jet aircraft – including ExIm Bank, ECGD (U.K.), COFACE (France), and Euler Hermes (Germany) – that they will not finance competing aircraft that will be principally located in their own or each other's countries. *See* Gerber, *Export-Import Bank, supra* note 265, at US Banking-12.

[269] U.S. and EU carriers, in particular, are critical of the rule as they face limited financing sources following the global economic crisis. *See* Gerber, *Export-Import Bank, supra* note 265, at US Banking-13.

[270] *See* OECD, *Sector Understanding on Export Credits for Civil Aircraft,* TAD/ASU(2011) 1 (Aug. 31, 2011) [hereinafter OECD, *2011 Understanding*].

[271] Thus far Australia, Brazil, Canada, the EU, Japan, Korea, New Zealand, Norway, Switzerland, and the United States have signed on to the 2011 Understanding, while China and Russia have opted to remain on the sidelines. *See id.* pt. I.

[272] *See* Press Release, OECD, Aircraft Sector Understanding: Signing Ceremony (Feb. 25, 2011).

[273] *See* OECD, *2011 Understanding, supra* note 270, app. II. The rate calculation and increases are set to be adjusted periodically based on market conditions and reflect a number of factors, including the borrower's risk classification.

principal funding tool. Moreover, the 2011 Understanding is intended to correct perceived defects in the previous agreement adopted in 2007. For instance, the new accord eliminates the 2007 Understanding's distinction between regional and large jets, with the former being previously eligible for broader financing options from government-backed institutions.[274] Further, the 2011 Understanding is intended to reduce the likelihood of participating States seeking to litigate aircraft export disagreements before the WTO while also upholding the OECD's WTO-delegated competence to design and implement trade-friendly export credit regimes.[275]

8.15.11. *Some Shortcomings of the 2011 Understanding*

The OECD's 2011 Understanding, which has been heavily criticized by a consortium of carriers using export credits, was unsurprisingly endorsed by many U.S. and EU carriers and by private financing institutions. As attractive as the Understanding may appear at first glance, a number of shortcomings can be identified. First, the document includes a broad "grandfather clause" that will allow aircraft orders financed before 2013 to be subject to the OECD's much more liberal export credit guidelines established in 2007.[276] Second, the 2011 Understanding may not be designed to take sufficient account of emerging regulatory incentives for airlines to purchase new, eco-friendly aircraft; if airlines feel compelled to rapidly upgrade their existing inputs in a more strict regulatory environment, there could be a considerable international backlash against the limitations established under the 2011 Understanding. Finally, as with any action taken by the OECD, there is the question of legality. Although nothing in international law prevents States from voluntarily agreeing to nonbinding accords, international law critics of a legalist bent are ever-wary of the expansion of so-called soft law. Their concern, perhaps misplaced, is that the existence of "*faux* law" like the 2011 Understanding undermines the legitimacy of "*bona fide* law" like the Cape Town Convention or the WTO's trade rules.

8.15.12. *Incentives for Compliance with the 2011 Understanding*

States may have other incentives (besides legality) for complying with the 2011 Understanding. It is not unlikely that the OECD will continue to act as a

[274] *Compare* OECD, *Sector Understanding on Export Credits for Civil Aircraft*, pt. II, ch.1, TAD/PG(2007) 4/Final (July 27, 2007), *with* OECD, *2011 Understanding*, *supra* note 270, pt. II, ch. 1.
[275] *See* Press Release, *supra* note 272.
[276] *See* OECD, *2011 Understanding*, *supra* note 270, pt. VI.

coordinating body for other matters of international economic concern: a State contemplating a defection from the 2011 Understanding may squander negotiating capital that it might otherwise wish to use at the OECD (or in another multilateral forum) in the future. Moreover, because the OECD is a relatively compact organization and the distribution of export credits is easily monitored, any State defecting from the 2011 Understanding risks sparking a chain reaction of defections. The EU, for example, may be satisfied that Emirates, a major international competitor of European airlines, is restricted by the 2011 Understanding from access to prior levels of export credits to purchase Boeing aircraft. But the EU could destabilize that development if, for instance, it were to furnish U.S. carriers with new export credits that breached the Understanding's maxima. Finally, it is likely that most (if not all) of the States that agreed to the 2011 Understanding believe that there is a domestic upside to doing so: their financial institutions want to restore competitiveness to the aircraft finance market, and their taxpayers will appreciate that national revenues no longer prop up lucrative transactions that benefit a small number of stakeholders (most of which, like airlines purchasing aircraft on credit, are foreign based).

8.15.13. *Beyond the 2011 Understanding*

However one assesses the position of the 2011 Understanding in international law, that instrument alone is unlikely to provide a complete solution to the export credit problem. A new shock to the global financial system could give the Understanding a short shelf life, and, as noted, changes in the airline industry's regulatory environment may lead to fresh lobbying for a relaxation of export credit rules (or, absent that, to direct government subsidies such as a "cash for clunkers"–style program to incentivize airlines to purchase "green" aircraft). Moreover, aircraft manufacturing giants Airbus and Boeing may also turn against the 2011 Understanding if it begins to impact their bottom line. As previously noted, more than 30% of these manufacturers' aircraft orders are supported by export credits. Still, if forecasts of a global $4.5 trillion demand for new commercial jet aircraft over the next two decades prove accurate,[277] limitations on the availability of export credits may not continue to stir controversy.

---

[277] *See* Parker, *supra* note 263, at 9.

Afterword

The European Union (EU) created a framework for aviation liberalization within its single market jurisdiction and has embarked on the task of establishing "horizontal agreements" (and a few comprehensive agreements) with the rest of the world. The EU is slowly but surely harmonizing more than 3600 bilateral agreements that exist between all the Member States and their aviation counterparts across the world. We could perhaps debate whether, particularly in the context of the U.S./EU open skies agreement, the EU used its leverage effectively. With respect to other third countries, the EU is frequently challenged to demonstrate the added value it creates vis-à-vis traditional bilateralism – to which the European Commission consistently replies that, in a global context, the Member States systemically diluted and fragmented Europe's negotiating clout.

The United States has likewise sought to export its version of open skies. Although at times criticized for having opened international aviation markets, but not the equally large continental U.S. market, for international competition, the United States is the uncontested leader in the liberalization of traditional closely regulated bilateral aviation markets.

However, dramatic changes are taking place in the global aviation marketplace, so that we must review past experiences and, if necessary, develop new concepts and solutions. After twenty years of U.S. open skies and a decade of the EU model, international aviation is anything but business as usual.

What has happened? To answer that question, my essay is divided in two parts. In the first part, I look at the intra-European market and the lessons it holds for what I call the "commoditization" of airline services – a phenomenon we see in regional markets worldwide. In the second part, I look more broadly at the market shifts that have taken place, and that are accelerating, in international and intercontinental services. In this second part, I call the reader's attention to the need for new global regulatory structures that can keep pace with these market changes.

As to the intra-European market, it is driven by *costs*. With more than 140 million passengers flying on low-cost carriers each year, market behavior and expectation on intra-European flights has changed. Low-cost carriers now cover approximately 45% of the European market.

Of course, traditional network carriers such as Lufthansa, Air France, KLM, Iberia, and others have announced, or already have developed, varying models of lower-cost enterprises that are to function as an additional product platform within each airline group. The bottom line is that traditional carriers that depend on intra-European routes must find – without an American-style Chapter 11 bankruptcy vehicle – ways of *reducing legacy costs*, because the short-haul product has been *commoditized*.

So what is next in the EU internal market? To avoid pure speculation, let me try to describe some vectors that could drive further developments.

The first vector is the general *perception* that low-cost carriers are really "low-cost" and can drive any competitor out of the market, either through an *absolute* low-cost system like Ryanair, or by adapting a *relative* low-cost system on a route-by-route basis like easyJet. This perception of "low-cost" as being the *ne plus ultra* in airline efficiency has given rise to the creation of airlines such as Germanwings and Iberia Express. They will seek to compete by unbundling and then rebundling the product elements to fit the brand. The objective is to minimize the effects of commoditization without jeopardizing brand loyalty.

This development is not unique to Europe. Carriers in Asia are following with keen interest whether an established airline, burdened by legacy costs, can actually develop from within its own structure a modern, low-cost subsidiary that can sustain itself with an "own" brand and an "own" product and pricing regime without cannibalizing the markets of its mother or sister companies belonging to the same group – and without simply further reducing yields. A fundamental question for the likes of ANA, JAL, Cathay Pacific, Qantas, Qatar, and so on, is: will it will be sufficient in the medium term to remain competitive by replacing "business class" with "economy plus," or are entirely new concepts and new business models required to withstand the growing competitive pressure?

These questions are of fundamental importance for airline consumers in the EU and elsewhere as the airline product commoditizes. They are an expression, too, of a growing realization that aviation is more than an infrastructure provider; aviation has a basic economic rationale and function. If the economic returns are insufficient for a given market, low-cost carriers will not operate there, and established airlines increasingly exit these kinds of markets. This trend has ramifications for an important (and traditional) characteristic of aviation – that "scheduled" operators are to provide regular and published services.

A second vector in the internal EU market is *consolidation* to generate economies of scale and scope. As was the case with Southwest in the United States, Europe's Ryanair is no longer a start-up, but rather a giant with 80 million passengers annually. Ryanair actually drives the rules of the game and is clearly seeking to maintain and even to strengthen its grip on the marketplace – in the future, perhaps, not only by relying on organic growth but also by turning to acquisitions. It is virtually a certainty that consolidation will have to occur if other players are going to continue to remain competitive in the internal EU market.

Moreover, as regional carriers like Ryanair and easyJet look outward to the international context beyond the EU, the most frequently debated question is the circumstances under which a new business model would need to be invented for their international long-haul operations. As they unbundle and rebundle their product, they will be reevaluating the willingness of passengers to self-connect. Self-connecting passengers on a large scale can actually generate totally new dynamics in international markets.

A third vector in Europe is a growing need for an *integrated European transport policy*. What is European aviation really about? Airlines seem to have the worst of both worlds: on the one hand, they are seen as a public service utility, offering scheduled services, but with inadequate investments into infrastructure and rising external costs; and on the other hand, they operate in a market that does not function properly because market entry barriers are too low and market exit barriers are too high. To complicate matters even further, EU Member States pursue different policies and with different priorities. A true single market does not yet exist because Europe consists of nations with their own separate economic and legislative histories, their own social legislation, and their own taxation systems. The Third Package in 1992 was an important step, but it was *liberalization without harmonization*. Now, particularly in the light of experience with other regions of the world, EU policymakers must develop an aviation policy that recognizes the role of air transport by promoting competition as a driver of consolidation, and by investing in infrastructure as a prerequisite for international competitiveness.

And this question of aviation policy leads me once again to the international marketplace, the world beyond Europe but which, of course, also includes Europe. The need for this kind of intensive policy thinking now exists throughout the global aviation community. Countries that have recognized the economic value of aviation and that are investing in infrastructure – such as Turkey, China, and the Gulf States – have demonstrably shown themselves able to prepare for the growth of aviation as a sector, and the growth of aviation as a driver of national economic growth. Evidently, continued expansion will ultimately have to be balanced against environmental and social concerns; but nations that are avoiding such political discussions fail to appropriately address the stakes in terms of their economic prospects and stability.

Indeed, while some nations squabble about transport priorities and what it means to have an aviation industry, the markets continue to evolve internationally. Arguably, the bilateral strategic alliance grew into a system of multilateral alliances, and even those appear now to be ceding relevance to new structures. Within the Star Alliance in Europe, for example, a partnership among equals has been partially replaced by quasi-mergers and acquisitions: Lufthansa has bought Austrian and Swiss, and a significant share of Brussels Airlines. Similarly, within Skyteam, transactions have taken place between Air France, KLM, and Alitalia; and within oneworld, Iberia and British Airways merged in a holding entity called International Airlines Group. Such strong structures have served to intensify cooperation with equally strengthened U.S. partners.

An additional piece of the puzzle has fallen into place with the increased presence of Gulf carriers within international alliances, as well as their involvement in acquisitions. Again, it is noteworthy that Lufthansa appears not to rely solely on an alliance relationship with fast-growing Turkish Airlines, but may also be interested in exploring ways of strengthening that cooperation beyond an alliance partnership as a strategic answer to the Gulf carriers.

Twenty years after the U.S./Netherlands open skies agreement, *globalization* has driven airlines out of their traditional bilateral paradigm. The key to success in such a global market is size and connectivity. If an airline has a sizable home market to feed its international network, it will seek to combine third and fourth freedom operations with fifth and sixth freedom routes. If it has a small home market, it will rely solely on its connectivity at its hub. But in all cases, the players seem now to believe that organic growth will not be sufficient to maintain a sustainably competitive position in the global market. That is a paradigm shift in international aviation in a mere twenty years!

International airlines (or, better said, airline groups), in my view, will strengthen their position in the markets that they dominate and strategically compete for growth in new markets through cooperation and acquisition. That will ultimately mean that smaller competitors will exit international routes, unless they operate in clearly defined niche markets with high barriers to entry. We will see the emergence of three or four international groups, functioning on the basis of equity swaps, acquisitions, mergers, or intense cooperation, sharing a large part of the international market – with significant competition in selected key markets, and competition for growth markets.

In view of these fundamental, dramatic market developments, we need political leadership! There was a vision underlying the negotiations that led to a U.S/EU open skies agreement and a (partial) open aviation area between the two regions. And as much as I acknowledge the need for political realism in applying agreements, the U.S./EU agreement's innovative Joint Committee should be motivated to turn a vision into a reality. The EU + North Atlantic + U.S. market is the single biggest global traffic market, and the aviation relationship between the EU and the United States should not be reduced to managing a treaty. I do fear that we are beginning to get used to *managing* the *acquis international*.

Surely, also, the time has come to review ownership and control provisions. It is not a dogma but a necessity to question whether these restrictions are still fit for purpose in light of the ongoing market developments I am describing. Ultimately we should strive to create one aviation market for the global economy, so let us start by reinforcing norms that set a framework for one North Atlantic market.

And this leads me to another phenomenon. Airlines are becoming increasingly upset about the competitive distortions created by differing levels of *external costs*. Even if they reduce their internal costs, how are they supposed to compete against other airlines that do not have to pay an aviation tax or that are subsidized by their governments? The *conditions of competition* have become highly relevant, not only the market access opportunities.

The question is how, in a globalized economic environment, the market conditions can be harmonized in order to enable fair international competition. The U.S./EU agreement provided tools to address that question with its Joint Committee. Does this historic agreement not mark the beginning of a new approach to cooperation on regulatory issues? Hopefully, we will see encouraging developments with respect to the emissions trading scheme. But the agreement also has, in its core, a commitment to an element of international cooperation on standards of competition. Ten years after the first EU-driven bilateral open skies agreements, we should look at whether broader conditions of competition on safety, environment, competition policy, state aids, consumer rights, security, and other regulatory matters should be harmonized – with the ultimate vision in mind that if they are not harmonized, airlines will not be able to compete under fair market conditions for the simple reason that there is not one market.

Many incremental steps would be necessary to create that one market. But the time has come to perceive the enormous momentum we now have in international aviation, and to take stock of the changes required to provide for a suitable framework for global aviation.

In summary, I will conclude with what I consider to be three crucial points. First, the EU Court of Justice and the Council of EU Transport Ministers did actually set the stage in 2002 for a new approach to international aviation by determining how sovereign Member States of the EU would coordinate their international aviation negotiations.

Second, the liberalization of the intra-European market, and the development of regulatory tools for the international negotiations that followed, acted as catalysts for dynamic market changes.

Third, the international markets have matured even further to the point that legal and political answers must be found to guide these dynamic market changes.

The changes that I have noted and forecasted are not unique to a single region; they are happening across the world and are in need of regulatory attention across the world. But global aviation, as yet, has no economic regulatory framework *with teeth*. It is time to move, as the industry itself has done, from a national and bilateral paradigm and to consider the most appropriate manner in which *global regulatory approaches* can address the challenges of a global airline marketplace.

Ulrich Schulte-Strathaus
Managing Director, Aviation Strategy & Concepts
Brussels, March 2013

Select Bibliography

BOOKS (AND CONTRIBUTED CHAPTERS TO BOOKS) LISTED
ALPHABETICALLY BY AUTHOR

AREEDA, PHILIP E. & HERBERT HOVENKAMP, ANTITRUST LAW (3D ED. 2006)

ARISTOTLE, ETHICA NICOMACHEA (L. Bywater ed., Oxford Univ. Press (1920))

AUST, ANTHONY, MODERN TREATY LAW AND PRACTICE (2000)

BANNER, STUART, WHO OWNS THE SKY?: THE STRUGGLE TO CONTROL AIRSPACE FROM THE WRIGHT BROTHERS ON (2008)

Basedow, Jürgen, *Verkehrsrecht und Verkehrspolitik als Europäische Aufgabe, in* EUROPÄISCHE VERKEHRSPOLITIK 1 (Gerd Aberle ed., 1987)

BASSIOUNI, M. CHERIF & EDWARD M. WISE, AUT DEDERE AUT JUDICARE: THE DUTY TO EXTRADITE OR PROSECUTE IN INTERNATIONAL LAW (1995)

BROWNLIE, IAN, PRINCIPLES OF PUBLIC INTERNATIONAL LAW (7th ed. 2008)

BUNKER, DONALD H., 1 INTERNATIONAL AIRCRAFT FINANCING (2005)

BURLEIGH, MICHAEL, BLOOD AND RAGE: A CULTURAL HISTORY OF TERRORISM (2009)

CALDWELL, LYNTON KEITH, INTERNATIONAL ENVIRONMENTAL POLICY AND LAW (1st ed. 1980)

CCH AVIATION LAW REPORTER (1947–)

CHENG, BIN, THE LAW OF INTERNATIONAL AIR TRANSPORT (1962)

Clarke, Claybourne Fox & Thiago Chagas, *Aviation and Climate Change Regulation, in* LEGAL ASPECTS OF CARBON TRADING: KYOTO, COPENHAGEN, AND BEYOND 606 (David Freestone & Charlotte Streck eds., 2009)

CONCISE ENCYCLOPEDIA OF ECONOMICS (David R. Henderson ed., 2007)

DAVIES, NORMAN, VANISHED KINGDOMS: THE RISE AND FALL OF STATES AND NATIONS (2012)

Dee, Philippa, *Services Liberalization Toward the ASEAN Economic Community, in* TRACING THE PROGRESS TOWARD THE ASEAN ECONOMIC COMMUNITY 28 (Shujiro Urata & Misa Okabe eds., 2010)

DEGAN, V. D., SOURCES OF INTERNATIONAL LAW (1997)

DIEDERIKS-VERSCHOOR, I. H. PH., AN INTRODUCTION TO AIR LAW (8th rev. ed. 2006)

DIEDERIKS-VERSCHOOR, I. H. PH., AN INTRODUCTION TO AIR LAW (Pablo M. J. Mendes de Leon ed., 9th rev. ed. 2012)

DOGANIS, RIGAS, FLYING OFF COURSE: AIRLINE ECONOMICS AND MARKETING (4th ed. 2010)

DOLZER, RUDOLF & CHRISTOPH SCHREUER, PRINCIPLES OF INTERNATIONAL INVESTMENT LAW (2008)

DONNELLY, JACK, REALISM AND INTERNATIONAL RELATIONS (2000)

ECONOMICS OF PUBLIC INTERNATIONAL LAW (Eric A. Posner ed., 2010)

EPSTEIN, RICHARD A., A THEORY OF STRICT LIABILITY: TOWARD A REFORMATION OF TORT LAW (1980)

EPSTEIN, RICHARD A., TORT LAW (1999)

EUROPEAN AIR LAW (Elmar Giemulla et al. eds., 1992–)

Gerber, Dean N., *Aircraft Financing*, ch. 7, *in* EQUIPMENT LEASING – LEVERAGED LEASING (Ian Shrank & Arnold G. Gough eds., 5th ed. 2012)

GERBER, DEAN N., et al., *Aircraft Financings Involving the Export-Import Bank of the United States, in* AIRCRAFT FINANCE ONLINE (2010)

GOEDHUIS, DANIEL, AIR LAW IN THE MAKING (1938)

GOLDHIRSCH, LAWRENCE B., THE WARSAW CONVENTION ANNOTATED: A LEGAL HANDBOOK (2d ed. 2000)

GOLDSMITH, JACK L. & ERIC A. POSNER, THE LIMITS OF INTERNATIONAL LAW (2005)

GOODE, ROY, COMMERCIAL LAW (2d ed. 1995)

GOODE, ROY, OFFICIAL COMMENTARY ON THE CONVENTION ON INTERNATIONAL INTERESTS IN MOBILE EQUIPMENT AND PROTOCOL THERETO ON MATTERS SPECIFIC TO AIRCRAFT EQUIPMENT (UNIDROIT rev. ed. 2008)

GOODE, ROY, HERBERT KRONKE, EWAN MCKENDRICK, & JEFFREY WOOL, TRANSNATIONAL COMMERCIAL LAW: INTERNATIONAL INSTRUMENTS AND COMMENTARY (2d ed. 2012)

GROTIUS, HUGO, THE FREEDOM OF THE SEAS (Ralph Van Deman Mogoffin trans., Oxford Univ. Press 1916) (1608)

HAANAPPEL, PETER P. C., RATEMAKING IN INTERNATIONAL AIR TRANSPORT: A LEGAL ANALYSIS OF INTERNATIONAL AIR FARES AND RATES (1978)

THE HAGUE CONVENTION ON JURISDICTION AND JUDGMENTS (Andreas F. Lowenfeld & Linda J. Silberman eds., 2001)

HANLEY, DONAL P., AIRCRAFT OPERATING LEASING: A LEGAL AND PRACTICAL ANALYSIS IN THE CONTEXT OF PUBLIC AND PRIVATE INTERNATIONAL AVIATION (2012)

HANLON, PAT, GLOBAL AIRLINES: COMPETITION IN A TRANSNATIONAL INDUSTRY (2D ED. 2002)

HARRIS, JAMES W., PROPERTY & JUSTICE (1996)

HAVEL, BRIAN F., BEYOND OPEN SKIES: A NEW REGIME FOR INTERNATIONAL AVIATION (2009)

Havel, Brian F., *A US Point of View on European ATM Developments, in* ACHIEVING THE SINGLE EUROPEAN SKY 107 (Pablo M. J. Mendes de Leon & Daniel Calleja Crespo eds., 2011)

Havel, Brian F. & Gabriel S. Sanchez, *International Air Transport Association, in* HANDBOOK OF TRANSNATIONAL ECONOMIC GOVERNANCE REGIMES (Christian Tietje & Alan Brouder eds., 2009)

HENKIN, LOUIS, HOW NATIONS BEHAVE (2d ed. 1979)

HOFFMANN, MATTHEW J., CLIMATE GOVERNANCE AT THE CROSSROADS: EXPERIMENTING WITH A GLOBAL RESPONSE AFTER KYOTO (2011)

Honnebier, B. Patrick, *The English Blue Sky Case – Topical International Aviation Finance Law Issues, in* 2011 IIASL ALUMNI BOOK (2d (rectified) ed. 2012)

Hsu, Chia-Jui & Yu-Chan Chang, *The Influence of Airline Ownership Rules on Aviation Policies and Carriers' Strategies, in* 5 PROCEEDINGS OF THE EASTERN ASIA SOCIETY FOR TRANSPORTATION STUDIES 557 (2005)

HUANG, JIEFANG, AVIATION SAFETY THROUGH THE RULE OF LAW: ICAO'S MECHANISMS AND PRACTICES (2009)

INAMA, STEFANO, RULES OF ORIGIN IN INTERNATIONAL TRADE (2009)

INTERNATIONAL ENCYCLOPEDIA OF THE SOCIAL SCIENCES (William A. Darity ed., 2d ed. 2008)

INTERNATIONAL INVESTMENT LAW AND COMPARATIVE PUBLIC LAW (Stephan W. Schill ed., 2010)

KAHN, ALFRED E., THE ECONOMICS OF REGULATION: PRINCIPLES AND INSTITUTIONS (1981)

KANE, ROBERT M., AIR TRANSPORTATION (2003)

KASARDA, JOHN & GREG LINDSAY, AEROTROPOLIS: THE WAY WE'LL LIVE NEXT (2011)

KASPER, DANIEL A., DEREGULATION AND GLOBALIZATION: LIBERALIZING INTERNATIONAL TRADE IN SERVICES (1988)

KEOHANE, ROBERT O., AFTER HEGEMONY: COOPERATION AND DISCORD IN THE WORLD POLITICAL ECONOMY (1984)

LAW AFTER GROUND ZERO (John Strawson ed., 2002)

LAWSON, ROBERT NEALE, A PLAN FOR THE ORGANIZATION OF A EUROPEAN AIR SERVICE (1936)

THE LEGAL ADVISORY PANEL OF THE AVIATION WORKING GROUP, PRACTITIONER'S GUIDE TO THE CAPE TOWN CONVENTION AND THE AIRCRAFT PROTOCOL (rev. ed. Nov. 2012)

Levine, Michael E., *Scope and Limits of Multilateral Approaches to International Air Transport, in* ORGANISATION FOR ECONOMIC CO-OPERATION AND DEVELOPMENT, INTERNATIONAL AIR TRANSPORT: THE CHALLENGES AHEAD 75 (1993)

LITIGATING THE AVIATION TORT CASE: FROM PRE-TRIAL TO CLOSING ARGUMENT (Andrew J. Harakas ed., 3rd ed. 2008)

LOWENFELD, ANDREAS F., AVIATION LAW: CASES AND MATERIALS (1972)

LOWENFELD, ANDREAS F., AVIATION LAW: CASES AND MATERIALS (2d ed. 1981)

LOWENFELD, ANDREAS F., INTERNATIONAL ECONOMIC LAW (2d ed. 2008)

LOWENFELD, ANDREAS F., INTERNATIONAL LITIGATION AND ARBITRATION (3d ed. 2005)

MAZOWER, MARK, GOVERNING THE WORLD: THE HISTORY OF AN IDEA (2012)

MENDES DE LEON, PABLO, CABOTAGE IN AIR TRANSPORT REGULATION (1981)

MIDDLEBURG, ANNEMARIE, PIRACY IN A LEGAL CONTEXT: PROSECUTION OF PIRATES OPERATING OFF THE SOMALI COAST (2011)

MONBIOT, GEORGE, HEAT: HOW TO STOP THE PLANET FROM BURNING (2007)

NEWHOUSE, JOHN, BOEING VERSUS AIRBUS: THE INSIDE STORY OF THE GREATEST INTERNATIONAL COMPETITION IN BUSINESS (2008)

THE OXFORD GUIDE TO TREATIES (Duncan B. Hollis ed., 2012)

PANDEY, MOHAN R., HOW BOEING DEFIED THE AIRBUS CHALLENGE: AN INSIDER'S ACCOUNT (2010)

PAUWELYN, JOOST, CONFLICT OF NORMS IN PUBLIC INTERNATIONAL LAW: HOW WTO LAW RELATES TO OTHER RULES OF INTERNATIONAL LAW (2003)

Poole, Robert W., Jr., *Toward Safer Skies, in* INSTEAD OF REGULATION: ALTERNATIVES TO FEDERAL REGULATORY AGENCIES 207 (Robert W. Poole ed., 1982)

Posner, Eric A., *The Decline of the International Court of Justice, in* INTERNATIONAL CONFLICT RESOLUTION 111 (Stefan Voigt et al. eds., 2006)

POSNER, ERIC A., THE PERILS OF GLOBAL LEGALISM (2009)

POSNER, ERIC A. & DAVID WEISBACH, CLIMATE CHANGE JUSTICE (2010)

POSNER, RICHARD A., ECONOMIC ANALYSIS OF LAW (8th ed. 2011)

POSNER, RICHARD A., THE ECONOMICS OF JUSTICE (1983)

POSNER, RICHARD A., PREVENTING SURPRISE ATTACKS (2005)

POSNER, RICHARD A., UNCERTAIN SHIELD: THE U.S. INTELLIGENCE SYSTEM IN THE THROES OF REFORM (2006)

QUIGLEY, CONOR, EUROPEAN UNION STATE AID LAW AND POLICY (2D ED. 2009)

RESTATEMENT (SECOND) OF TORTS (1977)

RESTATEMENT (THIRD) OF FOREIGN RELATIONS LAW OF THE UNITED STATES (1987)

ROBERTS, ANDREW, THE STORM OF WAR: A NEW HISTORY OF THE SECOND WORLD WAR (2009)

ROBINSON, DAVID E., CLIMATEGATE DEBUNKED: BIG BROTHER, MAINSTREAM MEDIA, COVER-UPS (2010)

SALACUSE, JESWALD W., THE LAW OF INVESTMENT TREATIES (2010)

SANDHOLTZ, WAYNE & ALEC STONE SWEET, EUROPEAN INTEGRATION AND SUPRANATIONAL GOVERNANCE (1998)

SAYERS, DOROTHY L., THE LOST TOOLS OF LEARNING (1961)

SCHARF, MICHAEL P. & PAUL R. WILLIAMS, SHAPING FOREIGN POLICY IN TIMES OF CRISIS (2010)

SCHERER, FREDERIC M., COMPETITION POLICIES FOR AN INTEGRATED WORLD ECONOMY (1994)

SCHLUMBERGER, CHARLES E., OPEN SKIES FOR AFRICA: IMPLEMENTING THE YAMOUSSOUKRO DECISION (2010)

SCHMITT, CARL, THE NOMOS OF THE EARTH IN THE INTERNATIONAL LAW OF THE JUS PUBLICUM EUROPAEUM (G. L. Ulmen trans., 2003) (1950)

SCHUMPETER, CHARLES A., CAPITALISM, SOCIALISM, AND DEMOCRACY (1975)

SHAW, MALCOLM N., INTERNATIONAL LAW (6th ed. 2008)

SPEISER, STUART M. ET AL., RECOVERY FOR WRONGFUL DEATH AND INJURY (3d ed. 1992)

STONE, RICHARD D., THE INTERSTATE COMMERCE COMMISSION AND THE RAILROAD INDUSTRY: A HISTORY OF REGULATORY POLICY (1991)

STORY, JOSEPH, COMMENTARIES ON THE CONFLICTS OF THE LAW (1834)

SVENDSEN, ADAM D. M., UNDERSTANDING THE GLOBALIZATION OF INTELLIGENCE (2012)

Sykes, Alan O., *International Trade: Trade Remedies, in* RESEARCH HANDBOOK OF INTERNATIONAL ECONOMIC LAW 62 (2007)

TERRORISM AND INTERNATIONAL LAW: ACCOUNTABILITY, REMEDIES, REFORM: A REPORT OF THE IBA TASK FORCE ON TERRORISM (Elizabeth Stubbins Bates et al. eds., 2011)

THE HAGUE CONVENTION ON JURISDICTION AND JUDGMENTS (Andreas F. Lowenfeld & Linda J. Silberman eds., 2001)

THE OXFORD GUIDE TO TREATIES (Duncan B. Hollis ed., 2012)

TIETENBERG, THOMAS H., EMISSIONS TRADING: PRINCIPLES AND PRACTICE (2006)

TRACHTMAN, JOEL P., ECONOMIC STRUCTURE OF INTERNATIONAL LAW (2008)

U.S. DEP'T OF STATE, TREATIES IN FORCE (2011)

U.S. DEP'T OF STATE, TREATIES IN FORCE (2004)

VON MISES, LUDWIG, HUMAN ACTION: A TREATISE ON ECONOMICS (4th ed. 1996)

WASSENBERGH, HENRY A., PUBLIC INTERNATIONAL AIR TRANSPORTATION LAW IN A NEW ERA (1976)

WEBER, LUDWIG, INTERNATIONAL CIVIL AVIATION ORGANIZATION: AN INTRODUCTION (2007)

WOODWARD, RICHARD, THE ORGANIZATION FOR ECONOMIC CO-OPERATION AND DEVELOPMENT (2009)

YERGIN, DANIEL & JOSEPH STANISLAW, THE COMMANDING HEIGHTS: THE BATTLE FOR THE WORLD ECONOMY (rev. ed. 2002)

YERGIN, DANIEL ET AL., FETTERED FLIGHT: GLOBALIZATION AND THE AIRLINE INDUSTRY (2000)

JOURNAL ARTICLES AND SCHOLARLY WORKING PAPERS
LISTED ALPHABETICALLY BY AUTHOR

Abbott, Kenneth W., *Modern International Relations Theory: A Prospectus for International Lawyers*, 14 YALE J. INT'L L. 335 (1989)

Abeyratne, Ruwantissa I. R., *The Decision of the European Court of Justice on Open Skies – How Can We Take Liberalization to the Next Level?*, 68 J. AIR L. & COM. 485 (2003)

Abeyratne, Ruwantissa I. R., *Ensuring Regional Safety in Air Transport*, 35 AIR & SPACE L. 249 (2010)

Abeyratne, Ruwantissa I. R., *Mental Distress in Aviation Claims – Emergent Trends*, 65 J. AIR L. & COM. 225 (2000)

Abeyratne, Ruwantissa I. R., *Regulatory Management of the Warsaw System of Air Carrier Liability*, 3 J. AIR TRANSPORT MGMT. 37 (1997)

Abeyratne, Ruwantissa I. R., *Responsibility and Liability Aspects of the Icelandic Volcanic Eruption*, 35 AIR & SPACE L. 281 (2010)

Abeyratne, Ruwantissa I. R., *The Role of the International Civil Aviation Organization (ICAO) in the Twenty-First Century*, 34 ANNALS AIR & SPACE L. 529 (2009)

Abeyratne, Ruwantissa I. R., *Trade in Air Transport Services: Emerging Trends*, 35 J. WORLD TRADE 1133 (2001)

Abramovsky, Abraham, *Multilateral Conventions for the Suppression of Unlawful Seizure and Interference with Aircraft Part 1: The Hague Convention*, 13 COLUM. J. TRANSNAT'L L. 381 (1974)

Andemariam, Senai W., Does the Montreal Convention of 1999 Require that a Notice be Given to Passengers? What is the Validity of Notice of a Choice of Forum Clause Under Montreal 1999?, 71 J. AIR L. & COM. 251 (2006)

Anderson, H. Edwin III, *The Nationality of Ships and Flags of Convenience: Economics, Politics, and Alternatives*, 21 TUL. MAR. L.J. 139 (1996)

Andrews, Christian & Vernon Nase, *Psychiatric Injury in Aviation Accidents Under the Warsaw and Montreal Conventions: The Interface Between Medicine and Law*, 76 J. AIR L. & COM. 3 (2011)

Arthurs, Harry, *Navigating the Transsystemic Madly Off in One Direction: McGill's New Integrated, Polyjural, Transsystemic Law Programme*, 50 McGILL L.J. 707 (2005)

Atwood, John, *The Status of the Mobile Equipment (Cape Town) Convention – Arrival of an International Registration System*, 39 UCC L.J. 1 (2006)

Baden, Naneen K., *The Japanese Initiative on the Warsaw Convention*, 61 J. Air L. & Com. 437 (1996)

The 2010 Beijing Convention and Protocol: Ushering in a New Legal Era for Aviation, 66 No. 1 I ICAO J. 6 (2011)

Bilokach, Volodymyr & Kai Huscherlatch, *Airline Alliances and Antitrust Policy: The Role of Efficiencies*, 21 J. Air. Transp. Mgmt. 76 (2012)

Boliver, Angie, *Square Pegs in a Round Hole? The Effects of the 2006 Cape Town Treaty Implementation and its Impact on Fractional Jet Ownership*, 72 J. Air L. & Com. 529 (2007)

Bonin, Jason R., *Regionalism in International Civil Aviation: A Reevaluation of the Economic Regulation of International Air Transport in the Context of Economic Integration*, 12 Singapore Y.B. Int'l L. & Contributions 113 (2008)

Boyle, Robert P. & Roy Pulsifer, *The Tokyo Convention on Offenses and Certain Other Acts Committed On Board Aircraft*, 30 J. Air L. & Com. 305 (1964)

Brown, Kriss E., Comment, *The International Civil Aviation Organization is the Appropriate Jurisdiction to Settle Hushkit Dispute Between the United States and the European Union*, 20 Penn St. Int'l L. Rev. 465 (2002)

Brueckner, Jan K., *Price vs. Quantity-Based Approaches to Airport Congestion Management*, 93 J. Pub. Econ. 681 (2009)

Busuttil, James J., *The Bonn Declaration on International Terrorism: A Non-Binding International Agreement on Aircraft Hijacking*, 31 Int'l & Comp. L.Q. 474 (1982)

Cheng, Bin, *The Role of Consultation in Bilateral International Air Services Agreements, as Exemplified by Bermuda I and Bermuda II*, 19 Colum. J. Transnat'l L. 183 (1981)

Coyle, John F., *Rethinking the Commercial Law Treaty*, 45 Ga. L. Rev. 343 (2011)

Crans, Berend, *The Implications of the EU Accession to the Cape Town Convention*, 35 Air & Space L. 1 (2010)

Cuming, Ronald C. C., *Considerations in the Design of an International Registry for Interests in Mobile Equipment*, 4 Unif. L. Rev. n.s. 275 (1999)

Cunningham, McKay, *The Montreal Convention: Can Passengers Finally Recover for Mental Injuries?*, 41 Vand. J. Transnat'l L. 1043 (2008)

Dean, Warren L., Jr. & Jeffrey N. Shane, *Alliances, Immunity and the Future of Aviation*, 22 No. 4 Air & Space Law. 1 (2010)

Decurtins, Cecilia, *The Air Transport Review at the WTO: Bilateralism versus Multilateralism* (June 14, 2007) (unpublished Ph.D. thesis, University of Geneva), http://www.unige.ch/cyberdocuments/theses2007/DecurtinsCG/these. pdf

Dempsey, Paul Stephen, *Aerial Piracy and Terrorism: Unilateral and Multilateral Responses to Aircraft Hijacking*, 2 Conn. J. Int'l L. 427 (1987)

Dempsey, Paul Stephen, *Flights of Fancy and Fights of Fury: Arbitration and Adjudication of Commercial and Political Disputes in International Aviation*, 32 Ga. J. Int'l & Comp. L. 231 (2004)

Dempsey, Paul Stephen, *The Rise and Fall of the Civil Aeronautics Board – Opening Wide the Floodgates of Entry*, 11 Transp. L.J. 91 (1979)

Dinwoodie, Graeme B., *A New Copyright Order: Why National Courts Should Create Global Norms*, 149 U. Penn. L.R. 469 (2000)

Downs, George W. & Michael A. Jones, *Reputation, Compliance, and International Law*, 31 LEGAL STUD. S95 (2002)

Easterbrook, Frank H., *Cyberspace and the Law of the Horse*, 1996 U. CHI. LEGAL F. 207

Easterbrook, Frank H., *Predatory Strategies and Counterstrategies*, 48 U. CHI. L. REV. 48 (1981)

Easton, John F., *Jennifer Trock, & Kent Radford, Post-Traumatic "Lésion Corporelle": A Continuum of Bodily Injury Under the Warsaw Convention*, 68 J. AIR L. & COM. 665 (2003)

Editorial, *Convention on International Recognition of Rights in Aircraft: Early Ratification Desirable*, 16 J. AIR L. & COM. 61 (1949)

Ensuring the Safety and Efficiency of Global Aviation, 66 ICAO J. 3 (2011)

Epstein, Richard A., *Toward a General Theory of Tort Law: Strict Liability in Context*, 3 J. TORT L. 6 (2010)

Ergas, Henry & Christopher Findlay, *New Directions in Australian Air Transport*, 10 AGENDA 27 (2003)

Feyissa, Hailegabriel G., *Ethiopian Law of International Carriage by Air: An Overview*, 5 No. 2 MIZAN L. REV. 215 (2011)

Firak, Nancy Lee & Kimberly A. Schmaltz, *Air Rage: Choice of Law for Intentional Torts Occurring in Flight Over International Waters*, 63 ALB. L. REV. 1 (1999)

Forrest, R. M., *Is Open Competition Preferable to Regulation?*, 6 AIR L. 7 (1981)

Fox, Eleanor M., *Toward World Antitrust and Market Access*, 91 AM. J. INT'L L. 1 (1997)

Fuller, Lon L., *The Case of the Speluncean Explorers*, 62 HARV. L. REV. 616 (1949)

García-Arboleda, José Ignacio, *Transnational Airlines in Latin America Facing the Fear of Nationality*, 37 AIR & SPACE L. 93 (2012)

Gardiner, Richard, *Revising the Law of Carriage by Air: Mechanisms in Treaties and Contract*, 47 I.C.L.Q. 278 (1998)

Gates, Sean & George LeLoudas, *From Rome to Montreal in 57 Years: Worth the Wait?*, 22 AIR & SPACE L. 1 (2009)

Gerber, David J., *Two Forms of Modernization in European Competition Law*, 31 FORDHAM INT'L L. J. 1235 (2007)

Gerber, Dean N., *The 2011 Aircraft Sector Understanding: Calming the Turbulent Skies*, 24 No. 1 AIR & SPACE LAW. 1 (2011)

Gertler, Z. Joseph, *Order in the Air and the Problem of Real and False Opinions*, 4 ANNALS AIR & SPACE L. 9319 (1979)

Goldsmith, Jack L., *Liberal Democracy and Cosmopolitan Duty*, 55 STAN. L. REV. 1667 (2003)

Goldsmith, Jack L. & Eric A. Posner, *Moral and Legal Rhetoric in International Relations: A Rational Choice Perspective*, 31 J. LEGAL STUD. S115 (2002)

Goldsmith, Jack L. & Eric Posner, *The New International Law Scholarship*, 34 GA. J. INT'L L. 463 (2006)

Goode, Roy, *The International Interest as an Autonomous Property Interest*, EUR. REV. PRIVATE L., 1–2004, at 18

Goode, Roy, *The Protection of Interests in Movables in Transnational Commercial Law*, 3 UNIF. L. REV. n.s. 453 (1998)

Gray, Donald G. & Auriol Marasco, *The Cape Town Convention: Where is Canada?*, 24 No. 2 AIR & SPACE LAW. 1 (2011)

Guillaume, Gilbert, *The Use of Precedent by International Judges and Arbitrators*, 2 J. Int. Disp. Settlement 5 (2011)

Haanappel, Peter P. C., *The External Aviation Relations of the European Economic Community and of the EEC Members into the Twenty-First Century, Part II*, 14 Air L. 122 (1989)

Hathaway, Oona & Scott J. Shapiro, *Outcasting: Enforcement in Domestic and International Law*, 121 Yale L.J. 252 (2011)

Havel, Brian F., *The Constitution in an Era of Supranational Adjudication*, 78 N.C. L. Rev. 257 (2000)

Havel, Brian F., *Mixed Signals on Foreign Ownership: An Assessment*, Issues Aviation L. & Pol'y (CCH) ¶ 25,341, at 13,125 (May 2005)

Havel, Brian F., *Rethinking the General Agreement on Trade in Services as a Pathway to Global Aviation Liberalization*, 44(1) Irish Jurist 95 (2009)

Havel, Brian F. & John Q. Mulligan, *The Triumph of Politics: Reflections on the Judgment of the Court of Justice of the European Union Validating the Inclusion of Non-EU Airlines in the Emissions Trading Scheme*, 37 Air & Space L. 3 (2012)

Havel, Brian F. & Jeremias Prassl, *Reforming Civil Aviation Regulation in the United Kingdom: The Civil Aviation Bill 2011–12*, 11 Issues Aviation L. & Pol'y 321 (2012)

Havel, Brian F. & Gabriel S. Sanchez, *The Emerging* Lex Aviatica, 42 Geo. J. Int'l L. 639 (2011)

Havel, Brian F. & Gabriel S. Sanchez, *Restoring Global Aviation's "Cosmopolitan Mentalité"*, 29 B.U. Int'l L.J. 1 (2011)

Havel, Brian F. & Gabriel S. Sanchez, *Toward an International Aviation Emissions Agreement*, 36 Harv. Envtl. L. Rev. 351 (2012)

Havel, Brian F. & Niels van Antwerpen, *The Dutch Ticket Tax and Article 15 of the Chicago Convention*, 34 Air & Space L. 141 (2009).

Havel, Brian F. & Niels van Antwerpen, *The Dutch Ticket Tax and Article 15 of the Chicago Convention (Continued)*, 34 Air & Space L. 447 (2009).

Heller-Roazen, Daniel, *Introduction to "The Concept of Piracy,"* 2 Human. 23 (2011)

Heyvaert, Veerle, *Regulatory Competition: Accounting for the Transnational Dimension of Environmental Regulation* (May 16, 2012) (unpublished paper presented to the Center for Socio-Legal Studies, Oxford)

Hill, Harriet Oswalt, Comment, *Bermuda II: The British Revolution of 1976*, 44 J. Air L. & Com. 111 (1978)

Honnebier, B. Patrick, *Clarifying the Alleged Issues Concerning the Financing of Aircraft Engines*, 56 Zeitschrift für Luft-und Weltraumrecht [Z.L.W.] 383 (2007)

Honnebier, B. Patrick, *The English "Blue Sky" Case Shows that the Aircraft Finance Practice Needs Uniform International Substantive Mortgage Laws as the Existing Conflict Rules Fail; The Cape Town Convention Solves the Existing Problems while the Geneva Convention is Obsolete*, 2011-2 Tijdschrift Vervoer & Recht 70

Honnebier, B. Patrick, *The Fully Computerized International Registry for Security Interests in Aircraft and Aircraft Protocol that will Become Effective Toward the Beginning of 2006*, 70 J. Air L. & Com. 63 (2005)

Honnebier, B. Patrick, *New Protocols and the Financing of Aircraft Engines*, 21 No. 1 Air & Space Law. 15 (2006)

Horan, Hubert, *"Double Marginalization" and the Counter Revolution Against Liberal Airline Competition*, 37 TRANSP. L.J. 251 (2010)

Huang, Jiefang, *Aviation Safety and ICAO (Mar. 18, 2009)* (unpublished Ph.D. thesis, Leiden University)

Huang Jiefang, *Aviation Safety, ICAO and Obligations Erga Omnes*, 8 No. 1 CHINESE J. OF INT'L L. 63 (2009).

Hudec, Robert E., *The New WTO Dispute Settlement Procedure*, 8 MINN. J. GLOBAL TRADE 1 (1999)

Jansson, Madeleine, *The Consequences of a Deletion of the Nautical Fault* 12–17 *(May 2007)* (unpublished M.A. thesis, Department of Law, Göteborg University)

Joyner, Christopher C., *International Extradition and Global Terrorism: Bringing International Criminals to Justice*, 25 LOY. L.A. INT'L & COMP. L. REV. 493 (2003)

Kaczorowski, Robert J., *The Common-Law Background of Nineteenth-Century Tort Law*, 51 OHIO ST. L. J. 1127 (1990)

Kane, Terry Richard, *Prosecuting International Terrorists in United States Courts: Gaining the Jurisdictional Threshold*, 12 YALE J. INT'L L. 294 (1987)

Klein, Herbert David, *Cujus Est Solum Ejus Est. . . Quousque Tandem?*, 26 J. AIR L. & COM. 237 (1959)

Koh, Harold, *Why Do Nations Obey International Law?*, 106 YALE L.J. 2599 (1997)

Kuhn, Arthur K., *The Beginnings of Aerial Law*, 4 AM. J. INT'L L. 109 (1910).

Kyser, Kevin, *Tarnished But Still Valuable: A History and Present State of the Gold Franc*, 16 CURRENTS: INT'L TRADE L.J. 82 (2007)

Levine, Michael E., *Airline Alliances and Systems Competition: Antitrust Policy Toward Airlines and the Department of Justice Guidelines*, 45 HOUS. L. REV. 333 (2008)

Levine, Michael E., *Airport Congestion: When Theory Meets Reality*, 26 YALE J. ON REG. 37 (2009)

Levine, Michael E., *Is Regulation Necessary? California Air Transportation and National Regulatory Policy*, 74 YALE L.J. 1416 (1965)

Lewis, Douglas R., *Air Cabotage: Historical and Modern-Day Perspectives*, 45 J. AIR L. & COM. 1059 (1980)

Linetsky, Vadim, *Economic Benefits of the Cape Town Treaty* (OCT. 18, 2009), http://www.awg.aero/assets/docs/economicbenefitsofCapeTown.pdf

Luft, Gal & Anne Korin, *Terrorism Goes to Sea*, 83 FOREIGN AFF. 61 (2004)

Macdonald, Roderick, *Unitary Law Re-form, Pluralistic Law Re-Substance: Illuminating Legal Change*, 67 LA. L. REV. 1113 (2007)

MacGibbon, I. C., *Estoppel in International Law*, 7 INT'L & COMP. L.Q. 468 (1958)

Mamounas, Joseph, *Controlling Foreign Ownership of U.S. Strategic Assets: The Challenge of Maintaining National Security in a Globalized and Oil Dependent World*, 13 LAW & BUS. REV. AM. 381 (2007)

Mankiewicz, Rene H., *The 1971 Protocol of Guatemala City to Further Amend the 1929 Warsaw Convention*, 38 J. AIR L. & COM. 519 (1972)

Manner, Jennifer A., *How to Avoid Airbus II: A Primer for the Domestic Industry*, 23 CAL. W. INT'L L.J. 139 (1992)

Meier-Kaienberg, Nils, *The WTO's "Toughest" Case: An Examination of the Effectiveness of the WTO Dispute Resolution Procedure in the Airbus-Boeing Dispute Over Aircraft Subsidies*, 71 J. AIR L. & COM. 191 (2006)

Mendelsohn, Allan I., *Recent Developments in the Forum Non Conveniens Doctrine*, 52 FED. LAW. 45 (2005)

Mendelsohn, Allan I., *The Value of the Poincaré Gold Franc in Limitation of Liability Conventions*, 5 J. MAR. L. & COM. 125 (1973)

Mendelsohn, Allan I. & Renee Lieux, *The Warsaw Convention Article 28, the Doctrine of Forum Non Conveniens, and the Foreign Plaintiff*, 68 J. AIR L. & COM. 75 (2003)

Mendes De Leon, Pablo & Werner Eyskens, *The Montreal Convention: Analysis of Some Aspects of the Attempted Modernization and Consolidation of the Warsaw System*, 66 J. AIR. L. & COM. 1155 (2001)

Michaels, Ralf, *Public and Private International Law: German Views on Global Issues*, 4 J. PRIVATE INT'L L. 121 (2008)

Müller-Rostin, Wolf, *The Montreal Convention of 1999: Uncertainties and Inconsistencies*, AVIATION Q. 218 (2000)

Naveau, Jacques, *Arbitral Award in the Dispute between the Belgian and Irish Civil Aviation Authorities over Services between Brussels and Dublin by Sabena and Aer Lingus, given at Dublin July 17, 1981*, 8 AIR L. 50 (1983)

Newton, Michael A., *Exceptional Engagement: Protocol I and a World United Against Terrorism*, 45 TEX. INT'L L.J. 323 (2009)

Norberg, Naomi, *Terrorism and International Criminal Justice: Dim Prospects for a Future Together*, 8 SANTA CLARA J. INT'L L. 11 (2010)

Ottley, Bruce L., *Airport Full-Body Scanners: Improved Security or Cause for Concern?*, 9 ISSUES AVIATION L. & POL'Y 221 (2009)

Peil, Michael, *Most Highly-Qualified Publicists: Who Are They and How Are They Used?*, 1 CAMBRIDGE J. INT'L & COMP. L. 136 (2013)

Plachta, Michael, *The Lockerbie Case: The Role of the Security Council in Enforcing the Principle Aut Dedere Aut Judicare*, 12 EUR. J. INT'L L. 125 (2001)

Pogust, Glenn, *The Warsaw Convention – Does It Create a Cause of Action?*, 47 FORDHAM L. REV. 366 (1978)

Polk, Frank L., *Cape Town and Aircraft Transactions in the United States*, 20 No. 3 AIR & SPACE LAW. 4 (2006)

Posner, Eric A., *Do States Have a Moral Duty to Obey International Law?*, 55 STAN. L. REV. 1901 (2003)

Posner, Eric A., *Human Rights, the Laws of War, and Reciprocity* (John M. Olin L. & Econ. WORKING PAPER NO. 537 (2D SER.), SEPT. 2010)

Posner, Eric A., *The International Court of Justice: Voting and Usage Statistics*, 99 AM. SOC'Y INT'L L. PROC. 130 (2005)

Posner, Eric A. & Miguel F. P. de Figueiredo, *Is the International Court of Justice Biased?*, 34 J. LEGAL STUD. 599 (2005)

Prassl, Jeremias, *The European Union and the Montreal Convention: A New Analytical Framework*, 12 ISSUES AVIATION L. & POL'Y 381 (2013)

Reinhardt, Dean N., *The Vertical Limit of State Sovereignty*, 72 J. AIR L. & COM. 65 (2007)

Rhyne, Charles S., *International Law and Air Transportation*, 47 MICH. L. REV. 41 (1948)

Salacuse, Jeswald W., *The Emerging Global Regime for Investment*, 51 HARV. INT'L L. J. 427 (2010)

Sanchez, Gabriel S., *An Institutional Defense of Antitrust Immunity for International Airline Alliances*, 62 CATH. U. L. REV. 139 (2012)

Schleusser, John M., *The Deception Dividend: FDR's Undeclared War*, 34 INT'L SECURITY 133 (2010)

Schmid, Alex, *Terrorism – The Definitional Problem*, 36 CASE W. RES. J. INT'L L. 375 (2004)

Schmid, Ronald & Elmar Giemulla, *Council Regulation (EC) No. 2027/97 on Air Carrier Liability in the Event of Accidents and Its Implications for Air Carriers*, 23 AIR & SPACE L. 98 (1998)

Schmitt, Carl, *The Concept of Piracy*, 2 *Human.* 27 (2011)

Schwab, William P., *Air Rage: Screaming for International Uniformity*, 14 TRANSNAT'L LAW. 401 (2001)

Schwartz, Warren F. & Alan O. Sykes, *The Economic Structure of Renegotiation and Dispute Settlement in the World Trade Organization*, 31 J. LEGAL STUD. S179 (2002)

Sheehan, W. M., COMMENT, *Air Cabotage and the Chicago Convention*, 63 HARV. L. REV. 1157 (1950)

Shelton, Dinah, *Human Rights and the Environment: What Specific Environmental Rights Have Been Recognized*, 35 DENV. J. INT'L L. & POL'Y 129 (2006)

Spanogle, Jr., John A., *The Arrival of International Private Law*, 25 GEO. WASH. J. INT'L L. & ECON. 477 (1992)

Steinberg, Andrew B. & Charles T. Kotuby, JR., *Bilateral Investment Treaties and International Air Transportation: A New Tool for Global Airlines to Redress Market Barriers*, 76 J. AIR L. & COM. 457 (2011)

Stephan, Paul B., *Global Governance, Antitrust, and the Limits of International Cooperation*, 38 CORNELL INT'L L.J. 173 (2005)

Sundahl, Mark J., *The "Cape Town Approach": A New Method of Making International Law*, 44 COLUM. J. TRANSNAT'L L. 339 (2006)

SYMPOSIUM, Rational Choice and International Law, 31 J. LEGAL STUD. S1 (2002)

Tan, Alan Khee Jin, *The ASEAN Multilateral Agreement on Air Services: En Route to Open Skies?*, 16 J. AIR TRANSP. MGMT. 289 (2010)

Tan, Alan Khee Jin, *Singapore's New Air Services Agreements with the E.U. and U.K.: Implications for Liberalization in Asia*, 73 J. AIR L. & COM. 351 (2008)

Trakman, Leon E., *Foreign Direct Investment: Hazard or Opportunity?*, 41 GEO. WASH. INT'L L. REV. 1 (2009)

Trakman, Leon E., *The Twenty-First Century Law Merchant*, 48 AM. BUS. L.J. 775 (2011)

Watson, Geoffrey R., *The Passive Personality Principle*, 28 TEX. INT'L L.J. 1 (1993)

Wiener, Jonathan Baert, *On the Political Economy of Global Environmental Regulation*, 87 GEO. L.J. 749 (1999)

Wilberforce, J. Richard Orme, *Crime in Aircraft*, 67 J. ROYAL AERONAUTICAL SOC'Y 175 (1963)

Witten, Samuel M., *The U.S.-U.K. Arbitration Concerning Heathrow Airport User Charges*, 89 AM. J. INT'L L. 174 (1995)

Woerth, Duane E., *Airline Labor Law in the Era of Globalization: The Need to Correct a Misreading of the Railway Labor Act*, ISSUES AVIATION L. & POL'Y (CCH) ¶ 30,011, at 16,011 (Oct. 2001)

Woll, Cornelia, *The Road to External Representation: The European Commission's Activism in International Air Transport*, 13 J. EUR. PUB. POL'Y 52 (2006)

Wood, Diane, *The Impossible Dream: Real International Antitrust*, 1992 U. CHI. LEGAL F. 277 (1992)

Wool, Mary Christina, *Nature's Trust: A Legal, Political and Moral Frame for Global Warming*, 34 B.C. ENVT'L. AFF. L. REV. 577 (2007)

Wool, J., *Lessor, Financier, and Manufacturer Perspectives on the New Third-Party Liability Convention*, 22 No. 4 AIR & SPACE LAW. 1 (2010)

Wool, Jeffrey, *Rethinking the Notion of Uniformity in the Drafting of International Commercial Law: A Preliminary Proposal for the Development of a Policy-Based Unification Model*, 2 UNIF. L. REV. N.S. 46 (1997)

York, Brower V., *International Air Law in the Americas*, 3 J. AIR L. 411 (1932)

PERIODICAL, SERVICE, AND NEWSPAPER ARTICLES LISTED ALPHABETICALLY BY AUTHOR

Avila, Frank, *2 Dozen Join NY JetBlue Lawsuit Over Pilot Scare*, ASSOCIATED PRESS, Sep. 27, 2012

Brûlé, Tyler, *Embassies with Wings*, FT.COM, Feb. 24, 2012

Cameron, Doug, *U.S. Airline Merger to Affect Alliances*, WSJ.COM, Feb. 14, 2013

Cha, Ariana Eunjung & Del Quentin Weber, *U.S., China Agree to Double Flights*, WASH. POST, May 24, 2007, at D1

Clark, Nicola & David Jolly, *Hungarian National Airline Halts Flights*, N.Y. TIMES, Feb. 3, 2012

Clark, Pilita, *Russia Threatens to Ban Austrian Airlines*, FIN. TIMES, Mar. 1, 2010, at 1

Cleveland, Paul A. & Thomas L. Tucker, *Privatizing Airline Safety and Security*, IDEAS ON LIBERTY, Nov. 2002, at 6

Europe Considers Suspending Airline Emissions Charge, ASSOCIATED PRESS, Sept. 12, 2012

EU-U.S. Security Agreement Allows Cheaper, Faster Air Cargo Operations, HOMELANDSECURITYNEWSWIRE.COM, June 5, 2012

5Q with Former State Department Official John Byerly, BUS. TRAVEL NEWS, Nov. 10, 2010

Flottau, Jens & Robert Wall, Russia May Block EU Carriers from Siberian Overflight in Emissions Trading Battle, AVIATION WEEK, Feb. 23, 2012

Heathrow: Government to Study Airport Expansion Plans, BBC News, Sept. 5, 2012, http://www.bbc.co.uk/news/uk-politics-19484126

Knibb, David, *Chile Trades Cabotage for 'Precedent Setting' Deal*, AIRLINE BUS., Apr. 1, 2003, at 14

Lewis, Barbara & Nina Chestney, *EU Airline Carbon Cash Should Help Fill Climate Fund*, REUTERS, May 16, 2012

MacLaggan, Corrie, *U.S. Charges JetBlue Pilot for Midair Meltdown*, REUTERS, Mar. 29, 2012

Martín, Hugo, *Airlines Cut Routes as Fuel Costs Climb; Ticket Prices Will Stay High and Planes Will Stay Crowded for the Near Future, FAA Report Says*, L.A. TIMES, Mar. 9, 2012, at B1

Michaels, Daniel & Susan Carey, *More Airline Mergers Leap Borders*, WALL ST. J., June 28, 2012, at B10

Miller, Lisa, *Airlines and Courts Are Cracking Down on Unruly Passengers as Assaults Rise*, WALL ST. J., Dec. 27, 1996, at A2

Moores, Victoria, *ICAO Sees EU ETS as Regional Issue*, AIR TRANSPORT WORLD DAILY NEWS (Oct. 1, 2012)

Mouawad, Jad, *For Air Cargo, A Screening Conundrum*, N.Y. TIMES, Dec. 21, 2010, at B1

Niththyananthan, Kaveri, *Lufthansa, ANA Get Antitrust Clearance*, WSJ.COM, June 1, 2011

Parker, Andrew, *Aerospace: A Dogfight for the Duopoly*, FIN. TIMES, Aug. 7, 2012, at 7

Parker, Andrew & David Gelles, *Brussels Renews Push in U.S. for Airline Mergers*, FIN. TIMES, Sept. 26, 2012, at 6

Plushnick-Masti, Ramit, *Texas Judge Rules Atmosphere, Air Is Public Trust*, ASSOCIATED PRESS, July 12, 2012

Pruzin, Daniel, *WTO Panel Ruling Slams Illegal Subsidies for Europe's Airbus in Case Brought by U.S.*, 27 INT'L TRADE REP. (BNA) 1029 (July 8, 2010)

Pruzin, Daniel, *WTO Publishes Final Ruling in Complaint Against Boeing Subsidies: EU, US Claim Win*, 28 INT'L TRADE REP. (BNA) 564 (Apr. 7, 2011)

Schuetze, Arno & Andreas Kröner, *NordLB Sells First Aircraft Covered Bond in Germany*, REUTERS, July 10, 2012

Sechler, Bob, *FedEx, UPS Get a Toehold in China's Express Delivery*, WALL ST. J., Sept. 11, 2012, at B1

Slaughter, Stanley, *Analysis: Time Running Out for Deal on Airline Emissions*, AIR & BUS. TRAVEL NEWS, Oct. 4, 2012

Stone, David, *New Zealand May Beat Australia to an Open EU Aviation Agreement*, N.Z. HERALD, Aug. 24, 2009

Suhartono, Harry & Tim Hepher, *Asia Plugs European Aircraft Lending Gap*, REUTERS, Feb. 17, 2012

Szalavitz, Maia, *10 Ways We Get the Odds Wrong*, PSYCHOL. TODAY, Jan. 1, 2008

Topham, Gwyn, *Transport: There's Only Room for One Hub, Says Heathrow*, THE GUARDIAN, Nov. 15, 2012, at 34

U.S. Airlines Fight For New Routes, SHANGHAI DAILY, July 25, 2007

Volcovici, Valeri, *U.S. Airline Industry Urges Obama to Block EU Carbon Scheme*, REUTERS, Sept. 18, 2012

Walker, Karen, *EU MP: Europe Will Not Back Down on ETS*, AIR TRANSPORT WORLD DAILY NEWS, Nov. 7, 2011

TELEVISION BROADCASTS

Nova: The Deadliest Plane Crash (PBS (U.S.) TELEVISION BROADCAST 2006)

The Plot to Bring Down Britain's Planes (CHANNEL 4 (U.K.) TELEVISION BROADCAST APR. 26, 2012)

SPEECHES, PRESENTATIONS, INTERVIEWS, AND BRIEFING PAPERS LISTED ALPHABETICALLY BY SPEAKER

Byerly, John R., Deputy Assistant Sec'y for Transp. Affairs, Dep't of State, Opening Remarks at the London AirFinance Journal Conference (May 18, 2009)

Kotaite, Assad, President, ICAO, Opening Address at the International Conference on Air Law on the Modernization of the Warsaw System (May 10, 1999)

Lobbenberg, Andrew, Airline Analyst, European Airline Equity Research, HSBC, interview with author

Mamdouh, Hamid, Director, Trade in Services, World Trade Organization, address at Sustainable Aviation Policies for America and the World: A Leadership Summit (Oct. 19, 2006)

Tilton, Glen, Chairman, Air Transport Association, Speech to UK Aviation Club (Feb. 11, 2010)

REPORTS, STUDIES, PAPERS, PRESS RELEASES, AND OTHER DOCUMENTS LISTED ALPHABETICALLY

Archick, Kristin, Cong. Res. Serv., RS 22030, U.S.-EU Cooperation Against Terrorism (2011)

Association of European Airlines, Towards a Transatlantic Common Aviation Area: AEA Policy Statement (1999)

Association of Southeast Asian Nations (ASEAN), Implementation Framework of the ASEAN Single Aviation Market (Dec. 16, 2011)

Bonn Declaration on International Terrorism, Pub. Papers 1308, July 17, 1978, *reprinted in* 17 I.L.M. 1285

Centre for Aviation, New LAN-TAM Parent Latam Emerges as a Leader Globally and a Powerful Force Across South America, June 28, 2012, http://centreforaviation. com/analysis/new-lan-tam-parent-latam-emerges-as-a-leader-globally-and-a-power ful-force-across-south-america-76917

Council for Trade in Services, Quantitative Air Services Agreements Review (QUASAR): Part B: Preliminary Results (Nov. 30, 2006)

Elias, Bart, Cong. Res. Serv., R 41515, Screening and Securing Air Cargo: Background and Issues for Congress (2010)

E-mail from Daniel Calleja, former Director for Air Transport, European Commission, to Brian F. Havel (Mar. 18, 2010, 17:49:00 CST) (copy on file with authors)

European Aviation Safety Agency, Assessment of Foreign Aircraft (EC SAFA Programme), http://www.easa.europa.eu/approvals-and-standardisation/safety-assess ment-of-foreign-aircraft-SAFA.php

European Commission & U.S. Department of Transportation, Transatlantic Airline Alliances: Competitive Issues and Regulatory Approaches (2010)

Federal Aviation Administration, International Aviation Safety Assessment Program, http:// www.faa.gov/about/initiatives/iasa/more/

Federal Aviation Administration, Task Force on Deterrence of Air Piracy Final Report, FAA-AM-78–35 (1978)

Institute of International Law, Krakow Session – 2005, Resolution of the Seventeenth Commission, Universal Criminal Jurisdiction with Regard to the Crime of Genocide, Crimes Against Humanity and War Crimes (Aug. 26, 2005)

Intergovernmental Panel on Climate Change (IPCC), Climate Change 2007: Impacts, Adaptation and Vulnerability (2007)

Intergovernmental Panel on Climate Change (IPCC), Climate Change 2007: Synthesis Report: Summary for Policymakers (2007)

International Air Transport Association, Agenda for Freedom, http://www.agenda-for-freedom.aero

International Air Transport Association, Agreement on the Measures to Implement the IATA Intercarrier Agreement, *reprinted in* 3 Av. L. Rep. (CCH) ¶ 27,952 [IATA Implementation Agreement]

International Air Transport Association, Fact Sheet: Environment, http://www.iata.org/pressroom/facts_figures/fact_sheets/pages/environment.aspx

International Air Transport Association, A Global Approach to Reducing Aviation Emissions (Nov. 2009), http://www.iata.org/SiteCollectionDocuments/Documents/Global_Approach_Reducing_Emissions_251109web.pdf.

International Air Transport Association, IATA Economics Briefing, The Economic Benefits Generated by Alliances and Joint Ventures (2012), http://www.iata.org/whatwedo/Documents/economics/Economics%20of%20JVs_Jan2012L.pdf

International Air Transport Association, Intercarrier Agreement on Passenger Liability, Oct. 31, 1995, *reprinted in* 3 Av. L. Rep. (CCH) ¶ 27,951 [IATA Intercarrier Agreement]

International Airlines Group, News Release, Issue of Debt (July 9, 2012)

International Civil Aviation Organization, Action of the Council, 71st Session, ICAO Doc. 8923-C/998, *reprinted in* 9 I.L.M. 1286 (1970)

International Civil Aviation Organization, Air Services Negotiation Conference, http://legacy.icao.int/ican2011/

International Civil Aviation Organization, Air Transport Bureau, Economic Policy & Infrastructure Management Section, Economic Regulation Template Air Services Agreement, http://legacy.icao.int/icao/en/atb/epm/Ecp/Tasa.htm.

International Civil Aviation Organization, Assembly Resolutions in Force, ICAO Doc. 9958 (2010)

International Civil Aviation Organization, Committee on Aviation Environmental Protection (CAEP), http://www.icao.int/environmental-protection/pages/CAEP.aspx

International Civil Aviation Organization, Composite Table (Status of Treaties and Status of States vis-à-vis Treaties), http://www.icao.int/Secretariat/Legal/Pages/TreatyCollection.aspx

International Civil Aviation Organization, Consolidated Conclusions, Model Clauses, Recommendations and Declarations, ATConf/5 (Mar. 31, 2003) (revised July 10, 2003)

International Civil Aviation Organization, Economic Commission, Regulation of International Air Transport Services, Report by the Council on Trade in Services, A33-WP/7 (Jun. 6, 2001)

International Civil Aviation Organization, Executive Committee Working Paper, Development of a Global Framework for Addressing Civil Aviation CO_2 Emissions, A37-WP/217 EX/39 (2010)

International Civil Aviation Organization, General Responsibilities of Each Regional Office, http://legacy.icao.int/icao/en/ro/roresp.htm

International Civil Aviation Organization, Guidance on the Implementation of Article 83*bis* of the Convention on International Civil Aviation, Cir. 295 LE/2 (Feb. 2003)

International Civil Aviation Organization, ICAO Aviation Security Programme, http://www2.icao.int/en/avsec/pages/default.aspx/

International Civil Aviation Organization, ICAO Policies on Charges for Airports and Air Navigation Services, ICAO Doc. 9082/7 (7th ed. 2004)

International Civil Aviation Organization, ICAO's Policies on Taxation in the Field of Air Transport, ICAO Doc. 8632 (1999)

International Civil Aviation Organization, International Conference on Air Law (Convention for the Unification of Certain Rules for International Carriage by Air), Montreal (May 10–28, 1999), Minutes, ICAO Doc. 9775-DC/2 (2001)

International Civil Aviation Organization, Manual on the Regulation of International Air Transport, ICAO Doc. 9626 (2d ed. 2004)

International Civil Aviation Organization, Offsetting Emissions from the Aviation Sector, ICAO Doc. 9951 (2011)

International Civil Aviation Organization, Policy and Guidance Material on the Economic Regulation of International Air Transport, ICAO Doc. 9587 (3rd ed. 2008)

International Civil Aviation Organization, Rules for the Settlement of Differences, ICAO Doc. 7782/2 (1975)

International Civil Aviation Organization, Scoping Study on the Application of Emissions Trading and Offsets for Local Air Quality in Aviation, ICAO Doc. 9948 (2011)

International Civil Aviation Organization, Special Subcommittee of the Legal Committee for the Modernization of the Tokyo Convention Including the Issue of Unruly Passengers Working Paper, Report of the Rapporteur of the Special Sub-Committee on the Preparation of an Instrument to Modernize the Convention on Offenses and Certain Other Acts Committed On Board Aircraft of 1963, LC/SC-MOT-WP/1 (2012)

International Civil Aviation Organization, Study on Aircraft Leasing, Air Transport Committee, 156th Session of the Council, 1999

International Civil Aviation Organization, Treaty Status, http://www.icao.int/secretariat/legal/List%20of%20Parties/Mtl99_EN.pdf

International Civil Aviation Organization, 2011: State of Global Aviation Safety (2011)

International Civil Aviation Organization, USOAP Continuous Monitoring Approach http://www.icao.int/safety/CMAForum/Pages/default.aspx

International Civil Aviation Organization, Worldwide Air Transport Conferences, http://legacy.icao.int/ICAN2009/docs/ICAO_Journal_ICAN2008_Vol64Num01_p21.pdf

International Law Association, Piracy: Sea and Air, Report of the Fifty-Fourth Conference (1970)

International Maritime Organization, Summary of Status of Conventions, http://www.imo.org/About/Conventions/StatusOfConventions/Pages/Default.aspx

International Monetary Fund, Factsheet: Special Drawing Rights (Aug. 24, 2012)

InterVISTAS-ga, The Economic Impact of Air Service Liberalization (2006)

Lang, Christian G. & Prager Dreifuss, *Forum Non Conveniens* in Continental Europe (unpublished paper, Aug. 2, 2009), http://www.prager-dreifuss.com/system/document_des/78/original/Forum_Non_Conveniens_Cont_Europe_.pdf?128937866

National Aeronautics and Space Administration, Goddard Space Flight Center, *NASA Study Finds Clock Ticking Slower on Ozone Hole Recovery*, June 29, 2006, http://www.nasa.gov/centers/goddard/news/topstory/2006/ozone_recovery.html

Office of Sec'y, Dep't of Transp. & Fed. Aviation Admin., Code-Share Safety Program Guidelines (2006)

Organisation for Economic Co-operation and Development, Principles for the Liberalisation of Air Cargo (2000)

Organisation for Economic Co-operation and Development, Sector Understanding on Export Credits for Civil Aircraft, TAD/PG (2007) 4/Final (July 27, 2007)

Organisation for Economic Co-operation and Development, Sector Understanding on Export Credits for Civil Aircraft, TAD/ASU (2011) 1 (Aug. 31, 2011)

Parker, Larry & John Blodgett, Cong. Res. Serv., RL 32721, Greenhouse Gas Emissions: Perspectives on the Top 20 Emitters and Developed Versus Developing Nations (2008)

Piermartini, Roberta & Linda Rousová, Liberalization of Air Transport Services and Passenger Traffic, WTO Staff Working Paper SRSD-2008–06 (Dec. 2008)

Pitmans Lawyers News, Shopping for Bankruptcy?, http://www.pitmans.com/news/shopping-for-bankruptcy

Press Release, American Civil Liberties Union, TSA Body Scanning Technology Strips Away Privacy (Oct. 1, 2009)

Press Release, Australian Competition and Consumer Commission, ACCC Grants Interim Authorisation to Alliance Between Qantas and Emirates (Jan. 17, 2013)

Press Release, Council of the European Union, Transport, Telecommunications and Energy: Transport Items, PRES/12/447 (Oct. 29, 2012)

Press Release, Europa, Air Transport: Commission Welcomes Agreement on Siberian Overflights (Dec. 1, 2011)

Press Release, Europa, Antitrust: Commission Market Tests Commitments from Eight Members of SkyTeam Concerning their Alliance Cooperation (Oct. 19, 2007)

Press Release, Europa, Antitrust: Commission Market Tests Commitments Proposed by BA, AA and Iberia Concerning Transatlantic Co-operation (Mar. 10, 2010)

Press Release, Europa, Antitrust: Commission Opens a Probe into Transatlantic Joint Venture between Air France-KLM, Alitalia and Delta and Closes Proceedings against Eight Members of SkyTeam Airline Alliance (Jan. 1, 2012)

Press Release, Europa, Commission Takes Action to Combat Aircraft Noise (Mar. 13, 1998)

Press Release, Europa, Stopping the Clock of ETS and Aviation Measures Following Last Week's International Civil Aviation Organization (ICAO) Council (Nov. 12, 2012)

Press Release, European Aviation Safety Agency, EASA Proposes New Harmonized Rules to Avoid Flight Crew Fatigue (Oct. 1, 2012)

Press Release, European Parliament, Parliament Gives Green Light to Air Passenger Data Deal with U.S. (Apr. 19, 2012)

Press Release, Federal Aviation Administration, FAA Issues Final Rule on Pilot Fatigue (Dec. 21, 2011)

Press Release, Global Industry Analysts, Inc., Global Aircraft Leasing Market to Reach $279 Billion by 2015 (Feb. 19, 2009)

Press Release, Organisation for Economic Co-operation and Development, Aircraft Sector Understanding: Signing Ceremony (Feb. 25, 2011)

Press Release, Organisation for Economic Co-operation and Development, Chile Signs Up as First OECD Member in South America (Jan. 11, 2010)

Skybrary, ICAO USOAP and Safety Performance, http://www.skybrary.aero/index. php/ICAO_USOAP_and_Safety_Performance

Tieleman, Katia, The Failure of the Multilateral Agreement on Investment (MAI) and the Absence of a Global Public Policy Network, Case Study for the UN Vision Project on Global Public Policy Networks (2000), http://www.gppi.net/fileadmin/ gppi/Tieleman_MAI_GPP_Network.pdf

Transatlantic Economic Council (TEC), Statement of the European Union and the United States on Shared Principles for International Investment (Apr. 12, 2012)

United Nations Blog, Most-ratified International Treaties (Sept. 24, 2012), http://blogs. un.org/blog/2012/09/24/most-ratified-international-treaties/

United Nations Conference on Environment and Development, Rio de Janeiro, Braz., June 3–14, 1992, Agenda 21, U.N. Doc. A/CONF. 151/26 (Aug. 12, 1992)

United Nations Conference on Environment and Development, Rio de Janeiro, Braz., June 3–14, 1992, Rio Declaration on Environment and Development, princ. 1, U.N. Doc. A/ CONF.151/26/Rev.1 (Aug. 12, 1992)

United Nations Framework Convention on Climate Change, Conference of the Parties, Durban, Nov. 28- Dec. 14, 2011, Draft Decision 1/CP.17, http://unfccc. int/files/meetings/durban_nov_2011/decisions/application/pdf/cop17_durbanplat form.pdf

United Nations General Assembly, Fragmentation of International Law: Difficulties Arising from Diversification and Expansion of International Law – Report of the Study Group of the International Law Commission, Doc. A/CN.4/L682 (Apr. 13, 2006)

U.S. General Accounting Office, Airline Competition: Impact of Changing Foreign Investment and Control Limits on U.S. Airlines, GAO/RCED-93–7 (1992)

World Economic Forum, Policies and Collaborative Partnership for Sustainable Aviation (2011)

World Trade Organization, Air Services Agreements Projector (2010), http://www.wto. org/asap/index.html

WTO Analytical Index: Agreement on Trade in Civil Aircraft, http://www.wto.org/ english/res_e/booksp_e/analytic_index_e/aircraft_01_e.htm

World Trade Organization, Council for Trade in Services, Quantitative Air Services Review (QUASAR): Part B: Preliminary Results, S/C/W/270/Add.1 (Nov. 30, 2006)

World Trade Organization, GATS Training Module, http://www.wto.org/english/tra-top_e/serv_e/cbt_course_e/signin_e.htm

World Trade Organization, The WTO Dispute Settlement Procedures: A Collection of the Relevant Legal Texts (2012)

Table of Authorities

TREATIES AND OTHER INTERNATIONAL AGREEMENTS
LISTED ALPHABETICALLY

Agreement Between the Government of Australia and the Government of the Argentine Republic Relating to Air Services (Mar. 11, 1992) (not in force)

Agreement between the Government of the United States of America and the [EU Commission] Regarding Application of Their Competition Laws, 1995 O.J. (L 95) (Sept. 23, 1991), *as corrected by* 1995 O.J. (L134) 1, *reprinted in* 4 Trade Reg. Rep. (CCH) ¶ 13,504, at 21,233-9

Agreement between Japan and the Republic of Uzbekistan for Air Services, Dec. 22, 2003, U.N. Reg. No. I-48368

Agreement between the United States of America and the European Union on the Use and Transfer of Passenger Name Records to the United States Department of Homeland Security, Dec. 8, 2011, 2012 O.J. (L 215) 5

Agreement Concerning Air Services, U.S.-U.K., June 22 & July 23, 1977, 28 U.S.T. 5367 [Bermuda II] (no longer in force)

Agreement on Air Transport between Canada and the European [Union] and its Member States, Dec. 17, 2009, 2010 O.J. (L 207) 32

Agreement on Certain Aspects of Air Services, Chile-EU, Oct. 31, 2006, 2006 O.J. (L 300) 46

Agreement on Mutual Legal Assistance between the European Union and the United States of America, June 25, 2003, T.I.A.S. 10-201.1, 2003 O.J. (L 181) 34

Agreement on Rules of Origin, Apr. 15, 1994, Marrakesh Agreement Establishing the World Trade Organization, 1868 U.N.T.S. 397 (1994)

Agreement on Subsidies and Countervailing Measures, Apr. 15, 1994, Marrakesh Agreement Establishing the World Trade Organization, 1869 U.N.T.S. 14 (1994)

Agreement on Trade in Civil Aircraft, *opened for signature* Apr. 12, 1979, 1186 U.N.T.S. 170, *reprinted as amended at* 1869 U.NT.S. 508

Agreement Relating to Air Services, U.S.-U.K., Feb. 11, 1946, 12 Bevans 726 [Bermuda I] (no longer in force)

Air Transport Agreement, U.S.-Austl., Mar. 31, 2008, [2008] ATNIF 3 (Austl.)

Air Transport Agreement, U.S.-Can., Mar. 12, 2007, *reprinted in* 3 Av. L. Rep. (CCH) ¶ 26,246a

Air Transport Agreement, U.S.-Eth., May 17, 2005, *reprinted in* 3 Av. L. Rep. (CCH) ¶ 26,300a

Air Transport Agreement, U.S.-EU, Apr. 30, 2007, 2007 O.J. (L 134) 4, 46 I.L.M. 470, as amended by Protocol to Amend the Air Transport Agreement, U.S.-EU, Mar. 25, 2010, 2010 O.J. (L 223) 3 [U.S./EU Air Transport Agreement]

Air Transport Agreement, U.S.-Gabon, Aug. 23, 2004, *reprinted in* 3 Av. L. Rep. (CCH) ¶ 26,310a

ASEAN Multilateral Agreement on Air Services, *opened for signature* May 20, 2009 [ASEAN MAAS]

Charter of the United Nations, *opened for signature* June 26, 1945, 3 Bevans 1153 (entered into force Oct. 24, 1945)

Clinton, William Jefferson, Letter Approving the Montreal Convention (Sept. 6, 2000), 106th Cong., 2d Sess., Treaty Doc. 106-45 (2000)

Convention for the Suppression of Unlawful Acts Against the Safety of Civil Aviation, *opened for signature* Sept. 23, 1971, 974 U.N.T.S. 178 (entered into force Jan. 26, 1973) [Montreal Convention]

Convention for the Suppression of Unlawful Seizure of Aircraft, *opened for signature* Dec. 16, 1970, 860 U.N.T.S. 105 (entered into force Oct. 14, 1971) [The Hague Convention]

Convention for the Unification of Certain Rules for International Carriage by Air, *opened for signature* May 28, 1999, 2242 U.N.T.S. 350 (entered into force Nov. 4, 2003) [Montreal Convention]

Convention for the Unification of Certain Rules Relating to International Carriage by Air, *opened for signature* Oct. 12, 1929, 137 L.N.T.S. 11, 49 Stat. 3000 (entered into force Feb. 13, 1933) [Warsaw Convention]

Convention on Biological Diversity, *opened for signature* June 5, 1992, 1760 U.N.T.S. 79 (entered into force Dec. 29, 1993)

Convention on Compensation for Damage Caused by Aircraft to Third Parties, ICAO Doc. 9919, *opened for signature* May 2, 2009 [General Risks Convention]

Convention on Compensation for Damage to Third Parties, Resulting from Acts of Unlawful Interference Involving Aircraft, *opened for signature* May 2, 2009, ICAO Doc. 9920 [Unlawful Interference Convention].

Convention on Damage Caused by Foreign Aircraft to Third Parties on the Surface, *opened for signature* Oct. 7, 1952, 310 U.N.T.S. 182 (entered into force Feb. 4, 1958) [Rome Convention]

Convention on the High Seas, *opened for signature* April 29, 1958, 450 U.N.T.S. 11 (entered into force Sept. 30, 1962)

Convention on International Civil Aviation, *opened for signature* Dec. 7, 1944, 61 Stat. 1180, 15 U.N.T.S. 295 (entered into force Apr. 7, 1947) [Chicago Convention]

Convention on International Interests in Mobile Equipment, *opened for signature* Nov. 16, 2001, 2307 U.N.T.S. 285 (entered into force Apr. 1, 2004) [Cape Town Convention]

Convention on the International Recognition of Rights in Aircraft, *opened for signature* Jun. 19, 1948, 4 U.S.T. 1830, 310 U.N.T.S. 151 [Geneva Convention]

Convention on Long-Range Transboundary Air Pollution, *opened for signature* Nov. 13, 1979, 1302 U.N.T.S. 217

Convention on the Marking of Plastic Explosives for the Purpose of Detection, *opened for signature* Mar. 1, 1991, 2122 U.N.T.S. 359 (entered into force June 21, 1998) [Plastic Explosives Convention]

Convention on Offenses and Certain Other Acts Committed on Board Aircraft, *opened for signature* Sept. 14, 1963, 704 U.N.T.S. 219 (entered into force Dec. 4, 1969) [Tokyo Convention]

Convention on the Settlement of Investment Disputes Between States and Nationals of Other States, *opened for signature* Mar. 18, 1965, 17 U.S.T. 1270, 575 U.N.T.S. 159 [ICSID Convention]

Convention on the Suppression of Unlawful Acts Related to International Civil Aviation, *opened for signature* Sept. 10, 2010, ICAO Doc. 9960 [Beijing Convention]

Convention Relating to the Regulation of Aerial Navigation, *opened for signature* Oct. 13, 1919, 11 L.N.T.S. 173 (entered into force May 31, 1920) [Paris Convention]

Convention, Supplementary to the Warsaw Convention, for the Unification of Certain Rules Relating to International Carriage by Air Performed by a Person Other Than the Contracting Carrier, ICAO Doc. No. 8181 (entered into force May 1, 1964)

Declaration Prohibiting Launching of Projectiles and Explosives from Balloons, *opened for signature* July 29, 1900, 1 Bevans 270 (entered into force Sept. 4, 1900)

Free Trade Agreement, U.S.-Austl., May 18, 2004, 118 Stat. 919

General Agreement on Trade in Services [GATS], Annex on Air Transport Services, Marrakesh Agreement Establishing the World Trade Organization,

Annex 1B, Legal Instruments – Results of the Uruguay Round, *opened for signature* Apr. 15, 1994, 1869 U.N.T.S. 183, *reprinted in* 33 I.L.M. 1125 (1993)

Ibero-American Convention, *opened for signature* Nov. 1, 1926, 45 Stat. 2409

International Air Services Transit Agreement, *opened for signature* Dec. 7, 1944, 59 Stat. 1693, 84 U.N.T.S. 389 [Two Freedoms Agreement]

International Air Transport Agreement, *opened for signature* Dec. 7, 1944, 59 Stat. 1701, 171 U.N.T.S. 387 [Five Freedoms Agreement]

International Convention for the Prevention of Marine Pollution from Ships, Nov. 2, 1973, 1340 U.N.T.S. 184, *as modified by* Protocol, Feb. 17, 1978, 1340 U.N.T.S. 61

International Convention for the Unification of Certain Rules Relating to Damage Caused by Aircraft to Third Parties on the Surface, *opened for signature* May 29, 1933, 192 L.N.T.S. 291 (entered into force Feb. 13, 1942)

International Declaration Prohibiting the Discharge of Projectiles and Explosives from Balloons, *opened for signature* Oct. 18, 1907, 1907 A.T.S. 14 (entered into force Nov. 27, 1909)

Kyoto Protocol to the United Nations Framework Convention on Climate Change, *opened for signature* Dec. 11, 1997, 2303 U.N.T.S. 162 (entered into force Feb. 16, 2005) [Kyoto Protocol]

Marrakesh Agreement Establishing the World Trade Organization, *opened for signature* Apr. 15, 1994, 1867 U.N.T.S. 154 [WTO Agreement]

Memorandum of Consultations and Draft Exchange of Notes concerning Modifications to the U.S./U.K. Air Services Agreement, *reprinted in* 3 Av. L. Rep. (CCH) ¶ 26,540j, at 23,923 (Jan. 2007)

Multilateral Agreement on the Liberalization of International Air Transportation, *opened for signature* May 1, 2001, 2215 U.N.T.S. 33 [MALIAT]

North American Free Trade Agreement, U.S.-Can.-Mex., Dec. 17, 1992, *reprinted in* 32 I.L.M. 289 (1993) (entered into force Jan. 1, 1994)

Pan American Convention on Commercial Aviation, *opened for signature* Feb. 20, 1928, 129 L.N.T.S. 223 [Havana Convention]

Protocol between the Government of the United States of America and the Government of the Russian Federation to Amend the Jan. 14, 1994 Air Transport Agreement, U.S.-Rus., Oct. 5, 2005

Protocol between the United States of America and the Federal Republic of Germany to Amend the Air Transport Agreement of July 7, 1995, with related Route Schedule, signed at Milwaukee, May 23, 1996

Protocol for the Suppression of Unlawful Acts of Violence at Airports Serving International Civil Aviation, *opened for signature* Feb. 24, 1988, 1589 U.N.T.S. 473 (entered into force Aug. 6, 1989) [Montreal Protocol]

Protocol Supplementary to the Convention for the Unification of Certain Rules Relating to Damage Caused by Foreign Aircraft to Third Parties on the Surface, *opened for signature* Sept. 29, 1938, ICAO Doc. 107-CD

Protocol to Amend the Air Transport Agreement, U.S.-EU, Apr. 25 & 30, 2010, 2010 O.J. (L 223) 3 [U.S./EU Protocol]

Protocol to Amend the Convention on Damage Caused by Foreign Aircraft to Third Parties on the Surface Signed at Rome on 7 October 1952, *opened for signature* Sept. 23, 1978, ICAO Doc. 9257 (entered into force July 25, 2002) [1978 Montreal Protocol]

Protocol to Amend the Convention for the Unification of Certain Rules Relating to International Carriage by Air, *opened for signature* Sept. 28, 1955, 478 U.N.T.S. 371 (entered into force Aug. 1, 1963) [The Hague Protocol]

Protocol to Amend the Convention for the Unification of Certain Rules Relating to International Carriage by Air, as Amended by The Hague Protocol, *opened for signature* Mar. 8, 1971, ICAO Doc. 8392 (1971) [Guatemala Protocol]

Protocols to Amend the Convention for the Unification of Certain Rules Relating to International Carriage by Air, *opened for signature* Sept. 25, 1975, *reprinted in* 22 I.L.M. 13 [Montreal Protocols 1, 2, 3, & 4]

Protocol to Amend the Jan. 14, 1994 Air Transport Agreement, U.S.-Rus., Oct. 5, 2005, *reprinted in* 3 Av. L. Rep. (CCH) ¶ 26,474d, at 22,977

Protocol to the Convention on International Interests in Mobile Equipment on Matters Specific to Aircraft Equipment, *opened for signature* Nov. 16, 2001, 2367 U.N.T.S. 517 (entered into force Mar. 1, 2006)

Protocol Supplementary to the Convention for the Suppression of Unlawful Seizure of Aircraft, *opened for signature* Sept. 10, 2010, ICAO Doc. 9959 [Beijing Protocol]

Resolutions for the Final Act of the International Civil Aviation Conference, Dec. 7, 1944, *reprinted in* 3 Av. L. Rep. (CCH) ¶ 28,012

Settlement Understanding, Ann. 2 to the WTO Agreement, *in* Final Act Embodying the Results of the Uruguay Round of Multilateral Trade Negotiations, *opened for signature* Apr. 15, 1994, 33 I.L.M. 1226

Statute of the International Court of Justice, *opened for signature* June 26, 1945, 59 Stat. 1031, 3 Bevans 1153, 33 U.N.T.S. 993

Treaty of Lisbon Amending the Treaty on European Union and the Treaty Establishing the European Communities, Dec. 13, 2007, 2007 O.J. (C 306) 1

Treaty on the Functioning of the European Union, Sept. 5, 2008, 2008 O.J. (C 115) 47, *reprinted in consolidated form at* 2010 O.J. (C 83) 47 [TFEU]

Treaty on Principles Governing the Activities of States in the Exploration and Use of Outer Space, including the Moon and Other Celestial Bodies, *opened for signature* Jan. 27, 1967, 610 U.N.T.S. 205

UNIDROIT Convention on International Financial Leasing, *opened for signature* May 28, 1988, *reprinted in* 27 I.L.M. 931

United Nations Convention on the Law of the Sea, *opened for signature* Dec. 10, 1982, 1833 U.N.T.S. 397 [UNCLOS]

United Nations Framework Convention on Climate Change, May 9, 1992, 1771 U.N.T.S. 107 (entered into force Mar. 21, 1994) [UNFCCC]

U.S.-Cuba Memorandum of Understanding on Hijacking of Aircraft and Vessels and Other Offenses. Feb. 15, 1973, U.S.-Cuba, 24 U.S.T. 737

U.S. Dep't. of State, 2012 U.S. Model Bilateral Investment Treaty, http://www.state.gov/documents/organization/188371.pdf [U.S. Model BIT]

U.S. Dep't of State, Air Transport Agreement Between the Government of the United States of America and the Government of [Country], http://www.state.gov/e/eb/rls/othr/ata/114866.htm (Jan. 12, 2012) [Model Open Skies Agreement]

U.S. Dep't of State, United States Model Bilateral Air Transport Agreement ("Open Skies Agreement"), *reprinted at* 35 I.L.M. 1479 (1996)

Vienna Convention on the Law of Treaties, *opened for signature* May 23, 1969, 1155 U.N.T.S. 331

Vienna Convention for the Protection of the Ozone Layer, *opened for signature* Mar. 22, 1985, T.I.A.S. No. 11,097, 1513 U.N.T.S. 293

INTERNATIONAL CIVIL AVIATION ORGANIZATION ASSEMBLY RESOLUTIONS LISTED CHRONOLOGICALLY

International Civil Aviation Organization, Air Navigation Bureau, *Making an ICAO Standard*, Assembly Res. A1-31, ICAO Doc. 4411 (A1-P/45) (1947)

International Civil Aviation Organization, *Consolidated Statement of Continuing ICAO Policies and Practices Related to Environmental Protection*, Assem. Res. A32-8 (2000), *compiled in Assembly Resolutions in Force*, ICAO Doc. 9790 (2001)

International Civil Aviation Organization, *Establishment of an ICAO Universal Safety Oversight Audit Programme*, Assem. Res. A32-11, *compiled in Assembly Resolutions in Force*, ICAO Doc. 9790 (2001)

International Civil Aviation Organization, *Declaration of Misuse of Civil Aircraft as Weapons of Destruction and Other Terrorist Acts Involving Civil Aviation*, Assem. Res. A33-1 (2001)

International Civil Aviation Organization, *Adoption of National Legislation on Certain Offenses Committed on Board Civil Aircraft (Unruly/Disruptive Passengers)*, Assem. Res. A33-4 (2001)

International Civil Aviation Organization, *Consolidated Statement of Continuing ICAO Policies and Practices Related to Environmental Protection*, Assem. Res. A33-7 (2001), *compiled in Assembly Resolutions in Force*, ICAO Doc. 9790 (2001)

International Civil Aviation Organization, *Consolidated Statement of Continuing ICAO Policies and Practices Related to Environmental Protection*, Assem. Res. A36-22 (2007), *compiled in Assembly Resolutions in Force*, ICAO Doc. 9902 (2007)

International Civil Aviation Organization, *Consolidated Statement of Continuing ICAO Policies and Practices Related to Environmental Protection – Climate Change*, Assem. Res. A37-19, *compiled in Assembly Resolutions in Force*, ICAO Doc. 9958 (2010)

U.S. FEDERAL AND STATE COURT CASES LISTED ALPHABETICALLY

Abdullah v. American Airlines, Inc., 181 F.3d 363 (3d Cir. 1999)

Air Crash at Taipei on Oct. 31, 2000, In re, 219 F. Supp. 2d 1069 (C.D. Cal. 2002)

Air Crash Disaster Near New Orleans, La. on July 9, 1982, In re, 821 F.2d 1147 (5th Cir. 1987) (en banc)

Air Disaster Near Cove Neck, N.Y., In re, 774 F. Supp. 725 (E.D.N.Y. 1991)

Air Fr. v. Saks, 470 U.S. 392 (1985)

Alleged Food Poisoning Incident, Mar., 1984, In re, 770 F.2d 3 (2d Cir. 1985)

Avero Belgium Ins. v. American Airlines, Inc., 423 F.3d 73 (2d Cir. 2005)

Baah v. Virgin Atl. Airways Ltd., 473 F. Supp. 2d 591 (S.D.N.Y. 2007)

Benjamins v. British European Airways, 572 F.2d 913 (2d Cir. 1978)

Best v. BWIA West Indies Airways, Ltd., 581 F. Supp. 2d 359 (E.D.N.Y. 2008)

Blansett v. Continental Airlines, Inc., 379 F.3d 177 (5th Cir. 2004)

Borham v. Pan Am. World Airways, Inc., No. 85 Civ. 6922, 1986 WL 2974 (S.D.N.Y. Mar. 5, 1986)

Boyd v. White, 276 P.2d 92, 128 Cal. App. 2d 641 (Cal. Dist. Ct. App. 1954)

Byrd v. Comair, Inc. (In re Air Crash at Lexington, Ky., Aug. 27, 2006), 501 F. Supp. 2d 902 (E.D. Ky. 2007)

Chan v. Korean Air Lines, Ltd., 490 U.S. 122 (1989)

Chubb & Son, Inc. v. Asiana Airlines, 214 F.3d 301 (2d Cir. 2000), *cert. denied*, 533 U.S. 928, 121 S. Ct. 2549 (2001)

Chubbs Ins. Co. of Eur. S.A. v. Menlo Worldwide Forwarding Inc., 634 F.3d 1023 (9th Cir. 2011)

Continental Ins. Co. v. Federal Express Corp., 454 F.3d 951 (9th Cir. 2006)

Day v. Trans World Airlines, Inc., 528 F.2d 31 (2d Cir. 1975)

Dooley v. Korean Air Lines Co., 524 U.S. 116 (1998)

Eastern Airlines, Inc. v. Floyd, 499 U.S. 530 (1991)

Eck v. United Arab Airlines, Inc., 360 F.2d 804 (2d Cir. 1966)

Ehrlich v. American Airlines, Inc., 360 F.3d 366 (2d Cir. 2004)

El Al Isr. Airlines, Ltd. v. Tseng, 525 U.S. 155 (1999)

Feeney v. America W. Airlines, 948 P.2d 110 (Colo. App. 1997)

Fujitsu Ltd. v. Federal Exp. Corp., 247 F.3d 423 (2d Cir. 2001)

Fulop v. Malev Hungarian Airlines, 175 F. Supp. 2d 651 (S.D.N.Y. 2001)

Hilton v. Guyot, 159 U.S. 113 (1895)

Hipolito v. Northwest Airlines, Inc., 2001 WL 861984 (4th Cir. 2001)

Hornsby v. Lufthansa German Airlines, 593 F. Supp. 2d 1132 (C.D. Cal. 2009)

Hosaka v. United Airlines, Inc., 305 F.3d 989 (9th Cir. 2002)

Husserl v. Swiss Air Transport Co., 388 F. Supp. 1238 (S.D.N.Y. 1975)

Kahn v. Trans World Airlines, Inc., 82 A.D.2d 696 (N.Y. App. Div. 1981)

Koninkljjke Luchtvaart Maatschappij N.V. KLM v. Tuller, 292 F.2d 775 (D.C. Cir. 1960)

Korean Air Lines Disaster of Sept. 1, 1983, *In re*, 932 F.2d 1475 (D.C. Cir. 1991)

Langadinos v. American Airlines, Inc., 199 F.3d 68 (1st Cir. 2000)

MacDonald v. Air Can., 439 F.2d 1402 (1st Cir. 1971)

Manufacturers Hanover Trust Co. v. Alitalia Airlines, 429 F. Supp. 964 (S.D. N.Y. 1977), *aff'd*, 573 F.2d 1292 (2d Cir. 1977)

Margosian v. U.S. Airlines, Inc., 127 F. Supp. 464 (E.D.N.Y. 1955)

Martinez Hernandez v. Air Fr., 545 F.2d 279 (1st Cir. 1976)

Matveychuk v. Deutsche Lufthansa AG, No. 08-CV-3108, 2010 WL 3540921 (E.D.N.Y. Sept. 7, 2010)

Maugnie v. Compangie Nationale Air Fr., 549 F.2d 1256 (9th Cir. 1977)

Missouri Pac. R.R. v. Elmore & Stahl, 377 U.S. 134 (1964)

Motorola, Inc. v. MSAS Cargo Int'l, Inc., 42 F. Supp. 2d 952 (N.D. Cal. 1998)

Nastych v. British Airways PLC, No. 09 Civ. 9082, 2010 WL 363400 (S.D.N.Y. Feb. 2, 2010)

O'Grady v. British Airways, 134 F. Supp. 2d 407 (E. D. Pa. 2001)

Olympic Airways v. Husain, 540 U.S. 644 (2004)

Padilla v. Olympic Airways, 765 F. Supp 835 (S.D.N.Y. 1991)

Paquete Habana, 175 U.S. 677 (1900)

Polanski v. KLM Royal Dutch Airlines, 378 F. Supp. 2d 1222 (S.D. Cal. 2005)

Price v. British Airways, No. 91 Civ. 4947, 1992 WL 170679 (S.D.N.Y. July 7, 1992)

Ramos v. American Airlines, Inc., No. 3:11cv207, 2011 WL 5075674 (W.D.N.C. Oct. 25, 2011)

Rodriguez v. Ansett Austl. Ltd., 383 F.3d 914 (9th Cir. 2004)

Rosman v. Trans World Airlines, Inc., 34 N.Y.2d 385 (N.Y. Ct. App. 1974)

Scala v. American Airlines, 249 F. Supp. 2d 176 (D. Conn. 2003)

Schaefer-Condulmari v. U.S. Airways Group, LLC, No. 09-1146, 2012 WL 2920375 (E.D. Pa. July 18, 2012)

Stone v. Continental Airlines, Inc., 905 F. Supp. 823 (D. Haw. 1995)

Sweis v. Trans World Airlines, Inc., 681 F. Supp. 501 (N.D. Ill. 1988)

Trans World Airlines, Inc. v. Franklin Mint Corp., 466 U.S. 243 (1984)

Twardowski v. American Airlines, Inc., 535 F.3d 952 (9th Cir. 2008)

Ugaz v. American Airlines, Inc., 576 F. Supp. 2d 1354 (S.D. Fla. 2008)

U.S. v. Causby, 328 U.S. 256 (1946)

U.S. v. Cordova, 89 F. Supp. 298 (E.D.N.Y. 1950)

U.S. v. Rezaq, 134 F.3d 1121 (D.C. Cir. 1998)

U.S. v. Yunis, 681 F. Supp. 896 (D.D.C. 1988), *aff'd*, 924 F.2d 1086 (D.C. Cir. 1991)

U.S. v. Zehe, 601 F. Supp. 196 (D. Mass 1985)

Vosburg v. Putney, 80 Wis. 523, 50 N.W. 403 (Wis. 1891)

Wallace v. Korean Air Lines, 214 F.3d 293 (2d Cir. 2000), *cert. denied* 531 U.S. 1144 (2001)

Watts v. American Airlines, Inc., No. 1:07-cv-0434, 2007 WL 3019344 (S.D. Ind. Oct. 10, 2007)

West Caribbean Airways, S.A., *In re*, 619 F. Supp. 2d 1299 (S.D. Fla. 2007)

Woodard v. Saginaw City Lines, Inc., 112 N.W.2d 512 (Mich. 1961)

Wyeth v. Levine, 555 U.S. 555 (2009)

Yahya v. Yemenia-Yemen Airways, No. 08-14789, 2009 WL 3424192 (E.D. Mich. Oct. 20, 2009)

Zicherman v. Korean Air Lines Co., 516 U.S. 217 (1996)

U.S. ADMINISTRATIVE (CAB/DOT/FAA) PROCEEDINGS LISTED ALPHABETICALLY

Air Canada, The Austrian Group, British Midland Airways Ltd., Continental Airlines, Inc., Deutsche Lufthansa Ag, Polskie Linie Lotniecze Lot S.A., Scandinavian Airlines System, Swiss International Air Lines Ltd., Tap Air Portugal, and United Air Lines, Inc., *Joint Application to Amend Order 2007-2-16 so as to Approve and Confer Antitrust Immunity*, Dkt. No. OST-2008-0234, Show Cause Order 2009-4-5 (Apr. 7, 2009)

Air Canada et al., *Final Order to Amend Order 2007-2-16 so as to Approve and Confer Antitrust Immunity*, Dkt. No. OST-2008-0234, Order 2009-7-10 (July 10, 2009)

Air Canada et al., *Joint Application to Amend Order 2007-2-16 so as to Approve and Confer Antitrust Immunity*, Dkt. No. OST-2008-0234, Order 2011-11-16 (Nov. 14, 2011)

Air Transport Association – Order on Reconsideration – International Air Carrier Liability Limits, Dkt. No. OST-2005-22617, Order 2006-10-14 (Oct. 26, 2006)

Alitalia-Linee Aeree Italiane-S.p.A., Czech Airlines, Delta Air Lines, Inc., KLM Royal Dutch Airlines, Northwest Airlines, Inc., and Société Air France, *Joint Application for Approval of and Antitrust Immunity for Alliance Agreements under 49 U.S.C. §§ 41308 and 41309*, Dkt. No. OST-2004-19214, Show Cause Order 2005-12-12 (Dec. 12, 2005)

Alitalia-Linee Aeree Italiane-S.p.A., Czech Airlines, Delta Airlines, Inc., KLM Royal Dutch Airlines, Northwest Airlines, Inc., & Société Air France, *Joint Application for Approval of and Antitrust Immunity for Alliance Agreements Under 49 U.S.C. §§ 41308 and 41309*, Dkt. No. OST-2007-28644, Show Cause Order 2008-4-17 (Apr. 9, 2008)

All Nippon Airways Co., Ltd., Continental Airlines, Inc. and United Airlines, Inc., *Joint Application under 49 U.S.C. §§ 41308–41309 for Approval of and Antitrust Immunity for Alliance Agreements*, Dkt. No. OST-2009-0350 (Dec. 23, 2009)

American Airlines, Inc., British Airways PLC, Finnair OYJ, Iberia Lineas Aereas De Espana, S.A., Royal Jordanian Airlines, *Joint Application Under 49 U.S.C. §§ 41308-41309 for Approval of and Antitrust Immunity for Alliance Agreements*, Dkt. No. OST-2008-0252, Order 2010-2-8 (Feb. 13, 2010)

American Airlines, Inc., British Airways PLC, Finnair OYJ, Iberia Lineas Aereas De Espana, S.A., Royal Jordanian Airlines, *Joint Application Under 49 U.S.C. §§ 41308-41309 for Approval of and Antitrust Immunity for Alliance Agreements*, Dkt. No. OST-2008-0252, Order 2010-7-8 (July 20, 2010)

The Austrian Group, British Midland Airways Limited, Deutsche Lufthansa AG, Polskie Linie Lotnicze S.A., Scandinavian Airlines System, Swiss International Air Lines Ltd., TAP Air Portugal, and United Air Lines, Inc., and United Air Lines, Inc. and Air Canada, *Joint Application under 49 U.S.C. §§ 41308 and 41309 for Approval of and Antitrust Immunity for Commercial Alliance Agreements*, Dkt. Nos. OST-2005-22922 and OST-96-1434, Show Cause Order (Dec. 19, 2006)

Comments of the Department of Justice on the Show Cause Order to Amend Order 2007-2-16 so as to Approve and Confer Antitrust Immunity, Docket DOT-OST-2008-0234 (June 26, 2009)

Computer Reservation Systems (CRS) Regulations, Dkt. No. OST-97-2881, Final Rule, 14 C.F.R. Part 255, 69 Fed. Reg. 976 (Jan. 7, 2004)

DHL Airways, Inc. (ASTAR), Dkt. No. OST-2002-13089, 2003 DOT Av LEXIS 1086 (Dec. 19, 2003)

Enhancing Airline Passenger Protections, Dkt. No. OST-2010-0140, Final Rule (Apr. 20, 2011)

In the Matter of Defining "Open Skies," Dkt. No. 48130, Order 92-8-13, 1992 DOT Av. LEXIS 568 (Dep't of Transp. Aug 5, 1992)

Northwest Airlines, Inc. and KLM Royal Dutch Airlines, *Joint Application for Approval and Antitrust Immunity of an Agreement Pursuant to Sections 412 and 414 of the Federal Aviation Act, as amended*, Dkt. No. 48342, Order 92-11-27 to Show Cause (Nov. 16, 1992)

Order of Civil Aeronautics Board Approving Increases in Liability Limitations of Warsaw Convention and Hague Protocol, May 13, 1966 (approving Agreement CAB 18900), 31 Fed. Reg. 7302 (1966), *reprinted in* 49 U.S.C. app. § 1502 (1988)

Statement of United States Air Transportation Policy, Dkt. No. 49844, 60 Fed. Reg. 21,841 (May 3, 1995)

Translux International Airlines, *Notice of Action Taken*, Dkt. No. OST-98-4329 (Nov, 25, 1998)

United Air Lines, Inc. and Asiana Airlines, Inc., *Joint Application for Approval and Antitrust Immunity for an Alliance Expansion Agreement*, Dkt. No. OST-03-14202, Order 2003-5-18 Granting Approval and Antitrust Immunity (May 14, 2003)

2007, 2008, and 2009 US-China Air Services and Combination Frequency Allocation Proceeding, OST-2007-28567

U.S.-Japan Alliance Case, Answer of the Association of Flight Attendants-CWA, Docket DOT-OST-2010-0059 (July 9, 2010)

U.S.-Japan Alliance Case, Dkt. No. OST-2010-0059, Final Order 2010-11-10 (Nov. 10, 2010)

Virgin America, *Petition of Alaska Airlines for Review of Citizenship*, Dkt. No. OST-2009-0037 (Feb. 10, 2009)

INTERNATIONAL COURT OF JUSTICE CASES LISTED ALPHABETICALLY

Legality of the Threat or Use of Nuclear Weapons, Advisory Opinion, 1996 I.C.J. 226 (July 8) [GA Opinion]

Legality of the Use by a State of Nuclear Weapons in Armed Conflict, Advisory Opinion, 1996 I.C.J. 66 (July 8) [WHO Opinion]

Questions of Interpretation and Application of the 1971 Montreal Convention Arising from the Aerial Incident at Lockerbie (Libya v. United States), Provisional Measures, 1992 I.C.J. 114 (Apr. 14)

COURT OF JUSTICE OF THE EUROPEAN UNION CASES LISTED ALPHABETICALLY

Case C-366/10, The Air Transport Ass'n of America, American Airlines, Inc., Continental Airlines, Inc., United Airlines, Inc. v. the Sec'y of State for Energy and Climate Change, 2010 O.J. C-260/12, referred by UK High Court of Justice, Q.B. Div. (Admin. Ct.)

Cases C-467/98, C-468/98, C-469/98, C-471/98, C-472/98, C-475/98, and C-476/98, Comm'n v. Denmark, Sweden, Finland, Belgium, Luxembourg, Austria, and Germany, 2002 E.C.R. I-090519 *et seq.*

Case C-466/98, Comm'n v. U.K., 2002 E.C.R. I-09427

Joined Cases C-509/09 & C-161/10, eDate Advertising v. X and Olivier Martinez v. MGN Ltd. (Oct. 25, 2011)

Summary of Commission Decision of 14 July 2010 relating to a proceeding under Article 101 of the Treaty of the Functioning of the European Union and Article 53 of the EEA Agreement (COMP/39.56 – British Airways/American Airlines/Iberia) 2010 O.J. (C 278) 14

EUROPEAN COURT OF FIRST INSTANCE CASES LISTED ALPHABETICALLY

Case C-344/04, International Air Transp. Ass'n v. Department for Transp., 2006 E.C.R. I-00403

Joined Cases C-317 & C-318/04, Parliament v. Council, 2006 E.C.R. I-4721

NATIONAL COURT CASES LISTED ALPHABETICALLY

Blue Sky One Limited & Or's v. Mahan Air & Ano'r [2010] EWHC 631 (Comm.) (Mar. 25, 2010) (U.K.)

Bury v. Pope, Cro. Eliz. 118, 78 Eng. Rep. 375 (1587) (U.K.)

Celestial Aviation Trading 71 Ltd. v. Paramount Airways Pvt. Ltd., [2010] EWHC 185 (Comm.) (Feb. 11, 2010) (U.K.)

Chaudhari v. British Airways [1997] EWCA 1413 (U.K.)

Cie Air Fr. v. Teichner, 39 Revue Francaise de Droit Aerien 232, 23 EUR. TR. L. 87 (Isr. 1984)

Coccia v. Turkish Airlines, 108 Foro It. 1 1586 (Corte Cost. 1985)

Connaught Laboratories Ltd. v. Air Canada, 23 O.R. 2d 176 (Ont. Sup. Ct. J.) (1978) (Can.)

Daddon v. Air Fr., 1 S. & B. Av. R. 141 (Isr. 1984).

Deep Vein Thrombosis and Air Travel Group Litigation, [2005] UKHL 72, [2005] 1 A.C. 495 (U.K.)

Emery Air Freight Corp. v. Nerine Nurseries Ltd., [1997] 3 N.Z.L.R. 723 (N.Z.)

Gal v. Northern Mountain Helicopters Inc., Dkt. No. 3491834918, 1998 B.C.T.C. LEXIS 1351 (B.C.T.C. (Can.), July 22, 1998)

Gallais c. Aéro Maritime, T.G.I. Seine, Apr. 28, 1954, R.F.D.A. 1954, 184 (Fr.)

King v. Bristow Helicopters & In Re Morris, [2002] UKHL 7, 1 Lloyd's Rep. 745 (U.K.)

Kuate v. Air Fr., Kenya Airways and others, Cour d'appel [CA] [regional court of appeal] Paris, 2011 (Fr.)

Laroche v. Spirit of Adventure (UK) Ltd., [2009] EWCA (Civ) 12 (Eng.)

Naval-Torres v. Northwest Airlines, Inc., 159 D.L.R. (4th) 67 (Ont. Gen. Div. (Can.) 1998)

Povey v. Qantas Airways Ltd., [2005] 223 C.L.R. 189 (Austl.)

Seagate Technology Int'l v. Changi Int'l Airport Servs. Pte Ltd., [1997] 3 S.L.R. 1 (Sing.)

Sidhu v. British Airways plc, [1997] 1 All E.R. 193 (U.K. H.L.)

The Queen v. Sec'y of State for the Env't, Transp. & the Regions, ex parte Omega Air Ltd., High Court of Justice (Q.B., Nov. 25, 1999) (Eng.)

NON-U.S. ADMINISTRATIVE PROCEEDINGS LISTED
ALPHABETICALLY

European Aviation Safety Agency, Opinion 05/2012, Nov. 22, 2012

European Communities – Measures Concerning Meat and Meat Products (Hormones), Original Complaint filed by the United States, Recourse to Arbitration by the European Communities under Article 22.6 of the DSU: Decision by the Arbitrators, WT/DS26/ARB (July 12, 1999)

Final Report and Comments of the Netherlands Aviation Safety Board on the Investigation into the Accident with the Collision of KLM Flight 4805, Boeing 747-206B, PH-BUF and Pan American Flight 1736, Boeing 747-121, N736PA at Tenerife Airport, Spain on 27 March 1977 (*Source:* ICAO Circular 153-AN/56)

World Trade Organization, Appellate Body Report, *European Communities and Certain Member States – Measures Affecting Trade in Large Civil Aircraft*, WT/DS316/AB/R (May 18, 2011)

World Trade Organization, Appellate Body Report, *United States – Measures Affecting Trade in Large Civil Aircraft (Second Complaint)*, WT/DS353/AB/R (Mar. 13, 2012)

U.S. FEDERAL LEGISLATION BY U.S. CODE SEQUENCE

11 U.S.C. § 1110
18 U.S.C. § 7
18 U.S.C. § 953
49 U.S.C. § 40102(a)
49 U.S.C. § 40109(g)
49 U.S.C. § 41101(a)
49 U.S.C. § 41102(a)
49 U.S.C. § 41308(b)
49 U.S.C. § 41309
49 U.S.C. § 41309(b)
49 U.S.C. § 41309(b)(1)
49 U.S.C. § 41309(b)(1)(A)
49 U.S.C. § 41309(b)(1)(B)
49 U.S.C. § 41703
49 U.S.C. § 44108(a)(3)
49 U.S.C. § 46502
49 U.S.C. § 46502(a)
49 U.S.C. § 46504
50 U.S.C. § 2170

U.S. FEDERAL LEGISLATION BY POPULAR NAME LISTED CHRONOLOGICALLY

1799 Logan Act, 1 Stat. 613
1926 Air Commerce Act, ch. 344, 44 Stat. 568.
1938 Civil Aeronautics Act, ch. 601, 52 Stat. 973
2001 Air Transport Safety and System Stabilization Act, Pub. L. No. 107-42, 115 Stat. 230
2007 Implementing Recommendations of the 9/11 Commission Act of 2007, Pub. L. No. 110-53, 121 Stat. 266
2009 Ensure Adequate Airline Competition Between the United States and Europe Act, H.R. 831, 111th Cong.

U.S. CODE OF FEDERAL REGULATIONS LISTED
BY CODE SEQUENCE

14 C.F.R. § 34.21 (2012)
14 C.F.R. § 36.103 (2005)
14 C.F.R. § 153 (2008)
14 C.F.R. § 212 (2008)
14 C.F.R. § 255 (2004)
14 C.F.R. § 257.5 (2005)

U.S. LEGISLATIVE HISTORY

Impact of Consolidation on the Aviation Industry, With a Focus on the Proposed Merger Between Delta Air Lines and Northwest Airlines: Hearing Before the Subcomm. on Aviation of the H. Comm. on Transp. & Infrastructure, 110th Cong. 202–12 (2008) (testimony of James J. O'Connell, Deputy Assistant Attorney Gen., Antitrust Dept. U.S. Dept. of Justice)

EUROPEAN COMMISSION REGULATIONS LISTED
CHRONOLOGICALLY

Regulation 2027/97, Air Carrier Liability in the Event of Accidents, 1997 O.J. (L 285) 1

Regulation 889/2002, Amending Regulation (EC) No. 2027/97 on Air Carrier Liability in the Event of Accidents, 2002 O.J. (L 140) 2

Regulation 261/2004, of the European Parliament and of the Council of 11 February 2004 Establishing Common Rules on Compensation and Assistance to Passengers in the Event of Denied Boarding and of Cancellation or Long Delay of Flights, and Repealing Regulation 295/91/EEC, 2004 O.J. (L 46) arts. 4–6

Regulation 773/2004, Relating to the Conduct of Proceedings by the Commission Pursuant to Articles 81 and 82 of the EC Treaty, 2004 O.J. (L 123) 18

Regulation 2111/2005, Establishment of a Community List of Air Carriers Subject to an Operating Ban within the Community and on Informing Air Transport Passengers of the Identity of the Operating Air Carrier, and Repealing Article 9 of Directive 2004/36/EC, 2005 O.J. (L 344) 15

Regulation 473/2006, Laying Down Implementing Rules for the Community List of Air Carriers Which Are Subject to an Operating Ban within the

Community Referred to in Chapter II of Regulation (EC) No. 2111/2005 of the European Parliament and of the Council, 2006 O.J. (L 84) 8

Regulation No. 1141/2011, Amending Regulation (EC) No. 272/2009 Supplementing the Common Basic Standards on Civil Aviation Security as Regards the Use of Security Scanners at EU Airports, 2011 O.J. (L 293) 22

OTHER EUROPEAN COMMISSION DOCUMENTS LISTED ALPHABETICALLY

Background Fact Sheet on the EU/US Large Civil Aircraft Agreement (Oct. 11, 2012)

Commission Decision 29/03/2005, *Approving the Standard Clauses for Inclusion in Bilateral Air Service Agreements Between Member States and Third Countries Jointly Laid down by the Commission and the Member States*, 2005 O.J. (C 943) 1

Summary of Commission Decision of 14 July 2010 relating to a proceeding under Article 101 of the Treaty of the Functioning of the European Union and Article 53 of the EEA Agreement (COMP/39.56 – British Airways/American Airlines/Iberia), 2010 O.J. (C 278) 14

EU COUNCIL REGULATIONS LISTED CHRONOLOGICALLY

Council Regulation (EC) 925/1999, Registration and Operation within the Community of Certain Types of Civil Subsonic Jet Aeroplanes which Have Been Modified and Recertificated as Meeting the Standards of Volume I, Part II, Chapter 3 of Annex 16 to the Convention on International Civil Aviation, Third Edition, July 1993, 1999 O.J. (L 115) 1

Council Regulation 1/2003, Implementation of the Rules on Competition Laid Down in Articles 81 and 82 of the Treaty, 2003 O.J. (L 1) 1

Council Regulation 411/2004, Repealing Regulation (EEC) No 3975/87 and Amending Regulations (EEC) No 3976/87 and (EC) No 1/2003, in Connection with Air Transport between the Community and Third Countries, 2004 O.J. (L 68) 1

Council Regulation 773/2004, relating to the Conduct of Proceedings by the EC Pursuant to Articles 81 and 82 of the European Community Treaty, 2004 O.J. (L 123) 18

Council Regulation 847/2004, Negotiation and Implementation of Air Service Agreements between Member States and Third Countries, 2004 O.J. (L 157) 7

Council Regulation 868/2004, Protection Against Subsidisation and Unfair Pricing Practices Causing Injury to Community Air Carriers in the Supply of Air Services from Countries Not Members of the European Community, 2004 O.J. (L 162) 1

Council Regulation 1008/2008, Common Rules for the Operation of Air Services in the European [Union], 2008 O.J. (L 293) 3

Council Regulation 1219/2012, Transitional Arrangements for Bilateral Investment Agreements between Member States and Third Countries, 2012 O.J. (L 351) 40

EU COUNCIL DIRECTIVES LISTED CHRONOLOGICALLY

Council Directive 2003/87, Establishing a Scheme for Greenhouse Gas Emission Allowance Trading within the Community and Amending Council Directive 96/61/EC, 2003 O.J. (L 275) 36

Council Directive 2004/36/CE, Safety of Third-Country Aircraft Using [Union] Airports, 2004 O.J. (L 143) 76

Council Directive 2008/101, Amending Directive 2003/87/EC so as to Include Aviation Activities in the scheme for Greenhouse Gas Emission Allowance Trading within the Community, 2009 O.J. (L 8) 9–11, 17, 19

EU LEGISLATIVE PROPOSALS AND REPORTS LISTED CHRONOLOGICALLY

European Commission, A *Community Aviation Policy Towards its Neighbours*, COM (2004) 74 final (Feb. 9, 2004)

European Commission, Communication from the Commission, *Developing the Agenda for the Community's External Aviation Policy*, COM (2005) 79 final (Mar. 11, 2005)

European Commission, Communication from the Commission to the European Parliament, The Council, The European Economic and Social Committee and the Committee of the Regions, *The EU's External Aviation Policy: Addressing Future Challenges*, COM (2012) 556 final (Sept. 27, 2012)

OTHER NATIONAL LAWS AND REGULATIONS (LISTED ALPHABETICALLY)

Air Navigation Act, 2002, §11A (Austl.)
Civil Aviation Act, 1949, 12 & 13 Geo. 6, c. 67, § 40 (Eng.)

Damage by Aircraft Act, 1952 No. 46, § 2 (N.S.W.) (Austl.)
Damage by Aircraft Act, 1999 § 10 (Austl.).
Law No. 274 of July 7, 1988 (It.)
Ley 2.564 de 1979, arts. 1 & 2 (Chile)
Transportation Act, S.C. 1996, c.10, §§ 55, 61(a)(1) (Can.)

Index

Aer Lingus, 265
Agreement on Large Civil Aircraft
　(U.S./EU), 384
Agreement on Subsidies and Countervailing
　Measures (WTO), 382, 385
Agreement on Trade in Civil Aircraft
　(WTO), 383
African Airlines Association, 23
African Union, 26, 71, 99, 115
Air Berlin, 338
Air Canada, 13, 88, 90, 108, 126, 150, 166. *See
　also* Star
Air Dolimiti, 151
Air Egypt, 48
Air France, 88, 139, 143, 149, 164, 171, 309, 394
Air France v. Saks, 284
Air France v. Teichner, 289
Air France/KLM, 93, 139, 143, 164. *See also*
　SkyTeam
Air Lease Corporation, 338
Air Line Pilots Association, 27
Air Navigation Commission (ICAO), 58,
　178, 181
Air rage, 215
Air services agreements, 12, 20, 25, 69, 83, 95,
　113, 123, 138, 208, 241; authorization and
　designation under, 100; capacity and
　frequency requirements, 5, 74, 94, 103; and
　Chicago Convention, 69; and competition
　law, 105, 114, 120; customs, duties, and
　charges, 106; dispute settlement, 106, 108;
　doing business assurances, 104; and the
　environment, 241; liberalization of, 70, 94,
　122; multilateralization of, 109, 113; and
　nationality rule, 125; open skies model of, 95;
　and pricing freedom, 74, 102; remaining

challenges to, 115; and security, 210; and
　subsidies, 119; and traffic rights, 68, 72, 79,
　96. *See also* bilateralism, cabotage, freedoms
　of the air, nationality rule, open skies
Air traffic management, 28, 40, 46, 51, 57, 63,
　106, 212, 221, 244
Air Transport Action Group, 23
Air Transport Agreement (U.S./EU), *see*
　U.S./EU Air Transport Agreement
Air Transport Committee (ICAO), 59
AirAsia (Malaysia-based airline), 145; and
　related entities, 145
Airbus, 329, 380; subsidization dispute with
　Boeing, 384
Aircraft, 6, 11, 20, 28, 30, 37, 42, 78, 110, 153, 173,
　325, 383; crimes against, 182; definition of, 31;
　leasing of, 337, 339; registration and
　nationality of, 47, 48, 54, 328, 334, 340. *See
　also* Chicago Convention, emissions,
　financing, nationality (aircraft)
Aircraft Protocol Group (Unidroit), 352
Airlines for America (A4A), 23, 147
Airports, 22, 35, 46, 57, 97, 104, 120, 165, 187, 220,
　242, 293, 304, 321; and capacity constraints,
　116, 152, 158, 221, 245; charges for use of, 44,
　114, 236, 347; crimes against, 174, 185, 207,
　212; and passenger screening, 214
Airports Council International (ACI), 27
Airspace sovereignty, 17, 40, 72, 176, 227;
　reasons behind treaty basis for, 43;
　relationship with international
　environmental law, 228. *See also* Chicago
　Convention
Airworthiness, 20, 31, 67, 180; Certificate of, 35,
　173, 176, 247, 340
Alitalia, 164, 273

All Nippon Airways, 82, 152; and antitrust immunity, 163; cooperative agreement with Lufthansa, 163. *See also* Star

Alliance, airline, 9, 95, 105, 122, 124, 147, 280, 304, 396; consolidation of, 149; definition of, 148; future of, 171; history of, 124, 148; industrial policy relating to, 170; reasons for, 150. *See also* antitrust immunity, code-sharing, metal neutrality, oneworld, SkyTeam, spillover, Star

American Airlines, 149, 153, 168; as successor to TWA, 101. *See also* Oneworld

Animus furandi, 183

Annex on Air Transport Services (WTO), 110, 112, 136

Annexes, Chicago Convention. *See* Chicago Convention

Antitrust and competition law, 4, 29, 56, 105, 114, 120, 124, 130, 152, 157; global harmonization of, 120

Antitrust immunity, 105, 148, 154, 171, 270; comparison of U.S. and EU approaches to, 158, 161, 170; and Department of Transportation (U.S.), 155; and domestic spillover, 162; and EU approach to, 156; and global immunity, 167; and metal neutrality, 159. *See also* alliance, code-sharing, oneworld, SkyTeam, spillover, Star

Association of Asia-Pacific Airlines, 23

Association of European Airlines, 23, 146; and 1999 policy paper, 27, 146

Association of Southeast Asian Nations (ASEAN), 26, 71, 94, 99, 121; single aviation market of, 114, 145

Australia, 70, 85, 90, 114, 213, 246; and aviation policy of, 52, 140; and Chicago Convention, 36

Australia/U.K. air services agreement, *see* U.K./Australia air services agreement

Australia/U.S. air services agreement, *see* U.S./Australia air services agreement

Austria/Russia air services agreement, *see* Russia/Austria air services agreement

Austrian Airlines, 93, 140

Aut dedere aut judicare, 193

Aviareto, 363

Aviation trade, exceptionalism of, 242

Aviation Working Group (Unidroit), 351

Banju Accord Group Safety Oversight Organization, 178

Bankruptcy and insolvency, 174, 332, 345, 351, 368, 371

Beijing Convention (security), 207; and related protocol, 208

Bermuda I Agreement (U.S./U.K.), 102, 108

Bermuda II Agreement (U.S./U.K.), 101, 108, 149

Best v. BWIA West Indies Airways, 279

Bilateral air services agreement, *see* air services agreements, bilateralism

Bilateral Investment Treaty, 92, 131, 136, 357

Bilateralism, 86, 99, 103, 109, 122, 393; defined as the "Chicago system," 70; and managed trade, 37, 74; as not ordained in Chicago Convention, 75

Blind sector transit, *see* freedoms of the air

Blue Sky v. Mahan Air, 333, 347, 376

Boeing, 7, 13, 46, 329, 333, 352, 380; subsidization dispute with Airbus, 384

Bonn Declaration on Hijacking, 209

Brazil, 90, 99, 140, 147

Bretton Woods institutions, 34

British Airways, 49, 53, 78, 88, 93, 101, 116, 120, 140, 142, 144, 149, 168, 305, 328, 341, 396. *See also* Oneworld

Brownlie, Ian (law professor), 8

Brunei, 113

Bunker, Donald (lawyer), 345

Cabotage, 6, 49, 72, 84, 92, 97, 111, 114, 140, 153, 278, 318; Australian approach to, 52, 85; current concerns about, 52; EU cabotage-free zone, 52; history and legal basis of, 50; distinguished from right of establishment, 85; labor opposition to, 85; in U.S./EU negotiations, 86. *See also* freedoms of the air

Canada, 77, 90, 99, 108, 246

Canada/EU air services agreement, *see* EU/Canada air services agreement

Canada/U.S. air services agreement, *see* U.S./Canada air services agreement

Canadian Airlines, 168. *See also* Oneworld.

Capacity (airline), 69, 103; and restraints in international air transport, 116

Cape Town Convention, 252, 347; and aircraft leases, 339; and aircraft objects, 360; applicability of, 361; as solution to issue in *Blue Sky* case, 336; and choice of law, 375; covered agreements, 359; and creditor protection, 366; customizability, 354; and events of default, 367; economic context of, 351; and export credit agency discounts, 355, 377; history of, 351; implementation in domestic law, 356; and insolvency, 371; international interest, autonomy of, 361; international interest, creation of, 360; international registry, 363; international law significance of, 358, 378; and jurisdiction, 375; and priority of nonconsensual rights (liens, etc.), 363; ratifications of Convention and Protocol, 377; relationship with Aircraft Protocol, 352; and remedies, including self-help, deregistration, interim relief, 357, 368, 370; role in financing, 356; summary of, 359; and use of declarations, 353, 367

Cargo Lion (Luxembourg airline), 143

Caribbean Aviation Safety and Security Oversight System, 178

Cathay Pacific (Hong Kong), 168, 245. *See also* Oneworld.

Central American Agency for Aeronautical Safety, 178

Chicago conference, 29, 30, 36, 70, 72, 77, 87, 95

Chicago Convention, 6, 11, 13, 19, 22, 24, 28, 34, 125, 135, 229, 234, 239, 242, 251, 275, 305, 313, 319, 327; and aircraft licensing, 47; and aircraft nationality registration, 328, 340, 344; airspace regulation, 43; airspace restrictions, 42; and airspace sovereignty, 40, 43, 72, 228; annexes to, 24, 31, 43, 57, 60, 64, 177, 215, 225, 230, 246, 340; and bilateralism, 75; as charter for ICAO, 55; concessionary basis of market access, 41, 72; and conflicting views of, 37, 72, 126; and coordination of State regulations, 35; cosmopolitanism of, 33; economic impact of, 40, 72; and environmental regulation, 221, 225, 235, 246; and liberalization, 29, 39, 41, 69, 70, 86, 92, 125, 210; and navigation, 46; negotiations for, 28, 36; and pre-history of, 30; preamble of, 33; and registration and nationality of aircraft, 47, 343; restricted zones, 42; and safety, 176, 181, 256; and security, 42, 185, 187, 192; and relationship to State laws and regulations, 44; success of, 34; and taxation, 44, 106, 236; and uniformity, 47, 231. *See also* airspace sovereignty, cabotage, International Civil Aviation Organization, Standards and Recommended Practices

Chile, aviation policy of, 52, 141; membership of MALIAT, 113

Chile/EU air services agreement, *see* EU/Chile air services agreement

China, 90, 140, 245; and response to EU ETS, 240

China/U.S. air services agreement, *see* U.S./China air services agreement

Choice of law, 14, 258, 313, 334, 348, 355, 365, 375

Civil Aeronautics Board (U.S.), 9, 29, 148, 154

Clayton Antitrust Act (U.S.), 4

Code-sharing, 105, 122, 148, 152, 158, 161, 164, 265, 278, 305; defined, 153; and liability of air carriers, 280

Comity, international, 23

Commercial Aircraft Corporation of China, 387

Committee on Aviation Environmental Protection (ICAO), 218, 230

Committee on Unlawful Interference (ICAO), 59

Competition law, *see* antitrust and competition law

Conflict of laws, *see* choice of law

Congestion pricing, 117; as alternative to slots, 117

Continental Airlines, 150, 166; alliance membership, 166; merger with United Airlines, 162

Convention on Biological Diversity, 223

Convention on International Civil Aviation, *see* Chicago Convention

Convention on International Interests in Mobile Equipment, *see* Cape Town Convention

Convention on the International Recognition of Rights in Aircraft, *see* Geneva Convention (financing)

Convention on Offenses and Certain Other Acts Committed on Board Aircraft, *see* Tokyo Convention

Convention Relating to the Regulation of Aerial Navigation, *see* Paris Convention

Convention for the Suppression of Unlawful Acts Against the Safety of Civil Aviation, *see* Montreal Convention (security).

Convention for the Suppression of Unlawful Seizure of Aircraft, *see* Hague Convention, The (security)

Convention for the Unification of Certain Rules for International Carriage by Air, *see* Montreal Convention (liability)

Convention for the Unification of Certain Rules Relating to International Carriage by Air, *see* Warsaw Convention

Cooperative Development of Operational Safety and Continuing Airworthiness Programmes (ICAO), 67
Coterminalization, 80
Council of the EU, 97
Council for Trade in Services (WTO), 52, 112
Court of Justice of the European Union, 25, 45, 97, 213, 240, 313
Coyle, John F. (law professor), 358
Crimes, aviation, 11, 18, 67, 175, 185, 194, 205, 211; jurisdiction over, 189; and passenger data, 212; and piracy, 182; reactive and proactive approaches to, 212. *See also* hijacking, jurisdiction, security
Cuis est solum, eius est usque ad caelum et ad inferos, 18
Customary international law, 12, 17, 20, 40, 132, 135; and international aviation law, 18, 43, 235
Czech Airlines, 164

Debt (financing), 13, 162, 330, 361; distinguished from equity, 325. *See also* financing
Delays, *see* passenger rights
Delta Air Lines, 149, 152, 163, 171, 195, 214, 234, 238, 388. *See also* SkyTeam
Department of Homeland Security (U.S.), 213
Department of Justice (U.S.), 150, 154, 166
Department of Transportation (U.S.), 76, 124, 148, 154, 270
DHL, 83
Directorate-General for Competition (EU), 159
Dispute settlement, 11, 21, 59, 64, 106, 134, 240, 248, 310, 383. *See also* air services agreements, International Civil Aviation Organization, World Trade Organization
Doctrinalism, 7
Dubai, *see* Emirates Airlines
DVT, air carrier liability for, 286

Easterbrook, Frank (judge), 4, 6
Eastern Airlines v. Floyd, 289
easyJet, 7
Economic analysis of law, 4, 9
El Al Israel Airlines v. Tseng, 290, 300
Emirates Airlines, 81, 96, 120, 145, 245, 389
Emissions, aviation, 5, 10, 16, 22, 27, 44, 57, 67, 176, 217, 235, 397; and airspace sovereignty, 227; global response to, 221; and multilateral treaty, 242; regional approach to, 218, 243

Emissions Trading Scheme (EU), 16, 22, 45, 218, 226, 234, 240, 249, 397; and issue of unilateralism, 235
Environmental law, 54, 85
Environmental law, international, 124, 222; and airspace sovereignty, 227; and economic growth, 225; future of, 227; overview of, 222; principles of, 224; and subject-specific regulatory regimes, 223
Equity (investment), 70, 75, 113, 129, 328, 330; distinguished from debt, 325. *See also* financing
Estoppel (in international law), 142
Ethiopia, 115
European Commission, 97, 100, 150, 165, 172, 213, 220, 247, 393; and airline alliances, 156; and emissions trading scheme, 220; and horizontal and vertical air services agreements, 97. *See also* European Common Aviation Area
European Common Aviation Area, 99, 113, 146
European Parliament, 213
European Union, 3, 7, 24, 29, 124, 156, 243, 342, 393; common airline licensing regime, 98, 139; and airline liability, 273; as cabotage-free zone, 52; external aviation policy of, 99; and foreign investment in airlines, 90, 129; and liberalization, 70; and passenger rights, 312; and safety, 256; and security, 174; single aviation market of, 7, 24, 83, 97, 139; and subsidy policy, 119. *See also* Court of Justice of the European Union, emissions trading scheme, European Commission, European Common Aviation Area
EU/Canada air services agreement, 114, 141
EU/Chile air transport agreement, 93
EU/U.S. Air Transport Agreement, *see* U.S./EU Air Transport Agreement
Export credits, *see* subsidies
Export/Import Bank (U.S.), 388
Extradition, 187, 193, 198, 204; as alternative to prosecution, 193

Fauchille, Paul (jurist), 30
Federal Aviation Act (U.S.), 302
Federal Aviation Administration (U.S.), 7, 23, 179, 256, 364
Federal Trade Commission (U.S.), 154
FedEx, 83, 215
Fernandes, Tony (airline entrepreneur), 148
Financing, aircraft, 5, 13, 16, 20, 47, 179, 325, 343, 355, 377; cash-based, 330; and choice of

law issues, 324; "contractual" and "property" effects of secured transactions distinguished, 332; debt-based, 330; and insolvency, 350; and leases, 337; macroeconomic climate for, 329; problem of aircraft mobility, 345; problem of nonuniform legal concepts, 346; protection of security interests generally, 345; relationship with subsidization, 380; role of Cape Town Convention in, 356. *See also* Cape Town Convention, leases, subsidies

Finnair, 168. *See also* Oneworld.

Five Freedoms Agreement, 37, 39, 73, 78, 87, 125

Flag of convenience, 129

Forum non conveniens, 305

France, 49, 79, 144, 149, 165, 263, 291, 308, 319, 388

Freedoms of the air, 73, 76, 96, 99, 110; first freedom, 77; second freedom, 77, 96; third freedom, 78, 127; fourth freedom, 78, 127; fifth freedom, 79, 86, 96, 113, 153, 305; anterior fifth freedom, 81; fifth freedom and blind sector transit, 80, 153; intermediate fifth freedom, 80; sixth freedom, 81, 96; seventh freedom, 82, 96, 111, 113, 128; seventh freedom for all-cargo services, 83; eighth freedom, 84; ninth freedom, 84; exchange of all nine freedoms in the EU, 97. *See also* cabotage, European Union

Frequencies, *see* capacity

Friendly, Henry (judge), 1

Gabon, 115

Gatwick Airport (U.K.), 169

GE Capital Aviation Services, 338

General Agreement on Tariffs and Trade (WTO), 34, 110, 382

General Agreement on Trade in Services (WTO), 25, 110, 109

General principles of law, 11, 19, 107

General Risks Convention, 320, 322

Geneva Convention (financing), 347, 380; as a choice of law treaty, 348; criticism of, 350; enforcement only by domestic courts, 349; and issue of insolvency, 350

Geneva Convention on the High Seas, 184

Germany, 79, 84, 96, 112, 120, 133, 139, 149, 304, 319, 388

Global warming, 217, 229, 246

Globalization, 2, 29, 227, 242, 396

Goldsmith, Jack (law professor), 147

Goode, Sir Roy (law professor), 328, 345, 354, 362, 371

Google Earth, 42

Government aid (financing), *see* subsidies

Group on International Aviation and Climate Change (ICAO), 218

Guadalajara Supplementary Convention (liability), 265

Guatemala City Protocol (liability), 266, 304

Hague Convention, The (security), 186, 201, 207, 210, 212; and extradition, 204; and hijacking offenses, 202; jurisdiction under, 203; limitations of, 204

Hague Peace Conference, The, 30

Hague Protocol, The (liability), 262, 267, 270, 274, 308; and successive carriage, 264; U.S. failure to ratify, 264; and wilful misconduct, 263

Haneda Airport (Japan), 118

Hard law, 12, 63, 223, 231. *See also* soft law

Havana Convention, 32

Heathrow Airport (U.K.), 80, 101, 116, 144, 169; and capacity constraints, 116

Henkin, Louis (law professor), 8

Hijacking, 18, 48, 67, 184, 191, 201, 206, 212, 288; distinguished from piracy, 182. *See also* Bonn Declaration on Hijacking, Hague Convention, The (security)

Homer (Greek poet), 182

Honnebier, Patrick (lawyer), 333

Horizontal agreements (EU), 97, 140

Huang, Jiefang (ICAO lawyer), 342

Hushkit dispute, 247

Husserl v. Swiss Air Transp. Co., 288

Iberia Airlines, 93, 140, 168, 394. *See also* Oneworld

Ibero-American Convention, 32

Iceland, 114

India, 90, 120, 245

Indonesia, 145

Institut de Droit International. 30

Intercarrier Agreement (IATA) (liability), 270, 294

Intergovernmental organizations, 23

Intergovernmental Panel on Climate Change, 229

Interlining, 27, 127, 158, 278. *See also* alliance, code-sharing

International Air Cargo Association, 23

International Air Carrier Association, 23

International Air Services Transit Agreement, *see* Two Freedoms Agreement

International Air Transport Agreement, *see* Five Freedoms Agreement

International Air Transport Association, 23, 26, 70, 352; and "Agenda for Freedom," 146; and Cape Town Convention, 352; and emissions regulation, 242; and liability agreements, 253, 269; and relationship with governments, 27; and standard contract of carriage, 259

International aviation law, 1, 3, 122; as freestanding body of law, 4; relationship with domestic law, 3, 6; scope and content, 4

International Aviation Safety Assessment (FAA), 179

International Chamber of Commerce, 27

International Civil Aviation Organization, 5, 24, 55, 67, 142, 173; Assembly of, 59; Assembly resolutions of, 59; continuing mission of, 67; Council of, 22, 58, 64, 106, 176; and dispute settlement, 22, 64, 106, 135; and economic regulation, 56; and the environment, 217, 228, 233, 246; future development of, 68; goals of, 55; Legal Affairs Bureau of, 60; Legal Committee of, 186, 262, 320; and new safety annex, 181; role in Cape Town Convention, 352; role in creating Montreal liability agreement, 275, 320; and safety audit program, 67, 180; and safety regulation, 173; Secretariat of, 60; and security, 185, 206, 208; subordinate bodies of, 58; and surface damage liability treaties, 315, 320; and technical coordination, 56. *See also* Air Navigation Commission, Air Transport Committee, Committee on Unlawful Interference, Standards and Recommended Practices

International Commission for Air Navigation, 177

International Court of Justice, 21, 106, 222, 240; and role in ICAO dispute settlement, 64

International Declaration Prohibiting Launching of Projectiles and Explosives from Balloons, 30

International Explosives Technical Commission, 207

International governmental organizations, 23

International investment law, 131, 137; and arbitration of investor/State disputes, 135; bilateral investment treaties, 136; definition of foreign investment, 133

International law, private, 14

International law, public, 11; compliance, 8, 178; relationship with domestic law, 3; sources of, 16. *See also* customary international law, dispute settlement, general principles of law, judicial decisions, treaties

International Maritime Organization, 222, 226

International Monetary Fund, 267

International nongovernmental organizations, *see* nongovernmental organizations

International Registry of Mobile Assets (Cape Town Convention), 363

International Tribunal for the Law of the Sea, 22

Interstate Commerce Commission (U.S.), 29

Investment, crossborder, in airlines, 127, 133, 137, 171. *See also* international investment law

Iran, 333

Ireland, 363, 372

Irrevocable Deregistration and Export Request Authorization (IDERA), 369, 377

Israeli Supreme Court, 289

Italian Constitutional Court, 273

Jamaica, 143

Japan, 90

Japan Air Lines, 82, 152. *See also* SkyTeam

Japan/U.S. air services agreement, *see* U.S./Japan air services agreement

Judicial decisions, international, 21

Jurisdiction, international criminal, 189, 196, 203; bases of (in aviation crimes treaties), 192; enforcement jurisdiction, 190; extraterritorial jurisdiction, 211; judicial jurisdiction, 189; passive personality and protective principles, 192, 211; and State of registration, 189; universal jurisdiction, 190. *See also aut dedere aut judicare*, crimes (aviation)

Jus cogens, 18, 183

Kallas, Siim (EU transport commissioner), 172

Karman Line, 41

Keynes, John Maynard (economist), 38

KLM Airlines, 93, 139, 143, 148; and Northwest Airlines investment, 148

Korean Air, 164

Krugman, Paul (economist), 120

Kyoto Protocol, 5, 226, 230, 233

LAN (Chilean airline), 143

Latin America, 31, 93, 122, 143; and liberalization, 144

Latin American and Caribbean Air Transport Association, 23
League of Nations, 34
Leases (aircraft), 337; finance and operating leases distinguished, 339; growing significance of, 338; wet leases, 344. *See also* financing
Legal Affairs Bureau (ICAO), *see* International Civil Aviation Organization
Legal Committee (ICAO), *see* International Civil Aviation Organization
Legal theory, 7
Lenin, Vladimir, 38
Levine, Michael (law professor), 9, 36
Lex ferenda, 221
Lex loci delicti, 15
Lex mercatoria, 148, 358
Lex registrii, 334, 348, 376
Lex situs, 334, 348
Liability, international air carrier, 251, 258, 276, 293, 318; caps on, 266; cargo carriage, 280; and EU, 273; and Japan, 272, 294; public versus private oversight of, 255; standards of, 294; and third-party surface damage, 255, 315, 321, 317. *See also* Montreal Convention (liability), Warsaw Convention, Warsaw System
Lockerbie (Pan Am bombing), 207
LOT Airlines (Poland), 127. *See also* Star
Lowenfeld, Andreas (law professor), 1
Lufthansa, 90, 96, 120, 125, 133, 140, 149, 163, 166, 238, 304, 394. *See also* Star
Luxembourg, 143

Mahan Air, 333
Malta Agreement (liability), 273
Mare liberum, 38, 73
Market-based measures (environmental regulation), 218, 230, 233, 244
Mergers, airline, 120, 125, 127
Metal neutrality, 159; contrasting U.S. and EU approaches to, 161; and viewpoint of organized labor, 162
Mexico, 374
Mises, Ludwig von (economist), 104
Montreal Agreement (U.S./IATA) (liability), 269
Montreal Convention (liability), 14, 253, 274, 306, 313, 320; absence of dispute settlement mechanism, 311; accident causing death or injury, 283, 286; and advance compensation, 298; bodily versus psychic injury, 287, 291; and cargo carriage, 280; and code-sharing, 280; consumer orientation of, 276; and delay liability, 311; embarking and disembarking, 292; enforceability by contracting States, 258; entry into effect, 308; "escalator" clause, 297; exclusivity of, 299; and insurance, 307; future evolution of, 313; judicial interpretation of, 314; jurisdiction under, 303, 309; legal effect of, 308; liability principles of, 276, 293, 311; and negligence of air carriers, 295; and procedural questions, 305; punitive damages under, 299; passenger right of recourse against non-carriers, 307; relationship to Warsaw Convention, 253, 277, 309; and State reservations, 310; scope of, 277; and successive carriage, 279; and ticketing, 282. *See also* International Civil Aviation Organization, liability
Montreal Convention (plastic explosives), 207
Montreal Convention (security), 186, 205; meaning of "aircraft in service," 206; offenses under, 205; and related protocol, 207
Montreal Protocol (surface damage liability), 320
Montreal Protocols (liability), 267
Most favored nation, 110
Multilateral Agreement on Air Services (ASEAN), 114, 145
Multilateral Agreement on Full Liberalisation of Passenger Air Services (ASEAN), 115
Multilateral Agreement on Investment, 137
Multilateral Agreement on the Liberalization of Air Transportation (MALIAT), 113
Multilateral Convention on Foreign Investment in Airlines, 142
Multilateralism, 109; with respect to aviation carbon emissions regulation, 235

National Aeronautics and Space Administration (NASA), 385
National treatment, 110, 134
Nationality (aircraft), 328, 340; and aircraft financing, 343; and Chicago Convention, 344; EU rules, 342; ICAO approach to, 342; nationality of aircraft and airlines distinguished, 341; relationship to aircraft registration and safety oversight, 343
Nationality rule, 18, 49, 69, 86, 123, 125, 147, 341; and aircraft financing, 328; defined as citizenship purity, 8, 129; and domestic law, 90, 128, 140; elements of, 69, 91, 126; organized labor, viewpoint of, 129; origins and purpose of, 126; protectionist effects of,

89, 127; recent application and destabilization by States, 92, 138, 142; relationship with security and strategic trade policy, 88, 130; and right of establishment, 140; trade effects of, 87, 128; and waivers of, 142. *See also* right of establishment

Navigation, *see* Chicago Convention

Netherlands, The Kingdom of the, 122, 144, 149, 240, 334, 396; as monist State, 356

Netherlands, The Kingdom of the, Supreme Court, 240

New Zealand, 70, 114; and Chicago Convention, 36; membership of MALIAT, 113

Night flight restrictions (in U.S./EU relations), 248

Noise pollution, aviation, 220, 246

Nongovernmental organizations, 4, 23, 218, 270

North American Free Trade Agreement, 5, 109, 136

Northwest Airlines, 163. *See also* KLM Airlines

Norway, 114

Obama, Barack (U.S. president), 168

Olympic Airways v. Husain, 286

Oneworld (alliance), 105, 149; regulatory review of, 168

Open Aviation Area, 7, 71

Open skies, 7, 10, 70, 93, 95, 101, 106, 112, 136, 142, 144, 243, 393; and airline alliances, 150; and liberalization, 70, 83, 110

Organization for Economic Cooperation and Development, 25, 355, 389; and air cargo transport liberalization, 26; control of export credits, 381

Outer Space Treaty, 41

Paretianism, international, 10

Paris Convention, 18, 31, 176; and establishment of international aerial navigation commission, 31

Passenger data, 212; passenger name records, 213; U.S./EU agreements concerning, 213; use for security purposes, 212

Passenger rights, 312

Pauwelyn, Joost (law professor), 239

Philippines, 145

Piracy, aviation, 18, 182; distinguished from terrorism, 183; as *jus cogens* crime, 185. *See also* crimes (aviation)

PK Airfinance (U.S.), 333

Posner, Eric (law professor), 147

Pricing (airline), 69, 102

Private international law, *see* international law, private

Private international aviation law, 251; definition of, 13; judicial enforcement of, 22

Private transnational aviation law, 15; and judicial enforcement of, 22

Procedures for Air Navigation Services, 178

Protocol to the Convention on International Interests in Mobile Equipment on Matters Specific to Aircraft Equipment, *see* Cape Town Convention

Public international aviation law, definition of, 11; overlap with private transnational aviation law, 15

Public international law, *see* international law, public

Qantas, 85, 124, 142, 168. *See also* Oneworld.

Railway Labor Act (U.S.), 4

Rational choice theory, 10

Ratione loci, 202

Ratione personae, 203

Ratione temporis, 206

Regional Economic Integration Organization (Cape Town Convention), 377

Regional Safety Oversight Organization (ICAO), 178

Renvoi doctrine, 334

Right of establishment, 53, 85, 91, 128, 140, 172; distinguished from cabotage, 85. *See also* cabotage, investment, nationality rule

Rio Declaration on Environment and Development, 224

Rome Convention (1933 and 1952) (surface damage liability), 315, 317

Rome Protocol (surface damage liability), 315. *See also* Montreal Protocol (surface damage liability)

Roosevelt, Franklin D. (U.S. president), 28

Rosman v. Trans World Airlines, 288

Royal Bank of Scotland, 328

Royal Jordanian Airlines, 168. *See also* Oneworld

Russia, 77, 246; and EU aviation relations, 140; and trans-Siberian overflights, 77

Russia/Austria air services agreement, 140

Ryanair, 7, 330, 389

Safety, aviation, 175; and Chicago Convention, 176; and Paris Convention, 176. *See also* International Civil Aviation Organization

Safety Assessment of Foreign Aircraft (EU), 180
SAS Airlines, 166. *See also* Star
Schiphol Airport (Netherlands), 333
Schmitt, Carl (jurist), 183
Schwartz, Warren (economist and lawyer), 386
Sector Understanding for Export Credits on Civil Aircraft (OECD), 355, 389
Security, aviation, 173, 182; and air cargo, 215; and passenger and cargo screening procedures, 214; State bilateral cooperation, 211. *See also* air rage, crimes, International Civil Aviation Organization, passenger data
September 11, 2001 (9/11), 43, 119, 174, 187, 207, 212
Shane, Jeffrey (IATA general counsel), 150
Sherman Antitrust Act (U.S.), 29
Singapore, membership of MALIAT, 113
Singapore Airlines, 245
SITA (Cape Town registry), 363
SkyTeam (alliance), 105, 149, 156, 161, 171, 180, 396; regulatory review of, 164
Slots, 116, 158, 168, 221; as alternative to congestion pricing, 117
Soft law, 12, 63, 223, 231, 390. *See also* hard law
South Asian Regional Initiative, 178
South Korea, 145
Southwest Airlines, 330
Sovereignty, airspace, *see* airspace sovereignty. *See also* Chicago Convention
Space law, 41
Special Drawing Rights, 267
Spillover (of airline alliance immunity), 162, 167
Standard Form of Agreement for Provisional Air Routes, 75
Standards and Recommended Practices, 20, 24, 57, 61, 177, 231; differences in legal effect of, 62, 232
Star (alliance), 105, 149, 151, 161, 171, 280, 396; regulatory review of, 166
State aid, *see* subsidies
Strict liability (civil), 271, 276, 281, 294, 307, 311, 316, 322
Strict liability (criminal), 194
Subsidies, 119, 327, 382; and aircraft manufacturing, 327, 380; and export credits, 381, 388; future prospects for, 387. *See also* Airbus, Boeing, Sector Understanding for Export Credits on Civil Aircraft (OECD)
Successive carriage, 264, 279
Sumitomo Mitsui, 328
Summers, Lawrence (U.S. government official), 168

Supreme Court (U.S.), 289
Surface damage liability, *see* liability
Swiss International Airlines, 166. *See also* Star
Sykes, Alan (economist and lawyer), 386

TACA (El Salvador-based airline), 144
TAM (Brazilian airline), 143
TAP Air Portugal, 166. *See also* Star
Terrorism, 188, 212; and aviation, 174; distinguished from piracy, 183; and U.N. efforts to define, 184
Thai Airways, 166. *See also* Star
Thailand, 145
Tiger Airways, 145
Tokyo Convention, 186, 194; aircraft commander powers, 199; jurisdiction under, 196; limitations of, 198; offenses under, 194; scope of, 195; weaknesses of, 198
Trade, managed, 36, 74. *See also* air services agreements
Traffic rights, *see* air services agreements, freedoms of the air
Transatlantic Business Dialogue, 27
Transit rights, *see* freedoms of the air
Transportation Security Administration (U.S.), 214
Treaties, 3, 11, 16, 19; and dualism, 357; and monism, 356; role in international aviation law, 19
Treaty on the Functioning of the European Union, 156
Treaty on Principles Governing the Activities of States in the Exploration and Use of Outer Space, *see* Outer Space Treaty
Trinidad and Tobago, 143
Two Freedoms Agreement, 37, 73, 77, 87, 125

Unidroit, 351
Unilateralism, 234; with respect to airline carbon emissions regulation, 235
United Airlines, 78, 128, 163, 166; as successor to PanAm, 101; and antitrust immunity, 163
United Kingdom, and Chicago Convention, 36; as dualist State, 357; and aircraft financing, 377
U.K./Australia air services agreement, 85
United Arab Emirates, 245
United Nations, 5, 17, 34; and actions related to prevention of terrorism, 174; General Assembly, 174; Security Council, 174
United Nations Convention on the Law of the Sea, 222

United Nations Framework Convention on Climate Change, 5, 223, 227. *See also* Kyoto Protocol

United Nations Universal Declaration of Human Rights, 12

United Parcel Service (UPS), 83, 215

United States, 3, 10, 15, 25, 76, 104, 108, 124, 136; and approach to airline industry regulation, 29; as cabotage market, 52; and the Chicago Convention, 28, 36, 72; and the environment, 220, 239; and financing, 341, 353, 364, 377; and foreign investment in airlines, 90, 129; and liability, 253, 263, 268, 275, 308; and liberalization, 70, 143; and open skies policy, 70, 83, 93, 144, 149; and response to EU ETS, 240; and review of airline alliances, 149; and safety, 63, 179; and security, 206, 211

U.S./Australia air services agreement, 142

U.S./Brazil air services agreement, 143

U.S./Canada air services agreement, 90, 100, 125

U.S./China air services agreement, 76, 103, 111

U.S./EU Air Transport Agreement, 27, 78, 82, 86, 93, 111, 114, 127, 138, 141, 149, 164, 248, 393, 397; and antitrust and competition law, 121; as demonstration model, 122; dispute settlement under, 107; and the environment 241, 243; and modification of nationality rule, 142; and noise regulation, 248; as plurilateral agreement, 114, 244; and amending Protocol, 243; role of joint committee appointed under, 243

U.S. Export-Import Bank, 355, 388

U.S./France air services agreement, 144

U.S./Japan air services agreement, 118, 128

U.S./Mexico air services agreement, 81

U.S. Model Open Skies Agreement, 138

U.S./Netherlands air services agreement, 144

U.S./Singapore air services agreement, 85

U.S./South Korea air services agreement, 89

Universal Safety Oversight and Audit Programme, 180. *See also* International Civil Aviation Organization

Unlawful Interference Convention, 321; State resistance to, 322

Vertical agreements (EU), 98

Vienna Convention on the Law of Treaties, 19, 233, 239

Vienna Convention for the Protection of the Ozone Layer, 223

Virgin Australia (formerly Virgin Blue), 85, 141

Volcanic ash crisis, 43, 119

Wallace v. Korean Air, 285

Warsaw Convention, 14, 252, 274; bodily versus psychic injury, 287; enforceability by contracting States, 258; exclusivity of, 300; history of, 258; integration with national law and contracts of carriage, 259; jurisdiction under, 303; principles of liability, 260; reform of, 262; relationship to Montreal Convention, 253; U.S. skepticism of, 261, 268; and willful misconduct, 263. *See also* Hague Protocol (The) (liability), Guadalajara Supplementary Convention (liability), Guatemala City Protocol (liability), Malta Agreement (liability), Montreal Protocols (liability), Montreal Agreement (U.S./IATA) (liability), Intercarrier Agreement (IATA) (liability)

Warsaw System, 253, 257, 271; and liability caps, 266

Westphalia, Treaty of, 17

Wilson, Woodrow (U.S. president), 34

Wool, Jeffrey (law professor and lawyer), 378

World Economic Forum, 27

World Trade Organization (WTO), 21, 25, 52, 222, 380; and air services trade, 25, 52, 71, 89, 109; and Airbus/Boeing dispute, 381, 384; and aircraft financing, 380; and dispute settlement, 21, 107, 109, 135, 383. *See also* General Agreement on Tariffs and Trade, General Agreement on Trade in Services, subsidies

Wright Brothers, 30

Yamoussoukro Declaration/Decision (African Union), 26, 71, 99, 115

Milton Keynes UK
Ingram Content Group UK Ltd.
UKHW051538210324
439908UK00007B/375